The Foundations of Behavioral Economic Analysis:
Volume 1

The Foundations of Behavioral Economic Analysis is also available in seven newly revised volumes published by Oxford University Press

PRAISE FOR "THE FOUNDATIONS OF BEHAVIORAL ECONOMIC ANALYSIS"

"*The Foundations of Behavioral Economic Analysis* is a masterpiece. It covers the whole field of behavioral economics. And it is also an easy read, as beautiful examples throughout lead readers to appreciate behavioral decisions from the perspective of their own lifetime experience."

George A. Akerlof, University Professor, Georgetown University, and 2001 Nobel Laureate in Economics.

"The publication of this book is a landmark occasion for the field of behavioral economics. Until now there has been no comprehensive survey of the field suitable for graduate students. Professor Dhami has thoroughly and rigorously filled that gap. The book will be placed in a handy place in my office since I plan to consult it regularly."

Richard H. Thaler, Charles R Walgreen Distinguished Service Professor of Economics and Behavioral Science, University of Chicago, and 2017 Nobel Laureate in Economics.

"The seven volumes of *The Foundations of Behavioral Economic Analysis* offer a fascinating mix of theory and evidence and represent the most comprehensive synthesis of behavioral economics at an advanced level. They will be very useful for advanced researchers as well as for graduate students in behavioral economics and beyond."

Ernst Fehr, Professor of Economics, University of Zurich.

"This series of seven volumes is a tour de force, a literal encyclopedia of behavioral economics. Its extraordinary breadth and depth, spanning all aspects from psychological foundations to the most recent advances and seamlessly integrating theory with experiments, will make it the must-have reference for anyone interested in this field, and more generally in where economics is headed. It will quickly become the standard textbook for all graduate courses in behavioral economics, and a much-thumbed companion for all researchers working at the frontier."

Roland Benabou, Theodore A. Wells' 29 Professor of Economics and Public Affairs, Princeton University.

"In *The Foundations of Behavioral Economic Analysis*, Sanjit Dhami offers the first summary and exposition of research in this rapidly growing and increasingly influential subfield. The coverage is comprehensive, extending even to the recent subtopics of behavioral welfare economics and neuroeconomics. The book is distinguished by its detailed yet readable coverage of theory and evidence and its balanced discussion of the philosophical and methodological differences and similarities between 'behavioral' and neoclassical approaches to microeconomics. Select undergraduates, graduate students, and interested scholars will all gain from this masterful book."

Vincent P. Crawford, Drummond Professor of Political Economy, University of Oxford, and Research Professor, University of California, San Diego.

"This is the most complete and stimulating series of books on behavioral economics. With elegance and unprecedented elaborateness, it ties together a wealth of experimental findings, rigorous theoretical insights and exciting applications across all relevant fields of behavioral research. Sanjit Dhami's work has been shaped by numerous comments of the leaders in the field. Now, in the years to come, it will be the standard that shapes how the next generation of students and researchers think about behavior and its science."

Axel Ockenfels, University of Cologne, Speaker of the Cologne Excellence Center of Social and Economic Behavior.

"The expansion of behavioral economics during the past quarter century has been remarkable, much of it concerning strategic interaction and using tools from game theory. Sanjit Dhami's amazing book, now available in a convenient multi-volume format, summarizes—and even defines—the field, broadly as well as in depth. His coverage of theory as well as of experiments is superb. *The Foundations of Behavioral Economic Analysis* will be an indispensable resource for students and scholars who wish to understand where the action is."

Martin Dufwenberg, Karl & Stevie Eller Professor and Director of the Institute for Behavioral Economics at the University of Arizona.

"*The Foundations of Behavioral Economic Analysis* will be a central textbook for behavioral economics. One key feature is its appealing focus on the interplay between theory and evidence. For researchers, it will be a great source of information, puzzles, and challenges for the many years to come. It is a major achievement."

Xavier Gabaix, Pershing Square Professor of Economics and Finance, Harvard University.

"This is a unique and truly remarkable achievement. It is a magnificent overview of behavioral economics, by far the best there is, and it should define the field for at least a generation. But it is much more than that. It is also a brilliant set of original discussions, with pathbreaking thinking on every important topic. An invaluable resource for policymakers, students, and professors—and if they want to try something really special, for everyone else."

Cass Sunstein, coauthor of Nudge and Founder and Director of the Program on Behavioral Economics and Public Policy, Harvard Law School.

"This is truly an amazing work. It is unique in both comprehensiveness and depth. The author is to be applauded for producing what will surely be the standard reference for both researchers and students. And breaking it into seven volumes will greatly enhance its usability. I highly recommend these volumes to any serious reader in behavioral economics."

Gary Charness, Professor of Economics, University of California, Santa Barbara.

The Foundations of Behavioral Economic Analysis: Volume 1

Behavioral Economics of Risk, Uncertainty, and Ambiguity

SANJIT DHAMI

OXFORD
UNIVERSITY PRESS

UNIVERSITY PRESS

Great Clarendon Street, Oxford, OX2 6DP,
United Kingdom

Oxford University Press is a department of the University of Oxford.
It furthers the University's objective of excellence in research, scholarship,
and education by publishing worldwide. Oxford is a registered trade mark of
Oxford University Press in the UK and in certain other countries

Published in the United States of America by Oxford University Press
198 Madison Avenue, New York, NY 10016, United States of America

British Library Cataloguing in Publication Data

Data available

Library of Congress Control Number: 2018954093

ISBN 978–0–19–883560–8

Printed and bound by
CPI Group (UK) Ltd, Croydon, CR0 4YY

To my Parents, wife Shammi, and son Sahaj

PREFACE TO VOLUME 1: BEHAVIORAL ECONOMICS OF RISK, UNCERTAINTY, AND AMBIGUITY

The Foundations of Behavioral Economic Analysis (henceforth, FBEA) was published by Oxford University Press in November 2016. It was the culmination of more than a decade of dedicated work. The book was quite well received and it was heartening to receive messages of support, encouragement, and appreciation from many quarters. Several reviews of FBEA have been published and they have praised the comprehensiveness, formal analysis, and the attention to empirical detail in the book. The book is increasingly taught around the world in behavioral and experimental economics courses in the leading economics departments. Encouragingly, it is also being used in more enlightened courses in economic theory, which was always an important objective of writing this book. The practice of ignoring the empirical evidence and the theoretical models in behavioral economics, in many courses in microeconomics, game theory, and contract theory, is one of the most retrogressive practices in the profession and a form of self-handicapping that is difficult to understand.

At 1796 pages (including unnumbered pages), FBEA is probably one of the longest economics books ever to have been published in a single volume. Binding the book was a major challenge, which Oxford University Press accomplished with great competence. Some friends have written on a lighter note about the physical size and the weight of the book. Samuel Bowles wrote to say that Herbert Gintis had presented him with a copy of the book on Christmas and that he had to hire a truck to take it home. In one of his reviews, Daniel Read congratulated me on writing the "War and Peace" of behavioral economics. Andrew Schotter wrote to say that he keeps one copy at home and another in his office in NYU to avoid carrying it on the New York subway. A friend who had purchased the paperback version took the drastic step of physically separating Part 4 on behavioral game theory (a good 320 pages long) to carry around with him. Xavier Gabaix is one of many readers who prefers the electronic version that makes issues of the size of the book irrelevant. However, at least some readers, and I am part of this group, tend to be old fashioned and prefer the printed version.

We did explore the idea of splitting FBEA into two volumes before it was published and this was put to an informal vote among 30 of the leading behavioral economists. They were almost equally split. OUP took the casting vote to decide on a single volume, understandably because there are not too many multiple volume mainstream texts in economics. As more feedback from the users of the book emerged, Adam Swallow, the commissioning editor at OUP, began exploring with me the possibility of splitting the book into multiple volumes. Just as publishing such a long book and making it available for teaching to several instructors prior to its publication was a novel and bold experiment in publishing, so too is the proposal to split it into multiple volumes. After extensive discussions at OUP, I was given the go ahead to pursue this exciting and unprecedented opportunity.

What we present to you here, after considerable thought, is a seven-volume book on behavioral economics that splits the nine-parts of FBEA into the following topics: Behavioral economics of risk uncertainty and ambiguity (Volume 1); Other-regarding preferences (Volume 2); Behavioral economics of time discounting (Volume 3); Behavioral game theory (Volume 4); Bounded rationality (Volume 5); Behavioral models of learning (Volume 6); Further topics in behavioral economics that include emotions, behavioral welfare economics, and neuroeconomics (Volume 7). Other possible splits of FBEA were possible (e.g., combining Volumes 1 and 3; and Volumes 2 and 4), but none of these proposals offers the clean separation into the main topics in behavioral economics that the current split offers.

We believe that these seven volumes improve on FBEA for several reasons aside from just better portability of the print edition. First, it is a welcome opportunity to correct several typos and errors, as well as to improve the clarity of the text in many places. Second, it allows the updating of some of the material to reflect important recent scholarship in the form of a 'guide to further reading' at the end of each volume. This allows me to introduce several new concepts and tie them back to the discussion in the main text. Third, it gives readers the option to buy individual volumes, depending on their current research and teaching interests. However, those with a serious interest in economics, certainly all university academics, ought to consider reading all of the seven volumes. Fourth, given how daunting the prospect of revising the 1800 page FBEA would have been, the split volumes increase the likelihood of a second edition to some, or all, of the volumes in due course.

For the benefit of readers who buy the separate volumes, or just a few of the volumes, we have taken several steps. Each of the volumes will have a new preface, a new introduction, and carry a reprint of the original preface in FBEA. This will give readers an opportunity to get acquainted with how and why this book came to be. The introductory chapter in FBEA covered important ground. In particular, the first 25 pages outlined the antecedents of behavioral economics, the role of scientific methodology, and the rationale for the experimental method. A lack of proper understanding and appreciation of these critical prerequisites may seriously hamper an understanding of the subject matter. For this reason, in each volume, we shall also print an edited version of the first 25 pages in FBEA. In these pages, I have also added a brief new subsection on replication of experiments. The remaining part of the introductory chapter in FBEA (pages 25–64) is printed only in Volume 1. I have taken care to remove as many typos and errors from the introduction of FBEA as I could find, and improved the clarity of the material in many places.

Readers will find that we have done many of the same things that we might have done in bringing out a second edition of FBEA in these seven volumes. We hope that our efforts in this direction will lead to a better understanding and appreciation of the subject matter of behavioral economics.

PREFACE TO THE FOUNDATIONS OF BEHAVIORAL ECONOMIC ANALYSIS

We print below the original preface to *The Foundations of Behavioral Economic Analysis* in Dhami (2016).

Neoclassical economics is a logically consistent and parsimonious framework of analysis that is based on a relatively small set of core assumptions, and it offers clear, testable, predictions. However, extensive and growing empirical evidence reveals human behavior that is difficult to reconcile within the typical neoclassical models. There has been a parallel development in rigorous theoretical models that explains better the emerging stylized facts on human behavior. These models have borrowed insights from psychology, sociology, anthropology, neuroscience, and evolutionary biology. Yet, these models maintain a distinct economic identity in terms of their approach, rigor, and parsimony. Collectively, these models form the subject matter of behavioral economics, which is possibly the fastest growing and most promising area in economics.

This book is an account of behavioral economics that starts with the basics and takes the reader to the research frontiers in the subject. Depending on how one chooses to use it, the book is suitable for courses at the advanced undergraduate, postgraduate, and research level in economics, and the related social sciences, including, but not restricted to, psychology, management, finance, political science, and sociology. The book should also serve as an essential reference book for anyone generally interested in behavioral economics at any level, and also serve to stimulate the interests of non-specialist academics, specialist academics who are looking for a bird's-eye view of the entire field, and policymakers looking for policy applications of behavioral economics. It would be desirable to assign this book as background reading to courses in economic theory. The book is also, in my view, the minimum subject matter that anyone who writes behavioral economics as their research interest, should be deeply familiar with.

In November 2003, two months after I joined the department of economics at the University of Leicester, I chanced upon an invitation to attend a talk by a colleague, Ali al-Nowaihi, on the subject of *prospect theory*. Ali, a mathematician by training, an economist by profession, and a keen student of the philosophy of science, put forward a Popperian view to evaluate economic theories. He argued that *expected utility theory* was decisively rejected by the evidence, and prospect theory was the most satisfactory decision theory currently available. As a purely neoclassically trained economist, I was troubled by the claims, but also extremely skeptical. For a start, prospect theory sounded like a strange name for a theory, and the evidence was largely "experimental," a data source, that I knew little about. As my defensive instincts started to kick in, I wondered if prospect theory really was so important, then surely my graduate courses, many taught by leading decision theorists, would have found some reason to mention it. Nor was there any mention of such a theory in conversations with colleagues at the two British universities where I had taught so far, or at seminars or conferences that I had attended.

However, rather than just dismiss Ali, a very likeable and respected figure in the department, I decided to put his seemingly extreme views to the test. One of my majors was in public economics, so I decided to conduct a prospect theory analysis of tax evasion in the hope of explaining the *tax evasion puzzles*, which had been outstanding for three decades (details in Part 1). There was already some preliminary work in this area that Ali had mentioned in passing, but none of the papers explained all the puzzles in one fell swoop, using all components of prospect theory. It took me just a few weeks to work out the results. To my utter amazement, prospect theory explained the qualitative and quantitative tax evasion puzzles. By contrast, the predictions based on an expected utility analysis were wrong by a factor of up to 100. This led to my first joint publication with Ali, with whom I have spent many years of fruitful collaboration since then.

This initial, and successful, encounter with prospect theory convinced me that I needed to explore behavioral economics in greater depth. Yet, around 2004, there was no definitive graduate text on behavioral economics. To be sure, there were many excellent sets of collected readings, and several insightful surveys and commentaries on selected aspects of behavioral economics that I eagerly read. In particular, while there were many excellent discussions of the experimental evidence, a full treatment of behavioral economic theory and its applications was missing. One could always pursue the journal articles, but the literature was already enormous, rapidly expanding, and scattered, which made it difficult to spot the links between the various models or to clearly visualize how the various pieces of the jigsaw fitted together. This book was motivated initially by the lack of a serious graduate book on the entire subject matter of behavioral economics, my desire to master behavioral economics, and to support my growing research agenda with Ali. In due course, and as the full range of the subject matter gradually dawned upon me, the scope of the book naturally became more ambitious and daring.

I strive to strike a balance between behavioral economic theory, the experimental evidence, and applications of behavioral economics. The choice of theoretical models in this book is dictated, first and foremost, by their ability to explain the empirical evidence. In some cases, where no decisive empirical evidence is available, I make a judgment on which models are more promising than others, although I give a wide berth to most models.

The main prerequisite for the book is training in the first two to three years of a reasonably good British or North American undergraduate degree in economics, or its equivalent. Any further concepts and techniques are introduced in the book, where needed. A prior course in behavioral economics is not a prerequisite for the book.

The book is divided into nine parts that cover decision making under risk, uncertainty, and ambiguity; other-regarding preferences; behavioral time discounting; models of behavioral game theory and learning; role of emotions in decision making; models of bounded rationality; judgment heuristics and mental accounting; behavioral welfare economics; and neuroeconomics. The book also considers a range of applications of the theory to most areas in economics that include microeconomics, contract theory, macroeconomics, industrial organization, labor economics, development economics, public economics, political economy, and finance. A set of exercises at the end of each part, except the part on neuroeconomics, serves to enhance the reader's understanding of the subject.

Behavioral economics is now a mainstream area in economics. One just has to look at the growing and large number of journal publications and Ph.D. theses every year; the Nobel Prizes to Herbert Simon, Daniel Kahneman, Robert Shiller, Alvin Roth, Vernon Smith, and George Akerlof; the John Bates Clarke medal to Matthew Rabin; the growing importance of behavioral economics among policymakers, as witnessed by the 2015 World Bank Development Report, and the formation of the behavioral insights team in the UK; and the choice of Richard Thaler as the incoming President of the American Economic Association.

It is fair to say that no self-respecting economics department can now afford to omit a course in behavioral economics from its undergraduate or graduate curriculum; indeed, doing so would be grossly unjust to its students and a retrogressive step. Nor can any academic economist, who wishes to retain professional honesty and a balanced opinion on the subject, afford to be unfamiliar with the subject matter of behavioral economics; I am often amused by the ignorance and arrogance of many who pass judgment on behavioral economics with supreme confidence, yet appear to have little understanding of it.

This book has taken more than ten years to write, and my debts are deep and profound. My first and foremost debt and gratitude is to my loving family without which this book could not have been written. To my parents, Manohar and Baljeet, for their unconditional lifelong love and support, and instilling in me the core values of honesty, commitment, and hard work. To my wife, Shammi, and my son, Sahaj, for their patience, sacrifice, unflinching support, and constant encouragement. When I started writing this book, Sahaj was in primary school, and in the month of its first publication, he could be packing his bags to join a university. I do not recommend this as the best template to encourage your son to write any books in the future. However, there are close parallels between Sahaj's educational journey from primary school to university, with my own journey in behavioral economics.

I owe a deep intellectual debt to my long-time coauthor and friend, Ali al-Nowaihi. I first learnt about prospect theory from him. I also owe my appreciation of methodology and the philosophy of science entirely to him. He has undertaken a larger burden of our joint research in the last few years, allowing me to be immersed in the book. For all these reasons, he is very much a coauthor of the book in spirit.

I am extremely grateful to many academics and Ph.D. students who unselfishly and generously contributed their time and efforts to reading drafts of various parts of the book. The participation of so many leading behavioral economists in the making of this book is unprecedented and has really made it into a public project for which I shall always be very grateful. Herbert Gintis, Martin Dufwenberg, and Vincent Crawford deserve special mention for being so very gracious with their inputs into most parts of the book, and very quickly responding to my queries.

Many others also played a critical role in the writing of this book and commented on material closer to their areas of interest, and/or offered valuable encouragement and advice. In particular, I wish to thank Mohammed Abdellaoui, Ali al-Nowaihi, Dan Ariely, Douglas Barrett, Björn Bartling, Karna Basu, Kaushik Basu, Pierpaolo Battigalli, Roland Bénabou, Florian Biermann, Gary Bolton, Subir Bose, David Colander, Andrew Colman, Patricio Dalton, Alexandra Dias, Florian Englmaier, Armin Falk, Ernst Fehr, Urs Fischbacher, Xavier Gabaix, Sayantan Ghosal, Uri Gneezy, Werner Güth, Shaun Hargreaves Heap, Fabian Herweg, Karla Hoff, Philippe Jehiel, David Laibson, George Loewenstein, Michel Marechal, Friederike Mengel, Joshua Miller, Axel Ockenfels, Amnon Rapoport, Ludovic Renou, Alvin Roth, Klaus Schmidt, Andrei Shleifer, Dennis Snower, Joe Stiglitz, Cass Sunstein, Richard Thaler, Jean-Robert Tyran, KlausWaelde, Peter Wakker, Eyal Winter, and Peyton Young. I owe a profound intellectual debt to many others who did not read the book manuscript but whose work has greatly inspired me. These include Daniel Kahneman, Amos Tversky, Colin Camerer, Matthew Rabin, Herbert Simon, Robert Shiller, and George Akerlof. I am also very grateful to two successive Heads of the economics department at Leicester, Steve Hall and Chris Wallace, who tried to free up as much of my time as possible for writing the book.

I would like to specially acknowledge the enormous amount of work put in by two extremely conscientious and able Ph.D. students, Teimuraz Gogsadze and Junaid Arshad. They closely read and commented on successive drafts of the manuscript at all stages, offered very useful advice, and served as excellent sounding boards for new ideas. Jingyi Mao came up with a very nice cover for the book in a burst of creativity, for which I am very grateful. Other Ph.D. students who carefully read and commented on selected parts of the manuscript include: Ala Avoyan, Nino Dognohadze, Sneha Gaddam, Narges Hajimoladarvish, Emma Manifold, Jingyi Mao, Alexandros Rigos, David Tsirekidze, Yongli Wang, Mengxing Wei, and Mariam Zaldastanishvili.

I would be remiss not to thank the large number of other researchers whose work has made this book possible. I must also sincerely apologize to authors who feel that their work has been inadequately cited or not given the importance they feel that it deserves. To such authors, I say, omission of your papers does not mean that I necessarily viewed your papers as unimportant. In mitigation, I do not intend my book to be a survey of all the experimental results on all topics in behavioral economics; there are already excellent sources with this objective. And, quite possibly, I was simply unaware of your important work, which is in keeping with the evidence on limited attention and bounded rationality that plays an important role in this book.

I am very grateful to the team at Oxford University Press who have done an excellent job at all stages of this book. In particular, I would like to thank Adam Swallow, the commissioning editor for economics and finance at OUP for his patience, good cheer, organizational skills, and sound advice. Scott Parris, the economics editor at the US office of OUP, who retired just as this book was about to come out, was the first to spot the importance of this project. He offered very valuable advice and encouragement throughout the writing stage and played a key role in my decision to go with OUP. I must also thank Niko Pfund, the President of Oxford University Press USA, for his continued interest in the manuscript over several years, despite his many other responsibilities. The production and marketing teams at OUP were a pleasure to work with. Jon Billam took on the challenge of copy-editing an unusually large book with great enthusiasm. I am also very grateful to Emma Slaughter, the production editor for the book; Kim Stringer, the indexer; Kim Allen, the proofreader; Carla Hodge-Degler who took over as production editor from Emma; and to Leigh-Ann Bard, the marketing manager for the book.

CONTENTS

LIST OF FIGURES

LIST OF TABLES

Introduction to Volume 1

We begin by giving a taxonomy of the kinds of situations that we are interested in Volume 1. In the simplest economic problem, a single decision maker plays a game against nature. Depending on the action chosen by the decision maker, nature induces a probability distribution over a set of possible outcomes. The probability distribution may be *objective* or *subjective*.

Suppose that we make the strong assumption that the set of outcomes is known. If the probability distribution of the relevant outcomes can be estimated objectively, then we have a situation of *risk*. I do not wish to enter into philosophical arguments about the nature of probability and prefer to use the term 'objective probabilities' in the sense that it is used in standard microeconomics books such as Mas-Colell et al. (2015, p. 168). This implies that there is common agreement among people on the magnitude of these probabilities. For instance, a probability of 0.5 of a heads up in an unbiased coin toss, or a probability of 1/6 of the number 3 coming up in a throw of a fair, six-sided, dice. However, in some cases, no objective probabilities may be available, e.g., the dice may be known to be biased, but different people may have different views on the degree of the bias. In this case, decision makers may be able to assign a *subjective probability distribution* over outcomes that satisfies the Kolgomorov axioms. This is a situation of *uncertainty*.

A third class of events arises when no objective probabilities are available, nor can we assign any reasonable and consistent subjective probabilities that satisfy the Kolgomorov axioms. However, in this case, decision makers may be able to assign reasonable subjective probabilities to outcomes arising from each *source* of potential information. A source has been defined as "a group of events that is generated by a common mechanism of uncertainty." Readers familiar with the Ellsberg paradox could think of the known and the unknown urns in the paradox as two different sources. When the decision maker's subjective probabilities are elicited by comparing the different sources, as in the Ellsberg paradox, then evidence suggests that no reasonable subjective probabilities can be assigned. Such a situation of *source-dependent uncertainty* is known as *ambiguity*.[1]

The central question in decision theory, taken up in Volume 1, is this: How does the decision maker make optimal action choices in the presence of risk, uncertainty, or ambiguity? However, the attentive reader would have realized that our strong assumption of known outcomes has

---

[1] A case could be made to dispense with the term 'ambiguity' and replace it by the more enlightening source-dependent uncertainty. However, the term ambiguity is now established and entrenched in the literature; for this reason, we continue to use it.

precluded Knightian uncertainty or true uncertainty (termed in common parlance as the problem of *unknown unknowns*). A situation of true uncertainty arises when the outcomes and probabilities are unknown and unimaginable. In terms of the Ellsberg paradox, true uncertainty would arise if one was unaware about how many colors/number of balls might be present in the unknown urn. The human eye can distinguish between ten million colors and the number of balls can be very large. So, if you are a classical purist who believes that this situation can be accommodated within classical subjective uncertainty, then try to imagine the possible colors and the Cartesian product of colors and the number of balls over which you must form a subjective distribution. It is far-fetched to imagine that humans could do this sort of thing, even if in principle we could allow for this possibility and the use of subjective uncertainty. As a practical matter, it is better to classify such a situation as one of true uncertainty.

The taxonomy of situations described above may be illustrated in the following colorful quote attributed to Donald Rumsfeld, the American secretary of state in 2002 (I have inserted the relevant situations of interest in square brackets):

"Reports that say that something hasn't happened are always interesting to me, because as we know, there are known knowns [risk and uncertainty]; there are things we know we know. We also know there are known unknowns [ambiguity]; that is to say we know there are some things we do not know. But there are also unknown unknowns [true uncertainty]—the ones we don't know we don't know. And if one looks throughout the history of our country and other free countries, it is the latter category that tend to be the difficult ones."

Economics has very little to offer by way of predictions for the important case of true uncertainty, and this book is no exception. This is a serious limitation of economics and of behavioral economics. One possible solution is to use heuristics, or simple rules of thumb, as a response to true uncertainty; see Dhami et al. (2018) for some development of this idea and for the references. We explore heuristics more fully in Volume 5. In what follows below, in Volume 1, we abstract away from situations of true uncertainty.

Chapter 1 considers the elements of neoclassical decision theory. We mainly focus on *expected utility theory* (EU). Our exposition of EU is slightly condensed because most readers are likely to have some familiarity with this material. We examine the preference foundations of EU and highlight the critical axioms that have been subject to empirical testing, particularly the *independence axiom*. We also discuss the celebrated result of Leonard J. Savage that derives a preference foundation for choices under uncertainty. The resulting representation of preference looks similar to EU and is called *subjective expected utility* (SEU). Thus, there is no essential problem in making choices under uncertainty, provided that we can assign subjective probabilities to the relevant events that satisfy the Kolgomorov axioms.

Most lay people would readily concede that probabilities have something to do with risk. However, under EU, risk attitudes are determined entirely by the shape of the utility function, which is not only counterintuitive but empirically false. Further, as shown by Matthew Rabin in a celebrated result, if the decision maker is risk averse over small stakes for all levels of income, then he will be unreasonably risk averse for large stakes. We also discuss various methods of eliciting the utility function under risk and uncertainty. In the rest of Chapter 1, we consider the main refutations of EU. We use the convenient device of a Marshak–Machina probability triangle to illustrate the nature of the refutations. It turns out that most refutations of EU lie along the edges of the probability triangle, but it is precisely along the edges that most important economic situations of interest also occur. Other refutations that we consider include *preference reversals, description invariance,* and *failure of the reduction of compound lotteries axiom.*

EU has two critical features. These are: (i) *linearity in probabilities*, and (ii) *utilities that depend only on final levels of outcomes*. In contrast, empirical evidence shows that decision makers engage in non-linear probability weighting, and their utility depends on changes in outcomes relative to some reference point that splits the outcome domain into gains and losses. Furthermore, their preferences, including risk preferences, differ fundamentally in these two domains. In Chapter 2, we consider a range of behavioral decision theories that relax at least one or both of these features of EU or even introduce new features; these theories explain the available evidence much better.

A central feature of most behavioral alternatives to EU is *non-linear probability weighting*. This is incorporated through the device of a *probability weighting function* that captures the way in which individuals mentally code objective or subjective probabilities. For aggregate data, one typically finds an *inverse S-shaped* probability weighting, i.e., low probabilities are overweighted and high probabilities are underweighted. At the individual level, however, there is a degree of heterogeneity: One observes convex, concave, and inverse S-shaped weighting.

Rank dependent utility (RDU) under risk and under uncertainty incorporates non-linear probability weighting, and in this class of models it is the most satisfactory alternative to EU. RDU replaces the (objective or subjective) probabilities in an EU functional by *decision weights* that are *cumulative transformations of probabilities*. Decision makers who use RDU never choose first order stochastically dominated options. It is possible to explain the Allais paradox under RDU and to give meaning to commonly used terms such as *optimism* and *pessimism* that play no direct role under EU. RDU is a significant improvement over EU, yet it cannot explain all the empirical evidence, particularly that arising from reference dependence.

Original prospect theory (OPT) and *cumulative prospect theory* (PT) incorporate non-linear probability weighting and *reference dependent* preferences; the second feature sets it apart from RDU. Reference dependence partitions the domain of outcomes into gain and loss domains. The utility function is concave in gains and convex in losses. Furthermore, losses bite more than equivalent gains, a phenomenon known as *loss aversion*, which is one of the most enduring features of human behavior. Human behavior turns out to be fundamentally different in the gain and the loss domains.

PT can be readily extended from risk to the cases of uncertainty and ambiguity. Using the essential insight of cumulative transformations of probabilities from RDU, Kahneman and Tversky altered OPT, which was published in 1979, to PT, which was published in 1992. This ensured that decision makers would not choose stochastically dominated options. However, the psychological richness in the editing phase of OPT, an essential and valuable feature of OPT, was also lost in this process. Evidence indicates that when stochastic dominance is obvious, people do not choose dominated options but when such dominance is less obvious, people may choose the dominated options. So rather than simply ruling out theories that allow for dominated options, we need to ask what is it that makes dominance transparent or opaque. This is an avenue that has been poorly explored.

Under EU, attitudes to risk are determined entirely by the shape of the utility function. However, under RDU, OPT, PT (and other theories that use non-linear weighting), attitudes to risk depend *jointly* on the shapes of the probability weighting function and the utility function. Attitudes to risk are even richer in PT as compared to RDU on account of gain and loss domains. One observes a *fourfold classification of risk* that can explain the simultaneous occurrence of insurance and gambling as well as many other phenomena. The neoclassical idea that risk is captured entirely by the shape of the utility function is no longer tenable and it is rejected by an immense body of empirical evidence.

In OPT and PT, the reference point is typically specified to be the *status quo*, a *fair* or *just* entitlement, or a *norm driven* entitlement, all of which are eminently reasonable. Indeed, there are strong evolutionary and social foundations for such reference points. However, under certain circumstances, the endowment of an individual may be stochastic (e.g., owning a stock that has risky returns). In this case, the reference point itself may be stochastic. This has led to the development of *third generation prospect theory* (PT^3) that can incorporate stochastic reference points. Another popular approach in recent years is the *Köszegi–Rabin* framework that allows the reference point to be *stochastic and endogenous* on account its rational expectations feature. Although this framework has gained widespread acceptance, rational expectations sits uneasily with the other evidence on human behavior that suggests bounded rationality of behavior. For this reason, stringent testing of theory is required; some of the emerging empirical evidence is not supportive of the theory, although expectations appear to enter into the calculation of reference points in many cases.

PT is the main, though not the only, decision theory under consideration in Chapter 2. The evidence suggests that it is the most satisfactory decision theory under risk and uncertainty.[2] We also discuss the elicitation of the various components of PT, give preference foundations for the theory, and note its limitations. We next consider a range of other behavioral decision theories that take account of factors that are not directly present in RDU, OPT, and PT. These theories include *regret theory*, the *theory of disappointment aversion*, the role of *salience* and *context* in making choices among risky alternatives, *case-based decision theory*, and *configural weights models*. Existing theories find it difficulty to explain human behavior for events of *very low probability*. In many situations of economic interest, one observes that a fraction of decision makers ignores events of very low probability, such as insurance against natural hazards, accidents caused by running red traffic lights, or driving and using mobile phones. We consider a modification of PT, *composite prospect theory* (CPT) that can account for such behavior. Our modification must await stringent empirical testing before it can be accepted.

The final topic in Chapter 2 considers the interaction between risk and time preferences, which has been, and will continue to be, an active area of research. We shall continue with this topic in Volume 3 of the book on behavioral time discounting.

Chapter 3 considers applications of behavioral theories of decision making. An important application is to the disparity between *willingness to accept* (WTA) of sellers who are endowed with an object and *willingness to pay* (WTP) for the same item by buyers. The disparity between WTA and WTP arises because sellers who are endowed with the object experience loss aversion when they part with it. However, loss aversion does not apply to parting with money, giving rise to the disparity. We also consider a range of other possible explanations of exchange disparities and factors that might weaken or enhance it.

Loss aversion is a fundamental trait of human nature that we share with close primate relatives. This includes chimpanzees and even capuchin monkeys that separated from the lineage that gave rise to humans some 35 million years ago. This suggests that the emergence of loss aversion precedes the evolutionary separation of humans from close primate relatives and that we are likely to be hardwired to exhibit it. An important implication of loss aversion is that there might be *no risk aversion beyond loss aversion*. In other words, economists picking out risk aversion in their data, might actually be picking out loss aversion.

---

[2] PT also applies to ambiguity, as we shall see below.

Some other applications that we consider in Chapter 3 are the following. In a two-horse race between EU and PT, we show that PT successfully explains the qualitative and quantitative tax evasion puzzles, but EU fails to do so. *Myopic loss aversion*, the empirically supported tendency to use very short horizons in evaluating gains and losses, explains several phenomena, e.g., the *equity premium puzzle* (high returns on equities relative to bonds that cannot be explained by plausible attitudes to risk aversion). We show that under PT, *Rabin's puzzle* that arises under EU (risk aversion over small stakes implies implausible risk aversion over larger stakes) is readily explained. We show that once goals and targets are recognized as reference points, PT is able to account for the relevance of goals in influencing human behavior that cannot be explained by EU and RDU. PT can also explain the backward-bending labour supply curve of New York taxi drivers. A range of applications of the finding of an inverse S-shaped probability weighting function are also given, although some of these, such as the *psychology of tail events*, are postponed to Volume 5. Finally, we apply PT to issues of optimal contracts, the formation of firms, and renegotiation of long-term contracts. These topics form a part of the exciting new literature on behavioral contract theory. Further developments in behavioral contract theory, based on other-regarding preferences, are given in Volume 2.

Chapter 4, the final chapter in Volume I, considers models of *ambiguity*. In order to maintain a common theme across the chapter, and for pedagogical reasons, we focus on the ability of alternative models to resolve the Ellsberg paradox. The discussion in the chapter distinguishes between *neoclassical models of ambiguity* and *behavioral models of ambiguity*. This is not just a convenient separation because most, but not all, neoclassical models of ambiguity reduce to EU under risk, while the behavioral models do not. This is problematic because the evidence is not supportive of EU. Further, the empirical evidence for neoclassical models of ambiguity aversion is mixed. In particular, we find ambiguity seeking for low probabilities and ambiguity aversion for higher probabilities. Furthermore, empirical evidence suggests the finding of *a-insensitivity* (see the guide to further reading at the end of Volume 1). Neoclassical models of ambiguity struggle to account for all these findings. For this reason, our discussion of the neoclassical models is brief. On the other hand, the behavioral models are more promising in terms of explaining the evidence, and these developments are taking place at a rapid pace.

Some of the neoclassical models that we consider are *Choquet expected utility*, *multiple priors models*, *two stage recursive models* that relax reduction of compound lotteries, and models of *second order beliefs* such as the *smooth ambiguity aversion model*. Among the behavioral models, we consider *support theory* and *source-based uncertainty*. Promising new empirical evidence suggests that prospect theory outperforms most of the standard neoclassical models. The contribution of behavioral economics to ambiguity has continued to expand in size, scope, and importance since the Foundations of Behavioral Economic Analysis was published in 2016. This is reflected in the new material at the end of Chapter 4 and in the guide to the more recent literature that follows it. This strengthens the case that prospect theory applies equally well to risk, uncertainty, and ambiguity.

Finally, we briefly outline some of the recent key papers and results since the publication of Dhami (2016) in a separate chapter at the end that is titled: A Guide to Further Reading. This material is referenced back to the relevant sections of Volume 1; it extends some of the key concepts and introduces some new ones such as ambiguity generated insensitivity (or a-insensitivity) index. The exercises for Volume 1 are situated at the end of this chapter.

Introduction to Behavioral Economics and the Book Volumes

The *neoclassical framework* in economics provides a coherent and internally consistent body of theory that offers rigorous, parsimonious, and falsifiable models of human behavior.[1] Augmented with auxiliary assumptions, it is flexible enough to analyze a wide range of phenomena. In actual practice, the neoclassical framework includes, but is not restricted exclusively to, consistent preferences, subjective expected utility, Bayes' rule to update probabilities, self-regarding preferences, emotionless deliberation, exponential discounting, unlimited cognitive abilities, unlimited attention, unlimited willpower, and frame and context independence of preferences.[2] Neoclassical economics is also typically underpinned by optimization-based solution methods and an equilibrium approach.

In principle, the neoclassical framework is capable of relaxing many of its standard assumptions. For instance, it can allow for reference dependence preferences, social preferences, frame dependent preferences, and non-exponential models of discounting. However, these extensions are rare in actual practice, and when they are made, the neoclassical framework typically does not have fundamental new insights to offer. For instance, adding reference dependent preferences generates few, if any, insights in the absence of a theory about how human behavior differs in the domains of gains and losses relative to a reference point. Similarly, adding other-regarding preferences without attempting to fit such a model to the behavior of humans, particularly to the evidence from experimental games, offers little progress. For these reasons, my use of the term *neoclassical economics* is shorthand for *the typical practice in neoclassical economics.*

The intellectual developments in neoclassical economics are impressive. However, its empirical success in predicting and explaining human behavior is modest. Indeed, an impressive, thorough and detailed body of experimental, neuroeconomic, and field evidence, based on several decades of work, raises serious concerns about the core assumptions and predictions of neoclassical models. This has been matched by impressive theoretical developments, drawing on insights from psychology, biology, anthropology, sociology, and other social sciences, that has come to be

---

[1] I avoid the loaded term *standard economics* to refer to *neoclassical economics* because this might give the latter a certain empirical sanctity.

[2] I have deliberately avoided the word 'rationality' in this description of the neoclassical framework because it would have to be precisely defined. See Dhami and al-Nowaihi (2018) for the various senses in which rationality is used in neoclassical economics.

known as *behavioral economics*. These models have had much greater empirical success relative to neoclassical models.[3]

There is a danger that one may propose definitions of behavioral economics that are either too broad and have ambiguous scope, or are too narrow with limited scope; each of these outcomes would be unfair for a newly emerging field. Any falsifiable theory that replaces/modifies any of the core features of neoclassical economics, by alternatives that have a better empirical foundation in human behavior is a potential member of the class of behavioral economic theories, if it can pass stringent empirical tests.

The aim of this book is to offer an account of formal behavioral economic theory, its applications, and a discussion of the underlying experimental and field evidence.[4] The standard toolkit in neoclassical economics is adequate for the study of behavioral economics. Most behavioral models adopt an optimization framework, are typically underpinned by axiomatic foundations, are parsimonious, rigorous, falsifiable, and internally consistent.[5]

We do not attempt to pit behavioral economics against neoclassical economics in a paradigmatic battle. As in every science, we progress by taking account of evidence that suggests a refinement and improvement of existing models. In this case, the relevant improvement appears to have the steepest gradient in the direction of constructively incorporating insights from other behavioral sciences. The book outlines a new research program that offers a constructive way forward for economics by highlighting developments in behavioral economic theory, which also uses core insights from neoclassical economics. It is likely that in due course, behavioral economics will cease to exist as a separate field within economics, and this will become the normal way in which we do economics.

A distinction is sometimes drawn between experimental economics and behavioral economics.[6] However, the activity of behavioral economists and experimental economists has turned out to be complementary and collaborative, as in the natural sciences. It is often difficult to spot the dividing line between their work. For instance, experimental economists not only test the predictions of economic models, but their results have often been critical in suggesting further developments in behavioral models. Behavioral theorists on the other hand, often suggest experiments that could test their proposed theories.

The introduction to these volumes is an important and critical separate chapter that I would encourage readers to peruse before plunging into the book. Section 1 briefly traces some of the historical developments that have led to modern behavioral economics. Section 2 considers important methodological issues that lie at the heart of how economists 'do' and 'should'

---

[3] Increasing the explanatory power of neoclassical economics is very worthwhile but Thaler (2015) adds another reason for studying behavioral economics in his inimitable style: "Behavioral economics is more interesting and more fun than regular economics. It is the un-dismal science."

[4] For a non-technical treatment of behavioral economics, the reader can consult the extremely readable and witty account by Thaler (2015) that offers a much more detailed historical account of developments in behavioral economics from the 1970s onwards from a personal perspective.

[5] I use the word "rigorous" purely for its practical appeal to most neoclassical economists but I agree with the sentiments expressed by Gintis (2009, p. xviii): "The economic theorist's overvaluation of rigor is a symptom of their undervaluation of explanatory power. The truth is its own justification and needs no help from rigor."

[6] Loewenstein (1999) gives a nice discussion of the methods in each of these areas and offers the following definition (p. F25): "BEs [behavioral economists] are methodological eclectics. They define themselves, not on the basis of the research methods that they employ, but rather their application of psychological insights to economics. In recent published research, BEs are as likely to use field research as experimentation...EEs [experimental economists] on the other hand, define themselves on the basis of their endorsement and use of experimentation as a research tool."

practice their craft. Section 3 considers the importance of the experimental method in behavioral economics. Section 4 offers brief comments about the organization of the seven volumes of this book. Section 5 outlines five theoretical ideas in behavioral economics, locating them within the larger literature, and evaluating them against the empirical evidence. Section 6 considers the empirical evidence on five interesting questions in behavioral economics. There are two appendices. Appendix A outlines the random lottery incentive mechanism that lies at the heart of the modern experimental method in economics. Appendix B asks you to think of 50 questions as a problem set, but I deliberately give you very little structure at this stage in order to enable a free-spirited approach to the answers. Rigorous answers to these questions can be found in the book.

1 Some antecedents of behavioral economics

While Adam Smith's justly celebrated book, *The Wealth of Nations*, is widely cited, his other book, *The Theory of Moral Sentiments*, has received less attention. *The Theory of Moral Sentiments* reads like an agenda for modern behavioral economics; it recognizes many behavioral phenomena such as loss aversion, altruism, emotions, willpower, and the planner–doer framework (Ashraf et al., 2005). Classical economists such as Jeremy Bentham wrote about the psychological underpinnings of utility and Francis Edgeworth wrote about social preferences (Camerer and Loewenstein, 2004). Bardsley et al. (2010) trace the beginnings of experimental economics to the classical economists such as David Hume, Stanley Jevons, and Francis Edgeworth; Jevon's marginal utility analysis derived its motivation from experimental observations about the relation between stimuli and sensations.

Two factors contributed to the gradual elimination of psychology from economics. First, around the turn of the twentieth century, there was "a distaste for the psychology of their period, as well as the hedonistic assumptions of Benthamite utility" (Camerer and Loewenstein, 2004). The second was the revealed preference approach popularized by Paul Samuelson that emphasized the observation of *choice behavior* rather than the psychological foundations for choice behavior (Bruni and Sugden, 2007). Glimcher and Fehr (2014, p. xviii) write: "It cannot be emphasized enough how much the revealed-preference view suppressed interest in the psychological nature of preferences, because clever axiomatic systems could be used to infer properties of unobservable preference from choice."

Important, and path-breaking, developments in behavioral economics took place in the 1950s and 1960s that included: violations of the independence axiom of expected utility theory (Allais, 1953); violations of subjective expected utility (Ellsberg, 1961; Markowitz, 1952); demonstration of the importance of bounded rationality (Simon, 1978; Selten, 1998);[7] and early work on quasi hyperbolic discounting (Phelps and Pollak, 1968). However, at that time, this work struggled to get the attention that it deserved.

An important catalyst for the development of behavioral economics was the decline of the behavioralist school in psychology, and the emergence of cognitive psychology. Cognitive psychology emphasized the role of mental processes in the understanding of tasks involving decision making, perception, attention, memory, and problem solving. Some cognitive psychologists naturally turned their attention to testing their models against the neoclassical framework.

---

[7] Simon (1978) refers to Herbert Simon's Nobel lecture that traces the historical development of bounded rationality through the 1950s and 1960s. Selten (1998) is an English-language version of a paper that appeared initially in German in 1962.

The two most important cognitive psychologists in this category were Daniel Kahneman and Amos Tversky, whose work in the 1970s helped kick-start modern behavioral economics. Along with Richard Thaler, who was an economist by training, and was struggling to make sense of several anomalies in neoclassical economics from the mid 1970s onwards, they are some of the earliest and most significant modern behavioral economists.

The second topic is the *role of experimental evidence in economics* that I consider in Section 3. The justification for this section is the continued skepticism of many economists about experimental economics, which constitutes an important part of the evidence base for behavioral economics. The following quote attributed to the Nobel Prize winner Gary Becker from a magazine interview (Camerer, 2015, p. 250) is probably not unrepresentative: "One can get excellent suggestions from experiments, but economic theory is not about how people act in experiments, but how they act in markets. And those are very different things. That may be useful to get suggestions, but it is not a test of the theory. The theory is not about how people answer questions. It is a theory about how people actually choose in market situations."

What follows is a somewhat long introduction, but this is a somewhat long book too. In mitigation, the first one third of the introduction largely deals with background material that reflects the somewhat unsettled nature of economics. My hope is that if a second edition of this book is ever written, then there would be enough convergence of views on this material so that I can safely omit it.

2 On methodology in economics

University degrees in Economics and the natural sciences typically do not require formal courses in methodology. Yet, while all the natural sciences subscribe to the scientific method and students of natural sciences instinctively know that this means, economics has taken a very different, and pernicious, direction that has little basis in the scientific method. Consider, for instance, the following quote from Gintis (2009, p. xvi) that nicely captures the essence of the problem:

Economic theory has been particularly compromised by its neglect of the facts concerning human behavior... I happened to be reading a popular introductory graduate text on quantum mechanics, as well as a leading graduate text in microeconomics. The physics text began with the anomaly of blackbody radiation, ... The text continued, page after page, with new anomalies... and new, partially successful models explaining the anomalies. In about 1925, this culminated with Heisenberg's wave mechanics and Schrödinger's equation, which fully unified the field. By contrast, the microeconomics text, despite its beauty, did not contain a single fact in the whole thousand-page volume. Rather the authors built economic theory in axiomatic fashion, making assumptions on the basis of their intuitive plausibility, their incorporation of the "stylized facts" of everyday life, or their appeal to the principles of rational thought.... We will see that empirical evidence challenges some of the core assumptions in classical game theory and neoclassical economics.

The actual practice of behavioral economics is influenced, directly or indirectly, by Popperian views on methodology (Popper, 1934, 1963). Popper begins by distinguishing between science and non-science. A scientific hypothesis must be falsifiable in the sense that it must specify the conditions under which the hypothesis can be rejected. Further, one can only refute theories but never prove that they are true. For instance, the observation of a million white swans is consistent with the hypothesis that "all swans are white" but does not prove that the hypothesis is true; for the very next observation could be a non-white swan.

The best recipe for the advancement of science, in the Popperian view, is to subject scientific hypotheses to stringent testing, i.e., expose the hypotheses to tests that are most likely to reject them. In the strict Popperian view, one observation that is contrary to a hypothesis rejects it. For instance, a single observation of a black swan rejects the hypothesis that all swans are white. Science progresses by advancing a new hypothesis that explains everything that a rejected hypothesis explained, but, in addition, it explains some new phenomenon that the rejected hypothesis could not. For an application of the Popperian position to economic contexts, see Blaug (1992), Hausman (1992), and Hands (2001).

One concern with the Popperian approach is that a test of a hypothesis is a joint test of the hypothesis and several auxiliary assumptions. Thus, a rejection may arise because the hypothesis is incorrect, or the auxiliary assumptions might have been rejected, or both; this is known as the *Duhem–Quine thesis* (DQT). For instance, in an experimental test that rejects mixed strategy Nash equilibrium, one might wonder if the rejection was caused by (1) one of several confounding factors, such as an inappropriate subject pool, unclear experimental instructions, and inadequate incentives, or (2) because subjects do not follow a mixed strategy Nash equilibrium. For this reason, a single refutation of a theory is not sufficient unless well replicated to account for all the main confounding factors that might be at play.

While the Popperian position is *prescriptive* (how should we best do science?), a *descriptive* view (how is science actually done?) was offered by Kuhn (1962). Kuhn noted that knowledge in science does not accumulate in a linear manner. He highlighted, instead, the role of periodic revolutions in science, or an abrupt transformation in the existing worldview, a *paradigm shift*. He distinguishes between three phases in the development of any science. In pre-science, there is no central paradigm, but there is an attempt to focus on a set of problems. In normal science, the longest of the three phases, there is the establishment of a central paradigm, great progress is made in answering many of the questions posed during pre-science, and much success is achieved in answering new questions. In a departure from the Popperian prescriptive position, in this phase, rejections of the paradigm are robustly challenged or ignored, and belief in the paradigm is unshakable. However, as anomalies gradually begin to accumulate, and reach a tipping point, a crises takes place in the paradigm. There is a sudden paradigm shift and a new paradigm that subsumes the old paradigm takes its place.

One prescriptive response to the DQT and to Kuhn's descriptive ideas, while retaining a Popperian approach, was proposed by Lakatos (1970) under the name: *The methodology of scientific research programs* (MSRP). Lakatos distinguished between a set of non-expendable statements or assumptions, which is the *hard core of a research program*, and a set of expendable auxiliary assumptions. In a distinctly non-Popperian recommendation, but reminiscent of the normal science phase of Kuhn, the hard core is insulated from refutation; this also addresses the DQT. For instance, Newtonian physics has a hard core that comprises the three laws of dynamics and a law of gravitation. Any refutation of the research program, in this phase, is then ascribed to a failure of the auxiliary assumptions, which are modified to explain the refutation.

One potential defense of this approach is that it allows for a period of time for the development of a new research program that can take account of the emerging refutations. However, a practical downside could be that proponents of a research program might engage in defensive methodology for far too long, and resist the development of a new research program that has a different hard core. To take account of this possibility, Lakatos termed a research program as *theoretically progressive* if refinements that take place by altering auxiliary assumptions but not the hard core, lead to the explanation of existing anomalies and to novel predictions. A research program is *empirically progressive* if the novel predictions are not refuted. Adherence to a hard core is only admissible if research programs are theoretically and empirically progressive.

Eventually anomalies play the most important part in giving rise to new research programs; Lakatos noted that all theories are born into and die in a sea of anomalies.[8] The reader may find below that the actual practice in behavioral and experimental economics appears to be closer to the Lakatosian view than the Popperian view.[9] For instance, in decision theory, the hard core may be thought to comprise completeness, transitivity, and first order stochastic dominance (Bardsley et al., 2010, p. 129). Indeed, neither expected utility theory nor the main behavioral alternatives such as rank dependent utility, theory of disappointment aversion, or prospect theory, are willing to relax the assumption of well-behaved preferences. This makes it difficult for most decision theories to explain framing effects, although prospect theory is potentially able to capture framing effects through changes in the reference point.

With this minimum background, consider "normal" practice in physics; I encourage the reader not to judge natural sciences by a few well-publicized outliers. In a letter to the *London Times*, dated November 28, 1919, Albert Einstein described his *theory of relativity* in comparison to *Newtonian physics*, to a lay audience. Einstein mentioned two predictions of his theory that had been confirmed (both in domains where his theory was most likely to fail, hence, these are "stringent tests"): (1) Revolution of the ellipses of the planetary orbits round the sun, which was confirmed for the orbit of Mercury. (2) The curving of light rays by the action of gravitational fields. He then mentioned one prediction that had not yet been confirmed (displacement of the spectral lines toward the red end of the spectrum in the case of light transmitted to us from stars of considerable magnitude); indeed, at the time Einstein published the theory of relativity it was not even clear how to test this prediction. Einstein then wrote (p. 4): "The chief attraction of the theory lies in its logical completeness. If a single one of the conclusions drawn from it proves wrong, it must be given up."

I invite the reader to pause for a moment to compare Einstein's approach with the "mainstream" views in economics that I have outlined above. Indeed, as Bardsley et al. (2010, p. 8) note: "But it is surprisingly common for economists to claim that the core theories of their subject are useful despite being disconfirmed by the evidence."

In light of this brief discussion on methodology and an illustration of best practice in the natural sciences, let us return to the "neglect of the facts concerning human behavior in economics" that Herbert Gintis highlights above. Why should such a situation have arisen? In order to understand this state of affairs, consider the following three representative views, written by some of the leaders in neoclassical economics.

Dekel and Lipman (2010, p. 264) write: "Hence the choice of a model will depend on the purpose for which the model is used, the modeler's intuition, and the modeler's subjective judgment of plausibility.... One economist may reject another's intuition, and, ultimately, the marketplace of ideas will make some judgments."

Gilboa et al. (2014, p. F. 516) write: "In particular, we agree that: economic models are often viewed differently than models in the other sciences; economic theory seems to value

---

[8] Closer to home, economists would remember the influential *anomalies feature* that Richard Thaler wrote for the *Journal of Economic Perspectives* from 1987 to 2006. Indeed, in the very first piece, Thaler, keenly aware of methodological issues, quoted from Thomas Kuhn.

[9] For a critique of the Lakatosian approach as applied to economics, see Hands (1991) and De Marchi and Blaug (1991).

generality and simplicity at the cost of accuracy; models are expected to convey a message much more than to describe a well-defined reality; these models are often akin to observations, or to gedankenexperiments; and the economic theorist is typically not required to clearly specify where his model might be applicable and how."

Rubinstein (2006, p. 882) writes: "As in the case of fables, models in economic theory are derived from observations of the real world, but are not meant to be testable. As in the case of fables, models have limited scope. As in the case of a good fable, a good model can have an enormous influence on the real world, not by providing advice or by predicting the future, but rather by influencing culture. Yes, I do think we are simply the tellers of fables, but is that not wonderful?"

None of these representative quotes stresses the centrality of the empirical evidence in rejecting economic models or the need to design stringent tests to refute them; in fact economic models are not even meant to be tested. They also take a relativist position (one economist may reject another's intuition, and, ultimately, the marketplace of ideas will make some judgments) and take the role of models in economics as conveying "messages" or telling "fables".

Modern economics has been heavily influenced by the *instrumental position* taken by Friedman (1953), which is partly reflected in the three quotes above. Friedman argued that we should not judge economic theories by the realism of their assumptions but rather, by the accuracy of their predictions. He writes (p. 14): "Truly important and significant hypotheses will be found to have 'assumptions' that are wildly inaccurate descriptive representations of reality, and, in general, the more significant the theory, the more unrealistic the assumptions....To be important, therefore, a hypothesis must be descriptively false in its assumptions." And shortly thereafter (p. 15) he writes: "To put this point less paradoxically, the relevant question to ask about the 'assumptions' of a theory is not whether they are descriptively 'realistic,' for they never are, but whether they are sufficiently good approximations for the purpose in hand."

A natural progression of Friedman's position can be found in Gilboa et al. (2014, F. 514): "Why does economic theory engage in relatively heavy technical analysis, when its basic premises are so inaccurate? Given the various violations of fundamental economic assumptions in psychological experiments, what is the point in deriving elaborate and carefully proved deductions from these assumptions? Why do economists believe that they learn something useful from analyzing models that are based on wrong assumptions?" Their answer to these questions is based on an identification of economic models with *case-based reasoning* rather than *rule-based reasoning*. Rule-based reasoning requires the formulation of general rules or theories. In contrast, case-based reasoning requires one to draw inferences based on similar past cases. The purpose of economic models, in this view, is to add to the bucket list of cases and analogies that can be used to draw inferences now, or at some point in the future.

These views give a fair bit of insight into contemporary thinking in economics about how we should go about practicing our craft. I also believe that acceptance of these views is widespread in the economics profession and many economists challenged on these views are surprised and outrightly dismissive. Initial intuition about economic models, whether motivated by existing empirical evidence, or a desire to make novel predictions, must begin from somewhere. Here, the role of initial conjectures as parables, useful stories, or fables to inform one's intuition about better and more complete models is surely important. But this cannot be the justification for continued reliance on a set of models that have faced persistent refutation, or to wish to shield them from refutation by seeking a special status for them.

Indeed, and it has to be said with great regret, many of the contemporary methodological views in economics are retrogressive and a license to engage in defensive methodology to protect the status quo. Friedman's approach has been much misused in economics. Consider the following entirely reasonable description of Friedman's approach to *model building* (as distinct from evaluating theories) in Gintis (2015, p. 223) that this book concurs with: "The goal of model-building [is] to create a tractable analytical structure, analyze the behavior of this structure, and test the fruitfulness of the results by comparing them with empirical data."[10]

The tendency to ignore or to discount experimental evidence in economics, despite its growing importance and prominence, when it contradicts neoclassical models is an indictment of the methodological approach taken in economics. Another important factor is that Friedman's instrumental position has been used as a license by some to make ad hoc auxiliary assumptions, and others to genuinely believe that their assumptions are literally true in an "as if" sense. Any empirical rejection of the "as if" assumptions is often rejected on the grounds that the evidence is flawed, untrustworthy, based on dubious experimental methods, or lacks external validity. This is a form of defensive methodology that is inimical to the progress of economics, and I urge the reader to resist it.

Behavioral economics offers an easier resolution of the "as if" approach. There is now compelling evidence, which shows that some of the central tenets of neoclassical economics are neither true in an "as if" sense, nor are their predictions always satisfactory when subject to stringent tests. So even on the grounds that Friedman favoured, *predictions of the relevant theory*, some of the central elements in neoclassical economics, such as self-regarding preferences, expected utility theory, exponential discounting, Bayes' Law, Nash equilibrium and its refinements, must either be significantly modified or abandoned. This book is replete with evidence that supports such a view. In particular, it is untenable to continue teaching the entire corpus of the existing status quo in economics on any scientific or logical grounds.

Schotter (2015) offers the following critique of Friedman's position. Suppose that assumptions x, y, and z lead to some theory T. Suppose also that one or more assumptions are violated by the empirical evidence, yet T makes a successful prediction. Then there are three possibilities. (1) The violated assumptions are superfluous for the theory, at least in the context where the theory was tested. (2) The violated assumptions counteract each other perfectly, so they do not affect the prediction. (3) The successful prediction is a fluke. Conversely, if the assumptions are correct and the model is complete then we expect T to make successful predictions anyway. Thus, it is difficult to justify a theory based on patently false assumptions. Schotter (2015, p. 63) observes, correctly: "after all, the assumptions are the theory."

My colleague, Ali al-Nowaihi, likes to give the following example that applies to birds who cannot swim (e.g., gannets can swim, so they are excluded). Birds fly, so one may theorize that they behave "as if" they understand the laws of aerodynamics. This is an admissible hypothesis, but then one must test the "as if" assumption. Given that air is basically a fluid, so birds might also be assumed to know the laws of hydrodynamics. If the "as if" presumption were true in this case, then birds released under water should try to swim, but they actually try to fly, and drown. Thus, the original "as if" supposition is false. If the "as if" assumptions are not tested properly, then we can never have any degree of confidence in the models based on these assumptions.

A common view in economics (shared unfortunately by some behavioral and experimental economists, I must add) appears to be that there is something rather difficult and unique about testing economic theories, relative to the natural sciences. So, at least implicitly, the argument

---

[10] Readers interested in pursuing this approach further can consult Godfrey-Smith (2006, 2009) and Wimsatt (2007).

goes, one needs to accord a "special status" to economic theories. Consider the following representative quote from Richard Lipsey's wonderful introduction to economics (Lipsey, 1979, p. 8) cited in Bardsley et al. (2010, pp. 6–7) that, I suspect, many economists would agree with: "Experimental sciences, such as chemistry and some branches of psychology, have an advantage because it is possible to produce relevant evidence through controlled laboratory experiments. Other sciences, such as astronomy and economics, cannot do this." A similar view is expressed in another celebrated text in economics (Samuelson and Nordhaus, 1985, p. 8): "Economists (unfortunately) ... cannot perform the controlled experiments of chemists or biologists because they cannot easily control other important factors. Like astronomers or meteorologists, they generally must be content largely to observe." This mainstream view is contestable, and must be contested. There appears to be a misunderstanding about the relative difficulty of testing theories in the natural sciences and in economics.

The view that testing of theories is somehow easy or easier in the natural sciences, as compared to economics, must surely be deeply offensive and insulting to experimenters in the natural sciences. The Higgs boson or Higgs particle was proposed by British physicist Peter Higgs in the early 1960s, and it took 50 years of incredibly hard efforts to confirm the particle in 2013. Particle physicists did not seek a *special status* for this theory that could insulate it from rejection. The enormously high energies required to test for the Higgs particle required the construction of a very expensive and complex experimental facility, CERN's Large Hadron Collider, that eventually confirmed the theory. Note also that Peter Higgs was made to wait 50-odd years and given the Nobel Prize in physics only after his theory was confirmed. He was not given the Nobel on any of the following criteria: elegant and beautiful theory, useful model that helped the intuition of particle physicists, or a fable or useful story that aids in the understanding of how the universe began.

Astronomers who dealt with the question of the distance of earth from distant objects, or the chemical composition of stars that are millions of light years away, did not also seek a special status for their subject. They got on with the difficult job of seeking the relevant measurements, often using indirect evidence and clever implications of theory. They were eventually successful after several decades of work. Are economists seriously arguing that their measurement problems are more difficult than the problems in the natural sciences? Cosmic microwave background radiation was first proposed in 1948, but experimentally confirmed due to an accidental discovery in 1964. DNA was first isolated in 1869, but it took the most part of a century to find the double-helix structure of DNA, and confirm it by experimental evidence in 1953. The germ theory of disease was proposed in the mid sixteenth century, yet confirmation of the theory occurred in the seventeenth century. The pool of such examples is very large. The process of discovery, measurement, and of testing the theory, can be a long and arduous one; seeking a special status for the subject is defeatist and put bluntly, lazy.

Economists opposed to lab/field data are likely to argue that the behavior of humans is too noisy, heterogeneous, and fickle, which is not a problem in the natural sciences (e.g., atoms are, after all, not subject to mood swings). This overstates the degree of difficulty in testing economic theories, relative to those in the natural sciences on at least two grounds.

1. Experimental economics has discovered systematic human behavior in many of the most important domains in economics. A small sample includes reference dependence, loss aversion, non-linear probability weighting, conditional cooperation, intention-based reciprocity, present-biased preferences, and the importance of emotions such as regret, guilt, and disappointment. These behaviors are also underpinned by neuroeconomic evidence.

Replication of standard experimental results is routine, and if similar subject pools and protocols are used, experiments produce replicable data. Examples are results from double auction experiments, and a range of games that demonstrate human prosociality, such as the ultimatum game, the gift exchange game, the trust game, and the public goods game; these examples can be multiplied manyfold, as the results in this book attest.

2. If indeed human behavior is inherently too noisy and heterogeneous, then economic theory needs to focus more efforts in this direction. When Brownian motion was discovered in 1827 by Robert Brown, in the behavior of pollen grains, physicists did not throw up their arms in despair. Important work in the late part of the nineteenth century, and by Einstein in the early twentieth century, paved the way for describing not only the mathematics of Brownian motion, but also predicting the probability distribution of particles in Brownian motion. Perhaps, in an analogous manner, economic theories need to predict the probability distribution of economic behavior, which can then be tested in experiments.

Experimental economics in the lab, and in the field, has made enormous progress in developing new econometric techniques for small samples, and in novel experimental methods. It has also deeply enhanced our understanding of human behavior and allowed for stringent testing of economic theory. This progress is inconsistent with the view that we should grant a special status to economic theories that exempts them from careful and stringent testing. The differences in experiments in economics and the natural sciences are much smaller relative to the differences in attitudes and institutions in the two fields of study. Progress in economics will be substantially enhanced if we learn from best practice elsewhere, and give up our implicit demand for special status.

3 The experimental method in economics

Work on experiments in behavioral economics gained momentum following the seminal work of Daniel Kahneman and Amos Tversky in the 1970s. However, a number of important experiments in economics were also conducted in the late 1940s, the 1950s, and the 1960s. These include Edward H. Chamberlin's testing of general competitive equilibrium (Chamberlin, 1948); Maurice Allais' work on demonstrating violations of the independence axiom in expected utility theory (Allais, 1953); Vernon Smith's work on induced value elicitation and double auction experiments in competitive settings (Smith, 1962); and Sidney Siegel's experiments on bargaining (Siegel and Fouraker, 1960). Other prominent figures who were either involved in experimental economics, or expressed an interest in it during the 1950s and 1960s included Ward Edwards, Reinhard Selten, Martin Schubik, Herbert Simon, Charles Plott, Donald Davidson, and Pat Suppes; for a brief historical sketch, see Guala (2008) and Bardsley et al. (2010).

Experimental economics is now mainstream by most yardsticks, particularly in terms of its presence in peer-reviewed journals in economics. In his early surveys on experimental economics, Roth (1987, 1988) hoped that experimental economics would perform three kinds of functions: Speaking to theorists (testing economic theory), searching for facts (generating novel empirical regularities that could be modeled by subsequent theory), and whispering in the ears of princes (offering reliable policy advice). Roth (2015) takes stock of experimental economics on these criteria and finds that it is thriving. One of his case studies, on bargaining behavior, is outlined in detail in Volume 4 of the book.

At one level, there has been a complete denial of the usefulness of experiments in economics. Friedman (1953, p. 10) views the domain of empirical testing in economics to be naturally occurring field data: "Unfortunately, we can seldom test particular predictions in the social sciences by experiments explicitly designed to eliminate what are judged to be the most important disturbing influences. Generally, we must rely on evidence cast up by the 'experiments' that happen to occur." A modern critique of the experimental method in economics is offered by Levitt and List (2007). They list several objections to experimental results that I address in subsequent sections.

(1) Participants in experiments are subjected to unprecedented experimental scrutiny. Since subjects may perceive that they are being watched over by the experimenter, they may give responses that the experimenter really desires (*experimenter demand effects*; see Zizzo, 2010) or they may not reveal their true underlying preferences. For instance, they worry that participants may engage in more prosocial behavior than they really intend to.

Whilst I reserve my detailed responses to later sections, I find it somewhat curious that if subjects are accused of being influenced by experimenter demand effects, say out of reciprocity, guilt, or shame, then they appear to exhibit social preferences (or emotions reflected in beliefs may directly enter their utility functions, as in psychological game theory), which is precisely what is being disputed by the critics.

(2) In actual practice, human decisions are context-dependent and influenced by cues, social norms, and past experiences. It is not clear that experiments can capture these factors. For instance, participants in experiments may import an inappropriate "outside context" into their responses in experiments.

(3) Actual human behavior is strongly affected by stake sizes in experiments. Experiments are typically conducted with small stakes, so they might not capture the richness of human behavior that arises from varying stakes.

(4) There could be self-selection biases caused by student volunteers who might be particularly prosocial, younger, more educated, and have a higher need for approval, as compared to the average human population. In contrast, people who self-select themselves into real market situations might be particularly suitable to do well in real markets.

(5) Choice sets in experiments might be particularly restrictive relative to the real world. For instance, there could be more prosocial options in experiments relative to the real world.

(6) The results of lab experiments may generalize poorly to real-world behavior for all of the reasons mentioned in (1) through (5), above. This issue of *external validity* of lab experiments is the main concern raised by the authors who write (p. 170): "Perhaps the most fundamental question in experimental economics is whether findings from the lab are likely to provide reliable inferences outside of the laboratory."

This discussion briefly encapsulates the modern case against experimental economics. Let us now briefly examine these claims.

3.1 *Experiments and internal validity*

Experiments allow for unprecedented control over the economic environment, hence, they have high *internal validity*, which is critical for stringent tests of economic theories. Internal validity is reduced when there are, for instance, selection issues, confounds in treatments, and unclear experimental instructions, all of which are carefully addressed in modern experimental work. Thus, in well-conducted experiments, the complicated identification strategies of field studies can be replaced by clever and much simpler experimental design.

For instance, suppose that a researcher is interested in testing if higher wages elicit higher effort in a firm; this is known as a *gift exchange game*. A field experiment is likely to be influenced by strategic behavior and reputational concerns of the workers and firms; field experiments, in general, are likely to have lower internal validity. However, in a lab experiment, these factors are easily controlled, allowing one to cleanly separate the relation between a fair wage and effort. The high degree of experimental control in lab experiments allows for replication of lab results. For the converse reason, the results of field experiments are more difficult, and sometimes impossible to replicate when one is given access to a unique field environment.

Experiments can also test the predictions of theory in a parameter space that might be difficult to observe in the field. This is similar to extreme stress tests of aircraft frames under conditions that are not normally encountered in the actual operation of the aircraft, or the exposure of bridge designs to extreme environmental conditions. In a nutshell, all this allows for more stringent tests of economic theory. Experiments are sometimes criticized on the grounds that the sample sizes are small. Falk and Heckman (2009) term this issue as a "red herring" on the grounds that there have been important developments in small sample econometrics, and many experiments do use large subject pools.

Camerer (2015) argues that there is no evidence of experimenter demand effects, despite the suspicion that there might be such effects; see also his discussion of the alternative inter- pretations of experimenter demand effects in Hoffman et al. (1998). There are several reasons why experimenter demand effects may be weak or non-existent. Such demand effects require two conditions. First, subjects must know the experimenter's preferred hypothesis. Second, they should be willing to sacrifice their own experimental earnings in order to favor the experimenter's preferred hypothesis.

On a-priori grounds, arguably, it is often quite hard for subjects to know the experimenter's preferred hypothesis. This arises particularly when (i) experimental instructions are carefully worded to prevent any such inference, and (ii) the experimenter might not be sure which of the competing hypotheses actually hold. However, if subjects can somehow guess the preferred hypothesis, then stakes can be raised to levels where they are too difficult to sacrifice for the sake of pleasing the experimenter. However, in most cases, the results with high stakes are not dramatically different from those with modest stakes (Camerer and Hogarth, 1999).[11] In three preference reversal experiments, Lambdin and Shaffer (2009) find that the percentage of subjects who were successfully able to guess the preferred hypothesis of the experimenter was 7%, 32%, and 3%.

The degree of anonymity in lab experiments can be varied, so it is an ideal environment to test for the effects of variation in the degree of anonymity (Bolton et al., 1998). One's actions are often observed by others in real-world situations, and in many field situations, where controlling for such scrutiny, and varying its level, is arguably even more difficult. The criticism of lab experiments on grounds of scrutiny (by the experimenter and other participants), also applies to field experiments, insofar as field subjects realize that they are in an experiment. Such experimenter demand effects may arguably, in many cases, be even stronger in field experiments, which are typically run in collaboration with governmental and semi-governmental bodies, and NGOs.

---

[11] Andersen et al. (2011) consider extremely high stakes ultimatum game experiments; the stakes vary from the equivalent of 1.6 hours of work to 1600 hours of work. The median offer by the proposer is to give 20% of the share to the respondent, but the rejection rate falls with the increase in the stake. In real life, we rarely make decisions involving 1600 hours of work, yet social preferences were not eliminated in the experiment.

It is indeed the case that when subjects are observed in dictator game experiments in the lab, they give higher amounts (Dana et al., 2007; Haley and Fessler, 2005). In many real-world giving situations, actions are also observed by others; for instance, church collections that take the form of passing along a collection plate/basket, or having to declare one's charitable contributions for tax purposes. However, the effect of being observed disappears if one introduces a minimal element of strategic interaction as, say, in an ultimatum game (Barmettler et al., 2012). A more important determinant of giving in dictator games is whether income is earned or not. Giving in dictator game experiments falls to about 4.3% of an endowment of $10, when income is earned, relative to about 15% of the endowment in the case of unearned income (Cherry et al., 2002); the figure of 4.3% is closer to the corresponding field benchmark of charitable giving in the US, which stands at about 1% of income (Camerer, 2015).

A commonly heard critique of behavioral models of social preferences is that if experimentally observed social preferences are so important, then, putting it rather starkly, why do we not observe people giving envelopes stuffed with money to others (Bardsley et al., 2010, p. 53)? When dictators in experiments give out of earned income, then the extent of giving is not too far off from the rate of charitable giving (4.3% versus 1% for the case of US; see above). In the real world, subjects give money for charitable and other good causes out of after-tax income, which is not the case in the lab. So imagine that in dictator games in the lab with earned income, the dictator was told: "Here is your endowment of $10, which you have earned. We are taking 30% off as taxes, which we will partly use for redistributive purposes to the recipient in the experiment. How much of the rest will you offer to the recipient?" It would be surprising if the 4.3% giving in lab dictator games does not get closer to the 1% figure for charitable giving in the field. Similar observations apply to proposer offers and responder rejections in lab experiments that do not include a tax redistributive component. If this is the case, then giving in experiments may also be tapping into the innate human desire to redistribute to others, that is, at least partly, codified institutionally in the social welfare state.

3.2 Subject pools used in lab experiments

It is not unusual in many quarters to dismiss experiments conducted on students, the typical lab subject pool, as having limited or no relevance to testing economic theories. There are several objections to this claim that we now outline.

Economic theory does not specify the subject pool on which its predictions are to be tested. Gilboa et al. (2014, p. F516) write "the economic theorist is typically not required to clearly specify where his model might be applicable and how." Clearly, one cannot have it both ways by not specifying a subject pool and then objecting to a particular subject pool. This view has been popularized in Vernon Smith's *blame the theory argument*. Writing in the context of incentives in experiments, Smith (2001) writes in his abstract: "The rhetoric of hypothesis testing implies that game theory is not testable if a negative result is blamed on any auxiliary hypothesis such as 'rewards are inadequate.' This is because either the theory is not falsifiable (since a larger payoff can be imagined, one can always conclude that payoffs were inadequate) or it has no predictive content (the appropriate payoff cannot be prespecified)."

One concern with the student subject population is that students might not have the necessary and relevant experience to conform to the predictions of the theory. However, one can allow lab subjects to gain experience in the lab by repeatedly making decisions; indeed, many lab experiments examine such learning effects and the effects of experience. We postpone a fuller discussion of these issues to Section 3.4, where we consider the external validity of lab experiments.

Students possess higher than average education and intelligence, which should be rather favorable to tests of neoclassical economic theory that requires economic agents to possess high levels of cognitive ability. It often comes as a surprise to the critics, but student subjects are much less prosocial relative to non-student subject pools (Falk et al., 2013; Carpenter and Seki, 2011; Anderson et al., 2013).[12] In a review of 13 studies that satisfy stringent tests of comparability, Fréchette (2015) finds that either there was very little difference between the behavior of students and professionals, or students were actually closer to the predictions of neoclassical theory. CEOs are often more trusting as compared to the student population (Fehr and List, 2004). More prosocial students do not self-select themselves as subjects in experiment (Cleave et al., 2012). Students who self-select themselves into experiments are motivated by monetary rewards (Abeler and Nosenzo, 2015), or interest in experimental lab tasks (Slonim et al., 2013). This evidence stands in contrast to the characterization of students in Levitt and List (2007) (based on two studies conducted in the 1960s) as scientific do-gooders who cooperate with experimenters to seek social approval.

3.3 *Stake sizes in experiments*

Economic theory does not specify the size of the stakes for which its predictions hold. Experimental economics is typically criticized for its low stakes. The evidence on stake size effects is mixed. However, many experimental results continue to hold, at least qualitatively, even with higher stakes (Slonim and Roth, 1998; Cameron, 1999). The most prominent effect of stakes arises when one moves from hypothetical payoffs to some strictly positive incentives. However, there is much less difference between moderate and high stakes; in particular, the main effect is a reduction in the variance of responses (Camerer and Hogarth, 1999).

There are two issues with high stakes, which are understated in many critiques of experimental economics. First, the vast majority of decisions that we make in real life are low stake decisions. How many times do we buy a car, a house, or a consumer durable such as a TV/laptop? Second, the main evidence for stake effects comes from experiments themselves. Third, as Thaler (2015) notes, the insistence on high stakes arises presumably because we are supposed to pay greater attention to economic decisions involving high stakes. But our success and expertise in making economic decisions is as much a matter of practice and learning. Since high stakes decisions are rare, we get limited opportunities to learn and make optimal decisions; the converse is true of low stakes decisions. Hence, there is no supposition that high stakes decisions should be closer to the predicted outcomes in neoclassical economics. So, he argues, correctly, that economists need to make up their minds whether they wish to insist on high stakes or low stakes as the appropriate test of their theories. Either way, experiments still offer the most natural environment to test the effect of stakes, which is an argument for more, not fewer, experiments.

3.4 *The issue of the external validity of lab findings*

Camerer (2015) distinguishes between the *policy view* and the *scientific view*. In the policy view, generalizability of lab findings to the field, or *external validity*, is essential. In the scientific

---

[12] However, student subjects might be more prosocial when it comes to volunteering time (Slonim et al., 2013).

view, all properly gathered evidence, including lab and field evidence, serves to enhance our understanding of human behavior. In this view, there is no hierarchical relation between lab and field evidence, and it is a mistake to pose the issue as if one had to make a choice between the two kinds of evidence. Camerer (2015, p. 251) explains cogently: "In this view, since the goal is to understand general principles, whether the 'lab generalizes to the field' (sometimes called 'external validity' of an experiment) is distracting, difficult to know (since there is no single 'external' target setting), and is no more useful than asking whether 'the field generalizes to the lab.'"

To understand Camerer's argument more fully, consider the following simple formalization in Falk and Heckman (2009). Suppose that we are interested in some variable Y that can be explained fully by the variables $X_1, X_2, \ldots, X_n$ and the "true" functional relation between them is given by $Y = g(X_1, X_2, \ldots, X_n)$, which is sometimes known as an *all causes model*. A researcher may be interested in examining the causal effect of X_1 on Y, holding fixed all other variables $\widehat{X} = (X_2, X_3, \ldots, X_n)$. For instance, in gift exchange experiments, Y is the level of effort of a worker and X_1 is the level of wage paid by the firm. The all causes model will typically include many factors in the vector $\widehat{X}$, such as the number of firms and workers, choice sets, payoff functions, incentives, demographic characteristics, regulatory environment, and moral and social characteristics of the parties involved.

When the relevant hypothesis is tested in the lab, the researcher estimates a model of the form $Y = f(X_1, X^L)$, rather than the all causes model $Y = f(X_1, \widehat{X})$, where $X^L \neq \widehat{X}$; X^L includes variables such as incentives given in the experiment, the endowments of subjects, the subject pool, context, and the structure of payoffs. One may also conduct field experiments in which one estimates a model of the form $Y = f(X_1, X^{F_1})$, where $X^{F_1} \neq \widehat{X}$, and typically $X^{F_1} \neq X^L$. Field experiments are conducted with a particular subject pool, such as sports card traders in List (2006).

The typical claim by critics of the experimental method is that $f(X_1, X^L)$ does not satisfy external validity, but $f(X_1, X^{F_1})$ does satisfy it. Now suppose that we are interested in examining the gift exchange relation in yet another population of subjects in the field, say, part time employees at General Motors. This gives rise to yet another estimated relation $Y = f(X_1, X^{F_2})$, where X^{F_2} reflects the set of variables and their characteristics in this field experiment. Is there any particular reason why the results based on the model $Y = f(X_1, X^{F_1})$ are more relevant, as compared to $Y = f(X_1, X^L)$, for predicting the causal effects of X_1 in the relation $Y = f(X_1, X^{F_2})$? Camerer (2015, p. 256) offers his assessment (expressed in our notation): "If the litmus test of 'external validity' is accurate extrapolation to X^{F_2}, is the lab X^L necessarily less externally valid than the field setting X^{F_1}? How should this even be judged?" Falk and Heckman (2009, p. 536) go slightly further: "The general quest for running experiments in the field to obtain more realistic data is therefore misguided. In fact, the key issue is what is the best way to isolate the effect of X_1 while holding constant $\widehat{X}$."

Since the criterion for external validity is unclear, it is best to treat lab and field evidence as complementary. Lab evidence allows for much tighter control of the variables in $\widehat{X}$. Field experiments allow for a larger variation in some aspects of $\widehat{X}$ (e.g., different subject pools with different demographic and social characteristics) while lab experiments allow for larger variation in other aspects of $\widehat{X}$ (e.g., exploration of the parameter space for values that can be hard or rare to find in the field). Lab experiments allow for greater replication because they are less costly and the economic environment in the lab can be more tightly controlled, while any specific field environment could be fairly unique.

We review the evidence for the generalizability of lab evidence to the field in many parts of this book. We end this section with the following bold claim from Camerer (2015, p. 277) made from studies where the lab and field evidence can be well matched: "There is no replicated evidence that experimental economics lab data fail to generalize to central empirical features of field data (when the lab features are deliberately closely matched to field features)." Readers interested in these issues can further consult Camerer (2015, pp. 281–5) for a list of studies that show a good association of lab behavior with field behavior in studies where it is more difficult to match the lab and the field evidence due to differences in the design or subject population.

Not everyone within the experimental economics community is willing to dismiss the importance of external validity. For instance, Kessler and Vesterlund (2015) believe that aiming for external validity is important, that qualitative experimental results have high degree of external validity, and that the concerns about external validity pertain only to quantitative experimental results. However, using a relatively large number of studies, Herbst and Mas (2015) show that peer effects on worker output in lab experiments and field studies from naturally occurring environments are quantitatively very similar. Hence, experiments appear to have external validity, even for quantitative estimates.

In light of the discussion above, the reader may perhaps appreciate better the view taken in this book that all sources of evidence, lab experiments, field experiments, and field data are equally valid and complementary in nature.

3.5 *The role of incentives in economics*

The norm in experimental economics is that all decisions made by subjects, or any elicitations of their underlying preferences in experiments, should be incentive compatible. It would currently be near impossible to get an experimental paper published in an economics journal if it did not respect incentive compatibility, preferably by using monetary rewards. In contrast, psychology does not require similar adherence to incentives. Camerer and Hogarth (1999) perform a meta-study of 74 studies, over the period 1990–8, in the leading economics journals: *American Economic Review*, *Econometrica*, *Journal of Political Economy*, and *Quarterly Journal of Economics*. Not a single experimental study in this sample was published without the use of incentives. In a meta-study over the period 1988–97, Hertwig and Ortmann (2001) found that only 26% of the articles published in a leading journal in psychology, the *Journal of Behavioral Decision Making*, used monetary task related incentives.

Economists have traditionally viewed effort as aversive and requiring scarce cognitive resources. Hence, they believe that people will exert effort only if the marginal disutility of effort is exceeded by the marginal utility of monetary incentives (*extrinsic motivation*). By contrast, psychologists have stressed the *intrinsic motivation* of subjects in experiments that does not require task related monetary incentives. Psychologists do pay subjects a show-up fee and/or course credit because it may be unethical to pay less than a minimum wage for a student's time and also because the fixed fee may elicit a reciprocal response by priming intrinsic motivation. Another difference between experiments in economics and psychology is that in the former, experimental practice is much more standardized and regulated (Hertwig and Ortmann, 2001). For instance, deception is taboo in economics experiments, but its practice is variable in psychology experiments.

Smith (1976) made an early recommendation for the use of incentives, based on his experience in double auction experiments. Employing monetary incentives in experiments is also a common recommendation by some of the pioneers in the field (Davis and Holt, 1993; Roth, 1995; Smith, 1991; Smith and Walker, 1993). The effectiveness of incentives, particularly in settings outside double auction experiments, is an empirical question. Several meta studies of the effect of incentives are now available, which show that the effect of monetary incentives on effort and performance in experiments is quite subtle. Neither of the following two extreme positions is supported by the evidence: Incentives make no difference and incentives remove all behavioral anomalies.

However, there is a caveat to these meta studies. Since the underlying preferences are unobserved, in experiments, task performance and incentive compatibility are measured by compliance with the predictions of the underlying theory. However, the underlying theory might itself be refuted by the evidence. One might then fall back on measuring the effect of incentives on the effort undertaken by the subjects (an input), rather than the performance in the task (the output); for a brief survey of these studies, see Bardsley et al. (2010, Chapter 6). However, in many tasks, effort might not improve performance. For instance, consider subjects in experiments engaged in non-trivial strategic interaction. In most games, it would be hard for the players to hit upon the Nash equilibrium purely by deduction, even if incentives were high.

The results reported in the careful meta-study by Camerer and Hogarth (1999) are particularly instructive. In many economic environments, such as choosing among risky gambles, market trading, and bargaining, the weight of the evidence (and the modal result) shows that increasing incentives does not change the average behavior. However, incentives often reduce the variance of outcomes. Incentives may sometimes harm the performance of subjects in experiments, for instance, subjects may choke under pressure (Ariely et al., 2009); their intrinsic motivation may be crowded out, and they may engage in too much payoff-reducing experimentation to avoid negative incentives such as punishments (Hogarth et al., 1991);[13] they may place too great a reliance on personal judgment, when relying on public information would have improved payoffs (Arkes et al., 1986); they may experience motivational crowding-out, e.g., in the presence of incentives, individuals do not feel responsible for their own behavior (Gneezy and Rustichini, 2000b); individuals might be insulted by the low level of incentives (Gneezy and Rustichini, 2000a). However, for another set of problems, mostly in judgment tasks, financial incentives affect average performance. Typically, the nature of these tasks is such that increased effort improves performance. Examples include memory retrieval tasks, tasks where recalling the play in previous rounds improves predictions, or mundane tasks such as piece-rate clerical work where one might be easily bored, e.g., counting the number of occurrences of a particular alphabet on a page of English text.

The meta-study by Bonner et al. (2000) supports the results of the Camerer–Hogarth study. They find that incentives have little effect in problem solving tasks, highest positive effects in tasks where effort improves performance (e.g., clerical tasks, pain endurance, or detecting typos on a page), and weak positive effects in judgment tasks. Hertwig and Ortmann (2001) find moderately positive effect of incentives. However, their sample size is small. Only 48 out of 186 studies (26%) that they considered used financial incentives. Of these, only ten explored the effect of monetary payments. One of their suggestions is to use different treatments that do use and do not use monetary incentives to build a better picture of the effect of incentives.

Clearly, a reduction in the variance of responses in the presence of incentives, in some experiments, is desirable on the grounds that it improves the statistical power of tests. However,

---

[13] For a formal model that shows the trade-off between intrinsic and extrinsic motivation, see Bénabou and Tirole (2003).

economics advocates a cost–benefit approach, and research funding for experiments is a scarce resource. Hence, one has to trade off the reduced variance against performing more experiments with bigger subject pools in the absence of monetary incentives. Greater variance of responses produces more outliers, but as Camerer and Hogarth (1999, p. 31) point out, there are alternative solutions: "Of course, other methods might work the same magic more cheaply. Trimmed means and robust statistical methods also reduce the influence of outliers."

So what explains the absolute adherence of experimental economists to incentives as a matter of norm? Bardsley et al. (2010, pp. 249–50) conjecture a cynical explanation: "A reason often given to psychologist's opposition to them is that incentives present an obstacle to less-experienced researchers who find it harder to secure research funding. It may be that economists are less concerned by the presence of such obstacles, or even that some actively promote the use of incentives as a barrier to entry." Many psychologists remain unconvinced of the arguments that experimenters in economics propose in favor of using incentives. For instance, Read (2005, p. 265) concludes his paper as follows: "... there is no basis for requiring the use of real incentives to do experimental economics."

The decision to employ incentives is a part of the experimental design. But as a practical matter, experimenters interested in publishing their work in economics journals have little choice in this matter. A second issue in the design of experiments is the level of incentives and the context. Gneezy and Rustichini (2000b) use four different levels of incentives, zero, low, medium, and high, to check for the level effect and conduct two different experiments to check for context effects. In one experiment, the IQ experiment, they find that incentives improve performance when one compares the levels low and high; but there was no difference between medium and high incentives. In the second experiment, the donations experiment, donations were highest when no incentives were given; in this case, intrinsic motivation is superior to extrinsic motivation. Using the same dataset, Rydval and Ortmann (2004) find that ability levels of individuals explained greater variation in performance relative to incentives. The assessment offered by Bardsley et al. (2010, p. 253) on the level of incentives is this: "The message seems to be that in terms of the impact on cognitive effort allocation the presence of task related incentives matters more than their level."

How can an experimental economist who has decided to run experiments using incentives ensure that the responses by the subjects are incentive compatible? Typically, incentive compatibility in experiments has been defined with respect to expected utility theory; however, the behavior of the majority of people is not consistent with expected utility theory. Hence, judging incentive compatibility is a vexed task. For instance, the leading method of ensuring incentive compatible choices, the *random lottery incentive scheme* (RLI), that we outline in Appendix A, depends crucially on the *independence axiom* of expected utility theory. However, if the decision maker does not follow expected utility but follows, say, rank dependent utility or prospect theory, then the independence axiom does not hold. Thus, choices are not guaranteed to be incentive compatible.

The evidence against expected utility is now overwhelming, as we do indeed explore in this book, and the independence axiom has been rejected in many empirical tests (e.g., *Allais paradox*). Bardsley et al. (2010) argue, however, that despite the rejection of the independence axiom, empirical evidence shows that the random lottery mechanism does not bias results. They write (p. 270): "it may simply be a happy coincidence that the RLI works, by engaging a particular mental heuristic that promotes unbiased task responses." Some readers might find this argument to be weak, and will wish to seek further clarification of the underlying mechanism that makes RLI an empirically attractive option.

Another popular incentive compatible mechanism in experiments that relies on an expected utility formulation is the *Becker–DeGroot–Marshak mechanism* (BDM) (Becker et al., 1964). This is typically employed in eliciting the willingness to pay and the willingness to accept for an object. Subjects in their roles as sellers are asked to state their valuation, v, for an object. A random price, p, is then drawn. If $p \leq v$, then a seller is not allowed to sell but if $p > v$, then the seller must sell. Subjects who follow expected utility should report their true valuations. To see this, suppose that the seller's valuation for an object is believed to be distributed randomly over the interval $[\underline{v}, \overline{v}]$, the true valuation is v, and the price is drawn randomly from the interval $[\underline{v}, \overline{v}]$, using the distribution F. Suppose that the seller chooses to declare a low valuation, $v_L < v$. In this case, the seller chooses to forgo a profitable opportunity to sell if the price turns out to be in the interval $(v_L, v]$ and the expected forgone profits are $\int_{v_L}^{v} (v - p) dF(p) > 0$. Thus, the seller never declares a low valuation. Now suppose that the seller declares a high valuation, $v_H > v$. In this case, the seller risks the potential expected loss $\int_{v}^{v_H} (v - p) dF(p) < 0$, so he never overstates his valuation. In short, the BDM is incentive compatible under expected utility. A direct implementation of the BDM has been found not to be incentive compatible (Bohm et al., 1997). However, suppose decision makers are presented with ascending or descending prices and must choose to trade or not at these prices. In the end, one of the trades is picked at random and paid off. There is some evidence that this version of the BDM may be incentive compatible (Braga and Starmer, 2005).

Similar calculations as employed in the BDM show that the *second price auction* (bidders bid simultaneously, and the winner pays the second highest bid) is also incentive compatible under expected utility. Bardsley et al. (2010, Chapter 6) review evidence which shows that the responses in BDM and the second price auction are sensitive to experience and, in later rounds, valuations are likely to converge to the true values. But the evidence on the incentive compatibility of variants of the *Vickery auctions* (which is a more general form of second price auctions) is mixed. They write (p. 274): "the efficacy of particular elicitation mechanisms can vary across different types of tasks. Indeed, whether an elicitation mechanism works may depend on the kind of research question that motivates its use."

To summarize, the discussion on incentive compatible elicitation mechanisms in experiments raises uncomfortable questions for the practice of experimental economics. First, predicted incentive compatibility relies on theories such as expected utility theory that have inadequate empirical support. Second, there are no universally agreed on mechanisms that will guarantee incentive compatibility in experiments and it very much comes down to a matter of judgment of the experimenter. Third, despite the firm insistence of experimental economists to use task related incentives, the theoretical response to these problems (e.g., the development of incentive compatibility under behavioral decision theories) appears to be inadequate.

3.6 *Is survey data of any use?*

Section 3.5 shows that there is often merit in the use of incentives, e.g., usefulness in double auction experiments, judgment tasks, effort related responses as in clerical tasks, and reduction in variation of responses. However, it is fair to say that the empirical case for the use of incentives in experiments is not as strong as is typically made out within the experimental economics community. Hence, one needs to consider other sources of data too in order to build a composite picture of human behavior. Most economists mistrust *survey data* and data based on *hypothetical questions* on the grounds that subjects are not incentivized to reveal their true preferences. This is due to the traditional belief in economics that people mainly have *extrinsic* rather than *intrinsic* motivation.

In the history of behavioral economics, the reliance on hypothetical questions and survey data often gave rise to deep insights that allowed for major advances. Two prominent examples include the work of Daniel Kahneman and Amos Tversky on prospect theory (Kahneman and Tversky, 1979) based on hypothetical questions in lab experiments, and the work of Daniel Kahneman, Richard Thaler, and Jack Knetsch on fairness motivations in humans (Kahneman et al., 1986) based on hypothetical questions posed in telephone surveys. Kahneman and Tversky (1979) is the second most cited paper in all of economics, the catalyst for the Nobel prize to Kahneman, and the source of prospect theory, which is currently the most satisfactory decision theory under risk, uncertainty, and ambiguity.[14] Yet the paper is based on hypothetical, non-incentivized, lab experiments. Any guesses if it would have been published in an economics journal today?

Another merit of studies based on hypothetical, non-incentivized, questions is that they can complement lab experiments in certain areas. Here, we consider two examples from the work of Daniel Kahneman and Amos Tversky.

Example 1 *Consider the identification of loss aversion (losses bite more than equivalent gains) in Kahneman and Tversky (1979). In lab experiments, it is not always easy to induce loss aversion over "large losses" because it is considered unethical in experimental economics to leave subjects out-of-pocket. The main alternative in lab experiments is to give subjects money upfront to ensure they are never out-of-pocket. However, this may contaminate their responses by the "house money effect" (gamblers who win money in a casino are more likely to gamble with it; as they say, easy come easy go). Hence, if the intrinsic motivation of subjects to answer lab questions can be trusted, then there is no harm in presenting them with hypothetical loss scenarios.*

Example 2 *Consider the following hypothetical, non-incentivized, lab questions from experiments conducted in a seminal paper by Kahneman and Tversky (1984). The percentage of subjects choosing each response is given in brackets.*

Imagine that the US is preparing for the outbreak of an unusual Asian disease, which is expected to kill 600 people. Two alternative programs to combat the disease have been proposed. Assume that the exact scientific estimates of the consequences of the programs are as follows:

Positive Framing: If program A is adopted, 200 people will be saved. If program B is adopted, there is a one-third probability that 600 people will be saved and a two-thirds probability that no people will be saved. Which of the two programs would you favor? (72% chose A, 28% chose B).

Negative Framing: If program C is adopted, 400 people will die. If program D is adopted, there is a one-third probability that nobody will die and a two-thirds probability that 600 people will die. Which of the two programs would you favor? (22% chose C, 78% chose D).

Relative to the status quo, positive framing presents data in terms of "lives saved," while negative framing presents the same data in terms of "lives lost." Options A and C are identical, and options B and D are also identical. Under frame-invariance, the typical assumption in neoclassical economics, if A is chosen over B then C must be chosen over D (and vice versa). However, in the domain of gains (lives saved relative to the status quo), the majority (72%) chose the safe option (A) over the risky option (B). In the domain of losses (lives lost relative to the status quo) the majority (78%) chose the risky option (D) over the safe option (C).

---

[14] The source for the "second most cited paper" claim is Table 2 in Kim et al. (2006).

This establishes several results. First, behavior is not frame-invariant. Second, the results are not consistent with expected utility. Third, subjects are risk averse in gains and risk seeking in losses; this is one of the important insights of prospect theory.[15]

These results have survived several challenges (e.g., choices over incentivized lotteries) and even professional physicians and World Bank staff behave in the same manner as lab subjects. Clearly this experiment cannot be run in the lab because it would be unethical to take a life.

Thaler (2015, p. 47) writes on the aversion to survey data: "This disdain [for survey data] is simply unscientific. Polling data, which just comes from asking people whether they are planning to vote and for whom, when carefully used by skilled statisticians ... yield remarkably accurate predictions of elections. The most amusing aspect of this anti-survey attitude is that many important macroeconomic variables are produced by surveys! ... 'jobs' data ... come from surveys conducted by the Census Bureau. The unemployment rate, ... is also determined from a survey that asks people whether they are looking for work. Yet using published survey data is not considered a faux pas in macroeconomics. Apparently economists don't mind survey data as long as someone other than the researcher collected it."

Happiness economics, which we consider in Volume 7 is based almost entirely on survey data. Policymakers appear to take serious interest in this area and survey measures of well-being and happiness are highly correlated, which is consistent with the standard that one might expect from incentivized responses. Furthermore, firms often use information gleaned from market surveys to introduce new products about which consumers have no prior experience, and alter the characteristics of existing products; the consequences of these decisions run into billions of pounds every year.

Consider an example where incentives make the problem even worse. Using hypothetical, non-incentivized questions, Lichtenstein and Slovic (1973) asked people to chose between a less risky *P*-bet (high probability of winning a low prize) and a more risky $-bet (a low probability of winning a high prize). When asked to choose directly between the two bets, most people chose the low risk option, the *P*-bet. Yet, most people assigned a higher certainty equivalent to the $-bet as compared to the *P*-bet. Thus, we have a case of *preference reversals* that cannot be explained by any model of consistent preferences. Grether and Plott (1979) suspected that the problem was caused by hypothetical choices. However, when they re-ran the experiments using incentivized subjects, the incidence of preference reversals worsened.

In sum, there are no grounds to outrightly reject survey data. Survey data has pitfalls, for instance, poll data sometimes gives misleading results, however the benefits of survey data outstrip the potential pitfalls. But other data sources also have limitations; hence, it is important to use all sources of data, surveys, experiments, and field evidence, to build a more complete picture of human behavior.

3.7 Replications in experimental economics

Replications of existing research in economics is not a hugely active area, and certainly less active relative to psychology, which has led to a replication crises in that subject because the

---

[15] To be more precise, there is a *fourfold classification of risk attitudes* under prospect theory that depends jointly on the shapes of the probability weighting function and the utility function. The details are given below in Chapter 2.

majority of studies could not be replicated.[16] Camerer et al. (2016) replicate 18 between-subjects lab experiments published in the two leading journals, *American Economic Review* and the *Quarterly Journal of Economics*, between 2011 and 2014. They find that for 11 out of the 18 studies (61.1%) there is a significant effect in the same direction ($P < 0.05$) as reported in the main finding of each study; three more studies are also close to being successful. The remaining studies fail the replication test on this criterion. Using another method of assessment, they construct 95% confidence intervals of the main effect size for each paper; 12 of the 18 replications (66.7%) fall within this confidence level. How high are these successful replication rates? This is a relative question, and we simply do not have enough studies in economics and in psychology to make a comparison. When compared with this small number of studies, the authors report that the stated replication rates in economics experiments are relatively higher, but could be improved further.

Replications are critical, but they are not the only yardstick on which we should judge research. After all, if the original research questions were uninteresting and the research design was flawed, the replication can, at best, do no better. There have been suggestions to raise the significance levels for new results (Benjamin et al., 2018). Furthermore, the dependence of preferences on context, frame, and culture is widely evidenced in behavioral economics. These findings suggest that research in behavioral economics may not always be easy to replicate unless a range of contextual, cultural, and frame-dependent factors are controlled for.

4 Approach and organization of the book

This book is an attempt to take stock of behavioral economics and aims to serve several purposes: A course text for advanced students in economics and other social sciences, a research handbook for behavioral economists, and an invitation to economists and other social scientists of all persuasions to explore this exciting new field. In its teaching role, the book would ideally be taught in a yearlong course in behavioral economics, supplemented by readings that reflect the interests of the instructor. A good example is a typical two-semester North American-style course that has 13 weeks of teaching in each semester; students meet each week for a two-hour lecture and a one-hour problem-solving class. This book tries to standardize the material in behavioral economics so that students can see behavioral economics as a coherent and widely applicable body of theory, much as they might see any other established area in economics. It is also intended to 'nudge' many idiosyncratic course outlines, that pass for behavioral and/or experimental economics at the moment, to adopt a more balanced approach.

Given the scope of the book, one can also construct a large number of coherent and interesting single-semester courses not just in behavioral economics but also in behavioral decision theory, behavioral macroeconomics, behavioral industrial organization, behavioral contract theory, topics in behavioral economics, and the like. I believe that the book should also be essential background reading for any advanced course in microeconomics in order to address Herbert Gintis' (2009, p. xvi) concern raised in Section 2, till the time that microeconomics books respond in a satisfactory manner to his suggestion.

---

[16] For replications in psychology, see, for instance: Open Science Collaboration. (2015). Estimating the reproducibility of psychological science. *Science* 349(6251). For a discussion of replications in several areas of economics, see the May 2017 issue (Volume 107, No. 5) of the *American Economic Review*.

Despite the size of the book, it is, I believe, the "minimum" amount of material that any academic who declares behavioral economics or experimental economics as their research interest, must have deep, rather than passing, familiarity with.

As the reader may have guessed from Sections 2 and 3, my main criterion for including models in this book is their consistency with the evidence, unless there is significant merit in using a model for pedagogical or other reasons. Most of the models that I use can typically explain at least as much as neoclassical models, but can also better explain data from other domains of human behavior. It is entirely possible, of course, to append auxiliary assumptions to standard neoclassical models to explain almost any set of stylized facts. However, I try to stay away from models in which these auxiliary assumptions are ad hoc fixes.

I encourage the reader to keep an open mind about behavioral economics models and judge models by the relevant empirical evidence. Models in behavioral economics are as theoretically rigorous as models in neoclassical economics, if rigor is an important criteria for the reader. Gilboa (2009, Section 7.1) may well be right that all models are ultimately wrong. Even if this statement were true, we must consistently strive to improve our models in the light of rejections, in order to make better predictions and improve our understanding of human behavior. The sequence of these improved models may or may not ever converge to the "true model." Yet, each time we reject a model and put in its place a new one that makes better predictions, we make progress.

The level of honesty that we need as a profession is captured in the words of the Nobel Prize-winning physicist Richard Feynman (1965, p. 158) that economists would do well to embrace: "But experimenters search most diligently, and with the greatest effort, in exactly those places where it seems most likely that we can prove our theories wrong. In other words, we are trying to prove ourselves wrong as quickly as possible, because only in that way can we find progress." The "all models is wrong critique" is unhelpful at best and, if used inappropriately, it is likely to hinder progress in the subject.

For many of the topics, the book is organized in the following general style. A neoclassical theory is outlined, followed by a review of the evidence for it. If the weight of the evidence is inconsistent with the theory, then the behavioral alternatives and the evidence for or against them is described. There is a range of applications in the book for many of the behavioral theories that the reader/instructor can choose from. In order to help readers who might not be familiar with the full range of topics in behavioral economics, I err on the side of longer introductions to most of the chapters. As a first pass, readers may wish to skim through the introductions to the various volumes and chapters, in order to get a bird's-eye view of the material. This should enable readers to draw up a priority list of topics that they would wish to read or teach in their courses. I deliberately shy away from offering such a list of topics to the reader, and like a good restaurant, prefer to fall back on offering a wide menu of tempting choices, hoping that you, the reader, will keep coming back, and spread the word.

Some readers may feel that it is presumptuous to include the word "foundations" in the title of this book. However, in justification, I believe that there is now a sufficiently rich body of lab and field evidence that is well described by models of behavioral economic theory. The richness of human behavior that we can account for with these models is unprecedented in modern economics. A few of the areas in behavioral economics, notably *neuroeconomics*, are very young and I have some hesitation in bringing this material under the rubric of a book that claims to describe the foundations of a subject. Yet, omitting this material is not an attractive option, and I have erred on the side of inclusion.

I also try to flag up material that is speculative, yet promising, or where the evidence base is not sufficiently established at this point in time. Behavioral economics continues to be work in progress and despite the huge increase in understanding attained over the last several decades, a lot needs to be done. Writing this introduction upon completion of the book, and reflecting on the material, I must confess that I have never personally felt so enriched, yet so ignorant, in my life. I hope that the serious, and just the plain curious, among you, come away with a similar sentiment after reading this book.

The book is organized into seven volumes structured into multiple chapters; there are exercises at the end of each volume. The order of the volumes reflects, at least partially, the historical development of the subject, and also bears some similarity with the organization of a typical course in microeconomics. Each volume begins with an introduction to the material in that volume, and each chapter has a separate, but more detailed, introduction.

The table of contents give a bird's-eye view of what is inside the book and I will not bore you with a semi-verbatim description. I should make a few broad comments though, about my organization of the material. I focus mainly on topics that readers may find to be in an unexpected location within the book.

The book opens with Volume 1 on *behavioral decision theory* because playing a game against nature under risk, uncertainty, and ambiguity, in a static setting, is one of the simplest economic problems; this abstracts from temporal and strategic concerns. However, there is an important overlap between risk preferences and time preferences, which is split between Volume 1 and Volume 3 on time preferences. Many readers might have wished to see a more thorough treatment of ambiguity. However, most of the modern developments in ambiguity are within the confines of the neoclassical models. An important behavioral literature on source-dependent preferences is now beginning to develop that highlights the role of prospect theory. The literature on behavioral models of ambiguity aversion has been gaining momentum in the last few years, as evidenced from our discussion in the guide to further reading at the end of Volume 1.

Microeconomics texts typically begin with a discussion of the properties of human preferences, which are regarded as the primitives of the model. Most evidence now indicates that there is a mixture of individuals with purely *self-regarding preferences*, as in neoclassical economics, and those with *other-regarding preferences*. Volume 2 considers the evidence on *human sociality* and behavioral models that take account of this evidence. There is also a discussion of the implications of social preferences for competitive general equilibrium, which typically comes much later in a microeconomics course. Two important topics that lie at the heart of human motivation in economics, *social identity* and *human virtues*, appear in a stand-alone chapter in Volume 2. The inclusion of these major topics should be less surprising than the fact that most microeconomics texts have somehow contrived to exclude them.

An explicit time dimension is not fundamental to the material in Volumes 1 and 2. In Volume 3, we consider the evidence on time preferences and *behavioral models of time discounting*. The treatment of time preferences is excessively narrow in neoclassical microeconomics texts. This is because the entire psychology of time preferences is captured by a single parameter, the discount rate, in the exponential discounted utility model—the main model of time preferences in neoclassical economics. This is not just unsatisfactory in light of the richness in observed time preferences, but exponential discounting is strongly rejected by the evidence, perhaps even more so than expected utility theory.

Volume 3 is the slimmest of the seven volumes but there is likely to be much that is new and unfamiliar to many readers. This will require investment in learning new machinery such as *subadditivity*, *attribute-based models* of time preferences, and *models of reference time preferences*. I advise the serious reader to persevere with Volume 3. It is worth telling an anecdote that the reader may wish to keep in mind when an unfamiliar topic is encountered in Volume 3. When George Loewenstein, one of the leaders in time discounting, first saw the material in Volume 3, he particularly commended me for including *subadditivity* (i.e., discounting depends on how one partitions a given interval of time). However, when another group of non-specialists read the same material as part of a group reading seminar in a leading university, they were put off by the "unusual and new" concept of subadditivity. The reason subadditivity is there in the book is because it is currently supported by the evidence; its current popularity/aesthetic appeal (or lack of it) are criteria that, for this book, are not relevant.

Volume 4, perhaps the longest of the seven volumes, is on *behavioral game theory*. Classical game theory revolutionized economics by forcing it to specify explicitly the economic environment, set of players, sequence of moves, and the mapping of histories to payoffs. Anyone comparing industrial organization theory before the advent of game theory with modern industrial organization theory will immediately notice the much greater clarity achieved by modern game theoretic models (think, e.g., of models of entry deterrence). Gintis (2009) advocates keeping game theory as the common toolkit for all social sciences despite pointing out serious shortcomings in classical game theory, for instance, the assumption of common priors and the justification for a Nash equilibrium. The approach in this book concurs with this sentiment. Despite widespread belief to the contrary, the evidence has not been too kind to classical models of game theory. This is particularly the case for observed behavior in the early rounds of a game, and for equilibrium refinements that require high cognitive requirements. In particular, it stretches the imagination to believe that players could arrive at a Nash equilibrium purely by a deductive process. For instance, the cooperation rate in many static prisoner's dilemma game experiments is about 60%; cooperation here is a dominated strategy, which in classical game theory, ought never to have been played.[17]

We consider at length the evidence for classical models of game theory and the leading behavioral alternatives. Many of the main behavioral alternatives, such as *level-k models*, the *cognitive hierarchy model*, and the *quantal response equilibrium*, relax the "equilibrium in beliefs" assumption, or the assumption that players play a best response. There are several other behavioral models of strategic interaction that are in the fray. While the empirical evidence is not always consistent with these models, the most heartening aspect of the discourse in behavioral game theory is that we are actually using empirical evidence to choose among the models. You cannot convince the leaders in this field, say, Vincent Crawford or Colin Camerer, about your proposal for a new solution concept in game theory by simply appealing to the aesthetic appeal of your proposed model, or its ability to tell a useful story, or a fable, if it is not supported by the evidence. I have decided to include the topic of *psychological game theory* in Volume 4. I anticipate that some instructors may have wished to place this topic in Volume 7 on emotions, because it also deals with *anger* and *guilt*, while other instructors may have wished to see it in Volume 2, because it also deals with intentions-based reciprocity. My relatively detailed treatment of this material reflects my preference to see this material given more prominence in modern behavioral economics.

Volume 5 considers *models of bounded rationality*, and I personally believe that it is of enormous significance for the future direction of behavioral economics. It is split into

---

[17] Social preferences alone cannot explain behavior of the players in the prisoner's dilemma game; see al-Nowaihi and Dhami (2015).

three chapters. The chapter on *judgment heuristics*, a topic that owes its origin and importance to Tversky and Kahneman (1973, 1974), brings into sharp focus the debate about the relative suitability of the *optimization approach*, and the *heuristic-based approach* to economic models.[18] This chapter is a must-read for anyone who believes that the standard neoclassical framework is satisfactory on the grounds that its predictions match the data in an 'as if' sense. The chapter on *mental accounting* considers work that Richard Thaler almost single-handedly pioneered. It deserves to see much more development and interest among theorists working in behavioral economics. The reader may not have expected a chapter on *behavioral finance* in Volume 5 but there is no better place to illustrate bounded rationality and the inefficiency of markets in the very market that is typically held up as a model of efficiency in neoclassical economics.

Volume 6 outlines the evidence on human learning and introduces traditional as well as the newer *behavioral models of learning*. I also give chapter-length treatments of *evolutionary game theory* and *stochastic social dynamics*. An appendix briefly introduces the reader to the necessary technical machinery on deterministic and stochastic dynamical systems. Some instructors would have wished to see the chapter on evolutionary game theory in Volume 4. One aim of this chapter is to provide evolutionary foundations for human sociality that we covered in Volume 2, and also introduce some newer and interesting topics, such as *gene-culture coevolution* that justify the location of this chapter in a volume on learning. Volume 6 is particularly instructive in evaluating the common claim that a Nash equilibrium arises if sufficient learning opportunities are provided to the subjects. A separate chapter-length treatment on stochastic social dynamics in Volume 6 might be unexpected, even for many behavioral economists who do not typically include this topic in their courses. However, I believe that this material needs to be taken more seriously, and all students of behavioral economics should have at least a basic familiarity with it.

The final volume, Volume 7, considers three different topics: emotions, behavioral welfare economics, and neuroeconomics.

Neoclassical economics typically focuses on cold and emotionless deliberation. Part 1 in Volume 7 considers the role of emotions in explaining economic phenomena. Instructors interested in teaching a course that focuses on emotions will need to combine the material here with that from other parts of the book, such as psychological game theory (Volume 4), models of regret and disappointment aversion (Volume 1), and issues of self-control and present-biased preferences (Volume 3). We also consider the Gul–Pesendorfer model of temptation that some readers might have preferred to situate in Volume 3, where issues of present-biased preferences are discussed. I have also placed the important policy relevant topic of *happiness economics* here, insofar as happiness may be considered as a type of emotion. The evidence base in happiness economics is typically constructed using survey data that not all economists are comfortable with (see Section 3.6 above), which has hampered its acceptability within academic economists. I urge economists to take this material more seriously, particularly given the correlations between various measures of well-being and happiness. Some readers may find *models of dual selves* to be somewhat out of place in this part; I partly share this concern but it was not immediately clear where better to situate this important topic.

Part 2 in Volume 7 considers issues in *behavioral welfare economics*, which is an area that is likely to experience more development in the future. If people have behavioral biases relative to the neoclassical model, then should we respect those biases or not? The debate is not just about

---

[18] For a discussion of alternative views on the optimization versus heuristics debate, the reader may consult the June 2013 issue of the *Journal of Economic Literature*, Volume 51, No. 2.

libertarianism and *paternalism*, but also about exactly what these terms mean in the presence of behavioral biases.

Part 3 in Volume 7 gives a very brief tour of *neuroeconomics* that highlights the neuroeconomic foundations of just a few selected aspects of human behavior from the first four volumes of the book. In particular, I make no attempt at completeness in the treatment of neuroeconomics; several excellent and more authoritative sources are available (e.g., Glimcher et al., 2009; Glimcher and Fehr, 2014).

There are some notable omissions from the book that are partly dictated by technological considerations such as the physical size of the book, the current importance of these topics in behavioral economics, and last but not least, by my own lack of competence in these areas. *Complexity theory* and its implications for public policy do not figure in this book; readers can pursue Mitchell (2009) for an introduction, followed by Colander and Kupers (2014) for policy issues. I have also omitted a discussion of *agent-based computational models*; readers can begin with Tesfatsion and Judd (2006) and Farmer and Foley (2009). I also give insufficient attention to the *epistemic foundations of equilibrium concepts* in classical and behavioral game theory; see Dekel and Siniscalchi (2015) for a recent review and Gintis (2009) for a critique of the epistemic foundations of classical game theory.

5 Five theoretical approaches in behavioral economics

I would now like to pick up the story of behavioral economics where I left off at the end of Section 1. I shall consider five case studies of theoretical models in behavioral economics, chosen from five different volumes of this book.[19] In each case, I also briefly comment on some/all of the following: the historical context of these models, reactions to these models in the profession, evidence on the models, applications, and lessons learnt. The reader should not construe that I consider the behavioral models not mentioned in this section as necessarily hierarchically inferior. An identical observation holds for the material in Section 6 below, where I consider five examples of behavioral evidence.

5.1 *A case study of prospect theory*

Two papers in the 1970s by Daniel Kahneman and Amos Tversky may be identified with the beginning of modern behavioral economics. In the first, Tversky and Kahneman (1974) proposed a radical, non-optimization approach to decision making in economics in which people use heuristics or simple rules of thumb; we discuss this work in Volume 5 and in Section 5.5 below. In the second, Kahneman and Tversky (1979) outlined a new theory of decision making under risk, uncertainty, and ambiguity that distilled in a simple, conservative, extension of expected utility theory, the main experimental insights from their own work and that of others. They called it *prospect theory* (PT), which is not a particularly illuminating name for the theory.[20]

---

[19] An idea whose development I wished to trace out in this section, since Gary Bolton pointed it out to me a few years ago, was the development of models of relative concerns for others that arose surprisingly from experiments on bargaining games conducted by Alvin Roth with others (for bargaining games, see Volume 4 of the book). However, Roth (2015) has recently described this story very lucidly, so I have omitted it (see Volume 4 of the book for details).

[20] If you are mystified by the name "prospect theory," as I was once, then you can seek a resolution to this mystery by reading p. 25 in Thaler (2015).

Consider a lottery that describes outcome and probability pairs in n states of the world,

$$L = (x_1, p_1; x_2, p_2; \ldots; x_n, p_n), \tag{1}$$

where $x_1 < x_2 < \ldots < x_n$ are monetary prizes (positive or negative) and $p_i \geq 0$ is the objective probability with which the prize x_i occurs, such that $\sum_{i=1}^{n} p_i = 1$. In the dominant decision theory in neoclassical economics, *expected utility theory* (EU), lottery L is evaluated by the function $EU(L) = \sum_{i=1}^{n} p_i u(x_i)$, where u is a utility function for monetary prizes. When well-defined subjective probabilities replace objective probabilities (uncertainty) then EU is referred to as *subjective expected utility*. Two features stand out in this formulation. First, utility derives from the final outcomes in each of the n states. Second, the objective is linear in probabilities. EU is underpinned by a compelling and plausible set of preference axioms (von Neumann and Morgenstern, 1944).[21] However, a very large body of evidence rejects the hypothesis that all humans follow EU (Kahneman and Tversky, 2000; Starmer, 2000; Wakker, 2010). Axiomatic plausibility on its own cannot be used as a criterion for the continued acceptability of a theory if the evidence rejects it. Indeed, the independence axiom is often rejected by the evidence; the Allais paradox is one of the earliest violations.

PT is a *descriptive* theory of choice that strives to explain actual human behavior not just for risk, but also for uncertainty and ambiguity. Like many behavioral theories, it also has rigorous axiomatic foundations. PT not only accounted for the known violations of EU, it helped to successfully predict and explain a range of new phenomena. In this sense, it satisfies the criteria of theoretical and empirical progress in the Lakatosian framework. A key idea in PT is *reference dependence*. This implies that humans derive utility from changes in outcomes relative to some reference outcome; if the outcome is equal to or greater than the reference outcome it is in the *domain of gains*, otherwise it is in the *domain of losses*.

One could renormalize all outcomes relative to a reference outcome under EU but this is hardly enlightening, because EU has little to offer towards an understanding of human behavior in the domain of gains and losses. In contrast, PT gives a rich account of the difference in human behavior in the domain of losses. A key idea that drives many results in behavioral economics is *loss aversion*, i.e., losses bite more than equivalent gains. Kahneman and Tversky (1979) report a median figure of loss aversion of 2.25. So, for instance, assuming linear utility, a monetary gain of 100 feels likes a utility gain of 100, while a monetary loss of 100 feels like a utility loss of 225 under PT; under EU, a loss of 100 would just feel like a utility loss of 100. Loss aversion is empirically very robust, and it may help some of us to understand our own past behavior.[22]

Furthermore, evidence shows that the utility function, v, under PT is concave in the domain of gains and convex in losses. This is shown in Figure 1 for the case of the following power form of utility

$$v(y) = \begin{cases} y^{\gamma^+} & \text{if } y \geq 0 \\ -\lambda(-y)^{\gamma^-} & \text{if } y < 0 \end{cases}, \gamma^+ > 0, \gamma^- > 0, \lambda > 1, \tag{2}$$

---

[21] Bleichrodt et al. (2016) suggest that the credit for discovering the independence axiom, which is critical for the axiomatic development of EU, should go instead to John F. Nash and Jacob Marshak.

[22] I undoubtedly received many gifts as a child that I only have a dim memory of, but I can never forget the five-rupee note that I lost at age 5, or the toy car given to me by an uncle from the US that was stolen on the very first day in school. Losing the toy car was certainly a far more painful and long-lasting experience as compared to the joy that I felt at receiving it. Loss aversion may be one explanation behind these feelings.

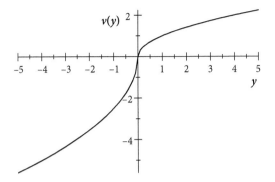

Figure 1 The power form of the utility function under prospect theory.

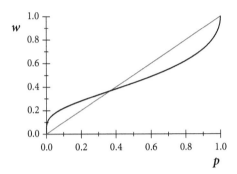

Figure 2 A plot of the Prelec function for $\beta = 1$ and $\alpha = 0.5$.

plotted for the case of the empirically observed values of $\gamma^+ = \gamma^- = 0.88$ and $\lambda = 2.25$ in Kahneman and Tversky (1979). Notice the kink at the reference point of zero and a sudden increase in slope as we enter into the domain of losses. This captures loss aversion, as reflected in the parameter λ in (2). Given the different shapes of the utility function in gains and losses (concave in gains, so risk averse, and convex in losses, so risk loving),[23] the reader should now readily make sense of the results in Example 2.

A third component of prospect theory is *non-linear probability weighting*; recall that under EU, probabilities are weighted linearly. In particular, at least for probabilities bounded away from the endpoints of the interval $[0,1]$, evidence suggests that low probabilities are subjectively overweighted, while high probabilities are subjectively underweighted. This is captured by a continuous, strictly increasing, *probability weighting function*, $w(p) : [0,1] \rightarrow [0,1]$ such that $w(0) = 0$ and $w(1) = 1$. Figure 2 shows a plot of the Prelec probability weighting function due to Prelec (1998); this is given by $w(p) = e^{-\beta(-\ln p)^{\alpha}}$, where $\alpha > 0, \beta > 0$. Arguably, Figures 1 and 2 are the two most important diagrams in Volume 1 of the book.

Suppose that an individual faces the following lottery in *incremental form*

$$\tilde{L} = (y_{-m}, p_{-m}; \ldots; y_0, p_0; \ldots; y_n, p_n),\tag{3}$$

---

[23] We have not, so far, said anything about non-linear probability weights, which, with the shape of the utility function, jointly determine attitudes to risk under PT (see below).

where $y_{-m} \leq \ldots \leq y_0 = 0 \leq \ldots \leq y_n$ are monetary outcomes, each expressed as an increment relative to a reference point r; so if the monetary outcome is x_i, then $y_i = x_i - r$. Here, we have m outcomes in the domain of losses and n outcomes in the domain of gains. Kahneman and Tversky (1979) proposed that a decision maker who follows PT, evaluates lottery $\widetilde{L}$ as $\Sigma_{i=-m}^{n} w(p_i)v(y_i)$, where v is the utility function under PT; an example is given in e.0.5.[24] However, it was soon realized that this could lead to stochastically dominated options being chosen.

Quiggin (1982) suggested a way out of this problem with his proposal of *rank dependent utility* (RDU) that alters EU in a minimal, but important way. A decision maker who follows rank dependent utility evaluates the lottery L in (1) as: $RDU(L) = \sum_{i=1}^{n} \pi_i u(x_i)$; π_i, known as the *decision weight* corresponding to outcome x_i, is simply a cumulative transformation of the probability weighting function given in Figure 2.[25] Crucially, the utility function, u, stays as it is under EU. RDU can explain everything that EU can (for the Prelec function, for $\alpha = \beta = 1$, we have $\pi_i = p_i$ so EU is a special case of RDU), disallows stochastically dominated choices, and can explain the celebrated Allais paradoxes.

Tversky and Kahneman (1992) incorporated insights from RDU into their 1979 version of prospect theory and came up with *cumulative prospect theory*.[26] Following convention, we call the 1979 version *original prospect theory* and the 1992 version, simply, *prospect theory* (PT), which we focus on below. Under PT, a decision maker evaluates the lottery in (3) as $PT(\widetilde{L}) = \Sigma_{i=-m}^{n} \pi_i v(y_i)$, where the decision weights, π_i, are constructed as under RDU but computed separately for gains and losses relative to the reference point. Decision makers who follow PT do not choose stochastically dominated options.

PT has been incredibly successful in understanding human behavior under risk, uncertainty, and ambiguity; for a book-length treatment, see Wakker (2010). Arguably, no other decision theory in economics has been so successful in explaining such a wide range of phenomena. A small sample of these applications is as follows. Why does the equity premium puzzle (too high a return on equities relative to bonds) exist (Benartzi and Thaler, 1995)? Why is it so hard to find a taxi on a rainy day in New York (Camerer et al. 1997)? Why do people pay taxes (Dhami and al-Nowaihi, 2007, 2010a)? Why is there a disparity between willingness to pay and willingness to accept (Thaler, 1980)? How does ex-ante competition serve as a reference point in the formation of ex-post contracts (Fehr et al. 2011)? Why are stabilizations delayed (Weyland, 1996)? Why are price elasticities asymmetric (Camerer, 2000)? Why do people hold on to loss-making stock for too long and sell winners too early (Odean, 1998)? Why are people influenced by goals (Locke and Latham, 1990)? Why do people simultaneously gamble and insure (Kahneman and Tversky, 1979)? Why are incentives low-powered (de Meza and Webb, 2007)? Why do markets price skewness in asset returns (Barberis, 2013)? Furthermore, most of what economists think of as *risk aversion* might well be just *loss aversion* (Novemsky and Kahneman, 2005). It is hard to think of an area in economics that has not been touched directly or indirectly by prospect theory.

EU is a special case of RDU, which in turn, is a special case of PT. Thus, PT can explain everything that the other theories can explain, but the converse is false. For the purists, PT has axiomatic foundations (Chateauneuf and Wakker, 1999) and the individual components of

---

[24] In the main, Kahneman and Tversky (1979) were interested in two-outcome lotteries but their model is generalizable to more than two outcomes.

[25] For readers who are itching for more information at this stage, before they get to Chapter 2, $\pi_n = w(p_n)$ and $\pi_i = w\left(\Sigma_{j=i}^{n} p_j\right) - w\left(\Sigma_{j=i+1}^{n} p_j\right)$ for $i = 1, 2, \ldots, n-1$.

[26] The work of Starmer and Sugden (1989) in suggesting a prospect theoretic type of functional ought also to be mentioned here.

prospect theory have axiomatic foundations, such as the utility function in Figure 1 (al-Nowaihi et al., 2008) and the Prelec probability function in Figure 2 (Prelec, 1998; al-Nowaihi and Dhami, 2006a). There is strong empirical support for the individual components of PT in choice data (Wakker, 2010), and in neural data (De Martino et al., 2006; Tom et al., 2007; Roiser et al., 2009). When a two-horse race is run between EU and PT, the predictions of EU are qualitatively and quantitatively unsatisfactory, while those of PT fit well the evidence (Dhami and al-Nowaihi, 2007). Mixture models indicate that there is possibly an 80%–20% split of people who follow PT and EU (Bruhin et al., 2010). Field evidence also supports PT, even among experienced subjects (Pope and Schweitzer, 2011; Fryer et al., 2012; Camerer, 2015).[27] Close primate relatives, such as capuchin monkeys, also exhibit loss aversion, suggesting that loss aversion already existed prior to the separation of the human line from other primate relatives, and is hardwired in us (Chen et al., 2006).

A non-economist reading this introduction would think that surely PT must be the main decision theory taught in microeconomics courses. Wrong! Most of the standard texts in microeconomics either omit any mention of PT, or refer to it only in passing (Varian, 1992; Mas-Colell et al., 1995; Jehle and Reny, 2011). Such a situation is unlikely to have arisen in the natural sciences, at least in modern times. Incredibly, it is still possible to get a degree in economics in many universities without having undertaken a study of prospect theory, or even a course in behavioral economics. So why this relative neglect of PT, despite its growing usefulness and importance, and the continued reliance on EU? One can conjecture several reasons.

1. The institutional structure in economics has a strong status-quo bias, partly because of homespun and self-serving methodological positions that do not recognize the primary role of evidence and of refutability (see discussion in Section 2 above). So, for instance, EU is often justified as telling a useful story of human behavior under risk and uncertainty or justified on the grounds that people behave "as if" they follow EU. An EU analysis also underpins many important results such as the existence of a Nash equilibrium and problems in mechanism design, thus, refutations of EU could be alarming for many economists. These defences of EU are untenable on scientific grounds.

2. Many economists appear to believe that EU is successful in making qualitative predictions, which justifies its use, while PT impinges mainly on quantitative results. However, a-priori, it is often not clear which qualitative predictions made under an EU analysis will be empirically supported. Within the same model, EU may make predictions that are qualitatively and quantitatively incorrect, while PT makes the correct predictions in each case (Dhami and al-Nowaihi, 2007, 2010a).

3. Economists critical of PT often argue that an exogenous reference point in PT is an unacceptable auxiliary assumption. In contrast, Kahneman and Tversky (1979) identified an endogenous reference point, the status quo, which is eminently sensible in most applications. As they also recognize, one's entitlement or bargaining power, historical norms, or the expected value of a lottery, may also prove to be compelling reference points. Every falsifiable theory makes auxiliary assumptions, which can and should be

---

[27] The List (2003) findings are commonly cited as showing that lab evidence on loss aversion does not generalize to the market; indeed, the title of the paper is: Does market experience eliminate market anomalies? However, the data in the paper shows that experience, whether in the lab or in the market, reduces loss aversion and the magnitudes of reduction are comparable. But even more importantly, significant loss aversion still remains despite market experience, as is established by many other empirical studies.

tested. Evidence shows that people do indeed have reference points. It is well known that rationality, by itself, has very little predictive power in the neoclassical model in the absence of auxiliary assumptions; see a nice discussion in Thaler (2015, Chapter 17). The current state of the art in neoclassical economics is not even remotely close to the position that "all auxiliary assumptions must be endogenized." Indeed it might not be sensible to aspire to do so.

One response to this criticism has been the development of a theory of *endogenous reference points*; roughly this is similar to imposing rational expectations on the formation of reference points (Köszegi and Rabin, 2006). This solution has served to satisfy many neoclassical theorists although it sits uneasily with the evidence on cognitive limitations that we review at length in this book. Whether endogenous reference points in the sense of Köszegi–Rabin is a step in the right direction is entirely an empirical question that its authors are aware of. Initial empirical evidence (reviewed in Chapter 2) is consistent with the model, but we must await more stringent tests of the theory before we can be more confident.

4. It is not uncommon to hear the following view from some quarters: "PT has more parameters than the other decision theories, so it is not surprising that it explains better?" Incidentally, it is conveniently glossed over that exactly the same a-priori argument applies to the use of EU over expected value theory that it replaced.

There are two main statistical methods of addressing this criticism. First, estimate the model for a subset of the sample and use the estimated parameters to test the predictions on the remaining data. Second, use statistical criteria that allow one to test the trade-off between a greater number of parameters and better explanatory power, even among non-nested models, such as the Akaike information criteria (AIC), or the Bayesian information criteria (BIC). One may then run a horse race between the alternative theories.

I am unaware of completed studies in the first category, but there are some in the second. In a horse race between eight theories including EU and RDU (but not PT), Hey and Orme (1994) conclude (p. 1321): "Expected utility (and its special case, risk neutrality) emerges from this analysis fairly intact . . . However, we should emphasize once more that this interpretation of our results needs to be taken with caution—since our sample of 80 subjects was in no sense representative." The overriding feeling from these results (see also the survey by Hey, 2014), is that victories for one decision theory over another are rather messy and require one to buy into functional restrictions, assumptions on the error processes, and data limitations that one is never entirely comfortable with.

It is not commonly realized that PT also applies to situations of ambiguity; this is shown explicitly in Tversky and Kahneman (1992). In a comprehensive and careful study, Kothiyal et al. (2014) run a horse race between 11 competing theories of ambiguity that include subjective expected utility, PT, and several theories that are natural extensions of expected utility to ambiguity; PT emerges as the clear winner in this competition. Erev et al. (2010) run an unusual choice prediction competition pitting several decision theories against each other, many of which are more popular in psychology. In choice tasks that involved predictions from actual decisions, a stochastic version of PT outperformed the other theories. In contrast, in choice tasks involving predictions from experience, models that relied on small samples from memory/experience performed best.

Under EU, attitudes to risk are captured entirely by the shape of the utility function. However, if we make any departure from linearity in probabilities in an EU-type functional, as e.g., in RDU or PT, then attitudes to risk are *jointly* determined by the shapes of the probability weighting function and the utility function. In particular, the *fourfold classification of risk* is one of the central insights of PT (Tversky and Kahneman, 1992), and despite subsequent empirical criticisms, it remains a robust finding (Fehr-Duda and Epper, 2012). Thus, under PT, one needs to elicit the probability weighting function and the utility functions separately. This can be accomplished by the trade-off method (Wakker and Deneffe, 1996; see Volume 1).

Using a cleverly designed elicitation domain, the trade-off method is valid for EU and RDU. Employing this procedure, Abdellaoui (2000) checked if people transform probabilities; in particular, this test is not subject to the criticism that RDU does better because it has a higher number of parameters. The test showed that people transformed probabilities, which is inconsistent with EU but consistent with RDU. Abdellaoui then conducted a stringent test of the difference between RDU and PT and found that the probability weighting function was different for gains and losses, which is consistent with PT but not RDU. He then checked for simple lotteries, a condition (the duality of probability weighting functions) that would have established that RDU and PT coincide, but this condition was rejected.[28]

A greater challenge to PT is posed by the following developments that appear to be lost in the rather narrow and confused mainstream critique of PT.

1. Michael Birnbaum has done a series of experiments whose results are not consistent with PT (Birnbaum, 2008). However, these results are not consistent with any of the other mainstream decision theories. His own proposals (e.g., *configural weights models*) are likely to appear ad hoc to many economists in the manner in which they allocate decision weights to outcomes. Further, there are no preference foundations of his proposed theory (see Volume 1). For simple lotteries, the predictions of configural weights models are identical to PT.

2. There could be potential interaction between probability weights and the size of outcomes (Fehr-Duda et al., 2010). These results hit at the very foundation of models where the relevant objective functions are separable in probabilities and outcomes, such as EU, RDU, PT, and most other known decision models.

3. As Kahneman and Tversky (1979) so presciently realized, human behavior near the end-points of the probability interval is variable. Some people treat very low probabilities as very salient (notice the steep slope of the Prelec function in Figure 2 as $p \to 0$). However, others simply ignore very low probabilities (but this cannot be captured in Figure 2). Since the probability weighting functions, such as the Prelec function, underlie many behavioral theories, such as RDU, PT, and configural weights models, this evidence is troublesome for all of them. The neglect of low probability events, at least for a sizeable fraction of the population, impinges on a wide range of phenomena, such as buying inadequate insurance for low probability natural hazards, running red traffic lights, deterrence effects of capital punishment, and driving and talking on mobile phones (see Volume 1 for details). One way of accounting for these phenomena is the proposal by Dhami and al-Nowaihi (2010b) to modify the Prelec function to a richer, axiomatically founded, probability weighting

---

[28] In personal communication, Mohammed Abdellaoui shared some findings of ongoing research that compares PT with alternative theories based on a comparison that takes account of the extra parameters under PT. These results are consistent with those reported above for Abdellaoui (2000).

function that allows both overweighting and underweighting of very tiny probabilities. Whether this proposal will work is an open empirical question.

The rather detailed case study of PT in this section is not only useful for those seeking insights into behavioral theories of decision making, but also to illustrate the approach that I take in this book. I shall ask uncomfortable questions of both neoclassical and behavioral models, highlight the progress that has been made, and, whenever possible, use empirical evidence to judge between alternative theories.

5.2 Human sociality and inequity averse preferences

The exclusive pursuit of self-interest and the lack of any consideration of character virtues in neoclassical economics, is at variance with the evidence.[29] Gintis (2009, p. 49) captures the heart of the issue: "Self-regarding agents are in common parlance called *sociopaths* ... We conclude from behavioral game theory that one must treat individuals' objectives as a matter of *fact*, not *logic*." Evidence indicates that humans: exhibit *altruism* and *envy*; have an inherent tendency to cooperate yet display *conditional reciprocity* (respond to kindness with kindness and unkindness with unkindness); are influenced by the kindness or otherwise of the *intentions* of others; and value human virtues such as "promises" for their own sake. Despite a great amount of evidence for *human sociality*, the acceptance of these forms of other-regarding behaviors is relatively slow among mainstream economics.

Many economists will probably dispute this criticism on the grounds that neoclassical economics allows people to have *other-regarding preferences*, and cite the rich tradition for this work (Veblen, 1899; Duesenberry, 1949). While this is certainly true, however, neoclassical economics has not generated models that can explain the richness of modern experimental findings on social preferences and human virtues, which is a minimum standard for aspiring contenders (Fehr and Schmidt, 2006). By contrast, behavioral economic theory has provided a rich range of models that are consistent with the evidence. Behavioral economics does not argue that human virtues, such as honesty and keeping one's promises, are absolutes. Human adherence to virtues also depends on the cost of being virtuous and on the behavior (virtuous or otherwise) of others, e.g., tax evaders feel less guilty if there is greater incidence of tax evasion in society.

Some of the earliest experiments on fairness concerns were conducted in the mid 1980s by Daniel Kahneman, Jack Knetsch, and Richard Thaler, based on telephone surveys in Canada.[30] Consider the following survey questions from Kahneman et al. (1991):

Question la. "A shortage has developed for a popular model of automobile, and customers must now wait two months for delivery. A dealer has been selling these cars at list price. Now the dealer prices this model at $200 above list price." Out of 130 respondents, 29% found the behavior of dealers acceptable, while 71% found it unacceptable.

Question lb. "A shortage has developed for a popular model of automobile, and customers must now wait two months for delivery. A dealer has been selling these cars at a discount of $200 below list price. Now the dealer sells this model only at list price." Out of 123 respondents, 58% found the behavior of dealers acceptable while 42% found it unacceptable.

---

[29] For a recent survey of experimental and field studies on character virtues in economics, see Dhami (2017).
[30] See the interesting background to these surveys in Thaler (2015, Ch. 14) and a discussion of the other experiments that they conducted.

This example illustrates a number of interesting points.

1. Under self-regarding preferences, the responses to the two questions should be similar, but they are different.
2. The two different economic environments in Q1a and Q1b may generate 'entitlements' or status-quo reference points, such that receiving less than the entitlement is considered unfair. The entitlement is not necessarily mutually agreed upon. In other contexts, this can give rise to a *self-serving bias* in negotiations, which can potentially account for strikes, wars, and bargaining failures (Babcock and Loewenstein, 1997).
3. This example highlights some issues that play no role in neoclassical economics: For instance, forgoing a discount is less aversive relative to a surcharge. This leads to a better understanding of many business practices. Consider, for instance, charging for credit card usage in the early days of credit cards (Thaler, 2015). Initially, there was a 3% *surcharge* on the use of credit card payments in retail stores, which a consumer could avoid by paying cash. The credit card companies successfully lobbied the retail price of a $1 item to be raised to $1.03. So cash buyers could pay a *discounted price* of $1, while card users could pay the *full price* of $1.03. Card users thus do not pay a surcharge for their purchase. As Thaler puts it (p. 18): "Paying a surcharge is out-of-pocket, whereas not receiving a discount is a 'mere' opportunity cost." Clearly direct out-of-pocket costs are more aversive relative to the more indirect concept of opportunity costs that is less well understood by many.

There is now overwhelming evidence of social preferences from lab and field data that has been widely replicated around the world with small and large stakes. Experimental games that have been used to build up the evidence base for social preferences include the *dictator game*, the *ultimatum game*, the *gift exchange game*, the *trust game*, and the *public goods game with and without punishment*.

Of the experimental games on human sociality, the *ultimatum game* (Güth et al., 1982) is the most replicated. In the ultimatum game, a proposer is given a fixed sum of money to split with the responder. The responder can then accept or reject. The backward induction outcome using classical game theory is that the proposer will offer the minimum divisible unit of money (e.g., 1 cent out of a dollar) to the responder; after all, something is better than nothing for the responder, so he accepts. By contrast, the average offer made by the proposer is 30–40 percent of the pie. Low offers are rejected by the responders who often invoke the "unfairness of low offers" as their justification for rejection; in neoclassical economics, people are amoral, so these considerations do not arise. The results survive with sensibly high stakes, but rejection rates fall with extremely high stakes, although proposers still offer 20% of the pie (see Volume 2 for details). These results have been replicated across the globe (Henrich et al., 2001) and reveal large cross-cultural differences in fairness norms.

The evidence from these experimental games shows that self-regarding preferences are not insignificant. However, a majority of the subjects also exhibit other-regarding preferences. A critical insight of this literature is that introducing a minority of individuals with other-regarding preferences in a pool of self-regarding individuals can potentially produce large changes (Fehr and Schmidt, 1999; Fehr and Gächter, 2000b; Dhami and al-Nowaihi, 2010d). Empirical success in many areas that traditionally relied on self-regarding preferences, e.g., contract theory and political economy, has been considerably enhanced by incorporating other-regarding preferences. Over many years, Herbert Gintis and Samuel Bowles have made a compelling case for incorporating reciprocity into economic models, based on its evolutionary foundations (Gintis, 2009; Bowles and Gintis, 2011).

How should one proceed in light of this empirical evidence? Economists have traditionally been justifiably worried about preference-manipulation to explain economic phenomena. However, these concerns do not, and should not, apply to the modern literature on other-regarding preferences. The main models of other-regarding preferences have been subjected to extensive and stringent empirical testing, and fit well the evidence from a range of experimental games. Yet, it is not unusual to hear the comments that the incorporation of other-regarding preferences will "compromise the hard-won discipline encapsulated in the neoclassical framework with self-regarding preferences," or that "other-regarding preferences are ad hoc," or that "they take the easy way out." There is no empirical basis for these arguments; and we seek to demonstrate this in Volume 2. Anyone who has been following the publications in the leading journals in economics in the last few years would have noticed that this state of affairs is fortunately changing.

Inequity aversion is an important human motivation. People chose to live in a welfare state with democratically elected governments where taxes finance redistribution to the poor and socially disadvantaged, and provide social insurance. Most of us will find it morally repugnant to live in a system without these features, even if we disagree on the exact levels of social redistribution. People also give their money and time to charitable causes; in the US, charitable donations alone account for 1% of GDP over and above redistributive taxes paid by people. Clearly, we are also driven by altruistic concerns. At the same time, we are envious of others who might be better-off than us. This is particularly the case when we believe that the higher income of others is not deserved; there is often a public outcry over high salaries and bonuses to top management in the financial sector especially at a time when they might be perceived as being responsible for a financial crises.

Fehr and Schmidt (1999) propose a simple, tractable, yet powerful model to capture these concerns. Suppose that n individuals are ordered in such a way that they have incomes $y_1 < y_2 < \ldots < y_n$. Then, the Fehr–Schmidt utility function of any individual i is given by

$$U_i = y_i - \frac{\alpha_i}{n-1} \sum_{j>i} (y_j - y_i) - \frac{\beta_i}{n-1} \sum_{j<i} (y_i - y_j), \alpha_i \geq 0, 0 \leq \beta_i < 1. \tag{4}$$

An individual is said to have *inequity averse preferences*, a form of other-regarding preferences, if at least one of β_i and α_i is non-zero. In contrast, the neoclassical model with self-regarding preferences requires $\beta_i = \alpha_i = 0$ for all i. The first term in (4) captures self-regarding preferences and the next two terms capture, respectively, disadvantageous and advantageous inequity. Most experiments find that $\beta_i < \alpha_i$, so individuals suffer relatively more from disadvantageous inequity; Eckel and Gintis (2010) review empirical estimates of the parameters from various studies. Empirically, $\beta_i < 1$ because we do not observe individuals throwing away their own incomes to reduce disutility from advantageous inequity. As with most other leading models in behavioral economics, this model has axiomatic foundations (Neilson, 2006). The Fehr–Schmidt model can be extended to a non-linear version, and this avenue has been fruitfully explored in several applications of the model.

Another popular model of inequity aversion is a model of *equity, reciprocity,* and *competition* (ERC), due to Bolton and Ockenfels (2000). Suppose that there are n players, $i = 1, 2, \ldots n$. The monetary payoff of player i is $y_i > 0$, and the sum of the total monetary payoffs is $S = \sum_{i=1}^{n} y_i$. The relative monetary payoff of player i is given by $r_i = y_i/S$. Then, the utility function of player i is given by

$$u^i (y_i, r_i). \tag{5}$$

u^i is twice continuously differentiable in y_i, r_i, and increasing and concave in y_i. For any given monetary payoff, u^i is maximized at $r_i = 1/n$ and is strictly decreasing and strictly concave in r_i around this point. Thus, individuals prefer to increase their monetary payoffs, yet for any monetary payoff, the individual prefers equal division; different individuals may view this trade-off differently, hence, the index i on the utility function. In the ERC model, individuals compare their payoff with the total payoff of others, but they do not care about interpersonal comparisons of their own payoffs with others (i.e., there is no notion of advantageous or disadvantageous inequity). In this sense, ERC has a less nuanced notion of inequality relative to the Fehr–Schmidt model.

The Fehr–Schmidt model is a bold one. It sticks its neck out and proposes a particular functional form that is eminently testable; this is quite distinct from the neoclassical approach, which argues that its underlying framework can potentially account for other-regarding preferences, yet does not specify how. The Fehr–Schmidt model has two eminently attractive features. First, it is able to explain the results from the key experimental games on human sociality such as the dictator game, ultimatum game, trust game, and public goods game with punishment; Volume 2 gives the details. Thus, it meets the minimum standard for any aspiring theory of other-regarding preferences. Second, it predicts cooperation and sharing in bilateral/small group encounters and self-regarding outcomes under market competition. For instance, in ultimatum games, the proposer offers the responder a share of the pie because advantageous inequity is aversive and the responder rejects low offers because disadvantageous inequity is aversive. Ex-post punishment of non-contributors by contributors in public goods games can also be explained by disadvantageous inequity suffered by contributors. By contrast, under self-regarding preferences, we should never observe such punishments because bygones are bygones; see Section 6.2 below for more details. However, in an ultimatum game with responder competition, low offers are not rejected by any responder, because another responder may accept the offer, removing the opportunity to punish the proposer for an unfair offer. Anticipating this, the proposer makes a low offer. In this case, the outcome is 'as if' individuals had self-regarding preferences although they really have other-regarding preferences.

The ERC model is also able to explain several important experimental results such as those from ultimatum games (including those under proposer competition), differences in the relative amounts given by proposers in ultimatum and dictator games, and the positive association between effort and rents in the gift exchange game. The ERC model also allows for asymmetric information, which gives it a wider domain of applicability. It can also explain better the data in three-player ultimatum games where a passive third party appears less cared-for relative to the predictions of the Fehr–Schmidt model (Bolton and Ockenfels, 1998). In other domains, it is less successful. Mean preserving spreads of payoffs leave a player's utility unaffected but this is not supported by the experimental results (Charness and Rabin, 2002). In public goods games with punishments, players with ERC utility will not punish non-contributors because they are not concerned with a comparison of individual payoffs. Anticipating this, non-contributors will not contribute. Hence, the ERC model predicts that the outcome of the public goods games with and without punishments should be identical, a finding that is rejected by the evidence (Fehr and Gächter, 2000a,b). The ERC model may perhaps give even more realistic predictions in cognitively challenging situations where players might not know the precise income distribution of others but still have a rough idea of their relative income.

Clearly, the Fehr–Schmidt model and the ERC model cannot explain all aspects of social preferences because they are not designed to do so. In many situations, inferring intentions is important. Most people would punish others for intentional unkindness, but not for unintentional unkindness. Even the law makes a distinction between murder and manslaughter. However, inferring intentions of others requires a specification of belief hierarchies and a rigorous analysis requires the use of *psychological game theory*, which, in contrast to classical game theory, allows beliefs to directly enter the utility function (Geanakoplos et al., 1989; Rabin, 1993; Dufwenberg and Kirchsteiger, 2004; Battigalli and Dufwenberg, 2009); see Volume 4 for the details. For instance, we may offer a tip to a taxi driver if we believe that he expects a tip, otherwise we feel guilty. The insights offered by Fehr–Schmidt preferences have been successfully combined with endogenous beliefs in the framework of psychological game theory (Falk and Fischbacher, 2006). In other domains, such as equal splits in ultimatum games, it appears that people follow certain *fairness norms* that are not directly captured either by the Fehr–Schmidt model or the ERC model (Rotemberg, 2008; Andreoni and Bernheim, 2009). The interested reader can pursue an empirical critique of both models in Cooper and Kagel (2015).

The Fehr–Schmidt model has led to several important theoretical advances in the literature on human sociality. For instance, it has played an important role in contract theory in the understanding of long-term contracts (Brown et al., 2004, 2012), and the choice of contracts in the presence of contractual incompleteness, such as the choice of bonus contracts over incentive contracts (Fehr et al., 2007). In each of these cases, the experimental evidence is consistent with the predictions of the underlying model.

Redistributive concerns are often center stage in national and local elections. In experimental games, people often prefer a smaller more equitably distributed cake to a larger less equitably distributed cake; these results fit well the Fehr–Schmidt model (Tyran and Sausgruber, 2006; Ackert et al., 2007). These empirical insights have led to new theoretical results in *behavioral political economy*, such as the existence of a Condorcet winner with inequity averse preferences, and the equilibrium redistributive tax when there is a mixture of voters who have self-regarding and Fehr–Schmidt preferences (Dhami and al-Nowaihi, 2010c,d). There has been progress in establishing key results on the effects of other-regarding preferences in a Walrasian competitive equilibrium (Dufwenberg et al., 2011); Fehr–Schmidt preferences provide an important example of a key separability assumption in this framework (Dhami and al-Nowaihi, 2010d). The standard machinery of stochastic dominance for self-regarding preferences (e.g., first and second order stochastic dominance and Lorenz dominance) does not apply when people have other-regarding preferences. However, the analogues of all these concepts for inequity averse preferences have been developed rigorously (Dhami and al-Nowaihi, 2013). Volume 2 describes the details of these developments.

5.3 *The quasi-hyperbolic model and self-control problems*

Temporal analyses of economic models, for descriptive and normative purposes, almost exclusively rely on the *exponential discounted utility* (EDU) model. The EDU model arose purely in response to technical considerations. Samuelson (1937) proposed the EDU model and it turned out to be the unique method of discounting among delay-discounting models that leads to *time consistent choices* (Strotz, 1956). Let $\mathbf{c}_0 = (c_0, c_1, \ldots, c_T)$ denote the real-valued *temporal consumption profile* of an individual at time $t = 0$. Under EDU, this consumption profile is evaluated by the following utility function,

$$U(\mathbf{c}_0) = \sum_{t=0}^{T} \delta^t u(c_t); \; \delta = \frac{1}{1+\theta}, \theta > 0. \tag{6}$$

The EDU model captures the key idea of impatience in a simple and parsimonious manner. However, a single parameter, the constant *discount rate*, θ, captures all relevant psychological considerations. In contrast to many who followed him, Samuelson was very careful in introducing his proposal. On the descriptive validity of his model he writes (p. 159), "It is completely arbitrary to assume that the individual behaves so as to maximize an integral of the form envisaged in (2) [i.e., the EDU model in (6)]." On the normative implications of EDU he writes (p. 161), "…any connection between utility as discussed here and any welfare concept is disavowed."

The evidence does not support the EDU model. Arguably, the EDU model is rejected even more strongly than expected utility theory. The evidence can be gleaned from many sources (Loewenstein and Prelec, 1992; Frederick et al., 2002). There are several anomalies of the EDU model that make it a poor candidate of choice on empirical grounds. For instance, empirical evidence shows that losses are discounted less than gains (*the sign effect*), greater magnitudes are discounted relatively less (*the magnitude effect*), discounting over an interval depends on how that interval is subdivided (*subadditive discounting*), temporal choices can be cyclical (*apparent intransitivity of preferences*), and choices may depend on the *shape of the consumption profile*, despite no changes in discounted utility. Furthermore, the discount rate depends on age (younger people are more impatient), intelligence (higher IQ is correlated with lower impatience), and addictions (gamblers, smokers, drug users, and heavy alcohol drinkers are more impatient).

In this section, we concentrate on an important anomaly of the EDU, namely, the rejection of the constant discount rate, sometimes known as the *common difference effect*. Consider the following example from Thaler (1981): "Most people prefer one apple today to two apples tomorrow but they prefer two apples in 51 days to one apple in 50 days." This *temporal preference reversal* violates constant discounting. A range of other examples highlight an increase in impatience when a future reward is shifted in date towards the present. For instance, short-lived New Year resolutions on smoking or drinking alcohol made with perfect sincerity at an earlier date, procrastination in undertaking various tasks or activities, splurging too much on consumption now, and saving inadequately for the future.

The sort of preferences exhibited in Thaler's apples problem are known as *present-biased preferences*. Consider outcome–time pairs of the form (z, t), where z is an outcome (possibly but not necessarily monetary), and t is time. Consider two possible outcomes z, z' and three time periods t, τ, t', all strictly positive. The decision maker considers alternative outcome–time pairs at time 0. Let $\succsim$ be a preference relation between outcome–time pairs (e.g., if $(8, 3) \succsim (10, 4)$, the 8 units received 3 periods from now are "at least as good as" 10 units received 4 periods from now). A great deal of evidence indicates *preference reversals* of the following form.

$$(z, t) \succsim (z', t') \text{ but } (z', t' + \tau) \succsim (z, t + \tau); \tau > 0, t' > t, z' > z. \qquad (7)$$

One may fix z, t, t' in an experiment and ask subjects to state a value of z' such that they are indifferent between (z, t) and (z', t'). A straightforward calculation can then be used to infer the implied discount rate. Early experiments by Thaler (1981) showed that the implied discount rates for a one-month, one-year, and ten-year horizon, were, respectively, 3.45, 1.2, and 0.19. Thus, individuals are more impatient the closer the reward is to the present.

Fundamental work was done by George Ainslie in fitting discount functions to human and non-human temporal choice data that is summarized in Ainslie (1992). Figure 3 plots the implied per-period discount rate when the future reward is received with various time delays, for one

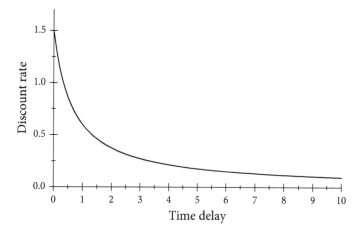

Figure 3 A plot of the discount rate for the one-parameter hyperbolic discounting function with varying time delay.

of his functional forms that fitted his data well; see Volume 3 for the details. As in Thaler's experiments, the discount rate is higher when the reward is more proximate to the present and the discount rate is hyperbolically declining, hence, the term *hyperbolic discounting*.

One behavioral response to the empirical data has been to suggest a two-parameter *general hyperbolic discount function* that nests EDU as a special case (Loewenstein and Prelec, 1992).[31] However, a much simpler version, *quasi hyperbolic discounting* or the (β, δ) form, based on initial work by Phelps and Pollak (1968), but popularized by Laibson (1994, 1997), has paved the way for major applications of present-biased preferences. Under quasi-hyperbolic discounting, the consumption profile $\mathbf{c}_0 = (c_0, c_1, \dots, c_T)$ is evaluated in the following manner.

$$U^0(\mathbf{c}_0) = u(c_0) + \beta \sum_{t=1}^{T} \delta^t u(c_t), \, 0 < \beta < 1, \delta = \frac{1}{1+\theta}, \theta > 0. \tag{8}$$

Here, δ plays the same role that it plays in the EDU model. The real bite comes from the term β that shrinks the utility from future consumption levels, relative to the present. This creates an additional *present bias for current consumption* over and above the impatience that is captured in the discount factor δ. This feature explains preference reversals such as in Thaler's apples example, which the reader can readily verify. Unlike the general form of hyperbolic discounting, under quasi-hyperbolic discounting, the discount rate jumps up discontinuously just as one approaches the current date; the reader can do a few quick plots to check this.

Empirical evidence typically shows declining discount rates as in Figure 3, which implies *present-biased preferences*. However, there is somewhat less agreement about whether discount rates just decline, or if they decline in a hyperbolic manner. A great deal of empirical evidence from the lab and the field is consistent with quasi-hyperbolic discounting (Viscusi et al., 2008; Fang and Silverman, 2009; Tanaka et al., 2010).

Quasi-hyperbolic discounting has given rise to a wide range of applications of behavioral time discounting and a real improvement in our understanding of temporal decisions; an

---

[31] See also al-Nowaihi and Dhami (2006b) for a simple axiomatic derivation of the general hyperbolic discount function that corrects some errors in the seminal work of Loewenstein and Prelec (1992).

entire chapter is devoted to these applications in Volume 3. Do individuals with present-biased preferences have adequate awareness that they might also exhibit a present bias in the future? This turns out to be a rather critical question whose consequences have been well explored (O'Donoghue and Rabin, 2001). In this context, it is best to think of individuals as a collection of *multiple selves*, each self coinciding with a distinct time period (e.g., a morning-self who presses the snooze button, overriding the decision to wake up early made by a night-self). Empirical evidence suggests that individuals lie somewhere between the two extremes of full awareness of future self-control problems, and no awareness of such problems; thus, they may termed as partial-naifs.

Partial-naivety about future self-control problems, in conjunction with quasi-hyperbolic preferences, makes interesting predictions in a range of problems (see Volume 3). There are important applications to macroeconomics, where one can derive the behavioral analogue of the Euler equation and explain several critical puzzles, for instance (Laibson, 1997, 1998): Why does consumption track income so closely? Why do individuals undersave for retirement? Why is there a sharp drop in consumption at retirement? Why do individuals hold illiquid assets and credit card debt simultaneously? Why is high consumption variability not associated with high consumption growth? What is the appropriate relation between intertemporal substitution and risk?

But there is also an equally important range of microeconomic questions that can be addressed with this framework: Why do many people procrastinate (O'Donoghue and Rabin, 2001)? Why do many people retire early (Diamond and Köszegi, 2003)? What are appropriate sin taxes (taxes on harmful activities to oneself or to society) in the presence of present bias (O'Donoghue and Rabin, 2006)? Why do smokers sometimes welcome an increase in the retail tax on cigarettes (Gruber and Mullainathan, 2005)? Why might some people buy expensive annual gym memberships, when a pay-per-visit contract would have saved them money (DellaVigna and Malmendier, 2004)? Why might farmers use fertilizers suboptimally (Duflo et al., 2011)? Hopefully these questions may whet your appetite to read Volume 3 in more detail.

Given the evidence, the rigorous axiomatic developments, and wide-ranging applications of present-biased preferences, the dominance of EDU might well be an interesting topic for a student of economic thought writing a dissertation in 2030. But I would be lying if I said that the current generation of behavioral economists do not find this state of affairs to be frustrating. There have been several criticisms of hyperbolic discounting. But whether time preferences are exactly hyperbolic or not will be eventually less important than whether they are present-biased.[32] Ultimately, a more complete picture of choice over temporal sequences might also need to relax the high degree of cognitive requirement that is embodied in all delay-discounting models. *Attribute-based models* that invoke choice heuristics may well outperform existing delay-discounting models (Ericson et al., 2015).

5.4 *Level-k and CH models: disequilibrium in beliefs in strategic interaction*

Non-cooperative game theory represents one of the most significant advances in economic theory. It has enabled economists to make very precise and testable predictions in strategic

---

[32] In this book we also consider several other theories of present-biased preferences. These include the *planner–doer model* (Shefrin and Thaler, 1981), *models of dual-selves* (Fudenberg and Levine, 2006), and the Gul–Pesendorfer model of *temptation preferences* (Gul and Pesendorfer, 2001).

situations. In the economics profession there is widespread acceptance and use of the main solution concept, *Nash equilibrium*. In a Nash equilibrium and its extensions, players play a best response to their beliefs, and the beliefs and actions of the players are mutually consistent. Furthermore, Bayes' rule is used to update beliefs, whenever possible.

How do the actions and beliefs of players come to be mutually consistent? The most common justifications are an appeal to an unmodeled, underlying, process of learning, or that a Nash equilibrium is simply a social norm. None of these arguments is satisfactory. First, as we show in Volume 6, the outcomes of experiments on learning do not necessarily converge to a Nash equilibrium. Second, many norms are not Nash equilibria, particularly in the domain of cooperative human outcomes. Furthermore, the epistemic conditions for a Nash equilibrium are too strong and there are no plausible epistemic conditions that justify common knowledge of rationality (Gintis, 2009).

Whether people do play a Nash equilibrium is an empirical matter. Let me cull out, very briefly, some interesting aspects of the evidence that is reviewed over several hundred pages in Volumes 4 and 6; I suppress the very large number of references.[33] In many games, the experimental evidence, particularly in the early rounds of a game, is not consistent with a Nash equilibrium. In many others, the outcomes do not converge to a Nash equilibrium, even when the experiments are repeated over a large number of rounds. Even in relatively simple games that involve more than two to three steps of iterated deletion of dominated strategies, the outcome is often not a Nash equilibrium. However, it is also the case that in more complicated games, experimental evidence is sometimes surprisingly consistent with a Nash equilibrium, such as in signaling game experiments. In other games where complexity and cognitive requirements are quite high, such as bargaining under one-sided asymmetric information, the evidence is inconsistent with a Nash equilibrium. Yet, rather miraculously, when the degree of complexity is raised even further, as in bargaining under two-sided asymmetric information, the evidence fits well with a Nash equilibrium. In some games, where the Nash equilibrium is incredibly difficult to compute, such as in traffic network games, one sometimes observes relatively quick convergence to the Nash equilibrium; see, for instance, Mak et al. (2015). In this game, there are 3.3 billion pure-strategy equilibria, yet, incredibly, all players coordinate to converge on one of these equilibria! In other fairly complex games, the outcome is not even close to a Nash equilibrium, e.g., players might be subject to a winner's curse in common value auctions.

In other cases, such as *market entry games*,[34] the number of entrants exactly matches that predicted by a Nash equilibrium. Kahneman (1988), who ran these experiments, exclaimed that "it looks like magic." However, it is now well known that behavioral theories, such as the *cognitive hierarchy model*, discussed in Volume 4, explain the evidence on market entry games equally well.

In sum, the case for focusing exclusive attention on a Nash equilibrium in economics is difficult to justify. In far too many cases, the behavioral alternatives provide a much superior explanation of the relevant evidence. One approach to relaxing the cognitive requirements embodied in a Nash equilibrium is to allow players to play noisy best replies, rather than strict best replies. This is the approach taken in *quantal response equilibrium* (QRE). A second approach, that we focus on briefly in this section, is *level-k* models (Nagel, 1995; Stahl and Wilson, 1995) and the closely related *cognitive hierarchy* model (Camerer et al., 2004).

---

[33] For an excellent, but slightly dated review of the evidence, see Camerer (2003a).

[34] In a market entry game, a set of firms with unit supply must simultaneously enter into a market with a fixed demand of $d > 0$ integer units. If just d firms enter, all firms make profits. If more than d firms enter, all firms earn zero, and if less than d firms enter, then the entrants earn a low but positive level of profits.

The classic game that is used to illustrate the level-k model is the *p-beauty contest*. Suppose that in a winner-take-all contest, each of n participants chooses a number, x_i, from the interval $[0,100]$. The winning guess is the number closest to $p\bar{x}$, where $p > 0$, and $\bar{x}$ is the mean guess. Let us assume that $p = \frac{2}{3}$. In a symmetric Nash equilibrium, all participants should choose the guess 0. This is easily checked. Conditional on the equilibrium guess of the other players, any player who chooses $0 + \varepsilon$, where $\varepsilon \in \{0, 1, \ldots, 100\}$, moves the target ($\frac{2}{3}\bar{x}$) upwards from 0 to $\frac{2}{3n}\varepsilon$. But for $n \geq 2$, the new target is still closer to 0 than to ε, so no profitable deviations are possible. Likewise, the reader can check that there is no symmetric pure strategy Nash equilibrium in guesses that is strictly positive, because it would be destroyed if one individual chooses a lower guess.[35]

In what follows, we shall, on empirical grounds, ignore Breitmoser's effect that was raised in the last footnote. The typical findings in p-beauty game experiments are shown in Figure 4 for $p = \frac{2}{3}$ and for a diverse subject pool, comprising high ability Caltech students, economics Ph.D. students, portfolio managers, and high school students. The results are in stark contrast to the Nash equilibrium prediction. The original experimental findings are due to Nagel (1995), the first replication was by Ho et al. (1998), and since then, the experiment has been replicated many times. In particular, a peculiar feature of the data is that there are spikes around guesses of 33, 22, 14, ... This is inconsistent with a Nash equilibrium.

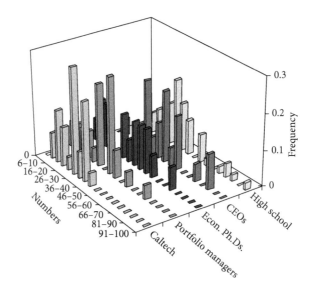

Figure 4 Distribution of choices by different subject pools in a p-beauty contest game.

Source: Reprinted from Trends in Cognitive Sciences, 7(5): 225–31. Colin F. Camerer, "Behavioural studies of strategic thinking in games." © 2003, with permission from Elsevier.

---

[35] Breitmoser (2012) questions the suitability of a level-k approach for the p-beauty contest. His main point is that by ignoring the effect of one's own guess on the average guess, the predictions of level-k models are misspecified. However, it appears to be the case, in most experiments, that subjects ignore the effects of their own actions on the average and the guesses of subjects in experiments are in conformity with the predictions of level-k models; see Volume 4 for the details.

Level-k models offer a parsimonious explanation of the spikes around 33, 22, 14,.... In a level-k model, players have types Lk, $k = 0, 1, \ldots, K$. Each type, except type $L0$, plays a best response, assuming that all other players are of type $Lk - 1$. The specification of type $L0$ depends on the problem and in some applications, this type is assumed to randomize equally among the available actions. In other domains, uniform randomization by type $L0$ players is behaviorally implausible, and one may have to modify it. For instance, in Crawford and Iriberri (2007b), type $L0$ players prefer the label-salient action in games where labels convey salience. The theory does not require type $L0$ players to physically exist; this type may simply represent a model of other players that type $L1$ players have in mind. The frequencies of the various types of players can be estimated from the data. Empirical studies show that the largest percentage of players is of types $L0$, $L1$, and $L2$. Players of type $L3$ or beyond, are rare.

Level-k models directly speak to the cognitive limitations of players and truncate the "infinite regress in beliefs" feature of classical game theory at some low, cognitively plausible, level. In particular, the solution concept that is proposed here is non-circular in the following sense that is well described by Selten (1998): "Basic concepts in game theory are often circular in the sense that they are based on definitions by implicit properties...Boundedly rational strategic reasoning seems to avoid circular concepts. It directly results in a procedure by which a problem solution is found."

Let us apply level-k models to the p-beauty contest game. Type $L0$ players simply randomize equally among the various guesses so their average guess is 50. Type $L1$ players play a best response to a guess of 50, which is $\frac{2}{3}50 = 33.3$. Type $L2$ players play a best response to a guess of 33.3, which is $\frac{2}{3}33.3 = 22.2$. Similarly, type $L3$ players choose $\frac{2}{3}22.2 = 14.8$. The level-k model predicts spikes at 33.3, 22.2, and 14.8, which matches well with the data in Figure 4. If we accept that type $L0$ players randomize equally among their choices, then this is an incredibly precise prediction that is confirmed by the data; however a richer model is likely to be needed to explain all the data in Figure 4. This model is a "disequilibrium in beliefs" model so that, ex-post, many players will be surprised at the outcome, because their initial beliefs about other players are not confirmed.

A perseverant classical game theorist may not accept these results, arguing that a Nash equilibrium is about learning through repeated play; so, if you played the p-beauty game several times, the Nash equilibrium prediction will hold. This argument does not hold for several reasons. First, even if subjects use simple rules of thumb in a repeated p-beauty contest, and play a best response to the observed mean in the last period, then under reasonable assumptions the outcomes can be shown to converge to a guess of zero. Second, unlike the repeated p-beauty contest, real-world environments are not stationary, so a repeated p-beauty contest is not a stringent test of the theory. Third, a Nash equilibrium does not explain the temporal pattern of guesses. In a ten-round repeated p-beauty contest where groups of three subjects are matched by cognitive ability, a level-k model describes well the temporal pattern of guesses (Gill and Prowse, 2015). In the final two rounds, the high cognitive ability group reaches the Nash equilibrium prediction 29% of the time; the corresponding figure for the mixed and low cognitive ability groups is, respectively, only 15% and 13%.

A particularly simple version of the p-beauty contest occurs when there are two players, $n = 2$. For $p = \frac{2}{3}$, the winning guess is simply the lower of the two guesses. Thus, the cognitive requirements in guessing a Nash equilibrium are substantially reduced. Yet, before the p-beauty contest was part of the folklore, when the experiments were run with professionals at conferences, the Nash outcome was not achieved for the vast majority of subjects. Four of these five conferences were economics conferences that included game theorists (Grosskopf and Nagel, 2008). 36.2%

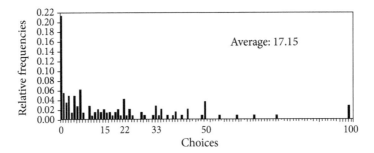

Figure 5 Choices of game theorist subjects in a p-beauty contest game.
Source: Bosch-Domènech et al. (2002) with permission from the American Economic Association.

of professionals and 9.85% of students chose the Nash outcome. However, any choice greater than zero is a weakly dominated strategy, which is chosen by 62.8% of professionals and 91.15% of students. There is no statistical difference between the cumulative distribution of choices in the cases $n = 2$ and $n > 2$ for both pools of players. The results from game theorist subjects in Figure 5 show that their behavior is similar to other humans, although 22% of the choices in this group conformed to the Nash outcome, the highest among the six groups considered (Bosch-Domènech et al., 2002).

The *cognitive hierarchy* (CH) model is similar to the level-k model. However, in the CH model, each type, $Lk, k = 1, 2, \ldots$, assumes that there is a distribution, typically Poisson, of players of all lower types, $Lk - 1, Lk - 2, \ldots, L0$. The predictions of the level-k model and the CH model are similar for a large class of games and it is very difficult to put one ahead of the other on empirical grounds (Crawford et al., 2013). When the early-round results of a large class of 55 games are pitted against the predictions of the CH model and the Nash equilibrium, then there are two findings (Camerer et al., 2004). Whenever the Nash equilibrium predicts well, CH predicts well too, and when the Nash equilibrium predicts poorly, CH predictions are more accurate. Field data supports the superior predictions of the CH model relative to a Nash equilibrium (Goldfarb and Yang, 2009; Goldfarb and Xiao, 2011). Level-k models are supported by a great deal of other evidence (Costa-Gomes et al., 2001; Costa-Gomes and Crawford, 2006).

The applications of level-k and CH models have grown enormously. These range from testing the significance of focal points when they come into conflict with label salience in symmetric and asymmetric games (Crawford et al., 2008); the role of preplay communication in enhancing coordination (Crawford, 2007); the explanation of the "magical" results in the market entry game that were originally thought of as a remarkable confirmation of Nash equilibrium (Camerer et al., 2004); and the explanation of the winner's curse in common-value auctions (Crawford and Iriberri, 2007a; Crawford et al., 2009).

Level-k models do not have a theory of level-0 players and the behavior of these players needs to be inferred from the data. So, a critic might argue, is it legitimate to use the same data to infer parameters of the behavior of level-0 players, and then use these estimated parameters to estimate the remaining parameters of interest? Crawford and Iriberri (2007b) solve this problem by first using a part of the sample to estimate the behavior of level-0 players. They then successfully make predictions for out-of-sample data (which in this case is a set of closely related games) that are confirmed.

Hargreaves Heap et al. (2014) question the issue of portability of level-k behavior across a wider range of games than are considered in Crawford and Iriberri (2007b). They do assume, however, that the specification of the level L0 players is identical across these games. In some games, particularly coordination games, *team reasoning* (see Volume 4) rather than level-*k* models appears to better describe the evidence. This should alert us to the importance of different contexts that may trigger different behavioral responses—in some kinds of games, level-*k* reasoning may be invoked, while in others, team reasoning may be invoked. Perhaps a hybrid of level-*k* and team reasoning models, provided team reasoning can be formally defined in a satisfactory manner, may explain the data even better; similar conclusions are reached by Crawford et al. (2008, p. 1448).

5.5 *The heuristics and biases program: radical behavioral economics*

The neoclassical approach views economic agents as Bayesian, subjective expected utility maximizing decision makers who have unlimited cognitive abilities and follow the rules of classical statistics. These economic agents also routinely engage in mathematical optimization, using the latest developments in mathematics, statistics, engineering, and computer science. This is one possible hypothesis of human behavior to start with. However, as always, its descriptive validity hinges on the empirical evidence. Following Milton Friedman's approach (see Section 2 above), and some may argue, its misuse, it is not an uncommon response in economics to handwave away the evidence and argue that real humans behave "as if" they were textbook economic agents in neoclassical theory.

The crucial significance of the *heuristics and biases program* of Daniel Kahneman and Amos Tversky was that they showed systematically that this "as if" view is inconsistent with the evidence (Tversky and Kahneman, 1974). *Heuristics* are any rules of thumb that individuals actually use, as distinct from normative recommendations. Heuristics are *fast*, in terms of the computation time required, and *frugal*, in terms of information requirements. The term *biases* in the program refers to the difference between actual human behavior and the predictions of neoclassical theory.

The heuristics and biases program, one of the most important advances in all of social science, created great disagreement among psychologists. Some of the attacks on Tversky and Kahneman were vicious, and even personal (see Volume 5 and Stanovich and West, 2000, p. 649).[36] Most economists ignored this work, and continue to do so, despite its ubiquitous presence around us in the media, public debates, and in behavioral finance. Luckily for behavioral economics, a young economist, reading this work in 1976 did not ignore it; he wrote about it recently (Thaler, 2015, p. 22): "As I read, my heart started pounding the way it might during the final minutes of a close game. The paper took me thirty minutes to read from start to finish, but my life had changed forever."

Tversky and Kahneman identified a range of judgment heuristics, which are underpinned by a great deal of evidence. Volume 5 gives the details. Here, we consider some aspects of this research program. Let us call a textbook neoclassical economic agent who follows the rules of classical statistics a *Bayesian*.

People are often asked to answer questions of the form: How likely is it that event A was generated by category/class/process B? In answering this question, people often use the

---

[36] Here are some quotes from published journal articles (references in Volume 5). 1. "it is Kahneman & Tversky, not their subjects, who have failed to grasp the logic of the problem." 2. "If a 'fallacy' is involved, it is probably more attributable to the researchers than to the subjects." 3. "In the examples of alleged base rate fallacy considered by Kahneman and Tversky, they, and not their experimental subjects, commit the fallacies."

representativeness heuristic, i.e., they give an answer based on how much event A looks like B.[37] Relative to a Bayesian, people often assign too high a probability that small samples share the properties of large samples. Such individuals behave as if they obeyed a *law of small numbers*, rather than the statistically correct, *law of large numbers*. This has important implications. For instance, individuals find it difficult to produce hypothetical sequences of random numbers; these sequences exhibit too much *negative autocorrelation* (Tversky and Kahneman, 1974; Bar-Hillel and Wagenaar, 1991; Rapoport and Budescu, 1997). This behavior produces the *gambler's fallacy*, i.e., avoiding bets on recent winning numbers in gambling or recent winners in the stock market (Clotfelter and Cook, 1993; Terrell, 1994; Odean, 1998).

People may often observe many consecutive, identical, outcomes. In this case, they may use the representativeness heuristic to infer that the sample is drawn from a population that contains a disproportionate share of such outcomes. Thus, they may expect more of these outcomes in the future; this *positive autocorrelation* in outcomes is known as the *hot hands fallacy*. Clearly, a Bayesian would also update in the same direction, however, under representativeness, individuals react more strongly. The hot hands phenomenon has been documented in sports, such as basketball or baseball, where players who score heavily in a game may be believed to be on a hot streak. Lotto stores that sell winning lotto tickets experience unusually high sales for up to 40 weeks following the lotto win, although the probability of purchasing a winning ticket from that store is unchanged (Guryan and Kearney, 2008). For an "animate" stochastic process that relies on human skills (e.g., basketball and baseball), one is more likely to observe a hot hands fallacy relative to an "inanimate" process (e.g., casino betting), where a gambler's fallacy is more likely to be observed (Ayton and Fischer, 2004). The law of small numbers can also explain the existence of overconfidence (Rabin, 2002).

Individuals use the *availability heuristic* when they judge the probability of an event by the ease with which similar events are accessible or "available" to the mind. Accessibility is easier for salient and vivid events, which highlights the importance of media coverage of events. There is a close link between the perceived frequency of deaths by various causes and proxies for the availability of such events in memory (Lichtenstein et al., 1978).

The *affect heuristic* identifies the role of emotions in human decisions (Loewenstein et al., 2001; Slovic et al., 2002). People often classify and tag events by their *affect*. For instance, a holiday in New York may leave a positive affect, if it was enjoyable but, *ceteris paribus*, a negative affect, if one was mugged during the holiday. The affect heuristic argues that the pool of these positive and negative affects determines our choices, rather than objective statistical probabilities of events, e.g., do I go to New York for my next holiday? The affect heuristic may economize on cognitive efforts in making a decision and quicken decision making, because it is easier to think "what do I feel about it?" rather than "what do I think about it?" (Kahneman, 2011). Even experts rate the risk of hazardous substances by the feeling of dread that these substances invoke (Fischhoff et al., 1978; Slovic et al., 1999). Loewenstein et al. (2001) make a powerful case for understanding choices among risky options in terms of their emotional impact.

Anchoring, the influence of initial suggestions as anchors on subsequent judgments, is one of the most robust and important heuristics. When anchors are self-generated, people adjust

---

[37] For instance, suppose that three successive balls are drawn with replacement from either urn A that has 1 red and 2 black balls or urn B, which has 2 red and 1 black balls; it is common knowledge that urn A is chosen with probability 0.6. The three sampled balls turn out to be 1 red and 2 black. What is the probability that the balls came from urn A? The statistically correct answer is 0.75, but an individual subject to the representativeness heuristics gives an answer greater than 0.75 and, in the extreme case, an answer of 1.

insufficiently towards the correct response, but when they are provided by others (e.g., the experimenter), people are often biased towards finding confirmatory evidence for them. In a famous experiment, the response of subjects to the question "how many African countries are there in the United Nations?" is influenced by the prior observed outcome of a random wheel of fortune that is rigged to come up with the numbers 10 or 65 (Tversky and Kahneman, 1974); clearly irrelevant information influences choice in this case. In field studies, experienced judges and estate agents are influenced by anchors (Northcraft and Neale, 1987; Englich and Mussweiler, 2001). Implausible and irrelevant anchors can have a significant effect on subjects' choices (Strack and Mussweiler, 1997). Regulation, such as caps on damages awarded to litigants, serves an anchoring role and influences the rate of pretrial settlements and the level of damages (Babcock and Pogarsky, 1999; Pogarsky and Babcock, 2001).

Anchoring has been documented in a wide range of contexts, such as poetry reading sessions (Ariely et al., 2006); violation of a basic implication of efficient markets (Mussweiler and Schneller, 2003); and first offers in price negotiation (Galinsky and Mussweiler, 2001). Anchoring has also been used to explain a range of other behavioral phenomena, such as hindsight bias, non-linear probability weighting, and preference reversals.

Bayes' rule fundamentally underpins modern economic theory. However, most people do not employ Bayes' rule when the relevant information is presented in a probability format. In particular, individuals routinely exhibit *base rate neglect*, i.e., give insufficient attention to the prevalence of a particular trait or feature in the overall population (Kahneman and Tversky, 1972; Bar-Hillel, 1980; Tversky and Kahneman, 1980). Consider the following problem, adapted from Casscells et al. (1978) that was given to students at Harvard Medical School. Suppose that a police Breathalyzer test discovers false drunkenness in 5% of the cases when the driver is sober. However, the Breathalyzers are always able to detect a truly drunk person with complete certainty. In the general population, 1/1000 of drivers engage in driving while drunk. Suppose that a driver is checked at random, and takes a Breathalyzer test, which shows that the driver is drunk. How high is the probability he or she really is drunk? The modal response was 95%, the mean response was 56%, and only a sixth of the students gave the correct answer, which is approximately 2%. Most people ignore the low base rate of 1/1000 of drivers who drink and drive.

Hindsight bias occurs when individuals make a prediction about some future event, but after they observe the actual outcome, their postdictive judgment (i.e., recall of their initial prediction) is too close to the actual outcome (Fischhoff, 1975). Thus, people give the impression as if "they knew it all along." This bias is extremely important in legal cases where the judge and jurors must infer if the defendant took enough preventive care in the past, having already observed the outcome of the defendant's decision. A meta-study finds that experts also exhibit the hindsight bias (Guilbault et al., 2004). In finance, hindsight bias reduces estimates of volatility, and people engage in less corrective activity of incorrect models (Biais and Weber, 2009).

Confirmation bias is an important heuristic in which people interpret the evidence in a self-serving manner so as to confirm their initially held views (Lord et al. 1979). Higher cognitive ability does not reduce this bias (Stanovich and West 2007). As one may expect, since confirmation bias vindicates initially held views, it can also explain the prevalence of overconfidence and underconfidence (Rabin and Schrag, 1999).

Some of the initial criticisms against the heuristics and biases approach could be easily refuted. These included: subject errors and misperceptions caused the biases, or that Kahneman and Tversky did not understand probability theory well enough. Other criticisms took longer to refute, some were already actually answered by Tversky and Kahneman in their published work, others helped to modify the theory without serious changes in the message. A prime example is the belief that if individuals are presented with information in *frequency format* rather than in a *probability format*, then human biases disappear (Gigerenzer and Hoffrage, 1995; Cosmides and Tooby, 1996). Empirical evidence, examined in some detail in Volume 5, supports two kinds of conclusions. (1) Natural frequency format reduces the extent of biases only for a few heuristics. For instance, in the best-case scenario for the frequency format, for base-rate neglect, less than half the subjects conform to Bayes' rule. (2) For the vast majority of heuristics, results for the probability format and the frequency format are comparable. Most real-world data of interest to economists are presented in a probability format, e.g., interest rate increases announced by central banks, interest rates quoted by mortgage providers, percentage changes in unemployment, crime, and GDP changes announced by various government agencies. Thus, the debate between the proponents of the natural frequency format and the probability format might be of more academic than substantive interest.

In his seminal work on bounded rationality, Herbert Simon argued that cognitive limitations preclude individuals from engaging in neoclassical optimization exercises. As Simon (1978, p. 347) famously put it: "But there are no direct observations that individuals or firms do actually equate marginal costs and revenues." Reinhard Selten has often argued that many economic problems are hard in the sense that they are *NP-Complete*. This means that the number of steps needed to solve a problem in any algorithm of the solution, grows exponentially with the size of the problem, as in the well-known traveling salesman problem. Moderately difficult problems in this class require very high computation time. It is a leap of faith to assume that humans can routinely solve these problems or act "as if" they could.

Herbert Simon's solution was to replace *optimization behavior* with *satisficing behavior*, i.e., individuals have an *aspiration level* and adjust gradually towards it (Simon, 1978, 2000; Selten, 2001); for supportive empirical evidence see Caplin et al. (2011). A second line in the literature is associated with the work of Gerd Gigerenzer and colleagues (Gigerenzer et al., 1999; Gigerenzer and Selten, 2001). The main thrust of this approach is that heuristics are not mistakes, but a rational response to bounded rationality, and heuristics often outperform selected optimization methods. However, the superiority of these fast and frugal heuristics is often demonstrated in domains where the relevant optimization benchmark is unclear. In contrast, Tversky–Kahneman were interested in domains where the relevant benchmark is completely clear. Furthermore, in the fast and frugal heuristics approach, the heuristics are typically experimenter provided; by contrast, in more complicated situations, it is not always clear what the relevant heuristics should be. Tversky–Kahneman are able, in contrast, to typically specify the environments in which their heuristics apply.

Gerd Gigerenzer's work has led to a heated debate with the Tversky–Kahneman approach and many commentators treat the two positions as adversarial. This has come to be known as the *great rationality debate* and it is outlined in Volume 5 (Stanovich and West, 2000; Stanovich, 2012). My own reading is that this debate is extremely muddled; the two approaches are complementary and often deal with quite different domains (for details, see Dhami et al., 2018). Both approaches need to be encouraged, but for entirely different reasons. Kahneman and Tversky's (1996, p. 584) frustration is well captured in this quote: "The position described by Gigerenzer is indeed easy to refute but it bears little resemblance to ours. It is useful to remember that the refutation of a caricature can be no more than a caricature of a refutation."

How would you feel about economics, and particularly about economists, if you were Daniel Kahneman? (1) Prospect theory, the most empirically satisfactory decision theory for risk, uncertainty, and ambiguity, has not yet made it into the mainstream economics curriculum, nearly 40 years after it was published. (2) The heuristics and biases approach was initially viciously attacked, continues to be ignored by most economists despite having the greatest relevance for their work, and then pitted unfairly and unnecessarily against Gerd Gigerenzer's approach. One can sense the underlying disappointment if one reads Kahneman (2011) between the lines. However, the literature on behavioral finance, and a new generation of economists, most notably led by Matthew Rabin, have rekindled interest in this approach. Volume 5 reports this work in detail.

6 Five examples of behavioral evidence

In this section, I consider five examples of behavioral evidence. This evidence often challenges some of the assumptions or implications of neoclassical models that are taken to be true on a-priori grounds. A more detailed account can be found later in the book.

6.1 *Does competitive market equilibrium survive fairness considerations?*

The development of the theory of competitive market equilibrium (CE) is one of the great intellectual achievements of modern economics. Empirical tests of a CE require a specification of the hypothetical Walrasian auctioneer that is a central part of the theory. Chamberlin (1948) ran some of the first CE experiments with Harvard students. He allowed students to interact freely in their roles as buyers and sellers in a market, and strike voluntary and mutually agreeable deals. This experimental protocol accords well with the intuition of many people about how competitive markets function. He found that prices did not converge to a CE. Modern experimentalists will disagree with many features of Chamberlin's experiments, despite their intuitive appeal. For instance, subjects were not incentivized and did not play the game anonymously without face-to-face interaction. I suspect strongly that Chamberlin's results will go through even if the subjects were incentivized; the main drivers of his result are the other elements of his experimental design. However, Chamberlin's results have unfortunately not had a fundamental impact on modern economics.

Vernon Smith (1962) used a novel method of inducing demands and supplies among subjects in experiments. This is known as *induced value methodology*, and is now a standard technique to induce preferences in experiments. Each buyer is given a card with a valuation on it that is privately known to the buyer only. The buyers cannot pay a price above their valuation. Similarly, sellers are given a card with a cost on it, and they are not permitted to sell below it. In a *double auction setting*, in each round, buyers place 'bids' and sellers post 'asks.' Buyer–seller pairs voluntarily trade within a given period; successful matches drop out for the remainder of the period. Subjects keep playing within the period until they strike no more voluntary deals, or the period ends. Within this setting, there is relatively quick convergence to a CE, a result that has been replicated many times (Davis and Holt, 1993; Kagel and Roth, 1995). This result also holds with zero intelligence robots (Gode and Sunder, 1993), which suggests that it is the underlying induced value methodology and the institution of double auctions that lead to a CE.

Vernon Smith's findings were readily accepted into economics, unlike Chamberlin's and Kahneman and Tversky's findings. However, Smith's results leave open the question whether we get the CE outcome in the absence of (i) the double auction setting, which is not a particularly pervasive institution, (ii) the induced value methodology, and (iii) in richer competitive market settings. Regarding (ii), Thaler (2015, p. 40) writes: "But I had some worries about this methodology [induced value methodology]. When you go to the store and decide whether to buy a jacket for $49, no one is telling you how much you are willing to pay for it. You have to decide that for yourself, and that value might depend on all sorts of issues." Indeed, in Thaler's own experiments on exchange asymmetries, when subjects had to assign a value to an owned object and an unowned but identical object, owners assigned higher values to owned items. In this section, we focus on (iii).

Fehr et al. (1998) tested for a CE by enriching the market environment to include issues of endogenous quality. In this case, the outcomes did not converge to a CE. It is worth exploring these findings and the subsequent literature. Suppose that risk-neutral sellers have some fixed cost, f, of producing a single unit of a good and they must choose the quality of the good from some interval $[q_0, q_1]$. The variable cost of producing alternative quality levels is given by the function $c(q)$ such that $c' > 0$, so higher quality is more costly to produce. Risk-neutral buyers have unit demands, know the seller's cost, and make price offers to the sellers. Hence, this is a one-sided oral auction with many buyers. Buyers prefer higher quality, and their valuation for one unit of the good is $v(q)$, such that $v' > 0$. Sellers observe the auction price, p, and then decide on non-enforceable quality that they will supply to the buyer. There are more sellers than buyers.

Since higher quality is costly to produce, if all parties have self-regarding preferences, then we should expect sellers to act opportunistically and supply the lowest quality, q_0. Anticipating this, buyers will offer the lowest price $p = v(q_0)$. Thus, in a competitive equilibrium, sellers make a profit equal to $v(q_0) - f - c(q_0)$, the utility of the buyer who wins the auction is $v(q_0) - p = 0$, and the utility of non-winning buyers is also zero. The parameters of the experiment are chosen so that $v(q_0) > f + c(q_0)$, where $f + c(q_0)$ is the minimum cost to the seller of supplying a unit of the good at the lowest quality, hence, it is the *reservation price* in the experiments.

The outcome will be very different if market participants have other-regarding preferences. In particular, if sellers are known to exhibit reciprocity, then buyers will offer prices in excess of the seller's reservation price, and the seller will reciprocate with higher quality. It is likely that in equilibrium, buyers and sellers derive, respectively, higher utility and higher profits relative to the predictions of a CE (with self-regarding preferences). This may be termed as the reciprocity treatment (RT). The parameters in the experiments were chosen so that reciprocal quality increases were associated with Pareto improvements. In order to check if reciprocity is the driving motive, a control treatment (CT) was also implemented in which the quality was publicly known to be exogenously fixed and the seller had no control over it.

There was intra-group homogeneity among the sellers and the buyers. The matched parties did not know each other's identities. While prices were publicly announced, the information on quality was revealed only to the two contracting parties. These features ensured that there were no reputational effects across different rounds of the game if parties were randomly rematched at the end of each round. For the RT, Figure 6 shows the response of quality (vertical axis, $[q_0, q_1] = [0, 0.7]$) to various levels of price (horizontal axis, in blocks of 10s, and ranging from 30 to 110). Numbers over the bars indicate the number of observations in each category. The main finding is that higher prices offered by buyers elicit higher quality by the sellers. Furthermore, in the RT, the average price offered by the buyers was twice the level of the reservation price. However, in the CT, where the quality was fixed exogenously, the prices go down to the sellers' reservation price, hence, sellers' reciprocal behavior is the main driver of departures from the CE outcome. When sellers were offered low prices, they reacted by offering the minimum quality, which is also consistent with the reciprocity hypothesis.

There is experimental evidence of correlation between competition, market institutions, and trust/reciprocity. In their seminal cross-cultural study of the ultimatum game, Henrich et al. (2001) found that the rejection rates of lower offers are higher in societies where there

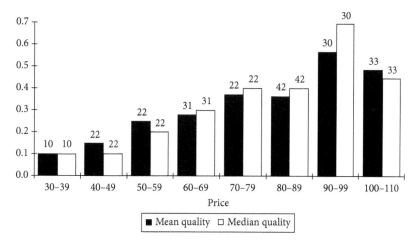

Figure 6 Response of quality to price in a competitive equilibrium.

Source: Reprinted from European Economic Review, 42(1): 1–34. Ernst Fehr, Georg Kirchsteiger, and Arno Riedl, "Gift exchange and reciprocity in competitive experimental markets." © 1998, with permission from Elsevier.

is predominance of buying/selling, working for a wage, and production is carried out on a cooperative basis (as in modern firms). However, causality can run both ways. In societies with greater trust and reciprocity, markets may tend to work well because it is easier to engage in information contracts. Conversely, markets may have an impact on sociality and, therefore, affect the willingness to trust and reciprocate. Given the current evidence, we cannot establish the direction of causality. Evidence shows that in the trust game, competition improves human sociality (Huck et al., 2012); this line of research needs to be developed further.

List (2006) seeks to address the issue of sellers' quality differences between lab and field experiments, based on data gathered from sports card dealers. In the typical marketplace for sports cards, dealers display their sports cards and buyers mill around, requesting cards of a particular quality and offering a price for that quality. In the field data, quality can often be hard to verify and sellers do not know if buyers will later engage in costly quality verification from a third party. Buyers and sellers are recruited by monitors from a sports card market to participate in an hour-long experiment. Buyers can offer either a low price, $20, or a high price, $65. In contrast to the field study, sellers in the lab know that the quality will be subsequently measured, a factor that may influence their quality supplied in the lab relative to the field.

The lab experiments were conducted in close proximity to the sports card market, hence, these experiments offer an unusually clean comparison of lab and field results. There were two kinds of subjects under study, local dealers (70% of the sample), and non-local dealers (30% of the sample). List (2006, pp. 5–6) used the results of this data to conclude that "even though the data collected from one-shot laboratory experiments suggest that social preferences are quite important among these agents, parallel treatments in the field suggest that such effects have minimal influence in naturally occurring transactions. In this sense, dealer behavior in the marketplace approaches what is predicted by self-interest theory."

Following Camerer (2015), let us re-examine the data arising from a within-subjects analysis, i.e., from instances where the same sports card seller or buyer generated data in the lab and in the field; clearly, this is the most meaningful comparison between the lab and the field. This also ties in nicely with the discussion on lab–field generalizability in Section 3, above. The results are

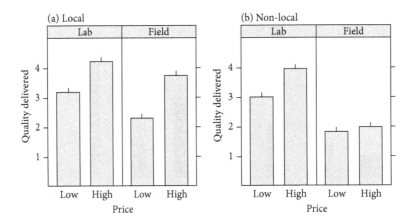

Figure 7 Response of quality to price for local and non-local dealers in the lab and in the field.

Source: Camerer, Colin F. (2015). "The promise and success of lab–field generalizability in experimental economics: a critical reply to Levitt and List." In G. R. Fréchette and A. Schotter (eds.), Handbook of Experimental Economic Methodology, pp. 249–96. Adapted from List, J. A. (2006). "The behavioralist meets the market: measuring social preferences and reputation effects in actual transactions." Journal of Political Economy 114(1) 1–37.

shown in Figure 7; some of this data is based on analysis that was not reported in List (2006). When data are pooled for local and non-local dealers, the quality level supplied (on a 1 to 5 scale) is lower in the field setting, relative to the lab, for each price level: 2.3 versus 3.1 when the price is $20, and 3.1 versus 4.1 when the price is $65. However, the response of quality to changes in price is similar in the lab and the field.

Interpreting the results of List (2006), Levitt and List (2008) argue that sports card dealers in the field behave more selfishly, and (p. 10) "increase quality little in response to a generous offer from the buyer." In their abstract, they say: "Economic models can benefit from incorporating insights from psychology, but behavior in the lab might be a poor guide to real-world behavior." Is this a reasonable conclusion for the more relevant case of within-subjects design? Using Figure 7, for field data, non-local dealers increase their quality in response to higher prices by just 0.13, but the corresponding figure for local dealers (who constitute 70% of the sample) is 1.40, which is significant. Levitt and List draw their strong conclusion because they only report the data for non-local dealers in their 2008 paper. Local dealers do offer higher quality in response to higher prices, hence, their behavior could be the outcome of social preferences.

Camerer (2015) conducts tests of statistical significance of the difference in quality between the lab and the field, for the within-subjects design, but the results are inconclusive. He notes: "To be crystal clear, I am not sure whether dealers behave differently in the lab and the field." List (2006) also gives data on the difference between actual quality supplied by sellers and the seller's claimed quality, a measure of the sellers' mendacity. Mendacious behavior is more common in the field, yet the statistical tests lack power to differentiate lab and field data.

6.2 Why do we not let bygones be bygones?

An important insight of neoclassical economics is that if self-regarding preferences are combined with classical game theory, then we should not observe costly ex-post punishments. This is because such punishments only reduce the size of an individual's payoff, so why punish? In other words, *let bygones be bygones.*

Consider a typical public goods game experiment. A group of n risk-neutral individuals are given an initial endowment of money, $y > 0$. They simultaneously decide on their respective contributions, $g_i \geq 0$, $i = 1,\ldots,n$, to a public good, giving rise to $G = \sum_{i=1}^{n} g_i$ units of the public good (the production technology for the public good is linear). The public good gives a return $r > 0$ per unit, to each individual. Thus, the utility of the ith individual is given by $y - g_i + rG$; typically $\frac{1}{n} < r < 1$, so that it is privately optimal to free-ride (i.e., $g_i = 0$), although the socially optimal solution is that everyone should contribute their entire endowment (i.e., $g_i = y$). Now introduce a costly ex-post punishment stage in which, at the end of the game, the individuals can observe the contributions of others, and engage in costly punishment of non-contributors. An individual who desires to punish another, gives up one monetary unit and the experimenter takes away three monetary units from the intended target of the punishment.

Classical game theory predicts that the punishment stage is irrelevant, because bygones are bygones. Looking ahead, rational players will realize that the punishment stage has no bite, hence, the public goods game with and without punishment is predicted to yield identical results. Fehr and Gächter (2000a) put this to the test. They ran ten rounds of a public goods game with punishment, followed by ten rounds without punishment (rounds 11–20), with $y = 20$ and $r = 0.4$. There were three different treatments. In the partner treatment, the same subjects were matched over all rounds. In the stranger treatment, they were randomly rematched in groups at the start of each round. The perfect stranger treatment is similar to the stranger treatment, but when subjects are rematched at the start of each round, the experimenter ensures that they have not been matched in any of the past rounds. The results are shown in Figure 8.[38]

The prediction of classical game theory, based on self-regarding preferences, is rejected by this evidence. Contributions are high in the presence of punishment for each of the three treatments

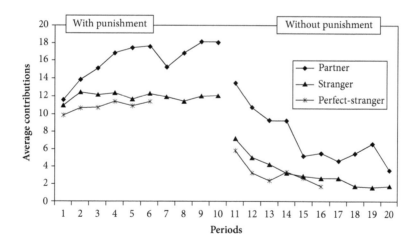

Figure 8 Public good contributions in the presence and absence of punishments.
Source: Fehr and Gächter (1999).

---

[38] One of the most versatile and sagacious social scientists of our times, Herbert Gintis, once mentioned to me that Figure 8 was one of the most important graphs that he had seen in his life.

(rounds 1–10), but decline rapidly once the punishment is removed, reaching near perfect free-riding levels (rounds 11–20). Furthermore, in the presence of punishments, there is a marked difference in the contributions in the three treatments. Contributions are near first-best levels in the partner treatment, but even in the perfect stranger treatment, subjects contribute about half their endowments. Subjects seem to anticipate that they will be punished if they contribute less, particularly when they are repeatedly matched with the same partners. This induces high levels of cooperation.

Punishments, in contrast to the predictions of classical game theory, perform a prosocial role. When the punishment option is removed, subjects begin with high levels of cooperation. However, once contributors observe low contributions in their groups by opportunistic players, they respond in the next round by contributing less. This leads to successive rounds of negative reciprocity and reduced contributions. The efficiency enhancing role of punishments has also been documented in other games, such as in the gift exchange game with punishment (Fehr et al., 1997); we consider this and other evidence in Volume 2.

Consider a few other related points about this analysis.

1. The fact that in the absence of punishment, we observe widespread free-riding does not save the theory with self-regarding preferences, because it cannot explain the pattern of decay in contributions. An explanation of this pattern requires a fraction of the players to exhibit conditional reciprocity (Fischbacher et al., 2001; Fehr and Fischbacher, 2005; Fischbacher and Gächter, 2010).

2. When the experiment is repeated outside Western countries, one also observes *antisocial punishment*, i.e., punishment of contributors by non-contributors who react to past punishments. Antisocial punishments are more likely to be found in societies where the indices for the *norms of civic cooperation* and *rule of law* are low (Herrmann et al., 2008). Experiments possibly overstate the role of punishments because in actual practice, punishments are institutionally meted. Democratic societies do not typically sanction private antisocial punishments. The human desire for prosocial punishments, and the efficiency enhancing role of prosocial punishments in most Western societies, possibly underpins public sanctions against antisocial punishment.

   In an important advance, Fehr and Williams (2015) allow subjects in experiments to voluntarily choose one of the following four institutions. (1) No punishments. (2) Fehr–Gächter type peer punishment. (3) As in (2), but with the additional opportunity for each individual to announce how much everybody should contribute. The average contributions are revealed at the end of each round. This captures the formation of social norms of contributions. (4) Centralized punishment by a democratically determined leader, plus social norms of contributions, as in (3). The main result is that virtually all subjects choose institutions (3) and (4). Furthermore, institution (4) wipes out antisocial punishment. We also review other results in Volume 2, which demonstrate that antisocial punishments are eliminated if, ex-ante, individuals choose the punishment institution by a referendum.

3. The efficiency enhancing role of costly punishments has also been debated using evolutionary arguments. In experiments, the net effect of costly punishments may be to reduce overall payoffs (Page et al., 2005). However, this is not the case if sufficiently large numbers of rounds of punishments are allowed. Gächter et al. (2008) have shown that if the credibility of the punishment threat is established, and if the punishment opportunity arises over sufficiently many rounds (10- and 50-round cooperation games

are considered), then punishments are efficiency enhancing; in fact, only 5–8 rounds of punishments may suffice to increase overall payoffs. Social punishments and reciprocity are also likely to have been essential to the formation of social norms of cooperative behavior (Gintis, 2009).

4. Subjects do not let bygones be bygones, which is a puzzle under self-regarding preferences. Punishments in the public goods experiments can be explained by Fehr–Schmidt preferences in which people have a concern for inequity aversion. Neural evidence is consistent with the view that individuals derive hedonic satisfaction from the act of punishing others who they believe have wronged them. A region of the brain, the striatum, that is associated with the brain's reward circuits, shows greater activity when social punishments are carried out (De Quervain et al., 2004). This also illustrates the powerful role of neural evidence in informing us about human motivations.

6.3 Are financial markets efficient?

Let us call the neoclassically rational agents in financial market *arbitrageurs*. Most neoclassical economic analyses allow for the possibility that some economic agents could be irrational, also known as *noise traders*, relative to arbitrageurs. Yet, it is argued, we can ignore noise traders due to two a-priori arguments.

1. The individual errors of *noise traders* will cancel in the aggregate.
2. Noise traders, if any, will lose money due to the arbitrage activity of arbitrageurs, hence, they will eventually exit the market.

Anyone who has done an introductory course in economics would have come across these plausible-sounding arguments. Most, including those teaching these arguments, are likely to have been convinced. Empirical evidence shows how flawed this a-priori reasoning can be. Formulating plausible a-priori hypotheses is essential in all science, as is testing them stringently, but the stringent testing bit appears to have received less attention, possibly motivated by bogus "as if" arguments.

The first argument has been debunked by the heuristics and biases approach of Kahneman and Tversky (Section 5.5, above). Individual errors of noise traders are often systematic and not random, so they can accumulate in one direction. For instance, individuals subject to the hindsight bias consistently underestimate volatility of stock prices, and fail to update their incorrect models fully (Biais and Weber, 2009). In the formation of *bubbles,* for instance, house price bubbles, individual beliefs can systematically depart from fundamental values for a sufficient length of time. In financial markets, the *disposition effect* caused by loss aversion may prevent people from selling stock below its purchase price precisely at a time when such arbitrage activity is required to equilibrate the market. Insofar as loss aversion is hardwired in individuals, they systematically engage in the disposition effect.

The second argument also turns out to be problematic. Consider the example of house price bubbles, and let prices exceed fundamental values. Yet, suppose that investor sentiment, as captured in the beliefs of noise traders, is that prices will continue to increase. If there are enough noise traders in the market, then arbitrageurs might be forced to bet their money in the direction of a price increase, which exacerbates the departure of price from fundamental values. The seminal work of De Long et al. (1990) shows that noise traders may make more profits than arbitrageurs, particularly if they are bullish, and they may continue to make money for a time, while arbitrageurs might not be able to hold on to loss-making positions for long enough. But, there are many other reasons why financial markets might not be efficient that we discuss next.

Traditional finance has been built on the foundations of the *efficient markets hypothesis* (EMH). It requires that at any instant in time, the price of a security must equal its fundamental value, which we may take to be the present discounted value of all future income flows from the security. Several theoretical arguments can be advanced for why the EMH need not hold. The demonstration of De Long et al. (1990) for market inefficiency based on noise trader risk provided an early theoretical challenge to the EMH. The full range of substitute securities that are required to guarantee EMH might not exist. Transaction costs of arbitrage (cost of finding mispricing information and brokerage fees for taking a short position) might also impede market efficiency.

The difficulty of beating the stock market is often cited as proof of its efficiency. EMH implies that there are no arbitrage opportunities; however, the absence of arbitrage opportunities does not logically imply that EMH holds. This is simply a confusion between necessary and sufficient conditions (Barberis and Thaler, 2003). EMH relies on instantaneous flows of information. Yet, evidence shows that some kinds of information may flow only gradually through the market, leading to a relationship between momentum and trading volumes of stocks, and aggressive trading, even when price equals fundamental values (Hong and Stein, 1999, 2007).

Professional arbitrageurs, such as mutual funds managers, invest on behalf of small and dispersed investors who have little financial expertise. However, the greater financial nous of professional arbitrageurs cannot be relied on to induce market efficiency (Shleifer and Vishny, 1997). Small investors only observe indirect signals of the ability of professional arbitrageurs, such as the end of year financial performance of professionals, and their performance relative to other professionals. This forces professional arbitrageurs to (i) liquidate their positions in loss-making assets too quickly before the year is out, which makes it difficult to counter the activity of noise traders, and (ii) to invest in relatively similar portfolios to avoid looking worse than the others, which is a form of *herding behavior* and can lead errors to accumulate in one direction. These distortions may even reduce the performance of professional arbitrageurs below that of passive investment strategies (Ippolito, 1989; Lakonishok et al., 1992).

A great deal of evidence from financial markets is inconsistent with the EMH. While substitute securities are essential for EMH, their prices can differ systematically, which is inconsistent with EMH. Particularly clean evidence of this effect comes from *Siamese-twin companies* that have merged in the past on an $x : y$ equity basis, yet may trade separately in different markets. If EMH holds, then their traded prices should be in the $x : y$ ratio, but they differ systematically from this ratio (Froot and Dabora, 1999). Security prices often react to no-news and many stock market crashes occur suddenly without any apparent changes in fundamental values (Cutler et al., 1991). The price of freshly inducted stocks into the S&P 500 index immediately jumps upwards, but no new information about the company has been revealed (Shleifer, 1986). The volatility in stock prices is excessive, relative to the predictions of EMH (Shiller, 1981).

Stale information can predict future prices. For instance, stocks that have done well over a long horizon give low subsequent returns and past losers give higher subsequent returns (De Bondt and Thaler, 1985). Over shorter horizons, a *momentum effect* has been observed; recent stock market performance of stocks can carry over to the future (Jegadeesh and Titman, 1993). All public information should immediately have been incorporated into stock prices, yet there is evidence of a *post-earnings-news drift* (Michaely et al., 1995). The decision to buy stocks depends on whether news about the performance of stocks is framed as *high, long-term, returns*, or a *more finely presented series of fluctuating short-term stock returns* (Benartzi and Thaler, 1995). The evidence from closed-end funds shows that there is a systematic difference between "net asset value" and the market price of shares, which is not consistent with the EMH (Lee et al., 1991).

The behavior of investors who follow prospect theory creates another reason for the inconsistency of evidence with the EMH, which assumes that investors follow expected utility theory. Recall the probability weighting function in Figure 2. This is central to the emerging topic of *psychology of tail events* (Barberis, 2013). Since individuals overweight small probabilities, the market will price skewness in the returns to assets (fat tails on the right of the returns distribution); although the probability of these returns is low, the probability is overweighted. If there is a small probability of returns on an asset collapsing, then this can potentially explain the equity premium puzzle (De Giorgi and Legg, 2012); since the low probability downside risk is overweighted, a premium must be paid to induce investors to hold it. Other aspects of prospect theory also mitigate against the EMH. Loss aversion contributes to two phenomena already discussed above, the disposition effect (Odean, 1998), and the equity premium puzzle (Benartzi and Thaler, 1995).

6.4 Is expert behavior consistent with neoclassical economics?

A common response to the anomalies of the neoclassical model is that its predictions apply only to experienced subjects who operate in domains familiar to them. A particularly good test of this response is to examine the behavior of experts in their own field. The available empirical evidence shows that experts are not immune to biases and exhibit some biases even more than lay people (Gilovich et al., 2002; Kahneman, 2003; Kahneman, 2011; and Tetlock, 2006). Tetlock (1999, p. 351) evaluates the evidence on the predictions of experts on political events as follows: "Across all seven domains, experts were only slightly more accurate than one would expect from chance .... Most respondents thought they knew more than they did. Across all predictions that were elicited, experts who assigned confidence estimates of 80% or higher were correct only 45% of the time ... Expertise thus may not translate into predictive accuracy, but it does translate into the ability to generate explanations for predictions that experts themselves find so compelling that the result is massive over-confidence."

Experts exhibit many of the biases that we outlined in Section 5.5. They exhibit greater *overconfidence* relative to lay people (Heath and Tversky, 1991; Frascara, 1999; Glaser et al., 2007a,b), and more experienced experts are even more overconfident (Kirchler and Maciejovsky, 2002). Managerial overconfidence may explain excessive merger activity, despite the fact that relatively few mergers are successful (Malmendier and Tate, 2005, 2008). Another manifestation of overconfidence is the predicted distributions of stock market returns by senior finance professionals; the predicted intervals are too narrow, and realized returns are within their 80% confidence intervals only 36% of the time (Ben-David et al., 2013). Mathematical psychologists exhibit the *law of small numbers* (Tversky and Kahneman, 1973). Experts' perceived riskiness of various hazardous substances is determined by their *affective response* (Slovic et al., 1999). The affective response of experts also determines the likelihood of reoffending that they assign to discharged mental patients (Slovic et al., 2000). Clinical psychologists *underweight the base rate* relative to a Bayesian decision maker (Meehl and Rosen, 1955). Finance professionals exhibit the *hindsight bias* (Guilbault et al., 2004; Biais and Weber, 2009).

Estate agents *anchor* on the list price when evaluating the value of properties (Northcraft and Neale, 1987). The anchoring heuristic has also been found to influence expert legal judgment (Chapman and Bornstein, 1996; Englich and Mussweiler, 2001; Englich et al., 2006). Judges exhibit the false consensus effect (Solan et al. 2008) and there have been various legal and institutional developments to minimize the effect of such biases (Rachlinski, 1998). In imputing the risk preferences of others, finance professionals are disproportionately influenced by their own risk preferences—this is the *false consensus effect* (Roth and Voskort, 2014). When presented with identical options, the responses of physicians are influenced by *framing effects*; their responses depend on whether outcomes are framed as gains or losses relative to a reference point (McNeil et al., 1982; Kahneman and Tversky, 1984). Physicians display limited attention and cognitive overload with the addition of extra choices, even when the total number of choices is relatively small (Redelmeier and Shafir, 1995).

6.5 *Do people play a mixed strategy Nash equilibrium?*

The ability to play a *mixed strategy Nash equilibrium* (MSE) is critical to the theoretical foundations of neoclassical economics; many critical results, such as existence results in game theory, depend on it (Nash, 1950). We have already noted that the epistemic conditions for playing a Nash equilibrium are extremely stringent, although these issues are inadequately highlighted in most game theory courses. Harsanyi (1973) interprets an MSE as the limiting behavior in a set of games that have pure strategy equilibria, but the payoffs are perturbed; this is the *purification agenda*. Yet, these results do not hold for an important range of games that economists are interested in, such as repeated games and principal–agent games, which limits the practical usefulness of this argument (Gintis, 2009, Chapter 6).

An extra layer of cognitive sophistication is required for an MSE relative to a pure strategy Nash equilibrium. Players must randomize among their pure strategies in such a manner that leaves their opponents exactly indifferent among the pure strategies in the support of their mixed strategies. It takes most undergraduates a while to internalize this breathtaking degree of sophistication, but most buy into the idea within a few weeks. However, the evidence on MSE is rarely presented in game theory courses. The history of science is replete with ideas that were ex-ante counterintuitive, yet surprisingly turned out to be true when confronted with the empirical evidence. Based on the available evidence, MSE cannot be classified into this category. The empirical argument is twofold: (i) Many people play a mixed strategy, but not an MSE. (ii) The best evidence supporting the MSE comes from professional sports, a domain that arguably is not the most suitable for reasons given below.

Consider the rather complicated choice facing a football penalty kicker. It requires choosing the height, direction, and swerve of the ball, as well as body feints and gestures. For simplicity, let us assume that the choice is either to kick to the left, or to the right of the goalkeeper. Clearly, over successive penalty shots, kickers would need to randomize somehow, otherwise, given the widespread use of video analysis of past games in modern sports, they will be ineffective. Similar comments apply to tennis serves, which are complicated by the spin, the angle, and the slice on the ball, but let us assume that the choice is to serve either to the left or to the right. In these domains, support is found for the MSE in professional soccer games (Palacios-Huerta, 2003) and in professional tennis matches (Walker and Wooders, 2001). However, in each case, there is serial dependence in the actions (penalty kicks and tennis serves) that is not detected by the opponents, thus, they are not able to exploit it. Serial dependence is not surprising, given the difficulty that humans have in generating random sequences of numbers (see Section 5.5, above). However, leaving aside the modelling of other complexities in penalty kicks and tennis serves that are mentioned above, serial dependence is strictly not consistent with an MSE.

The results on MSE in a sports context are clearly important because they give us a concrete domain in which MSE is reasonably successful. However, the main skills employed by professional sportsmen in playing mixed strategies are motor skills and hand–eye–foot coordination. The development of these skills has an evolutionary basis in hunting, and in intergroup conflict, where they were probably critical for physical survival. Indeed, with practice, humans can achieve a high level of these skills, as evidenced by professional sportsmen. There is less basis to believe that motor skills come into play in important economic decisions such as choosing between alternative pension plans, portfolios of assets, savings decisions, choice of a university course or degree, tax evasion decisions, number of hours to work, or in dealing with self-control issues. Data from professional sports may, thus, have low external validity in establishing conclusive evidence for an MSE.

The ability to play an MSE in a sports context does not translate into an ability to play MSE in other contexts, i.e., the ability to play mixed strategies is not portable. The initial evidence was supportive of the portability of MSE (Palacios-Huerta and Volij, 2008); however, this was overturned by the results in Wooders (2010). In a carefully conducted study, Levitt et al. (2010) appear to have largely settled the debate by providing a clear negative answer to the question of the portability of MSE.

The serial dependence in football kicks and tennis serves suggests that subjects may be using some mixing heuristics that were not explicitly tested in the empirical model. This is an important consideration. In an influential experiment to test an MSE, O'Neill (1987) employed a two-player zero-sum game in which each player had four strategies (Ace, 2, 3, and Joker) and there was a unique MSE (details in Volume 4). The experimental results, on the face of it, provided stunning confirmation of an MSE. The marginal frequencies of play by the row and column players appeared close to the MSE, as did the win percentages of each player. However, in an exemplary piece of empirical work, Brown and Rosenthal (1990) showed that O'Neill's findings constituted an unequivocal rejection of MSE. Indeed, several plausible heuristic-based models could account for the observed empirical results. Despite the proximity of the empirical frequencies of play with the MSE predictions, a chi-square test rejected MSE at any level of significance. Furthermore, they showed that the O'Neill design had insufficient power to distinguish between MSE and the alternative explanations.

There is some evidence that an MSE is more likely to be supported by the evidence when it predicts uniform randomization over the available pure strategies (Slonim et al., 2003). However, moving away from this special case and from sports contexts, the evidence often does not support an MSE. Using an extensive empirical analysis, Mookherjee and Sopher (1994, 1997) conclude in their 1994 paper (p. 109) that: "The rejection of the minimax theory at the aggregate level, and not just at the level of individual decision making, implies that it cannot even be treated as an acceptable as if theory."

Suppose that a game has a unique MSE and it is played repeatedly over a finite number of rounds. One expects players to draw repeatedly in each round from a multinomial distribution that reflects the MSE of the game. However, a common finding is that there is serial correlation in such play. One defence of the MSE is that although players can play an MSE in a static game, they are unable to draw randomly from the relevant multinomial distribution in repeated play. In order to test for this possibility, subjects were given a randomizing device, yet they exhibited serial correlation in play (Shachat, 2002). A reasonable interpretation is that subjects do play mixed strategies, but not in the proportions predicted by MSE. We consider several empirical studies of MSE in Volume 4.

In the *equilibrium in beliefs* interpretation of MSE, each player plays a pure strategy (but never a mixed strategy) and the proportion of players who play each pure strategy is identical to the predicted MSE. Thus, each player acts as if he faces an opponent who plays a mixed strategy (Binmore, 1991). However, the evidence that people do play mixed strategies (although typically not the MSE) also rejects the equilibrium in beliefs interpretation of MSE.

7 Appendix A: The random lottery incentive mechanism

Consider the *random lottery incentive mechanism* (RLI) that is widely employed to pay subjects in experiments. Suppose that expected utility maximizing subjects in an experiment perform n tasks from a set of tasks $T = \{t_1, \ldots, t_n\}$. Let task t_i involve choosing from a set of lotteries, $\mathcal{L}_i$ and define $\mathcal{L} = \cup_i \mathcal{L}_i$ as the set of all lotteries considered in the n tasks. Consider a subject in the experiment whose preferences over pairs of elements in $\mathcal{L}$ are represented by $\succeq$. At the beginning of the experiment, subjects are told that one of the tasks will be picked at random once all tasks are completed, and their choice in that task will be paid to them for real. Let us abstract from issues of a possible show-up fee for the experiment that we have already commented on above.

Suppose that in any task, t_i, the most preferred lottery of the subject is L_i^*. Conditional on the incentive structure described above, should the subject choose L_i^*? An elicitation method is incentive compatible if the answer is yes. The probability that task i is chosen to be rewarded at the end of the experiment is $\frac{1}{n}$. With the complementary probability $1 - \frac{1}{n}$, any of the other $n - 1$ tasks might be chosen to be rewarded. Let the choice made by the subject on any task $t_j, j \neq i$ be L_j. Let us denote by $(L_1, p_1; \ldots; L_i^*, p_i; \ldots; L_n, p_n)$ the compound lottery in which lottery L_j is played with probability p_j. From the *independence axiom* of expected utility theory that should be familiar to most undergraduates in economics (see Chapter 1 for details), we know that since $L_i^* \succeq \widehat{L}_i$ for all $\widehat{L}_i \in \mathcal{L}_i$, it follows that

$$\left(L_1, \frac{1}{n}; \ldots; L_i^*, \frac{1}{n}; \ldots; L_n, \frac{1}{n}\right) \succeq \left(L_1, \frac{1}{n}; \ldots; \widehat{L}_i, \frac{1}{n}; \ldots; L_n, \frac{1}{n}\right) \text{ for all } \widehat{L}_i \in \mathcal{L}_i. \tag{9}$$

In words, the independence axiom says that if $L_i^* \succeq \widehat{L}_i$ then the decision maker prefers any mixture of lotteries that gives L_i^* over an identical mixture that contains $\widehat{L}_i$ in its place. Thus, the subject will choose L_i^* in task t_i. We can show this to be true for all tasks $t_j \in T$. Thus, RLI is incentive compatible.

8 Appendix B: In lieu of a problem set

This section poses 50 problems that you will encounter in this book. The problems are tailored to the material presented in the introduction. If you are already familiar with a particular problem, just move on to the next one. The problems range from straightforward applications of the material in the introduction to slightly more challenging ones. I deliberately avoid giving too much structure to the problems, so that you can try to solve them by writing your own models in a free-spirited manner. If you wish to use the neoclassical model to solve a problem, then think carefully about the auxiliary assumptions that you might need to invoke. In particular, do ask yourself if the auxiliary assumptions that you use are ad hoc or not. You will encounter the solutions to these problems, and many others, as you progress through the book; this will also give you an opportunity to check your initial responses.

1. Many taxi drivers quit too early on rainy days in New York when the effective wage rate is actually very high. In other words, why is it so hard to find a taxi on a rainy day in New York?

2. Why do owners of objects, humans, or chimps, value them more than non-owners (under neoclassical economics, everyone should value objects at their opportunity cost)?

3. If people play Russian roulette, why are they likely to pay more to reduce the number of bullets from 1 to 0, as compared to from 4 to 3 (check that under expected utility these two choices should be equally valuable)?

4. From 1926 to about the mid 1980s, the annual real return on stocks has been about 7% with a standard deviation of 20%, while the annual real return on treasury bills has been less than 1%. In neoclassical economics, a coefficient of relative risk aversion of about 30 can explain these findings, but the actual coefficient is around 1. *This is the equity-premium puzzle*. How can you explain the equity-premium puzzle?

5. A decision maker has initial wealth, w. Suppose that at all levels of wealth, he prefers to keep his wealth rather than play the lottery L_1 : win $11 or lose $10 with equal chance, for any w. Then, under expected utility theory, the decision maker will prefer the lottery L_1 to the lottery L_2 : lose $100 and win an infinite amount with equal probability (*Rabin's paradox*). Thus risk aversion over small stakes, under expected utility theory, implies implausible risk aversion over large stakes. Does expected utility correctly encapsulate the risk attitudes of an individual? Can you think of modifications to expected utility that will explain Rabin's paradox?

6. For an amateur tax evader, the actual probability of audit is 1–3% and the penalty for being caught is (i) return of evaded taxes, plus (ii) fine at the rate of 1–2 times evaded tax. A quick back of the envelope calculation will show that this implies a return on tax evasion of about 96–98%. If you are an expected utility maximizer and have a coefficient of relative risk aversion of about 70 or above, you will pay your taxes; but, empirically, the coefficient is about 1. Since there are very few assets with this return, why do people pay any taxes?

7. Why do people not buy insurance against very low probability events such as natural hazards, even when insurance is better than actuarially fair and the losses of insurance firms are underwritten by the government?

8. In everyday conversations about risky decisions, people speak of *optimism, pessimism, disappointment*, and *regret* (think only of pure risk in a simple game against nature). Can neoclassical decision theory under risk account for these emotions?

9. In recessions, why do firms typically prefer to lay-off workers rather than cut wages?

10. Why do most people find a cut in the nominal wage of 5% under zero inflation to be more unfair relative to a nominal wage increase of 2% under 7% inflation? What are the implications for macroeconomics?

11. In experiments on redistributive taxes, why do people often choose a smaller, more equally distributed, cake as compared to one in which they get a larger share of a very unequally distributed cake?

12. Should we generally expect any difference in outcomes relative to the neoclassical case if a minority of players have other-regarding preferences (i.e., also care about payoffs of others in addition to their own)? You may think of optimal contracts (static and finitely

repeated) between a principal and two agents in a production task where both agents are essential. One of the agents has self-regarding preferences, but the other has other-regarding preferences; the principal does not know who's who.

13. Why are individuals often willing to punish third-parties for observed norm violations between other players even when their own payoffs have not been affected?

14. Why do workers often respond to higher wage offers of firms by working harder, even in 'static games', where they could take the money and run? Why, in these static problems, may firms choose to offer high wages that exceed the opportunity cost of hiring workers? How might you distinguish the predictions of this model from the model of efficiency wages?

15. Why may firms sometimes choose to offer non-enforceable bonus contracts to workers in preference to enforceable incentive contracts, even in static problems? And why might the choice of effort by workers under bonus contracts be relatively higher as compared to that under incentive contracts?

16. Why do moral suasion, trust, and giving workers a goal/sense of purpose or a particular company identity, often outperform monetary incentives?

17. Why do people not lie maximally even when their behavior is guaranteed to remain completely anonymous? And why do we teach children not to lie, act morally rather than opportunistically, and help those who are less fortunate, rather than the neoclassical prescriptions about human behavior (maximize your payoffs/utility subject to technological constraints, but ignore any moral or ethical considerations relative to payoff maximization)?

18. Consider Akerlof and Kranton's (2005, p. 9) description of the following initiation process at the US West Point military academy. "On plebes' first day...they strip down to their underwear. Their hair is cut off. They are put in uniform. They then must address an older cadet, with the proper salute...must stand and salute and repeat, and stand and salute and repeat, until they get it exactly right, all the while being reprimanded for every tiny mistake." How would an economist brought up on the theory of incentives and organizations make sense of this initiation ceremony?

19. Why does the law make a distinction between murder and manslaughter, assigning much lower punishments for manslaughter for the same harm to the victim?

20. Most people would prefer one apple today to two apples tomorrow, but they prefer two apples in 51 days to one apple in 50 days. How can you explain this preference reversal?

21. Discounting over an entire time interval $[t, \bar{t}]$ in one go, turns out to be smaller, relative to discounting over n successive sub-intervals $[t, t_1], [t_1, t_2], \ldots, [t_{n-1}, \bar{t}]$; this is known as *subadditive discounting*. Under exponential discounting, the two answers should be identical. What modifications do you think are needed to the exponential discounting model to explain this empirical finding?

22. Why does the data (e.g., for the US) show a sharp drop in consumption at retirement?

23. Why do people simultaneously hold illiquid assets and credit card debt?

24. Why do people procrastinate so much?

25. Why do people often pay more for an annual gym membership when they could save money on a pay-as-you-go basis?

26. In normal form games in which a Nash equilibrium can be found with more than 2–3 steps of iterated elimination of dominated strategies, the experimental evidence often shows that the outcome is not a Nash equilibrium. Does this evidence cause you to have

any reservations about equilibrium concepts in classical game theory or a desire to modify them? If so, how?

27. Why do we observe far more cooperation in a one-shot prisoner dilemma game (about 60% of the time) relative to the prediction of classical game theory that predicts no cooperation under the assumption that people have self-regarding preferences? Bear in mind that the prisoners' dilemma game is possibly the most widely used game in the social sciences as a metaphor for human cooperation (or the lack of it), so this is not an unimportant result that can be ignored.

28. Empirical evidence shows that in centipede games, the backward induction outcome (play down at the first node) is played less than 10% of the time. In six-node centipede games, in a majority of the cases, players move across to at least the fourth node. How can you explain these findings? Does your explanation have testable implications?

29. If you are unconvinced by the experimental method, can you come up with a few "stringent" non-experimental tests of classical game theory using real-world data?

30. Why do bargaining negotiations often stall with adverse consequences for both parties (union strikes, wars, family gridlocks over issues) even when issues of asymmetric information are not salient? This is particularly the case in conditions where the classical alternating offers bargaining game predicts an immediate bargaining solution without delay.

31. You live in Italy and as most folks who live there, you typically don't tip cab drivers. However, one week you go abroad, and take a taxi to a friend's house who lives in the countryside in a country where there is a norm for tipping taxi drivers. A 70-year-old meek-looking and frail taxi driver delivers you safely to your destination. Would you honor the norm of tipping him or just walk away? Suppose you answered that you would pay the tip. Is your behavior consistent with classical game theory? If not, then which feature of classical game theory could be altered to explain your tipping behavior?

32. Why are winners of common value auctions often 'cursed' in the sense that they make far less money than they anticipated?

33. Eyetracking data from a three-round, two-player bargaining game whose structure is hidden from view, but searchable by using mouse clicks, reveals the following. Most subjects search for payoffs and the size of the cake to be divided in each round, forward from the first round rather than backward from the third round. Furthermore, subjects trained in backward induction do search backwards more often. Does this in any way make you uneasy about equilibrium concepts in classical game theory, or would you simply discount this evidence?

34. Why do interrogators often conduct around-the-clock interrogation of suspects?

35. Why might many people end up marrying or proposing marriage/seeking divorce without sufficient deliberation, or buy consumer durables in haste? Can you think of any legal interventions that take such human behavior into account? Would such legal interventions be necessary for the typical individual in the neoclassical framework?

36. Why are we typically happy to buy consumer durables on installments, yet prefer to prepay for a holiday?

37. Why do smokers and alcoholics often pay money at rehab clinics to get rid of their addictions? Recall that the typical model of addiction in neoclassical economics assumes that people choose to get rationally addicted, taking account of the relevant costs and benefits now, and in the future.

38. Why do many cigarette smokers report an increase in happiness following an increase in excise duty on cigarettes (based on US and Canadian data)?

39. A town is served by two hospitals. In the larger hospital, about 45 babies are born each day, and in the smaller hospital, about 15 babies are born each day. As you know, about 50% of all babies are boys. However, the exact percentage varies from day to day. For a period of one year, each hospital recorded the days on which more than 60% of the babies born were boys. Which hospital do you think recorded more such days? 53 students in the sample said that both hospitals are equally likely to have recorded such days and 21 students each chose the larger and the smaller hospital, respectively. Are the students behaving like the agents in neoclassical economics (sometimes known as *Econs*)? If not, what does their behavior reveal?

40. Why do sales at lotto stores that have sold a winning ticket soar in the immediate weeks following the lotto win (this positive effect on sales persists for up to 40 weeks following the lotto win)? How can you test the hypothesis that "the winning store just produced more interest among the local population to buy more lotto tickets, so that this finding is perfectly consistent with neoclassical economics"?

41. Why do so many mergers fail, yet we often observe waves of mergers from time to time?

42. Why do people find it more difficult to make a choice when the set of choices expands (people choose easily among three types of jams, but often struggle to choose among 27 types of jams)?

43. There is much cross-country variation in organ donation rates in European countries (98% in Austria, but 12% in Germany; 99.9% in France, but 17.7% in the UK; 85.9% in Sweden, but 4.25% in Denmark). It turns out that in countries with high organ donation rates, people are automatically enrolled in the organ donation program, but can opt-out if they wish. The situation is exactly the reverse in countries with low organ donation rates, where people can opt-in if they wish. Can this empirical fact be explained under neoclassical economics? If you answer yes, then be careful in stating your auxiliary assumptions and think of the evidence for these assumptions.

44. There are only two cab companies in the city, Green and Blue; 85% of the cabs are Green. There was an accident last night. A witness comes forward to testify that the cab involved in the accident was Blue. In similar conditions, the reliability of the witness is 80%, i.e., the probability that he gets it wrong is 20%. What is the probability that the actual cab involved in the accident was Blue? The median and modal response was 80%. Are the students behaving like the agents in neoclassical economics? If not, what does their behavior reveal?

45. Why do buyers of a new car often find that the particular model they drive suddenly appears more common on the roads?

46. Why do marketing people play on alternative ways of framing information that has identical information-content? Why for instance, may swimsuit models be placed next to sports cars in advertisements, when the main role of advertisement in the neoclassical framework is to convey information to potential buyers?

47. Why do sales drop if publicly known sales taxes are displayed on price stickers rather than being added at the check-out counter?

48. Why might the financial market price skewness in asset returns?

49. Why are so many financial crises accompanied by no-news (i.e., no information related to fundamental values)?

50. Consider the probability of success that entrepreneurs assign to their startups. In one empirical study, only 5% of startup entrepreneurs believe that their odds are any worse than comparable enterprises and a third believe that their success is assured. Based on French data, 56% expect 'development' and only 6% of startup entrepreneurs expect 'difficulty'; three years on, the respective figures are 38% and 17%. Empirically, only half of all startups survive beyond three years and the high failure rate among startups is widely reported in the popular press. How can we square these figures with the supposed rationality of participants in corporate finance? How should we react to this sort of evidence?

REFERENCES FOR INTRODUCTION

Abdellaoui, M. A. (2000). Parameter-free elicitation of utility and probability weighting functions. *Management Science* 46(11): 1497–512.

Abeler, J. and Nosenzo, D. (2015). Self-selection into laboratory experiments: pro-social motives versus monetary incentives. *Experimental Economics* 18(2): 195–214.

Ackert, L. F., Martinez-Vazquez, J., and Rider, M. (2007). Social preferences and tax policy design: some experimental evidence. *Economic Inquiry* 45(3): 487–501.

Ainslie, G. W. (1992). *Picoeconomics*. Cambridge: Cambridge University Press.

Akerlof, G. A. and Kranton, R. E. (2005). Identity and the economics of organizations. *Journal of Economic Perspectives* 19(1): 9–32.

Allais, M. (1953). La psychologie de l'homme rationnel devant le risque: critique des postulats et axiomes de l'école Américaine. *Econometrica* 21: 503–46.

al-Nowaihi, A. and Dhami, S. (2006a). A simple derivation of Prelec's probability weighting function. *Journal of Mathematical Psychology* 50(6): 521–4.

al-Nowaihi, A. and Dhami, S. (2006b). A note on the Loewenstein–Prelec theory of intertemporal choice. *Mathematical Social Sciences* 52(1): 99–108.

al-Nowaihi, A. and Dhami, S. (2015). Evidential equilibria: heuristics and biases in static games of complete information. *Games* 6(4): 637–77.

al-Nowaihi, A., Bradley, I., and Dhami, S. (2008). A note on the utility function under prospect theory. *Economics Letters* 99(2): 337–9.

Andersen, S., Ertaç, S., Gneezy, U., Hoffman, M., and List, J. A. (2011). Stakes matter in ultimatum games. *American Economic Review* 101(7): 3427–39.

Anderson, J., Burks, S. V., Carpenter, J. et al. (2013). Self-selection and variations in the laboratory measurement of other-regarding preferences across subject pools: evidence from one college student and two adult samples. *Experimental Economics* 16: 170–89.

Andreoni, J. and Bernheim, B. D. (2009). Social image and the 50-50 norm: a theoretical and experimental analysis of audience effects. *Econometrica* 77(5): 1607–36.

Ariely, D., Bracha, A., and Meier, S. (2009). Doing good or going well? Image motivation and monetary incentives in behaving prosocially. *American Economic Review* 99(1): 544–55.

Ariely, D., Loewenstein, G., and Prelec, D. (2006). Tom Sawyer and the construction of value. *Journal of Economic Behavior and Organization* 60: 1–10.

Arkes, H. R., Dawes, R. M., and Christensen, C. (1986). Factors influencing the use of a decision rule in a probabilistic task. *Organizational Behavior and Human Decision Processes* 37: 93–110.

Ashraf, N., Camerer, C. F., and Loewenstein, G. (2005). Adam Smith, behavioral economist. *Journal of Economic Perspectives* 19(3): 131–45.

Ayton, P. and Fischer, I. (2004). The hot hand fallacy and the gambler's fallacy: two faces of subjective randomness? *Memory and Cognition* 32: 1369–78.

Babcock, L. and Loewenstein, G. (1997). Explaining bargaining impasse: the role of self-serving biases. *Journal of Economic Perspectives* 11(1): 109–26.

Babcock, L. and Pogarsky, G. (1999). Damage caps and settlement: a behavioral approach. *Journal of Legal Studies* 28: 341–70.

Barberis, N. (2013). The psychology of tail events: progress and challenges. *American Economic Review* 103(3): 611–16.

Barberis, N. and Thaler, R. H. (2003). A survey of behavioral finance. In G. M. Constantinides, M. Harris, and R. M. Stulz (eds.), *Handbook of the Economics of Finance, Volume 1*. 1st edition Amsterdam: Elsevier, pp. 1053–128.

Bardsley, N., Cubitt, R., Loomes, G., Moffatt, P., Starmer, C., and Sugden, R. (2010). *Experimental Economics: Rethinking the Rules*. Princeton, NJ: Princeton University Press.

Bar-Hillel, M. (1980). The base rate fallacy in probability judgements. *Acta Psychologica* 44: 211–33.

Bar-Hillel, M. and Wagenaar, W. A. (1991). The perception of randomness. *Advances in Applied Mathematics* 12: 428–54.

Barmettler, F., Fehr, E., and Zehnder, C. (2012). Big experimenter is watching you! Anonymity and prosocial behavior in the laboratory. *Games and Economic Behavior* 75(1): 17–34.

Battigalli, P. and Dufwenberg, M. (2009). Dynamic psychological games. *Journal of Economic Theory* 144(1): 1–35.

Becker, G. M., Degroot, M. H., and Marschak, J. (1964). Measuring utility by a single-response sequential method. *Systems Research* 9: 226–32.

Bénabou, R. and Tirole, J. (2003). Intrinsic and extrinsic motivation. *Review of Economic Studies* 70(3): 489–520.

Benartzi, S. and Thaler, R. H. (1995). Myopic loss-aversion and the equity premium puzzle. *Quarterly Journal of Economics* 110(1): 73–92.

Ben-David, I., Graham, J., and Harvey, C. (2013). Managerial miscalibration, *Quarterly Journal of Economics* 128(4): 1547–84.

Benjamin, D. J., Berger, J. O., Johannesson, M., Nosek, B. A., Wagenmakers, E. J., Berk, R., Morgan, S. L. (2018). Redefine statistical significance. *Nature Human Behaviour* 2(1): 6–10.

Biais, B. and Weber, M. (2009). Hindsight bias, risk perception and investment performance. *Management Science* 55(6): 1018–29.

Binmore, K. (1991). *Playing for Real: A Text on Game Theory.* Oxford: Oxford University Press.

Birnbaum, M. H. (2008). New paradoxes of risky decision making. *Psychological Review* 115(2): 463–501.

Blaug, M. (1992). *The Methodology of Economics, Or, How Economists Explain.* Cambridge and New York: Cambridge University Press.

Bleichrodt, H., Li, C., Moscati, I., and Wakker, P. P. (2012). Nash was a first to axiomatize expected utility. *Theory and Decision* 81: 309–12.

Bohm, P., Lindén, J., and Sonnegård, J. (1997). Eliciting reservation prices: Becker-DeGroot-Marschak mechanisms vs. markets. *Economic Journal* 107: 1079–89.

Bolton, G. E. and Ockenfels, A. (1998). Strategy and equity: an ERC-analysis of the Guth–van Damme game. *Journal of Mathematical Psychology* 42(2): 215–26.

Bolton, G. E. and Ockenfels, A. (2000). ERC: a theory of equity, reciprocity, and competition. *American Economic Review* 90(1): 166–93.

Bolton, G. E., Zwick, R., and Katok, E. (1998). Dictator game giving: rules of fairness versus acts of kindness. *International Journal of Game Theory* 27(2): 269–99.

Bonner, S. E., Hastie, R., Sprinkle, G. B., and Young, S. M. (2000). A review of the effects of financial incentives on performance in laboratory tasks: implications for management accounting. *Journal of Management Accounting Research* 13: 19–64.

Bosch-Domènech, A., Montalvo, J. G., Nagel, R., and Satorra, A. (2002). One, two, (three), infinity,…newspaper and lab beauty-contest experiments. *American Economic Review* 92(5): 1687–701.

Bowles, S. and Gintis, H. (2011). *A Cooperative Species: Human Reciprocity and Evolution.* Princeton, NJ: Princeton University Press.

Braga, J. and Starmer, C. (2005). Preference anomalies, preference elicitation and the Discovered Preference Hypothesis. *Environmental and Resource Economics* 32: 55–89.

Breitmoser, Y. (2012). Strategic reasoning in p-beauty contests. *Games and Economic Behavior* 75(2): 555–69.

Brown, J. N. and Rosenthal, R. W. (1990). Testing the minimax hypothesis: a re-examination of O'Neill's game experiment. *Econometrica* 58(5): 1065–81.

Brown, M., Falk, A., and Fehr, E. (2004). Relational contracts and the nature of market interactions. *Econometrica* 72(3): 747–80.

Brown, M., Falk, A., and Fehr, E. (2012). Competition and relational contracts: the role of unemployment as a disciplinary device. *Journal of the European Economic Association* 10(4): 887–907.

Bruhin, A., Fehr-Duda, H., and Epper, T. (2010). Risk and rationality: uncovering heterogeneity in probability distortion. *Econometrica* 78(4): 1375–412.

Bruni, L. and Sugden, R. (2007). The road not taken: how psychology was removed from economics, and how it might be brought back. *Economic Journal* 117: 146–73.

Camerer, C. F. (2000). Prospect theory in the wild: evidence from the field. In D. Kahneman and A. Tversky (eds.), *Choices, Values and Frames.* Cambridge: Cambridge University Press, pp. 288–300.

Camerer, C. F. (2003a). *Behavioral Game Theory: Experiments in Strategic Interaction.* Princeton, NJ: Princeton University Press.

Camerer, C. F. (2003b). Behavioural studies of strategic thinking in games. *Trends in Cognitive Sciences* 7(5): 225–31.

Camerer, C. F. (2015). The promise and success of lab–field generalizability in experimental economics: a critical reply to Levitt and List. In G. R. Fréchette and A. Schotter (eds.), *Handbook of Experimental Economic Methodology*. Oxford: Oxford University Press. pp. 249–95.

Camerer, C. F., Babcock, L., Loewenstein, G., and Thaler, R. H. (1997). Labor supply of New York City cabdrivers: one day at a time. *Quarterly Journal of Economics* 112(2): 407–41.

Camerer, C. F., Dreber, A., Forsell, E., Ho, T.-H., Huber, J., Johannesson, M., Kirchler, M., Almenberg, J., Altmejd, A., Chan, T., et al. (2016). Evaluating replicability of laboratory experiments in economics. *Science* 351(6280): 1433–6.

Camerer, C. F., Ho, T.-H., and Chong, J.-K. (2004). A cognitive hierarchy model of games. *Quarterly Journal of Economics* 119(3): 861–98.

Camerer, C. F. and Hogarth, R. M. (1999) The effects of financial incentives in experiments: a review and capital–labor–production framework. *Journal of Risk and Uncertainty* 19(1–3): 7–42.

Camerer, C. F. and Loewenstein, G. (2004). Behavioral economics: past, present, future. In C. F. Camerer, G. Loewenstein, and M. Rabin, (eds.), *Advances in Behavioral Economics*. New York: Russell Sage, pp. 3–51.

Cameron, L. A. (1999). Raising the stakes in the ultimatum game: experimental evidence from Indonesia. *Economic Inquiry* 37(1): 47–59.

Caplin, A., Dean, M., and Martin, D. (2011). Search and satisficing. *American Economic Review* 101(7): 2899–922.

Carpenter, J. P. and Seki, E. (2011). Do social preferences increase productivity? Field experimental evidence from fishermen in Toyama Bay. *Economic Inquiry* 49(2): 612–30.

Casscells, W., Schoenberger, A., and Graboys, T. B. (1978). Interpretation by physicians of clinical laboratory results. *New England Journal of Medicine* 299: 999–1000.

Chamberlin, E. H. (1948). An experimental imperfect market. *Journal of Political Economy* 56(2): 95–108.

Chapman, G. B. and Bornstein, B. H. (1996). The more you ask for, the more you get: Anchoring in personal injury verdicts. *Applied Cognitive Psychology* 10: 519–40.

Charness, G. and Rabin, M. (2002). Understanding social preferences with simple tests. *Quarterly Journal of Economics* 117(3): 817–69.

Chateauneuf, A. and Wakker, P. P. (1999). An axiomatization of cumulative prospect theory for decision under risk. *Journal of Risk and Uncertainty* 18(2): 137–45.

Chen, M. K., Lakshminaryanan, V., and Santos, L. (2006). How basic are behavioral biases? Evidence from capuchin monkey trading behavior. *Journal of Political Economy* 114(3): 517–32.

Cherry, T., Frykblom, P., and Shogren, J. (2002). Hardnose the dictator. *American Economic Review* 92(4) 1218–21.

Cleave, B. L., Nikiforakis, N., and Slonim, R. (2012). Is there selection bias in laboratory experiments? The case of social and risk preferences. *Experimental Economics* 16(3): 372–82.

Clotfelter, C. T. and Cook, P. J. (1993). The gambler's fallacy in lottery play. *Management Science* 39: 1521–25.

Colander, D. and Kupers, R. (2014). *Complexity and the Art of Public Policy: Solving Society's Problems from the Bottom Up*. Princeton, NJ: Princeton University Press.

Cooper, D. J. and Kagel, J. H. (2015). Other-regarding preferences: a selective survey of experimental results. In J. H. Kagel and A. E. Roth (eds.), *The Handbook of Experimental Economics, Volume 2*. Princeton University Press, forthcoming.

Cosmides, L. and Tooby, J. (1996). Are humans good intuitive statisticians after all? Rethinking some conclusions from the literature on judgment under uncertainty. *Cognition* 58: 1–73.

Costa-Gomes, M., Crawford, V. P., and Broseta, B. (2001). Cognition and behavior in normal-form games: an experimental study. *Econometrica* 69(5): 1193–235.

Costa-Gomes, M. A. and Crawford, V. P. (2006). Cognition and behavior in two-person guessing games: an experimental study. *American Economic Review* 96(5): 1737–68.

Crawford, V. P. (2007). Let's talk it over: coordination via preplay communication with level-k thinking. Mimeo, UCLA Department of Economics.

Crawford, V. P., Costa-Gomes, M. A., and Iriberri, N. (2013). Structural models of non-equilibrium strategic thinking: theory, evidence, and applications. *Journal of Economic Literature* 51(1): 5–62.

Crawford, V. P., Gneezy, U., and Rottenstreich, Y. (2008). The power of focal points is limited: even minute payoff asymmetry may yield large coordination failures. *American Economic Review* 98(4): 1443–58.

Crawford, V. P. and Iriberri, N. (2007a). Level-k auctions: can a nonequilibrium model of strategic thinking explain the winner's curse and overbidding in private-value auctions? *Econometrica* 75(6): 1721–70.

Crawford, V. P. and Iriberri, N. (2007b). Fatal attraction: salience, naïveté, and sophistication in experimental hide-and-seek games. *American Economic Review* 97(5): 1731–50.

Crawford, V. P., Kugler, T., Neeman, Z., and Pauzner, A. (2009). Behaviorally optimal auction design: an example and some observations. *Journal of the European Economic Association* 7(2–3): 377–87.

Cutler, D., Poterba, J., and Summers, L. (1991). Speculative dynamics. *Review of Economic Studies* 58: 529–46.

Dana, J., Weber, R. A., and Kuang, J. X. (2007). Exploiting moral wriggle room: experiments demonstrating an illusory preference for fairness. *Economic Theory* 33: 67–80.

Davis, D. D. and Holt, C. A. (1993). *Experimental Economics*. Princeton, NJ: Princeton University Press.

De Bondt, W. and Thaler, R. H. (1985). Does the stock market overreact? *Journal of Finance* 40: 793–808.

De Giorgi, E. G. and Legg, S. (2012). Dynamic portfolio choice and asset pricing with narrow framing and probability weighting. *Journal of Economic Dynamics and Control* 36(7): 951–72.

De Long, J. B., Shleifer, A., Summers, L., and Waldmann, R. (1990). Noise trader risk in financial markets. *Journal of Political Economy* 98: 703–38.

De Marchi, N. and Blaug, M. (eds.) (1991). *Appraising Economic Theories: Studies in the Methodology of Research Programmes*. Cheltenham: Edward Elgar.

De Martino B., Kumaran D., Seymour B., and Dolan R. J. (2006). Frames, biases, and rational decision-making in the human brain. *Science* 313: 684–7.

de Meza, D. and Webb, D. C. (2007). Incentive design under loss aversion. *Journal of the European Economic Association* 5(1): 66–92.

De Quervain, D., Fischbacher, U., Treyer, V., et al. (2004). The neural basis of altruistic punishment. *Science* 305(5688): 1254–8.

Dekel, E. and Lipman, B. L. (2010). How (not) to do decision theory. *Annual Review of Economics* 2: 257–82.

Dekel, E. and Siniscalchi, M. (2015). Epistemic game theory. In H. P. Young and S. Zamir (eds.), *Handbook of Game Theory with Economic Applications, Volume 4*. Amsterdam: Elsevier, pp. 619–702.

DellaVigna, S. and Malmendier, U. (2004). Contract design and self-control: theory and evidence. *Quarterly Journal of Economics* 119(2): 353–402.

Dhami, S. (2017). Human ethics and virtues: rethinking the Homo-economicus model. CESifo Working Paper No. 6836. Forthcoming in *Handbook of Ethics and Economics*. Oxford: Oxford University Press.

Dhami, S. and al-Nowaihi, A. (2007). Why do people pay taxes? expected utility versus prospect theory. *Journal of Economic Behavior and Organization* 64(1): 171–92.

Dhami, S. and al-Nowaihi, A. (2010a). Optimal income tax taxation in the presence of tax evasion: expected utility versus prospect theory. *Journal of Economic Behavior and Organization* 75(2): 313–37.

Dhami, S. and al-Nowaihi, A. (2010b). A proposal to combine "prospect theory" and "cumulative prospect theory." University of Leicester. Discussion Papers in Economics 10/11.

Dhami, S. and al-Nowaihi, A. (2010c). Existence of a Condorcet winner when voters have other-regarding preferences. *Journal of Public Economic Theory* 12(5): 897–922.

Dhami, S. and al-Nowaihi, A. (2010d). Redistributive policy with heterogeneous social preferences of voters. *European Economic Review* 54(6): 743–59.

Dhami, S. and al-Nowaihi, A. (2013). Stochastic dominance for Fehr–Schmidt preferences. University of Leicester, Discussion Papers in Economics. Working Paper No. 13/09.

Dhami, S. and al-Nowaihi, A. (2018). Rationality in Economics: Theory and Evidence. CESifo Working Paper No. 6872. Forthcoming in *Handbook of Rationality*. Cambridge, MA: MIT Press.

Dhami, S., al-Nowaihi, A., and Sunstein, C. (2018). Heuristics and public policy: decision making under bounded rationality. Discussion Paper No. 06/2018, Harvard Law School, John M. Olin Centre for Law, Economics and Business.

Diamond, P. and Koszegi, B. (2003). Quasi-hyperbolic discounting and retirement. *Journal of Public Economics* 87(9–10): 1839–72.

Duesenberry, J. S. (1949). *Income, Saving, and the Theory of Consumer Behavior*. Cambridge, MA: Harvard University Press.

Duflo, E., Kremer, M., and Robinson, J. (2011). Nudging farmers to use fertlizer: theory and experimental evidence from Kenya. *American Economic Review* 101(6): 2350–90.

Dufwenberg, M., Heidhues, P., Kirchsteiger, G., et al. (2011). Other-regarding preferences in general equilibrium. *Review of Economic Studies* 78(2): 613–39.

Dufwenberg, M. and Kirchsteiger, G. (2004). A theory of sequential reciprocity. *Games and Economic Behavior* 47(2): 268–98.

Eckel, C. C. and Gintis, H. (2010). Blaming the messenger: notes on the current state of experimental economics. *Journal of Economic Behavior and Organization* 73(1): 109–19.

Ellsberg, D. (1961). Risk, ambiguity, and the Savage axioms. *Quarterly Journal of Economics* 75(4): 643–69.

Englich, B. and Mussweiler, T. (2001). Sentencing under uncertainty: anchoring effects in the courtroom. *Journal of Applied Social Psychology* 31: 1535–51.

Englich, B., Mussweiler, T., and Strack, F. (2006). Playing dice with criminal sentences: the influence of irrelevant anchors on experts' judicial decision makings. *Personality and Social Psychology Bulletin* 32(2): 188–200.

Erev, I., Ert, E., and Roth, A. E. (2010). A choice prediction competition: choices from experience and from description. *Journal of Behavioral Decision Making* 23: 15–47.

Ericson, K. M. M., White, J. M., Laibson, D., and Cohen, J. D. (2015). Money earlier or later? Simple heuristics explain intertemporal choices better than delay discounting does. *Psychological Science* 26(6): 826–33.

Falk, A. and Fischbacher, U. (2006). A theory of reciprocity. *Games and Economic Behavior* 54(2): 293–315.

Falk, A. and Heckman, J. J. (2009). Lab experiments are a major source of knowledge in the social sciences. *Science* 326: 535–8.

Falk, A., Meier, S., and Zehnder, C. (2013). Do lab experiments misrepresent social preferences? The case of self-selected student samples. *Journal of the European Economic Association* 11(4): 839–52.

Fang, H. M. and Silverman, D. (2009). Time-inconsistency and welfare program participation: evidence from the NLSY. *International Economic Review* 50(4): 1043–77.

Farmer, J. D. and Foley, D. (2009). The economy needs agent-based modelling. *Nature* 460: 685–6.

Fehr, E. and Fischbacher, U. (2005). Human altruism: proximate patterns and evolutionary origins. *Analyse & Kritik* 27(1): 6–47.

Fehr, E. and Gächter, S. (1999). Cooperation and punishment in public goods experiments. University of Zurich, Institute for Empirical Research in Economics, Working Paper 10.

Fehr, E. and Gächter, S. (2000a). Cooperation and punishment in public goods experiments. *American Economic Review* 90(4): 980–94.

Fehr, E. and Gächter, S. (2000b). Fairness and retaliation: the economics of reciprocity. *Journal of Economic Perspectives* 14(3): 159–81.

Fehr, E., Gächter, S., and Kirchsteiger, G. (1997). Reciprocity as a contract enforcement device: experimental evidence. *Econometrica* 65(4): 833–60.

Fehr, E., Hart, O., and Zehnder, C. (2011). Contracts as reference points: experimental evidence. *American Economic Review* 101(2): 493–525.

Fehr, E., Kirchsteiger, G., and Riedl, A. (1998). Gift exchange and reciprocity in competitive experimental markets. *European Economic Review* 42(1): 1–34.

Fehr, E., Klein, A., and Schmidt, K. M. (2007). Fairness and contract design. *Econometrica* 75(1): 121–54.

Fehr, E. and List, J. A. (2004). The hidden costs and returns of incentives: trust and trustworthiness among CEOs. *Journal of the European Economic Association* 2(5): 743–71.

Fehr, E. and Schmidt K. (1999). A theory of fairness, competition and cooperation. *Quarterly Journal of Economics* 114(3): 817–68.

Fehr, E. and Schmidt, K. (2006). The economics of fairness, reciprocity and altruism: Experimental evidence and new theories. In S.-C. Kolm and J. M. Ythier (eds.), *Handbook of the Economics of Giving, Altruism and Reciprocity, Volume 1.* Amsterdam: Elsevier.

Fehr, E. and Williams, T. (2015). The endogenous emergence of efficient sanctioning institutions. Mimeo, Department of Economics, University of Zurich.

Fehr-Duda, H. and Epper, T. (2012). Probability and risk: foundations and economic implications of probability-dependent risk preferences. *Annual Review of Economics* 4: 567–93.

Feynman, R. (1965). *The Character of Physical Law.* Cambridge, MA: MIT Press.

Fischbacher, U. and Gächter, S. (2010). Social preferences, beliefs, and the dynamics of free-riding in public goods experiments. *American Economic Review* 100(1): 541–56.

Fischbacher, U., Gächter, S., and Fehr, E. (2001). Are people conditionally co-operative? Evidence from a public goods experiment. *Economics Letters* 71(3): 397–404.

Fischhoff, B. (1975). Hindsight ≠ foresight: the effect of outcome knowledge on judgment under uncertainty. *Journal of Experimental Psychology: Human Perception and Performance* 1: 288–99.

Fischhoff, B., Slovic, P., Lichtenstein S., Read S., and Combs, B. (1978). How safe is safe enough? A psychometric study of attitudes toward technological risks and benefits. *Policy Sciences* 9: 127–52.

Fouraker, L. E. and Siegel, S. (1963). *Bargaining Behavior.* New York: McGraw-Hill.

Frascara, J. (1999). Cognition, emotion and other inescapable dimensions of human experience. *Visible Language* 33: 74–87.

Fréchette, G. R. (2015). Laboratory experiments: professionals versus students. In G. R. Fréchette and A. Schotter (eds.), *Handbook of Experimental Economic Methodology.* Oxford: Oxford University Press, pp. 360–90.

Frederick, S., Loewenstein, G., and O'Donoghue, T. (2002). Time discounting and time preferences: a critical review. *Journal of Economic Literature* 40(2): 351–401.

Friedman, M. (1953). *The Methodology of Positive Economics.* Chicago, IL: University of Chicago Press.

Froot, K. and E. Dabora (1999). How are stock prices affected by the location of trade? *Journal of Financial Economics* 53: 189–216.

Fryer, R. G., Levitt, S. D., List, J. A., and Sadoff, S. (2012). Enhancing the efficacy of teacher incentives through loss aversion: a field experiment. NBER. Working Paper 8237.

Fudenberg, D. and Levine, D. K. (2006). A dual-self model of impulse control. *American Economic Review* 96(5): 1449–76.

Gächter, S., Renner, E., and Sefton, M. (2008). The long-run benefits of punishment. *Science* 322: 1510.

Galinsky, A. D. and Mussweiler, T. (2001). First offers as anchors: the role of perspective-taking and negotiator focus. *Journal of Personality and Social Psychology* 81(4): 657–69.

Geanakoplos, J., Pearce, D., and Stacchetti, E. (1989). Psychological games and sequential rationality. *Games and Economic Behavior* 1(1): 60–79.

Gigerenzer, G. and Hoffrage, U. (1995). How to improve Bayesian reasoning without instruction: frequency formats. *Psychological Review* 102: 684–704.

Gigerenzer, G. and Selten, R. (2001). Rethinking rationality. In G. Gigerenzer and R. Selten (eds.), *Bounded Rationality: The Adaptive Toolbox. Dahlem Workshop Report.* Cambridge, MA: MIT Press, pp. 1–12.

Gigerenzer, G., Todd, P. M., and the ABC Research Group (1999). *Simple Heuristics That Make Us Smart.* New York: Oxford University Press.

Gilboa, I. (2009). *Theory of Decision Under Uncertainty.* Cambridge: Cambridge University Press.

Gilboa, I., Postlewaite, A., Samuelson, L., and Schmeidler, D. (2014). Economic models as analogies, *Economic Journal* 124: F513–33.

Gill, D. and Prowse, V. (2015). Cognitive ability, character skills, and learning to play equilibrium: a level-k analysis. Forthcoming in *Journal of Political Economy.*

Gilovich, T., Griffin, D., and Kahneman, D. (2002). *Heuristics and Biases: the Psychology of Intuitive Judgment.* New York: Cambridge University Press.

Gintis, H. (2009). *The Bounds of Reason: Game Theory and the Unification of the Behavioral Sciences.* Princeton, NJ: Princeton University Press.

Gintis, H. (2015). Modeling homo-socialis: a reply to critics. *Review of Behavior Economics* 2: 211–37.

Glaser, M., Langer, T., Reynders, J., and Weber, M. (2007a). Framing effects in stock market forecasts: the difference between asking for prices and asking for returns. *Review of Finance* 11: 325–57.

Glaser, M., Langer, T., and Weber, M. (2007b). On the trend recognition and forecasting ability of professional traders. *Decision Analysis* 4: 176–93.

Glimcher, P. W., Camerer, C. F., Fehr, E., and Poldrack, R. A. (2009). *Neuroeconomics*. Amsterdam: Academic Press, Elsevier Inc.

Glimcher, P. W. and Fehr, E. (eds.) (2014). *Neuroeconomics*. Amsterdam: Elsevier Inc.

Gneezy, U. and Rustichini, A. (2000a). A fine is a price. *Journal of Legal Studies* 29(1): 1–17.

Gneezy, U. and Rustichini, A. (2000b). Pay enough or don't pay at all. *Quarterly Journal of Economics* 115(3): 791–810.

Gode, D. K. and Sunder, S. (1993). Allocative efficiency of markets with zero intelligence traders: market as a partial substitute for individual rationality. *Journal of Political Economy* 101(1): 119–37.

Godfrey-Smith, P. (2006). The strategy of model-based science. *Biology and Philosophy* 21: 725–40.

Godfrey-Smith, P. (2009). Models and fictions in science. *Philosophical Studies* 143: 101–16.

Goldfarb, A. and Xiao, M. (2011). Who thinks about the competition? Managerial ability and strategic entry in US local telephone markets. *American Economic Review* 101(7): 3130–61.

Goldfarb, A. and Yang, B. (2009). Are all managers created equal? *Journal of Marketing Research* 46(5): 612–22.

Grether, D. M. and Plott, C. (1979). Economic theory of choice and the preference reversal phenomenon. *American Economic Review*. 69(4): 623–38.

Grosskopf, B. and Nagel, R. (2008). The two-person beauty contest. *Games and Economic Behavior* 62(1): 93–9.

Gruber, J. H. and Mullainathan, S. (2005). Do cigarette taxes make smokers happier? *B.E. Journals: Advances in Economic Analysis and Policy* 5(1): 1–45.

Guala, F. (2008). Experimental economics, history of. In S. N. Durlauf and L. E. Blume (eds.), *The New Palgrave Dictionary of Economics*. 2nd edition. Basingstoke: Palgrave Macmillan.

Guilbault, R. L., Bryant, F. B., Brockway, J. H., and Posavac, E. J. (2004). A meta-analysis of research on hindsight bias. *Basic and Applied Social Psychology* 26: 103–17.

Gul, F. and Pesendorfer, W. (2001). Temptation and self control. *Econometrica* 69(6): 1403–36.

Guryan, J. and Kearney, M. S. (2008). Gambling at lucky stores: empirical evidence from state lottery sales. *American Economic Review* 98(1): 458–73.

Güth, W., Schmittberger, R., and Schwarze, B. (1982). An experimental analysis of ultimatum bargaining. *Journal of Economic Behavior and Organization* 3(4): 367–88.

Haley, K. J. and Fessler, D. M. T. (2005). Nobody's watching? Subtle cues affect generosity in an anonymous economic game. *Evolution and Human Behavior* 26(3): 245–56.

Hands, D. W. (1991). The problem of excess content: economics, novelty, and a long Popperian tale. In M. Blaug and N. DeMarchi (eds.), *Appraising Economic Theories*. Cheltenham: Edward Elgar, pp. 58–75.

Hands, D. W. (2001). *Reflections Without Rules: Economic Methodology and Contemporary Science Theory*. Cambridge: Cambridge University Press.

Hargreaves Heap, S., Rojo-Arjona, D., and Sugden, R. (2014). How portable is level-0 behavior? A test of level-k theory in games with non-neutral frames. *Econometrica* 82(3): 1133–51.

Harsanyi, J. C. (1973). Games with randomly disturbed payoffs: a new rationale for mixed-strategy equilibrium points. *International Journal of Game Theory* 2(1): 1–23.

Hausman, D. (1992). *The Inexact and Separate Science of Economics*. Cambridge: Cambridge University Press.

Heath, C. and Tversky, A. (1991). Preference and belief: ambiguity and competence in choice under uncertainty. *Journal of Risk and Uncertainty* 4: 5–28.

Henrich, J., Boyd, R., Bowles, S., et al. (2001). Cooperation, reciprocity and punishment in fifteen small-scale societies. *American Economic Review* 91: 73–8.

Herrmann, B., Thöni, C., and Gächter, S. (2008). Antisocial punishment across societies. *Science* 319(5868): 1362–7.

Herbst, D. and Mas, A. (2015). Peer effects on worker output in the lab generalize to the field. Forthcoming in *Science*.

Hertwig, R. and Ortmann, A. (2001). Experimental practices in economics: a methodological challenge for psychologists? *Behavioral and Brain Sciences* 24(3): 383–403.

Hey, J. D. (2014). Choice under uncertainty: empirical methods and experimental results. In M. J. Machina and W. K. Viscusi (eds.), *Handbook of the Economics of Risk and Uncertainty Volume 1*. Oxford: North Holland, pp. 809–50.

Hey, J. D. and Orme, C. (1994). Investigating generalizations of expected utility theory using experimental data. *Econometrica* 62(6): 1291–326.

Ho, T., Camerer, C. F., and Weigelt, K. (1998). Iterated dominance and iterated best response in experimental "p-beauty contests." *American Economic Review* 88(4): 947–69.

Hoffman, E., McCabe, K. A., and Smith, V. L. (1998). Behavioral foundations of reciprocity: experimental economics and evolutionary psychology. *Economic Inquiry* 36: 335–52.

Hogarth, R. M., Gibbs, B. J., McKenzie, C. R. M., and Marquis, M. A. (1991). Learning from feedback: exactingness and incentives. *Journal of Experimental Psychology: Learning, Memory and Cognition* 17: 734–52.

Hong, H. and Stein, J. (1999). A unified theory of underreaction, momentum trading, and overreaction in asset markets. *Journal of Finance* 54: 2143–84.

Hong, H. and Stein, J. (2007). Disagreement and the stock market. *Journal of Economic Perspectives* 21: 109–28.

Huck, S., Lünser, G. K., and Tyran, J.-R. (2012). Competition fosters trust. *Games and Economic Behavior* 76(1): 195–209.

Ippolito, R. A. (1989). Efficiency with costly information: a study of mutual fund performance, 1965–1984. *Quarterly Journal of Economics* 104(1): 1–23.

Jegadeesh, N. and Titman, S. (1993). Returns to buying winners and selling losers: implications for stock market efficiency. *Journal of Finance* 48: 65–91.

Jehle, G. J. and Reny, P. J. (2011). *Advanced Microeconomic Theory*. 3rd edition. Upper Saddle River, NJ: Prentice Hall.

Kagel, J. H. and Roth, A. E. (1995). *The Handbook of Experimental Economics*. Princeton, NJ: Princeton University Press.

Kahneman, D. (2003). Maps of bounded rationality: psychology for behavioral economics. *American Economic Review* 93(5): 1449–75.

Kahneman, D. (2011). *Thinking Fast and Slow*. New York: Farrar, Strauss, Giroux.

Kahneman, D., Knetsch, J. L., and Thaler, R. H. (1986). Fairness as a constraint on profit seeking: entitlements in the market. *American Economic Review* 76(4): 728–41.

Kahneman, D., Knetsch, J. L., and Thaler, R. H. (1991). Anomalies: the endowment effect, loss aversion, and status quo bias. *Journal of Economic Perspectives* 5(1): 193–206.

Kahneman, D. and Tversky, A. (1972). On prediction and judgment. *Oregon Research Institute Bulletin* 12(4).

Kahneman, D. and Tversky, A. (1979). Prospect theory: an analysis of decision under risk. *Econometrica* 47(2): 263–91.

Kahneman, D. and Tversky, A. (1984). Choices, values, and frames. *The American Psychologist* 39: 341–50.

Kahneman, D. and Tversky, A. (1996). On the reality of cognitive illusions: a reply to Gigerenzer's critique. *Psychological Review* 103: 582–91.

Kahneman, D. and Tversky, A. (2000). *Choices, Values and Frames*. Cambridge: Cambridge University Press.

Kessler, J. B. and Vesterlund, L. (2015). The external validity of laboratory experiments: the misleading emphasis on quantitative effects. In G. R. Fréchette and A. Schotter (eds.), *Handbook of Experimental Economic Methodology*. Oxford: Oxford University Press, pp. 391–406.

Kim, E. H., Morse, A., and Zingales, L. (2006). What has mattered to economics since 1970. *Journal of Economic Perspectives* 20: 189–202.

Kirchler, E. and Maciejovsky, B. (2002). Simultaneous over- and underconfidence: evidence from experimental asset markets. *Journal of Risk and Uncertainty* 25: 65–85.

Köszegi, B. and Rabin, M. (2006). A model of reference-dependent preferences. *Quarterly Journal of Economics* 121(4): 1133–65.

Kothiyal, A., Spinu, V., and Wakker, P. P. (2014). An experimental test of prospect theory for predicting choice under ambiguity. *Journal of Risk and Uncertainty* 48(1): 1–17.

Kuhn, T. S. (1962). *The Structure of Scientific Revolutions.* Chicago, IL: University of Chicago Press.

Laibson, D. (1994). Essays in hyperbolic discounting. MIT, Ph.D. Dissertation.

Laibson, D. (1997). Golden eggs and hyperbolic discounting. *Quarterly Journal of Economics* 112(2): 443–78.

Laibson, D. (1998). Life-cycle consumption and hyperbolic discount functions. *European Economic Review* 42(3–5): 861–71.

Lakatos, I. (1970). Falsification and the methodology of scientific research programmes. In I. Lakatos and A. Musgrave (eds.), *Criticism and the Growth of Knowledge.* Cambridge: Cambridge University Press.

Lakonishok, J., Shleifer, A., and Vishny, R. W. (1992). The impact of institutional trading on stock prices. *Journal of Financial Economics* 32: 23–44.

Lambdin, C. G. and Shaffer, V. A. (2009). Are within-subjects designs transparent? *Judgement and Decision Making* 4(7): 554–66.

Lee, C. M. C., Shleifer, A., and Thaler, R. H. (1991). Investor sentiment and the closed-end fund puzzle. *Journal of Finance* 46: 76–110.

Levitt, S. D. and List, J. A. (2007). What do laboratory experiments measuring social preferences reveal about the real world? *Journal of Economic Perspectives* 21(2): 153–74.

Levitt, S. D. and List, J. A. (2008). Homo economicus evolves. *Science* 319: 909–10.

Levitt, S. D., List, J. A., and Reiley, D. H. (2010). What happens in the field stays in the field: professionals do not play minimax in laboratory experiments. *Econometrica* 78(4): 1413–34.

Lichtenstein, S. and Slovic, P. (1973). Response-induced reversals of preference in gambling: an extended replication in Las Vegas. *Journal of Experimental Psychology* 101(1): 16–20.

Lichtenstein, S., Slovic, P., Fischhoff, B., Layman, M., and Combs, B. (1978). Judged frequency of lethal events. *Journal of Experimental Psychology: Human Learning and Memory* 4: 551–78.

Lipsey, R. G. (1979). *An Introduction to Positive Economics.* 5th edition. London: Weidenfeld and Nicholson.

List, J. A. (2003). Does market experience eliminate market anomalies? *Quarterly Journal of Economics* 118(1): 41–71.

List, J. A. (2006). The behavioralist meets the market: measuring social preferences and reputation effects in actual transactions. *Journal of Political Economy* 114(1): 1–37.

Locke, E. A. and Latham, G. P. (1990). *A Theory of Goal Setting and Task Performance.* Englewood Cliffs, NJ: Prentice-Hall.

Loewenstein, G. F. (1999). Experimental economics from the vantage-point of behavioural economics. *Economic Journal* 109(453): 25–34.

Loewenstein, G. F. and Prelec, D. (1992). Anomalies in intertemporal choice: evidence and an interpretation. *Quarterly Journal of Economics* 107(2): 573–97.

Loewenstein, G. F., Weber, E. U., Hsee, C. K., and Welch, E. S. (2001). Risk as feelings. *Psychological Bulletin* 127: 267–86.

Lord, C. G., Ross, L., and Lepper, M. R. (1979). Biased assimilation and attitude polarization: the effects of prior theories on subsequently considered evidence. *Journal of Personality and Social Psychology* 37(11): 2098–109.

McNeil, B. J., Pauker, S. G., Sox, H. C., Jr., and Tversky, A. (1982). On the elicitation of preferences for alternative therapies. *New England Journal of Medicine* 306: 1259–62.

Mak, V., Gisches, E. J., and Rapoport, A. (2015). Route vs. segment: an experiment on real-time travel information in congestible networks. *Production and Operations Management* 24(6): 947–60.

Malmendier, U. and Tate, G. (2005). CEO overconfidence and corporate investment. *Journal of Finance* 60: 2661–700.

Malmendier, U. and Tate, G. (2008). Who makes acquisitions? CEO overconfidence and the market's reaction. *Journal of Financial Economics* 89: 20–43.

Markowitz, H. (1952). The utility of wealth. *Journal of Political Economy* 60(2): 151–8.

Mas-Collel, A., Whinston, M. D, and Green, J. R. (1995). *Microeconomic Theory.* New York: Oxford University Press.

Meehl, P. E. and Rose, A. (1955). Antecedent probability and the efficiency of psychometric signs, patterns or cutting scores. *Psychological Bulletin* 52: 194–216.

Michaely, R., Thaler, R. H., and Womack, K. (1995). Price reactions to dividend initiations and omissions. *Journal of Finance* 50: 573–608.

Mitchell, M. (2009). *Complexity: A Guided Tour*. Oxford: Oxford University Press.

Mookherjee, D. and Sopher, B. (1994). Learning behavior in an experimental matching pennies game. *Games and Economic Behavior* 7(1): 62–91.

Mookherjee, D. and Sopher, B. (1997). Learning and decision costs in experimental constant sum games. *Games and Economic Behavior* 19(1): 97–132.

Mussweiler, T. and Schneller, K. (2003). What goes up must come down: how charts infuence decisions to buy and sell stocks. *Journal of Behavioral Finance* 4(3): 121–30.

Nagel, R. (1995). Unraveling in guessing games: an experimental study. *American Economic Review* 85(5): 1313–26.

Nash, J. F. (1950). Equilibrium points in n-person games. *Proceedings of the National Academy of Sciences of the United States of America* 36(1): 48–9.

Neilson, W. S. (2006). Axiomatic reference-dependence in behavior toward others and toward risk. *Economic Theory* 28(3): 681–92.

Northcraft, G. B. and Neale, M. A. (1987). Experts, amateurs, and real estate: An anchoring-and-adjustment perspective on property pricing decisions. *Organizational Behaviour and Human Decision Processes* 39: 84–97.

Novemsky, N. and Kahneman, D. (2005). The boundaries of loss aversion. *Journal of Marketing Research* 42(2): 119–28.

Odean, T. (1998). Are investors reluctant to realize their losses? *Journal of Finance* 53: 1775–98.

O'Donoghue, T. and Rabin, M. (2001). Choice and procrastination. *Quarterly Journal of Economics* 116(1): 121–60.

O'Donoghue, T. and Rabin, M. (2006). Optimal sin taxes. *Journal of Public Economics* 90(10–11): 1825–49.

O'Neill, B. (1987). Nonparametric test of the minimax theory of two-person zerosum games. *Proceedings of the National Academy of Sciences of the United States of America* 84(7): 2106–9.

Page, T., Putterman, L., and Unel, B. (2005). Voluntary association in public goods experiments: reciprocity, mimicry and efficiency. *Economic Journal* 115(506): 1032–53.

Palacios-Huerta, I. (2003). Professionals play minimax. *Review of Economic Studies* 70(2): 395–415.

Palacios-Huerta I. and Volij, O. (2008). Experientia docet: professionals play minimax in laboratory experiments. *Econometrica* 76(1): 71–115.

Phelps, E. and Pollak, R. A. (1968). On second best national savings and game equilibrium growth. *Review of Economic studies* 35(2): 185–99.

Pogarsky, G. and Babcock, L. (2001). Damage caps, motivated anchoring and bargaining impasse. *Journal of Legal Studies* 30: 143–59.

Pope, D. and Schweitzer, M. (2011). Is Tiger Woods loss averse? Persistent bias in the face of experience, competition, and high stakes. *American Economic Review* 101(1): 129–57.

Popper, K. (1934). *Logik der Forschung* (Hutchinson & Company published the translation by Karl Popper titled *The Logic of Scientific Discovery* in 1959).

Popper, K. (1963). *Conjectures and Refutations: The Growth of Scientific Knowledge*. London: Routledge & Kegan Paul.

Prelec, D. (1998). The probability weighting function. *Econometrica* 66(3): 497–527.

Quiggin, J. (1982). A theory of anticipated utility. *Journal of Economic Behavior and Organization* 3(4): 323–43.

Rabin, M. (1993). Incorporating fairness into game theory and economics. *American Economic Review* 83(5): 1281–302.

Rabin, M. (2002). Inference by believers in the law of small numbers. *Quarterly Journal of Economics* 117: 775–816.

Rabin, M. and Schrag, J. (1999). First impressions matter: a model of confirmatory bias. *Quarterly Journal of Economics* 114(1): 37–82.

Rachlinski, J. J. (1998). A positive psychological theory of judging in hindsight. *University of Chicago Law Review* 65: 571–625.

Rapoport, A. and Budescu, D. V. (1997). Randomization in individual choice behavior. *Psychological Review* 104: 603–17.

Read, D. (2005). Monetary incentives, what are they good for? *Journal of Economic Methodology* 12(2): 265–76.

Redelmeier, D. A. and Shafir, E. (1995). Medical decision making in situations that offer multiple alternatives. *Journal of the American Medical Association* 273(4): 302–5.

Roiser, J. P., De Martino, B., Tan, G. C. Y., et al. (2009). A genetically mediated bias in decision making driven by failure of amygdala control. *Journal of Neuroscience* 29(18): 5985–91.

Rotemberg, J. J. (2008). Minimally acceptable altruism and the ultimatum game. *Journal of Economics and Organizational Behavior* 66: 457–76.

Roth, A. E. (1987). Laboratory experimentation in economics. In T. Bewley (ed.), *Advances in Economic Theory, Fifth World Congress*. Cambridge: Cambridge University Press, pp. 269–99.

Roth, A. E. (1988). Laboratory experimentation in economics: a methodological overview. *Economic Journal* 98: 974–1031.

Roth, A. E. (1995). Introduction to experimental economics. In J. H. Kagel and A. E. Roth (eds.), *The Handbook of Experimental Economics*. Princeton, NJ: Princeton University Press, pp. 3–109.

Roth, A. E. (2015). Is experimental economics living up to its promise? In G. R. Fréchette and A. Schotter, (eds.), *Handbook of Experimental Economic Methodology*. Oxford: Oxford University Press, pp. 13–40.

Roth, B. and Voskort, A. (2014). Stereotypes and false consensus: how financial professionals predict risk preferences. *Journal of Economic Behavior and Organization* 107: 553–65.

Rubinstein, A. (2006). Dilemmas of an economic theorist, *Econometrica* 74(4): 865–83.

Rydval, O. and Ortmann, A. (2004). How financial incentives and cognitive abilities affect task performance in laboratory settings: an illustration. *Economics Letters* 85: 315–20.

Samuelson, P. A. (1937). A note on measurement of utility. *Review of Economic Studies* 4(2): 155–61.

Samuelson, P. A. and Nordhaus, W. (1985). *Economics*. New York: McGraw Hill.

Schotter, A. (2015). On the relationship between economic theory and experiments. In G. R. Fréchette and A. Schotter (eds.), *Handbook of Experimental Economic Methodology*. Oxford: Oxford University Press, pp. 58–85.

Selten, R. (1998). Features of experimentally observed bounded rationality. *European Economic Review* 42(3–5): 413–36.

Selten, R. (2001). What is bounded rationality? In G. Gigerenzer and R. Selten (eds.), *Bounded Rationality: The Adaptive Toolbox*.

Dahlem Workshop Report. Cambridge, MA: MIT Press, pp. 1–12.

Shachat, J. M. (2002). Mixed strategy play and the minimax hypothesis. *Journal of Economic Theory* 104(1): 189–226.

Shefrin, H. M. and Thaler, R. H. (1988). The behavioral life-cycle hypothesis. *Economic Inquiry* 26(4): 609–43.

Shiller, R. (1981). Do stock prices move too much to be justified by subsequent changes in dividends? *American Economic Review* 71: 421–36.

Shleifer, A. (1986). Do demand curves for stocks slope down? *Journal of Finance* 41: 579–90.

Shleifer, A. and Vishny, R. (1997). The limits of arbitrage. *Journal of Finance* 52: 35–55.

Siegel, S. and Fouraker, L. E. (1960). *Bargaining and Group Decision Making*. New York: McGraw-Hill.

Simon, H. A. (1978). Rational decision-making in business organizations. Nobel Memorial Lecture, December 8, 1978.

Simon, H. A. (2000). Bounded rationality in social science: today and tomorrow. *Mind and Society* 1(1): 25–39.

Slonim, R. and Roth, A. E. (1998). Learning in high stakes ultimatum games: an experiment in the Slovak Republic. *Econometrica* 66(3): 569–96.

Slonim, R. L., Roth A. E., and Erev, I. (2003). Regularities in play of zero-sum games with unique mixed-strategy equilibria. Mimeo, Case Western Reserve University.

Slonim, R., Wang, C., Garbarino, E., and Merret, D. (2013). Opting-in: participation bias in economic experiments. *Journal of Economic Behavior and Organization* 90: 43–70.

Slovic, P., Finucane, M., Peters, E., and MacGregor, D. G. (2002). The affect heuristic. In T. Gilovich, D. Griffin, and D. Kahneman (eds.), *Heuristics and Biases: The Psychology of Intuitive Judgment*. New York: Cambridge University Press, pp. 397–420.

Slovic, P., MacGregor, D. G., Malmfors, T., and Purchase, I. F. H. (1999). *Influence of Affective Processes on Toxicologists' Judgments of Risk (Report No. 99-2)*. Eugene, OR: Decision Research.

Slovic, P., Monahan, J., and MacGregor, D. G. (2000). Violence risk assessment and risk communication: the effects of using actual cases, providing instruction, and employing probability versus frequency formats. *Law and Human Behavior* 24: 271–96.

Smith, V. L. (1962). An experimental study of competitive market behavior. *Journal of Political Economy* 70: 111–37.

Smith, V. L. (1976). Experimental economics: induced value theory. *American Economic Review* 66: 274–9.

Smith, V. L. (1991). Rational choice: the contrast between economics and psychology. *Journal of Political Economy* 99: 877–97.

Smith, V. L. (2001). From old issues to new directions in experimental psychology and economics. *Behavioral and Brain Sciences* 24(3): 428–9.

Smith, V. L. and Walker, J. M. (1993). Monetary rewards and decision cost in experimental economics. *Economic Inquiry* 31: 245–61.

Solan, L., Rosenblatt, T., and Osherson D. (2008). False consensus bias in contract interpretation. *Columbia Law Review* 108(5): 1272–300.

Stahl, D. O. and Wilson, P. (1995). On players' models of other players: theory and experimental evidence. *Games and Economic Behavior* 10: 218–54.

Stanovich, K. E. (2012). On the distinction between rationality and intelligence: implications for understanding individual differences in reasoning. In K. Holyoak and R. Morrison (eds.), *The Oxford Handbook of Thinking and Reasoning*. New York: Oxford University Press, pp. 343–65.

Stanovich, K. E. and West, R. F. (2000). Individual differences in reasoning: implications for the rationality debate [Target article and commentaries]. *Behavioral and Brain Sciences* 23: 645–726.

Stanovich, K. E. and West, R. F. (2007). Natural myside bias is independent of cognitive ability. *Thinking & Reasoning* 13(3): 225–47.

Starmer, C. (2000). Developments in non-expected utility theory: the hunt for a descriptive theory of choice under risk. *Journal of Economic Literature* 38(2): 332–82.

Starmer, C. and Sugden, R. (1989). Probability and juxtaposition effects: an experimental investigation of the common ratio effect. *Journal of Risk Uncertainty* 2(2): 159–78.

Strack, F. and Mussweiler, T. (1997). Explaining the enigmatic anchoring effect: mechanisms of selective accessibility. *Journal of Personality and Social Psychology* 73: 437–46.

Strotz, R. H. (1955–6). Myopia and inconsistency in dynamic utility maximization. *Review of Economic Studies* 23(3): 165–80.

Tanaka, T., Camerer, C. F., and Nguyen, Q. (2010). Risk and time preferences: linking experimental and household survey data from Vietnam. *American Economic Review* 100(1): 557–71.

Terrell, D. (1994). A test of the gambler's fallacy: evidence from pari-mutuel games. *Journal of Risk and Uncertainty* 8: 309–17.

Tesfatsion, L. and Judd, K. L. (eds.) (2006). *Handbook of Computational Economics, Volume 2: Agent-Based Computational Economics*. Amsterdam: North-Holland.

Tetlock, P. E. (1999). Theory-driven reasoning about possible pasts and probable futures in world politics: are we prisoners of our preconceptions? *American Journal of Political Science* 43(2): 335–66.

Tetlock, P. E. (2006). *Expert Political Judgment: How Good Is It? How Can We Know?* Princeton, NJ: Princeton University Press.

Thaler, R. H. (1980). Toward a positive theory of consumer choice. *Journal of Economic Behavior and Organization* 1: 39–60.

Thaler, R. H. (1981). Some empirical evidence of dynamic inconsistency. *Economics Letters* 8(3): 201–7.

Thaler, R. H. (2015). *Misbehaving: The Making of Behavioral Economics*. New York: W. W. Norton.

Tom, S. M., Fox, C. R., Trepel, C., and Poldrack, R. A. (2007). The neural basis of loss aversion in decision-making under risk. *Science* 315: 515–18.

Tversky, A. and Kahneman, D. (1973). Availability: a heuristic for judging frequency and probability. *Cognitive Psychology* 5(2): 207–32.

Tversky, A. and Kahneman, D. (1974). Judgment under uncertainty: heuristics and biases. *Science* 185: 1124–30.

Tversky, A. and Kahneman, D. (1980). Causal schemas in judgments under uncertainty. In M. Fishbein (ed.), *Progress in Social Psychology*. Hillsdale, NJ: Erlbaum, pp. 49–72.

Tversky, A. and Kahneman, D. (1992). Advances in prospect theory: cumulative representation of uncertainty. *Journal of Risk and Uncertainty* 5(4): 297–323.

Tyran, J.-R. and Sausgruber, R. (2006). A little fairness may induce a lot of redistribution in a democracy. *European Economic Review* 50(2): 469–85.

Varian, H. (1992). *Microeconomic Analysis*. New York: W. W. Norton.

Veblen, T. (1899). *The Theory of the Leisure Class. An Economic Study of Institutions*. Random House.

Viscusi, K. W., Huber, J., and Bell, J. (2008). Estimating discount rates for environmental quality from utility-based choice experiments. *Journal of Risk and Uncertainty* 37(2–3): 199–220.

von Neumann, J. and Morgenstern, O. (1944). *Theory of Games and Economic Behavior*. Princeton, NJ: Princeton University Press.

Wakker, P. P. (2010). *Prospect Theory for Risk and Ambiguity*. Cambridge: Cambridge University Press.

Wakker, P. P. and Deneffe, D. (1996). Eliciting von Neumann–Morgenstern utilities when probabilities are distorted or unknown. *Management Science* 42(8): 1131–50.

Walker, M. and Wooders, J. (2001). Minimax play at Wimbledon. *American Economic Review* 91(5): 1521–38.

Weyland, K. (1996). Risk taking in Latin American economic restructuring: lessons from prospect theory. *International Studies Quarterly* 40(2): 185–207.

Wimsatt, C. W. (2007). *Re-Engineering Philosophy for Limited Beings*. Cambridge, MA: Harvard University Press.

Wooders, J. (2010). Does experience teach? Professionals and minimax play in the lab. *Econometrica* 78(3): 1143–54.

Zizzo, D. J. (2010). Experimenter demand effects in economic experiments. *Experimental* 13(1): 75–98.

CHAPTER 1

The Evidence on Human Choice under Risk and Uncertainty

1.1 Introduction

Suppose that a decision maker takes some action that leads to an *objective probability distribution* over a set of known outcomes. This is a situation of *risk*. In this chapter, we briefly consider the elements of the neoclassical approach to decision making in such situations, *expected utility theory* (EU), and the empirical evidence for EU. Most readers of this book would be familiar with EU. For this reason, no more than an outline of the basic elements is provided.[1]

Section 1.2 outlines the basic framework of EU, with particular emphasis on its preference foundations (von Neumann and Morgenstern, 1944). We also consider *attitudes to risk* that, for EU, are determined entirely by the shape of the utility function. Although most people may believe that probabilities have something to do with risk, they play no role in EU in determining risk attitudes. We also give the basic definitions of *stochastic dominance* for later use. The axioms that lead to an EU representation of preferences are also known as the *axioms of rationality*. Ultimately the validity of these axioms is an empirical matter.

In contrast to risk, under *uncertainty* no objective probabilities that are universally agreed upon can be identified. Section 1.3 considers the basic model of uncertainty in economics, *subjective expected utility* or SEU (de Finetti, 1937; Savage, 1954). This approach underpins the *Bayesian approach to uncertainty*.

Section 1.4 considers a topic of considerable applied interest. Namely, the problem of eliciting the utility function of an EU decision maker under risk (McCord and de Neufville, 1986), and uncertainty (Wakker and Deneffe, 1996).

Section 1.5, the heart of the chapter, describes the violations of EU. Section 1.5.1 focuses on the evidence arising from the violation of the *independence axiom*, one of the main axioms of rationality. These violations take two forms, the *common ratio effect*, and the *common consequence effect* (Allais, 1953). The common ratio violation takes place when scaling down the probabilities in two-outcome lotteries by a common factor leads to a reversal in preferences. The common consequence violation takes place when two pairs of lotteries each have a common consequence, yet the decision maker exhibits a form of preference reversal.

---

[1] The interested reader may wish to consult any advanced undergraduate or graduate text in economics; see, for instance, Varian (1992) and Mas-Collel et al. (1995). A more formal treatment can be found in Fishburn (1982b).

Section 1.5.2 introduces a particularly useful device to study the implications of violations of the axioms of rationality: the *Marshak–Machina probability triangle*. The independence axiom that underpins EU implies that the indifference curves in the probability triangle are parallel straight lines. However, one observes both *fanning-in* and *fanning-out* of indifference curves, which violates the independence axiom. Furthermore, empirical evidence suggests that the violations of EU are more pronounced along the edges of the probability triangle as compared to the interior of the triangle. These violations in many cases arise from non-linear weighting of probabilities that is particularly pronounced close to the edges of the probability triangle.

Section 1.5.3 briefly considers alternative theories that explain the evidence in the probability triangle by relaxing the independence axiom; for instance *weighted utility theory* (Chew and MacCrimmon, 1979). Theories that have the best chance of explaining the evidence incorporate both fanning-in and fanning-out of indifference curves in the probability triangle. An example is the theory of *disappointment aversion* (Gul, 1991) that we consider in more detail in the next chapter.

Section 1.5.4 considers Rabin's (2000a) *calibration theorem*. Consider an EU decision maker who has an increasing and concave utility function. Rabin showed that if this decision maker turns down a moderate stake gamble (say, 50–50 chance of losing 10 and gaining 11), then the decision maker will turn down the following equiprobable gamble: lose 100 and win an infinite amount. Clearly this is absurd, but it is a logical outcome under EU. We shall see in Chapter 3 that this paradox does not arise under prospect theory.

EU assumes that the choice among pairs of mathematically equivalent lotteries does not depend on how the information in the lotteries is framed, also known as the assumption of *description invariance*. Section 1.5.5 considers a classic problem from Tversky and Kahneman (1981) that powerfully illustrates a violation of description invariance. This problem also illustrates that decision makers are risk loving (respectively, risk averse) when they perceive themselves to be in losses (respectively, gains), a finding of considerable importance that we study more closely in the subsequent chapters.

Section 1.5.6 considers the widely documented phenomenon of *preference reversal* (Lichtenstein and Slovic, 1971). Suppose that we have two lotteries: A *P*-bet has a high probability of winning a low prize and a $-bet has a low probability of winning a high prize. When decision makers have to directly choose between the two bets, they prefer the *P*-bet. However, at the same time they exhibit a higher certainty equivalent for the $-bet. We also consider attempts to explain preference reversals.

Section 1.5.7 closes the chapter by demonstrating that the reduction of compound lotteries axiom typically does not hold. This has far reaching implications for the validity of EU and will play an important role in providing one potential explanation of the Ellsberg paradox in Chapter 4.

1.2 The elements of classical decision theory

Let $X = \{x_1, x_2, \ldots, x_n\}$ be a fixed, finite, set of real numbers such that $x_1 < x_2 < \ldots < x_n$. One may interpret X as the set of all possible levels of wealth of the decision maker. We define a *lottery*, or *gamble*, as

$$L = (x_1, p_1; x_2, p_2; \ldots; x_n, p_n), \tag{1.1}$$

where $p_1, p_2, \ldots, p_n$, are the respective probabilities corresponding to the outcomes $x_1, x_2, \ldots, x_n$, such that $p_i \in [0,1]$ and $\sum_{i=1}^{n} p_i = 1$. The lottery $(x_i, 1)$ denotes an outcome x_i received with certainty, so we sometimes simply denote it as x_i. The lottery in (1.1) is sometimes also known as a *simple lottery*. Given two simple lotteries, L_1 and L_2, a lottery of lotteries, say, $(L_1, p; L_2, 1-p)$, where $p \in (0,1)$, is known as a *compound lottery*; the special case, $(L, p; 0, 1-p)$ is sometimes denoted by (L, p).

A situation of *risk* arises when the probabilities are objectively known. In contrast, when probabilities are not objectively known, then we have a situation of *uncertainty*. We focus on risk first.

Let the set of all lotteries of the form (1.1) be denoted by $\mathcal{L}$. Suppose that the decision maker must choose a lottery from some set $\mathcal{L}' \subset \mathcal{L}$. The fundamental question in decision theory is: Which lottery will the decision maker choose? This is also the simplest possible setting. It is "as if" the decision maker is simply playing a game against nature. Nature chooses the set of lotteries and the decision maker simply picks one or more elements from the set. In game theory, by contrast, the decision maker, in addition, has to take account of the behavior of others.

1.2.1 *Preference foundations of expected utility theory (EU)*

The most widely used theory under risk in economics is *expected utility theory* (EU).[2] Many behavioral models in decision theory build on the EU model and the lessons learnt from the empirical anomalies, relative to the EU predictions. We first briefly review the foundations of EU.

The decision maker is endowed with a binary preference relation over $\mathcal{L}$, denoted by $\succeq$; it is interpreted as "at least as good as." So, for $L_1, L_2 \in \mathcal{L}$, $L_2 \succeq L_1$ means that the lottery L_2 is "at least as good as" the lottery L_1, or L_2 is "weakly preferred" to L_1. The notations $L_2 \succeq L_1$ and $L_1 \preceq L_2$ are equivalent, just as $5 < 7$ or $7 > 5$, and one may use either of the two; similar comments apply to "strict preference," e.g., $L_2 \succ L_1$ and $L_1 \prec L_2$ are equivalent.

We now represent preferences in a more convenient form. Consider the following conditions, or axioms, on preferences. We assume that all lotteries belong to the set $\mathcal{L}$, and a typical member of this set is given in (1.1).

Axiom 1.1   *(Order) Order requires the following two conditions.*

   a. *Completeness: For all lotteries L_1, L_2, either $L_2 \succeq L_1$ or $L_2 \preceq L_1$.*
   b. *Transitivity: For all lotteries L_1, L_2, L_3, $L_3 \succeq L_2$ and $L_2 \succeq L_1 \Rightarrow L_3 \succeq L_1$.*

Two further binary relations between lotteries can be defined in terms of $\preceq$:

$$\begin{cases} \text{Indifference:} & L_1 \sim L_2 \Leftrightarrow L_2 \succeq L_1 \text{ and } L_1 \succeq L_2. \\ \text{Strict preference:} & L_2 \succ L_1 \Leftrightarrow \text{it is not the case that } L_1 \succeq L_2. \end{cases}$$

Axiom 1.2   *(Best and worst) $x_n \succ x_1$ (i.e., $(x_n, 1) \succ (x_i, 1)$).*

Axiom 1.3   *(Continuity) For each lottery, L, there is a $p \in [0,1]$ such that $L \sim (x_1, 1-p; x_n, p)$.*

---

[2] For the preference foundations of EU, the interested reader can consult Kreps (1990), Varian (1992), and Mas-Collel et al. (1995). Kreps (1990) already makes a strong case for exploring alternatives to EU. For a more advanced and definitive treatment of EU, see Fishburn (1982b).

Axiom 1.4 *(Independence) For all lotteries L_1, L_2, L, and all $p \in [0,1]$, $L_2 \succeq L_1 \Leftrightarrow$ $(L_2, p; L, 1-p) \succeq (L_1, p; L, 1-p)$.*

Axiom 1.5 *(Reduction, or law of compounding lotteries) Let p_1, p_2, $p \in [0,1]$. Let $L_1 \sim$ $(x_i, 1-p_1; x_j, p_1)$ and $L_2 \sim (x_i, 1-p_2; x_j, p_2)$. Then*

$$(L_1, p; L_2, 1-p) \sim \left((x_i, 1-p_1; x_j, p_1), p; (x_i, 1-p_2; x_j, p_2), 1-p\right)$$
$$\sim \left(x_i, (1-p_1)p + (1-p_2)(1-p); x_j, pp_1 + (1-p)p_2\right).$$

From Axiom 1.2, a decision maker strictly prefers receiving the highest outcome with certainty to receiving the lowest outcome with certainty. The continuity property in Axiom 1.3 asserts that every lottery is equivalent to a simple lottery obtained by probabilistically mixing the highest outcome, x_n, and the lowest outcome, x_1. The independence axiom, Axiom 1.4, is the most crucial. It requires that if a lottery, L_2, is preferred to a lottery, L_1, then mixing each with a third lottery, L, (with the same positive mixing probability, p) does not alter the preference.

"Rationality" has a precise meaning in decision theory that is given in the next definition.[3]

Definition 1.1 *(Axioms of rationality): The following axioms: Order, best and worst, continuity, independence, and reduction, collectively, are termed as the axioms of rationality. If a binary relation $\succeq$ on $\mathcal{L}$ satisfies the axioms of rationality, then it is called a rational ordering of $\mathcal{L}$.*

Definition 1.2 *(Representation): Let $\succeq$ be a binary relation on $\mathcal{L}$ and let $U : \mathcal{L} \to \mathbb{R}$ such that for all $L_1, L_2 \in \mathcal{L}$, $L_2 \succeq L_1$ if, and only if, $U(L_2) \geq U(L_1)$. Then U is said to represent $\succeq$ and we say that $\succeq$ is induced by U.*

Definition 1.3 *(von Neumann–Morgenstern expected utility function): A utility function $U : \mathcal{L} \to \mathbb{R}$ has the 'expected utility form' (or the von Neumann–Morgenstern form) if we can assign a real number, $u(x_i)$, to each possible outcome, x_i, such that for the lottery L in (1.1), we can write*

$$U(L) = \sum_{i=1}^{n} p_i u(x_i). \tag{1.2}$$

We now state the main result, the existence of a von Neumann–Morgenstern expected utility representation.

Proposition 1.1 *(von Neumann and Morgenstern, 1944): Suppose that the binary relation, $\succeq$, on the set of lotteries $\mathcal{L}$, satisfies the axioms of rationality. Then there is a function, $U : \mathcal{L} \to \mathbb{R}$, such that, for all $L_1, L_2, L \in \mathcal{L}$,*

(a) $U(x_1) \leq U(L) \leq U(x_n)$ and $U(x_1) < U(x_n)$,
(b) $L_2 \succeq L_1$ if, and only if, $U(L_2) \geq U(L_1)$,
(c) the utility function is of the von Neumann–Morgenstern form.

Proposition 1.1(a) shows that a constant utility function will not suffice. Proposition 1.1(b) shows that a utility function exists that represents the underlying preferences and Proposition 1.1(c) shows that it takes the familiar form under EU that is linear in probabilities.

---

[3] Notice that rationality does not imply other literal meanings of the word such as welfare or efficiency maximizing choices or preferences that are self regarding or other regarding, etc.

Among the set of available lotteries, $\mathcal{L}$, the *EU criterion* requires that the decision maker chooses the one that gives the highest expected utility. The converse of Proposition 1.1 also holds. Namely that if a function U with the properties listed in Proposition 1.1 exists, then $\preceq$ satisfies the axioms of rationality. An important property of the EU functional is that it is invariant with respect to positive affine transformations. Thus, the utility function $\widehat{U}(L) = \sum_{i=1}^{n} p_i[a + bu(x_i)]$, where $a \in \mathbb{R}$ and $b > 0$, represents the same preferences as does U in (1.2).

The axioms of rationality appear intuitive and plausible. A violation of the axioms of rationality is not a form of irrationality or madness. The axioms are no more than assumptions about human behavior, and their reasonableness must be tested by empirical evidence. A large number of rigorous tests have rejected the axioms of rationality. The challenge for behavioral economics is to produce a behavioral decision theory that is, on the one hand, in conformity with the evidence and, on the other hand, sufficiently tractable.

> **Remark 1.1** *EU has two main features:*
>
> (i) *Linearity in probabilities. Formally, this means that $EU(L_1, p; L_2, 1-p) = pEU(L_1) + (1-p)EU(L_2)$. This assumption is fundamental to many areas in economics. For instance, it is required in the proof of the existence of a mixed strategy Nash equilibrium. However, extensive empirical evidence shows that it is violated. Most non-EU decision theories relax the linearity assumption.*
>
> (ii) *In most applications of EU, utility typically depends on the final wealth level in each state of the world. Redefining outcomes under EU relative to a reference outcome (or any outcome) is not inconsistent with the axioms of EU. Doing so would partition the domain of outcomes into gains (outcomes greater than the reference point) and losses (outcomes lower than the reference point). However, EU offers no insights about human behavior in the domain of gains and losses. By contrast, empirically observed behavior of decision makers is fundamentally different in the domain of gains and losses. Indeed, differences in behavior in gains and losses are not only an essential driver of many important results in other decision theories such as prospect theory, but there is empirical confirmation of these predictions.*

1.2.2 Attitudes to risk under EU

The EU criterion contrasts with the earlier *expected value maximization criterion* (EV), which evaluates the lottery $L = (x_1, p_1; x_2, p_2; \ldots; x_n, p_n)$ as $EV(L) = \sum_{i=1}^{n} p_i x_i$.

Consider a decision theory in which the utility function $\overline{U}$ is able to represent preferences over lotteries, e.g., under EU, $\overline{U} = U$. In other cases, $\overline{U}$ could be the utility representation under rank dependent utility or under prospect theory.

> **Definition 1.4** *(Certainty equivalent): Consider the lottery $(C_L, 1)$, where $C_L \in \mathbb{R}$. If a solution exists to the equation $\overline{U}(C_L) = \overline{U}(L)$, then C_L is known as the certainty equivalent of the lottery L.*

Notice that the definition of a certainty equivalent holds for any decision theory that admits a utility representation of preferences over lotteries, although the value of certainty equivalent under alternative decision theories is likely to differ. We now state the meaning of risk aversion; an individual who would rather accept a sure amount that is lower than the expected value of the lottery, in order to avoid playing the lottery, is said to be risk averse.

Definition 1.5 *(Risk aversion): A decision maker is 'risk neutral' if $C_L = EV(L)$, 'risk averse' if $C_L < EV(L)$, and 'risk loving' if $C_L > EV(L)$.*

In this section, we only consider an expected utility representation of preferences $(\overline{U} = U)$. The next proposition states a well-known result that you are asked to prove in one of the exercises.

Proposition 1.2 *Under expected utility theory, the properties of risk neutrality, risk aversion, and risk seeking are equivalent, respectively, to a linear, concave, and convex utility function.*

Risk aversion arising from a concave utility function underpins many important economic phenomena. For instance, the study of insurance, the design of contract schemes in principal–agent problems, the optimal rates of taxes, and determination of wage rates.

The EV criterion restricts decision makers to be risk neutral, hence, lotteries that have the same EV but appear different in their risk characteristics are equally preferred by the EV criterion. Daniel Bernoulli showed in 1738 that a famous paradox, the *St. Petersburg paradox*, cannot be resolved by the EV criterion but can be resolved by the EU criterion (you are asked to prove this in one of the exercises). The EU criterion can solve the St. Petersburg paradox because it allows for risk aversion. However, risk preferences are incorporated in EU through the shape of the utility function alone, rather than through probabilities. By contrast, many psychologists would typically argue that risk should be incorporated through probabilities rather than the shape of the utility function.

We can also compare the desirability of two lotteries that have the same outcomes but different probability distributions over them. Consider lotteries of the form $L = (x_1, p_1; x_2, p_2; \ldots; x_n, p_n)$, where the outcomes $x_1 < x_2 < \ldots < x_n$ belong to the set of real numbers. Under any distribution function P over this set of incomes, the probability of outcome x_i is denoted by $p_i \geq 0$, $\sum_{i=1}^{i=n} p_i = 1$. The *cumulative probability distribution* is given by $P_0 = 0$, $P_j = \sum_{i=1}^{i=j} p_i$. Denote by Π, the set of all such distributions over X. The *cumulative of the cumulative distribution* is given by $\widetilde{P}_0 = 0$, $\widetilde{P}_j = \sum_{i=1}^{i=j} P_i$, $j = 1, 2, \ldots, n$. Let $\widetilde{\Pi}$ be the set of all such distributions. The average, or mean, of $x_1, x_2, \ldots, x_n$, under the distribution $P \in \Pi$ is $\mu_P = \sum_{i=1}^{i=n} p_i x_i$. Let u be the utility function for sure outcomes $(x_i, 1)$.

Notation 1.1 *Denote by* **u**, *the class of all non-decreasing utility functions.*

We state here the basic results on *first order stochastic dominance* and *second order stochastic dominance* in the case of discrete outcomes; the continuous analogues can be picked up from any advanced microeconomics book. We shall need the results for the discrete case to prove some of the results below.

Definition 1.6 *(First order stochastic dominance): Let $P, Q \in \Pi$. Then P first order stochastically dominates Q ($P \succeq_1 Q$) if $P_j \leq Q_j$ for $j = 1, 2, \ldots, n$. If, in addition, the inequality is strict for some j, then P strictly first order stochastically dominates Q ($P \succ_1 Q$).*

Definition 1.7 *We say that the outcome levels are equally spaced if for some positive real number, δ, $x_{i+1} - x_i = \delta$ for $i = 1, 2, \ldots, n-1$.*[4]

---

[4] This is not restrictive because we can always introduce extra income levels, each with probability zero, to achieve equal spacing. For example, the incomes $y_1 = 5$, $y_2 = 7$, $y_3 = 11$, are not equally spaced. Let $P_1 = \frac{1}{3}$, $P_2 = \frac{2}{3}$, and $P_3 = 1$. Consider $y_1 = 5$, $y_2 = 7$, $y_3 = 9$, $y_4 = 11$, which are equally spaced, and $Q_1 = \frac{1}{3}$, $Q_2 = \frac{2}{3}$, $Q_3 = \frac{2}{3}$, and $Q_4 = 1$. Both P and Q describe the same reality.

Definition 1.8 *(Second Order Stochastic dominance): Suppose that incomes are equally spaced (Definition 1.7).[5] Let $P,Q \in \Pi$. Then P second order stochastically dominates Q ($P \succeq_2 Q$) if $\widetilde{P}_j \le \widetilde{Q}_j$ for $j = 1,2,\ldots,n$ and if $\mu_P \ge \mu_Q$.[6] If, in addition, one of these inequalities is strict, then P strictly second order stochastically dominates Q ($P \succ_2 Q$).*

So far, the definitions of first order and second order dominance are purely statistical. We now explore their economic content. The results should be familiar to most advanced undergraduates in economics, so the proofs are omitted; readers interested in the continuous case can consult Mas-Collel et al. (1995).

Proposition 1.3 *Let $P,Q \in \Pi$. Then $P \succeq_1 Q$ if, and only if, for any $u \in \mathbf{u}$,*

$$\sum_{i=1}^{i=n} p_i u(x_i) \ge \sum_{i=1}^{i=n} q_i u(x_i), \tag{1.3}$$

and $P \succ_1 Q$ if, and only if, the inequality in (1.3) is strict for all strictly increasing $u \in \mathbf{u}$.

Choosing the non-decreasing function $u(x) = x$ as a candidate function in Proposition 1.3, we get that if $P \succeq_1 Q$ ($P \succ_1 Q$), then $\mu_P \ge \mu_Q$ ($\mu_P > \mu_Q$).

Proposition 1.4 *Let $P,Q \in \Pi$. Then $P \succeq_2 Q$ if, and only if, for any concave $u \in \mathbf{u}$,*

$$\sum_{i=1}^{i=n} p_i u(x_i) \ge \sum_{i=1}^{i=n} q_i u(x_i), \tag{1.4}$$

and $P \succ_2 Q$ if, and only if, the inequality in (1.4) is strict for all strictly increasing and strictly concave $u \in \mathbf{u}$.

It is also possible to give an alternative definition of first order stochastic dominance with a discrete set of outcomes that holds fixed the probability distribution but alters the spread of the outcomes in X. Let $L_2 \succeq_1 L_1$ and $L_2 \succ_1 L_1$ denote that the lottery L_2 first order stochastically dominates L_1, respectively, in a weak and strict sense.

Definition 1.9 *Let $L_1 = (x_1,p_1;\ldots;x_n,p_n)$ and $L_2 = (y_1,p_1;\ldots;y_n,p_n)$, then*

(a) $x_i \le y_i, i = 1,2,\ldots,n \Rightarrow L_2 \succeq_1 L_1$,

(b) $x_i \le y_i, i = 1,2,\ldots,n$ and $x_i < y_i$ for some $i \Rightarrow L_2 \succ_1 L_1$. (1.5)

The reader may construct a few examples that satisfy the conditions in Definition 1.9 and compare the distribution functions of the relevant lotteries to establish stochastic dominance.

1.3 Subjective expected utility theory (SEU)

Let there be n mutually exclusive *events* $E_1,E_2,\ldots,E_n$ that form a partition of some relevant sample space, S. The objective probabilities of these events are not known. The decision maker assigns *subjective probabilities* $\mu(E_1),\mu(E_2),\ldots,\mu(E_n)$ to these events such that $\mu(E_i) \ge 0$ for all

---

[5] Often 'equal spacing' is not stated as part of the definition of second order stochastic dominance. But then it has to be stated in the Propositions. We find it more convenient to state it in the definition. The equal spacing assumption is not needed in the continuous case.

[6] Often the condition $\mu_P \ge \mu_Q$ is not included as part of the definition of second order stochastic dominance. But then it needs to be included in the statement of the relevant Propositions. It is slightly simpler to include $\mu_P \ge \mu_Q$ as part of the definition of second order stochastic dominance.

i and $\sum_{i=1}^{n} \mu(E_i) = 1$. This is a situation of *uncertainty* because, although objective probabilities are not known, well-defined and consistent subjective probabilities exist. Now suppose that a decision maker needs to evaluate a special kind of lottery of the form

$$f = (E_1, x_1; E_2, x_2; \ldots; E_n, x_n), \tag{1.6}$$

where the decision maker receives the outcome x_i if the event E_i occurs, $i = 1, 2, \ldots, n$. For pedagogical simplicity, let the outcomes be monetary, such as income or wealth. The object in (1.6) is also known as a *Savage act*. For any partition of a sample space, S, into a set of *mutually exclusive* events $\{E_1, E_2, \ldots, E_n\}$, a Savage act, f, maps states of the world to outcomes, i.e., $f : S \to X$; sometimes the notation $f(E_i) = x_i$, $i = 1, \ldots, n$ is also used.

One of the earliest justifications for the use of subjective utility was given in the work of de Finetti (1937). Denote the set of all Savage acts of the form in (1.6) by F, and define a binary relation over F by $\succeq$ that denotes "at least as good as." The addition operator, $+$, applied to elements of the set F implies state by state addition of outcomes. For instance, let $f_1, f_2, f_3 \in F$:

$$f_1 = (E_1, x_1; E_2, x_2), f_2 = (E_1, y_1; E_2, y_2), f_3 = (E_1, z_1; E_2, z_2) \tag{1.7}$$

then,

$$f_1 + f_3 = (E_1, x_1 + z_1; E_2, x_2 + z_2), f_2 + f_3 = (E_1, y_1 + z_1; E_2, y_2 + z_2). \tag{1.8}$$

We now define the analogue of the independence axiom of EU under uncertainty, which is termed as *additivity*.

Definition 1.10

(i) (*Additivity*): Suppose that we have Savage acts $f_1, f_2, f_3 \in F$ such that $f_1 \succeq f_2$. Then additivity implies that $f_1 + f_3 \succeq f_2 + f_3$.

(ii) (*Monotonicity*): Let $f_1 = (E_1, x_1; E_2, x_2; \ldots; E_n, x_n)$, $f_2 = (E_1, y_1; E_2, y_2; \ldots; E_n, y_n)$. Suppose that $x_i \geq y_i$ for $i = 1, 2, \ldots, n$. Then monotonicity implies that $f_1 \succeq f_2$.

Suppose that in addition to additivity, $\succeq$ is a weak order (transitive and complete), and *monotonicity* holds. Let f be as defined in (1.6) and $g = (E_1, y_1; E_2, y_2; \ldots; E_n, y_n)$, where $f, g \in F$. Then (under a further continuity assumption) de Finetti (1937) obtained the following remarkable result (for details, see Wakker 2010 and Gilboa 2009).

$$f \succeq g \Leftrightarrow \sum_{i=1}^{n} \mu(E_i) x_i \geq \sum_{i=1}^{n} \mu(E_i) y_i.$$

Thus, the individual acts so as to maximize the *expected value of a lottery*. Furthermore, the numbers $\mu(E_1), \mu(E_2), \ldots, \mu(E_n)$, which may be interpreted as *subjective probabilities*, are *unique*.

In many contexts, expected value maximization might not be very attractive.[7] Despite the drawbacks of the expected value criterion, de Finetti's (1937) result provided the basis and initial

---

[7] Consider the binary Savage acts, f_1, f_2, f_3 in (1.7) and their addition, defined in (1.8). Let the individual be declared bankrupt if his income in any state falls below some monetary level b. Suppose that all monetary

impetus for using subjective probabilities in a formal manner. For small-stake experiments, expected value might not necessarily be a bad approximation.

Let $f(E_i), g(E_i)$ denote the respective outcomes under the Savage acts f, g, when the event E_i occurs. Define a function $u : S \to R$ that it is unique up to a positive affine transformation; $u(f(E_i))$ has the interpretation of the utility of the outcome $f(E_i)$. The following functional has the interpretation of *subjective expected utility* from the Savage act f.

$$V(f) = \sum_{i=1}^{n} \mu(E_i)u(f(E_i)), \tag{1.9}$$

where $\mu(E_i) \geq 0 \,\forall i$ and $\sum_{i=1}^{n} \mu(E_i) = 1$. This is the sense in which EU can be plausibly extended to subjective beliefs. Risk can now be seen as a special case of uncertainty when there exists an objective probability p_i such that $p_i = \mu(E_i)$ for $i = 1, \ldots, n$. When new information arrives, the decision maker engages in Bayesian updating to update his prior beliefs into a set of posterior beliefs that comprise the new, unique, additive probability measure.

In one of the most brilliant results in all of social science, Savage (1954) derived the following representation of preferences of the individual. For any two Savage acts, f, g:

$$f \succeq g \Leftrightarrow \sum_{i=1}^{n} \mu(E_i)u(f(E_i)) \geq \sum_{i=1}^{n} \mu(E_i)u(g(E_i)), \tag{1.10}$$

where μ is a unique additive probability measure such that $\mu(E_i) \geq 0$ for all i and $\sum_{i=1}^{n} \mu(E_i) = 1$.[8] Savage (1954) provides an axiomatic foundation of *subjective expected utility* (SEU), also sometimes known as the *Bayesian approach to uncertainty* because beliefs are updated in a Bayesian manner.[9] In addition to the standard axioms of completeness and transitivity, the substantive new axiom in the Savage framework is the *sure thing principle* that is the analogue of the independence axiom under EU.[10]

> **Definition 1.11** *(Sure thing principle): Consider the following pairwise choices between four Savage acts, $f_1, f_2, f_3, f_4 \in F$ that are defined over the events E_1, E_2, E_3; let y, x_1, x_2, x_3, x_4 be the possible outcomes.*
>
> $$f_1 = (E_1, y; E_2, x_2; E_3, x_3), f_2 = (E_1, x_1; E_2, x_2; E_3, x_3),$$
> $$f_3 = (E_1, y; E_2, x_2; E_3, x_4), f_4 = (E_1, x_1; E_2, x_2; E_3, x_4).$$
>
> *The sure thing principle holds if $f_1 \succ f_2 \Leftrightarrow f_3 \succ f_4$.*

Definition 1.11 is easily extended to more events and outcomes. The remarkable thing about Savage's axiomatic framework is that the axioms make no assumptions about objects such as probabilities. However, the actual representation of preferences in (1.10) is similar to that under EU except that the (unique) objects $\mu(E_i)$, $i = 1, \ldots, n$, have the interpretation of subjective probabilities.

We now define *probabilistic sophistication*, a term that we require in Chapter 4.

---

outcomes in (1.7), (1.8) are greater than b except for $x_1 + z_1$, which is below b. Then the individual might express the preference $f_2 + f_3 \succsim f_1 + f_3$ which violates additivity.

[8] μ is an additive probability measure if $\mu(\cup_{i=1}^{n} E_i) = \sum_{i=1}^{n} \mu(E_i)$.

[9] While Savage's preference foundations have received the most attention, there are others; see Ramsey (1931), de Finetti (1937), and Anscombe and Aumann (1963).

[10] There are two further axioms that allow one to make a distinction between beliefs of the individual and the individual's tastes. For a discussion of these axioms, see Karni (2003) and Gintis (2009, Section 1.5).

Definition 1.12 *Lotteries or Savage acts, as defined in (1.6), are known as event contingent lotteries.*[11] *By contrast, lotteries written in the standard form, $L = (x_1, p_1; \ldots; x_n, p_n)$, such that $p_i \geq 0$ and $\sum_{i=1}^{n} p_i = 1$, are known as probability contingent lotteries.*

Suppose that the decision maker assigns the probability p_i to the event E_i, $i = 1, \ldots, n$. Then the decision maker may consider the lotteries $(x_1, p_1; \ldots; x_n, p_n)$ and $(E_1, x_1; E_2, x_2; \ldots; E_n, x_n)$ to be identical and treat them interchangeably; this is known as probabilistic sophistication and summarized in the next definition.

Definition 1.13 *(Probabilistic sophistication): Consider Definition 1.12. The decision maker is said to be probabilistically sophisticated when event contingent lotteries can be replaced by probability contingent lotteries. The subjective probabilities in probability contingent lotteries constitute a probability measure. However, there is no presumption, under probabilistic sophistication, that in comparing two lotteries, the decision maker uses SEU. For instance, the decision maker may also follow any of the non-expected utility theories. Furthermore, the decision maker is indifferent between two event contingent lotteries that lead to the same probability contingent prospect.*[12]

In Chapter 4 we will consider an example in which the *Ellsberg paradox* implies a violation of probabilistic sophistication.

1.4 Eliciting the utility function under EU

In this section, we consider the elicitation of the underlying utility function when the decision maker follows EU. We consider the two cases of known and unknown probabilities.

1.4.1 *The case of known probabilities*

Suppose that probabilities and outcomes are known. Consider any two outcomes such that $x_l < x_h$. Then, we can choose the following convenient normalization.

$$u(x_l) = 0, \ u(x_h) = 1. \tag{1.11}$$

Example 1.1 *Consider a set of outcomes $x_1 \leq x_2 \leq \ldots \leq x_n$, where at least one of the inequalities is strict. Let x_l be the lowest outcome and x_h the highest. Suppose that there is a utility function v such that $v(x_l) < v(x_h)$. We wish to renormalize the utility function such that the utility from the lowest outcome is 0 and the utility from the highest outcome is 1. Recall that if v represents the decision maker's preferences under EU, then so does $u = a + bv$, $a \in \mathbb{R}$ and $b > 0$ (invariance to positive affine transformations). Solving the two simultaneous equations $u(x_1) = 0 = a + bv(x_1)$ and $u(x_n) = 1 = a + bv(x_n)$ gives the required values of $a = -bv(x_l)$ and $b = \frac{1}{v(x_h) - v(x_l)}$.*

---

[11] One could give a more formal measure theoretic construction if required, but our discussion here is at a heuristic level only.

[12] The axiomatic justification of probabilistic sophistication can be found in Machina and Schmeidler (1992), Epstein and LeBreton (1993), Sarin and Wakker (2000), Abdellaoui and Wakker (2005), Chew and Sagi (2006), and Grant et al. (2008).

We now offer the decision maker, lotteries of the form

$$L = (x_l, 1 - p; x_h, p), \; x_l < x_h \tag{1.12}$$

and compute the certainty equivalent, x, of the lottery. Under EU, and using (1.11), this is given by the solution to

$$u(x) = (1 - p)u(x_l) + pu(x_h) = p. \tag{1.13}$$

From (1.13) we can find the utility of the decision maker at the certainty equivalent as simply the known probability of the best outcome. The requirement that a solution exists to (1.13) is called *standard gamble solvability*. This procedure for eliciting the utility function is also known as the problem of eliciting standard gamble probability (SG) with respect to the outcomes x_l, x_h. Suppose that the decision maker's preferences are a *weak order* (complete and transitive) and the following condition, known as *standard gamble dominance*, holds:[13]

$$(x_l, 1 - p; x_h, p) \succ (x_l, 1 - q; x_h, q) \text{ for } p > q.$$

Then it can be shown that p in (1.13) is unique.[14] When p is unique, then keeping fixed x_l and x_h, we can vary x, generating corresponding values of p that ensure (1.13) is satisfied; this reveals the underlying utility function.

Under SG, as shown in (1.13), the decision maker compares a risky choice (the RHS of the first equality) with a riskless choice (LHS of the first equality). McCord and de Neufville (1986) have criticized this approach and argued for eliciting the utility function from more general risky choices. In the SG method, if individuals are not EU maximizers and evaluate probabilities non-linearly, then because high probabilities are underweighted, forcing probabilities to be linear will overestimate the concavity of the utility function for high probabilities.[15] Furthermore, a strong *certainty effect* could magnify the problems created on account of the riskless choice in the SG method.[16] In order to control for the certainty effect, McCord and de Neufville (1986) propose an improvement in the SG method by calculating the value of x such that

$$(x, \lambda; a, 1 - \lambda) \sim ((x_l, 1 - p; x_h, p), \lambda; a, 1 - \lambda), \tag{1.14}$$

where $a \in \mathbb{R}$ and $\lambda \in (0, 1)$. The indifference in (1.14) is arrived at by asking a series of questions from subjects in experiments that pit the two lotteries against each other and using the tipping point where the preferences flip from one direction to the other, as the point of indifference. This remark applies to all the indifference elicitations here and in Section 2.5.

For an EU maximizer, the indifference in (1.14) implies that

$$\lambda u(x) + (1 - \lambda) u(a) = \lambda \left[(1 - p)u(x_l) + pu(x_h) \right] + (1 - \lambda) u(a). \tag{1.15}$$

---

[13] For $x_l = x_1$ and $x_h = x_n$ standard gamble dominance is equivalent to monotonicity.

[14] See exercise 2.6.3 in Wakker (2010).

[15] For instance, it has been shown that EU is violated for health outcomes (Rutten-van Mölken et al., 1995; Stalmeier and Bezembinder, 1999). One would then expect that measurements of utility of health outcomes based on the SG method would lead to biased estimates of utility. This was shown by Bleichrodt et al. (2007).

[16] The certainty effect refers to relatively greater sensitivity to marginal changes in probability around zero as one approaches the certainty of an outcome.

Using (1.11), we get from (1.15) that $u(x) = p$, which is identical to (1.13). When one applies EU, one expects the SG method and the method of McCord and de Neufville (1986) to give identical results. This is called *standard gamble equivalence*. In practice, however, the results differ, possibly because individuals in fact use non-linear weighting of probabilities.[17]

1.4.2 *The case of unknown probabilities*

Now suppose that probabilities are unknown, i.e., they are not objectively given. This is a more difficult problem because both probabilities and the utility function are unknown. We now give a simple method of eliciting utilities and probabilities in this case.[18] The basis of this elicitation is the *trade-off method* that is given in Wakker and Deneffe (1996); for the relevant preference foundation, see Section 2.6.1. This section will also help us to address the problem of eliciting probability weights and utilities under rank dependent utility and under cumulative prospect theory.

Suppose that there are two possible events E_1 and E_2 with unknown objective probabilities. The decision maker, however, forms subjective beliefs $\mu(E_1) \geq 0$ and $\mu(E_2) \geq 0$ such that $\mu(E_1) + \mu(E_2) = 1$, and evaluates the lottery $(E_1, x_1, ; E_2, x_2)$ as in *subjective expected utility* (SEU) (see Section 1.3), i.e.,

$$\mu(E_1)u(x_1) + \mu(E_2)u(x_2). \tag{1.16}$$

This form of evaluation can be extended to finitely many outcomes.

Suppose that an initial monetary reward y_0 is given. Consider the following sequence of lotteries that elicit a value $y_j, j = 1, 2, 3, 4$, in order to ensure the indifference relation

$$\left(E_1, y_j, ; E_2, a\right) \sim \left(E_1, y_{j-1}, ; E_2, b\right), \tag{1.17}$$

where $a, b \in \mathbb{R}$ and E_1, E_2 are given. Thus, y_1, y_2, y_3, y_4 are to be elicited using (1.17), over four iterations.

Using (1.16), (1.17) we get equalities of the form:

$$\mu(E_1)u(y_j) + \mu(E_2)u(a) = \mu(E_1)u(y_{j-1}) + \mu(E_2)u(b); \; j = 1, 2, 3, 4. \tag{1.18}$$

On rearranging, we get

$$\mu(E_1)\left[u(y_j) - u(y_{j-1})\right] = \mu(E_2)\left[u(b) - u(a)\right]; \; j = 1, 2, 3, 4. \tag{1.19}$$

Using the fact that the RHS in (1.19) is identical for all four iterations, we get the following system of equations.

$$u(y_4) - u(y_3) = u(y_3) - u(y_2) = u(y_2) - u(y_1) = u(y_1) - u(y_0). \tag{1.20}$$

---

[17] It can be shown (See Theorem 2.6.3 in Wakker, 2010, p. 62) that EU is equivalent to $\succeq$ being a weak order in the presence of the following conditions (defined above in this subsection). (1) Standard gamble solvability. (2) Standard gamble dominance. (3) Standard gamble equivalence.

[18] The interested reader can consult Wakker (2010, Ch. 4) for a more detailed discussion.

In (1.20), we have successfully eliminated the unknown probabilities. As in Example 1.1, normalize so that $u(y_0) = 0$ and $u(y_4) = 1$. This gives rise to the following system of three equations in three unknowns:

$$1 - u(y_3) = u(y_3) - u(y_2)$$
$$u(y_3) - u(y_2) = u(y_2) - u(y_1)$$
$$u(y_2) - u(y_1) = u(y_1).$$

Solving these equations simultaneously we get,

$$u(y_0) = 0; u(y_1) = \frac{1}{4}; u(y_2) = \frac{1}{2}; u(y_3) = \frac{3}{4}; u(y_4) = 1.$$

Recall that only y_0 is given, while y_1, y_2, y_3, y_4 are elicited from the choices made by the decision maker. By generating sufficiently many points such as these, one can recover the underlying utility function. By extending the number of iterations, and adjusting the value of y_0, one can extend the domain over which the utility function is elicited.

Once the utility function is elicited, then the subjective probabilities of an event E in the sample space can be found. Suppose that the decision maker is asked for a value of x such that the following indifference relation holds.

$$x \sim (E, y; E^c, 0), \tag{1.21}$$

where E^c is the complement of E. Under SEU, the indifference relation in (1.21) implies that $u(x) = \mu(E)u(y)$ (because $u(0) = 0$). Since the utility function has already been elicited, $\mu(E) = u(x)/u(y)$ is the required answer. In actual practice, there are problems, however. Consistency might be violated (i.e., subjective probabilities might not add up to 1) and the utility function might not have been fitted (in the first stage) corresponding to the outcome x.

Another method for finding the relevant subjective probabilities is the *method of matching probabilities*. Here, the decision maker is asked to state the probability such that

$$(E, 1; E^c, 0) \sim (1, p; 0, 1 - p). \tag{1.22}$$

Notice the difference in the representation of the two lotteries under uncertainty (LHS) and certainty (RHS). In (1.22), p is said to be the matching probability. If SEU holds, then the unknown probability $\mu(E) = p$.

1.5 Violations of expected utility theory

In this section we show that a great deal of evidence is inconsistent with the predictions of EU; indeed, it would not be unfair to say that EU is rejected by the evidence.[19]

---

[19] Strictly speaking, a *refutation* is an empirical finding that rejects any of the axioms of EU. A *violation* of EU occurs when the empirical evidence rejects an auxiliary assumption of EU. We use these terms interchangeably in this section. Readers can consult the excellent discussions in Kahneman and Tversky (1979), Kahneman and Tversky (2000), Starmer (2000), and Wakker (2010).

1.5.1 *Violations of the independence axiom*

We first show a violation of the independence axiom, originally due to Allais (1953). Example 1.2, below, draws on Kahneman and Tversky (1979) who showed that the Allais paradox can be explained by assuming that decision makers overweight low probabilities and underweight high probabilities. In contrast, EU is linear in probabilities (Remark 1.1).

> **Example 1.2** *(Allais paradox as a 'common ratio violation'. Problems 3 and 4 in Kahneman and Tversky, 1979) Consider a decision maker with initial wealth, x_0, and utility function u. Outcomes are in units of Israeli pounds.*
>
> *Problem 3: (95 subjects) Choose between the two lotteries*
>
> $$b_1 = (x_0, 0; x_0 + 3000, 1) \text{ and } b_2 = (x_0, 0.2; x_0 + 4000, 0.8),$$
>
> *80% chose b_1, and 20% chose b_2.*
> *Problem 4: (95 subjects) Choose between the two lotteries*
>
> $$b_3 = (x_0, 0.75; x_0 + 3000, 0.25) \text{ and } b_4 = (x_0, 0.8; x_0 + 4000, 0.2),$$
>
> *35% chose b_3, and 65% chose b_4.*
> *Denoting by $\prec_{EU}$ the binary EU preference relation, the prediction of EU is,*
>
> $$b_1 \prec_{EU} b_2 \Leftrightarrow b_3 \prec_{EU} b_4. \tag{1.23}$$
>
> *The proof of (1.23) is as follows. Since EU preferences are invariant to a positive affine transformation, we can assume $u(x_0) = 0$. Hence, the expected utility of the 2 pairs of lotteries in each problem is:*
>
> $$EU(b_1) = u(x_0 + 3000), \ EU(b_2) = 0.8u(x_0 + 4000). \tag{1.24}$$
> $$EU(b_3) = 0.25u(x_0 + 3000), \ EU(b_4) = 0.2u(x_0 + 4000). \tag{1.25}$$
>
> *From (1.24) we get that*
>
> $$b_1 \prec_{EU} b_2 \Leftrightarrow u(x_0 + 3000) < 0.8u(x_0 + 4000).$$
>
> *Dividing both sides by 4, we get*
>
> $$0.25u(x_0 + 3000) < 0.2u(x_0 + 4000) \Leftrightarrow b_3 \prec_{EU} b_4.$$
>
> *Hence, $b_1 \prec_{EU} b_2 \Rightarrow b_3 \prec_{EU} b_4$. A similar argument shows that $b_3 \prec_{EU} b_4 \Rightarrow b_1 \prec_{EU} b_2$. Hence, (1.23) holds. However, since a majority of subjects chose b_1 over b_2 and b_4 over b_3, at least some decision makers must have violated (1.23) and, hence, EU.*
> *In Allais' original presentation to Leonard Savage, Paul Samuelson, and others in Paris in 1952 (in units of millions of 1952 Francs), $b_1 = (100, 1)$, $b_2 = (500, 0.98)$, $b_3 = (100; 0.01)$, and $b_4 = (4000; 0.0098)$. To quote from Allais: "The author of this memoir, who is perfectly familiar with Samuelson's arguments, unhesitatingly prefers lottery [b_1] to lottery [b_2] and lottery [b_4] to lottery [b_3] and he thinks that most of his readers will share his preference; yet to the best of his knowledge, he believes that he is not irrational. He is perfectly aware that 2 chances in 100,000 is a non-negligible quantity, but his view is that this quantity does not offset for him the reduction in the possible gain from 500 to 100 million, whereas for him by contrast, the achievement of certainty by raising the chance of winning from 98% to 100% is well worth this reduction" (Allais and Hagen 1979, p. 102).*

Savage (like Allais) initially chose b_1 over b_2 *and* b_4 over b_3. However, after an EU calculation, Savage concluded that he had made a mistake. Savage's response was that EU is needed to guide us to correct decision making. Of course, both positions may be correct. Savage may be right to conclude that decision makers should be trained in EU. Allais may be right to conclude that, in fact, most decision makers do not follow EU.

The Allais paradox can be explained as follows. In problem 4, the decision maker codes the probability 0.2 as close to 0.25 (and 0.75 as close to 0.80). Hence, he prefers b_4 to b_3 because it gives him a higher outcome (4000 instead of 3000). By contrast, in problem 3, the decision maker does not code the probability 0.8 as close to 1; the certain outcome in lottery b_1 is particularly salient (this is an example of the *certainty effect*). In other words, he *underweights* the probability 0.8 in lottery b_2. Hence, *non-linear weighting of probabilities* is a potential explanation of the Allais paradox but EU does not allow it. However, it is not simply a matter of arbitrarily using non-linear transformations of probabilities. We show below that unless carefully applied, non-linear weighting can also allow stochastically dominated options to be chosen.

When the Allais paradox first appeared, it was thought to be an isolated example for a long time. However, it was realized later that the Allais paradox was part of a family of paradoxes that took two forms, the *common ratio violation* form, and the *common consequence violation* form. Both forms violate the independence axiom of EU (Axiom 1.4) and have been widely replicated. There is some evidence that professional traders also exhibit Allais-type violations but to a lesser extent than students, who are the main subject pool of these experiments; see List and Haigh (2005).

Definition 1.14 *(Common ratio violation) Consider two probabilities $p, P \in (0,1]$ and two prizes z, Z; typically, $p < P$ and $0 < z < Z$. Let $\mu \in (0,1)$. Recall our convention that (x, p) denotes the lottery $(x, p; 0, 1 - p)$. Consider a choice between the following pairs of lotteries.*

$$b_1 = (z, P) \text{ and } b_2 = (Z, p), \qquad (1.26)$$
$$b_3 = (z, \mu P) \text{ and } b_4 = (Z, \mu p). \qquad (1.27)$$

The 'common ratio violation' occurs if a decision maker prefers b_1 over b_2 and b_4 over b_3 (or b_2 over b_1 and b_3 over b_4). The name 'common ratio' derives from the fact that the ratio of probabilities for the outcomes in each of the two choices is the same, i.e., P/p.

Example 1.2, above, is a special case of this violation if we assume that the returns on the asset are not integrated with the existing wealth level x_0. Empirical evidence is consistent with non-integration of assets or, at best, partial integration (Andersen et al., 2012). Fafchamps et al. (2014) find no evidence that subjects in experiments integrate asset returns in the lab with their real-life income/wealth, although winnings in one round may influence subsequent risk attitudes. One explanation is that subjects create different *mental accounts* for the lab and non-lab earnings; see Volume 5 for mental accounting.

Assuming non-integration and using the notation of Definition 1.14, in Example 1.2 $p = 0.8$, $P = 1$, $z = 3000$, $Z = 4000$, and $\mu = 1/4$. For other experimental tests of the common ratio violation, see, for instance, Chew and Waller (1986) and MacCrimmon and Larsson (1979). Blavatskyy (2010) reports a reverse common ratio violation effect that takes place when the probability p in Definition 1.14 drops below 0.5. The pattern of violation of EU that is observed is then the reverse of the normal one that we observe with the Allais paradox.[20]

---

[20] Blavatskyy (2011) suggests an explanation based on the *stochastic expected utility theory* of Blavatskyy (2007) and the *perceived relative argument model* of Loomes (2008).

We already know, from Example 1.2, that an observation of a common ratio violation is a refutation of EU. We now consider the question of which axiom (or axioms) might be responsible for the refutation.

Proposition 1.5 *The common ratio violation is a violation of the independence axiom, or the reduction axiom, or of both axioms.*

Proof: Assume that $b_1 \succ b_2$, so $(z, P) \succ (Z, p)$. Hence, $(z, P) \succeq (Z, p)$. From the independence axiom (Axiom 1.4) we get that $((z, P), \mu; 0, 1 - \mu) \succeq ((Z, p), \mu; 0, 1 - \mu)$, which, given our notation, can be denoted as $((z, P), \mu) \succeq ((Z, p), \mu)$. From the reduction axiom (Axiom 1.5) it follows that $((z, P), \mu)$ and $((Z, p), \mu)$ are equivalent to $(z, \mu P)$ and $(Z, \mu p)$, respectively. Hence, $(z, \mu P) \succeq (Z, \mu p)$, i.e., $b_3 \succeq b_4$. Thus, the observation of a common ratio violation, namely, $b_1 \succ b_2$ *and* $b_4 \succ b_3$ is a rejection of the independence axiom, given the other axioms of EU. Alternatively, we may view the observation of a common ratio violation as a rejection of the reduction axiom, given the other axioms of EU, an observation that is missed by many texts in microeconomics. ∎

We now move on to another generic class of paradoxes, associated with the *common consequence violation*, which was also given by Allais (1953).

Definition 1.15 *(Common consequence violation) Let A, B, C, D be lotteries and $\mu \in (0, 1)$. Suppose that we have the following four compound lotteries, a_1, a_2 and a_3, a_4, that are compared in a pairwise manner: a_1 with a_2 and a_3 with a_4.*

$$a_1 = (A, \mu; D, 1 - \mu); \; a_2 = (B, \mu; D, 1 - \mu), \tag{1.28}$$

$$a_3 = (A, \mu; C, 1 - \mu); \; a_4 = (B, \mu; C, 1 - \mu). \tag{1.29}$$

The 'common consequence violation' occurs if a decision maker prefers a_1 over a_2 and a_4 over a_3 (or a_2 over a_1 and a_3 over a_4). The following restrictions are typically imposed on the lotteries A, B, C, D: (1) The lottery A gives a sure prize of x, i.e., $A = (x, 1)$. (2) The lottery B has some outcomes that are greater than x and others that are less than x. (3) Lottery D first order stochastically dominates lottery C.

The independence axiom implies either of the following two scenarios. Since D is common in the first pair in (1.28) and C is common in the second pair in (1.29), it follows that: (1) If A is preferred to B, then subjects must choose a_1 over a_2 and a_3 over a_4. If, on the other hand, B is preferred to A, then subjects must prefer a_2 over a_1 and a_4 over a_3. Thus, the observation of a "common consequence violation," namely, the empirically observed preference of a_1 over a_2 and a_4 over a_3, is a refutation of EU, and, in particular, of the independence axiom.

Example 1.3 *(Allais paradox as a common consequence violation. Problems 1 and 2 from Kahneman and Tversky, 1979) Let a decision maker have initial wealth, x_0, and utility function, u. All lotteries are in units of Israeli pounds.*
Problem 1: (72 subjects) Choose between

$$a_1 = (x_0, 0; x_0 + 2400, 1) \; and \; a_2 = (x_0, 0.01; x_0 + 2400, 0.66; x_0 + 2500, 0.33).$$

Problem 2: (72 subjects) Choose between

$$a_3 = (x_0, 0.66; x_0 + 2400; 0.34) \; and \; a_4 = (x_0, 0.67; x_0 + 2500, 0.33).$$

82% of the subjects chose a_1 in problem 1 and 83% of the subjects chose a_4 in problem 2. Each of these preferences was significant at the 1% level.

Example 1.3 can be recast as a common consequence violation as defined in Definition 1.15. To see this, let $\mu = 0.34$ and define the following lotteries.

$$A = (x_0 + 2400, 1); B = \left(x_0 + 2500, \frac{33}{34}; x_0; \frac{1}{34}\right);$$

$$C = (x_0, 1); D = (x_0 + 2400, 1).$$

Then the pairwise comparison lotteries (1.28), (1.29) can be written, in full standard form, as follows.

$$a_1 = (A, 0.34; D, 0.66) = (x_0, 0; x_0 + 2400, 1; x_0 + 2500, 0), \tag{1.30}$$

$$a_2 = (B, 0.34; D, 0.66) = (x_0, 0.01; x_0 + 2400, 0.66; x_0 + 2500, 0.33), \tag{1.31}$$

$$a_3 = (A, 0.34; C, 0.66) = (x_0, 0.66; x_0 + 2400, 0.34; x_0 + 2500, 0), \tag{1.32}$$

$$a_4 = (B, 0.34; C, 0.66) = (x_0, 0.67; x_0 + 2400, 0; x_0 + 2500, 0.33). \tag{1.33}$$

1.5.2 *The probability triangle and violations of the axioms of rationality*

The lotteries, b_1, b_2, b_3, b_4 in (1.26), (1.27) can be written in the following alternative but equivalent notation.

$$b_1 = (0, 1 - P; z, P; Z, 0) \text{ and } b_2 = (0, 1 - p; z, 0; Z, p),$$
$$b_3 = (0, 1 - \mu P; z, \mu P; Z, 0) \text{ and } b_4 = (0, 1 - \mu p; z, 0; Z, \mu p).$$

Using Definition 1.14, we can illustrate the common ratio violation through a useful device, *the probability triangle* (also known as the *Marshak–Machina probability triangle*). Order the three outcomes in Definition 1.14 as $0 < z < Z$ and suppose that we denote their respective probabilities by p_1, p_2, and p_3. Since p_1, p_3 are the probabilities of outcomes 0 and Z respectively, the probability of the outcome z is simply calculated as a residual, $p_2 = 1 - p_1 - p_3$. Hence, we need only two independent probabilities, p_1, p_3. Expressing the lotteries, b_1, b_2, b_3, b_4, in terms of the ordered pair (p_1, p_3), corresponding to the outcomes $0, Z$ (probability of z being calculated as a residual) we get:

$$(p_1, p_3): b_1 = (1 - P, 0); b_2 = (1 - p, p); b_3 = (1 - \mu P, 0); b_4 = (1 - \mu p, \mu p). \tag{1.34}$$

The probability triangle corresponding to this case is shown in Figure 1.1. We measure p_1 along the horizontal axis and p_3 along the vertical, such that $p_1, p_3 \in [0, 1]$ (by definition, $p_2 = 1 - p_1 - p_3$). Along the *left edge* of the diagram, $p_1 = 0$, so we get combinations of p_2, p_3 such that $p_2 + p_3 = 1$. Along the *hypotenuse* of the triangle, $p_2 = 0$, so we get combinations of p_1, p_3 such that $p_1 + p_3 = 1$. Along the *lower edge* of the diagram $p_3 = 0$, so we get combinations of p_1, p_2 such that $p_1 + p_2 = 1$.

The lotteries in (1.26), (1.27), expressed in terms of the ordered pair (p_1, p_3) in (1.34), can be represented in the probability triangle. We now draw the indifference curves corresponding to these lotteries within the probability triangle. Consider the generic lottery

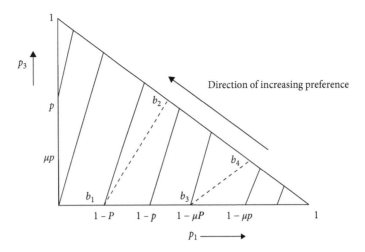

Figure 1.1 Illustration of the common ratio effect in a probability triangle.

$(0, p_1; z, 1 - p_1 - p_3; Z, p_3)$; we would like to find all combinations of (p_1, p_3) that (for fixed outcomes) generate identical levels of utility, $\bar{u}$, i.e.,

$$p_1 u(0) + (1 - p_1 - p_3) u(z) + p_3 u(Z) = \bar{u}. \tag{1.35}$$

From (1.35), the equation of the indifference curves in the probability triangle is,

$$p_3 = \frac{\bar{u} - u(z)}{u(Z) - u(z)} + \frac{u(z) - u(0)}{u(Z) - u(z)} p_1. \tag{1.36}$$

The outcomes $0, z, Z$, and $\bar{u}$ are held fixed, hence, (1.36) is the equation of a straight line. Since $0 < z < Z$, and u is a non-decreasing function, it follows that the slope, $[u(z) - u(0)] / [u(Z) - u(z)]$ is constant and positive. Hence, under EU, the indifference curves are all parallel, positively sloping, straight lines. Furthermore, for a fixed p_1, higher points in the probability triangle (corresponding to higher values of p_3) represent higher values of $\bar{u}$, and lie on a higher indifference curve. The reader can now prove the following two propositions to gain useful practice with the probability triangle (part of the second proposition summarizes some results that we have already proved above).

Proposition 1.6 *The axioms of rationality (see Definition 1.1) translate into various features of the probability triangle. Completeness (see Axiom 1.1a) implies that any two points in the probability triangle lie either on the same indifference curve or different indifference curves. Transitivity (Axiom 1.1b) ensures that no two indifference curves intersect. Independence (Axiom 1.4) implies that indifference curves are parallel straight lines.*

Proposition 1.7 *In the probability triangle, the following properties hold.*

(i) The indifference curves under EU are parallel, positively sloping, straight lines.
(ii) Upward shifts (in the northwest direction) of the indifference curves increase utility.
(iii) Steeper indifference curves are associated with greater risk aversion.

Using the fact that $P > p, \mu \in (0,1)$, and the machinery developed above, the lotteries in (1.34) can now be expressed in the probability triangle in Figure 1.1. Two sets of indifference curves are shown, bold and dotted. The bold indifference curves correspond to EU; these are parallel, straight lines. From Figure 1.1, it is immediate that under EU, decision makers should either choose (1) b_1 over b_2 and b_3 over b_4 (this is the case shown in Figure 1.1), or (2) b_2 over b_1 and b_4 over b_3 (this would require relatively flatter indifference curves in Figure 1.1). A similar illustration can be given for the common consequence violation.

The evidence in the case of the common ratio violation is that the majority of decision makers choose b_1 over b_2 and b_4 over b_3. These choices provide a clue to the behavior of decision makers relative to the predictions of EU. In order to explain the evidence, as one moves towards the southeast corner of the probability triangle, the indifference curves must flatten out, i.e., the decision maker becomes less risk averse (see Proposition 1.7(iii)). This is called the *fanning-out hypothesis* and it is a necessary condition to explain the common consequence violation and the common ratio violation. By contrast, the independence axiom in EU forces the indifference curves to be parallel, hence, they cannot fan out. Figure 1.1 shows two dotted indifference curves that demonstrate fanning-out.

1.5.3 *Some attempts to relax the independence axiom*

A number of theoretical models, underpinned by preference foundations, are able to incorporate fanning-out. These models relax the independence axiom, which leads to Allais-type violations. We briefly mention some of these models here to give a flavor of the arguments.[21] One model that generates fanning-out but retains the linearity of indifference curves is the *weighted utility theory* of Chew and MacCrimmon (1979).[22] In this case, the utility arising from the lottery $L = (x_1, p_1; \ldots; x_n, p_n)$ is given by[23]

$$U(L) = \frac{\sum_{i=1}^{n} p_i \phi(x_i) u(x_i)}{\sum_{i=1}^{n} p_i \phi(x_i)},$$

where $\phi : \mathbb{R} \to \mathbb{R}_+$. Weighted utility theory uses a weak form of the independence axiom, called *weak independence*; Starmer (2000) raises concerns about the intuitive appeal of this axiom.

> **Definition 1.16** *(Weak Independence) Suppose that for lotteries $L_1, L_2 \in \mathcal{L}$, $L_1 \prec L_2$. Then, for each $p \in (0,1)$, there is a unique $q \in (0,1)$ such that for all $L_3 \in \mathcal{L}$,*
>
> $$\left(L_1, q; L_3, 1-q\right) \prec \left(L_2, p; L_3, 1-p\right).$$

Another theory that allows for fanning-out is the theory of *disappointment aversion*; see for instance, Bell (1985) and Loomes and Sugden (1986).[24] In this formulation, for a lottery $L = \left(x_1, p_1; \ldots; x_n, p_n\right)$ such that $x_1 < x_2 < \ldots < x_n$, the decision maker derives the utility

---

[21] The interested reader can consult Starmer (2000), Sugden (2004), and Wakker (2010) for more details.

[22] For various axiomatic foundations of weighted utility theory, see Chew and MacCrimmon (1979), Chew (1983), and Fishburn (1983).

[23] Two other models that retain linearity of the indifference curves but also permit fanning-out are the *implicit expected utility model* of Dekel (1986) and the *implicit weighted utility model* of Chew (1989).

[24] See Section 2.10.2 for a more detailed exposition of disappointment aversion.

$$D(L) = \sum_{i=1}^{n} p_i \left[u(x_i) + D\left(u(x_i) - \overline{U}\right) \right]. \tag{1.37}$$

In (1.37), $\overline{U}$ is the utility that the decision maker expects from the lottery, say, the certainty equivalent of the lottery. $u(x_i)$ is the utility that actually arises when the outcome is x_i. If $u(x_i) - \overline{U} > 0$, the decision maker experiences *elation*. *Disappointment* is experienced if $u(x_i) - \overline{U} < 0$. *Disappointment aversion* is built into the model by assuming that $D(x)$ is concave for $x < 0$ and convex for $x > 0$.

It turns out that linearity of indifference curves in the probability triangle is equivalent to the *betweenness axiom* that weakens the independence axiom by requiring the indifference curves to be straight lines, not necessarily parallel.

> **Definition 1.17** *(Betweenness): Given two lotteries a_1, a_2, if $a_2 \prec a_1$, then betweenness implies that for all $p \in (0,1)$, $a_2 \prec (a_1, p; a_2, 1-p) \prec a_1$.*

To visualize betweenness, think of straight line indifference curves in a probability triangle. Suppose that a_1 lies on a higher indifference curve than a_2. Then all linear combinations of a_1, a_2 lie on an indifference curve no higher than the indifference curve on which a_1 lies and no lower than the indifference curve on which a_2 lies. If the binary relation is one of indifference, betweenness implies that if $a_1 \sim a_2$, then for all $0 \le p < 1$, $a_1 \sim (a_1, p; a_2, 1-p) \sim a_2$. This is also immediately seen by looking at one of the straight-line indifference curves in the probability triangle. If the lotteries a_1, a_2 lie on the same indifference curve, then the decision maker is also indifferent between all linear combinations of a_1, a_2 because they too lie on the same indifference curve. However, while betweenness implies (and is implied by) linear indifference curves, it does not impose the restriction that the indifference curves be parallel in the probability triangle.

Now suppose that we relax betweenness and consider the two cases: concave indifference curves (i.e., quasi-convex preferences), and convex indifference curves (i.e., quasi-concave preferences). These cases are shown in Figures 1.2 and 1.3, respectively. In each diagram, the dotted line connecting the two lotteries, a_1, a_2, among which the decision maker is indifferent, represents all possible linear combinations of a_1, a_2, i.e., lotteries of the form $(a_1, p; a_2, 1-p)$. When the indifference curves are concave, then any lottery of the form $(a_1, p; a_2, 1-p)$ lies on a lower indifference curve. Hence, the decision maker is averse to randomizing among a_1, a_2. The converse applies in Figure 1.3 where the indifference curves are convex, and the decision maker prefers to randomize.

The possibilities shown in Figures 1.2 and 1.3 are not the only ones. For instance, Chew et al. (1991) propose a model that is quadratic in probabilities. In this model, the utility from a lottery $L = (x_1, p_1; \ldots; x_n, p_n)$ is written as follows.

$$Q(L) = \sum_{i=1}^{n} \sum_{j=1}^{n} p_i p_j v(x_i, x_j). \tag{1.38}$$

The utility function in (1.38) is generated by a weakened form of the independence axiom called *mixture symmetry*, which we define next.

> **Definition 1.18** *(Mixture asymmetry) Mixture symmetry requires that for all lotteries, a_1, a_2, if $a_1 \sim a_2$, then for all $0 \le p < 1$, $(a_1, p; a_2, 1-p) \sim (a_2, p; a_1, 1-p)$.*

In the probability triangle, the indifference curves generated by (1.38) can exhibit both concavity and convexity over different domains. In other words, these indifference curves exhibit

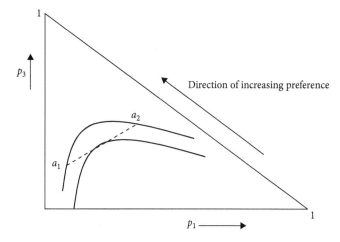

Figure 1.2 Concave indifference curves.

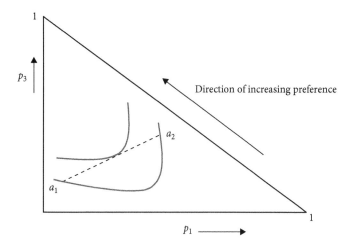

Figure 1.3 Convex indifference curves.

both fanning-in and fanning-out. The *theory of disappointment* in Gul (1991) incorporates both these features.

We now turn briefly to the empirical evidence.[25] Empirical evidence for fanning-out is, at best, mixed. The results do not change if we use real or hypothetical gambles (Camerer, 1995, p. 634). In a careful empirical study, Chew and Waller (1986) reported violations of the independence axiom in the common consequence and the common ratio forms. They also found that betweenness is not consistent with their data. Other studies have also subsequently cast doubt on the betweenness axiom. It is not easy, however, to discern a pattern to these violations;

---

[25] For more detailed surveys, see Camerer (1995), Starmer (2000), Sugden (2004), and Wakker (2010).

for a review of nine studies see Camerer and Ho (1994). Fanning-out is found when the gambles are unattractive but not when they are attractive; in the probability triangle, these are respectively the southeast and northwest corners (Camerer, 1989).

Fanning-in has been found in several parts of the probability triangle. For instance, along the *lower edge* (Starmer and Sugden, 1989a; Battalio et al., 1990), northwest corner (Conlisk, 1989), lower edge and southeast corner (Prelec, 1990), and moving up along the left edge (Starmer, 1992). While it is difficult to establish a pattern, it would seem that there is sufficient evidence of fanning-in. This, however, casts doubt on fanning-out as an explanation of the common consequence and the common ratio violations.

In the light of this evidence, theories which incorporate both fanning-in and fanning-out appear to have a better chance of explaining the data. This includes theories such as those proposed by Gul (1991) and Neilson (1992); however, the lack of evidence supporting the betweenness axiom, which both these papers assume, is a cause for concern.

Violations of EU are less pronounced, but still significant, in the interior of the probability triangle as compared to the edges (Conlisk, 1989; Camerer, 1992; Harless, 1992). This is most likely caused by non-linear weighting of probabilities and the certainty effect. However, a reduction in violations towards the interior of the probability triangle does not rescue EU. We shall see below that many economically important events involve events that occur towards the boundary of the probability triangle.

There is also evidence that some salient aspects of the behavior of human decision makers under risk might be shared with that of other animals. For instance, it has been found that rats also violate betweenness. They have indifference curves that fan-in and fan-out and that exhibit the common ratio violation.[26] There are also evolutionary reasons why animals may neglect events of very low probability.[27] Hence, many violations of EU arise from a shared evolutionary history of mammals.

1.5.4 Attitudes to risk for small and large stakes: Rabin's paradox

In a fundamental result, Rabin (2000a) showed that under EU risk aversion over small stakes implies implausibly high risk aversion over large stakes. A more accessible treatment of the issues can be found in Rabin (2000b).[28] We first state the result informally. Suppose that the utility function of a decision maker who follows EU is increasing and concave. Then if the decision maker is risk averse for a small stakes gamble, it implies he/she is implausibly risk averse for large scale gambles.

Let a decision maker have initial wealth, w. Define three lotteries, L_0, L_1, L_2 as follows. $L_0 = (w, 1)$, $L_1 = (w - 10, 0.5; w + 11, 0.5)$, and $L_2 = (w - 100, 0.5; w + m, 0.5)$, where m is any positive level of wealth. Consider assumption A1.

A1. Suppose that for all levels of w the decision maker expresses the preference

$$L_1 \prec L_0. \tag{1.39}$$

---

[26] See Battalio et al. (1985), Kagel et al. (1990), and MacDonald et al. (1991).

[27] I am grateful to Herbert Gintis for bringing this to my attention. Evolutionary dynamics show that very small probabilities will be ignored because (a) the rate of false positives will be high and (b) the cost of maintaining the neural machinery to detect and react to low probability events is too high; see Heiner (1983).

[28] Wakker (2005) not only gives a particularly lucid account of these results but also discusses the context of subsequent remarks and some confusions in the literature.

Under EU, (1.39) implies that

$$u(w) > 0.5u(w - 10) + 0.5u(w + 11),\tag{1.40}$$

where $u(w)$ is the utility from outcome w. Since the expected value of lottery L_1 is higher, yet $L_1 \prec L_0$, thus, the decision maker is risk averse over small stakes.[29] Under EU this implies that the utility function u must be concave. Rabin's (2000a) central insight is to show that for arbitrarily large values of m, the decision maker must then have the preferences

$$L_2 \prec L_1,\tag{1.41}$$

i.e., by turning down a lottery that offers infinite wealth with probability 0.5, the decision maker expresses an unreasonable amount of risk aversion. We now give a heuristic proof of Rabin's result.

Rewriting (1.40) we get

$$u(w + 11) - u(w) < u(w) - u(w - 10).\tag{1.42}$$

At this stage, the reader may find it useful to visualize an increasing, concave, utility function u at three values: $w - 10$, w, $w + 11$. The following sequence of steps can then be constructed:

$$u'(w + 11) < \frac{u(w + 11) - u(w)}{11} \text{ (from concavity of } u\text{)},$$

$$\frac{u(w + 11) - u(w)}{11} < \frac{u(w) - u(w - 10)}{11} \text{ (since (1.42) holds)},$$

$$= \frac{10}{11} \frac{[u(w) - u(w - 10)]}{10},$$

$$\leq \frac{10}{11} u'(w - 10) \text{ (from concavity of } u\text{)}.\tag{1.43}$$

$$\Rightarrow u'(w + 11) < \frac{10}{11} u'(w - 10).$$

In other words, over an interval of length 21, marginal utility drops by $\frac{10}{11}$ of the original value. Thus, each unit of money between w and $w + 11$ is valued, on average, at most $\frac{10}{11}$ of each unit of money, on average, between $w - 10$ and w.

Table 1.1   Drop in marginal utility for successive intervals in Rabin's calibration theorem.

Interval size	21	210	2100	21000	210000
Final to initial marginal utility	0.90909	0.38554	73×10^{-6}	4.0487×10^{-42}	1.1834×10^{-414}

---

[29] The expected value of the lottery L_1 is $w + 0.5$ but the certainty equivalent is less than w, hence, the decision maker is risk averse.

Table 1.1 shows this drop as the interval size increases successively (recall that m can be as large as we want it to be). Successive numbers in the second row of Table 1.1 are derived from the sequence $\left(\frac{10}{11}\right)^1$, $\left(\frac{10}{11}\right)^{10}$, $\left(\frac{10}{11}\right)^{100}$,...

The problem is that under EU, the marginal utility drops off too rapidly. Consequently, and this is crucial to Rabin's results, for extremely large rewards, the marginal utility of the large reward relative to a relatively small loss becomes so miniscule that the lottery has little attraction for the decision maker, hence, accounting for the preferences shown in (1.41). Thus, if an EU decision maker is risk averse for small stake gambles (which is reasonable), then the same decision maker is absurdly risk averse for large stake gambles (which is unreasonable). By contrast, there is no puzzle under prospect theory (see Section 3.6).

> **Example 1.4** *Let us now consider a concrete example to illustrate Rabin's paradox under EU.[30] If the utility function, u, is not bounded above, then, clearly, $u(\infty) = \infty$, hence, $\frac{1}{2}u(w+\infty) = \infty$. It follows that for any real numbers, w and x, i.e., for any finite level of wealth, w, and any finite loss, x,*
>
> $$EU(L_2) = \frac{1}{2}u(w-x) + \frac{1}{2}u(w+\infty) = \infty > u(w).$$
>
> *Thus, any decision maker who follows EU will accept the gamble L_2. Hence, the utility function must be bounded above. Consider the utility function*
>
> $$u(w) = 1 - e^{-w}, \tag{1.44}$$
>
> *Thus, $u'(w) > 0$ and $u''(w) < 0$. Under the utility function in (1.44), the preference $L_1 \prec L_0$ for any level of initial wealth, w, implies that*
>
> $$\frac{1}{2}\left(1 - e^{-(w-10)}\right) + \frac{1}{2}\left(1 - e^{-(w+11)}\right) < 1 - e^{-w} \Leftrightarrow 11013 > 1.$$
>
> *Hence, assumption A1 holds for the utility function in (1.44). We now wish to show that for this utility function, it is also the case that $L_2 \prec L_1$, i.e., the decision maker turns down a lottery that offers infinite wealth with a probability of 0.5. The preference $L_2 \prec L_1$ for any level of initial wealth, w, implies that*
>
> $$\frac{1}{2}u(w-100) + \frac{1}{2}u(w+\infty) < \frac{1}{2}u(w-10) + \frac{1}{2}u(w+11).$$
>
> *For the utility function in (1.44) we have*
>
> $$u(w+\infty) = 1 - e^{-(w+\infty)} = 1 \text{ and } u(w-100) = 1 - e^{-(w-100)}.$$
>
> *It follows that the preference $L_2 \prec L_1$ implies*
>
> $$\frac{1}{2}\left(1 - e^{-(w-100)}\right) + \frac{1}{2}\left(1 - e^{-(w+\infty)}\right) < \frac{1}{2}\left(1 - e^{-(w-10)}\right) + \frac{1}{2}\left(1 - e^{-(w+11)}\right)$$
>
> *or $e^{100} > e^{10} + e^{-11}$, which is true. Hence, under Assumption A1, an EU decision maker exhibits the absurd preference $L_2 \prec L_1$ (Rabin's paradox).*

---

[30] I am grateful to Ali al-Nowaihi for suggesting this example.

1.5.5 *Violations of description invariance*

In the typical applications of EU, alternative methods of describing lotteries are assumed not to have any effect on choices. This is known as *description invariance* or the absence of *framing effects*. Description invariance is not required by the axioms of EU. By contrast, empirical evidence shows that human behavior is frame- and context-dependent. As we shall see below, in Example 1.5, a particular violation of description invariance served as a building block of a non-EU theory, prospect theory, that we study in more detail below. This example also illustrates the relative risk attitudes of subjects when they perceive that they are in a *gain situation* as compared to a *loss situation* (these terms are formally defined later).

> **Example 1.5** *(Tversky and Kahneman, 1981): Imagine that the US is preparing for the outbreak of an unusual Asian disease, which is expected to kill 600 people. Two alternative programs to combat the disease have been proposed. Assume that the exact scientific estimates of the consequences of the programs are as follows:*
> *Positive Framing: If program A is adopted, 200 people will be saved. If program B is adopted, there is a one-third probability that 600 people will be saved and a two-thirds probability that no people will be saved. Which of the two programs would you favor?*
> *Negative Framing: If program C is adopted, 400 people will die. If program D is adopted, there is a one-third probability that nobody will die and a two-thirds probability that 600 people will die. Which of the two programs would you favor?*
> *Under positive framing, the solution is framed in terms of lives saved (a gain situation). The result was that 72% of the subjects chose A, the safe program, and 28% chose the risky program B. For the case of negative framing, i.e., lives lost (a loss situation), 22% voted for C and 78% for D, the risky program. The options in each frame are identical. In each frame, two hundred lives are saved for sure in the first option (options A and C) and two hundred lives are expected to be saved in the second option (options B and D). While the aim of Kahneman and Tversky was to show that individuals are risk averse for gains and risk loving for losses, an issue of critical importance in prospect theory (see Chapter 2), the framing of the same question leads to completely different choices.*

In this book, we shall review overwhelming evidence of framing effects, which shows that description invariance is not supported. Among the main decision theories, only prospect theory is able to handle framing effects by altering the *reference point*.

1.5.6 *Preference reversals*

The basic preference reversal problem is that under one elicitation method, lottery A is preferred to lottery B, while under another method, B is preferred to A; this result also holds for experienced decision makers (Lichtenstein and Slovic, 1971).[31] Consider two probabilities $p < P$, two outcomes $z < Z$, and the following pair of lotteries.

$$P\text{-bet} = (0, 1 - P; z, P), \ \$\text{-bet} = (0, 1 - p; Z, p). \tag{1.45}$$

---

[31] For the literature circa late 1980s, see Tversky and Thaler (1990).

The names P-bet and $-bet come from the fact that the first lottery has a higher probability of winning, while the second has a higher prize. The decision maker must make a choice between the two bets in two different tasks.

1. In the first task, decision makers directly choose between the P-bet and the $-bet.
2. In the second task, decision makers are asked to assign certainty equivalents to the P-bet and the $-bet, respectively, C_P and $C_\$$.

The typical empirical finding in a large number of studies is that the P-bet is chosen over the $-bet in the first task and $C_P < C_\$$ in the second task (Lichtenstein and Slovic, 2006).[32] These findings of *preference reversals* contradict EU (or equivalently, the axioms of rationality).

The empirical findings from tasks 1 and 2 imply that: $-bet\sim C_\$ \succ C_P \sim P$-bet$\succ$$-bet, which is a failure of transitivity. Theories that allow for violation of transitivity such as regret theory (Loomes and Sugden, 1982) can potentially explain these findings. Other attempts to explain preference reversals include abandoning the reduction principle (Segal, 1988), and abandoning the independence axiom (Holt, 1986; Karni and Safra, 1987). Tversky and Thaler (1990) argue that none of these attempts can fully account for preference reversals. Tversky et al. (1990) put the various explanations to the test and find that it is violations of *procedure invariance* that explain the finding of preference reversals. Gintis (2009, p. 238) expresses the view that the expected value of the lotteries used in preference reversal experiments is too close to permit firm conclusions to be drawn. Lichtenstein and Slovic (2006) offer a more recent survey of the literature.

If transitivity does not hold, then there can be no preference foundations for utility functions. For this reason, most economists may feel uneasy about abandoning transitivity. Insofar as intransitivity arises from changing the frame, context, or reference point, one may consider preferences over objects, conditional on a given frame, context, or reference point. Such conditional preferences would then be transitive. This idea is formally pursued in Sugden (2003). However, the resulting utility representation is linear in probabilities, as in subjective expected utility, hence, it would contradict the burgeoning evidence on non-linear probability weighting (Fehr-Duda and Epper, 2012).

We shall show in Chapter 2 that preference reversals can also be explained using the *third generation of prospect theory* due to Schmidt et al. (2008). Preference reversals can also arise under *ambiguity* but they are of a different nature; see Trautmann et al. (2011).

1.5.7 Is the reduction axiom supported by the evidence?

Under EU, decision makers are able to reduce a compound lottery (where the outcomes themselves are lotteries) to a simple lottery of the form $L = (x_1, p_1; \ldots; x_n, p_n)$ (see the *reduction axiom*, Axiom 1.5, above). However, empirical evidence is not supportive of the reduction axiom (Bernasconi and Loomes, 1992; Conlisk, 1989; Miao and Zhong, 2012). Harrison et al. (2012) find mixed support for the hypothesis. In simple one outcome choice problems there is support for the reduction axiom but in multichoice problems, the axiom does not hold.

Abdellaoui et al. (2014) find that the reduction axiom does not hold. They compute the certainty equivalent of compound lotteries, C_c, and the certainty equivalent of their associated reduced form lotteries, C_r. They term the difference between the two certainty equivalents,

---

[32] Also see Hershey and Schoemaker (1985) and Johnson and Schkade (1989).

$C_r - C_c$, as the *compound risk premium*. If the difference is zero, the reduction axiom holds; if the difference is positive, the decision maker is *compound risk averse*; and if the difference is negative, the decision maker is compound risk seeking. They find that the difference is non-zero and most individuals are compound risk averse, i.e., they are more unwilling to play the compound lottery relative to the equivalent reduced lottery.

It also turns out that there are important links between the decision maker's attitudes to ambiguity aversion and the compound risk premium. Halevy (2007) found the presence of compound risk premium as a necessary condition for non-neutral ambiguity attitudes. Indeed, he proposed that the failure of the reduction axiom is an important explanation of the Ellsberg paradox (see Chapter 4). Abdellaoui et al. (2014) find support for this view but their evidence suggests a weaker link between ambiguity aversion and compound risk premium. We postpone a discussion of models of ambiguity to Chapter 4.

CHAPTER 2

Behavioral Models of Decision Making

2.1 Introduction

Under expected utility theory (EU), decision makers *weight probabilities linearly*, and in each state of the world they derive utility from the *final levels of wealth*. In this chapter, we relax both these features of EU and consider the main behavioral decision theories under risk and uncertainty. Theories of ambiguity are considered in Chapter 4.

The behavioral decision theories considered in this chapter include *rank dependent utility* (RDU), *original prospect theory* (OPT), *cumulative prospect theory* (PT), and theories of *regret and disappointment aversion*. We also consider the more recent behavioral theories such as *third generation prospect theory*, *prospect theory with endogenous reference points*, and *composite prospect theory* (CPT). The behavioral decision theories explain the evidence much better than EU. The continued use of EU in large swathes of contemporary research in economics remains an enduring puzzle for most behavioral economists.

The linear weighting of probabilities under EU leads to many puzzles. For instance, Chapter 1 described the Allais paradox that is highly suggestive of *non-linear probability weighting*; evidence reviewed in this chapter gives further support to non-linear probability weighting. A *probability weighting function* reflects the mental representation of objective or subjective probabilities by a decision maker. It is central to almost all alternatives to EU. Section 2.2 introduces the basics, with particular emphasis on the *Prelec probability weighting function* (Prelec, 1998), although several other weighting functions are also outlined.

Empirical evidence shows heterogeneity in probability weighting functions for individual decision makers. One observes convex weighting, concave weighting, and *inverse S-shaped weighting* (Fehr-Duda and Epper, 2012). However, once we pool this information, at the aggregate level, the typical finding is that of an *inverse S-shaped* probability weighting, i.e., low probabilities are overweighted and high probabilities are underweighted. It turns out that one cannot simply replace probabilities under EU/SEU by probability weighting functions because this may lead to violation of first order stochastic dominance (Fishburn, 1978); we shall show this formally.

Section 2.3 introduces RDU under risk (Quiggin, 1982) and under uncertainty (Schmeidler, 1989). The idea under RDU is to replace the probabilities in an EU functional by *decision weights* that are *cumulative transformations of probabilities*. Decision makers who use RDU do not choose first order stochastically dominated options. RDU can explain several puzzles that EU cannot—the Allais paradox is a prominent example. Not surprisingly, preference foundations of RDU relax the independence axiom in EU. One implication of inverse S-shaped probability weighting under RDU is that since low probabilities are overweighted, financial markets may price the skewness of asset returns; these issues are also considered in Volume 5 (Barberis, 2013).

Under EU, attitudes to risk, for instance, the degree of risk aversion, depend entirely on the shape of the utility function. However, under RDU, attitudes to risk depend *jointly* on the shapes of the probability weighting function and the utility function. This also holds for other behavioral decision theories that use non-linear probability weighting. For instance, under RDU, if the probability weighting function is convex throughout, then the decision maker can be shown to be *pessimistic* in the sense that he assigns relatively higher decision weights to lower outcome. A decision maker with a weighting function that is concave throughout, on the other hand, can be shown to be *optimistic* and places relatively higher decision weights on higher outcomes.

In what follows, we abbreviate the *original prospect theory* of Kahneman and Tversky (1979) by OPT and *cumulative prospect theory* of Tversky and Kahneman (1992) by PT. The main difference between these theories is the way that they account for non-linear probability weighting. Following convention, unless we wish to make a distinction between the two theories, we shall use the abbreviation PT for both theories.[1]

Both EU and RDU assume that decision makers derive utility from *final levels* of variables of interest, such as wealth. These theories can account for utility that is derived from changes in outcomes relative to a *reference point*. However, since EU/SEU/RDU do not have insights about how behavior in the domain of gains and losses may differ, incorporating a reference point in these theories is not very illuminating.

In contrast, PT appeals to robust psychological evidence to argue that decision makers derive utility from *changes* in variables of interest relative to some *reference point*. While it is usually argued that the reference point under PT is exogenous, Kahneman and Tversky justified the status quo as a useful reference point. In other cases, a social norm of fairness, or a legal entitlement may serve as reference points. The reference point partitions the domain of outcomes into *gains* and *losses*. Furthermore, there are robust differences in behavior in gains and losses. For example, decision makers exhibit *loss aversion*: losses bite more than equivalent gains. Section 2.4 considers PT under risk when the reference point is a fixed, non-stochastic, entity. Section 2.4.1 shows that the extension of PT to uncertainty is straightforward.

The utility function of the decision maker under PT (unlike EU/SEU/RDU) is *concave in gains* and *convex in losses*. Thus, a central insight of PT, based on robust evidence, is that attitudes to risk are fundamentally different in the two domains. Section 2.4.2 shows that risk attitudes under PT are even richer than RDU, since they are jointly determined by the shapes of the utility function and the probability weighting function, and we distinguish between gains and losses. Under PT, one observes a *four-fold pattern of attitudes to risk aversion* (Tversky and Kahneman, 1992). Although decision makers can choose stochastically dominated options under OPT they cannot do so under PT. The reason is that PT borrows its machinery on non-linear probability weighting from RDU in which decision makers never choose dominated options.

While PT is the most satisfactory and influential account of human behavior under risk and uncertainty (Wakker, 2010), it is work in progress. Section 2.4.4 considers some common

---

[1] Daniel Kahneman won the Nobel prize for PT in 2003. Amos Tversky, who would almost surely have shared this prize, had sadly died by that time, and the Nobel prize cannot be conferred posthumously.

criticisms of PT that are misplaced. In contrast, Section 2.9 considers more serious criticisms of PT that an even more complete theory of decision making may wish to address in due course.

Section 2.5 considers the applied problem of eliciting the utility function and the probability weighting function under PT (Wakker and Deneffe, 1996; Abdellaoui, 2000; Bleichrodt and Pinto, 2000; Köbberling and Wakker, 2003; Abdellaoui et al., 2007). In this section, we also consider the various definitions of loss aversion, as well as a brief discussion of some of the parameter estimates under PT.

Section 2.6 considers the preference foundations of PT in three different subsections. Section 2.6.1 considers the preference foundations of PT based on the *trade-off consistency method* (Chateauneuf and Wakker, 1999; Köbberling and Wakker, 2003). The trade-off consistency method is one of the most profound and practical achievements in behavioral decision theory. This method is able to provide a unified account of the preference foundations of PT, RDU, and EU in terms of risk and uncertainty.[2] Next, we consider the preference foundations of the two most widely used components in applied PT: the *Prelec probability weighting function,* and the *power form of utility* that fit well the experimental data.

Section 2.6.2 considers the preference foundations of the Prelec function (al-Nowaihi and Dhami, 2006). Section 2.6.3 considers the preference foundations of the power form of utility (al-Nowaihi et al., 2008). In particular, we show that under the axiom of *preference homogeneity,* not only does the utility function take the power form, but it also implies loss aversion, identical powers of utility in the domain of gains and losses, and identical probability weighting functions in the domain of gains and losses.

A decision maker's endowment may be stochastic. For instance, houses, consumer durables, financial assets, and other personal belongings may suffer a loss in value with some probability, arising on account of, say, changes in market value, theft, accidents, and other natural hazards. Thus, expectations of the loss may influence one's reference point. We now consider two ways in which stochastic reference points have been incorporated into PT.

The first proposal, in Section 2.7, considers *third generation prospect theory,* PT[3] (Schmidt et al., 2008). *Reference dependent expected utility* (Sugden, 2003) is a special case of this model. PT[3] proposes a representation of preferences over *Savage acts.*[3] The representation is similar to PT, except that the utility function is now defined over outcomes and a *stochastic reference point.* This framework can explain disparities between *willingness to pay* (WTP) and *willingness to accept* (WTA), sometimes also known as the *endowment effect* (see Chapter 3). It can also explain *preference reversals.*

The second proposal, in Section 2.8, considers the Köszegi–Rabin framework for *endogenous stochastic reference points* (Köszegi and Rabin, 2006, 2007, 2009). They distinguish between three equilibrium concepts— the two main concepts differ in the timing of actual decisions, prior to the resolution of uncertainty. Conditional on a stochastic reference point, the decision maker makes ex-ante choices for future states of the world, which, in equilibrium, are confirmed to be optimal, ex-post. The initial choices then become self-fulfilling; this is the sense in which reference points are endogenous.

We consider several illustrative examples of this framework to convey the insights of the two main equilibrium concepts. In particular, in Section 2.8.1 we consider the newsvendor problem

---

[2] Our discussion is necessarily condensed. For a more detailed account, see the masterful treatment by one of the leaders in this area, Wakker (2010).

[3] Given a set of uncertain events that form a partition of the sample space, a Savage act specifes the outcome for the decision maker, for each uncertain event; see Chapter 1 for a more formal definition.

(Herweg, 2013) and in Section 2.8.2, the backward bending labour supply curve. In Section 2.8.3, we consider the empirical evidence, which is consistent with the predictions of the Köszegi-Rabin framework (Abeler et al. 2011; Ericson and Fuster, 2011). On the one hand, the Köszegi-Rabin framework appeals to those who were uneasy with the traditional justifications for a reference point in PT (e.g., status quo, social norms, and other legal or social entitlements). However, on the other hand, this framework has extremely high cognitive requirements, which sit uneasily with the main thrust of behavioral models. The authors are fully aware of these difficulties, and are at pains to highlight them, but no practical alternatives to the rational expectations requirement that could be used in applied work have been proposed. Whatever the merits of these arguments, empirical evidence must be the final arbiter. Future research must consider even more stringent tests of the framework; this is likely to be an area of continued importance.

Section 2.9 considers some limitations of PT. In Section 2.9.1, we consider the critique based on several papers by Michael Birnbaum and associates; for a summary, see Birnbaum (2008). These experiments consider the implications of splitting outcomes or probabilities that, under PT, are not predicted to alter the choice between lotteries. Yet, empirically, this is found to be violated. However, this evidence appears to reject most decision theory models. The associated theoretical alternatives suggested by this literature that go under the name of *configural weights models* are considered in a later section; however, these are not without problems either.

Section 2.9.2 considers an implication of PT, *gain–loss separability* (Wu and Markle, 2008). Suppose that we split two mixed lotteries,[4] A and B, into their respective gain and loss components. If the decision maker prefers each of the components of A over the corresponding components of B, then, under PT, he should also prefer A to B. Yet this is found to be violated. However, these results need to be replicated with a wider range of probabilities and payoffs to judge not just how general they are, but also to discover the underlying mechanisms.

Section 2.9.3 considers the *stake size effect*, that cannot be accounted for by any theory that separates utilities from probabilities.[5] The stake size effect refers to the observed change in relative risk aversion as the stake size in the domain of gains goes up. In an important advance, it has been shown that the stake size effect arises not from the utility function but from the probability weighting function (Fehr-Duda et al., 2010). This suggests that the development of theories that are non-separable in probabilities and outcomes might be a fruitful area of research in the future.

Most non-stochastic decision theories of choice typically predict an unambiguous choice of one lottery over another. However, the typical experimental finding is a dispersion of choices across subjects for pairs of lotteries. One possible resolution is to introduce arbitrary noise or errors into the choices of subjects. Although not uncommon in empirical work, this is neither intellectually satisfying, nor well founded unless one has good reasons for preferring one noise structure to another. A second resolution, is to allow for the possibility that different individuals may follow different decision theories. This has led to the exploration of heterogeneity in preferences using a *mixture model approach* (Bruhin et al., 2010; Fehr-Duda et al., 2010; Conte et al., 2011). The main empirical finding is the presence of *preference heterogeneity*. For instance, in three separate datasets, Bruhin et al. (2010) find the respective shares of EU and RDU/PT preferences to be 20% and 80%. By contrast, the shares of SEU types are much higher in the absence of a mixture model approach that relies instead on noisy choices (Hey, 2014).

---

[4] Mixed lotteries contain at least one outcome each in the domain of gains and losses.
[5] These theories include EU, RDU, OPT, PT with fixed and stochastic reference points, PT^3, CPT, and disappointment aversion.

Section 2.10 considers a range of other behavioral theories of decision making. These theories offer additional insights into decision making that we have not considered so far. Section 2.10.1 considers *regret theory* (Bell, 1982; Fishburn, 1982a; Loomes and Sugden, 1982). The idea is that in any state of the world, the decision maker derives utility not only from his own choice but also from the forgone outcomes from other choices that were not made. Regret theory allows for the violation of transitivity. One can also explain the Allais paradox using regret theory. However, the evidence is not always consistent with the pattern of intransitivity predicted by the theory (Starmer, 2000).

Section 2.10.2 considers the *theory of disappointment aversion* (Gul, 1991). This is a theory of endogenous reference points because the decision maker treats the certainty equivalent of the lottery under consideration as his reference point. All outcomes in the lottery that are less than the certainty equivalent are coded as loss outcomes, and all outcomes that are greater than the certainty equivalent are coded as gain outcomes. Non-linear probability weights are then used to form decision weights. However, the construction of decision weights is different from RDU and PT. The resulting model may, however, be observationally similar to RDU (Fehr-Duda and Epper, 2012).

Section 2.10.3 considers the role of *salience* and *context* in making choices among risky alternatives (Bordalo et al., 2012). In this case, the decision maker compares pairwise outcomes in each choice and assigns salience to the outcomes, using a salience function that depends on the relative and the absolute sizes of the outcomes. The outcomes are then ranked by salience and decision weights assigned to the outcomes. More salient outcomes receive higher decision weights. This theory can explain the Allais paradox, preference reversals, and context dependent preferences.

In Section 2.10.4, we consider *case-based decision theory* (Gilboa and Schmeidler, 1995, 1997, 2001). The model is based on an extremely plausible idea. Namely, that in deciding on our current actions, we first identify the environment, or situation. Next, we look at past actions taken in various environments and compare the current environment–action pairs to all environment–action pairs in the past using a *similarity function*. Such a comparison may suggest the optimal action that we must take today. Under certain conditions, the long-run behavior of this process converges to one that would be chosen by an expected utility maximizer. However, the evidence strongly indicates that expected utility is refuted (see Chapter 1). A drawback of case-based decision theory is that it does not allow one to construct hypothetical cases. Indeed, it would seem that since no environment is likely to be an exact replica of another, one's ability to construct hypothetical cases (perhaps also based on past environment–action pairs) is critical in constructing an even better theory. However, some emerging evidence is consistent with the theory (Pape and Kurtz, 2013; Bleichrodt et al., 2017).

Section 2.10.5 considers *configural weights models* that can explain the evidence that we outline in Section 2.9.1 (Birnbaum, 2008). We consider a range of models in this class. These include the *rank affected multiplicative weights model*, the *transfer of attention in exchange model*, and the *gains decomposition utility model*. Unlike most other behavioral models that we consider, there are no preference foundations for these models. Further, the construction of decision weights in these models are likely to appear arbitrary to many economists. Perhaps for this reason, this class of models has not yet gained prominence in economics.

Section 2.11 considers the extremely important, but often neglected issue of the behavior of decision makers towards *events of very low probability*. In a range of situations, one observes that a fraction of decision makers ignore events of very low probability, which can lead to serious consequences for the decision maker.[6] Examples, with well-documented empirical support include the following (al-Nowaihi and Dhami, 2010a): reluctance to buy insurance against low probability natural hazards; running red traffic lights; driving and talking on mobile phones; and not wearing non-mandatory seat belts. Existing theories cannot explain human behavior in these cases. EU certainly cannot explain it but the problem is even worse when one uses a typical probability weighting function (such as the Prelec function) in any of the non-EU theories such as RDU and PT. The reason is that the typical probability weighting function is too steep near the origin, so, such probabilities should be tremendously salient rather than be ignored.

In other words, EU and most non-EU theories (except OPT) predict that nobody should run red traffic lights, or refrain from wearing seat belts in vehicles, or drive and talk on mobile phones simultaneously, or refrain from buying insurance against even the most unlikely natural hazard. In Section 2.11.1, we argue that Kahneman and Tversky (1979) were well aware of these issues in OPT. In the *editing phase* in OPT, a fraction of the decision makers simply omit very low probability events from the lotteries that they are presented with. In the next step, the *evaluation phase*, decision makers choose among alternatives that have been edited in the first phase.

Our main explanation of human behavior for low probability events is based on *composite prospect theory* (CPT) (al-Nowaihi and Dhami, 2010a). In CPT, a fraction of the decision makers use a standard, inverse S-shaped, probability weighting function, e.g., the Prelec function. However, the remaining fraction use the *composite Prelec function* (CPF), which is an axiomatically founded modification of the Prelec function. Decision makers who use the CPF, significantly underweight very low probability events (unlike the Prelec function). Although CPT can explain human behavior in all the above mentioned puzzles of human behavior for very low probability events, it awaits empirical testing.

The outcomes of most human decisions are *uncertain* and take *time* to materialize. Yet, it is usual practice to treat *risk preferences* and *time preferences* separately. An emerging literature makes a strong case to integrate the two. Section 2.12 considers the relation between risk and time preferences. We also give a complementary discussion of this topic in Volume 3.

The usual method of integrating risk and time preferences is to offer decision makers a sequence of dated payoffs, but future payoffs materialize with a probability less than one. In Section 2.12.1, we use this method, and first consider evidence which suggests that neither EU, nor any of the mainstream behavioral alternatives can explain the experimental choices (Andreoni and Sprenger, 2012b). However, it is crucial to specify how one reduces lotteries that have a time dimension. Using a plausible method of reduction, the portfolio method, one can explain the experimental findings in Andreoni and Sprenger (2012b) if the decision maker follows RDU (Epper and Fehr-Duda, 2014a).

Section 2.12.2 introduces the concept of *intertemporal risk aversion*. Section 2.12.3 lays out the agenda for future research for the study of the interaction between risk and time preferences (Epper and Fehr-Duda, 2014b). Some features of this agenda are as follows. Decision makers appear more risk tolerant for events in the more distant future. The decision making process, for instance, whether dated lotteries are reduced in one go or sequentially reduced, influences choices. The timing of the resolution of uncertainty matters too. The extent of discounting depends on the degree of riskiness of lotteries. Finally, behavior differs whether lotteries are

---

[6] Peter Wakker (personal communication) points out that Buffon (1977, p. 72) argued that all probabilities less than .0001 be treated as "morally" equal to zero.

reduced first in the time dimension or the risk dimension. Suppose that an observer observes the choices of a decision maker when outcomes are delayed, and when the probability that they will materialize, falls over time. Sections 2.12.4 and 2.12.5 consider the resulting effects on the observed probability weighting function in terms of factors such as its elevation, subproportionality, and elasticity (Epper and Fehr-Duda, 2014b).

2.2 Probability weighting functions

Under EU, decision makers weight probabilities linearly (see Remark 1.1). In contrast, empirical evidence suggests non-linear weighting of probabilities. There is fairly widespread agreement in the empirical literature on the shape of the non-linear weighting for probabilities that are bounded away from the end points of the interval [0, 1]. However, there are unresolved issues about the precise shape of non-linear weighting close to the end points of the probability interval [0, 1], an issue that only the more recent literature has focused on. To separate these issues, and based on the empirical evidence, it is useful to consider the following two hypotheses, H1 and H2. Most behavioral decision theory proceeds under the assumption of H1. However, a more nuanced picture is given in H2.

H1: Decision makers overweight small probabilities and underweight large probabilities, no matter how small or how large they are.[7]

H2: There are two kinds of decision makers:

(H2a) A fraction $\mu \in [0, 1]$ of decision makers (i) ignore events of extremely low probability and, (ii) treat extremely high probability events as certain.[8] For all other (non-extreme) probabilities they behave as in H1, i.e., they overweight small probabilities and underweight large ones.

(H2b) A fraction $1 - \mu$ of the decision makers behave as in H1 for all levels of probabilities.

Classical non-EU theories largely subscribe to H1 (or assume that $\mu = 0$ in hypothesis H2). In contrast, hypothesis H2 has been largely ignored despite a compelling case for it in Kahneman and Tversky's (1979) original prospect theory, and in the *bimodal perception of risks* model (Viscusi, 1998). We follow the chronological order of developments so, for the moment, we focus only on H1. In Section 2.11, we examine the evidence for H2 and outline al-Nowaihi and Dhami's (2010a) *composite prospect theory* (CPT) that is able to account for H2.

We have already conjectured that the Allais paradox can be resolved under non-linear probability weighting. As a compelling illustration of the importance of non-linear probability weighting, consider the following example from Kahneman and Tversky (1979, p. 283). Suppose that one is compelled to play Russian roulette using a revolver that can potentially fire six rounds, but all rounds are not loaded.[9] One would be willing to pay much more to reduce the number

---

[7] For the evidence, see Kahneman and Tversky (2000), Starmer (2000), and Appendix A in Wakker (2001). For the necessary and sufficient conditions required for inverse S-shaped probability weighting functions, see Tversky and Wakker (1995). There is also emerging evidence of the neuro-biological foundations for such behavior (Berns et al., 2008); see Volume 7 for a more detailed discussion.

[8] In the context of the take-up of insurance for low probability natural hazards, the results from one set of experiments by Kunreuther et al. (1978) are consistent with $\mu = 0.8$.

[9] Readers may remember the game of Russian roulette from the 1978 film, the Deer Hunter. In this potentially lethal game, fewer than six rounds in a revolver are loaded, the cylinder is spun, and an individual places the muzzle against his/her head, and pulls the trigger.

of bullets from one to zero (elimination of risk) than from four to three (reduction, but not elimination, of risk). However, in each case, the reduction in the probability of a bullet firing is 1/6 and, so, under EU, the decision maker should be willing to pay the same amount. The payment of different amounts suggests non-linear weighting of probabilities.

For any lottery L, let $E(L)$ be the expected value of the lottery and let C_L be the certainty equivalent. Then, we can define the *relative risk premium* as

$$RRP = \frac{E(L) - C_L}{|E(L)|}. \tag{2.1}$$

There are three possibilities: Risk aversion corresponds to $RRP > 0$, risk neutrality to $RRP = 0$, and risk seeking/loving to $RRP < 0$. Fehr-Duda and Epper (2012) compute the RRP for a student population recruited from two major Swiss universities in 2006, and a representative population of Swiss German-speaking adults. Lotteries of the form $(x_1, 1 - p; x_2, p)$ are used, where $0 \leq x_1 < x_2$. The results are shown in Figure 2.1; relative risk premium, RRP, is plotted on the vertical axis and the probability of the highest outcome, p, is plotted on the horizontal axis. Clearly, the RRP is probability dependent. Thus, risk preferences of the decision maker depend on probabilities. This is inconsistent with EU because under EU, risk preferences arise solely through the shape of the utility function.

Definition 2.1 *(Probability weighting function): By a probability weighting function, we mean a strictly increasing function $w : [0,1] \xrightarrow{onto} [0,1]$.*

To fix ideas, readers may, for the moment, consider $w(p)$ as the subjective weight placed by decision makers on the objective probability, p (these ideas carry over to non-negative subjective probabilities that sum up to 1). The proof of the next proposition is left as an exercise.

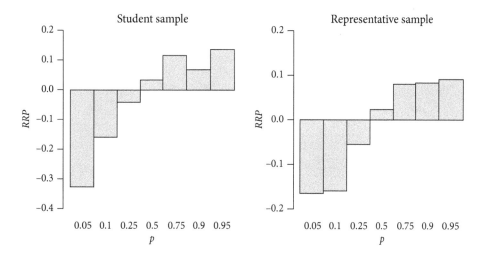

Figure 2.1 Relative risk premium for the Student and the Representative population.

Source: Reproduced with permission of Annual Review of Economics, Volume 4. Helga Fehr-Duda and Thomas Epper, "Probability and risk: foundations and economic implications of probability-dependent risk preferences." © 2012 by Annual Reviews http://www.annualreviews.org.

Proposition 2.1 *A probability weighting function has the following properties:*
(a) $w(0) = 0$, $w(1) = 1$. (b) w has a unique inverse, w^{-1}, and w^{-1} is also a strictly increasing function from $[0,1]$ onto $[0,1]$. (c) w and w^{-1} are continuous.

In order to distinguish between the hypotheses H1 and H2, we will need to look at the behavior of alternative probability weighting functions for probabilities close to the endpoints of $[0,1]$. In particular, we need to speak meaningfully about the steepness of the probability weighting function around $p = 0$ and $p = 1$. The next two definitions introduce the relevant concepts.

Definition 2.2 *(al-Nowaihi and Dhami, 2010a): A probability weighting function, $w(p)$,*
(i) infinitely overweights infinitesimal probabilities if, for $\gamma > 0$, $\lim_{p \to 0} \frac{w(p)}{p^{\gamma}} = \infty$, and (ii)
infinitely underweights near-one probabilities if $\lim_{p \to 1} \frac{1-w(p)}{1-p} = \infty$.[10]

Definition 2.3 *(al-Nowaihi and Dhami, 2010a): A probability weighting function, $w(p)$,*
(i) zero-underweights infinitesimal probabilities if, for $\gamma > 0$, $\lim_{p \to 0} \frac{w(p)}{p^{\gamma}} = 0$, and (ii) zero-
overweights near-one probabilities in the sense that $\lim_{p \to 1} \frac{1-w(p)}{1-p} = 0$.

For aggregate data (and for non-extreme probabilities), the data typically suggests an *inverse S-shaped probability weighting function*. Figure 2.2 shows the estimated probability weighting function using non-parametric estimates corresponding to the data in Figure 2.1.

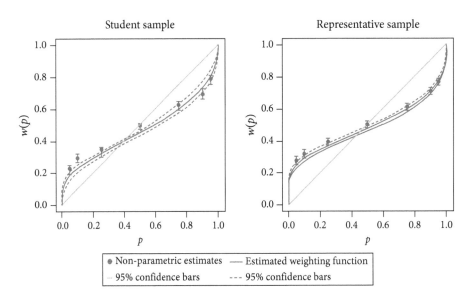

Figure 2.2 Non-parametrically estimated probability weighting functions for the Student and Representative population based on aggregate data.

Source: Reproduced with permission of Annual Review of Economics, Volume 4. Helga Fehr-Duda and Thomas Epper, "Probability and risk: foundations and economic implications of probability-dependent risk preferences." © 2012 by Annual Reviews http://www.annualreviews.org.

---

[10] In particular, for $\gamma = 1$, Definition 2.2(i) implies that $\lim_{p \to 0} \frac{w(p)}{p} = \infty$.

2.2.1 *Prelec's probability weighting function*

A large number of probability weighting functions have been proposed in the literature. The most popular of these functions is the Prelec (1998) function. The Prelec function is parsimonious, tractable, and has axiomatic foundations. Depending on parameter values, we will see that it is either consistent with H1 or the special case of H2 with $\mu = 1$. We now turn to a detailed examination of the Prelec weighting function, reminding readers that the comments we make here apply to most probability weighting functions (the so-called *standard weighting functions*, which we define, below).[11] Furthermore, an understanding of the Prelec function will be critical to appreciating the recent developments that take account of hypothesis H2; see Section 2.11.3.

> **Definition 2.4** *(Prelec, 1998): By the Prelec function, we mean the probability weighting function $w(p) : [0,1] \rightarrow [0,1]$ given by*
>
> $$w(0) = 0, \, w(1) = 1, \tag{2.2}$$
>
> $$w(p) = e^{-\beta(-\ln p)^{\alpha}}, \, 0 < p \leq 1, \alpha > 0, \beta > 0. \tag{2.3}$$
>
> *Sometimes the special case of $\beta = 1$ is known as Prelec-I and the case of $\beta \neq 1$ is known as Prelec-II to distinguish between the one-parameter and the two-parameter family of distributions.*

The Prelec function only requires that $\alpha > 0$, $\beta > 0$. In order to distinguish between H1 and H2, it is critical whether α is smaller or larger than 1. For this reason, we make a distinction between the *Prelec function* and the *standard Prelec function*; Prelec (1998) prefers the latter for reasons we give below.

> **Definition 2.5** *(Standard Prelec function): By the standard Prelec probability weighting function, we mean the Prelec function, defined in (2.2) and (2.3), but with $0 < \alpha < 1$.*

> **Remark 2.1** *For $\alpha = \beta = 1$ we get $w(p) = p$ as in EU. Since an infinite number of α, β values are possible and just one pair of values coincides with the special case of EU, it would be quite remarkable if human behavior could be represented by just that one pair of values. Indeed, the evidence clearly rules out this possibility. It is even more remarkable that many economists still stubbornly wish to cling on to EU.*

A simple proof that is omitted gives rise to the following result.

> **Proposition 2.2** *The Prelec function (Definition 2.4) satisfies the properties listed in Proposition 2.8.*

The roles of α, β in the Prelec weighting function are highlighted next.

1. (Role of α) The parameter α controls the convexity/concavity of the Prelec function. If $\alpha < 1$, then the Prelec function is strictly concave for low probabilities but strictly convex for high probabilities. In this case, it is *inverse S-shaped*, as in the curve $w(p) = e^{-(-\ln p)^{0.5}}$ (i.e., $\alpha = 0.5, \beta = 1$), which is sketched as the *thick curve* in Figure 2.3. The converse holds if $\alpha > 1$, in which case the Prelec function is *S-shaped*. An example is the curve $w(p) = e^{-(-\ln p)^{2}}$ ($\alpha = 2, \beta = 1$), sketched in Figure 2.3 as the *light curve*.

---

[11] The interested reader can also consult al-Nowaihi and Dhami (2011) for more details.

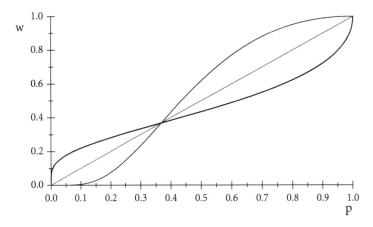

Figure 2.3 Plots of $w(p) = e^{-(-\ln p)0.5}$ and $w(p) = e^{-(-\ln p)^2}$.

The straight line in Figure 2.3 is the 45° line $w(p) = p$ ($\alpha = \beta = 1$) corresponding to the case of EU.

2. (Role of β) Between the region of strict convexity ($w'' > 0$) and the region of strict concavity ($w'' < 0$), there is a point of inflexion ($w'' = 0$). The parameter β controls the location of the inflexion point, relative to the 45° line. For $\beta = 1$, the point of inflexion is at $p = e^{-1}$ and lies on the 45° line, as in Figure 2.3. However, if $\beta < 1$, then the point of inflexion lies above the 45° line, as in the curve $w(p) = e^{-0.5(-\ln p)^2}$ ($\alpha = 2, \beta = 0.5$). For this example, the fixed point, $w(p^*) = p^*$, is at $p^* \simeq 0.14$ but the point of inflexion, $w''(\tilde{p}) = 0$, is at $\tilde{p} \simeq 0.20$.

Some useful results about the Prelec function are given next. The reader is asked to prove them in the exercises.

Proposition 2.3 *For $\alpha = 1$, the Prelec probability weighting function (Definition 2.4) takes the form $w(p) = p^\beta$. It is strictly concave if $\beta < 1$, but strictly convex if $\beta > 1$. In particular, for $\alpha = \beta = 1$, $w(p) = p$ (as under EU).*

Proposition 2.4 *(al-Nowaihi and Dhami, 2010a): Suppose that $\alpha \neq 1$. Then, the Prelec function has the following properties.*

(a) *It has exactly three fixed points: 0, $p^* = e^{-\left(\frac{1}{\beta}\right)^{\frac{1}{\alpha-1}}}$, and 1. For $\beta = 1$, $p^* = e^{-1}$.*
(b) *It has a unique inflexion point, $\tilde{p} \in (0,1)$ at which $w''(\tilde{p}) = 0$.*
(c) *If $\alpha < 1$, it is strictly concave for $p < \tilde{p}$ and strictly convex for $p > \tilde{p}$ (inverse S-shaped).*
(d) *If $\alpha > 1$, it is strictly convex for $p < \tilde{p}$ and strictly concave for $p > \tilde{p}$ (S-shaped).*
(e) *The inflexion point, $\tilde{p}$, lies above, on, or below, the 45^0 line, respectively, if β is less than, equal to, or greater than one.*

Table 2.1, graphs the Prelec function $w(p) = e^{-\beta(-\ln p)^\alpha}$, for various values of α, β.

Corollary 2.1

(i) *Suppose that $\alpha \neq 1$. Then $\tilde{p} = p^* = e^{-1}$ (i.e., the point of inflexion, $\tilde{p}$, and the fixed point, p^*, coincide) if, and only if, $\beta = 1$.*

Table 2.1 Representative graphs of the Prelec function.

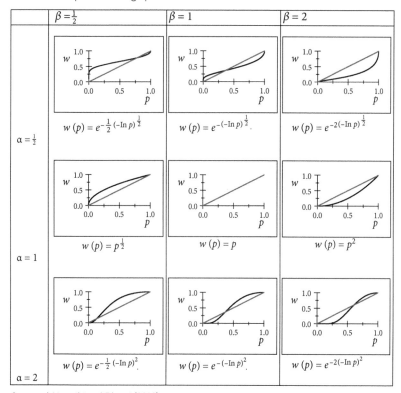

	$\beta = \frac{1}{2}$	$\beta = 1$	$\beta = 2$
$\alpha = \frac{1}{2}$	$w(p) = e^{-\frac{1}{2}(-\ln p)^{\frac{1}{2}}}$	$w(p) = e^{-(-\ln p)^{\frac{1}{2}}}$.	$w(p) = e^{-2(-\ln p)^{\frac{1}{2}}}$
$\alpha = 1$	$w(p) = p^{\frac{1}{2}}$	$w(p) = p$	$w(p) = p^2$
$\alpha = 2$	$w(p) = e^{-\frac{1}{2}(-\ln p)^2}$.	$w(p) = e^{-(-\ln p)^2}$.	$w(p) = e^{-2(-\ln p)^2}$

Source: al-Nowaihi and Dhami (2011).

(ii) *If $\beta = 1$, then:*

(a) *If $\alpha < 1$, then w is strictly concave for $p < e^{-1}$ and strictly convex for $p > e^{-1}$ (inverse S-shape; see the thick curve in Figure 2.3).*

(b) *If $\alpha > 1$, then w is strictly convex for $p < e^{-1}$ and strictly concave for $p > e^{-1}$ (S-shape; see the light curve in Figure 2.3).*

For the thick curve in Figure 2.3 (and first row in Table 2.1), where $\alpha < 1$, the slope of $w(p)$ becomes very steep near $p = 0$. By contrast, for the thin curve in Figure 2.3 (and last row in Table 2.1), where $\alpha > 1$, the slope of $w(p)$ becomes shallow near $p = 0$; in this case low probabilities are underweighted. We now tie these observations with the notion of steepness of a probability weighting function at extreme probabilities (Definitions 2.2, 2.3).

Proposition 2.5

(a) *For $\alpha < 1$ and $\gamma > 0$, the Prelec (1998) function: (i) infinitely overweights infinitesimal probabilities, i.e., $\lim_{p \to 0} \frac{w(p)}{p^\gamma} = \infty$, and (ii) infinitely underweights near-one probabilities, i.e., $\lim_{p \to 1} \frac{1-w(p)}{1-p} = \infty$.*

(b) *For $\alpha > 1$ and $\gamma > 0$, the Prelec function: (i) zero-underweights infinitesimal probabilities, i.e., $\lim_{p \to 0} \frac{w(p)}{p^{\gamma}} = 0$, and (ii) zero-overweights near-one probabilities, i.e., $\lim_{p \to 1} \frac{1 - w(p)}{1 - p} = 0$.*

We have made a distinction between the *Prelec function* ($\alpha > 0$) and the *standard Prelec function* ($0 < \alpha < 1$). Prelec (1998) himself favors the case $0 < \alpha < 1$, and it is this case which is standard in non-EU theories such as rank dependent utility and prospect theory. According to Prelec (1998, p. 505), for the case $\gamma = 1$, the infinite limit in Proposition 2.12(a) captures the qualitative change as we move from impossibility to improbability. On the other hand, this contradicts hypothesis H2a, i.e., the observed behavior that many people simply ignore events of very low probability. These problems are avoided for $\alpha > 1$. However, for $\alpha > 1$, the Prelec function is S-shaped, see Proposition 2.4(d) and Figure 2.3, which conflicts with hypotheses H1 and H2b. This suggests that we need a richer account of decision making under risk for events when near-zero and near-one probabilities are involved; *composite prospect theory*, outlined in Section 2.11.3, is one attempt to give such an account.

When aggregate data is taken into account, most weighting functions appear to be inverse S-shaped. However, there is substantial heterogeneity at the individual level with the two most common shapes being convex and inverse S-shape.[12] Fehr-Duda and Epper (2012) give estimates of the Prelec function for two different populations—a student population and a representative population (see description, above). For the student population, $\alpha = 0.513$ and $\beta = 0.958$, and for the representative population, $\alpha = 0.423$ and $\beta = 0.868$.

Definition 2.6 *(Subproportionality and certainty effect): A feature of most probability weighting functions, at least over a range $[\widehat{p}, 1]$, $\widehat{p} \geq 0$, is subproportionality, i.e.,*

$$\frac{w(p)}{w(q)} > \frac{w(\lambda p)}{w(\lambda q)}, \, 0 < \lambda < 1, \widehat{p} \leq q < p \leq 1. \tag{2.4}$$

If $\widehat{p} = 0$ and $0 < q$, then w is subproportional over the entire probability range. The certainty effect arises when $p = 1$. In this case, we have

$$w(\lambda q) > w(\lambda)w(q).$$

Probability weighting functions that have the feature of subproportionality, can typically explain the common ratio effect. In addition, inverse S-shaped probability weighting functions that cut the diagonal from above can explain the common consequence effect and the simultaneous existence of insurance and gambling.[13]

There are other probability weighting functions also; we now briefly consider the main ones.

OTHER PROBABILITY WEIGHTING FUNCTIONS

1. The Tversky and Kahneman (1992) probability weighting function is

$$w(p) = \frac{p^{\tau}}{\left[p^{\tau} + (1 - p)^{\tau} \right]^{\frac{1}{\tau}}}, \, 0.279 < \tau < 1. \tag{2.5}$$

This probability weighting function is not subproportional for small values of p, hence, it cannot account for the common ratio effect for small probabilities. A smaller value

---

[12] See, for instance, Gonzalez and Wu (1999), Stott (2006), van de Kuilen and Wakker (2011), Fehr-Duda and Epper (2012).

[13] Friedman and Savage (1948) proposed a utility function with concave and convex segments to explain the simultaneous occurrence of insurance and gambling but this does not explain why risk preferences of individuals are sensitive to probabilities at different levels of payoffs (see Figure 2.1).

of τ induces a more pronounced departure from linearity. One potential drawback of this function is that the point of intersection with the diagonal is not independent of the curvature parameter, τ (recall that this problem does not arise with the Prelec function).

2. Karmakar (1979) proposed the following weighting function

$$w(p) = \frac{p^\tau}{p^\tau + (1-p)^\tau}, \, 0 < \tau < 1. \tag{2.6}$$

This function is not subproportional for low values of p but it intersects the diagonal at $p = 0.5$, which is independent of τ (unlike the Tversky–Kahneman function).

3. The Goldstein and Einhorn (1987) linear-in-log-odds probability weighting function is given by

$$w(p) = \frac{\delta p^\eta}{\delta p^\eta + (1-p)^\eta}, \, p \in [0,1], \delta \geq 0, \eta \geq 0. \tag{2.7}$$

In this specification, η is responsible for the curvature and a smaller value of η induces a more pronounced departure from the EU case, $w(p) = p$. The parameter δ controls elevation; an increase in δ increases the elevation of the weighting function. The standard EU case corresponds to $\delta = \eta = 1$.

Fehr-Duda and Epper (2012) argue that the one-parameter weighting functions do not fit the data as well as the two-parameter family of functions. Gonzalez and Wu (1999) show that the Prelec function in (2.3) and the Goldstein–Einhorn function in (2.7) fit the data equally well.

2.2.2 *Stochastic dominance under non-linear probability weighting*

If hypotheses H1 and H2 are important, then it may seem natural to replace the linear weighting under EU with non-linear weighting. However, the next example shows that this is not straight-forward.

Example 2.1 *(Simple non-linear probability weighting): One alternative to EU is the decision weighted form of utility in which we define:*

$$\widetilde{U}(x_1,p_1;\ldots;x_n,p_n) = \Sigma_{i=1}^n w(p_i)u(x_i), \tag{2.8}$$

where $w(p_i)$ is the probability weight of outcome x_i. Early attempts at formulating these kinds of utility functions include Edwards (1954, 1962) and Handa (1977). One problem with this utility function is that the choices generated by it might be stochastically dominated. This is shown in Example 2.2 (Fishburn, 1978).

Example 2.2 *(Problems with non-linear weighting of probabilities): Consider the lottery $L = (x,p;y,1-p)$, $0 < p < 1$. Let $w : [0,1] \to [0,1]$ be a probability weighting function. Let u be a utility function for sure outcomes and let $\widetilde{U}$ be the utility function in (2.8). By definition,*

$$\widetilde{U}(L) = w(p)u(x) + w(1-p)u(y).$$

Let preferences induced by $\widetilde{U}$ be denoted by $\prec_{\widetilde{U}}$

(a) *For the special case, $x = y$, we get $\widetilde{U} = [w(p) + w(1-p)]u(x)$. In general, for non-EU theories, $w(p) + w(1-p) \neq 1$. For probabilities bounded away from the end points of the interval $[0,1]$, we typically have $w(p) + w(1-p) < 1$.*[14]

---

[14] For instance, for the Prelec probability weighting function, and for values of the parameters $\alpha = 0.5$ and $\beta = 1$ the statement $w(p) + w(1-p) < 1$ is true for all probabilities in the range $[0.03, 0.97]$.

Hence, $(x,p;x,1-p) \prec_{\widetilde{U}} (x,1)$. But any "sensible" theory of risk should give $(x,p;x,1-p) \sim_{\widetilde{U}} (x;1)$.

(b) Take $y = x + \epsilon$, $\epsilon > 0$. Then, first order stochastic dominance for discrete outcomes (Definition 2.9) implies that $(x,1) \prec_1 (x,p;x+\epsilon,1-p)$. Now, $\widetilde{U}(x,p;x+\epsilon,1-p) = w(p)u(x) + w(1-p)u(x+\epsilon)$. Assuming u is continuous and $w(p) + w(1-p) < 1$, we get

$$\lim_{\epsilon \to 0} \widetilde{U}(x,p;x+\epsilon,1-p) = w(p)u(x) + w(1-p)u(x)$$
$$= [w(p) + w(1-p)]u(x) < \widetilde{U}(x).$$

Hence, for sufficiently small $\epsilon > 0$, $\widetilde{U}(x,p;x+\epsilon,1-p) < \widetilde{U}(x)$. Thus, we have that $(x,1) \prec_1 (x,p;x+\epsilon,1-p)$ but $\widetilde{U}(x,p;x+\epsilon,1-p) < \widetilde{U}(x,1)$. Hence, first order stochastic dominance is violated. We discuss the approaches taken to deal with this problem in various non-EU theories, below.

2.3 Rank dependent utility theory (RDU)

To summarize the story so far, that is relevant for this section: Hypothesis H1, above, highlighted the tendency for decision makers to overweight small probabilities and underweight large probabilities. EU is unable to take account of H1 because it weights probabilities in a linear manner. Example 2.1 captures the early attempts to introduce non-linear weighting, by transformation of *point probabilities*. However, decision makers could choose stochastically dominated options in these theories (Example 2.2), which was not an attractive option for most economists.

Rank dependent utility theory (RDU), relying on the work of Quiggin (1982, 1993), proposed the first satisfactory solution to the problem of non-linear probability weighting. Unlike Example 2.2, Quiggin suggested transformation of *cumulative probabilities*. EU and RDU are otherwise similar, except for cumulatively transformed probabilities. This was a major advance over EU, because it could resolve several paradoxes of EU, e.g., the Allais paradox. Further, decision makers who use RDU do not choose stochastically dominated options.

We now introduce *decision weights* that play a key role in most non-EU theories.

Definition 2.7 (Decision weights): Consider the lottery $(x_1,p_1;\ldots;x_n,p_n)$. Let w be the probability weighting function. For RDU, the decision weights, π_i, are defined as follows.

$\pi_n = w(p_n)$,
$\pi_{n-1} = w(p_{n-1} + p_n) - w(p_n)$,
$\ldots$
$\pi_i = w\left(\Sigma_{j=i}^n p_j\right) - w\left(\Sigma_{j=i+1}^n p_j\right)$,
$\ldots$
$\pi_1 = w\left(\Sigma_{j=1}^n p_j\right) - w\left(\Sigma_{j=2}^n p_j\right) = w(1) - w\left(\Sigma_{j=2}^n p_j\right) = 1 - w\left(\Sigma_{j=2}^n p_j\right)$.

From Definition 2.7, we get that,

$$\pi_j \geq 0 \text{ and } \Sigma_{j=1}^n \pi_j = 1. \tag{2.9}$$

The logic and intuition for decision weights in Definition 2.7 is made clear later in this section.

Definition 2.8 *Consider the lottery* $L = (x_1, p_1; \ldots; x_n, p_n)$, *where* $x_1 < \ldots < x_n$. *Let* w *be the probability weighting function. Let* π_i, $i = 1, \ldots, n$, *be given by Definition 2.7. The decision maker's rank dependent utility from L, is given by*

$$RDU(L) = \Sigma_{i=1}^{n} \pi_i u(x_i). \tag{2.10}$$

From (2.10), an implication of models of RDU is that two outcomes that differ in rank but have the same probability will typically have different decision weights assigned to them.

2.3.1 *Attitudes to risk under RDU*

Under EU, attitudes to risk are captured by the shape of the utility function. For instance, a concave utility function implies and is implied by risk aversion. Typically, for psychologists, and many economists, the notion that risk is captured by the shape of the utility function alone, does not seem a palatable one. Indeed, it seems natural to associate the notion of riskiness also with probabilities. An important implication of RDU is that the utility function and the decision maker's perception of objective probabilities *jointly* determine attitudes to risk.[15]

Example 2.3 *Suppose that a decision maker is offered the lottery* $L = (0, 1 - p; 1, p)$, $0 < p < 1$, *so the expected value is* $EL = p$. *Suppose that the decision maker follows RDU, the weighting function is convex, say,* $w(p) = p^2$, *and the utility function is linear, i.e.,* $u(x) = x$. *Under EU, such a decision maker is risk neutral. Using Definition 2.8, under RDU, $RDU(L) = w(p) = p^2$. Since, $u(x) = x$, the certainty equivalent of the lottery under RDU, C_L, equals p^2. Risk aversion requires that the certainty equivalent of a lottery is lower than the expected value of the lottery for all lotteries, hence,*

$$C_L < EL \Leftrightarrow p^2 < p \Leftrightarrow p < 1,$$

which is true. In other words, the finding of risk aversion can equally well be explained by a linear utility function and a convex probability weighting function. In this example, the decision maker would have been risk loving if $w(p) = \sqrt{p}$, *which illustrates the importance of the probability weighting function in determining risk attitudes under RDU.*

The discussion, below, shows that decision weights in Definition 2.7 have a simple, intuitive, explanation.

Example 2.4 *(Curvature of weighting function and optimism, pessimism): The curvature of w is also sometimes interpreted in terms of the optimism or pessimism of the decision maker; these terms have no natural analogue in EU. To see this, assume that w is convex throughout. Suppose that we have the balanced risk lottery* $L = (x_1, 0.5; x_2, 0.5)$; $x_1 < x_2$. *Using Definition 2.8, under RDU*

$$RDU(L) = u(x_1)[1 - w(0.5)] + u(x_2)w(0.5). \tag{2.11}$$

Since $w(0) = 0, w(1) = 1$ (see Definition 2.1) and w is assumed to be convex throughout, so $w(0.5) < 0.5$. Thus, in (2.11), the weight on $u(x_1)$ is higher than the weight on $u(x_2)$ despite identical objective probabilities. In other words, the decision maker is pessimistic in placing a higher weight on the lower outcome. The converse (optimism) would apply if w

---

[15] See Chateauneuf and Cohen (1994) for an early theoretical demonstration of this idea.

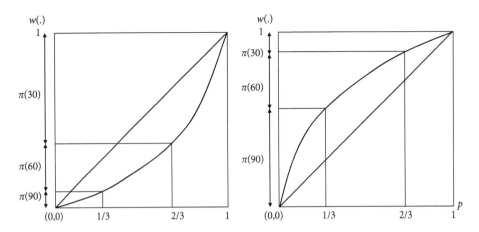

Figure 2.4 An illustration of pessimism (left panel) and optimism (right panel) as the shape of the probability weighting function varies.

were concave throughout; in this case, the decision maker puts a higher decision weight on the higher outcome, despite both outcomes being equiprobable.

Let us delve a bit further into the relation between decision weights and probability weights. Consider the lottery $(30, 1/3; 60, 1/3; 90, 1/3)$. Using Definition 2.7, the decision weights corresponding to the three outcomes are

$$\pi(30) = 1 - w(2/3); \pi(60) = w(2/3) - w(1/3); \pi(90) = w(1/3). \tag{2.12}$$

Figure 2.4 plots a convex weighting function (LHS panel) and a concave weighting function (RHS panel). The magnitudes of the decision weights corresponding to each of the three outcomes, as calculated in (2.12), are marked on the vertical axis. For the convex case, the magnitudes of the decision weights decrease as the outcome increases, $\pi(90) < \pi(60) < \pi(30)$; this reflects *pessimism*. If such a weighting function is combined with a concave utility function, it enhances risk aversion. The converse happens when the weighting function is concave. Here larger outcomes are given greater decision weights, $\pi(90) > \pi(60) > \pi(30)$; this reflects *optimism*. Combined with a concave utility function, optimism reduces risk aversion.

> **Example 2.5** *(Elevation of probability weighting function and optimism): Consider a decrease in the elevation of the probability weighting function, e.g., an increase in β in the Prelec function (Definition 2.4). This change is associated with a lower degree of optimism. To see this, consider the lottery $L = (x_1, 1 - p; x_2, p)$, $x_1 < x_2$. The rank dependent utility of this lottery is given by*
>
> $$RDU(L) = w(p)[u(x_2) - u(x_1)] + u(x_1).$$
>
> *Following a decrease in elevation, $w(p)$ decreases, which reduces RDU by reducing the decision weight that the decision maker puts on the higher outcome. A similar insight holds under prospect theory if all outcomes are in the domain of gains.*

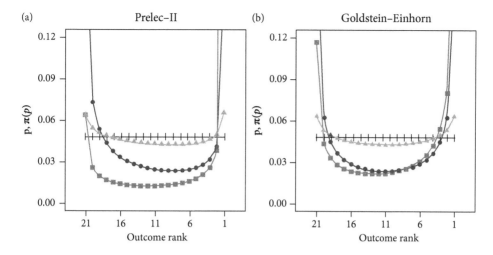

Figure 2.5 Shapes of decision weights when there are multiple outcomes under RDU. Panel (a) shows the Prelec-II function and Panel (b) shows the Goldstein–Einhorn function. + denotes the uniform objective probability distribution. • denotes the case $\alpha = \eta = 0.2$, $\beta = \delta = 1$. ▲ denotes the case $\alpha = \eta = 0.9$, $\beta = \delta = 1$. ■ denotes the case $\alpha = \eta = 0.2$, $\beta = \delta = 0.3$.

Source: Reproduced with permission of Annual Review of Economics, Volume 4. Helga Fehr-Duda and Thomas Epper, "Probability and risk: Foundations and economic implications of probability-dependent risk preferences." © 2012 by Annual Reviews http://www.annualreviews.org.

What is the shape of decision weights when there are several outcomes and we have an inverse S-shaped probability weighting function? Following simulations reported in Fehr-Duda and Epper (2012), the typical shape is shown in Figure 2.5. We have 21 ranked outcomes with a uniform probability distribution over them, plotted for two weighting functions—the Prelec-II function and the Goldstein–Einhorn function (see Definition 2.4 and (2.7)); recall that $0 < \alpha < 1$ gives the inverse S-shape under the Prelec function, and a similar role is played by the parameter η in the Goldstein–Einhorn function. Extreme outcomes are accorded extreme decision weights, while the intermediate outcomes are accorded relatively flat weights. This enhances the salience of extreme outcomes, a feature that explains several puzzles in finance (see Section 2.11).

> **Remark 2.2** *Several axiomatizations of RDU allow for additive separability between terms that multiply utility with probability weights, e.g., Abdellaoui (2002) and Wakker (1994). In order to ensure concavity or convexity of the weighting function, these contributions introduce additional global auxiliary conditions such as probabilistic risk aversion. See in particular, Wakker (2001) who allows for a preference axiomatization of convex capacities. This allows for a weighting function that is either concave or convex throughout. Diecidue et al. (2009) introduce local conditions that allow for probabilistic risk aversion to vary over the probability interval [0, 1]. For one set of parameter values, they can address hypothesis H1, while for the complementary set of parameter values, they can address hypothesis H2a. However, their proposal was not designed with a view to simultaneously addressing H1 and H2.*

A decision maker who follows RDU never chooses stochastically dominated lotteries. We state here the formal result without proof.[16] Let $x_1 < x_2 < \ldots < x_n$ be a set of outcomes. Consider two lotteries, L_p, L_q, corresponding to two different distribution functions P, Q over the outcomes,

$$L_p = (x_1, p_1; \ldots; x_n, p_n), \quad L_q = (x_1, q_1; \ldots; x_n, q_n).$$

Suppose that the decision weights (Definition 2.7) for the lotteries L_p, L_q are denoted respectively by π_{pi} and π_{qi}, $i = 1, 2, \ldots, n$.

Let W be the set of all probability weighting functions, i.e.,

$$W = \left\{ w : [0,1] \to [0,1], \, w(0) = 0, \, w(1) = 1, \, w \text{ is non-decreasing} \right\}. \tag{2.13}$$

Definition 2.9 *Under RDU, the lottery, L_p, is preferred to another lottery, L_q, written $L_p \succeq_{RDU} L_q$, if and only if*

$$\Sigma_{i=1}^{n} \pi_{pi} u(x_i) \geq \Sigma_{i=1}^{n} \pi_{qi} u(x_i), \text{ for all } u \in \mathbf{u} \text{ and for all } w \in W,$$

where $\mathbf{u}$ is the class of all non-decreasing utility functions and π_{pi}, π_{qi} are decision weights for lotteries L_p and L_q. If, in addition, the inequality is strict for some $u \in \mathbf{u}$, then we say that L_p is strictly preferred to L_q, written as $L_p \succ_{RDU} L_q$.

Proposition 2.6 *(Quiggin, 1993; al-Nowaihi and Dhami, unpublished notes)*

(a) *$P \succeq_1 Q$ if, and only if, $L_p \succeq_{RDU} L_q$, for all $u \in \mathbf{u}$ and for all $w \in W$.*
(b) *$P \succ_1 Q$ if, and only if, (i) $L_p \succeq_{RDU} L_q$, for all $u \in \mathbf{u}$ and for all $w \in W$, and (ii) $L_p \succ_{RDU} L_q$, for some $u \in \mathbf{u}$ and for some $w \in W$.*

Note that Proposition 2.6 under RDU is very similar to Proposition 1.3 under EU. In both cases, decision makers do not choose stochastically dominated lotteries.

2.3.2 RDU under uncertainty

Recall our discussion of subjective expected utility (SEU) under uncertainty in Section 1.3. We now consider RDU under uncertainty. Consider the Savage act (see Section 1.3 for the definition),

$$f = (E_1, x_1; E_2, x_2; \ldots; E_n, x_n),$$

where $\cup_{i=1}^{n} E_i = S$, the sample space. Suppose also that the outcomes are ordered as $x_1 < x_2 < \ldots < x_n$. We briefly describe how Schmeidler (1989) formulated a more general rank dependent theory to deal with uncertainty (and not just risk, which was Quiggin's (1982) contribution).

Definition 2.10 *A subjective probability weighting function (or event weighting function), $\widetilde{w} : E \to \mathbb{R}$ where $E \subseteq S$ has the following properties:*

---

[16] Formal and full proofs are somewhat hard to find, although see Quiggin (1993). The formal results below draw on unpublished joint research conducted by Ali al-Nowaihi and Sanjit Dhami.

(1) $\widetilde{w}(\varnothing) = 0$, where $\varnothing$ is the empty set.
(2) If $E_i \subset E_j$, then $\widetilde{w}(E_i) \leq \widetilde{w}(E_j)$.
(3) $\widetilde{w}(S) = 1$.

$\widetilde{w}$ need not be additive, i.e., for mutually exclusive sets E_i, E_j, $\widetilde{w}(E_i \cup E_j)$ need not equal $\widetilde{w}(E_i) + \widetilde{w}(E_j)$.

The objective function for *rank dependent utility under uncertainty* is defined as:

$$U(f) = \sum_{j=1}^{n} \pi_j u(x_j).$$

The decision weights under uncertainty, π_j, are defined as follows:

$$\pi_j = \widetilde{w}(E_j \cup E_{j+1} \cup \ldots \cup E_n) - \widetilde{w}(E_{j+1} \cup E_{j+2} \cup \ldots \cup E_n).$$

RDU under risk is a special case of Schmeidler's (1989) framework when the probability of event E_j equals its objective probability and probabilistic sophistication (Definition 1.13) holds.

The Ellsberg paradox (see Chapter 4) can be explained under RDU if one relaxes the assumption of probabilistic sophistication. The assumption of probabilistic sophistication allows us to write

$$\widetilde{w}(E) = w(p(E)), \tag{2.14}$$

where w is the probability weighting function under risk and $p(E)$ denotes the objective probability of event E. The non-linearity of $\widetilde{w}$ can now be seen immediately. Let E_i, E_j be mutually exclusive events, then, under probabilistic sophistication:

$$\begin{aligned}
\widetilde{w}(E_i \cup E_j) &= w(p(E_i \cup E_j)) \\
&= w(p_i + p_j) \\
&\neq w(p_i) + w(p_j) = \widetilde{w}(E_i) + \widetilde{w}(E_j).
\end{aligned}$$

The first line is true by definition, the second follows because E_i and E_j are mutually exclusive events, and the third because w is non-linear. In the discussion of RDU under risk, we showed how various shapes of the probability weighting function, w, can denote optimism or pessimism. Similar notions hold for the event weighting function, $\widetilde{w}$. For instance, pessimism can be shown to be equivalent to the inequality $\widetilde{w}(E_i \cup E_j) \geq \widetilde{w}(E_i) + \widetilde{w}(E_j)$ (see exercise 10.4.2 in Wakker, 2010).

The most interesting aspect of the formulation of rank dependent utility under uncertainty, aside from its generality, is that the empirical evidence on the shape of w carries over to the shape of $\widetilde{w}$. Indeed, the inverse S-shape is even more vivid under $\widetilde{w}$. We omit a discussion of the empirical findings. The interested reader can consult Hogarth and Kunreuther (1989), Kilka and Weber (2001), and Abdellaoui et al. (2005).

2.3.3 *Drawbacks of RDU*

RDU offers a distinct improvement over EU. Since EU is a special case of RDU when $w(p) = p$, RDU explains everything that EU does but the converse is false. RDU is able to explain the Allais paradoxes. An exercise asks you to do the relevant calculations. However, RDU cannot explain all the facts, as the next example shows.

Example 2.6 *(A refutation of both EU and RDU): Consider Problems 11 and 12 from Kahneman and Tversky (1979).*

Problem 11. In addition to whatever you own (x_0), you have been given 1000. You are now asked to choose between

$$A = (x_0 + 1000, 0.5; x_0 + 2000, 0.5) \text{ and } B = (x_0 + 1000, 0; x_0 + 1500, 1).$$

A is chosen by 16%, while B is chosen by 84%. Using Definition 2.8, under RDU, the evidence, thus, suggests that for most subjects,

$$[1 - w(0.5)]u(x_0 + 1000) + w(0.5)u(x_0 + 2000) < u(x_0 + 1500). \tag{2.15}$$

Problem 12: In addition to whatever you own (x_0), you have been given 2000. You are now asked to choose between

$$C = (x_0 + 1000, 0.5; x_0 + 2000, 0.5) \text{ and } D = (x_0 + 1500, 1; x_0 + 2000, 0)$$

C is chosen by 69% of the subjects, while D is chosen by 31%. Using Definition 2.8, under RDU, the empirical evidence indicates that for most subjects,

$$[1 - w(0.5)]u(x_0 + 1000) + w(0.5)u(x_0 + 2000) > u(x_0 + 1500). \tag{2.16}$$

Clearly, (2.15) contradicts (2.16), violating RDU. The main reason for this violation is that RDU does not take account of shifts in the "reference point" of the decision maker, when the endowment changes from $x_0 + 1000$ to $x_0 + 2000$. We shall see below in Example 2.9 that prospect theory, which takes account of such changes in reference points, can account for this puzzle.

RDU is unable to explain many important phenomena whose explanation rests on features that are central to prospect theory such as *loss aversion* and *reference dependence*. Examples include explanations of the equity premium puzzle, tax evasion puzzles, disposition effect, backward bending labor supply curve, endowment effect, asymmetric price elasticities, and exchange asymmetries. These phenomena have a straightforward explanation under prospect theory, as we shall see below.

2.4 Prospect theory (PT)

Remark 1.1, above, listed the two main features of EU: linearity in probabilities and utility that does not differ in the domain of gains and losses. RDU relaxed the first feature by introducing non-linear probability weighting. Prospect theory goes a step further and relaxes both features of EU. There are two main versions of prospect theory.[17] *Original prospect theory* (OPT) is due to Kahneman and Tversky (1979) and *cumulative prospect theory*, or simply *prospect theory* (PT), is due to Tversky and Kahneman (1992).[18] Our focus here will be on PT. Section 2.11.1, below, gives a brief treatment of OPT.

---

[17] See also *third generation prospect theory* in Section 2.7, and *composite prospect theory* in Section 2.11.3.
[18] Starmer and Sugden (1989b) also introduced non-linear probability weights in a prospect theory framework. Although this is rarely mentioned, Tverksy and Kahneman (1992) also extend prospect theory to ambiguity, using the framework suggested by Schmeidler (1989).

Under PT (and OPT), the carriers of utility are not final levels of wealth, but deviations of actual wealth levels from a *reference point*, an idea that is well established in psychology. Evidence indicates that when exposed to external stimuli, such as temperature, brightness, and pain, individuals are more sensitive to *changes* rather than *levels* (Helson, 1964). In order to fix ideas on reference dependence, consider the following well-known experiment: Put your right hand in cold water and your left hand in warm water until both hands have had time to adjust to the temperature. Then, simultaneously take out both hands and dip them in lukewarm water. Although both hands experience the identical lukewarm temperature, the right hand feels warm and the left hand feels cold.

Strictly speaking, the view that the reference point is exogenous under PT needs to be qualified. Kahneman and Tversky were fully aware that the *status quo* turns out to be a useful reference point in many applications. Other possible choices could be an *expected outcome*, a *fair outcome*, or a *legal entitlement*; clearly the context dictates the appropriate reference point. The reference point could also be state-dependent wealth, average wealth, desired wealth, or it could even be made endogenous by using the rational expectations of future wealth (see Section 2.8). For a discussion, see Kahneman and Tversky (2000), Köszegi and Rabin (2006), and Schmidt et al. (2008). Abeler et al. (2011) find that expectations of income serve as reference points and determine effort provision. Falk and Knell (2004) show how individuals might attempt to endogenize their reference points with a view to taking account of self-improvement and self-enhancement.

If the outcome turns out to be better (respectively worse) as compared to the reference point, then the decision maker is said to be in the *domain of gains* (respectively *losses*). Experimental and field evidence suggests that utility is evaluated differently in the domain of gains and losses. For instance, Example 1.5, due to Tversky and Kahneman (1981), demonstrated that decision makers are risk averse in the domain of gains and risk loving in the domain of losses. Using Australian data, Page et al. (2012) showed that following a natural disaster (floods), individuals who suffer a loss of at least 50% of their property values are more likely to accept risky gambles.

Extensive evidence, that we review below, also indicates that losses bite more than equivalent gains. This phenomenon, known as *loss aversion*, accounts for a large number of puzzles that could not be explained using EU and RDU. Finally, under PT (but not under OPT), decision makers transform probabilities non-linearly, in a manner similar to RDU, to produce decision weights. The difference from RDU is that, under PT, these transformations are applied separately in the domain of gains and losses.

We now give a more formal treatment of PT.[19] To take account of reference dependence, we first define lotteries in *incremental form*.

Definition 2.11 (*Lotteries in incremental form or prospects*) *We say that a lottery is presented in incremental form if it is represented as:*

$$L = \left(y_1, p_1; y_2, p_2; \ldots; y_n, p_n\right),\tag{2.17}$$

where

$$y_i = x_i - x_0, \; i = 1, 2, \ldots, n,\tag{2.18}$$

---

[19] A feature of the ideas in OPT/PT is that they may appear self-evident. For an interesting account of the application of these ideas to Greek mythology, see Orwin (1994) and Ober (2012).

is the increment (positive, negative, or zero) in wealth, x_i, relative to reference wealth, x_0. The reference wealth may be fixed at some given level, e.g., when wealth is simply the status-quo level, or it may be stochastic, as in the models described below in Sections 2.7 and 2.8. Lotteries represented in the incremental form are sometimes also known as "prospects."

In PT, the *utility function* is sometimes termed as a *value function*. However, we speak of utility under PT in the normal sense that readers would understand the term in EU and RDU, and reserve the term value function for the objective function under PT.

Definition 2.12 *(Utility function under PT; Tversky and Kahneman, 1979). Let $Y \subset \mathbb{R}$ be the set of wealth levels relative to a reference point, as in (2.18). A utility function, v, is a mapping $v : Y \to \mathbb{R}$ that satisfies the following:*

1. *v is continuous.*
2. *v is strictly increasing.*
3. *$v(0) = 0$ (reference dependence).*
4. *v is concave for $y \geq 0$ (declining sensitivity for gains).*
5. *v is convex for $y \leq 0$ (declining sensitivity for losses).*
6. *$-v(-y) > v(y)$ for $y > 0$ (loss aversion).[20]*

There are several alternative concepts of loss aversion in PT; these are discussed in Section 2.5.2. Tversky and Kahneman (1992) propose the following power form of the utility function.[21]

$$v(y) = \begin{cases} y^{\gamma} & \text{if} \quad y \geq 0 \\ -\lambda(-y)^{\gamma} & \text{if} \quad y < 0 \end{cases}, \tag{2.19}$$

where γ and λ are constants such that $0 < \gamma < 1$, and $\lambda > 1$ is known as the *coefficient of loss aversion*. One may also impose separate powers in the domain of gains and losses, respectively, γ^+ and γ^-. Tversky and Kahneman (1992) estimated that $\gamma^+ \simeq \gamma^- = \gamma = 0.88$ and $\lambda \simeq 2.25$.

The properties in Definition 2.12, are illustrated in Figure 2.6, which is a plot of (2.19) for $\lambda = 2.5, \gamma = 0.5$.

Suppose that we have a total of $m + 1 + n$ outcomes such that there are m distinct outcomes in the domain of losses, n distinct outcomes in the domain of gains, and there is 1 reference outcome. Consider the following lottery in incremental form (Definition 2.11) that represents these outcomes and the associated probabilities

$$L = (y_{-m}, p_{-m}; y_{-m+1}, p_{-m+1}; \ldots; y_{-1}, p_{-1}; y_0, p_0; y_1, p_1; y_2, p_2; \ldots; y_n, p_n), \tag{2.20}$$

where y_i is defined in (2.18). The restriction on probabilities is given by

$$\sum_{i=-m}^{n} p_i = 1, p_i \geq 0, i = -m, -m+1, \ldots, n. \tag{2.21}$$

---

[20] Notice that this formulation makes sense because of properties 2 and 3 of the utility function.
[21] For the axiomatic foundations of this utility function, see Section 2.6 below.

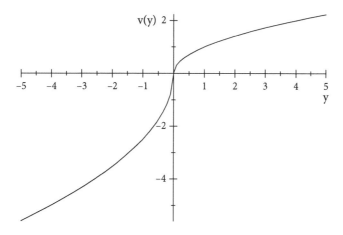

Figure 2.6 The utility function under prospect theory.

It is pedagogically more convenient to refer to the y_i values as "outcomes" rather than using the more cumbersome but accurate expression "outcomes relative to the reference point." We shall follow this convention, below. The restriction on outcomes is given by

$$y_{-m} < y_{-m+1} < \ldots < y_{-1} < y_0 = 0 < y_1 < y_2 < \ldots < y_n, \tag{2.22}$$

where $y_0 = 0$ is the *reference outcome* (the reference point is x_0). Thus, in PT, outcomes are ordered from worst, y_{-m}, to best, y_n.

> **Definition 2.13**   *(Set of lotteries): Denote by $\mathcal{L}_P$, the set of all lotteries of the form given in (2.20), subject to the restrictions (2.21), (2.22).*

In order to compute the decision weights for gains under PT, we apply the usual RDU calculations, as in Definition 2.7, starting at the positive extreme and using a probability weighting function, w^+, for the domain of gains. However, for losses, we start at the negative extreme, and use a probability weighting function, w^-, for the domain of losses.

> **Remark 2.3**   *Abdellaoui (2000) and Abdellaoui et al. (2005) find that there is no significant difference in the curvature of the weighting function for gains and losses. For the Prelec function (see Definition 2.4), we know that the parameter α controls the curvature. However, the elevation (which in the Prelec function is controlled by the parameter β) can be different in the domain of gains and losses.*

> **Definition 2.14**   *(Tversky and Kahneman, 1992). For PT, the decision weights, π_i, are defined as follows:*
> $$\pi_n = w^+ (p_n)$$
> $$\pi_{n-1} = w^+ (p_{n-1} + p_n) - w^+ (p_n) \ldots$$
> $$\pi_i = w^+ \left(\Sigma_{j=i}^n p_j \right) - w^+ \left(\Sigma_{j=i+1}^n p_j \right) \ldots$$
> $$\pi_1 = w^+ \left(\Sigma_{j=1}^n p_j \right) - w^+ \left(\Sigma_{j=2}^n p_j \right)$$
> $$\pi_{-m} = w^- (p_{-m})$$
> $$\pi_{-m+1} = w^- (p_{-m} + p_{-m+1}) - w^- (p_{-m}) \ldots$$

$$\pi_{-j} = w^- \left(\Sigma_{i=-m}^{-j} p_i \right) - w^- \left(\Sigma_{i=-m}^{-j-1} p_i \right) \cdots$$
$$\pi_{-1} = w^- \left(\Sigma_{i=-m}^{-1} p_i \right) - w^- \left(\Sigma_{i=-m}^{-2} p_i \right)$$

We now define the objective function of a decision maker who follows PT. This objective function is called the *value function*.

Definition 2.15 *(The value function; Starmer and Sugden, 1989a; Tversky and Kahneman, 1992): The value of the lottery $L \in \mathcal{L}_P$ to the decision maker is given by*

$$V(L) = \Sigma_{i=-m}^n \pi_i v(y_i). \tag{2.23}$$

Under RDU, there are no separate domains of gains and losses, so the decision weights add up to one (see (2.9)). Under PT, this does not hold (Proposition 2.7, below). However, since $v(0) = 0$, the corresponding decision weight, π_0, can be chosen arbitrarily to ensure that decision weights add up to one.

Proposition 2.7 *Under PT, if all outcomes are in the domain of gains or in the domain of losses, then the decision weights add up to one, otherwise they do not.*

In most examples in this section, the Prelec (1998) probability weighting function will be used because it appears to be the one with the strongest empirical support. To quote from Stott (2006, p. 102): "the most predictive version of [cumulative prospect theory] has a power value curve, a single parameter risky weighting function due to Prelec (1998) and a Logit stochastic process." Under PT, w^+ and w^- are allowed to differ; however, we will typically make the simplifying assumption that $w^+ = w^- = w$; see Prelec (1998).

2.4.1 A brief note on PT under uncertainty

PT can be easily extended to uncertainty along the lines described in Section 2.3.2, so we shall be brief. The main difference is that we need to work with lotteries in incremental form. Consider the following Savage act

$$L = (E_{-m}, y_{-m}; \ldots; E_{-1}, y_{-1}; E_0, y_0; E_1, y_1; \ldots; E_n, y_n), \tag{2.24}$$

where (2.22) holds; $y_0 = 0$ is the outcome relative to the reference point, and $E_{-m}, \ldots, E_0, \ldots, E_n$ are $m + n$ disjoint events whose union forms the sample space. Denote by $\overline{\mathcal{L}}_P$ the set of all lotteries of the form given in (2.24). Denote the event weighting function (Definition 2.10) for gains by $\widetilde{w}^+$ and that for losses by $\widetilde{w}^-$.

Definition 2.16 *For PT under uncertainty, the decision weights, π_i, are defined as follows:*
$$\pi_n = \widetilde{w}^+(E_n)$$
$$\pi_{n-1} = \widetilde{w}^+(E_{n-1} \cup E_n) - \widetilde{w}^+(E_n) \cdots$$
$$\pi_i = \widetilde{w}^+ \left(\cup_{j=i}^n E_j \right) - \widetilde{w}^+ \left(\cup_{j=i+1}^n E_j \right) \cdots$$
$$\pi_1 = \widetilde{w}^+ \left(\cup_{j=1}^n E_j \right) - \widetilde{w}^+ \left(\cup_{j=2}^n E_j \right)$$
$$\pi_{-m} = \widetilde{w}^-(E_{-m})$$
$$\pi_{-m+1} = \widetilde{w}^-(E_{-m} \cup E_{-m+1}) - \widetilde{w}^-(E_{-m}) \cdots$$
$$\pi_j = \widetilde{w}^- \left(\cup_{i=-m}^j E_i \right) - \widetilde{w}^- \left(\cup_{i=-m}^{j-1} E_i \right) \cdots$$
$$\pi_{-1} = \widetilde{w}^- \left(\cup_{i=-m}^{-1} E_i \right) - \widetilde{w}^- \left(\cup_{i=-m}^{-2} E_i \right)$$

As in the case under risk, since $v(y_0) = v(0) = 0$, the decision weight corresponding to the reference outcome, π_0, can be chosen arbitrarily.

The objective function of the decision maker who uses PT under uncertainty is defined next.

Definition 2.17 *(The value function): The value of the lottery $L \in \overline{\mathcal{L}}_P$ to the decision maker who follows PT is given by*

$$V(L) = \Sigma_{i=-m}^{n} \pi_i v(y_i).\tag{2.25}$$

2.4.2 Attitudes to risk under prospect theory

Under EU, $w(p) = p$, so the attitudes to risk are completely determined by the shape of the utility function. Under PT (and OPT), the utility function is concave in the domain of gains and convex in the domain of losses. From this, it might be tempting to conclude that a decision maker who uses PT is risk averse in the domain of gains and risk loving in the domain of losses. Such an inference would be incorrect. The reason is that in PT (and in most non-EU theories), attitudes to risk are determined not only by the shape of the utility function but also by the shape of the probability weighting function, $w(p)$.

Example 2.7 *Suppose that a decision maker who uses PT faces the lottery $L = (0, 1-p; y, p)$ in incremental form, where $y > 0$. Using Definition 2.12, $v(0) = 0$. Let the utility function be given by $v(y) = \sqrt{y}$ and let the weighting function be the Prelec function, $w(p) = e^{-\beta(-\ln p)^{\alpha}}$, with $\alpha = 0.5$, $\beta = 1$. Using Definition 2.15,*

$$V(L) = [1 - w(p)]\sqrt{0} + w(p)\sqrt{y} = w(p)\sqrt{y}.$$

The expected value of the lottery is $EL = py$. The certainty equivalent of the lottery, C_L, can be calculated as follows:

$$w(p)\sqrt{y} = \sqrt{C_L},$$
$$\Rightarrow C_L = yw(p)^2.$$

The decision maker is risk loving if $C_L > EL$ and risk averse if $C_L < EL$.

$$C_L \gtreqless EL \Leftrightarrow yw(p)^2 \gtreqless py \Leftrightarrow w(p)^2 \gtreqless p.\tag{2.26}$$

For the special case of EU, $w(p) = p$. Since $p \in [0,1]$, for EU, $w(p)^2 \leq p$ and so $C_L \leq E$. Thus, assuming a concave utility function under EU (in this case, $v(y) = \sqrt{y}$) is sufficient to guarantee risk aversion. However, for PT and for the Prelec function, $w(p)^2 > p$ for low p and $w(p)^2 < p$ for high p. In particular, for the parameter values chosen in this example,

$$w(p)^2 \gtreqless p \Leftrightarrow -2(-\ln p)^{0.5} - \ln p \gtreqless 0.$$

Thus, for $p^* = 0.0183$, $w(p^*)^2 = p^*$, for $p < 0.0183$, $w(p)^2 > p$ (i.e., the decision maker is risk loving despite a concave utility function), and for $p > 0.0183$, $w(p)^2 < p$ (i.e., the decision maker is risk averse).

The result in Example 2.7 is more general, and stated next.

Claim 2.1 *Suppose that a PT decision maker has the utility function in Definition 2.12, and faces the incremental form lottery $L = (0, 1-p; y, p)$, where $y > 0$. For small probabilities in the domain of gains, the decision maker is risk loving, while for higher probabilities, the decision maker is risk averse.*

We leave it to the reader to construct an analogous example in the domain of losses to support the following claim.

Claim 2.2 *Suppose that a PT decision maker has the utility function in Definition 2.12, and faces the incremental form lottery $L = (y, p; 0, 1 - p)$, where $y < 0$. The decision maker is risk averse for low probabilities and risk loving for higher probabilities.*

The next example presents some experimental evidence supporting Claims 2.1, 2.2. Put together, these claims lead to a *fourfold classification of risk attitudes* under PT, which is one of the salient contributions of PT.

Example 2.8 *(The fourfold pattern of attitudes to risk; Tversky and Kahneman, 1992): Let C, E denote the certainty equivalent and the expected value, respectively, of a lottery. Table 2.2 shows values of C, E for lotteries of the form $(x, p; 0, 1 - p)$, i.e., outcome x with probability p or 0 with probability $1 - p$ for low and high p in the domain of gains $(x > 0)$ and losses $(x < 0)$. Comparing the values of C and E, we see that for low probabilities, there is risk seeking in the domain of gains but risk aversion in the domain of losses. For moderate or high probabilities, we see risk aversion in the domain of gains but risk seeking in the domain of losses. This pattern is hard to explain under EU or RDU, but is easily explained by PT. Thus, the attitudes to risk in PT are much richer than under EU or RDU.*

In subsequent studies the fourfold pattern of risk has been tested using two kinds of methods. The first method is a *choice-based elicitation procedure* in which subjects are directly asked to choose between the lottery and its expected value. A risk averse decision maker should prefer the expected value to the lottery and a risk seeking decision maker should prefer to play the lottery. The second method is a *price-based elicitation procedure* in which subjects are asked to state their maximum willingness to pay for the lottery if all outcomes are in gains and maximum willingness to pay to avoid playing the lottery if all outcomes are in the domain of losses. Harbaugh et al. (2002) and Harbaugh et al. (2010) use this method for a particularly simple class of lotteries of the form $L = (x, p)$. They find evidence for the fourfold classification of risk in the price-based elicitation procedure but not in the choice-based task, where subjects appear to be risk neutral.

Fehr-Duda and Epper (2012) raise the following three objections about the findings in Harbaugh et al. (2010) that are more widely applicable.

1. They are skeptical about the findings of approximate risk neutrality in the choice-based tasks. They argue (p. 583) that these findings are not surprising: "Because it is so obvious that expected value equals outcome times probability, people may interpret the experiment as a test of their intelligence or numeracy rather than as a preference elicitation task." For

Table 2.2 The fourfold classification of risk attitudes under prospect theory.

Probability	Domain of Gains	Domain of loses
Low	$(100, 0.5; 0, 0.95)$	$(-100, 0.05; 0, 0.95)$
	$C = 14, E = 5$	$C = -8, E = -5$
High	$(100, 0.95, 0, 0.05)$	$(-100, 0.95; 0, 0.05)$
	$C = 78, E = 95$	$C = -84, E = -95$

instance, an experimental subject, when asked for a choice between the lottery $(50, 0.10)$ and the expected value of the lottery, 5, may choose indifference between the two options.

2. A second issue they raise about the findings from lotteries of the form $L = (x, p)$ is that one cannot separately disentangle the parameters of the probability weighting function and the utility function, unless specific functional forms are used. They conclude (p. 583) with a cautionary note for experimental economists: "Therefore, we strongly recommend using multi-outcome prospects, with more than one nonzero outcome, over a wide range of probabilities to be able to generate a sufficiently rich database."

3. Finally, the lotteries used in Harbaugh et al. (2010) deal with probabilities in the set $\{0.1, 0.4, .0.8\}$. We know from our discussion in Section 1.5 that violations of EU are more pronounced along the boundaries of the probability triangle. Indeed, in the interior of a probability triangle for, say, RDU, the indifference curves appear approximately linear. Figure 2.7 illustrates the situation for a three-outcome lottery—the horizontal axis shows the probability, p_3, of the worst outcome and the vertical axis, the probability, p_1, of the best outcome.[22] The indifference curves in the probability triangle are for RDU. In the left panel the indifference curves are drawn over the entire relevant space. The right panel shows the same indifference curves but the boundaries have been truncated; the indifference curves in the interior now appear approximately linear.

Rieger et al. (2014) compare risk attitudes in 53 countries. They calculate the relative risk premium for gains and losses. There is strong support for risk aversion in gains and risk seeking in losses. The average relative risk premium in gains is 0.70 (risk aversion) and, in losses it is -0.46 (risk seeking). Individuals in richer countries are more risk averse in gains but also more risk seeking in losses. There are also gender effects—women are more risk averse in gains but they are also more risk seeking in losses.

We also consider the evidence on the fourfold classification of risk elsewhere; see, for instance, Section 2.9.3 and Figure 2.13 for confirmatory evidence.

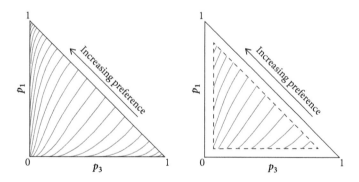

Figure 2.7 Indifference curves under RDU over the full range of probabilities (left panel) and with the boundaries truncated (right panel).

Source: Reproduced with Permission of Annual Review of Economics, Volume 4. Helga Fehr-duda and Thomas Epper, "Probability and risk: foundations and economics implications of probability-appendent risk preferences." © 2012 by Annual Reviews http://www.annualreviews.org.

---

[22] Unlike our notational convention in the rest of Volume 1, here the three outcomes are ordered as $x_3 < x_2 < x_1$.

2.4.3 A violation of EU and RDU that can be explained by PT

Recall Example 2.6 for which EU and RDU were both refuted. We now show that this example is consistent with PT because PT takes account of changes in the reference point, which EU and RDU do not.

> **Example 2.9** *(Support for PT against EU and RDU). Suppose that the decision maker has the utility function $v(y) = (y)^{0.6}$ and uses the Prelec probability weighting function $w(p) = e^{-(-\ln p)^{0.65}}$. Consider Example 2.6 that constituted a refutation of EU and RDU. Problem 11 in Example 2.6 involved the following choice*
>
> $$A = (x_0 + 1000, 0.5; x_0 + 2000, 0.5) \ versus \ B = (x_0 + 1000, 0; x_0 + 1500, 1).$$
>
> *Let us take a status-quo interpretation of reference points. Thus, for Problem 11, the reference point is the endowment point, $x_0 + 1000$ and so $y = x - (x_0 + 1000)$. Thus, the value function for each of these lotteries is given, respectively, by*
>
> $$V(A) = 1000^{0.6} e^{-(-\ln 0.5)^{0.65}} = 28.692.$$
> $$V(B) = 500^{0.6} = 41.628.$$
>
> *PT predicts that lottery B is preferred over lottery A, which is true for most subjects. Problem 12 in Example 2.6 considered the following choice,*
>
> $$C = (x_0 + 1000, 0.5; x_0 + 2000, 0.5) \ versus \ D = (x_0 + 1500, 1; x_0 + 2000, 0).$$
>
> *In this case, the reference point is $x_0 + 2000$ and so $y = x - (x_0 + 2000)$. Thus, the value function corresponding to each of these lotteries is*
>
> $$V(C) = -2.25(1000)^{0.6} e^{-(-\ln 0.5)^{0.65}} = -64.558.$$
> $$V(D) = -2.25(500)^{0.6} = -93.662.$$
>
> *PT predicts that C should be chosen over D, which is true for a majority of the subjects.*

2.4.4 Some erroneous criticisms of PT

We now consider some of the common criticisms of PT that are either misplaced or overstated.

1. *PT is only an "as if" theory*: All the mainstream decision theories that we have looked at, EU/RDU/PT, are 'as if' theories. Each of these theories involves a relatively high degree of cognitive sophistication. There is no supposition that the mental processes of decision makers mirror closely any of these theories, and the theories make no assumptions about cognitive processes. However, evidence from neuroeconomics confirms various aspects of PT, such as reference dependence, loss aversion, and non-linear probability weighting (see Volume 7 for details).

   So why does PT explain the evidence from many diverse problems so well, even if it is an "as if" theory? The answer probably lies in the individual components of PT that have strong empirical support. These components include reference dependence, loss aversion, diminished sensitivity to gains and losses, shape of the utility functions in the domain of gains and losses, and inverse S-shaped probability weighting functions. Thus, in many cases, the "as if" assumption actually turns out to be justified when one uses PT. By contrast, the empirically observed violations of EU, considered above, show that the "as if" supposition does not often hold in the case of EU.

2. *PT performs better only because it has additional parameters*: Another commonly heard criticism of PT is that "these theories have more parameters than EU and RDU, so it is 'no surprise' that they have greater explanatory power."

   Proponents of EU who make this criticism will find that EU is subjected to a similar criticism. EU has more parameters than expected value maximization (EV), so if the "no surprise" argument has any intrinsic merit, it would also apply to the better explanatory power of EU relative to EV (e.g., the St. Petersburg paradox). It is in the nature of scientific progress that one discovers new anomalies that existing theory cannot explain. One then needs to construct a new theory that explains everything that the old theory can explain, and also has the ability to explain the new anomalies. It may be unavoidable that the new theory has a larger number of parameters. The intellectual victory of EU over EV when the St. Petersburg paradox arose is a good example. A trivial example can also be used to make the same point. Suppose that one observes a scatter of points that is unmistakably quadratic. Then fitting a straight line rather than a curve through the points may be parsimonious, yet hardly satisfactory.

   The "no surprise" argument would have intellectual merit if the new theory explains less than the old theory particularly out-of-sample, is intractable, and lacks parsimony. This is not the case with PT. PT is elegant, tractable, based on robust psychological foundations, and relatively parsimonious. It explains everything that EU and RDU can explain; the converse is false.

   A theory with more parameters may explain better the in-sample data but not necessarily the out-of-sample data. Indeed, one can use statistical tests that allow us to trade off greater explanatory power against the larger number of parameters (e.g., the Akaike information criterion and the Bayesian information criterion). This methodology is routinely used to test alternative models of learning (see Volume 6). PT does not predict better than the alternative theories, just because it has a larger number of parameters (Abdellaoui, 2000; Dhami, 2016, pp. 30–1).

   One can separately elicit the parameters of the utility and the weighting functions, parametrically or non-parametrically, under PT; Section 2.5 is devoted to this endeavor. The results strongly support the functional forms under PT. Mixture models that allow for the presence of both EU and PT decision makers find that the vast majority of subjects (80% in the study of Bruhin et al. (2010) reviewed in Section 2.9.4) follow PT. On these grounds, EU is simply a mis-specified theory for most decision makers and the extra parameters under PT are supported by the empirical evidence.

3. *PT has an arbitrary reference point, which makes it vacuous*: Not only is it difficult to specify a universal reference point, it might not be desirable to do so.

   (a) PT is not unique among mainstream theories in not being able to strictly specify all components. For instance, Bayesian statistics does not specify a prior distribution but teaches us a method of updating a prior to a posterior distribution. This inability to specify a prior is not taken as a fatal shortcoming. Another example is that the predictions of neoclassical theory are often very sparse unless one is willing to specify explicitly, preferences and technology. A good example is general equilibrium theory; see, for instance, section 17.E in Mas-Collel et al. (1995) titled "Anything goes...." Indeed, the real bite in the predictions from many neoclassical models comes from actually specifying preferences and technology. This is hardly considered to be fatal for neoclassical economics.

(b) What if human behavior is actually "sufficiently rich" in terms of the reference point? "Sufficiently rich" does not imply infinitely rich or random. Indeed, many candidates for a reference point seem very salient across many problems and contexts. Of these, the *status quo* or a fair/just entitlement (even if the fairness is subjective) is one of the most salient. In actual applications, this is often able to guide the researcher to a suitable reference point.

In many contexts, a natural reference point arises on closer examination. For instance, in their explanation of the tax evasion puzzles (see Section 3.5 below), Dhami and al-Nowaihi (2007, 2010b) assume the "legal after-tax liabilities" to be the reference point for a potential tax evader; this has the flavor of a status-quo point. Their calibrated results, based on this suggestion match closely the data from the problem.

(c) There has been progress in endogenous specifications of the reference point; see, for instance, the discussion in Section 2.8 on the Köszegi–Rabin framework. In this framework, the reference point is determined within the model, in a manner that is consistent with rational expectations. The advantage is that this framework is not subject to the potential criticism of an arbitrary reference point. The disadvantage is that the required cognitive sophistication of the decision makers is very high.

A more serious criticism of PT comes from the evidence on human behavior for events of very low and very high probabilities. This is dealt with in Section 2.11.3 below. Indeed, newer theories that are able to handle events of very low and very high probabilities, such as *composite prospect theory* (see Section 2.11.3), rely heavily on the insights of PT because PT captures fundamentally important insights about human behavior. Other serious criticisms are discussed in Section 2.9. These have to do with the evidence from configural weights models, violations of gain–loss separability, the absence of "regret" in PT, and the interaction between probability weights and stake size.

2.5 Elicitation of utility and probability weighting functions in PT

In this section, we briefly consider some of the methods of elicitation under PT as well as some of the parameter estimates in the literature; for a more detailed discussion, see Wakker (2010).

2.5.1 *Elicitation of the utility function under PT*

In order to elicit the utility function under PT, let us suppose that the reference point is zero and proceed in the four steps suggested in Abdellaoui et al. (2007).

I. Determining probabilities p_l, p_g : $w^-(p_l) = \frac{1}{2}$ and $w^+(p_g) = \frac{1}{2}$, where w^- and w^+ are, respectively, probability weighting functions in the domain of losses and gains.

Suppose that, relative to the reference point, we are given (i) three outcomes in the loss domain, $l_0 < l < l^*$, and (ii) some level of probability p. Now we elicit two levels of outcomes in the loss domain, l_1 and l_2, such that $l_2 < l_1 < l_0 < l < l^*$. We first find the utility midpoints using the method of Abdellaoui (2000) and Köbberling and Wakker (2003).

Suppose that the following indifferences hold

$$\left(l_1, p; l^*, 1-p\right) \sim \left(l_0, p; l, 1-p\right). \tag{2.27}$$

$$\left(l_2, p; l^*, 1-p\right) \sim \left(l_1, p; l, 1-p\right). \tag{2.28}$$

Under PT, for $i = 0, 1$, $\left(l_{i+1}, p; l^*, 1-p\right) \sim \left(l_i, p; l, 1-p\right)$ implies that

$$w^-(p)v(l_{i+1}) + \left(1 - w^-(p)\right)v\left(l^*\right) = w^-(p)v(l_i) + \left(1 - w^-(p)\right)v(l), \tag{2.29}$$

where v is the utility function under PT. Rewriting (2.29),

$$v(l_i) - v(l_{i+1}) = \frac{\left(1 - w^-(p)\right)}{w^-(p)}\left(v\left(l^*\right) - v(l)\right). \tag{2.30}$$

The right hand side is independent of the indices, i, $i+1$, thus, for $i = 0, 1$, and using (2.27), (2.28), we have

$$v(l_0) - v(l_1) = v(l_1) - v(l_2). \tag{2.31}$$

Thus,

$$v(l_1) = \frac{1}{2}[v(l_0) + v(l_2)], \tag{2.32}$$

is the utility midpoint of $v(l_0)$ and $v(l_2)$. Once the values l_1 and l_2 are elicited, then we find the probability p_l such that $(l_1, 1) \sim (l_2, p_l; l_0, 1 - p_l)$. This indifference implies that

$$v(l_1) = w^-(p_l)v(l_2) + \left(1 - w^-(p_l)\right)v(l_0). \tag{2.33}$$

Substituting (2.32) into (2.33) we get the required value

$$w^-(p_l) = \frac{1}{2}. \tag{2.34}$$

We now proceed to the domain of gains. We begin with a probability p and three outcomes in the domain of gains $g_0 > g > g^*$. Now we elicit two levels of gains g_1 and g_2 such that $g_2 > g_1 > g_0 > g > g^*$. Suppose that the following indifferences hold

$$\left(g^*, 1-p; g_1, p\right) \sim \left(g, 1-p; g_0, p\right). \tag{2.35}$$

$$\left(g^*, 1-p; g_2, p\right) \sim \left(g, 1-p; g_1, p\right). \tag{2.36}$$

Having elicited g_1 and g_2 we can now proceed analogously to the domain of losses to find a probability p_g such that

$$w^+(p_g) = \frac{1}{2}. \tag{2.37}$$

II. Eliciting utility in the loss domain.

Pick an outcome y_l in the domain of losses and normalize $v(y_l) = -1$. We now elicit the outcome $l_{0.5}$ in the domain of losses such that $(l_{0.5}, 1) \sim (y_l, p_l; 0, 1 - p_l)$, where p_l is found in (2.34). Under PT, this indifference implies that

$$v(l_{0.5}) = w^-(p_l)v(y_l).$$

Substituting (2.34) and $v(y_l) = -1$ we get

$$v(l_{0.5}) = -\frac{1}{2}.$$

We can now proceed to elicit the utility function in the interval $[y_l, 0]$. For instance, elicit an outcome $l_{0.25}$ such that $(l_{0.25}, 1) \sim (l_{0.5}, p_l; 0, 1 - p_l)$. This indifference implies that

$$v(l_{0.25}) = w^-(p_l)v(l_{0.5}) = -\frac{1}{4}.$$

Similarly we can find $l_{0.125}$ such that $(l_{0.125}, 1) \sim (l_{0.25}, p_l; 0, 1 - p_l)$, so $v(l_{0.125}) = w^-(p_l)v(l_{0.25}) = -\frac{1}{8}$, and so on.

III. Linking utility in the loss domain with utility in the gain domain.

We now relate utility in the loss domain from Step II with utility in the gain domain. This is an important step in the framework of Abdellaoui et al. (2007), which allows for the measurement of loss aversion.[23] We consider three indifferences.

(a) Consider one of the elicited outcomes in the interval $[y_l, 0]$ in Step II, say, l_s with the corresponding utility function $v(l_s) = -s$ (e.g., $v(l_{0.25}) = -0.25$). We now find an outcome l in the loss domain such that $(l_s, 1) \sim (l, 0.5; 0, 0.5)$. This implies that $v(l_s) = w^-(0.5)v(l)$, so

$$-s = w^-(0.5)v(l). \tag{2.38}$$

(b) Now elicit an outcome in the domain of gains, g, such that $(0, 1) \sim (l, 0.5; g, 0.5)$. This implies that $0 = w^-(0.5)v(l) + w^+(0.5)v(g)$. Using (2.38) we get

$$w^+(0.5)v(g) = s. \tag{2.39}$$

(c) Elicit the outcome g_s in the domain of gains so that $(g_s, 1) \sim (g, 0.5; 0, 0.5)$. This implies that $v(g_s) = w^+(0.5)v(g)$. Using (2.39), we get that $v(g_s) = s$. Thus, in terms of utility, the outcome g_s in the domain of gains is the mirror image of the outcome l_s in the domain of loss.

IV. Eliciting utility in the gain domain.

We now determine utility in the gain domain in the interval $[0, g_s]$, where g_s was determined in Step III. We elicit $g_{0.5} \in [0, g_s]$ such that $(g_{0.5}, 1) \sim (0, 1 - p_g; g_s, p_g)$. This gives rise to the condition $v(g_{0.5}) = w^+(p_g)v(g_s)$. Using (2.37) and $v(g_s) = s$ we get $v(g_{0.5}) = \frac{s}{2}$. Proceeding in an analogous manner, we can generate utility in the gains domain for other values in the interval $[0, g_s]$ such as $g_{0.25}, g_{0.125}$.

---

[23] In the trade-off method of Wakker and Deneffe (1996), one cannot measure simultaneously the utility in the domain of gains and losses, thus making it difficult to measure loss aversion.

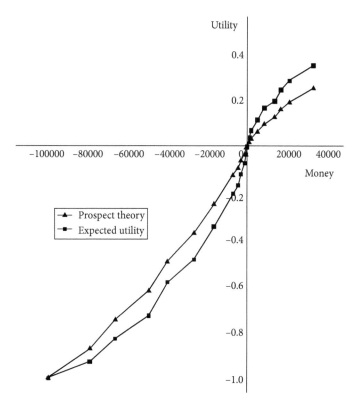

Figure 2.8 Non-parametric estimates of utility for gains and losses under PT and EU based on median data. Source: Abdellaoui et al. (2007). Reproduced with permission. © INFORMS http://www.informs.org.

Figure 2.8 shows a non-parametric utility function fitted to the data from Abdellaoui et al. (2007) for EU and for PT. The non-parametric curve is concave in gains and convex in losses.[24] The degree of concavity and convexity is more pronounced relative to several other studies.[25] At the individual level, the most common pattern was an S-shaped utility function. Only one individual out of 48 behaved in a manner consistent with the typical assumption in EU of a concave utility function throughout. Similar results are obtained by Abdellaoui et al. (2013) when they elicit the preferences of private bankers and fund managers. This serves to contribute towards the external validity of lab experiments in such domains.

Figure 2.9 fits the power form of utility in (2.19) to the same data. The coefficient γ in the domain of gains is 0.75 and in the domain of loss it is 0.74. The curve has an extremely good fit and most points lie very close to the fitted curve.

One disadvantage of non-parametric estimation is that there might be substantial error propagation. Further, the procedure is not very efficient in the sense that too many iterations are

---

[24] The finding of risk seeking behavior in the domain of losses does not allow us to conclude that the utility function is convex. This is because risk seeking in the domain of losses might also arise due to the shape of the probability weighting function; see Section 2.4.2 and Abdellaoui et al. (2007).

[25] For instance, Tverksy and Kahneman (1992), Fennema and van Assen (1998), Abdellaoui (2000), and Schunk and Betsch (2006).

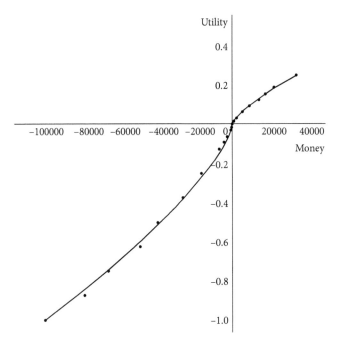

Figure 2.9 Parametric estimates of the power form of utility for gains and losses under PT based on median data.

Source: Abdellaoui et al. (2007). Reproduced with permission. © INFORMS http://www.informs.org.

needed, imposing greater cognitive requirements on the subjects. In response to these concerns, Abdellaoui et al. (2008) propose a parametric estimation method with the power form of utility. They confirm all the individual features of prospect theory: Concavity of utility in the domain of gains, convexity in the domain of losses, loss aversion, and inverse S-shaped probability weighting.

2.5.2 *Elicitation of loss aversion under PT*

There are many different definitions of loss aversion.[26] These definitions typically rely on the utility function and not on the probability weighting function. Hence, the elicitation of the utility function in Section 2.5.1 sets the stage for the elicitation of loss aversion.

The original definition of loss aversion, due to Kahneman and Tversky (1979), is given in Definition 2.12, i.e.,

$$\frac{-v\left(-y\right)}{v(y)} > 1; y > 0.$$

When the utility function takes the power form in (2.19), loss aversion is simply

$$\lambda = \frac{-v(-1)}{v(1)}.$$

---

[26] For some work on the behavioral foundations of loss aversion, see Peters (2012).

Köbberling and Wakker (2005) consider the implications of an alternative definition of loss aversion. In this definition, suggested originally but informally by Benartzi and Thaler (1995), for a general utility function v,

$$\lambda = \frac{v'_\uparrow(0)}{v'_\downarrow(0)},\tag{2.40}$$

where $v'_\uparrow(0)$ and $v'_\downarrow(0)$ are, respectively, the left hand side and the right hand side limits around 0.

The Wakker and Tversky (1993) definition of loss aversion requires a greater slope of the utility function at any loss outcome relative to the slope at the absolute value of the loss, i.e.,

$$v'\left(-y\right) > v'\left(y\right), \forall y > 0.$$

Neilson (2002) proposed the following requirement for a loss averse decision maker

$$\frac{v(-x)}{-x} \geq \frac{v\left(y\right)}{y}, x > 0, y > 0.$$

Once the utility function has been estimated using the technique in Section 2.5.1, then any of these definitions can be applied to estimate loss aversion.

There are also some definitions of loss aversion that rely on the probability weighting function.

> **Definition 2.18**   *(Kahneman and Tversky, 1979): Let $\prec$ be a binary preference relation over lotteries. An individual is loss averse if $\left(y, 0.5; -y, 0.5\right) \prec (z, 0.5; -z, 0.5)$ where $y > z \geq 0$.*

In OPT, Kahneman and Tversky (1979) defined loss aversion as the tendency of people to reject symmetric 50–50 bets (set $z = 0$ in Definition 2.18). Schmidt and Zank (2005) extend Definition 2.18 to the concept of *strong loss aversion*. As one might expect from Definition 2.18, in a comparison of the lotteries $\left(y, 0.5; -y, 0.5\right)$ and $(z, 0.5; -z, 0.5)$ under prospect theory, the weighting function plays a critical role. Thus, loss aversion, in this definition, involves a condition between changes in utility and the magnitude of probability weights.

Abdellaoui et al. (2007) summarize some of the estimates of loss aversion, based on aggregate data from previous studies; see Table 2.3. The estimates from separate studies are sometimes not comparable because some report median values, while others report mean values.[27] Based on this small set of results, the Tversky and Kahneman (1992) estimate of 2.25 is quite representative. The estimates in Table 2.3 are for aggregate data. Abdellaoui et al. (2007) also report their own estimates from individual data, based on various definitions of loss aversion.[28] Using the Kahneman and Tversky (1979) definition, they detect the presence of loss aversion at the aggregate and the individual level; 39 out of 47 subjects are loss averse. Using the Wakker and Tversky (1993) definition, 30 out of 36 are loss averse. In the Köbberling and Wakker (2005) definition, 35 out of 47 subjects are loss averse. The mean estimates of loss aversion for these three studies are, respectively, 2.04, 1.71, and 8.27.

---

[27]   In Table 2.3, median values are reported by Fishburn and Kochenberger (1979), Tversky and Kahneman (1992), and Bleichrodt et al. (2001).

[28]   Estimates of loss aversion at the individual level are also provided in Bleichrodt and Pinto (2002) and Schmidt and Traub (2002) although these studies find a lower proportion of loss averse subjects.

Table 2.3 Estimates of loss aversion in various studies. The two estimates in Bleichrodt et al. (2001) are based on two different datasets. The two estimates in Booij and van de Kuilen (2009) are based on high and low monetary amounts.

Study	Definition of loss aversion	Estimate
Fishburn and Kochenberger (1979)	$\frac{v'(-y)}{v'(y)}$	4.8
Tversky and Kahneman (1992)	$\frac{-v(-1)}{v(1)}$	2.25
Bleichrodt et al. (2001)	$\frac{v(-y)}{v(y)}$	2.17, 3.06
Schmidt and Traub (2002)	$\frac{v'(-y)}{v'(y)}$	1.43
Pennings and Smidts (2003)	$\frac{v'(-y)}{v'(y)}$	1.81
Booij and van de Kuilen (2009)	$\frac{v'_{\uparrow}(-y)}{v'_{\downarrow}(y)}$	1.79, 1.74

Source: Abdellaoui et al. (2007).

A large number of estimates of loss aversion have come from studies that examine exchange disparities. We consider these estimates separately in Section 3.2.1. Section 3.4 considers the concept of *myopic loss aversion.*

2.5.3 *Elicitation of the probability weighting function under PT*

One can either estimate the probability weighting function parametrically or non-parametrically. Table 2.4 shows some parameter estimates reported in Bleichrodt and Pinto (2000) for three main probability weighting functions.

For several reasons, one might be interested in non-parametric estimation of the probability weighting function. Consider the trade-off method proposed by Wakker and Deneffe (1996). Suppose that we begin with three outcomes in the domain of gains, $R > r > x_0$ such that $(R, 1) \succeq (x_0, 1)$. The outcome x_1 is then elicited such that

$$\left(x_0, 1 - p; R, p\right) \sim \left(x_1, 1 - p; r, p\right). \tag{2.41}$$

Under PT, the indifference in (2.41) implies that

$$\left(1 - w(p)\right) v(x_0) + w(p)v(R) = \left(1 - w(p)\right) v(x_1) + w(p)v(r). \tag{2.42}$$

Now the outcome x_2 is elicited such that

$$\left(x_1, 1 - p; R, p\right) \sim \left(x_2, 1 - p; r, p\right)$$

which implies that

$$\left(1 - w(p)\right) v(x_1) + w(p)v(R) = \left(1 - w(p)\right) v(x_2) + w(p)v(r). \tag{2.43}$$

From (2.42) and (2.43)

$$\left(1 - w(p)\right) \left(v(x_2) - v(x_1)\right) = w(p) \left(v(R) - v(r)\right). \tag{2.44}$$

Table 2.4 Estimates of the parameters of various probability weighting functions.

Probability weighting function	Parameter estimates
Tversky–Kahneman (1992) $$w(p) = \frac{p^\tau}{[p^\tau + (1-p)^\tau]^{\frac{1}{\tau}}}$$	Tversky–Kahneman (1992): $\tau = 0.61$ (gains), $\tau = 0.69$ (losses) Camerer and Ho (1994): $\tau = 0.56$ (gains) Wu and Gonzalez (1996): $\tau = 0.71$ (gains) Abdellaoui (2000): $\tau = 0.60$ (*gains*), $\tau = 0.70$ (losses)
Goldstein–Einhorn (1987) $$w(p) = \frac{\delta p^\eta}{\delta p^\eta + (1-p)^\eta}$$	Wu and Gonzalez (1996): $\delta = 0.84$, $\eta = 0.68$ (gains) Gonzalez and Wu (1999): $\delta = 0.77$, $\eta = 0.44$ (gains) Tversky and Fox (1995): $\delta = 0.77$, $\eta = 0.69$ (gains) Abdellaoui (2000): $\delta = 0.65$, $\eta = 0.60$ (gains) Abdellaoui (2000): $\delta = 0.84$, $\eta = 0.65$ (losses)
Prelec (1998) $$w(p) = e^{-(-1np)^\alpha}$$	Wu and Gonzalez (1996): $\alpha = 0.74$ (gains)

Source: Bleichrodt and Pinto (2000).

Notice that the RHS of (2.44) is independent of x_1 and x_2. One can now continue these iterations of indifferences. For instance, the next stage would be to find an x_3 such that $(x_2, 1 - p; R, p) \sim (x_3, 1 - p; r, p)$. In general, for any x_i and x_{i-1}, the analogue of (2.44) is

$$(1 - w(p))(v(x_i) - v(x_{i-1})) = w(p)(v(R) - v(r)). \qquad (2.45)$$

Since the RHS is independent of x_i and x_{i-1}, iterating the process k times, we get

$$v(x_1) - v(x_0) = v(x_2) - v(x_1) = v(x_3) - v(x_2) = \ldots = v(x_k) - v(x_{k-1}). \qquad (2.46)$$

Normalize $v(x_0) = 0$ and $v(x_k) = 1$. From the first equality in (2.46), we get $v(x_1) = \frac{1}{2}v(x_2)$. From the second equality, we get $v(x_2) = \frac{2}{3}v(x_3)$. In general, for the jth equality, we get $v(x_j) = \frac{j}{j+1}v(x_{j+1})$, and from the last equality, we get $v(x_{k-1}) = \frac{k-1}{k}v(x_k) = \frac{k-1}{k}$. Rolling back the iterations, we get $v(x_{k-2}) = \frac{k-2}{k-1}v(x_{k-1}) = \frac{k-2}{k-1}\frac{k-1}{k} = \frac{k-2}{k}$. This establishes the pattern of recursion, so that we have

$$v(x_j) = \frac{j}{k}, j = 1, 2, \ldots, k. \qquad (2.47)$$

Once we obtain the utility function in this manner (or in the manner suggested in Section 2.5.1), we can follow Abdellaoui (2000). Choose any $x_j \in \{x_0, x_1, \ldots, x_k\}$ (these are the first stage elicited values), and then elicit the probability q such that

$$(x_0, 1 - q; x_k, q) \sim (x_j, 1),$$

which, under PT, implies that

$$(1 - w(q))v(x_0) + w(q)v(x_k) = v(x_j).$$

Using $v(x_k) = 1$, $v(x_0) = 0$, and $v(x_j) = j/k$, we get

$$w(q) = \frac{j}{k}.$$

Now we select another element from $\{x_0, x_1, \ldots, x_k\}$ and repeat the procedure to get the probability weight associated with another probability value and so on for each point in $\{x_0, x_1, \ldots, x_k\}$. Bleichrodt and Pinto (2000) apply this procedure to health outcomes (rather than monetary prizes). They find strong evidence of an inverse S-shaped probability weighting function at the individual and the aggregate levels. As to the shapes of the weighting function at the individual level, they find that 10.9% of the subjects had a concave weighting function, 0% had a linear weighting function, 4.4% had a convex weighting function, and 83.7% had an inverse S-shaped weighting function.

2.6 The axiomatic foundations of PT

We briefly consider the preference foundations of various elements of PT in this section. The interested reader can consult Wakker (2010) for a comprehensive treatment. Since the Prelec (1998) probability weighting function (see Definition 2.4) and the power form of utility (see Equation 2.19) are used extensively, the reader is specifically given a flavor of their preference foundations.

2.6.1 *Foundations of PT in terms of the trade-off consistency method*

In this section we consider the preference foundations of PT based on the *trade-off consistency method* (Chateauneuf and Wakker, 1999; Köbberling and Wakker, 2003).[29] This method gives the preference foundations for EU, RDU, and PT under *risk* as well as under *uncertainty*. Our presentation here is based on Chateauneuf and Wakker (1999).[30]

For pedagogical simplicity, let $X = \mathbb{R}$ be the set of monetary outcomes.[31] The reference point is normalized to 0. A typical prospect is given by $L = (y_1, p_1; y_2, p_2; \ldots; y_n, p_n)$ (see Definition 2.11, with $x_0 = 0$), where $y_1 < y_2 < \ldots < y_n$ are outcomes in X and $p_1, p_2, \ldots, p_n$ are probabilities such that $p_i \geq 0$ and $\sum_i p_i = 1$. Let $\mathcal{L}_P$ be the set of all such prospects.

Let $\succeq$ be a preference relation over $\mathcal{L}_P$ and let $\succ$ and $\sim$ be the strict preference and indifference relations. Sure outcomes y_i are equivalent to the prospect $(y_i, 1)$. An outcome $y_i > 0$ is a gain,

---

[29] On the penultimate line of the second paragraph on p. 94 of his book, Wakker (2010) credits Pfanzagl (1968, Remark 9.4.5) with the recommendation of the trade-off tool. The interested reader can consult Wakker (2010) for a detailed statement of the relevant theorems and the references. For the preference foundations of PT in the continuous case, see Kothiyal et al. (2011).

[30] For other axiomatizations of prospect theory, see Tversky and Kahneman (1992), Wakker and Tversky (1993), Chateauneuf and Wakker (1999), Zank (2001), Wakker and Zank (2002), Köbberling and Wakker (2003), Schmidt (2003), Schmidt and Zank (2007, 2008). All these axiomatizations assumed an exogenous reference point. For axiomatizations of the rank dependent model, see Quiggin (1981, 1982), Yaari (1987), Schmeidler (1989), Luce (1991), Luce and Fishburn (1991), Abdellaoui (2002), and Luce and Marley (2005). For axiomatic extensions of the RDU model see Green and Jullien (1988), Chew and Epstein (1989a), and Segal (1989, 1993). These sets of papers provide links between EU and RDU as well as showing the connection between RDU and the betweenness axiom.

[31] The framework can be extended to more general spaces that do not restrict attention to monetary outcomes and higher dimensional spaces such as $\mathbb{R}^m$ where elements of X are m dimensional bundles of goods, etc.

while $y_i < 0$ is a loss. Since we have assumed that X is the set of monetary outcomes and the reference point is 0, $\succeq$ corresponds in a natural way with $\geq$.

If $\succeq$ is a *weak order* (i.e., complete and transitive), then we can find a preference representation such that for any two prospects $L_1, L_2 \in \mathcal{L}_P$ we have $L_1 \succeq L_2 \Leftrightarrow V(L_1) \geq V(L_2)$. Let $x = (x_1, x_2, \ldots, x_n) \in X^n$ and fix the prospect $L_1 = (y_1, p_1; \ldots; y_n, p_n)$. Preferences $\succeq$ are *continuous* if for all $x \in X^n$ and fixed probabilities $p_1, p_2, \ldots, p_n$, the following two sets are closed

$$\{x : (x_1, p_1; \ldots; x_n, p_n) \succeq L_1\}, \ \{x : (x_1, p_1; \ldots; x_n, p_n) \preceq L_1\}.$$

Let $L_1 = (y_1, p_1; \ldots; y_n, p_n)$ and $L_2 = (x_1, p_1; \ldots; x_n, p_n)$. Then, $\succeq$ satisfies *stochastic dominance* if $x_i \succeq y_i$ for $i = 1, 2, \ldots, n$ implies $L_2 \succeq L_1$ and if, in addition, $x_i \succ y_i$ for at least one i we have $L_2 \succ L_1$ (see Definition 1.9 and note that $x_i \succeq y_i \Leftrightarrow x_i \geq y_i$).

Suppose that we are given an arbitrary prospect $L = (y_1, p_1; \ldots; y_n, p_n)$. Then, we define a new prospect $\alpha_j L$ which replaces the jth outcome in L, y_j, by α_j, i.e.,

$$\alpha_j L = (y_1, p_1; \ldots; y_{j-1}, p_{j-1}; \alpha_j, p_j; y_{j+1}, p_{j+1}; \ldots; y_n, p_n); y_{j-1} < \alpha_j < y_{j+1}.$$

Definition 2.19 *Let there be four outcomes (all in gains or all on losses) a, b, c, d. Consider the preference relation $\succ^*$ such that $ab \succ^* cd$ (also written as $[a; b] \succ^* [c; d]$) if there exist prospects $L_1 = (y_1, p_1; y_2, p_2; \ldots; y_n, p_n), L_2 = (x_1, p_1; x_2, p_2; \ldots; x_n, p_n)$ (with identical probabilities) and an index $j = 1, \ldots, n$, such that*

$$a_j L_1 \succeq b_j L_2 \ \text{and} \ c_j L_1 \prec d_j L_2.$$

Example 2.10 *Suppose that $L_1 = (80, 0.3; y_2, 0.7)$ and $L_2 = (90, 0.3; x_2, 0.7)$. Then, using Definition 2.19, $[1; 0] \succ^* [9; 8]$ if*

$$(80, 0.3; 1, 0.7) \succeq (90, 0.3; 0, 0.7) \ \text{and} \ (80, 0.3; 9, 0.7) \prec (90, 0.3; 8, 0.7).$$

Recall that v is the utility function under PT (Definition 2.12). The next lemma illustrates the usefulness of the preference relation $\succ^*$ for utility differences.

Lemma 2.1 *Suppose that the decision maker follows PT. Then*

$$[a; b] \succ^* [c; d] \Rightarrow v(a) - v(b) > v(c) - v(d).$$

Proof: Let $L_1 = (y_1, p_1; \ldots; y_n, p_n)$ and $L_2 = (x_1, p_1; \ldots; x_n, p_n)$. Given Definition 2.19, the decision weights in the prospects $(a_j L_1, b_j L_2)$ and $(c_j L_1, d_j L_2)$ only differ at the jth place; denote this decision weight by π_j. Then $a_j L_1 \succeq b_j L_2 \Leftrightarrow V(a_j L_1) \geq V(b_j L_2)$ or (using Definition 2.15)

$$\pi_j(v(a) - v(b)) \geq \Sigma_{i \neq j} \pi_i v(x_i) - \Sigma_{i \neq j} \pi_i v(y_i). \tag{2.48}$$

Analogously $c_j L_1 \prec d_j L_2$ implies that

$$\pi_j(v(c) - v(d)) < \Sigma_{i \neq j} \pi_i v(x_i) - \Sigma_{i \neq j} \pi_i v(y_i). \tag{2.49}$$

Using (2.48), (2.49) we get

$$v(a) - v(b) > v(c) - v(d). \ \blacksquare$$

In the elicitation of the utility function under PT, see (2.47), notice that the elicited utility differences are constant. This is an implication of Lemma 2.1. To see this, the procedure elicits values $x_0, x_1, x_2, \ldots$ such that $[x_{j+1}; x_j] \sim^* [x_1; x_0]$ so $[x_{j+1}; x_j] \succeq^* [x_1; x_0]$ and $[x_{j+1}; x_j] \preceq^* [x_1; x_0]$, which implies, from Lemma 2.1, that $v(x_{j+1}) - v(x_j) = v(x_1) - v(x_0)$, as claimed.

In order to ensure that this elicitation process does not run into contradictions, we impose the next condition.

> **Definition 2.20** *(Trade-off consistency[32]): Under trade-off consistency there cannot exist outcomes a, b, c, d such that $[a; b] \succ^* [c; d]$ and $[c; d] \succeq^* [a; b]$.*

The main result is given in the next proposition.

> **Proposition 2.8** *(Chateauneuf and Wakker, 1999): Assuming trade-off consistency, the following two statements are equivalent.*
>
> *(i) Cumulative prospect theory holds with a continuous utility function.*
> *(ii) The preference relation $\succeq$ satisfies the following conditions.*
>
> > *(a) Weak ordering.*
> > *(b) Continuity.*
> > *(c) Stochastic dominance.*
> > *(d) Trade-off consistency.*

For an extension of this framework under risk to issues of uncertainty, a richer set of results, and a discussion of the related literature, see Köbberling and Wakker (2003), and Wakker (2010). The existing axiomatizations listed above, presuppose a reference point. Schmidt and Zank (2012) propose an alternative set of axioms to get a PT representation that does not impose a reference point. They rely on the idea of diminishing sensitivity around a reference point to endogenously identify a reference point.

2.6.2 Foundations of the Prelec weighting function

Under EU, one can use the reduction axiom to reduce compound lotteries to simple lotteries by using the product rule of probabilities. Under non-linear probability weighting, this method no longer works and we need something to replace the product rule of probabilities. Alternative preference foundations of the Prelec function propose different forms of the product rule.

Let X be the set of *outcomes*. Since outcomes are monetary losses or gains in all our applications, we may take X to be the set of real numbers, $\mathbb{R}$.[33] We assume that the preferences of the decision maker are described by a real-valued function $u : X \to \mathbb{R}$; $y \in X$ being preferred to $x \in X$ if, and only if, $u(y) \geq u(x)$. Three axiomatizations of the Prelec (1998) probability weighting function (see Definition 2.4) have been proposed. These are by Prelec (1998), Luce (2001), and al-Nowaihi and Dhami (2006). The main results are stated below to give readers a flavor of the literature.

---

[32] This condition is referred to as sign-comonotonic trade-off consistency in Wakker and Tversky (1993).

[33] If outcomes are bundles of goods, then X can be taken to be a subset of $\mathbf{R}^n$. For more complex outcomes, X can be taken to be an appropriate topological vector space.

We shall find it convenient to use the following notation: $(x;p_1,p_2)$ is the lottery (x,p_1) received with probability p_2. It is straightforward to extend this notation, iteratively, to $(x;p_1,p_2,p_3)$.

> **Definition 2.21** *(Reduction invariance; Luce, 2001): The probability weighting function, w, satisfies reduction invariance if, for all $x \in X$, $p_1,p_2,q \in [0,1]$, $\lambda > 0$, $(x;p_1,p_2) \sim (x;q) \Rightarrow (x;p_1^\lambda,p_2^\lambda) \sim (x;q^\lambda)$.*

> **Theorem 2.1** *(Luce, 2001): The probability weighting function, w, satisfies reduction invariance if, and only if, it is the Prelec function.*

> **Definition 2.22** *(Power invariance, al-Nowaihi and Dhami, 2006): The probability weighting function w satisfies power invariance if, for all $x \in X$, $p,q \in [0,1]$, $\lambda > 0$, $(x;p,p) \sim (x;q) \Rightarrow (x;p^\lambda,p^\lambda) \sim (x;q^\lambda)$ and $(x;p,p,p) \sim (x;q) \Rightarrow (x;p^\lambda,p^\lambda,p^\lambda) \sim (x;q^\lambda)$.*

Comparing Definitions 2.21 and 2.22, we see that *power invariance* is simpler in that it requires two probabilities (p,q) instead of three (p_1,p_2,q). On the other hand, *power invariance* requires two stages of compounding, instead of the single stage of *reduction invariance*. By contrast, *compound invariance* of Prelec (1998) involves no compounding but four probabilities and four outcomes.[34] We thus have a menu of testing options.

> **Theorem 2.2** *(al-Nowaihi and Dhami, 2006): The probability weighting function, w, satisfies power invariance if, and only if, it is the Prelec function.*

> **Corollary 2.2** *(al-Nowaihi and Dhami, 2006): Power invariance is equivalent to reduction invariance of Luce (2001) and compound invariance of Prelec (1998).*

2.6.3 Foundations of the power form of utility

Recall the power form of utility given in (2.19). We now discuss the preference foundations of this utility function due to al-Nowaihi et al. (2008).

Let $(x;p)$ stand for the *simple lottery* that pays $x \in \mathbb{R}$ with probability $p \in [0,1]$ and 0 otherwise. Let us use slightly different notation for lotteries in incremental form (Definition 2.11). Let

$$(\mathbf{x};\mathbf{p}) = (x_{-m}, x_{-m+1},\ldots,x_0, x_1,\ldots,x_n; p_{-m}, p_{-m+1},\ldots,p_0, p_1,\ldots,p_n)$$

stand for the lottery that pays $x_i \in \mathbb{R}$ with probability $p_i \in [0,1]$, where $\sum_{i=-m}^{n} p_i = 1$ and $x_{-m} \leq x_{-m+1} \leq \ldots \leq x_{-1} \leq x_0 = 0 \leq x_1 \leq x_2 \leq \ldots \leq x_n$. If $\mathbf{x} = (x_1,x_2,\ldots,x_n)$, then $-\mathbf{x} = (-x_1,-x_2,\ldots,-x_n)$ and $\mathbf{x}^r = (x_n,x_{n-1},\ldots,x_1)$. Thus $(-\mathbf{x}^r;\mathbf{p}^r)$ stands for the lottery that pays $-x_i$ with probability p_i. If each $x_i \geq 0$ and, for some i, $p_i x_i > 0$, then we call $(\mathbf{x};\mathbf{p})$ a *positive lottery*. For instance, if $(\mathbf{x};\mathbf{p}) = (-7,0,4;0.2,0.5,0.3)$, then $(-\mathbf{x};\mathbf{p}) = (7,0,-4;0.2,0.5,0.3)$ and $(-\mathbf{x}^r;\mathbf{p}) = (-4,0,7;0.3,0.5,0.2)$.

> **Definition 2.23** *(Tversky and Kahneman, 1992): The decision maker exhibits preference homogeneity if for all lotteries $(\mathbf{x};\mathbf{p})$, if c is the certainty equivalent of $(\mathbf{x};\mathbf{p})$, then, for all $k \in \mathbb{R}_+$, kc is the certainty equivalent of $(k\mathbf{x};\mathbf{p})$.*

---

[34] *Compound invariance* of Prelec (1998) is as follows. For all outcomes $x, y, x', y' \in X$, probabilities $p, q, r, s \in [0,1]$ and compounding integers $n \geq 1$: If $(x,p) \sim (y,q)$ and $(x,r) \sim (y,s)$; then $(x',p^n) \sim (y',q^n)$ implies $(x',r^n) \sim (y',s^n)$.

Definition 2.24 below, is an attempt to extend Tversky and Kahneman's (1992) concept of loss aversion to more general lotteries.

Definition 2.24 *Loss aversion holds for positive lotteries if, for some $\lambda > 1$, $\frac{|V(-\mathbf{x}^r; \mathbf{p}^r)|}{V(\mathbf{x}; \mathbf{p})} = \lambda$, for all positive lotteries, where V is the value function in prospect theory, given in (2.23). We call λ the coefficient of loss aversion.*

In the extreme case, where all outcomes are in gains, $V\left(-\mathbf{x}^r; \mathbf{p}^r\right)$ flips all outcomes to the domain of losses. The ratio $\frac{|V(-\mathbf{x}^r; \mathbf{p}^r)|}{V(\mathbf{x}; \mathbf{p})}$ captures the loss to gain utility under PT, which is a more general measure of loss aversion. In applications of PT and empirical implementations of PT, it is common to assume that in the power form of utility (see (2.19)), $\gamma^+ = \gamma^-$ and that the weighting function is identical in the domain of gains and losses ($w^- = w^+$). The next theorem provides the necessary justification.

Theorem 2.3 *(al-Nowaihi et al., 2008): (a) If preference homogeneity holds for simple lotteries, then the utility function for riskless outcomes, v, takes the form given in (2.19):*

$$v(x) = x^{\gamma^+}, \text{ for } x \geq 0, \ v(x) = -\lambda(-x)^{\gamma^-}, \text{ for } x < 0, \text{ where } \gamma^+ > 0, \gamma^- > 0, \lambda > 0. \quad (2.50)$$

Conversely, if the value function for riskless outcomes takes the form (2.50), then preference homogeneity holds for all lotteries.
(b) If the utility function (2.50) for riskless outcomes exhibits loss aversion, then $\lambda > 1$ and $\gamma^+ = \gamma^-$.
(c) If preference homogeneity and loss aversion both hold for simple lotteries, then the utility function for riskless outcomes takes the form (2.50) with $\lambda > 1$, $\gamma^+ = \gamma^-$, and $w^- = w^+$. Conversely, if the utility function for riskless outcomes takes the form (2.50) with $\lambda > 1$, $\gamma^+ = \gamma^-$, and $w^- = w^+$, then preference homogeneity holds for all lotteries and loss aversion holds for all positive lotteries.

2.7 Third generation PT and stochastic reference points

Schmidt et al. (2008) propose an extension of PT to the case of stochastic reference points. They call their descriptive theory of decision making, *third generation prospect theory*, or PT^3. Their framework addresses situations where individuals are endowed with a lottery and must choose between alternative actions that typically induce different probability distributions over outcomes. For instance, the decision maker who buys a house has an endowment in which his house may suffer harm due to fire or other natural hazards with some probability. His choice of action, for instance, to buy insurance, induces another probability distribution over the relevant outcomes.

Consider a set of states of nature $S = \{s_1, s_2, \ldots, s_m\}$. State $s_i \in S$ has an objective probability of occurrence, $0 \leq p_i \leq 1$ such that $\sum_{i=1}^{m} p_i = 1$. There is a set of state-contingent consequences from one's chosen action. The consequences, in any state, lie in the compact set $X = [a, b] \in \mathbb{R}$. To fix ideas, consider each of these consequences as terminal wealth. Suppose that F is the set of all *Savage acts*, where any $f \in F$ is a mapping $f : S \to X^m$; so $f(s_i) \in X$ is the outcome received by the decision maker when the state is s_i (see Section 1.3 for Savage acts).

Suppose that $r \in F$ is some *reference Savage act*; think of the reference act as the *state-wise entitlement* expected by the decision maker. Then, for $f, g \in F, f \succeq_r g$ denotes the preference of the decision maker for f over g when his reference act is r. In contrast to this *state-contingent reference act*, PT considers the special case when r is a *constant act*, i.e., $r(s_i) = r(s_j)$ for any $s_i, s_j \in S$.

Schmidt et al. (2008) propose the following preference representation. Suppose that a decision maker has the reference act r and wishes to compute his utility from the act f. Let

$$v(f(s_i), r(s_i)) = v(f(s_i) - r(s_i))$$

denote the utility in state s_i under the act f when the reference act is r. The function v is given in Definition 2.12, and a parametric form is given in (2.19). Thus, v is increasing and $v(r(s_i), r(s_i)) = 0$. Order the states in S in such a way that $f(s_i) - r(s_i)$ is increasing. Let S^+ be the set of states for which $f(s_i) - r(s_i) \geq 0$ and S^- be the set of states for which $f(s_i) - r(s_i) < 0$. Then the utility of the decision maker from the act f when his reference act is r is given by

$$V(f, r) = \sum_{s_i \in S^-} \pi(s_i; f, r) v(f(s_i), r(s_i)) + \sum_{s_i \in S^+} \pi(s_i; f, r) v(f(s_i), r(s_i)), \qquad (2.51)$$

where $\pi(s_i; f, r)$ is the decision weight corresponding to the state s_i. The decision weights are constructed as in Definition 2.14, separately cumulated in the domain of gains (S^+) and losses (S^-). The utility function V represents preferences in the sense that $f \succeq_r g \Leftrightarrow V(f, r) \geq V(g, r)$. As under PT, a decision maker who has these preferences does not choose stochastically dominated options. This implies that if for $f, g \in F$, $f(s_i) \geq g(s_i)$ for all $s_i \in S$, with strict inequality in at least one state, then $V(f, r) > V(g, r)$. EU, RDU, PT are all special cases of this framework. Sugden's (2003) *reference dependent subjective expected utility theory* (RDSEU) is also a special case when $\pi(s_i; f, r) = p_i$.

Schmidt et al. (2008) suggest the following parametric form. For the utility function, v, they suggest the parametric form in (2.19) and for the probability weighting function (that feeds into the calculations of decision weights) they propose the Tversky and Kahneman (1992) probability weighting function given in (2.5) with an identical weighting function in the domain of gains and losses. As parameter values they suggest the following. The parameter of loss aversion, $\lambda \in [1, 2.5]$, the utility function parameter in (2.19), $\gamma \in [0.5, 1]$, and the weighting function parameter in (2.5), $\tau \in [0.5, 1]$.

This framework can explain (i) the WTA/WTP disparity (see Section 3.2), provided the coefficient of loss aversion, $\lambda > 1$, and (ii) preference reversals (Section 1.5.6). Let us consider the WTA/WTP disparity. We first define *non-reversible preferences*. These preferences imply that if one prefers the act f over g when the reference act is g, one must continue to do so even if the reference act is altered to f.

Definition 2.25 *The preferences of a decision maker are said to be non-reversible if $f \succeq_g g \Rightarrow f \succeq_f g$. Preferences are said to be strictly non-reversible if $f \succeq_g g \Rightarrow f \succ_f g$, where $\succ$ is the strict preference relation.*

Proposition 2.9 *(Schmidt et al., 2008): (a) Strict non-reversibility implies the WTA/WTP disparity.*
(b) The parameterized version of PT^3 satisfies strict non-reversibility if the parameter of loss aversion $\lambda > 1$.

Proof: In this case, the reference act is the constant act (e.g., possession or non-possession of a mug in all states). Let r be a constant act such that $r(s_i) = z$ for all $s_i \in S$ and let $r \sim_g g$. Clearly

z is the WTA of the act g. Now suppose that r' is another constant act such that $r'(s_i) = z'$ for all $s_i \in S$ and let $r' \sim_{r'} g$. A moment's reflection reveals that z' is the WTP for the act g. Suppose preferences are strictly non-reversible. Then $r \sim_g g \Rightarrow r \succeq_g g$ and $g \succeq_g r$. But due to strict non-reversibility, $r \succeq_g g \Rightarrow r \succ_r g$. So $r \succ_r g \sim_{r'} r'$, thus, WTA > WTP.

(b) Left to the reader as an exercise. ∎

2.8 Stochastic reference points in PT under rational expectations

Köszegi and Rabin (2006) argue that existing evidence in support of the status quo as a reference point comes from experiments where the status quo is expected to remain unchanged in the future. However, when future values of the relevant variables of interest, say, income or wealth, are uncertain, then expectations about the future may be critical in the formation of the reference point. Recent evidence supports the idea that expectations can influence reference points (Ericson and Fuster, 2011). In one set of experiments, they endowed subjects with a mug and then probabilistically offered them a chance of exchanging the mug with a second object, a pen. When the probability of exchanging the mug for the pen was low, they found that subjects were less willing to exchange their mugs when they had an opportunity to do so.

We now explain the basic framework in Köszegi and Rabin (2006). Suppose that $c \in \mathbb{R}$ is the level of consumption. Different values of consumption could correspond to, say, dated values of consumption or to the levels of consumption in different states of the world. Let $r \in \mathbb{R}$ be a reference point.

Suppose that the actions of a decision maker lead to stochastic draws of consumption c with some distribution function F. Define the expected utility of the decision maker, conditional on a fixed reference point r as

$$U(F \mid r) = E_c u = \int u(c \mid r) dF(c),$$
(2.52)

where u is a utility function of consumption, conditional on the reference point, and F is induced by a particular action of the decision maker.

The reference point r may capture the beliefs of the decision maker about the possible outcomes, hence, a fixed reference point may not be reasonable. Since the consumption outcomes are stochastic, the reference point, r, may also be stochastic (as in Section 2.7) with a distribution function, G. It arguably reflects the decision maker's most recent beliefs about future outcomes. To quote from Köszegi and Rabin (2006): "Specifically, a person's reference point is her probabilistic beliefs about the impending outcome between the time she first focused on a decision and shortly before the time of consumption."

The expected utility of the decision maker when the reference point is stochastic is given by

$$U(F \mid G) = E_c E_r u = \int \left[\int u(c \mid r) dG(r) \right] dF(c).$$
(2.53)

This approach is similar to theories of disappointment aversion (Bell, 1985; Loomes and Sugden, 1986; Gul 1991; see Section 2.10.2). In these theories, one compares the consumption outcomes with a reference lottery that equals the certainty equivalent of the lottery. By contrast, in the Köszegi–Rabin framework, we compare each consumption outcome with each possible element of the reference lottery as in (2.53).

In PT, the utility function depends only on *gain–loss utility*, i.e., the utility of an outcome relative to the reference point. By contrast, in the Köszegi–Rabin framework, the conditional utility, *u*, depends on (i) the absolute level of *consumption utility*, and (ii) *gain–loss utility*, in the following manner.

$$u(c \mid r) = m(c) + l(c \mid r). \tag{2.54}$$

Remark 2.4   *In a more general model, one may consider an N-dimensional vector of consumption, $c = (c_1, c_2, \ldots, c_N) \in \mathbb{R}^N$ and an N-dimensional vector of reference points, $r = (r_1, r_2, \ldots, r_N) \in \mathbb{R}^N$. The analogue of (2.54) in this case is given by:*

$$m(c) = \sum_{j=1}^{N} m_j(c_j) \text{ and } l(c \mid r) = \sum_{j=1}^{N} l_j(c_j \mid r_j), \tag{2.55}$$

where m_j and l_j denote, respectively, consumption utility and gain–loss utility. For $j = 1, 2, \ldots, N$, each m_j is a differentiable and strictly increasing function. Both components of utility, m and l, are additively separable across the N dimensions. The gain–loss utility across each dimension is assumed identical, and it has the following form

$$l_j(c_j \mid r_j) = \mu \left(m_j(c_j) - m_j(r_j) \right). \tag{2.56}$$

However, for the case of (2.54) we have

$$l(c \mid r) = \mu \left(m(c) - m(r) \right). \tag{2.57}$$

Example 2.11   *John faces the consumption lottery $(c_1, p_1; c_2, p_2)$, where $c_1 < c_2$ and $p_1 + p_2 = 1$. Denote the probability distribution over these consumption levels by F. In theories of disappointment aversion, the reference point r is given by $\bar{r}$, the certainty equivalent, hence, the distribution G is degenerate at $\bar{r}$. The decision maker's utility in this case is given by*

$$U = \sum_{i=1}^{2} p_i v(c_i \mid \bar{r}),$$

where v is the standard utility function under PT (see Definition 2.12).
However, in the Köszegi–Rabin framework, uncertainty about the future induces a stochastic reference point. Suppose that the reference point r has the distribution G, such that $r = r_1$ with probability q_1 and $r = r_2$ with probability q_2 and $q_1 + q_2 = 1$. Then John's expected utility in (2.53) is given by

$$U(F \mid G) = p_1 \left[\sum_{j=1}^{2} q_j u(c_1 \mid r_j) \right] + p_2 \left[\sum_{j=1}^{2} q_j u(c_2 \mid r_j) \right]. \tag{2.58}$$

Substituting (2.54) and (2.57) in (2.58) we get

$$U(F \mid G) = \sum_{i=1}^{2} p_i m(c_i) + p_1 \left[\sum_{j=1}^{2} q_j \mu \left(m(c_1) - m(r_j) \right) \right]$$
$$+ p_2 \left[\sum_{j=1}^{2} q_j \mu \left(m(c_2) - m(r_j) \right) \right]. \tag{2.59}$$

The first term in (2.59) is standard expected utility and the next two terms capture gain–loss utility for each realization of the consumption level, weighted by the probability of its occurrence. For instance, in the second term in (2.59), when the realized consumption level is

c_1, *John compares his consumption with both possible realizations of the stochastic reference point; it is possible that he is elated in one of the comparisons and disappointed in the other. He performs a similar comparison in the third term when realized consumption is c_2. Notice that in this approach, probability is weighted linearly, as under expected utility theory. This assumption is contrary to the strong evidence on non-linear probability weighting that we review extensively (Fehr-Duda and Epper, 2012).*

The properties of gain–loss utility, μ, are as follows.

Definition 2.26 *The gain–loss utility, $\mu(x)$, is continuous, differentiable for all $x \neq 0$, and strictly increasing. It has the following properties.*

(i) *(Reference dependence) $\mu(0) = 0$.*

(ii) *(Large stakes loss aversion) For $0 < x < y$, $\mu(y) - \mu(x) < \mu(-x) - \mu(-y)$.*[35]

(iii) *(Small stakes loss aversion) Let $\mu'_+(0) = \lim_{x \to 0^+} \mu'(x)$ and $\mu'_-(0) = \lim_{x \to 0^-} \mu'(x)$. Then $\frac{\mu'_-(0)}{\mu'_+(0)} = \lambda > 1$, where λ is the parameter of loss aversion.*

(iv) *(Diminishing sensitivity) For $x > 0$, $\mu''(x) \leq 0$ and for $x < 0$, $\mu''(x) \geq 0$.*

The properties listed in Definition 2.26 are similar to those in Definition 2.12, except for the difference between small and large stakes loss aversion. For alternative definitions of loss aversion, see Section 2.5.2. For small stakes gambles, it is assumed that μ is linear,

$$\mu(y) = \begin{cases} \eta y & \text{if } y \geq 0 \\ \eta \lambda y & \text{if } y < 0 \end{cases}, \eta > 0, \lambda > 1. \tag{2.60}$$

In applying (2.53), one has to specify how the expectations about the reference point are formed. While the appropriate specification of a reference point is ultimately an empirical question, as a first pass, Köszegi and Rabin make the extreme assumption that the expectations of the decision maker are fully consistent with rational expectations in a manner that we specify below.

The next proposition formalizes two intuitive ideas that follow from Definition 2.26. First, if one's reference point is low, then most realized outcomes are in the domain of gains, hence, the decision maker's utility will be higher. Since the reference point is stochastic, a natural formalization of a "lower reference point" is to compare two distributions of reference points in which one distribution first order stochastically dominates the other. The dominated distribution gives a higher probability of lower reference points, hence, this should be the one that the decision maker should prefer. Second, individuals have a status-quo bias in the following sense. If a decision maker prefers the consumption bundle c to c', when the reference point is c', then the decision maker also prefers c to c' if the reference point is c. This is related to the idea of non-reversible preferences in Definition 2.25.

Proposition 2.10 *(Köszegi and Rabin, 2006): Let μ satisfy the conditions in Definition 2.26.*

(i) *Suppose that the distribution of consumption is given by F. Consider two distributions of the reference point, G and G', such that G' first order stochastically dominates G. Then $U(F \mid G) \leq U(F \mid G')$, where U is defined in (2.53).*

---

[35] Suppose that μ is linear such that $\mu(x) = x$ for $x > 0$ and $\mu(x) = 2x$ for $x < 0$. Let $x = 5$ and $y = 10$ then $\mu(y) - \mu(x) = 5$ and $\mu(-x) - \mu(-y) = 10$.

(ii) Suppose that $c, c' \in \mathbb{R}$ and $c \neq c'$. Then

$$u(c \mid c') \geq u(c' \mid c') \Rightarrow u(c \mid c) \geq u(c' \mid c). \tag{2.61}$$

The next example illustrates Proposition 2.10.

Example 2.12   *Suppose that in Example 2.11, $c_1 = 0$, $c_2 = 1$, $p_1 = p_2 = 0.5$. Let the reference point be $r_1 = 0$ with probability q_1 and $r_2 = 1$ with probability q_2. Suppose that μ is linear as in (2.60) and $m(x) = x$, then, from (2.59), the utility function of the decision maker is*

$$U(F \mid G) = \frac{1}{2} + \frac{1}{2} \eta \left(q_1 - q_2 \lambda \right).$$

Now consider another distribution of reference points, G' that dominates G. Under G', the probability of reference point $r = 1$ is $q_2' > q$ and $r = 0$ is $q_1' < q_1$. Then $U(F \mid G) - U(F \mid G') = \frac{1}{2} \eta \left[(q_1 - q_1') + \lambda \left(q_2' - q_2 \right) \right] > 0$, as predicted by Proposition 2.10(i). The proof of Proposition 2.10(ii) is relatively straightforward. Let $u(c \mid c') \geq u(c' \mid c')$ and suppose that $u(c \mid c) < u(c' \mid c)$. Then, a few simple calculations show that substituting the values of $u(c \mid c)$, $u(c' \mid c)$ lead to a contradiction.

From (2.54), $u(c \mid r) = m(c) + l(c \mid r)$. Thus, the utility function in the Köszegi–Rabin framework differs from the standard PT utility function in having the first term, $m(c)$, that depends on the absolute level of consumption. When large stakes are involved, then changes in utility are driven more by the first term, i.e., changes in marginal utility that economists are typically used to thinking about. However, when small stakes are involved, m is likely to be linear, so one may wonder if the Köszegi–Rabin utility function $u(c \mid r)$ behaves in a manner that is similar to gain–loss utility in prospect theory. This is formalized in the next result.

Proposition 2.11   *(Köszegi and Rabin, 2006): Suppose that stakes are small so that consumption utility, m, is linear and gain–loss utility μ satisfies the conditions in Definition 2.26. Then, there exists a utility function v that also satisfies the conditions in Definition 2.26 such that for all $c \in \mathbb{R}$ and $r \in \mathbb{R}$ we have*[36]

$$u(c \mid r) - u(r \mid r) = v(c - r).$$

However, for large stakes, when m is non-linear, Proposition 2.11 does not hold.

A *choice set*, D_k, $k = 1, 2, \ldots$ is a set of probability distributions over $\mathbb{R}$ (possibly degenerate), so $D_k \in \Delta \mathbb{R}$. Suppose that the decision maker expects to choose $F_k^* \in D_k$. The decision maker's beliefs are represented by a distribution Q over the choice sets $\{D_k\}_{k \in \mathbb{N}}$ such that q_k is the probability that choice set D_k occurs and F_k^* is chosen.[37] Thus, the decision maker's expected choice, prior to the resolution of uncertainty is

$$\sum_{j \in \mathbb{N}} q_j F_j^*.$$

---

[36] When the consumption and the reference point are drawn from $\mathbb{R}^N$ then under the conditions of Proposition 2.11, there exist utility functions $(v_1, v_2, \ldots, v_N) \in \mathbb{R}^N$ that also satisfy the conditions in Definition 2.26 such that for all $c = (c_1, c_2, \ldots, c_N) \in \mathbb{R}^N$ and $r = (r_1, r_2, \ldots, r_N) \in \mathbb{R}^N$ we have $u(c \mid r) - u(r \mid r) = \sum_{j=1}^{N} v_j(c_j - r_j)$.

[37] We consider here the case where the decision sets are sequences, $\{D_k\}_{k \in \mathbb{N}}$. For an extension to the continuous case, $\{D_k\}_{k \in \mathbb{R}}$, see Köszegi and Rabin (2006, 2007).

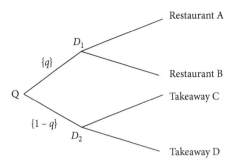

Figure 2.10 The case of two choice sets.

We now define three different kinds of equilibrium concepts, depending on how far in advance of the resolution of uncertainty the decision maker makes his choice. But first it is worth going through an example that clarifies the various constructions involved.

> **Example 2.13** *Consider, the example shown in Figure 2.10. In this case, there are two choice sets, D_1 and D_2. Each choice set is a degenerate probability distribution over meals.[38] Choice set D_1 gives a choice of eating out at one of two restaurants A or B. Choice set D_2 gives a choice of two takeaway meals to be eaten at home—C or D. In richer descriptions, each choice could be a probability distribution over a set of restaurants or a set of takeaway meals. Suppose that the decision maker knows that if he eats out (the choice set D_1), he prefers restaurant B (decision F_1^*), and if he eats at home (the choice set D_2), he prefers takeaway C (decision F_2^*). The decision maker's beliefs are represented by a distribution Q over the choice sets $\{D_1, D_2\}$, such that D_1 and D_2 are believed to occur with respective probabilities q and $1 - q$.*

Consider, first, situations where decisions are made sufficiently in advance of the actual outcomes, such as in insurance decisions. In this case, the individual gets enough time to be *acclimatized* to the decision. If $\left\{F_k^* \in D_k\right\}_{k \in \mathbb{N}}$ are the choices, then the individual regards $\sum_{j \in \mathbb{N}} q_j F_j^*$ as the reference point (or reference distribution). In this case, the relevant equilibrium is a *choice acclimating personal equilibrium* (CPE).

> **Definition 2.27** *(Köszegi and Rabin, 2007, p. 1058) Suppose that $\{D_k\}_{k \in \mathbb{N}}$ is a sequence of choice sets. Then $\left\{F_k^* \in D_k\right\}_{k \in \mathbb{N}}$ is choice acclimating personal equilibrium (CPE) if for each D_k,*
>
> $$U\left(F_k^* \mid \sum_{j \in \mathbb{N}} q_j F_j^*\right) \geq U\left(F_k' \mid q_k F_k' + \sum_{j \in \mathbb{N}/k} q_j F_j^*\right) \text{ for all } F_k' \in D_k.$$

Thus, once the decision made by the decision maker becomes the reference point, then, in a CPE, for each choice set, no other decision in the choice set can make the decision maker better off. This is the sense in which rational expectations are used to close the model. In particular, the decision maker correctly forecasts the economic environment and his own reaction in each possible state of the environment and then maximizes utility conditional on these "correct" expectations. We give several applications of a CPE below, but first, let us continue with Example 2.13 for a simple illustration of Definition 2.27.

---

[38] We assume that the meals can be translated into some units on the real line.

Example 2.14 *Consider Example 2.13. The selection $\{F_1 = B, F_2 = C\}$ described in Example 2.13 is a CPE if the following two conditions are met.*

$$U(B \mid qB + (1-q)C) \geq U(A \mid qA + (1-q)C). \tag{2.62}$$

$$U(C \mid qB + (1-q)C) \geq U(D \mid qB + (1-q)D). \tag{2.63}$$

Notice that in each of (2.62) and (2.63), if the decision maker deviates from one of the planned choices, then the new choice becomes a part of the stochastic reference point. This is a central feature of a CPE.

In contrast to a CPE, a second possibility is that the decision maker makes his decision too close to the actual resolution of uncertainty (e.g., buying insurance for a travel plan in order to take advantage of some last minute travel deals). In this case, the relevant equilibrium notion is one of an *unacclimating personal equilibrium* (UPE).

Definition 2.28 *(Köszegi and Rabin, 2007, p. 1056) Suppose that $\{D_k\}_{k \in \mathbb{N}}$ is a sequence of choice sets. Then $\left\{F_k^* \in D_k\right\}_{k \in \mathbb{N}}$ is an unacclimating personal equilibrium (UPE) if for each D_k,*

$$U\left(F_k^* \mid \sum_{j \in \mathbb{N}} q_j F_j^*\right) \geq U\left(F_k' \mid \sum_{j \in \mathbb{N}} q_j F_j^*\right) \text{ for all } F_k' \in D_k.$$

In Köszegi and Rabin (2006, p. 1143) a UPE is simply described as a "personal equilibrium" (PE).

The two equilibrium concepts, CPE and UPE (Definitions 2.27 and 2.28) differ only in the treatment of the reference point when one deviates from a planned decision. However, theory does not specify the length of time needed for acclimatization, which could be a potential issue in experimental tests of the theory.

Example 2.15 *Consider Example 2.13. The selection $\{F_1 = B, F_2 = C\}$ described in Example 2.13 is a UPE, if the following two conditions are met.*

$$U(B \mid qB + (1-q)C) \geq U(A \mid qB + (1-q)C). \tag{2.64}$$

$$U(C \mid qB + (1-q)C) \geq U(D \mid qB + (1-q)C). \tag{2.65}$$

The main difference from the conditions in (2.62) and (2.63) is that the reference point is now attuned only to the choices $F_1 = B$ and $F_2 = C$ that occur with respective probabilities q and $1 - q$.

What is the relevant equilibrium concept when a UPE leads to multiple equilibria? Unlike cases of multiple equilibria in strategic interaction, the setting of a game against nature is much simpler. The relevant refinement, embodied in a *preferred personal equilibrium* (PPE), is that restricting to the set of UPE, the decision maker picks the sequence $\{F_k\}_{k \in \mathbb{N}}$ that gives him the highest ex-ante expected utility.

Definition 2.29 *(Köszegi and Rabin, 2006, p. 1144) Suppose that $\{D_k\}_{k \in \mathbb{N}}$ is a sequence of choice sets. Then $\{F_k \in D_k\}_{k \in \mathbb{N}}$ is a preferred personal equilibrium (PPE) if $\{F_k \in D_k\}_{k \in \mathbb{N}}$ is a UPE and for all UPE sequences $\left\{F_k' \in D_k\right\}_{k \in \mathbb{N}}$ we have that*

$$U\left(\sum_{j \in \mathbb{N}} q_j F_j \mid \sum_{j \in \mathbb{N}} q_j F_j\right) \geq U\left(\sum_{j \in \mathbb{N}} q_j F_j' \mid \sum_{j \in \mathbb{N}} q_j F_j'\right).$$

Let us now consider a simple example that illustrates the difference between a CPE and a UPE.

Example 2.16 *Suppose that a decision maker has current wealth w and he faces the lottery $L = (w - 100, 0.5; w, 0.5)$, thus, with probability 0.5, the decision maker faces a potentially large loss. The decision maker can pay an insurance premium of 55 and obtain, instead, the lottery $L' = (w - 55, 1)$. Denote the probability distributions over outcomes in the lotteries L and L' by respectively, F and F'. Should the decision maker buy insurance?*

(a) *Consider first a CPE. In this case, there is significant time between the actual decision and the resolution of uncertainty. So, if the decision maker does not buy insurance, his reference point is the lottery L and if he buys insurance, the reference point is the lottery L'. In a CPE, it is profitable to buy insurance if*

$$U(F \mid F) \leq U(F' \mid F'), \tag{2.66}$$

where U is defined in (2.53) to (2.57). Let consumption utility be linear, so $m(x) = x$ and let μ be given by (2.60). Then, (2.66) can be written as

$$\frac{1}{2}\left[(w - 100) + \frac{1}{2}\eta\lambda(-100)\right] + \frac{1}{2}\left[w + \frac{1}{2}\eta(100)\right] \leq w - 55, \tag{2.67}$$

where the LHS and RHS of (2.67) give, respectively, $U(F \mid F)$ and $U(F' \mid F')$. In computing $U(F' \mid F')$, note that the outcome under the lottery F' is a certain outcome so there is no gain–loss utility. However, gain–loss utility plays a critical role in the computation of $U(F \mid F)$. When the outcome is $w - 100$, the decision maker suffers a loss relative to the reference outcome w. Analogously, when the outcome is w, there is a feeling of gain relative to the reference outcome $w - 100$.

(b) *Consider now the case of a UPE. Buying insurance is a UPE, if having initially planed to buy the insurance, the individual finds it optimal to carry out the initial plan to buy rather than not buy insurance. Hence, in a UPE, it is profitable to buy insurance if*

$$U(F \mid F') \leq U(F' \mid F'). \tag{2.68}$$

$U(F' \mid F')$ *is already given by the RHS of (2.67). However, $U(F \mid F')$ is given by*

$$U(F \mid F') = \frac{1}{2}[w - 100 - 45\eta\lambda] + \frac{1}{2}[w + 55\eta]. \tag{2.69}$$

If we are now willing to specify the values of λ and η, then we can carry out the relevant comparisons for each of the two equilibria.

Example 2.17 *(Stochastic dominance and CPE[39]): One undesirable feature of a CPE is that the decision maker may choose stochastically dominated options. Let us use the gain–loss function of the form given in (2.61):*

$$\mu(y) = \begin{cases} 0 & \text{if } y \geq 0 \\ \widehat{\lambda}y & \text{if } y < 0 \end{cases}, \widehat{\lambda} = \eta(\lambda - 1) \geq 0.$$

[39] I am grateful to Fabian Herweg for suggesting this example.

The decision maker is loss averse if $\widehat{\lambda} > 0$ and loss neutral if $\widehat{\lambda} = 0$. Consider the following two lotteries

$$A = (10, p; 20, 1 - p); B = (10, 1), \ 0 < p < 1.$$

Clearly, lottery A first order stochastically dominates B (the distribution function for lottery A lies everywhere below that for B). In a CPE, using a condition analogous to (2.66), the decision maker prefers lottery B to lottery A if

$$p10 + (1 - p)20 - p(1 - p)\eta(\lambda - 1)10 < 10$$

or, $B \succ A$ is equivalent to

$$\frac{1}{p} < \eta(\lambda - 1).$$

The LHS attains a minimum value of 1. Thus, if $\widehat{\lambda} = \eta(\lambda - 1) < 1$, then the preference for the stochastically dominated option ($B \succ A$) can never arise for any p. For this reason, applications of this framework often make such an assumption. On the other hand, if $\widehat{\lambda} = \eta(\lambda - 1) > 1$, then for some values of p, a decision maker chooses the stochastically dominated option in a CPE.[40]

What is the relation between the Köszegi–Rabin framework and PT[3]? Schmidt et al. (2008, p. 207) argue that when the Köszegi–Rabin framework is recast in terms of Savage acts, it has an undesirable implication. Consider two acts f and g, and the probabilities of each state are the same but for at least some $s_i \in S$ it is the case that $f(s_i) \neq g(s_i)$. Since the probabilities are identical across states, the Köszegi and Rabin framework would treat these two acts as identical, yet under PT[3] these acts are not identical (see (2.51)).

There are at least two issues for applied economists in testing the Köszegi and Rabin framework. First, it is not clear how much time should elapse before the decision maker has become acclimatized to his decision, hence, the choice between a CPE and a UPE can be unclear. Since the predictions of a CPE and a UPE may be different, this is an important consideration in making the theory falsifiable. A second issue is the "strength" of empirical tests. Empirical tests that simply demonstrate "expectations driven reference points" are consistent with the Köszegi and Rabin framework, but not stringent enough to reject it. For instance, such tests may not be able to distinguish between the Köszegi–Rabin framework and theories of disappointment aversion. A stringent test must, therefore, incorporate the rational expectations built into the Köszegi and Rabin framework. It is worth bearing this in mind when you read Section 2.8.3.

In the remaining subsections we give examples of a CPE and a UPE as well as the empirical evidence for this class of models.

2.8.1 An example of a choice acclimating equilibrium (CPE): The newsvendor problem

We now consider an example of a CPE in a newsvendor problem, due to Herweg (2013). At the beginning of a *trading period* (say, a day) a newsvendor orders a quantity $q \geq 0$ of newspapers at a unit wholesale price, w; this is the only decision made by the newsvendor. The vendor is uncertain

---

[40] This may create technical problems. For instance, non-concavities of the target function (Herweg, 2013) or non-existence of a contract that implements certain actions (Herweg et al., 2010).

about the demand for newspapers, x, which is known to be distributed over the interval $[\underline{x},\overline{x}]$ with density f and distribution F. The retail price of newspapers is $p \geq 0$ per unit. During the trading period, the ordered quantity q cannot be replenished. Any unsold newspapers, $q - x$, are sold at a scrap price of $s \geq 0$ per unit. We assume that

$$0 \leq s < w < p. \tag{2.70}$$

Thus, the vendor always makes a profit on any newspapers that are sold and a loss on any newspapers that are unsold. This allows gain–loss utility to play an important role in the vendor's decisions. The ex-post state-dependent profits of the vendor are

$$\pi(q,x) = \begin{cases} \pi_L(q,x) = (p-w)x + (q-x)(s-w) & \text{if} \quad x < q \\ \pi_H(q,x) = (p-w)q & \text{if} \quad x \geq q \end{cases}. \tag{2.71}$$

Ex-ante, the newsvendor cannot know for certain what his profits will be. However, using the distribution of possible demand levels, F, and (2.71), the expected profit of the newsvendor is $E\pi(q,x) = \int_{\underline{x}}^{q} \pi_L(q,x)dF(x) + \int_{q}^{\overline{x}} \pi_H(q,x)dF(x)$. From (2.71)

$$\pi_L = (p-s)x - (w-s)q, \tag{2.72}$$

hence, we can rewrite expected profits as

$$E\pi(q,x) = \left[-(w-s)qF(q) + (p-s)\int_{\underline{x}}^{q} x\,dF(x) \right] + (p-w)q(1-F(q)). \tag{2.73}$$

The classical solution maximizes $E\pi(q,x)$ by a suitable choice of q. The first order condition is sufficient because the objective function is strictly concave. The solution, $q = q^*$, is given by

$$F(q^*) = \frac{p-w}{p-s} \in (0,1). \tag{2.74}$$

Suppose now that the newsvendor has the Köszegi–Rabin utility, U, defined in (2.53) to (2.57). Thus, the ex-post utility of the newsvendor for a fixed q, x, r is given by

$$U = \pi(q,x) + \mu(\pi(q,x) - r), \tag{2.75}$$

where r is the reference point and the gain–loss utility is assumed to take the particularly simple form

$$\mu(y) = \begin{cases} 0 & \text{if} \quad y \geq 0 \\ \lambda y & \text{if} \quad y < 0 \end{cases}, \quad \lambda \in [0,1]. \tag{2.76}$$

The restriction $\lambda \in [0,1]$ ensures that the newsvendor's objective function is concave. The reference point itself is determined as in the Köszegi–Rabin framework. We assume that the choices are made sufficiently in advance of the outcome so that the concept of the choice acclimating personal equilibrium (CPE) in Definition 2.27 applies.

Suppose that the newsvendor has ordered some quantity, q, and a particular level of demand x has materialized. If the decision maker has acclimatized with the decision (CPE), the reference point, r, in (2.75) is $\pi(q,z)$ where z has the distribution function $F(z)$. Thus, conditional on given levels of q,x, the utility of the newsvendor is

$$U = \pi(q,x) + \int_{\underline{x}}^{\overline{x}} \mu\left(\pi(q,x) - \pi(q,z)\right) dF(z),\tag{2.77}$$

where μ is defined in (2.76). There are two possibilities.

I. $(x < q)$: For any particular choice of q, followed by any realization of demand such that $x < q$, the material utility of the newsvendor is $\pi_L(q,x) = \left[(p-s)x - (w-s)q\right]$ defined in (2.72). The reference point is given by $\pi(q,z)$ and z has the distribution function $F(z)$. There are two subcases to consider: $z < q$ and $z \geq q$. When $z < q$, μ is defined on the term $\pi_L(q,x) - \pi_L(q,z) = (p-s)(x-z)$. For any $z \geq q$, μ is defined on the term $\pi_L(q,x) - \pi_H(q,z) = (p-s)(x-q) < 0$. Thus, the gain–loss utility (second term in (2.77)) is

$$\int_{\underline{x}}^{x} \mu\left((p-s)(x-z)\right) dF(z) + \int_{x}^{q} \mu\left((p-s)(x-z)\right) dF(z) + \int_{q}^{\overline{x}} \mu\left((p-s)(x-q)\right) dF(z).\tag{2.78}$$

Using the first row of (2.76), the first term in (2.78) is zero. Using the second row in (2.76), the second term equals $-\lambda(p-s)\int_x^q (z-x)dF(z)$ and the third equals $-\lambda(p-s)(q-x)(1-F(q))$. Hence, the Köszegi–Rabin utility of the newsvendor for a particular realization of x, when $x < q$ is given by

$$U^-(q,x) = \left[(p-s)x - (w-s)q\right] - \lambda(p-s)\int_x^q (z-x)dF(z) - \lambda(p-s)(q-x)(1-F(q)).\tag{2.79}$$

II. $(x \geq q)$: In this case, the realized demand exceeds the ordered supply. From (2.76), gain–loss utility $\mu(y) = 0$ if $y \geq 0$. Hence, the vendor will be able to sell his entire stock, q at a price p per unit. Thus, his material utility is given by $\pi_H = (p-w)q$ (see (2.71)) and there is no gain–loss utility. Thus, his Köszegi–Rabin utility for a particular realization of x, when $x \geq q$ is given by

$$U^+(q,x) = (p-w)q.\tag{2.80}$$

The utility levels in (2.79), (2.80) are for fixed levels of x (either side of q). However, ex-ante, the newsvendor does not know the realization of x. Thus, his expected utility is $EU(q) = \int_{\underline{x}}^{q} U^-(q,x)dF(x) + \int_{q}^{\overline{x}} U^+(q,x)dF(x)$. Substituting U^- and U^+ from (2.79), (2.80), we get

$$EU(q) = \int_{\underline{x}}^{q} [(p-s)x - (w-s)q - \lambda(p-s)\int_x^q (z-x)dF(z)$$
$$- \lambda(p-s)(q-x)(1-F(q))]dF(x) + (p-w)q(1-F(q)).\tag{2.81}$$

The vendor with Köszegi-Rabin preferences chooses q in order to maximize $EU(q)$ in (2.81).[41] Since $0 \leq \lambda \leq 1$, $EU(q)$ is strictly concave. The reader can also check that corner solutions can

---

[41] When $\lambda = 0$, the solution is given by (2.74).

be ruled out. This leaves only an interior solution $q = \widehat{q}$, given by the solution to the first order condition.

$$EU'(\widehat{q}) = 0 \Rightarrow (p - w) - (p - s) F(\widehat{q}) - \lambda(p - s)F(\widehat{q})(1 - F(\widehat{q})) = 0. \qquad (2.82)$$

Evaluating the first order condition (2.82) at $q = q^*$, where q^* is given in (2.74), we get

$$EU'(q^*) = -\lambda(p - w)\left(\frac{w - s}{p - s}\right) < 0. \qquad (2.83)$$

Since $EU(q)$ is strictly concave ($EU''(q) < 0$), we get from (2.83) that $\widehat{q} < q^*$, i.e., a newsvendor with Köszegi–Rabin preferences finds it optimal to order a lower quantity. This reduction in the optimal quantity is driven by the loss aversion of the newsvendor. To see this, implicitly differentiate (2.82) with respect to λ to get

$$\frac{\partial \widehat{q}}{\partial \lambda} = \frac{(p - s)F(\widehat{q})(1 - F(\widehat{q}))}{EU''(\widehat{q})} < 0.$$

A loss averse newsvendor hedges his bet in the face of demand uncertainty by lowering the ordered amount, q, relative to the case where no loss aversion exists. If the actual demand turns out to be lower than expected, then with a lower q, a loss averse newsvendor suffers a smaller loss in utility on account of loss aversion.

2.8.2 An example of an unacclimating personal equilibrium (UPE): The taxi drivers' problem

We consider the phenomenon of the backward bending labor supply of New York cab drivers in Chapter 3. Here, we consider a stylized model of such a situation.[42] A taxi driver has the material utility

$$m(w, e) = we - \frac{1}{2}e^2, \qquad (2.84)$$

where $w \geq 0$ is the market determined wage level, and $e \in [0, \bar{e}]$ is the taxi driver's effort level, measured in terms of number of hours worked. For any realization of the wage level, w, the taxi driver maximizes his material utility by a suitable choice of e. Since this is a strictly concave problem over a compact domain, the solution is given by

$$e^*(w) = w.$$

Thus, the labor supply curve is upward sloping.[43]

Suppose that the taxi driver has the Köszegi–Rabin utility in which the gain–loss utility applies to the income and effort dimensions (i.e., Remark 2.4 applies and $N = 2$). Suppose that

---

[42] We present a simplified version of the taxi driver problem using the unpublished notes of Fabian Herweg. See also Köszegi and Rabin (2006) for a related application.

[43] In a more general model under EU, there are well-known opposing income and substitution effects such that the labor supply can be upward or downward sloping.

there are two wage levels w_H, w_L ($w_H > w_L$) that arise with respective probabilities $p, 1 - p$. The driver expects to put in effort $e_H \geq 0$ when the wage is w_H, and effort $e_L \geq 0$ when the wage is w_L. We also assume that the decision is made sufficiently close to the actual realization of the outcomes, so that the relevant solution concept is an unacclimating personal equilibrium, UPE (Definition 2.28).

Definition 2.30 *The taxi driver has an income target, $\overline{w}$, if $w_H e_H = w_L e_L = \overline{w}$.*

Suppose that the taxi driver has an income target, as specified in Definition 2.30. Since $w_H > w_L$, one implication of having an income target is that $e_H < e_L$. So the driver works less when the wage is higher.

Since the driver plans to exert effort level e_j when wage is $w_j, j = H, L$, his stochastic *reference point for income* is

$$r_I = \begin{cases} w_H e_H & \text{with probability } p \\ w_L e_L & \text{with probability } 1 - p \end{cases},$$

and the *reference point for cost of effort* is

$$r_C = \begin{cases} \frac{1}{2} e_H^2 & \text{with probability } p \\ \frac{1}{2} e_L^2 & \text{with probability } 1 - p \end{cases}.$$

Suppose that the realized wage is w, and the driver exerts the effort level e. Then, the Köszegi–Rabin utility of the driver is:[44]

$$V(e \mid w, r_I, r_C) = \left[we - \frac{1}{2} e^2 \right] + \left[p\mu \left(we - w_H e_H \right) + (1 - p)\mu \left(we - w_L e_L \right) \right]$$

$$+ \left[p\mu \left(-\frac{1}{2} e^2 + \frac{1}{2} e_H^2 \right) + (1 - p)\mu \left(-\frac{1}{2} e^2 + \frac{1}{2} e_L^2 \right) \right]. \tag{2.85}$$

The first term in (2.85) is material utility $m(w, e)$. The second term is gain–loss utility from income. The actual income we is compared to the reference income $w_H e_H$ with probability p, and to the reference income $w_L e_L$ with probability $1 - p$. The third term is gain–loss utility from the effort level. The actual cost of effort $\frac{1}{2} e^2$ is compared to the reference cost $\frac{1}{2} e_H^2$ with probability p, and to the reference cost $\frac{1}{2} e_L^2$ with probability $1 - p$.

In a UPE, the planned choices of the driver are consistent with actual choices. Hence, we now check if the driver would like to carry out the planned choices in each state. Suppose that the driver exerts the effort level e. Then there are three cases to consider.

C1. $e \leq e_H < e_L$. In terms of gain–loss utility, the driver is in the gain dimension with respect to effort in both states.

C2. $e_H < e \leq e_L$. The driver is in the gain dimension with respect to the low wage state and in the loss dimension with respect to the high wage state.

C3. $e_H < e_L < e$. The driver is in the loss dimension in both states.

---

[44] It is more convenient in this example to replace the notation for the utility function U in the Köszegi–Rabin framework with the new notation V that keeps track of the effort level and the wage level in each case.

The second dimension of gain–loss utility arises with respect to the income level, so we need to check actual income against reference income, i.e., $w_i e \gtrless \overline{w}, i = H, L$. We consider the various cases separately and assume that gain–loss utility, μ, takes the linear form, given in (2.60) with $\eta = 1$.

Case I. The high wage state, w_H: Suppose that the realized wage is w_H. We need to consider each of the subcases, C1, C2, and C3.

C1. $e \le e_H < e_L$: In this case, since actual effort is lower than both levels of planned effort, so $w_i e < \overline{w}$ for $i = H, L$. Thus, the driver is in the loss dimension with respect to income and in the gain dimension with respect to effort. Using $w_H e_H = w_L e_L = \overline{w}$, the Köszegi–Rabin utility in (2.85) is

$$V(e \mid w_H, r_I, r_C) = \left[w_H e - \frac{1}{2} e^2 \right] + \left[-\lambda p \left(\overline{w} - w_H e \right) - \lambda (1-p) \left(\overline{w} - w_H e \right) \right]$$
$$+ \left[\frac{p}{2} \left(e_H^2 - e^2 \right) + \frac{(1-p)}{2} \left(e_L^2 - e^2 \right) \right]. \tag{2.86}$$

The first term is material utility, the second is gain–loss utility in the income domain, and the third is gain–loss utility in the effort domain. From (2.86), the first and second order derivatives with respect to e are: $V' = w_H (1 + \lambda) - 2e$ and $V'' = -2 < 0$. Since this is a high wage state, w_H, a UPE requires that the driver does wish to carry out his original plan of working at least e_H hours. Since $V'' < 0$, and $V' > 0$ for small values of e, a sufficient condition for ruling out the case $e < e_H$ is that $V' \mid_{e=e_H} \ge 0$ or $w_H (1 + \lambda) - 2e_H \ge 0$. Also $w_H e_H = \overline{w}$, so $e_H = \overline{w}/w_H$. In conjunction, these conditions imply that a sufficient condition for ruling out $e < e_H$ is

$$V' \mid_{e=e_H} \ge 0 \Leftrightarrow \overline{w} \le \frac{1+\lambda}{2} w_H^2. \tag{2.87}$$

Higher loss aversion, λ, is more conducive to the satisfaction of (2.87).

C2. $e_H < e \le e_L$: In this case, $\overline{w} = w_H e_H < w_H e$ and $w_H e \le w_H e_L = \overline{w}$. Thus, in the income dimension, the driver is in the domain of gains when wage is high and in the domain of losses when wage is low. In the effort dimension, the driver is in gains with respect to the low wage reference state and in losses with respect to the high wage reference state. Thus, using $w_H e_H = w_L e_L = \overline{w}$, the analogue of (2.86) is

$$V(e \mid w_H, r_I, r_C) = \left[w_H e - \frac{1}{2} e^2 \right] + \left[p \left(w_H e - \overline{w} \right) - \lambda (1-p) \left(\overline{w} - w_H e \right) \right]$$
$$+ \left[-\lambda \frac{p}{2} \left(e^2 - e_H^2 \right) + \frac{1-p}{2} \left(e_L^2 - e^2 \right) \right]. \tag{2.88}$$

In this case, one can check that $V' = w_H \left[1 + \lambda - p(\lambda - 1) \right] - e[2 + p(\lambda - 1)]$ and $V'' < 0$. In this case, $e_H < e$, so to rule it out we require $V' \mid_{e=e_H} \le 0$. A simple calculation shows that if the following condition holds, then we cannot have $e_H < e$:

$$V' \mid_{e=e_H} \le 0 \Leftrightarrow \overline{w} \ge \frac{w_H^2 \left(1 + \lambda - p(\lambda - 1) \right)}{2 + p(\lambda - 1)}. \tag{2.89}$$

C3. $(e_H < e_L < e)$. In this case, the driver is in the domain of gains with respect to income and in the domain of losses with respect to cost of effort in both reference states. Thus, his Köszegi–Rabin utility is

$$V(e \mid w_H, r_I, r_C) = \left[w_H e - \frac{1}{2} e^2 \right] + \left[p \left(w_H e - \overline{w} \right) + (1-p) \left(w_H e - \overline{w} \right) \right]$$
$$- \left[\lambda \frac{p}{2} \left(e^2 - e_H^2 \right) + \lambda \frac{1-p}{2} \left(e^2 - e_L^2 \right) \right]. \tag{2.90}$$

A simple calculation shows that $V' = 2w_H - e(1+\lambda)$, $V'_{e=0} > 0$, and $V'' < 0$. Using $e_H = \overline{w}/w_H$, and in order to keep to the planned effort levels (i.e., effort e_H when wage is w_H), we require that

$$V' \mid_{e=e_H} \leq 0 \Leftrightarrow \overline{w} \geq \frac{2w_H^2}{1+\lambda}. \tag{2.91}$$

However, if (2.89) holds, then so too does (2.91) because with $\lambda > 1$, $\min \left\{ \frac{2}{1+\lambda}, \frac{(1+\lambda-p(\lambda-1))}{2+p(\lambda-1)} \right\} = \frac{2}{1+\lambda}$. Hence, we can rule out any departure from the planned effort level in the high wage state by using (2.87) and (2.91). The result can be summarized as follows.

Proposition 2.12   *There exists a reference income, $\overline{w}$, satisfying*

$$w_H^2 \frac{2}{1+\lambda} \leq \overline{w} \leq \frac{1+\lambda}{2} w_H^2 \tag{2.92}$$

such that the taxi driver finds it optimal to carry out his planned effort level in the high wage state.

Case II. The low wage state, w_L.
In the low wage state, w_L, one needs to check, analogously to Case I, all three subcases in C1, C2, and C3. The analogue of Proposition 2.12 in this case is given next.

Proposition 2.13   *There exists a reference income $\overline{w}$ and functions $a(w_L, \lambda)$ and $b(w_L, \lambda)$ satisfying*

$$a(w_L, \lambda) \leq \overline{w} \leq b(w_L, \lambda), \tag{2.93}$$

such that the taxi driver finds it optimal to carry out his planned effort level in the low wage state.

We leave the proof of Proposition 2.13 to the reader. Putting Propositions 2.12 and 2.13 together we get the final result.

Proposition 2.14   *There exists a UPE with an income target, $\overline{w}$, if the target jointly satisfies (2.92) and (2.93). The state-contingent effort levels are $e_i = \overline{w}/w_i$, $i = L, H$.*

We have derived in this example the conditions under which a wage target is justified. But we have not derived the optimal wage target from the set of all wage targets. In order to compute the optimal wage target, one may proceed as suggested in the definition of a PPE (Definition 2.29). For each wage target, compute the utility from the wage target, and then choose the target that maximizes this utility.[45]

---

[45] In personal communication, Fabin Herweg points out that there exist also other UPEs that are not income target effort plans. It may well be that the PPE is one of these non-target UPEs.

2.8.3 *Some empirical evidence for Köszegi-Rabin preferences*

In Abeler et al. (2011), subjects perform a repetitive and tedious task that has no intrinsic value to the experimenter. They count the number of zeros in a table of 150 randomly ordered digits that are either 1 or 0. In the first stage, subjects were paid a piece rate of 10 cents for each correct table; the payment was received with probability 1. In the second task, they could decide how long they wanted to work, up to a maximum allowed time of 60 minutes.

Subjects in the second task received their accumulated earnings at the piece rate of 20 cents per correct table. However, the payment was received with probability 0.5, and with probability 0.5, they received a fixed payment, $f > 0$. In the LO treatment, $f = f_{LO} = 3$ euros and in the HI treatment, $f = f_{HI} = 7$ euros. Let w be the piece rate per correct table, e the number of correct tables (proxy for effort), and $\phi(e)$ the cost of effort function, such that $\phi' > 0$ and $\phi'' > 0$. Consider the predictions of three different classes of model.

1. Absence of a reference point: Consider the canonical textbook model and the following additively separable utility function

$$U(e,f,w) = \left[0.5u(we) + 0.5u(f)\right] - \phi(e),$$

   where u is a continuous, differentiable, strictly increasing, and concave utility function. Individuals choose e to maximize U, given w,f. The first order condition $wu'(we) = 2\phi'(e)$ is independent of f and it can be solved for the optimal effort level, e^*, which is predicted to be independent of f. In particular, when $u(x) = x$, the solution is given by

$$\phi'(e^*) = \frac{w}{2}, \tag{2.94}$$

   where the LHS is the marginal cost of effort and the RHS is the marginal benefit.

2. Exogenous reference point: Suppose that there is no reference point for effort,[46] linear weighting of probabilities for simplicity, and the reference wage is exogenously given by w_r. Then, under prospect theory,

$$V(e,f,w) = \left[0.5v(we - w_re) + 0.5v(f - w_r)\right] - \phi(e).$$

   The first order condition is $(w - w_r)v' = 2\phi'(e)$. The optimal effort level is predicted to be independent of f.

3. Endogenous reference: Suppose that the reference point is given as in the Köszegi–Rabin framework, so that the utility function is defined in (2.53) to (2.57). In particular, let us consider the linear case, so $m(c) = c$, and gain–loss utility is also linear as in (2.60). We assume that the relevant equilibrium concept is a CPE (Definition 2.27). We also assume that there is no reference point for effort but there is a reference point for wage income. There are two cases: $we < f$ and $we > f$.

   3.1. The decision maker chooses e such that $we < f$. Prior to the resolution of uncertainty about the state, the consumption utility is $m(we) = we$ with probability 0.5

---

[46] This result is unchanged even if there is a positive but exogenous reference point for effort.

and $m(f) = f$ with probability 0.5. Each of these possible levels of consumption with the associated probabilities also serve as the reference points.

$$r = \begin{cases} we & \text{with probability } 0.5 \\ f & \text{with probability } 0.5 \end{cases}.$$

Each consumption level must now be compared with this stochastic reference point, and then we must aggregate over all consumption levels (see (2.53)). Denoting the Köszegi–Rabin utility in this case by U^-, we have

$$U^-(e \mid r) = \frac{1}{2}\left[we - \phi(e) + \frac{1}{2}\eta\lambda\left(we - f\right)\right] + \frac{1}{2}\left[f - \phi(e) + \frac{1}{2}\eta(f - we)\right].$$
(2.95)

In the first term in (2.95), the realization of consumption utility is we. Relative to the reference point we, the decision maker experiences no gain or loss. However, relative to the reference point f, the decision maker experiences a loss. In the second term, the realization of consumption utility is f. In this case, the decision maker feels a gain relative to the potential consumption level we, and no gain or loss relative to the consumption level, f. Let $\widehat{e}_-$ be the optimal effort level when $we < f$. The first order condition, which is sufficient, is given by

$$\phi'(\widehat{e}_-) = \frac{w}{2} + \frac{w}{4}\eta\left(\lambda - 1\right) = \phi'(e^*) + \frac{w}{4}\eta\left(\lambda - 1\right),$$
(2.96)

where e^* is the optimal effort in the absence of a reference point, see (2.94). From (2.96), if there were no loss aversion, $\lambda = 1$, then $\phi'(\widehat{e}_-) = \phi'(e^*)$. Recall from (2.60) that $\lambda > 1$, so in the presence of loss aversion, $\phi'(\widehat{e}_-) > \phi'(e^*)$, thus, given $\phi'' > 0$, we have $\widehat{e}_- > e^*$. By implication, $we^* < f$.

3.2. The decision maker chooses e such that $we > f$. Denoting the Köszegi–Rabin utility in this case by U^+, the expression analogous to (2.95) is given by

$$U^+(e \mid r) = \frac{1}{2}\left[we - \phi(e) + \frac{1}{2}\eta\left(we - f\right)\right] + \frac{1}{2}\left[f - \phi(e) + \frac{1}{2}\eta\lambda(f - we)\right].$$

The optimal effort level, in this case, $\widehat{e}_+$, is given by the solution to the following first order condition

$$\phi'(\widehat{e}_+) = \frac{w}{2} - \frac{w}{4}\eta\left(\lambda - 1\right) = \phi'(e^*) - \frac{w}{4}\eta\left(\lambda - 1\right).$$
(2.97)

In this case, the marginal benefit of effort at the optimal point is lower relative to the canonical model; $\phi'(\widehat{e}_+) < \phi'(e^*)$, so $\widehat{e}_+ < e^*$. Since $f < w\widehat{e}_+$ and $\widehat{e}_+ < e^*$, it follows that $we^* > f$. In this case, loss aversion serves to reduce effort below e^*.

Thus, once we allow for an endogenous reference point, the fixed payment f has an effect on effort, while in the other cases it has no effect. As f increases to a high enough level as in case 3.1, so $we^* < f$, we should, on average, observe an increase in effort under endogenous reference point. An increase in f increases the loss-aversion adjusted cost of $we < f$, hence, individuals exert more effort. This can be stated as a testable hypothesis:

H1: Average effort is higher when $f = f_H$, relative to the case $f = f_L$.

A second implication is as follows. The presence of gain–loss utility increases effort by increasing the marginal benefit of effort if $we < f$. The magnitude of this increase depends on the strength of loss aversion, λ. Gain–loss utility also reduces the marginal utility of effort when $we > f$ and, so, reduces optimal effort. In sum, loss aversion pushes effort in the direction of $we = f$. In the limit, as $\lambda \to \infty$, the first order conditions give $\widehat{we}_- = \widehat{we}_+ = f$; thus it is always optimal for the decision maker to stop exerting effort as soon as wage income equals f. Thus, f has the most powerful effect on effort in this case. This gives rise to the second testable hypothesis.

H2: The probability of stopping at $we = f_{LO}$ is higher when $f = f_{LO}$ relative to the case $f = f_{HI}$. Similarly, the probability of stopping at $we = f_{HI}$ is higher when $f = f_{HI}$ relative to the case $f = f_{LO}$. These effects are enhanced by an increase in loss aversion.

Figure 2.11 shows the histogram of earnings at which individuals stopped for two different treatments, $f_{LO} = 3$ and $f_{HI} = 7$. Individuals make fairly dispersed choices. However, there are sharp spikes at $f_{LO} = 3$ in the LO treatment, and at $f_{HI} = 7$ in the HI treatment; 15% and 16.7% of the subjects make these respective choices. These are also the modal choices in each treatment and are statistically different. By contrast, in the LO treatment, only 3.3% stop at an earning of 7 euros and in the HI treatment, only 1.7% stop at an earnings of 3 euros.

The results are even sharper when we consider stopping values in some range that is close to the predicted value. For instance, 30% of the subjects stop in the earnings range of 2–4 euros in the LO treatment and 38.3% stop in the earnings range of 6–8 euros in the HI treatment. Average effort levels are higher under the HI treatment as compared to the LO treatment. Using a proxy for loss aversion, based on binary lottery choices, subjects who exhibit higher loss aversion are

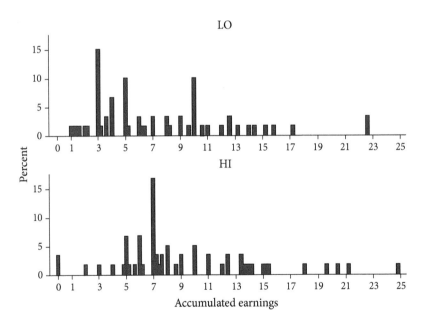

Figure 2.11 Histogram of accumulated earnings (in euros) at which a subject stopped.

Source: Abeler et al. (2011), with permission from the American Economic Association.

more likely to stop when their earnings are closer to f. The authors take their results as support for Köszegi–Rabin preferences and for the importance of expectations in the formation of reference points.

In the experiments of Abeler et al. (2011), subjects were not told that they were randomly assigned to one of two cases, $f = 3$ or $f = 7$. Hence, they might have inferred the value of their likely effort from the fixed payment, f, giving rise to a treatment effect. Ericson and Fuster (2011) correct for this feature and perform new experiments to test the Köszegi–Rabin framework. Their first experiment is described in Figure 2.12. Experimental subjects are endowed with a mug. They then get an opportunity (Op) to exchange the mug for a pen with probability p. With probability $1 - p$, there is no opportunity to exchange (Nop) and they end the experiment with a mug. If there is an opportunity to exchange, then they can exchange with a pen or elect to keep the mug. The decision maker has to commit ex-ante (prior to getting the opportunity to exchange) if he would like to exchange the mug for a pen.

Let u_P be the utility from owning a pen and u_M be the utility from owning a mug; we assume $u_P > u_M$. Under expected utility, committing ex-ante to exchange the mug for the pen gives the expected utility $pu_P + (1 - p)u_M$ and committing not to exchange gives u_M. Thus, exchange is better than no-exchange if $u_P > u_M$, which is independent of p.

Under expected utility and status-quo reference points, we can show that p does not have an effect on the decision to exchange. Here, the reference point is u_M because the decision maker is endowed with a mug. If the decision maker commits to exchange, his ex-ante utility is $p(u_P - u_M) + (1 - p)(u_M - u_M)$, and if he does not, it is $u_M - u_M = 0$. Thus, exchange is preferred if $u_P > u_M$, which is independent of p.

Under Köszegi–Rabin utility, we show below that p plays a role in the exchange decision. Hence, one can use experiments to compare the relative predictions of these theories. For pedagogical simplicity, we choose the CPE concept.

I. Suppose that the decision maker plans, ex-ante, to exchange the mug for the pen.

Let the realized utility of the decision maker be u_i, $i = P, M$ at any of the terminal nodes in Figure 2.12 (at the upper node in Figure 2.12, this is u_P, and at the lower node it is u_M). Then the Köszegi–Rabin utility, at that node, taking into account the stochastic reference point, r (u_P with probability p and u_M with probability $1 - p$), is

$$U(u_i \mid r) = u_i + \left[p\mu(u_i - u_P) + (1 - p)\mu(u_i - u_M) \right], \tag{2.98}$$

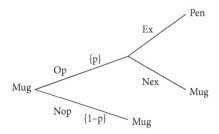

Figure 2.12 Decision tree for experiment 1 in Ericson and Fuster (2011).

Source: Keith M. Marzill Ericson and Andreas Fuster, "Expectations as endowments: evidence on reference-dependent preferences from exchange and valuation experiments," The Quarterly Journal of Economics (2011) 126(4): 1879–907, by permission of Oxford University Press.

where μ is given in its linear form in (2.60). For ease of exposition, we shall assume $\eta(\lambda - 1) > 1$ (this can be easily implemented in experiments).

The ex-ante Köszegi–Rabin utility at the initial node in Figure 2.12, given the decision to "exchange," is $U^{Ex} = pU(u_P \mid r) + (1-p)U(u_M \mid r)$, where U is defined in (2.98). Thus, using μ, given in (2.60), and $u_P > u_M$, we get

$$U^{Ex} = p\big[u_P + (1-p)\eta(u_P - u_M)\big] + (1-p)\big[u_M - p\lambda\eta(u_P - u_M)\big],$$

or,

$$U^{Ex} = u_M + p(u_P - u_M)\big(1 - (1-p)\eta(\lambda - 1)\big). \tag{2.99}$$

II. Suppose the ex-ante plan is not to exchange the mug.

In this case, the decision maker is always left with a mug in the end. The CPE equilibrium concept requires that the reference point in this case is u_M in all states. Thus, gain–loss utility is zero. The ex-ante Köszegi–Rabin utility in the case of "no-exchange" is simply $U^{Nex} = u_M$. Thus, the ex-ante plan to exchange the mug dominates if $U^{Ex} > U^{Nex}$, or

$$u_M + p(u_P - u_M)\big(1 - (1-p)\eta(\lambda - 1)\big) > u_M.$$

or,

$$p > p^* = 1 - \frac{1}{\eta(\lambda - 1)}. \tag{2.100}$$

By assumption, $\eta(\lambda - 1) > 1$, hence, $0 < p^* < 1$. From (2.100), as the probability of exchanging the mug, p, increases, the decision maker is more likely to choose to exchange. Thus, in equilibrium, a higher expectation of exchange does lead to greater exchange. By contrast in the other models, p should not influence the exchange decision.

Köszegi and Rabin (2007) show that a decision maker is more risk averse when he anticipates a risk and has the possibility to insure against that risk, relative to the case where he does not anticipate the risk. A related result can be found in Köszegi and Rabin (2009) in a life-cycle consumption model. In this model, an increase in consumption today reduces the expectation of consumption tomorrow, hence, it reduces the reference point tomorrow. This is in contrast to models of habit formation where an increase in consumption today increases the reference point for consumption tomorrow by increasing the habitual consumption level.

In the Ericson and Fuster (2011) experiments, two treatments were considered: Treatment T^L where $p = 0.1$ and treatment T^H where $p = 0.9$. The findings are as follows. In treatment T^L, 22.% of the subjects chose to exchange the mug, while in treatment T^H, this figure is 55.6%; these differences are statistically significant.[47] Probit regressions that include treatment and gender indicators also confirm this result. In Treatment T^L, where $p = 0.1$, the decision maker who wishes to exchange his mug experiences a greater risk so the typical decision maker appears more risk averse by choosing not to exchange; this exemplifies the remark on the Köszegi and Rabin (2007) result alluded to in the last paragraph.

---

[47] See also Smith (2008) for experimental evidence that supports the prediction of an endowment effect based on the Köszegi–Rabin framework.

Heffetz and List (2014) modify several aspects of the experimental design in Ericson and Fuster (2011). They find that the expectations effects predicted by the Köszegi–Rabin framework are quite weak.

2.9 Limitations of PT

We now consider evidence that is inconsistent with PT in some contexts. This evidence is also inconsistent with all other mainstream decision theories in economics, such as EU and RDU.

2.9.1 *The evidence and critique from configural weights models*

We first consider the work of Michael Birnbaum and his associates who have conducted experiments that contradict the predictions of OPT (Kahneman and Tversky, 1979). Many of these experiments exploit the heuristics used in the editing phase of OPT (see Section 2.11.1), which are not a part of PT (Tversky and Kahneman, 1992). The following terminology should be helpful in understanding the experimental results.

1. (Branches) For any lottery, such as $L = (x_1, p_1; x_2, p_2; \ldots; x_n, p_n)$, the ith *branch* is the ordered pair (x_i, p_i). In a two branch lottery $L = (x_1, p_1; x_2, p_2)$, $x_1 < x_2$, (x_2, p_2) is sometimes known as the *upper branch* and (x_1, p_1) is known as the *lower branch*.
2. (Coalescing) Under EU, RDU, and PT if the same outcome occurs more than once in a lottery, we can simply add up the corresponding probabilities and write a lottery in *coalesced* form. For instance, the lottery $(50, 0.2; 50, 0.3; 75, 0.5)$, also known as a *split lottery*, can be written in the coalesced form $(50, 0.5; 75, 0.5)$. Under EU, RDU, PT, the decision maker should be indifferent among the split and the coalesced forms. Depending on which branch of a lottery is split up we get *upper coalescing* (branch with the highest outcome is split) and *lower coalescing* (branch with the lowest outcome is split).
3. (Consequence monotonicity) If one outcome in a gamble is improved, then this should be preferred by the decision maker. Thus, if more is preferred to less, then the lottery $(200, 0.5; 0, 0.5)$ should be preferred to $(100, 0.5; 0, 0.5)$.
4. (Branch independence) Suppose that there are two lotteries L_1, L_2 such that (1) $L_1 \succeq L_2$, (2) there is a common branch in the two lotteries, say, (x_i, p_i) for some i, and (3) the outcomes in each lottery are all distinct. Branch independence implies that if, in both lotteries, we replace branch i with another branch (y_i, p_i), $x_i \neq y_i$ it is still the case that $L_1 \succeq L_2$. Consider the following additional property: (4) All corresponding probabilities are identical, i.e., for any i if (x_i, p_i) is the ith branch of L_1 and (y_i, q_i) is the ith branch of L_2, then $p_i = q_i$. When all four properties hold, we have the case of *restricted branch independence* (RBI).

Experiments indicate that coalescing lotteries can alter choices among lotteries.[48] Consider, for instance, the choice between the following two pairs of lotteries.

$$A = (50, 0.05; 50, 0.10; 100, 0.85) \text{ versus } B = (7, 0.05; 100, 0.10; 100, 0.85).$$
$$A' = (50, 0.15; 100, 0.85) \text{ versus } B' = (7, 0.05; 100, 0.95).$$

---

[48] See, for instance, Starmer and Sugden (1993), Humphrey (1995, 1998, 2000), Birnbaum (1999, 2004a, 2007).

In this pair of choices, if coalescing holds, then lotteries A, A' are identical and lotteries B, B' are also identical. Under EU, RDU, or PT, $A \succeq B$ implies $A' \succeq B'$. In contrast, for 200 subjects, Birnbaum (2004a) found that for 63% of the subjects, $B \succeq A$ and for 80% of the subjects, $A' \succeq B'$, which violates EU, RDU, and PT for a majority of the subjects.

Now consider a choice between the following two lotteries, C, D, where C first order stochastically dominates D,

$$C = (12, 0.05; 14, 0.05; 96, 0.90) \text{ versus } D = (12, 0.10; 90, 0.05; 96, 0.85).$$

Birnbaum and Navarrete (1998) found that 70% of the undergraduate students in their sample chose D over C.[49] Birnbaum (2004b) found that these results are not due to subject error in reporting their true preferences. Further, he showed that splitting the branches of a tree in a particular manner can reduce violations of stochastic dominance. Consider, for instance, C', D' that, in coalesced form, are identical to C, D respectively (so C' also first order stochastically dominates D'),

$$C' = (12, 0.05; 14, 0.05; 96, 0.05; 96, 0.85) \text{ versus } D' = (12, 0.05; 12, 0.05; 90, 0.05; 96, 0.85).$$

In C', relative to C, the top branch has been split, while in D', relative to D, the bottom branch is split. The splitting is done in such a way that the corresponding probabilities of all branches, when outcomes are ordered monotonically, are identical. This is known as the *canonical split form*. Birnbaum (2004b) found that 71% of the subjects violated stochastic dominance in a choice between C, D but only 5.6% did so when the choice was between C', D'.

Birnbaum (2008) reports the following two pairs of lotteries from Birnbaum (2001).[50]

$$E = (0, 0.50; 68, 0.07; 92, 0.43) \text{ versus } F = (0, 0.52; 92, 0.48).$$
$$E' = (0, 0.50; 68, 0.07; 97, 0.43) \text{ versus } F' = (0, 0.52; 92, 0.05; 97, 0.43).$$

RDU and PT imply that $F \succeq E$ if and only if $E' \succeq F'$ (the reader should check this). In contrast, out of a sample of 1438 respondents, for 66%, $E \succeq F$, while for 62%, $E' \succeq F'$, which contradicts RDU/PT.[51]

Birnbaum and Chavez (1997) find violations of restricted branch independence (RBI) but the direction of these violations is opposite to that predicted by PT.

2.9.2 *Violations of gain-loss separability*

Consider a lottery, as in (2.20), that is expressed in incremental form,

$$A = \left(y_{-m}, p_{-m}; y_{-m+1}, p_{-m+1}; \ldots; y_{-1}, p_{-1}; 0, p_0; y_1, p_1; y_2, p_2; \ldots; y_n, p_n\right),$$

where the reference outcome is identical to the reference point. We shall make use of the observation that in prospect theory, $v(0) = 0$, so we can assign any probability to an outcome of zero. Let the sum of probabilities in the domain of losses and gains be denoted, respectively, by $p_- = \sum_{i=-1}^{-m} p_{-i}$ and $p_+ = \sum_{j=0}^{n} p_j$. Denote by A^- and A^+, respectively, the negative and

---

[49] Birnbaum et al. (1999) found similar results on a new dataset.
[50] These lotteries were designed to test the property of *upper tail independence* in Wu (1994).
[51] See also Birnbaum (2005) for newer experiments that also arrive at similar findings.

positive components of A, having adjusted for the probability of a zero outcome in each case such that the respective probabilities in each component add upto 1.

$$A^- = \left(y_{-m}, p_{-m}; \ldots; y_{-1}, p_{-1}; 0, p_+\right), A^+ = \left(0, p_-; y_1, p_1; \ldots; y_n, p_n\right).$$

The probabilities in each of the lotteries in incremental form, A^- and A^+, add up to one. Using Definition 2.15, we can write the value function for lottery A as

$$V(A) = V\left(A^-\right) + V\left(A^+\right), \tag{2.101}$$

where $V\left(A^-\right)$ and $V\left(A^+\right)$ give the value function under PT corresponding to the two lotteries A^- and A^+. Consider another lottery in incremental form, B, with negative and positive components B^- and B^+; the reference point probability is adjusted so that probabilities of each component add up to 1. The decision maker is given a choice between the two pairs of prospects (i) A^+ and B^+, and (ii) A^- and B^-. Suppose that the following preference pattern is observed,

$$A^+ \succeq B^+, A^- \succeq B^-. \tag{2.102}$$

(2.102) implies that $V\left(A^+\right) \geq V\left(B^+\right)$ and $V\left(A^-\right) \geq V\left(B^-\right)$. Adding these two inequalities and using (2.101) we get

$$V(A) \geq V(B) \Leftrightarrow A \succeq B. \tag{2.103}$$

The pattern of preferences in (2.102), (2.103) constitute the property of *gain–loss separability* and it is satisfied by EU/RDU/OPT/PT. Wu and Markle (2008) give experimental evidence to reject gain–loss separability. They took the following lotteries

$$A^+ = (0, 0.5; 4200, 0.5), \ B^+ = (0, 0.25; 3000, 0.75),$$
$$A^- = (0, 0.5; -3000, 0.5), \ B^- = (0, 0.75; -4500, 0.25).$$

In a within-subjects experimental design, they found that for a clear majority of subjects $B^+ \succeq A^+$, $B^- \succeq A^-$, yet for a slight majority of subjects, it was found that $A \succeq B$.

2.9.3 Interaction between probability weights and stake sizes

The *stake size effect* refers to the observed change in relative risk aversion as the stake size in the domain of gains goes up; the idea goes back at least to Markowitz (1952). Empirical evidence suggests that the stake size effect arises from probability weighting rather than from the utility function. This calls into question the assumed separability between probabilities and outcomes that is assumed in EU, RDU, and PT.

The stake size effect has been verified in many studies but the stakes in these studies have typically not been very high or the high stakes have been hypothetical.[52] However, in the context of decision theory, doubts have been expressed about the use of hypothetical stakes relative to incentive compatible elicitation mechanisms.[53]

---

[52] See, for instance, Hogarth and Einhorn (1990), Bosch-Domenech and Silvestre (1999), and Weber and Chapman (2005).

[53] See, for instance, Beattie and Loomes (1997), Camerer and Hogarth (1999), and Holt and Laury (2002, 2005).

Not surprisingly, some of the high stakes experiments have come from subjects in developing countries; these studies report a significant stake effect in the domain of gains (Binswanger, 1981; Kachelmeier and Shehata, 1992). Post et al. (2008) consider data with very high stakes from the TV show *Deal or no Deal* and they report changes in risk aversion depending on the initial expectations and changes in the resolution of uncertainty. They offer support for PT over EU in explaining the observed facts.

What is the source of the stake size effect? Most empirical studies have attempted to identify the source as the utility function. However, some empirical studies have identified the role of probability weighting.[54] An important advance was made by Fehr-Duda et al. (2010) who dispensed with hypothetical rewards and considered lotteries in the domain of gains and losses. We now consider their work.

Experiments were conducted in Beijing in 2005 with 56 two-outcome lotteries—28 in the domain of gains and 28 in the domain of losses. One of the lotteries each in the domain of gains and losses was then randomly selected and played for real. In order to allow for lotteries in the loss domain, subjects were given initial endowments that covered the maximum possible loss. Outcomes and probabilities varied widely in the experiment and high stake lotteries were constructed from the low stake lotteries by scaling up the amounts by integer values.

It was assumed that the subjects used RDU (which nests EU as a special case). The functional forms used were as follows. The utility is of the power form as in (2.19), and the probability weighting function is the two-parameter Goldstein–Einhorn function given in (2.7). A finite mixture model was used to detect the presence of decision makers with heterogeneous preferences.[55]

Substantial heterogeneity in choices was found. About 27% of the subjects were expected utility types (labeled EUT types in Figure 2.13); they exhibited linear probability weighting functions and linear utility functions, so they are essentially expected value maximizers. The remaining 73% were non-expected utility types (labeled Non EUT types in Figure 2.13) and their probability weighting functions departed significantly from linearity. The experimental results for the two types of decision makers, separated by the gain and loss domains, and by stakes (high and low), are shown in Figure 2.13. On the vertical axis we have the relative risk premium (see 2.1). The main results arising from Figure 2.13 are as follows.

1. Fourfold classification of risk: The fourfold classification of risk that is explained above in Section 2.4.2 holds. For each type of decision maker, for high and low stakes gains that are of low probability, we have $RRP < 0$ (see (2.1) for the definition of RRP), hence, the decision maker is risk seeking. However, for higher probabilities in the domain of gains, for both EUT and non-EUT types, $RRP > 0$, so the decision maker is risk averse. The reverse picture emerges in the loss domain. Here, for both high and low stakes, $RRP > 0$ for small probabilities (risk aversion) and $RRP < 0$ for high probabilities (risk seeking).

2. The stake size effect: For any probability, p, in Figure 2.13, the stake size effect can be seen to hold for both types of decision makers (EUT and non-EUT) in the domain of gains. In the domain of gains, RRP is higher at each level of probability (except $p = 0.95$) when stakes are high as compared to when the stakes are low. However, no clear pattern on the stake size effect emerges in the domain of losses.

---

[54] See, for instance, Camerer (1992), Kachelmeier and Shehata (1992), Tversky and Kahneman (1992), and Etchart-Vincent (2004).

[55] The model is not designed to pick out prospect theory preferences because there are no mixed gambles, so loss aversion cannot be detected.

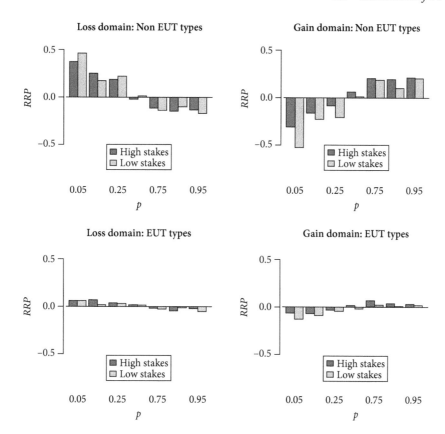

Figure 2.13 Median relative risk premium (RRP) for different types of decision makers as the probability, *p*, is varied.

Source: Journal of Risk and Uncertainty, 40(2): 147–80 (2010) "Rationality on the rise: why relative risk aversion increases with stake size." Helga Fehr-Duda, Adrian Bruhin, Thomas Epper, and Renate Schubert, Figure 2. © Springer Science + Business Media, LLC 2010, with kind permission from Springer Science and Business Media.

What causes the stake size effect to be prominent for gains but not for losses? The curvature of the utility function captured by the parameter γ does not vary with the stake size for both types of decision makers. Statistically, one cannot reject the hypothesis that the curvature of the utility function is stake-invariant. Since the only other component of the objective function is probability weights, it seems likely that this causes the stake size effect. This intuition is confirmed statistically.

The Goldstein–Einhorn function is a two-parameter family of probability weighting functions, hence, the inference about the contribution of probability weighting to the stake size effect must be based on the joint contribution of the two parameters, δ and η (see equation (2.7)). This is achieved by constructing 95% confidence bands based on the percentile bootstrap method, and using 2000 replications.

The probability weighting function for the EUT types is approximately linear, so in Figure 2.14 we report only the results in the gain and loss domains for the non EUT types. The probability weighting functions for high and low stakes in the domain of losses are quite similar, but there is a more marked difference in the domain of gains. In terms of the estimated parameters in the

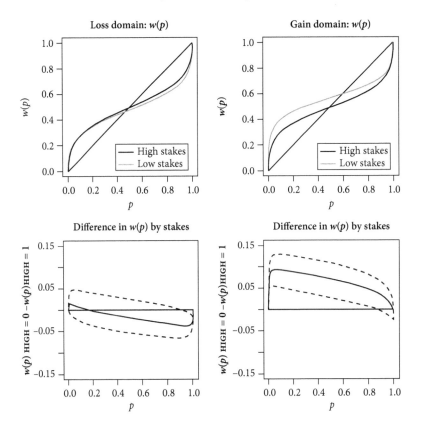

Figure 2.14 Stake dependent probability weights in the domain of losses and gains (upper panel) and 95% confidence bands based on the percentile bootstrap method (lower panel).

Source: Journal of Risk and Uncertainty, 40(2): 147–80 (2010) "Rationality on the rise: why relative risk aversion increases with stake size." Helga Fehr-Duda, Adrian Bruhin, Thomas Epper, and Renate Schubert, Figure 3. © Springer Science + Business Media, LLC 2010, with kind permission from Springer Science and Business Media.

domain of gains, δ, which captures the elevation of the Goldstein–Einhorn function, decreases from 1.304 to 0.913 as stakes increase. This corresponds to a lower degree of optimism. At the same time, η goes up with stakes, which mitigates slightly the inverse S-shape of the weighting function.

In the lower panel of Figure 2.14, if the confidence band includes the zero line, then we cannot reject the null hypothesis of stake-independent probability weights; this is the case in the domain of losses. There is also no noticeable difference between probability weights by stake in the domain of losses. However, in the domain of gains we can reject the hypothesis that the probability weighting function is stake independent (lower panel of Figure 2.14).

Not much is known about the determinants of probability weights but there have been several suggestions in the literature. These include differences in probability weights in the domain of gains and losses,[56] dependence on the timing of the resolution of uncertainty,[57] role of

---

[56] See, for instance, Abdellaoui (2000) and Bruhin et al. (2010).
[57] See, for instance, Noussair and Wu (2006) and Abdellaoui, Diecidue, and Öncüler (2011).

emotions,[58] and the *affect heuristic*.[59] Fehr-Duda et al., (2011) consider the effect of *incidental moods* on probability weighting by estimating a probability weighting function of the Goldstein–Einhorn form. Their subjects are asked if their day has been better or worse than normal on a scale of 0 (worse) to 5 (promising) and their probability weights for lotteries are elicited. Women who were in a better mood tended to weight probabilities more optimistically. No effect was found for men, most of whom behaved in a manner consistent with expected utility maximization.

2.9.4 *Heterogeneity in preferences*

Given a choice between two lotteries, non-stochastic versions of EU and most behavioral decision theories predict a preference for either of the two lotteries (unless one is indifferent between the two). In contrast, in most experiments, we observe heterogeneity in choices in the sense that there is a fraction of subjects who prefer each lottery. Experimental economists have tried to accommodate this stylized fact by allowing for subjects in experiments to make noisy decisions. The interested reader can consult Hey (2014) for a detailed and readable account of the various issues that we only briefly touch on here.

Suppose that subjects in experiments are asked to make a choice between two lotteries, L_1 and L_2. If the utility function V represents the decision maker's preferences in some decision theory, then we should observe L_1 to be chosen over L_2 if $V(L_1) > V(L_2)$. In this case, one typically conducts a test of differences in proportions to determine if the predictions of the relevant theory hold (Kahneman and Tversky, 1979). However, for whatever reasons, subjects in experiments may not state their preferences accurately, so they may exhibit a preference for L_1 over L_2 if $V(L_1) > V(L_2) + \varepsilon$, where ε is some random variable. This error term may be assumed to be common across all subjects in experiments (Camerer, 1989), or might vary by subjects in experiments (Carbone and Hey, 1994), or might even vary by the questions asked in experiments.

By assuming a specific error structure, one can engage in more sophisticated testing such as maximum likelihood rather than a simple test of proportions. For instance, Hey and Orme (1994) assumed that ε is normally distributed, while Carbone and Hey (1994) assume that ε has an extreme value distribution. Hey's (2014, p. 821) reading of the evidence based on experiments, which allow for noisy choices is this: "SEU is not bad, and where it is, then it is Rank Dependent that is better." But in other studies, there is strong support for prospect theory (Kothiyal et al., 2014; Abdellaoui, 2000; Erev et al., 2010).

One complication in models that are based on a uniform error structure across individuals is that the propensity to make decision errors varies with observed characteristics (von Gaudecker et al., 2011). Andersen et al. (2012) show that ignoring such heterogeneity may result in spurious correlation between background variables and risk attitudes. In particular, they show that cognitive ability is related to noisy decision making and that this can cause both positive and negative relationships between risk attitudes and cognitive ability, depending on the construction of the elicitation task.

---

[58] See, for instance, Walther (2003) who showed that anticipation of elation and disappointment lead to departures from linear probability weighting. The literature on regret aversion and disappointment aversion also identifies the effect of anticipated emotions on the shape of the probability weighting funtion; see, for instance, Bell (1982), Loomes and Sugden (1986), and Gul (1991). For other empirical evidence, see Fehr-Duda et al. (2011).

[59] See, for instance, Rottenstreich and Hsee (2001).

An even more satisfactory method of testing is to allow for a mixture of types in the experimental population who follow different behavioral decision theories. In addition, subjects may engage in noisy choices. Identifying heterogeneity in types, based on a *mixture model approach* has been an active area of research in recent years. In Fehr-Duda et al. (2010) that we considered above (Section 2.9.3), the evidence reveals a mixture of types in the population. About 23% are expected value maximizers, while the behavior of the remaining 73% is consistent with non-linear probability weighting.

Several recent papers ask the question: Is there a mixture of individuals in the population who follow different decision theories?[60] Harrison and Rutström (2009) calculated the probability that choices made by decision makers in their experiments are consistent with EU or with PT. They found that each of these two decision theories is equally likely to account for the observed choices. However, the authors recognize that these proportions are likely to vary with the task, context, and demographics of the subjects in experiments.[61]

Bruhin et al. (2010) use a finite mixture model and run three sets of experiments—two in Zurich and one in China. Across the three experiments, they find that about 20% follow expected value maximization, or EU maximization with risk neutrality. The remaining 80% exhibit non-linear probability weighting; 30% exhibit pronounced non-linear probability weighting and 50% somewhat less pronounced weighting. These proportions are roughly similar across the three experiments. Interestingly, these proportions (20% EU and 80% PT) are very similar to those found by Conte et al. (2011) who also use finite mixture models for British subjects in experiments, although there are several differences in the procedures followed by the two studies.

Figure 2.15 shows the estimated probability weighting functions for the student and the representative population in the study by Fehr-Duda and Epper (2012) that we have described above. For the student population (left panel of Figure 2.15), 80% exhibit a pronounced departure from linearity, of the inverse S-shaped form (Type I), while the remaining appear to be expected value maximizers (Type II). For the representative sample (right panel of Figure 2.15), 67% exhibit the inverse S-shaped form and have a more elevated probability weighting function (Type I), so they are more optimistic. The remaining 33% also exhibit a pronounced departure from linearity but they underweight probabilities significantly over a large range of higher probabilities (Type II). There are no expected value types in the representative sample. These results make a strong case for moving away from models of decision theory with linear probability weighting.

Mixture models would seem to have a better chance of explaining the dispersion in experimental results relative to any of the theories on their own. Heterogeneity in risk preferences can also arise in other dimensions. For gender based heterogeneity in risk attitudes, see Eckel and Grossman (2008), and Croson and Gneezy (2009); women are often more risk averse than men.[62] Dohmen et al. (2012) consider the intergenerational transmission of risk attitudes. Dohmen et al. (2011) uncover substantial heterogeneity of risk attitudes that depend on gender, age, parental background, and even height. Dohmen et al. (2010) find that lower cognitive ability is correlated with higher risk aversion as well as greater time impatience.

---

[60] See Hey and Orme (1994) for an earlier paper that revealed substantial heterogeneity between individuals.
[61] For evidence from diverse geographical regions, see Harrison et al. (2010).
[62] For a review of several studies of gender differences in risk seeking, which support the finding that men are more risk taking than women, see Charness and Gneezy (2012).

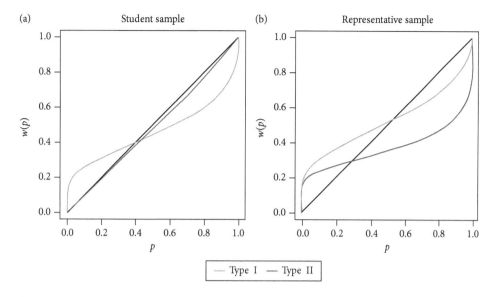

Figure 2.15 Two types of decision makers for the student and the representative population.

Source: Reproduced with permission of Annual Review of Economics, Volume 4. Helga Fehr-Duda and Thomas Epper, "probability and risk: foundations and economic implications of probability-dependent risk preferences." © 2012 by Annual Reviews http://www.annualreviews.org.

2.10 A selection of other behavioral theories

In this section, we consider some of the other important theories of behavioral decision making.

2.10.1 *Regret theory*

The ideas of *regret*, and its counterpart, *rejoice*, are not directly incorporated into EU/RDU/OPT/PT. In a recent book, Kahneman (2012, p. 288) lists the absence of the emotions of regret and disappointment as one of the blind spots of prospect theory. *Regret theory* tries to plug this gap.[63]

Suppose that there are n states of the world, $s_1, s_2, \ldots, s_n$, that can arise, respectively, with the objective probabilities $p_1, p_2, \ldots, p_n$. Suppose that a decision maker can take two possible actions, A_1 and A_2, each of which induces an outcome for each possible state. Let action A_1 induce outcomes $x_1, x_2, \ldots, x_n$ and action A_2 induce the outcomes $y_1, y_2, \ldots, y_n$. Suppose that outcomes are real numbers, say, levels of wealth.

Each state s_i is associated with a regret–rejoice function $R(x_i, y_i)$, where x_i, y_i are the respective outcomes under actions A_1 and A_2. When $R > 0$, the decision maker rejoices, and when $R < 0$, the decision maker regrets. If action A_1 is taken, the function $R(x_i, y_i)$ has the following properties:[64]

---

[63] Important early ideas that formed the basis of subsequent developments in this area are Bell (1982), Fishburn (1982a), and Loomes and Sugden (1982).

[64] Not all of these properties appeared in the early versions of regret theory. For instance, P2 and P4 were introduced by Loomes and Sugden (1987).

P1. $R(x_i, y_i)$ is positive if $x_i > y_i$, negative if $y_i > x_i$ and zero if $x_i = y_i$.

P2. $R(x_i, y_i)$ is increasing in the first argument and decreasing in the second.

P3. R is skew symmetric (or antisymmetric), i.e., $R(x_i, y_i) = -R(y_i, x_i)$.

P4. (Regret aversion) If $x > y > z > 0$ (where ">" means greater than), then

$$R(x,y) + R(y,z) < R(x,z). \tag{2.104}$$

From P1, in state s_i, the decision maker rejoices from taking action A_1 when it gives a relatively higher outcome ($x_i > y_i$). If $x_i > y_i$, rejoicing increases as the gap between x_i and y_i widens (property P2). P3 imposes strict symmetry into the model. The early formulations of regret theory allowed only for pairwise comparisons among tuples of the form x_i, y_i. Hence, transitivity could be easily shown to be violated. Loomes and Sugden (1987) then introduced property P4 that enabled comparisons between outcome triples.

In regret theory, action A_1 is preferred to action A_2 if, and only if,

$$\sum_{i=1}^{n} p_i R(x_i, y_i) > 0. \tag{2.105}$$

Regret theory is equivalent to EU in the special case where $R(x_i, y_i) = u(x_i) - u(y_i)$.

Regret aversion leads to fanning-out of the indifference curves in the probability triangle; see Sugden (1986). Hence, it is able to explain the Allais paradox. The early versions of regret theory can also easily account for intransitivity. Some early evidence indicated that the pattern of observed intransitivity was consistent with the predictions of regret theory (Loomes et al., 1989, 1991). However, subsequent evidence on observed patterns of intransitivity has been inconsistent with the predictions of regret theory (Starmer and Sugden, 1998). Furthermore, preferences under regret theory do not require that the decision maker should be indifferent between stochastically equivalent prospects (one of the exercises gives an example of such prospects). And so, regret theory is also able to account for violations of monotonicity. Some of these issues are further developed in exercises.

Bleichrodt et al. (2010) use the trade-off method to devise two separate tests for regret theory. Their two methods give similar results. In each case, they find support for an implication of regret aversion—namely that the regret function is convex. For a recent evaluation of regret theory, its ability to explain several facts that are puzzling for other decision theories, and a review of the relevant empirical evidence, see Bleichrodt and Wakker (2014).

2.10.2 *The theory of disappointment aversion*

Gul (1991) proposed a model of *disappointment aversion* in which decision makers distinguish between outcomes in a lottery that cause ex-post *elation* and *disappointment*. The reference point relative to which outcomes cause elation and disappointment is the *certainty equivalent* of the lottery. More formally, consider the lottery $L = (x_1, p_1; \ldots; x_n, p_n)$ such that $x_1 < \ldots < x_n$. Denote the certainty equivalent of this lottery by C_L. Suppose that

$$x_1 < \ldots < x_{k-1} \leq C_L < x_k < \ldots < x_n.$$

If the ex-post outcome is $x \leq x_{k-1}$ the decision maker feels disappointed and if it is $x > x_{k-1}$, then the decision maker feels elated. Define $q = \sum_{i=k}^{n} p_i$ as the sum of elation probabilities and

$1 - q$ as the sum of disappointment probabilities. A *disappointment-averse* decision maker then evaluates the lottery L as follows (Gul, 1991, Theorem 1):

$$U(L) = \sum_{j=1}^{k-1} \pi_j^D u(x_j) + \sum_{i=k}^n \pi_i^E u(x_i), \tag{2.106}$$

where u is a utility function, π_j^D is the decision weight accorded to the jth disappointing outcome, and π_i^E to the ith elating outcome. For $\theta > -1$, we define:

$$\pi_i^E = \left(\frac{q}{1 + (1-q)\theta} \right) \frac{p_i}{q} = \frac{p_i}{1 + (1-q)\theta}, k \le i \le n. \tag{2.107}$$

$$\pi_j^D = \left(1 - \frac{q}{1 + (1-q)\theta} \right) \frac{p_j}{1-q} = (1+\theta) \frac{p_j}{1 + (1-q)\theta}, 1 \le j \le k-1. \tag{2.108}$$

The parameter θ measures the sensitivity of the decision maker towards disappointment. To see this, suppose that an elating outcome, $i \ge k$, and a disappointing outcome, $j \le k-1$, have identical probabilities $p_i = p_j = p$, then $\pi_j^D = (1+\theta)\pi_i^E$. When $\theta > 0$, the decision weight assigned to a disappointing outcome is magnified relative to the case if it were actually an elating outcome. In the special case of $\theta = 0$, we get the formulation under EU, i.e., $\pi_i^E = p_i$ and $\pi_j^D = p_j$. The greater is θ, the more risk averse the decision maker may appear to be to an outside observer. The construction of the model has similarities with prospect theory because the certainty equivalent of the lottery plays the role of an endogenous reference point.[65]

Let us compare the model of disappointment aversion with RDU for the case of binary lotteries, $L_1 = (x_1, 1-p; x_2, p)$, where $x_1 < x_2$. In this case, the certainty equivalent of L_1 lies between x_1 and x_2. Thus, x_1 is the disappointing outcome and x_2 is the elating outcome. Using (2.106), (2.107), (2.108), and defining $\widetilde{w}(p) = \frac{p}{1+(1-p)\theta}$ and $\widetilde{w}(1-p) = \frac{1-p}{1+(1-p)\theta}$ we get[66]

$$U(L_1) = (1+\theta)\widetilde{w}(1-p)u(x_1) + \widetilde{w}(p)u(x_2). \tag{2.109}$$

Define a new probability function $w(p) = \frac{p}{1+(1-p)\theta}$ that is convex and subproportional (see Definition 2.6) for $\theta > 0$. Then (2.109) can be written as

$$U(L_1) = [1 - w(p)]u(x_1) + w(p)u(x_2). \tag{2.110}$$

(2.110) is observationally equivalent to the utility function under RDU. But there are other differences between the two theories. Consider a three-outcome lottery $L_1 = (x_1, p_1; x_2, p_2; x_3, p_3)$, $x_1 < x_2 < x_3$ and $p_1 + p_2 + p_3 = 1$. Fehr-Duda and Epper (2012) show that in a probability triangle with p_1 on the horizontal axis and p_3 on the vertical axis, the indifference curves under disappointment aversion are linear and they fan-out in the bottom half and fan-in in the top half. This contrasts with the indifference curves under RDU which are non-linear. The reason is that under disappointment aversion, the betweenness axiom is satisfied but it does not hold under RDU. Furthermore, consider a concave utility function. Then under RDU, the decision maker

---

[65] See Routledge and Zin (2010) for a two-parameter generalization of the model of disappointment aversion.

[66] Note that the reference point, the certainty equivalent of the lottery, C_L, is endogenous, and given by $u(C_L) = U(L|C_L)$, so in the general case, there is a fixed point to solve for (though not in the case with just two outcomes).

can be risk averse or risk seeking, depending on the shape of the probability weighting function. However, under disappointment aversion and $\theta > 0$, the decision maker can only be globally risk averse with a concave utility function; see Fehr-Duda and Epper (2012).

Abdellaoui and Bleichrodt (2007) find that Gul's model of disappointment aversion is too parsimonious and data suggests that disappointment aversion is not constant but variable.[67] Gill and Prowse (2012) find evidence for the general class of models of disappointment aversion, which they classify to include, Gul's disappointment aversion model, regret aversion, and the Köszegi–Rabin endogenous reference point model. They conduct a novel experiment in which two players sequentially choose effort levels in a tournament setting. Given their assumptions, the second mover's choice of effort is independent of the first mover's effort choice. Some of the results appear to be sensitive to the specification of the cost of effort function. Empirically, they find that the second mover's choice is influenced by the first mover's choice, which is consistent with models of disappointment aversion.

2.10.3 *Salience and context in decision theory*

We now consider an alternative model of decision making under risk that highlights the *salience* of outcomes (Bordalo et al., 2012). Let $S = \{s_1, \ldots, s_n\}$ be the set of possible states. State $s_i \in S$ occurs with probability $p_i \geq 0$, and $\sum_{i=1}^{n} p_i = 1$. Consider two lotteries or choices $\{L_1, L_2\}$, and let x_s^j be the payoff in state $s \in S$ when lottery $L_j, j = 1, 2$ is chosen. Let $x_s = \left(x_s^1, x_s^2\right)$ be the payoffs in the two choices when the state is s; $x_s^{\min}$ and $x_s^{\max}$ give the minimum and maximum payoffs in state s. Sometimes we shall denote x_s^{-i} as the payoff of lottery $L_j, j \neq i$, in state s.

We consider binary choices between lotteries, but the theory can be extended to multiple lotteries. In most behavioral alternatives to EU, whether a particular outcome is overweighted (more salient) or underweighted (less salient) depends on the probability associated with the outcomes, e.g., the Prelec (1998) probability weighting function overweights low probabilities and underweights high probabilities. In Bordalo et al. (2012), salience is a feature of the relative monetary payoffs of the two lotteries in each state.

> **Definition 2.31** *The salience of state s for lottery L_i, $i = 1, 2$, is given by a continuous and bounded salience function, $\sigma \left(x_s^i, x_s^{-i}\right)$, that has the following properties.*
>
> (a) *Ordering: Let $s, \tilde{s} \in S$. If $\left[x_s^{\min}, x_s^{\max}\right] \subset \left[x_{\tilde{s}}^{\min}, x_{\tilde{s}}^{\max}\right]$, then $\sigma \left(x_s^i, x_s^{-i}\right) < \sigma \left(x_{\tilde{s}}^i, x_{\tilde{s}}^{-i}\right)$.*
>
> (b) *Diminishing sensitivity: Suppose that in some state s, the outcomes in both lotteries are strictly positive, i.e., $x_s^i > 0$, $i = 1, 2$. Then, for any $\epsilon > 0$,*
>
> $$\sigma \left(x_s^i + \epsilon, x_s^{-i} + \epsilon\right) < \sigma \left(x_s^i, x_s^{-i}\right).$$
>
> (c) *Reflection: Let $s, \tilde{s} \in S$ and $x_s^i > 0$, $x_{\tilde{s}}^j > 0$, then*
>
> $$\sigma \left(x_s^i, x_s^{-i}\right) < \sigma \left(x_{\tilde{s}}^i, x_{\tilde{s}}^{-i}\right) \Leftrightarrow \sigma \left(-x_s^i, -x_s^{-i}\right) < \sigma \left(-x_{\tilde{s}}^i, -x_{\tilde{s}}^{-i}\right).$$

Ordering implies that a state is more salient if the distance between the two payoffs increases. Diminishing sensitivity implies that a state is less salient if, preserving the distance between the two outcomes, the outcomes are further away from zero. So zero plays the role of a reference point

---

[67] Camerer and Ho (1994) and Hey and Orme (1994) also report findings that are negative for models of disappointment aversion.

in this analysis. Reflection implies that salience is preserved under sign changes of outcomes. The last two properties also capture the notion of *context* in the model.

A decision maker in neoclassical theory, such as EU, treats all states as equally salient (in the sense defined above). However, in this model decision makers may assign higher probability weights to more salient states relative to less salient ones. Following Gennaioli and Shleifer (2010), we may term such decision makers as *local thinkers*.

Before we see how local thinkers make decisions, consider an example of a salience function that satisfies all the conditions in Definition 2.31.

$$\sigma\left(x_s^i, x_s^{-i}\right) = \frac{\left|x_s^i - x_s^{-i}\right|}{\left|x_s^i\right| + \left|x_s^{-i}\right| + \theta}; \theta > 0. \tag{2.111}$$

In (2.111), ordering is captured by the term in the numerator, and diminishing sensitivity by the denominator. Ordering and diminishing sensitivity are the two most important properties used in this model. Another property, *symmetry*, is intuitive when there are only two lotteries. Symmetry implies that $\sigma\left(x_s^i, x_s^{-i}\right) = \sigma\left(x_s^{-i}, x_s^i\right)$ and is satisfied by (2.111).

Example 2.18 *(Salience of states in the Allais paradox): Consider the Kahneman and Tversky (1979) version of the Allais paradox in its common consequence form (Definition 1.3). The decision maker chooses between the two lotteries*

   $L_1(z) = (0, 0.01; z, 0.66; 2500, 0.33)$ *and* $L_2(z) = (2400, 0.34; z, 0.66), z > 0.$

Since z is the common consequence, under EU different values of z should be irrelevant to the choice between L_1 and L_2. However, when $z = 2400$, most decision makers choose the safe lottery, $L_2(2400)$, and when $z = 0$ decision makers choose the risky lottery, $L_1(0)$. Let $z = 2400$, denote the three states by s_1, s_2, s_3, and rewrite $L_2(2400) = (2400, 0.01; 2400, 0.66; 2400, 0.33)$. Then, the three state-dependent outcome tuples in the two lotteries are $x_1 = (0, 2400), x_2 = (2400, 2400), x_3 = (2500, 2400)$ with associated probabilities $p_1 = 0.01$, $p_2 = 0.66$, $p_3 = 0.33$. We now consider the relative salience of these states. Using diminishing sensitivity,

$$\sigma(0 + 100, 2400 + 100) < \sigma(0, 2400). \tag{2.112}$$

Using the ordering property,

$$\sigma(2400, 2500) < \sigma(100, 2500). \tag{2.113}$$

From (2.112), (2.113),

$$\sigma(2400, 2500) < \sigma(0, 2400). \tag{2.114}$$

Also, by the ordering property,

$$\sigma(2400, 2400) < \sigma(2400, 2500). \tag{2.115}$$

From (2.114), (2.115), the relative salience of the three states is given by

$$\sigma(2400, 2400) < \sigma(2400, 2500) < \sigma(0, 2400). \tag{2.116}$$

If we wish to invoke symmetry, then we can also write the middle term as $\sigma(2500, 2400)$. We leave it to the reader to describe the salience of the various states when $z = 0$.

Definition 2.32 *Let $s, \widetilde{s} \in S$. Then state s is relatively more salient for lottery L_i (relative to lottery L_j) if $\sigma\left(x_s^i, x_s^{-i}\right) > \sigma\left(x_{\widetilde{s}}^i, x_{\widetilde{s}}^{-i}\right)$. Using this method we can rank the n states in the order of salience for lottery L_i. Let this ranking be $k_s^i \in \{1, 2, \ldots, n\}$ where a lower number denotes higher salience. Then, given the salience rankings of states, for lottery L_i, a "local thinker" transforms the relative probabilities of states s and $\widetilde{s}$, $\frac{p_s}{p_{\widetilde{s}}}$, as follows*

$$\frac{p_s^i}{p_{\widetilde{s}}^i} = \delta^{k_s^i - k_{\widetilde{s}}^i}\left(\frac{p_s}{p_{\widetilde{s}}}\right), \delta \in (0, 1], \tag{2.117}$$

where the ratio of transformed probabilities is denoted by $\frac{p_s^i}{p_{\widetilde{s}}^i}$. We normalize $\sum_{s \in S} p_s^i = 1$. The decision weight associated with the state s for lottery L_i is given by

$$p_s^i = p_s \omega_s^i, \text{ where } \omega_s^i = \frac{\delta^{k_s^i}}{\sum_{r \in S} \delta^{k_r^i} p_r}. \tag{2.118}$$

By definition,

$$\sum_{s \in S} p_s^i = \sum_{s \in S} \omega_s^i p_s = \sum_{s \in S} p_s \left(\frac{\delta^{k_s^i}}{\sum_{r \in S} \delta^{k_r^i} p_r}\right)$$

$$= \frac{1}{\sum_{r \in S} \delta^{k_r^i} p_r} \sum_{s \in S} p_s \delta^{k_s^i}$$

$$= 1.$$

Thus, the average distortion in probabilities must be zero (because $\sum_{s \in S} p_s = 1$). From (2.117), if state s is relatively more salient than state $\widetilde{s}$, then $k_s^i < k_{\widetilde{s}}^i$, so $\delta^{k_s^i - k_{\widetilde{s}}^i} > 1$, thus, the transformed probability of state s is also relatively higher. Conversely, if s is relatively less salient, then the transformed probability of that state is relatively lower. The size of δ is a measure of how much the probabilities are transformed. If $\delta = 1$, then $\delta^{k_s^i - k_{\widetilde{s}}^i} = 1$, so there is no distortion of probabilities and we have the case of EU; by contrast when $\delta < 1$, the decision maker is a local thinker. From (2.118), if $\delta^{k_s^i}$ is higher than the average $\sum_{r \in S} \delta^{k_r^i} p_r$, i.e., $\omega_s^i > 1$, then state s receives a higher decision weight; in other words it is relatively more salient. Thus, unlike some other behavioral theories, e.g., RDU, OPT, PT, the distortion in probabilities does not depend on the size of the probabilities, but rather on the salience of the outcomes in different states. Thus, low probability states are only overweighted if they are salient, otherwise not.

Definition 2.33 *The objective function of a "local thinker" for the lottery L_i, denoted by $V^{LT}(L_i)$ is given by*

$$V^{LT}(L_i) = \sum_{s \in S} p_s^i u(x_s),$$

where $u(x_s)$ is the utility of outcome x_s.

Let us revisit Example 2.18. Empirical evidence shows that most decision makers prefer $L_2(2400)$ to $L_1(2400)$. The explanation based on the framework of a local thinker is along the following lines. From (2.116), the most salient state for lottery $L_1(2400)$ is the one in which the outcome is 0, despite the fact that the outcome 0 occurs with a very small probability of 0.01. This leads to a substantial overweighting of this outcome (as is the case under RDU/OPT/PT, but for an entirely different reason). Thus, the decision maker prefers the lottery $L_2(2400)$ to $L_1(2400)$.

The model can explain the Allais paradox, preference reversal, and certain context dependent choices. Bordalo et al. (2013a) apply this model to explain four puzzles in finance. For instance, they can explain why the prices of assets with skewed returns are so high; the reason is that skewed returns are relatively more salient. For an alternative account, based on inverse S-shaped probability weighting functions, under RDU/PT, see Section 3.9. They can also explain the equity premium puzzle because downside risk is more salient than upside risk, an implication that does the job of loss aversion under PT. Bordalo et al. (2013b) apply the theory to consumer choice. They consider various attributes of consumer goods such as quality, price, and context. They then determine the consumer's willingness to pay for the good, depending on which attributes are more salient.

There is strong empirical support for the separate components of prospect theory that is also able to explain most of the phenomena that this theory of salience can explain. Hence, what is needed are empirical tests that stringently pit the predictions of the two theories against each other in domains where these predictions differ.

2.10.4 *Case-based decision theory*

One criticism of the Bayesian approach is that it is agnostic about the source of beliefs. One possible response to this criticism is the *case base decision theory* approach developed in Gilboa and Schmeidler (1995, 1997, 2001).[68] A central construct in this theory is a *similarity function*. When evaluating a new choice, individuals use a similarity function to compare it with all other *cases* in their database. The degree of similarity with other cases as well as the historical outcomes associated with choices made in the other cases then guide individuals in forming beliefs about their new choice.

The essence of the idea can be explained as follows. Suppose that an individual has some action set $A = \{a_1, \ldots, a_n\}$. There is also some universal set of *cases*, or possible situations, $C = \{c_1, \ldots, c_m\}$. Suppose that, at some instant in time, an individual has experience with the subset of cases $\overline{C} = \{c_1, \ldots, c_n\}$, $n \leq m$. Denote the utility arising from taking action a_i (in the past) in case c_j by u_{ij}. Then, for all i, j, the memory of the individual is given by $\Omega = \{A, \overline{C}, C, \{u_{ij}\}\}$. Suppose now that some new case arises, say, $c_k \in C$, $c_k \notin \overline{C}$. What action should the decision maker take?

Define an exogenously given similarity function $s(c_j, c_k)$, $c_j \in \overline{C}$. This captures the similarity between the new case, c_k, and any case $c_j \in \overline{C}$. Suppose that the decision maker wishes to evaluate the utility from taking action a_i under the new case, c_k. Let $M_i \subset C$ be the subset of cases in which action a_i was taken in the past. Then the utility from taking action a_i in case c_k, given M_i, is denoted by $U(a_i \mid c_k, M_i)$; this is sometimes called a *similarity weighted utility*:

$$U_i = U(a_i \mid c_k, M_i) = \sum_j s(c_j, c_k) u_{ij}; \ c_j \in M_i. \tag{2.119}$$

In (2.119), all cases in which action a_i was not taken in the past are irrelevant for the calculation and assigned zero utility, which is taken to be the *default aspiration level* of the decision maker. The chosen action a^* then satisfies

$$a^* \in \arg\max_{a_i \in A} U_i. \tag{2.120}$$

---

[68] For axiomatizations, see Billot et al. (2005) and Gilboa et al. (2006).

One implication of this framework is that if an action was never taken in the past, then it might never be taken in the future. However, because the aspiration utility level is zero, if all actions taken in the past yield negative utility, then the decision maker randomly chooses an action from among the set of actions not tried in the past. In this case, an action that was never chosen in the past can get chosen.

Gilboa and Schmeidler (1997) ask: What does the behavior of a case-based decision maker converge to in the long run? To answer this question, they postulate dynamics for the aspiration level as well as a specific form of the similarity function. In particular, this similarity function rules out the possibility that the outcome of an act reveals any information that is relevant for the evaluation of another act.[69] Based on these assumptions they find that the long-run behavior of the decision maker is optimal in the sense that it converges to one that would be chosen by an expected utility maximizer.

Guerdjikova (2008) shows that the optimality result fails if the specific similarity function used by Gilboa and Schmeidler (1997) is altered. She goes on to show how a modification of the similarity function and the dynamics of the aspiration levels can ensure the achievement of optimality. Extensive empirical evidence is required to sharpen and test these models. Using agent-based computational methods, Pape and Kurtz (2013) find evidence in support of case-based decision theory. Bleichrodt et al. (2017) also report evidence that is supportive of the theory.

Two further issues that need to be addressed are as follows. First, individuals often construct *hypothetical cases* and case studies in their minds before making choices, yet such cases are not a part of the existing theory. These hypothetical cases/actions might be completely unrelated to past cases/actions or payoffs, yet, be crucial in making current choices. Indeed, the ability to construct complex and informative hypothetical cases may be unique to humans. Second, the convergence of the model to an expected utility framework needs to address the issue of the empirical rejection of the expected utility model that we have considered at length above.

2.10.5 *Configural weights models*

We now briefly outline some *configural weights models* that have been proposed to deal with the violations of PT outlined in this section, followed by an assessment.[70] Like other non-EU alternatives, these models also weight probabilities in a non-linear manner. In these models, one first writes down the decision tree corresponding to the problem.

> **Definition 2.34** (*Lotteries and ranks*): *Consider some lottery,* $L = (x_1, p_1; \ldots; x_n, p_n)$ *where* $x_1 \geq \ldots \geq x_n$.[71] *Outcome* x_j *is then said to have rank* j, $j = 1, \ldots, n$.

---

[69] One can immediately think of many examples to convince oneself that this is quite a strong assumption. For instance, a car accident while being drunk may convince an individidual to avoid drinking while operating other forms of machinery.

[70] The interested reader may consult Birnbaum (2008) for an exhaustive set of references and a detailed survey of these models.

[71] Note that configural weights models write the successive outcomes in a lottery (reading from left to right) in decreasing order. This convention is used only in this section in the book.

THE RANK AFFECTED MULTIPLICATIVE WEIGHTS MODEL (RAM)

In the *rank affected multiplicative weights model* (RAM), the utility from lottery, L, is:[72]

$$RAM(L) = \frac{\sum_{i=1}^{n} a(i,n,s)t(p_i)u(x_i)}{\sum_{j=1}^{n} a(j,n,s)t(p_j)}. \tag{2.121}$$

Indices i,j denote the *rank* of the outcome (see Definition 2.53) and s is the *augmented sign* of the branch's consequence (positive, zero, or negative). The weighting function under RAM, $t(p)$, is an increasing function of p that takes the form,

$$t(p) = p^{\nu}; 0 < \nu < 1. \tag{2.122}$$

The utility function $u(x)$ typically takes the power form,

$$u(x) = x^{\beta}; 0 < \beta < 1. \tag{2.123}$$

$a(i,n,s)$ is the *rank and sign augmented branch weight* corresponding to the outcome that has rank i. The sign s of an outcome can be positive, negative, or zero. For two branch gambles ($n = 2$), e.g., the lottery $L = (100, 0.5; 0, 0.5)$, the lower outcome ($\$0$) has branch weight $a = 2$ and the higher outcome has branch weight $a = 1$. For $n \geq 3$, the branch weights are simply the ranks of the outcomes for that branch. For example, for the set of of outcomes, $x_1 \geq \ldots \geq x_{n-1} \geq x_n$ the weights are, respectively, $1, 2, \ldots, n-1, n$. Thus, lower outcomes are given higher weights, which is one of the main features of the model. The presence of the sign, s, of the outcome in $a(i,n,s)$ allows one to alter the branch weight, depending on the sign. Finally, using (2.122), we get

$$\lim_{p \to 0} \frac{t(p)}{p^{\nu}} = 1. \tag{2.124}$$

TRANSFER OF ATTENTION IN EXCHANGE MODELS (TAX)

Transfer of attention in exchange models (TAX) assume that the decision maker has a fixed and limited amount of attention. Hence, it is assumed, as in RAM models, that the decision maker transfers weight from higher ranked to lower ranked outcomes. Consider a *three-branch* lottery, L, given by $L = (x_1, p_1; x_2, p_2; x_3, p_3)$, $x_1 \geq x_2 \geq x_3$. Then, the utility of lottery L to the decision maker under TAX is given by

$$TAX(L) = \frac{w_1 u(x_1) + w_2 u(x_2) + w_3 u(x_3)}{w_1 + w_2 + w_3}, \tag{2.125}$$

where,

$$w_1 = t(p_1) - \frac{2}{4}\delta t(p_1); w_2 = t(p_2) - \frac{1}{4}\delta t(p_2) + \frac{1}{4}\delta t(p_1); w_3 = t(p_3) + \frac{1}{4}\delta t(p_1) + \frac{1}{4}\delta t(p_2); \tag{2.126}$$

---

[72] The reader may consult Birnbaum (1997) for the details.

$t(p)$ is given in (2.122) and $\delta > 0$ is some constant. In this version of the TAX model, also known as the *special TAX model*, due to Birnbaum and Stegner (1979), one transfers a fixed amount of probability weight from a higher outcome, proportionately, to lower outcomes. Thus, $w_1 + w_2 + w_3 = t(p_1) + t(p_2) + t(p_3)$. From w_1 given in (2.126), it follows that the weight on the highest outcome, x_1, is reduced by $\frac{2}{4}\delta t(p_1)$, and each of the lower two outcomes gains one half of this weight. Similarly, the middle ranked outcome, x_2, sheds weight $\frac{1}{4}\delta t(p_2)$, which is gained by the worse outcome, x_3.

THE GAINS DECOMPOSITION UTILITY MODEL (GDU)

In the GDU model, multi-branch lotteries are reduced to simple, two-branch, lotteries.[73] For instance, consider the binary lottery $L_2 = (x_1, p; x_2, 1 - p)$ such that $x_1 \geq x_2$. Then, under the *gains decomposition utility model* (GDU), the utility of this binary lottery is:

$$GDU(L_2) = w(p)u(x_1) + \big(1 - w(p)\big)u(x_2). \qquad (2.127)$$

Notice that the decision weights are formed exactly as under RDU. Three-branch lotteries such as $L_3 = (x_1, p_1; x_2, p_2; x_3, 1 - p_1 - p_2)$, $x_1 \geq x_2 \geq x_3$, are then evaluated as follows. First, define the lottery

$$L_4 = \left(x_1, \frac{p_1}{p_1 + p_2}; x_2, 1 - \frac{p_1}{p_1 + p_2} \right),$$

which offers a binary choice between the two best outcomes with the probabilities normalized to add up to one. Next, consider the lottery

$$L_5 = \big(L_4, p_1 + p_2; x_3, 1 - p_1 - p_2\big),$$

which offers a binary choice between the worst outcome x_3 in lottery L_3 and the lottery L_4. The worth of the lottery L_3 to the decision maker under the GDU model is

$$GDU(L_3) = w(p_1 + p_2)GDU(L_4) + \big[1 - w(p_1 + p_2)\big]u(x_3).$$

The weighting functions used in this theory are the standard weighting functions. Thus, $\lim_{p \to 0} \frac{w(p)}{p^\gamma} = \infty$ (see Definition 2.41).

AN EVALUATION OF THE CONFIGURAL WEIGHTS MODELS

Section 2.9.1 described several anomalies of EU/RDU/OPT/PT. These included coalescing, stochastic dominance, pattern of RBI, and upper tail independence. The configural weights models are able to explain these anomalies (Birnbaum, 2008). So what are economists to make of these models, which seem to be the only ones that can explain the relevant evidence?

1. The main difference in predictions between PT and the configural weights models arises in the case of *event splitting* (see Section 2.9.1); see Birnbaum (2008). This occurs when there are two identical outcomes in a lottery. This does not apply when all outcomes in a lottery are distinct, as for instance is the case with most of our applications (see Chapter 3).

---

[73] For the GDU model, see Luce (2000), and Marley and Luce (2001, 2005).

2. For lotteries of the form $(x, p; y, 1 - p)$, where $x < 0 < y$, Birnbaum (2008) reports that PT and TAX give close results. In many cases in economics, one is interested in binary decisions, often associated with binary outcomes, such as to pay or not pay taxes, to insure or not insure, to quit or not to quit one's job. So, for TAX to offer different predictions, we need lotteries with at least three outcomes.

3. More generally, it is difficult to distinguish between PT and TAX within the probability triangle. Hence, where PT is successful (e.g., the experiments reported by Kahneman and Tversky (1979), Tversky and Kahneman (1992) and, more generally, events that can be represented in the probability triangle), TAX is also successful. But for the "new" paradoxes, TAX succeeds where PT fails.

4. In many applications that involve use of hypothesis H2 (i.e., behavior for near-zero probabilities), configural weights models fail (see, e.g., (2.124)) as do EU, RDU, and PT, while *composite prospect theory* (CPT) succeeds in these cases (see Section 2.11). In these cases, the configural weights models can benefit by incorporating hypothesis H2 and the insights generated by composite prospect theory (described in Section 2.11).

5. To many economists, the practice of transferring an arbitrary amount of weight from a higher outcome to a lower outcome (see, e.g., (2.126)) will appear unattractive and mechanical. Proponents of configural weights models will argue that the weight to be transferred is calculated to fit the existing data; see Birnbaum (2008). But this begs the question of uniqueness; is there a unique way to transfer weight from the upper to the lower branches that leads to a successful prediction? This is the sense in which these models may appear arbitrary to some. It is also not clear what restrictions on preferences give rise to the RAM and TAX models or even if these restrictions are reasonable; by contrast the behavioral theories typically have rigorous preference foundations.

Overall, economists are likely to be intrigued by the evidence from configural weights models but not persuaded by the configural weights models that have been proposed to explain the evidence. Explaining the evidence gathered in this literature remains a challenge for behavioral decision theory.

2.11 Human behavior for extreme probability events

Many behavioral economists believe that for situations of risk, uncertainty, and ambiguity, RDU, OPT, and PT are the most satisfactory alternatives to EU (Wakker, 2010). Recall hypotheses H1 and H2 from Section 2.2. RDU and PT only take account of hypothesis H1; however, no decision theory accounts for the more general hypothesis H2 in a satisfactory manner. al-Nowaihi and Dhami (2010a) propose a modification of PT, *composite prospect theory* (CPT), that is able to account for H2. They also show how RDU can be modified to produce *composite rank dependent utility theory* (CRDU) that can also explain H2, but it is less satisfactory as compared to CPT. For the benefit of the readers we reproduce H2 here:

H2: There are two kinds of decision makers:

(H2a) A fraction $\mu \in [0, 1]$ of decision makers (i) ignore events of extremely low probability, and (ii) treat extremely high probability events as certain.[74] For all other (non-

---

[74] In the context of the take-up of insurance for low probability natural hazards, the results from one set of experiments by Kunreuther et al. (1978) are consistent with $\mu = 0.8$.

extreme) probabilities they behave as in H1, i.e., they overweight small probabilities and underweight large ones.

(H2b) A fraction $1 - \mu$ of the decision makers behave as in H1 for all levels of probabilities.

We may also view H2 as a *bimodal perception of risk*. Namely, that some individuals ignore very low probabilities altogether. Others do not ignore very low probabilities, particularly in the domain of losses; see for instance, McClelland et al. (1993) in an insurance context. Similar arguments can be constructed from the work of Viscusi (1998). Kunreuther et al. (1978) argue that the bimodal response to low probability events is pervasive in field studies. In their OPT, Kahneman and Tversky (1979) were acutely aware of H2.

The bimodal perception of risks framework and OPT (see Section 2.11.1 below) do not specify the size of μ. It is likely that μ depends on the context and the type of problem and that it can be influenced by the media, family, friends, and public policy. The size of μ is also likely to be influenced by emotions, experience, time available to make a decision, bounded rationality, framing, incentive effects, and so on.[75] For the purposes of our exposition we shall simply take μ as given. The endogeneity of μ is likely to be a fruitful avenue for future work.

2.11.1 *Original prospect theory (OPT)*

The only decision theory that incorporates hypothesis H2 is Kahneman and Tversky's (1979) *original prospect theory* (OPT). OPT makes a distinction between an *editing* and an *evaluation/decision* phase. From our perspective, the most important aspect of OPT is that decision makers decide *which improbable events to treat as impossible and which probable events to treat as certain*. Kahneman and Tversky (1979) employ an objective function similar to (2.23) in Definition 2.15, with one main difference: they use point transformations of probabilities, $\pi_i = w(p_i)$. From Example 2.2, we know that decision makers who use such a transformation can choose stochastically dominated options (Fishburn, 1978). Based on $\pi_i = w(p_i)$, and taking account of H2, they drew their decision weights function (or probability weighting function), $\pi(p)$, as in Figure 2.16; for our purposes the exact shape is less important than the gaps at the endpoints.

Kahneman and Tversky (1979, pp. 282–3) summarize the evidence for H2, as follows.

The sharp drops or apparent discontinuities of $\pi(p)$ at the end-points are consistent with the notion that there is a limit to how small a decision weight can be attached to an event, if it is given any weight at all. A similar quantum of doubt could impose an upper limit on any decision weight that is less than unity... the simplification of prospects can lead the decision maker to discard events of extremely low probability and to treat events of extremely high probability as if they were certain. Because people are limited in their ability to comprehend and evaluate extreme probabilities, highly unlikely events are either ignored or overweighted, and the difference between high probability and certainty is either neglected or exaggerated. Consequently $\pi(p)$ is not well-behaved near the end-points.

In this quote, Kahneman and Tversky are very explicit about human behavior near $p = 0$. Such events, in their words, are either *ignored* by some fraction μ of individuals (H2a) or *overweighted* by the complementary fraction $1 - \mu$ (H2b). This is what creates the gaps at the end points in

---

[75] See Ch. 4 (Anomalies on the demand side) in Kunreuther and Pauly (2005).

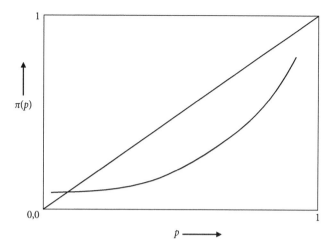

Figure 2.16 A hypothetical probability weighting function.
Source: Kahneman and Tversky (1979, p. 282) with permission of The Econometric Society.

Figure 2.16. However, the informal and heuristic approach of OPT is not always practical in dealing with H2.

We briefly describe some of the other simplifications or heuristics undertaken in the editing phase of OPT, although these do not necessarily deal with extreme probabilities. *Coalescing* or *combination* is the property that if an outcome appears more than once in a lottery, its probabilities can be added. For instance, the lottery (30, 0.2; 30, 0.3; 75, 0.5), also known as a *split lottery*, is equivalent to the lottery written in the coalesced form as (30, 0.5; 75, 0.5). The *cancellation heuristic* is used to eliminate common components among the lotteries being compared. The *dominance heuristic* is used to recognize and eliminate lotteries that are stochastically dominated. At the end of the *editing phase*, the decision maker converts lotteries into incremental form as in Definition 2.11 (probabilities can be normalized to add up to one if needed). In the *evaluation phase*, the decision maker evaluates these lotteries as in Example 2.1 above.

OPT was heavily criticized for the feature that decision makers could choose stochastically dominated options (Examples 2.1, 2.2). In response to these difficulties, Tversky and Kahneman (1992) modified OPT to *cumulative prospect theory* (PT) by incorporating the insight of *cumulative transformation of probabilities* from RDU. Hence, they needed a probability weighting function, $w(p)$, that, unlike the one in Figure 2.16, was *defined* for the entire probability domain $[0, 1]$ (otherwise Definition 2.14 could not be applied). Modifying OPT to PT meant eliminating the psychologically rich *editing phase*, which may have been a difficult choice for its authors. Furthermore, since PT lacks the relevant editing phase, it cannot account for H2a.

2.11.2 *The evidence on behavior under low probability events*

In this section we present a brief overview of the evidence for hypothesis H2. The interested reader can consult al-Nowaihi and Dhami (2010a) for the details. In all the anomalies arising from low probability events in this section, the most natural explanation is that a fraction of the individuals behave as in H2a. Thus, they ignore the very low probability of the potentially high levels of harm that might be caused by their actions (actions with low levels of harm are not as interesting). We note that under EU, but particularly under RDU and PT, decision makers place too great a salience on low probability events because for most probability weighting functions, $lim_{p\to 0} \frac{w(p)}{p} = \infty$ (see Proposition 2.5).

INSURANCE FOR LOW PROBABILITY EVENTS

Kunreuther et al. (1978) provide striking evidence that decision makers buy inadequate non-mandatory insurance against low probability natural hazards, e.g., earthquakes, floods, and hurricane damage in areas prone to these hazards.[76] EU predicts that a risk averse decision maker facing an actuarially fair premium will, in the absence of transactions costs, buy full insurance for all probabilities, however small. Kunreuther et al. (1978, Chapter 7) presented subjects with varying potential losses with various probabilities, and fixed expected loss. Subjects faced actuarially fair, unfair, or subsidized premiums. In each case, they found that as the probability of the loss decreases, there is a point below which the take-up of insurance drops dramatically.[77]

The lack of interest in buying insurance for low probability natural hazards arose despite active government attempts to (i) provide subsidy to overcome transaction costs, (ii) reduce premiums below their actuarially fair rates, (iii) provide reinsurance for firms, and (iv) provide the relevant information. Furthermore, insurees were aware of the losses due to natural hazards (many overestimated them). Moral hazard issues (e.g., expectation of federal aid in the event of disaster) were not found to be important.

Arrow's own reading of the evidence in Kunreuther et al. (1978) is that the problem is on the demand side rather than on the supply side. Arrow writes (Kunreuther et al., 1978, p. viii), "Clearly, a good part of the obstacle [to buying insurance] was the lack of interest on the part of purchasers." Kunreuther et al. (1978, p. 238) write: "Based on these results, we hypothesize that most homeowners in hazard-prone areas have not even considered how they would recover should they suffer flood or earthquake damage. Rather they treat such events as having a probability of occurrence sufficiently low to permit them to ignore the consequences." This behavior is in close conformity to H2a.

THE BECKER (1968) PARADOX

A celebrated result, the *Becker (1968) proposition*, states that the most efficient way to deter crime is to impose the "*severest possible penalty, F, with the lowest possible probability of detection and conviction, p.*" By reducing p, society can economize on the costs of enforcement, such as policing and trial costs. But by increasing F, which is relatively less costly, the deterrence effect of the punishment is maintained. In an appropriately specified model, one can prove the following proposition

> **Proposition 2.15** *(Dhami and al-Nowaihi, 2013): Under EU, risk-neutrality or risk-aversion, potentially infinitely severe punishments,[78] and a utility that is unbounded below,*

---

[76] In the foreword, Arrow (Kunreuther et al., 1978, p. vii) writes: "The following study is path breaking in opening up a new field of inquiry, the large scale field study of risk-taking behavior." The reader can also consult similar but more recent evidence in Kunreuther and Pauly (2004, 2005).

[77] These results were shown to be robust to changes in subject population, changes in experimental format, order of presentation, presenting the risks separately or simultaneously, bundling the risks, compounding over time, and introducing "no claims bonuses."

[78] For instance, ruinous fines, slavery, torture, extraction of body parts (all of which have been historically important), and modern capital punishment.

the Becker proposition implies that crime would be deterred completely, however small the
probability of detection and conviction.

Kolm (1973) memorably phrased this proposition as: *it is efficient to hang offenders with*
probability zero. Empirical evidence strongly suggests that the behavior of a significant number
of people does not conform to the Becker proposition. This is known as the *Becker paradox.* For
instance, Levitt (2004) shows that the estimated contribution of capital punishment in deterring
crime in the US, over the period 1973–91, was zero.[79]

Under RDU and PT, because decision makers heavily overweight the small probability of
a punishment (see Proposition 2.5), they can be shown to be deterred by Becker type punishments even more as compared to EU and so the Becker paradox remains; see Dhami and
al-Nowaihi (2013) for a formal proof. There are several competing explanations for the Becker
paradox but none of them are ultimately satisfactory; see al-Nowaihi and Dhami (2010a) for
the details.

A natural explanation for the Becker paradox is that a fraction μ of individuals ignore (or
heavily underweight) the very low probability of getting caught (as in H2a), so they commit a
crime despite high levels of punishment.

EVIDENCE FROM JUMPING RED TRAFFIC LIGHTS

Consider the act of running a red traffic light. There is at least a *small probability* of an accident.
al-Nowaihi and Dhami (2010a) show that the nature of this problem is very similar to the
Becker proposition, except that the consequences are *self-inflicted* and potentially have *infinite costs,* such as loss of one's life. Indeed, under EU, we should not expect anyone to run
red traffic lights. Decision makers using RDU and PT should be even more reluctant to run red
traffic lights because of the feature $lim_{p\to 0}\frac{w(p)}{p} = \infty$ (see Proposition 2.5) in most probability
weighting functions.

Bar-Ilan and Sacerdote (2001, 2004) estimate that there are 260,000 accidents per year in the
US caused by red-light running with implied costs of car repair alone of the order of $520 million
per year. Clearly, this is an activity of economic significance and it is implausible to assume that
running red traffic lights are simply "mistakes." Using Israeli data, Bar-Ilan (2000) calculated
that the expected gain from jumping one red traffic light is, at most, one minute (the length of a
typical light cycle). Given the known probabilities, they find that if a slight injury causes a loss
greater or equal to 0.9 days, a risk-neutral person who follows EU will be deterred by that risk
alone. However, the corresponding numbers for the additional risks of serious and fatal injuries
are 13.9 days and 69.4 days respectively, which should ensure complete compliance with the law.
However, evidence is to the contrary.

Clearly, EU combined with risk aversion struggles to explain this evidence. So too do RDU
and PT. A plausible explanation for observed red traffic light running is that a fraction μ of
individuals run red traffic lights because they ignore or seriously underweight the very low
probability of an accident (as under H2a).

OTHER EXAMPLES OF HYPOTHESIS H2

Consider the usage of hand-held mobile phones in moving vehicles. A user of mobile phones
faces potentially *infinite punishment* (e.g., loss of one's and/or the family's life) with *low probabil-*

---

[79]   See also Radelet and Ackers (1996) and Polinsky and Shavell (2007).

ity, in the event of an accident.[80] Evidence from the UK indicates that up to 40% of individuals drive and talk on mobile phones (The Royal Society for the Prevention of Accidents, 2005). Pöystia et al. (2005) report that two thirds of Finnish drivers and 85% of American drivers use their phone while driving, which increases the risk of an accident by two to sixfold. Hands-free equipment, although now obligatory in many countries, seems not to offer essential safety advantages.

People were initially reluctant to use non-mandatory seat belts in cars despite publicly available evidence that seat belts save lives. Prior to 1985, in the US, only 10–20% of motorists wore seat belts voluntarily (Williams and Lund, 1986). Car accidents may be perceived by individuals to be *very low probability events*, particularly if individuals are overconfident of their driving abilities.[81] Although accidents are *potentially fatal*, many people seem to ignore the low probability of facing such events.

Even as evidence accumulated on the dangers of breast cancer (*low probability, potentially fatal, event*[82]) women only sparingly took up the offer of breast cancer examination. In the US, this changed only after the greatly publicized events of the mastectomies of Betty Ford and Happy Rockefeller; see Kunreuther et al. (1978, pp. xiii, 13–14). Hence, the fraction of individuals to whom stylized fact H2(a) applies, μ, is not static.

CONCLUSION FROM THESE DISPARATE CONTEXTS

Two main conclusions arise from these examples. First, human behavior for low probability events cannot be easily explained by most decision theories. EU and the associated auxiliary assumptions are unable to explain the stylized facts. RDU and PT make the problem even worse because $lim_{p \to 0} \frac{w(p)}{p} = \infty$ (see Proposition 2.12). Second, a natural explanation for these phenomena is that many individuals (the fraction, μ) simply ignore or seriously underweight very low probability events, even when the consequence is a huge loss.

2.11.3 *Composite Prospect Theory*

The theoretical solution offered by al-Nowaihi and Dhami (2010a) to incorporate hypothesis H2 is a proposal for a new probability weighting function—the *composite Prelec probability weighting function* (CPF). The CPF is generated by *smooth pasting* three standard Prelec functions; see Figure 2.17 for the general shape of a CPF. In Figure 2.17, decision makers heavily underweight very low probabilities in the range $[0, p_1]$ in the sense that is made clear in Remark 2.5.

Remark 2.5 *The CPF zero-underweights infinitesimal probabilities, i.e.,* $\lim_{p \to 0} \frac{w(p)}{p} = 0$,

and zero-overweights near-one probabilities, i.e., $\lim_{p \to 1} \frac{1-w(p)}{1-p} = 0$. *This contrasts with the*

standard Prelec function where $\lim_{p \to 0} \frac{w(p)}{p} = \infty$ *and* $\lim_{p \to 1} \frac{1-w(p)}{1-p} = \infty$ *(see Proposition 2.5).*

---

[80] Extensive evidence suggests that the perceived probability of an accident might be even lower than the actual probability because drivers are *overconfident* of their driving abilities. Taylor and Brown (1988) suggest that up to 90% of car accidents might be caused by overconfidence.

[81] People assign confidence intervals to their estimates that are too narrow and 90% of those surveyed report that they have above-average levels of intelligence and emotional ability (Weinstein, 1980).

[82] We now know that the *conditional* probability of breast cancer if there is such a problem in close relatives is not low. However, we refer here to data from a time when such a link was less well understood.

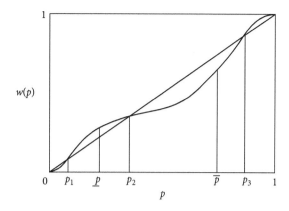

Figure 2.17 The composite Prelec weighting function (CPF).

Decision makers who use the CPF ignore very low probability events by assigning low subjective probability weight, w, to them, hence, conforming with H2a. By contrast, decision makers who use the standard Prelec function heavily overweight very low probabilities (see Proposition 2.5), and so they conform to H2b. Events in the interval $[p_3, 1]$ are overweighted in the CPF, as suggested by Kahneman and Tversky (1979, pp. 282–3). In the middle segment, $p \in [\underline{p}, \overline{p}]$, the CPF is inverse S-shaped, identical to a standard Prelec function. al-Nowaihi and Dhami (2010a) show formally that CPF is *flexible* and has preference foundations. The standard Prelec function is a special case of the CPF.

A BRIEF, MORE FORMAL TREATMENT OF THE CPF

The CPF takes three segments from three different Prelec functions (see Definition 2.4) and joins them up in a continuous manner. The two points, $\underline{p}, \overline{p}$, in Figure 2.17 are the cutoff points between the three Prelec functions. Define,

$$\underline{p} = e^{-\left(\frac{\beta}{\beta_0}\right)^{\frac{1}{\alpha_0 - \alpha}}}, \ \overline{p} = e^{-\left(\frac{\beta}{\beta_1}\right)^{\frac{1}{\alpha_1 - \alpha}}}. \tag{2.128}$$

Definition 2.35   *(al-Nowaihi and Dhami, 2010a): By the composite Prelec weighting function we mean the probability weighting function $w : [0,1] \to [0,1]$ given by*

$$w(p) = \begin{cases} 0 & if & p = 0 \\ e^{-\beta_0(-\ln p)^{\alpha_0}} & if & 0 < p \leq \underline{p} \\ e^{-\beta(-\ln p)^{\alpha}} & if & \underline{p} < p \leq \overline{p} \\ e^{-\beta_1(-\ln p)^{\alpha_1}} & if & \overline{p} < p \leq 1 \end{cases} \tag{2.129}$$

where $\underline{p}$ and $\overline{p}$ are given by (2.128) and

$$0 < \alpha < 1, \ \beta > 0; \ \alpha_0 > 1, \ \beta_0 > 0; \ \alpha_1 > 1, \ \beta_1 > 0, \beta_0 < 1/\beta^{\frac{\alpha_0 - 1}{1 - \alpha}}, \ \beta_1 > 1/\beta^{\frac{\alpha_1 - 1}{1 - \alpha}}. \tag{2.130}$$

The restrictions $\alpha > 0$, $\beta > 0$, $\beta_0 > 0$, and $\beta_1 > 0$, in (2.130), are required by the axiomatic derivations of the Prelec function; see al-Nowaihi and Dhami (2006). The restriction

$\beta_0 < 1/\beta^{\frac{\alpha_0-1}{1-\alpha}}$ and $\beta_1 > 1/\beta^{\frac{\alpha_1-1}{1-\alpha}}$ ensure that the interval $(\underline{p},\overline{p})$ is not empty. The interval limits are chosen so that the CPF in (2.129) is continuous across them.

Proposition 2.16 *(al-Nowaihi and Dhami, 2010a): The composite Prelec function (Definition 2.55) is a probability weighting function in the sense of Definition 2.1.*

Define p_1, p_2, p_3 (see Figure 2.17) as follows:

$$p_1 = e^{-\left(\frac{1}{\beta_0}\right)^{\frac{1}{\alpha_0-1}}}, p_2 = e^{-\left(\frac{1}{\beta}\right)^{\frac{1}{\alpha-1}}}, p_3 = e^{-\left(\frac{1}{\beta_1}\right)^{\frac{1}{\alpha_1-1}}}. \tag{2.131}$$

Proposition 2.17 *(al-Nowaihi and Dhami, 2010a): (a) $p_1 < \underline{p} < p_2 < \overline{p} < p_3$. (b) $p \in \left(0,p_1\right) \Rightarrow w\left(p\right) < p$. (c) $p \in \left(p_1,p_2\right) \Rightarrow w\left(p\right) > p$. (d) $p \in \left(p_2,p_3\right) \Rightarrow w\left(p\right) < p$. (e) $p \in \left(p_3,1\right) \Rightarrow w\left(p\right) > p$.*

By Proposition 2.17, a CPF overweights low probabilities in the range $\left(p_1,p_2\right)$ and underweights high probabilities in the range $\left(p_2,p_3\right)$, thus, it is inverse S-shaped in the middle. But, in addition, and unlike all the standard probability weighting functions, it underweights near-zero probabilities in the range $\left(0,p_1\right)$, and overweights near-one probabilities in the range $\left(p_3,1\right)$ as required in H2a.

The restrictions $\alpha_0 > 1, \alpha_1 > 1$ in (2.130) ensure that a CPF has the following properties, that help explain human behavior for extremely low probability events.

Proposition 2.18 *For the CPF (Definition 2.35), $\forall \gamma > 0$, the CPF (i) zero-underweights infinitesimal probabilities, i.e., $\lim\limits_{p \to 0} \frac{w(p)}{p^\gamma} = 0$, and (ii) zero-overweights near-one probabilities, i.e., $\lim\limits_{p \to 1} \frac{1-w(p)}{1-p} = 0$.*

The CPF has not yet been empirically estimated, so its ability to explain H2 is still an open question. The larger number of parameters in the CPF relative to any of the standard weighting functions can pose difficulties in estimation. Indeed, as Peter Wakker points out in personal communication, one needs to conduct proper statistical tests such as Akaike's criterion for weighing the pros and the cons of additional parameters. We welcome such tests. However, most economic situations of interest where the CPF has real bite are low probability events. Over this range, a CPF is simply a Prelec function with $\alpha > 1$. Hence, at a very minimum, one might wish to estimate if for *low probabilities* we observe a separation of decision makers into two groups: One with a Prelec parameter $\alpha > 1$ and another with $\alpha < 1$. Clearly, these low probabilities must be lower relative to those that are used in the standard experiments, say, one in 10,000 or one in 20,000. These could be the approximate chances of a house being burgled in some area, or the probability of suffering an accident while driving and talking on a mobile phone.

DEFINITIONS OF CPT AND CRDU

We now give definitions of *composite prospect theory* (CPT) and *composite rank dependent utility* (CRDU).

Definition 2.36 *(Composite prospect theory (CPT), al-Nowaihi and Dhami, 2010a): Under CPT, a fraction $1 - \mu$ of the population uses cumulative prospect theory, PT, with any of its standard probability weighting functions, such as the standard Prelec function, so $\lim_{p\to0} \frac{w(p)}{p} = \infty$. This fraction conforms to hypothesis H2b. The remaining fraction, μ,* uses PT but replaces the standard probability weighting function with the composite Prelec probability weighting function, CPF, for which $\lim_{p \to 0} \frac{w(p)}{p} = 0$ (see Propositions 2.5 and 2.18). This fraction conforms to H2a.

From Definition 2.36, for the respective fractions μ and $1 - \mu$, the decision weights in Definition 2.14 are calculated by using, respectively, the CPF and the standard probability weighting function. Once these probability weights are calculated, the objective function in Definition 2.15 is used to compute the utility from any lottery in incremental form.

> **Definition 2.37** *(Composite rank dependent utility (CRDU); al-Nowaihi and Dhami, 2010a) In CRDU, RDU replaces PT in Definition 2.36.*

From Definition 2.37, we use the appropriate probability functions (CPF for the fraction μ and any standard function for the fraction $1 - \mu$) to calculate the decision weights in Definition 2.7, followed by the calculation of the value of the objective function in Definition 2.8.

Other than the probability weighting functions, CPT and CRDU share all other elements with PT and RDU, respectively. In this sense, both are conservative extensions of existing and established theories. However, the extension enables the explanation of hypothesis H2, which is more general than H1. Thus, we have the nested structure: CPT can explain everything that PT can, which in turn can explain everything that RDU can, which in turn can explain everything that EU can, which in turn explains everything that expected value maximization (EV) can. However, the converse is false in each case.[83]

CRDU could be thought of as a special case of CPT in the absence of a reference point.[84] However, this rules out the psychologically powerful and robust notions of loss aversion and reference dependence, which have strong explanatory power in a variety of contexts and are too important to be ignored.[85] This is likely to weaken the explanatory power of CRDU relative to CPT.

CPT has potential applications to a wide range of economically important problems such as insurance, and crime and punishment. Some of these applications are considered in the exercises.

2.12 Risk preferences and time preferences

In economics, it is typical to give a separate treatment of risk preferences and time preferences and assume that these two kinds of preferences are unrelated. Yet, the outcomes of most human decisions are uncertain and take time to materialize, which is suggestive of a potential link between the two. An emerging literature has tried to grapple with the complex interaction between these two entities. The contributions have been both theoretical and empirical.[86] Issues

---

[83] See al-Nowaihi and Dhami (2010a) for these claims. CPT can also incorporate the insight from *third generation prospect theory* of Schmidt et al. (2008). One may also refer to CPT as *fourth generation prospect theory* if one prefers this kind of terminology.

[84] This requires, of course, that we collapse lotteries in incremental form in CPT back to ordinary lotteries first (i.e., add the reference point to each outcome), and then apply CRDU.

[85] See, for instance, the applications discussed in Camerer (2000), Kahneman and Tversky (2000), and Barberis and Thaler (2003).

[86] For the theoretical contributions, see, for instance, Halevy (2008), Walther (2010), Baucells and Heukamp (2012), and Epper and Fehr-Duda (2014b). For the empirical contributions, see, for instance, Andreoni and Sprenger (2012b) and Epper and Fehr-Duda (2014a).

of time discounting are considered more fully in Volume 3 where we also consider the effect of uncertainty on time preferences. In this section, we consider some of the theoretical and empirical contributions that explore the links between these two areas but with greater focus on risk preferences.

2.12.1 *Can non-linear probability weighting explain temporal behavior under risk?*

We begin by considering the contribution by Andreoni and Sprenger (2012b). In order to separate the role of risk and time preferences, they use a test method known as *convex time budgets*. This method and the basic research question here is adapted from their earlier work in Andreoni and Sprenger (2012a). At date 0, subjects are allocated 100 tokens. They can allocate integer amounts between an earlier date, t, or a later date, $t + k$. A generic allocation is denoted by $(n, 100 - n)$, where $0 \leq n \leq 100$. These tokens can then be exchanged for cash at dates t and $t + k$, respectively, at exchange rates of a_t and a_{t+k} per token. Two values of k are considered: $k = 28$ and $k = 56$.

In the experiments, $a_{t+k} = \$0.2$ per token and $a_t = \frac{a_{t+k}}{1+r}$, where r is the gross interest rate over k days.[87] The interest rate was varied from 0% to 2116.6% in discrete steps. Suppose that we refer to the income realized at any date as the consumption at that date. The future is uncertain in the sense that the payments at t and $t + k$, respectively, are honored with probabilities p_1 and p_2 that are independent of each other. If the payments at both dates go through, then the consumption stream is given by

$$\left(c_t, c_{t+k}\right) = \left(na_t, (100 - n)a_{t+k}\right). \tag{2.132}$$

Using $a_t = \frac{a_{t+k}}{1+r}$, the budget constraint of the consumer, expressed in date $t + k$ units, is given by[88]

$$(1 + r)c_t + c_{t+k} = 100a_{t+k}. \tag{2.133}$$

Given the uncertainty in the payments, the decision maker faces the following prospect:

$$L(p_1, p_2) = \left(\left(c_t, c_{t+k}\right), p_1 p_2; (c_t, 0), p_1(1 - p_2); \left(0, c_{t+k}\right), (1 - p_1)p_2; (0, 0), (1 - p_1)(1 - p_2)\right). \tag{2.134}$$

In order to evaluate the utility of the consumer, we follow the *portfolio approach* in Chew and Epstein (1990). There are at least two other approaches—the *separable case* and the *recursive case*; see Appendix A1 in Epper and Fehr-Duda (2014a). Andreoni and Sprenger (2012b) use the separable case. The separable and recursive cases do not correctly predict the behavior in the left panel of Figure 2.19, while the portfolio case correctly predicts it, as we show below. It is worth noting how the three cases reduce lotteries when both time and risk are present; see the self-explanatory Figure 2.18.

In this section, we shall consider only the portfolio case. Denote the *intertemporal discounted utility* from the consumption profile $\left(c_t, c_{t+k}\right)$ by $D(t)v(c_t) + D(t + k)v(c_{t+k})$, where D is a

---

[87] The standardized daily net interest is, therefore, $(1 + r)^{1/k} - 1$.
[88] We could alternatively have expressed the budget constraint in date t units as $c_t + \frac{c_{t+k}}{(1+r)} = 100a_t$.

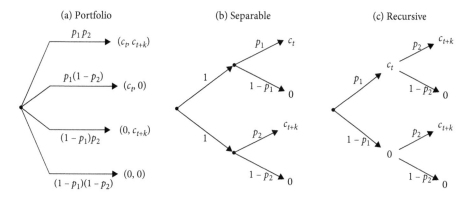

Figure 2.18 Reduction of lotteries when both time and risk are present, in three different cases.
Source: Epper and Fehr-Duda (2014a) with permission from the American Economic Association.

discount function that is differentiable throughout, is strictly decreasing in time, and has continuous partial derivatives up to order two. v is a utility function such that

$$v(0) = 0, v' > 0 \text{ and } v'' < 0. \tag{2.135}$$

In a baseline condition, $(1,1)$, the prospect is $L(1,1)$ and it is compared to a scaled down version (λ, λ), with the corresponding prospect $L(\lambda, \lambda)$, where $0 < \lambda < 1$, in order to check for the common ratio effect. Two different risk conditions are considered, $(1, q)$ and $(q, 1)$. In each case, their respective scaled down conditions $(\lambda, \lambda q)$ and $(\lambda q, \lambda)$ are also considered to check for the common ratio effect under risk.

> **Proposition 2.19** *In any delay-discounting model (exponential discounting is a special case), where the decision maker follows expected utility, suppose that the optimal number of tokens purchased by the decision maker is n^*.*
>
> (i) *The optimal number of tokens, n^*, and the optimal consumption levels, c_t^* and c_{t+k}^*, do not change when p_1 and p_2 are scaled up or down by a common factor.*
> (ii) *The optimal number of tokens, n^*, and optimal consumption c_t^*, decrease as the interest rate, r, goes up.*

Proof: (i) In any delay-discounting model, the utility of the prospect in (2.134), given $v(0) = 0$, is given by

$$V_D = p_1 p_2 \left[D(t)v(c_t) + D(t+k)v(c_{t+k}) \right] + p_1(1-p_2)D(t)v(c_t) + (1-p_1)p_2 D(t+k)v(c_{t+k}). \tag{2.136}$$

The decision maker optimally chooses c_t and c_{t+k}, subject to the constraint in (2.133). Substituting c_{t+k} from (2.133) in (2.136), we get the following unconstrained problem in which the decision maker chooses c_t; the number of tokens can then be recovered from (2.132). The unconstrained problem is

$$c_t^* \in \underset{0 \leq c_t \leq 100a_t}{\arg\max} \ V_D = p_1 D(t)v(c_t) + p_2 D(t+k)v(100a_{t+k} - (1+r)c_t).$$

Using (2.132), the optimal number of tokens is $n^* = \frac{c_t^*}{a_t}$. V_D is a strictly concave function on a compact set, so the condition for a unique maximum value, c_t^*, is given by

$$\frac{v'(c_t)}{v'(c_{t+k})} = (1+r)\frac{D(t+k)}{D(t)}\frac{p_2}{p_1}. \tag{2.137}$$

(2.137) is the key condition that unlocks the main comparative statics in the model. A scaling of p_1 and p_2 by a common factor λ does not alter the ratio $\frac{p_2}{p_1}$. Thus, both sides of (2.137) are unaffected, leaving c_t^* (and n^*) unchanged.

(ii) Given that v is strictly concave, any increase in the LHS must relatively increase $v'(c_t)$, or equivalently, reduce c_t. As r increases, the RHS of (2.137) increases so c_t^* falls and $n^* = \frac{c_t^*}{a_t}$ also falls. ∎

Based on Proposition 2.19 we expect the following pairs of conditions to give identical results in terms of the optimal consumption levels: (i) $(1,1)$ and (λ,λ). (ii) $(1,q)$ and $(\lambda,\lambda q)$. (iii) $(q,1)$ and $(\lambda q,\lambda)$. A representative set of results is shown in Figure 2.19, which reports the average consumption level of decision makers at date t, $\bar{c}_t$, as a function of $(1+r)\frac{p_2}{p_1}$.[89]

Figure 2.19 shows that Proposition 2.19 is violated. For instance, in the left panel of Figure 2.19, the average optimal level of consumption is predicted to be identical in the two conditions $(1,1)$ and $(0.5,0.5)$, yet average consumption is initially higher in the $(1,1)$ condition and then

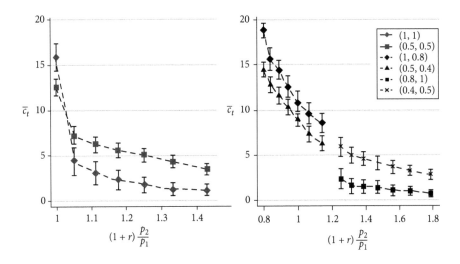

Figure 2.19 Average consumption, $\bar{c}_t$, in various conditions. In the left panel, the delay is $k = 28$ days, and we compare the two conditions $(1, 1)$ and $(0.5, 0.5)$. In the right panel, we consider a delay of $k = 56$ days, and we compare the conditions $(1, 0.8)$ versus $(0.5, 0.4)$ and $(0.8, 1)$ versus $(0.4, 0.5)$.

Source: Epper and Fehr-Duda (2014a) with permission from the American Economic Association.

[89] Andreoni and Sprenger (2012b) give the full set of results, i.e., first for $k = 26$ they give a comparision of the three pairs of conditions listed above, for $\lambda = 0.5$ and $q = 0.8$. Then they repeat the same comparison for $k = 52$. By contrast, we report in Figure 2.19, a comparison between the first pair for $k = 26$ and a comparison for the remaining two pairs for $k = 52$.

drops below the level for the $(0.5, 0.5)$ condition, i.e., the curves cross over. This result has been replicated by Cheung (2014) and Miao and Zhong (2012). In the $(1, 1)$ condition, where there is complete certainty of payment, about 80% of the allocations are at one corner ($n^* = 100$ or $n^* = 0$). But in the risky condition, $(0.5, 0.5)$, subjects try to diversify and only 26.1% are at a corner solution.

Consider the right panel of Figure 2.19 where $q = 0.8$ and $\lambda = 0.5$. First consider the conditions $(1, q)$ versus $(\lambda, \lambda q)$. The average consumption in the $(0.5, 0.4)$ condition is always lower than the $(1, 0.8)$ condition. The converse is true in a comparison of the conditions $(q, 1)$ and $(\lambda q, \lambda)$ (i.e., the conditions $(0.8, 1)$ and $(0.4, 0.5)$).

Andreoni and Sprenger (2012b) argue that models of non-linear probability weighting, such as RDU, cannot explain these results either. Their preferred explanation is models where the common ratio property (see (2.137)) does not hold; models in this category include those by Kreps and Porteus (1978), Chew and Epstein (1989b), and Epstein and Zin (1989). However, reworking through the same set of results, Epper and Fehr-Duda (2014a) show that the results can be explained by RDU if the decision maker cares for portfolio risk rather than employ the separable case that is used by Andreoni and Sprenger (2012b); see Figure 2.18.

Consider a RDU decision maker who faces the lottery in (2.134). There are four possible outcomes, but each outcome is a pair of consumption values. How are these pairs to be ranked? Consider the binary relation $\prec$ such that $(c_t, 0) \prec (0, c_{t+k})$ means that c_{t+k} received at date $t + k$ is "ranked higher" than c_t received at date t. It is reasonable to assume that

$$\begin{cases} (0, c_{t+k}) \prec (c_t, 0) & \text{if} \quad D(t + k)v(c_{t+k}) < D(t)v(c_t) \\ (c_t, 0) \prec (0, c_{t+k}) & \text{if} \quad D(t)v(c_t) < D(t + k)v(c_{t+k}) \end{cases}. \tag{2.138}$$

With this definition, it is always the case that $(0, 0) \prec (c_t, 0) \prec (c_t, c_{t+k})$ and $(0, 0) \prec (0, c_{t+k}) \prec (c_t, c_{t+k})$. Depending on which row of (2.138) applies, we get two possibilities, I and II.

$$\begin{cases} I: & (0, 0) \prec (0, c_{t+k}) \prec (c_t, 0) \prec (c_t, c_{t+k}) \\ II: & (0, 0) \prec (c_t, 0) \prec (0, c_{t+k}) \prec (c_t, c_{t+k}) \end{cases}. \tag{2.139}$$

The lottery in (2.134) gives the associated probability of each of the outcomes in cases I and II in (2.139). Let w be a probability weighting function. The decision weights (see Definition 2.7) of the lowest and the highest outcomes in cases I and II are identically given by

$$\pi(0, 0) = 1 - w(p_1 + p_2 - p_1 p_2), \pi(c_t, c_{t+k}) = w(p_1 p_2). \tag{2.140}$$

The decision weights for the two intermediate outcomes in cases I and II are:

$$\begin{cases} I: & \pi_I(0, c_{t+k}) = w(p_1 + p_2 - p_1 p_2) - w(p_1), \pi_I(c_t, 0) = w(p_1) - w(p_1 p_2) \\ II: & \pi_{II}(c_t, 0) = w(p_1 + p_2 - p_1 p_2) - w(p_2), \pi_{II}(0, c_{t+k}) = w(p_2) - w(p_1 p_2) \end{cases}. \tag{2.141}$$

Let the utility function of an outcome continue to be given by v, with the conditions in (2.135). Given the decision weights in (2.140) and (2.141), we can now define the objective function of the decision maker who follows RDU in the two cases in (2.138), $V_R^i, i = I, II$.

$$V_R^i = \pi_i(0, c_{t+k})D(t + k)v(c_{t+k}) + \pi_i(c_t, 0)D(t)v(c_t)$$
$$+ \pi(c_t, c_{t+k})[D(t)v(c_t) + D(t + k)v(c_{t+k})], i = I, II.$$

A decision maker who follows RDU, maximizes his objective function V_R^i, $i = I, II$, subject to the constraint in (2.133). The first order condition, the analogue of (2.137), is given by

$$\frac{v'(c_t)}{v'(c_{t+k})} = (1+r)\frac{D(t+k)}{D(t)}\varphi(p_1, p_2), \tag{2.142}$$

where,

$$\varphi(p_1, p_2) = \begin{cases} \frac{w(p_2)}{w(1)} & \text{if } p_1 = 1 \\ \frac{w(1)}{w(p_1)} & \text{if } p_2 = 1 \\ \varphi_I(p_1, p_2) = \frac{w(p_1 p_2) + w(p_1 + p_2 - p_1 p_2) - w(p_1)}{w(p_1)} & \text{if } p_1 \neq 1, p_2 \neq 1, (0, c_{t+k}) \prec (c_t, 0) \\ \varphi_{II}(p_1, p_2) = \frac{w(p_2)}{w(p_1 p_2) + w(p_1 + p_2 - p_1 p_2) - w(p_2)} & \text{if } p_1 \neq 1, p_2 \neq 1, (c_t, 0) \prec (0, c_{t+k}) \end{cases} \tag{2.143}$$

Let us compare average consumption under EU and RDU (delay-discounting in each case), i.e., we compare (2.137) and (2.142). The relevant comparison is between the terms $\frac{p_2}{p_1}$ and $\varphi(p_1, p_2)$.

We now consider the first order condition (2.142) for the three cases: (i) $(1, 1)$ versus (λ, λ), (ii) $(1, q)$ versus $(\lambda, \lambda q)$, and (iii) $(q, 1)$ versus $(\lambda q, \lambda)$. Some illustrative results for the case of the Prelec function (Definition 2.4) with $\alpha = 0.5$ and $\beta = 1$, and for $\lambda = 0.5$ and $q = 0.8$ are summarized in Table 2.5.

We are now interested in the empirical findings encapsulated in Figure 2.19.

I. Baseline condition: Consider first the comparison between the conditions $(1, 1)$ and (λ, λ). The illustrative example in Table 2.5 (first column) is consistent with the crossover of the two curves in the left panel of Figure 2.19 ($\varphi_{II}(0.5, 0.5) < \varphi(1, 1) < \varphi_I(0.5, 0.5)$). Now consider the more general case. For most probability weighting functions, including the Prelec function, that are inverse S-shaped, there is an initial concave segment, followed by a convex segment. The point of inflection that separates these segments is typically well below the probability of 0.5, which is used in the experiments in Andreoni and Sprenger (2012b), hence, we are in the convex region of the weighting function. Assuming a convex probability weighting function, we get

$$w(ap_1 + (1-a)p_2) < aw(p_1) + (1-a)w(p_2), 0 < a < 1. \tag{2.144}$$

From (2.143)

$$\varphi_I(\lambda, \lambda) = \frac{w(\lambda^2) + w(2\lambda - \lambda^2) - w(\lambda)}{w(\lambda)}, \varphi_{II}(\lambda, \lambda) = \frac{w(\lambda)}{w(\lambda^2) + w(2\lambda - \lambda^2) - w(\lambda)}. \tag{2.145}$$

Table 2.5 Various computations to explain the relevant empirical findings in different conditions.

Conditions $(1,1)$ and $(0.5,0.5)$	Conditions $(1,0.8)$ and $(0.5,0.4)$	Conditions $(0,8.1)$ and $(0.4,0.5)$
$\frac{p_1}{p_2} = 1$	$\frac{p_1}{p_2} = 1.25$	$\frac{p_1}{p_2} = 0.8$
$\varphi(1,1) = 1$	$\varphi(1,0.8) = 0.624$	$\varphi(0,8.1) = 1.604$
$\varphi_I(0.5,0.5) = 1.053$	$\varphi_I(0.5,0.4) = 0.912$	$\varphi_I(0.4,0.5) = 1.166$
$\varphi_{II}(0.5,0.5) = 0.950$	$\varphi_{II}(0.5,0.4) = 0.858$	$\varphi_{II}(0.4,0.5) = 1.097$

Source: Epper and Fehr-Duda (2014a).

From (2.144), (2.145) we get

$$\varphi_I(\lambda,\lambda) > \varphi(1,1) = 1 > \varphi_{II}(\lambda,\lambda). \tag{2.146}$$

When $(0,c_{t+k}) \prec (c_t,0)$ we have $\varphi_I(\lambda,\lambda) > 1$, thus, the RHS of (2.142) is greater under the condition (λ,λ) relative to the condition $(1,1)$. Since v is concave, it follows that c_t is relatively lower under the condition (λ,λ). On the other hand, in the condition $(c_t,0) \prec (0,c_{t+k})$ we have that $1 > \varphi_{II}(\lambda,\lambda)$ so c_t is greater under the condition (λ,λ) relative to the condition $(1,1)$. This implies the crossing over of the two curves that we observe in the left panel of Figure 2.19.

II. Differential risk conditions: Consider first the comparison $(1,q)$ versus $(\lambda,\lambda q)$ (the other comparison is $(q,1)$ versus $(\lambda q,\lambda)$). In this case, from (2.143)

$$\begin{cases} \varphi_I(\lambda,\lambda q) = \frac{w(\lambda^2 q) + w(\lambda + \lambda q - \lambda^2 q) - w(\lambda)}{w(\lambda)} \\ \varphi_{II}(\lambda,\lambda q) = \frac{w(\lambda q)}{w(\lambda^2 q) + w(\lambda + \lambda q - \lambda^2 q) - w(\lambda q)} \end{cases}. \tag{2.147}$$

In the experiments of Andreoni and Sprenger (2012b), $\lambda = 0.5$ and $q = 0.8$. Most probability weighting functions are quite flat over this range. Thus, let us use a linear approximation $w(p) \approx \widehat{w}(p) = a + bp$, $a > 0$, $b > 0$. Suppose that we apply this approximation to $\varphi_I(\lambda,\lambda q)$ in (2.147), then we get $\frac{a+b\lambda q}{a+b\lambda} = \frac{\widehat{w}(\lambda q)}{\widehat{w}(\lambda)}$. The same approximation applies to $\varphi_{II}(\lambda,\lambda q)$, thus,

$$\varphi_I(\lambda,\lambda q) \approx \frac{\widehat{w}(\lambda q)}{\widehat{w}(\lambda)} \approx \varphi_{II}(\lambda,\lambda q). \tag{2.148}$$

Thus, $\frac{\varphi_I(\lambda,\lambda q)}{\varphi_{II}(\lambda,\lambda q)} \approx 1$. From the RHS of (2.142), optimal consumption c_t is, thus, almost unchanged as the rank of outcomes change between $(0,c_{t+k}) \prec (c_t,0)$ and $(c_t,0) \prec (0,c_{t+k})$. From the subproportionality condition in Definition 2.6, applied to the function $\widehat{w}$ for $p = 1$ (this is the special case of the certainty effect), we get that $\frac{\widehat{w}(\lambda q)}{\widehat{w}(\lambda)} > \widehat{w}(q)$, so

$$\frac{w(\lambda q)}{w(\lambda)} \approx \frac{\widehat{w}(\lambda q)}{\widehat{w}(\lambda)} > \widehat{w}(q) \approx w(q). \tag{2.149}$$

For the condition $(1,q)$ we have, from (2.143),

$$\varphi(1,q) = \frac{w(q)}{w(1)} = w(q). \tag{2.150}$$

From (2.148)–(2.150) we get that

$$\varphi_I(\lambda,\lambda q) \approx \varphi_{II}(\lambda,\lambda q) > w(q) = \varphi(1,q). \tag{2.151}$$

Using (2.151) we get that the RHS in (2.142) is relatively higher in the condition $(\lambda,\lambda q)$ relative to the condition $(1,q)$ throughout the domain (even as we move across the two possibilities $(0,c_{t+k}) \prec (c_t,0)$ and $(c_t,0) \prec (0,c_{t+k})$). This feature is also present in the illustrative example as shown in the second column in Table 2.5. Thus, we expect average date t consumption, $\bar{c}_t$, to be relatively higher in the condition $(1,q)$, exactly as we have in the right panel of Figure 2.19. We leave it to the reader to show analogously that a comparison of the conditions $(q,1)$ and $(\lambda q,\lambda)$ is also consistent with the right panel of Figure 2.19.

Thus, if we use the portfolio method, the results of Andreoni and Sprenger (2012b) are consistent with a decision maker who follows RDU in evaluating uncertain dated streams of consumption goods using the delay discounting model.

2.12.2 *Intertemporal risk aversion*

Epper and Fehr-Duda (2014b) make preliminary progress in operationalizing *intertemporal risk aversion*, based on the work of Richard (1975) and Bommier (2007). Intertemporal risk aversion refers to the desire of decision makers to diversify consumption across time; empirical evidence can be found in Cheung (2014) and Miao and Zhong (2012). Suppose that $c_t \in \{\underline{c}_t, \overline{c}_t\}$ and $c_{t+k} \in \{\underline{c}_{t+k}, \overline{c}_{t+k}\}$, where $\underline{c}_t < \overline{c}_t$ and $\underline{c}_{t+k} < \overline{c}_{t+k}$. Define the prospects

$$L^- = \left((\overline{c}_t, \underline{c}_{t+k}), 0.5; (\underline{c}_t, \overline{c}_{t+k}), 0.5 \right), \; L^+ = \left((\overline{c}_t, \overline{c}_{t+k}), 0.5; (\underline{c}_t, \underline{c}_{t+k}), 0.5 \right). \tag{2.152}$$

The prospect L^+ is not as well diversified as prospect L^-. This leads to the following definition.

Definition 2.38 *(Intertemporal risk aversion): A decision maker is intertemporally risk averse if $L^+ \prec L^-$, where $\prec$ is the "strictly preferred to" binary relation.*

Let the discount function be D and instantaneous utility function be v. Define

$$V_D\left(x_t, y_{t+k}\right) = D(t)v(x_t) + D(t+k)v(y_{t+k}),$$

and assume, as in (2.138), that

$$\left(x_t, y_{t+k}\right) \prec \left(x'_t, y'_{t+k}\right) \; \Leftrightarrow \; V_D\left(x_t, y_{t+k}\right) < V_D\left(x'_t, y'_{t+k}\right). \tag{2.153}$$

We now wish to express the preference $L^+ \prec L^-$ for decision makers who follow RDU. It is not clear if $(\overline{c}_t, \underline{c}_{t+k}) \prec (\underline{c}_t, \overline{c}_{t+k})$ or $(\underline{c}_t, \overline{c}_{t+k}) \prec (\overline{c}_t, \underline{c}_{t+k})$. Thus, in specifying the utility function of a RDU decision maker, V_R (Definitions 2.7 and 2.8), we need to consider two possibilities.

$$V_R(L^-) = \begin{cases} (1 - w(0.5))\, V_D\left(\overline{c}_t, \underline{c}_{t+k}\right) + w(0.5)\, V_D\left(\underline{c}_t, \overline{c}_{t+k}\right) & \text{if } \left(\overline{c}_t, \underline{c}_{t+k}\right) \prec \left(\underline{c}_t, \overline{c}_{t+k}\right) \\ (1 - w(0.5))\, V_D\left(\underline{c}_t, \overline{c}_{t+k}\right) + w(0.5)\, V_D\left(\overline{c}_t, \underline{c}_{t+k}\right) & \text{if } \left(\underline{c}_t, \overline{c}_{t+k}\right) \prec \left(\overline{c}_t, \underline{c}_{t+k}\right) \end{cases}. \tag{2.154}$$

The ranking of outcomes under the prospect L^+ is unambiguous, hence, using Definitions 2.7 and 2.8

$$V_R(L^+) = (1 - w(0.5))\, V_D\left(\underline{c}_t, \underline{c}_{t+k}\right) + w(0.5)\, V_D\left(\overline{c}_t, \overline{c}_{t+k}\right). \tag{2.155}$$

Comparing (2.154) and (2.155) we get

$$V_R(L^-) - V_R(L^+) = \begin{cases} (1 - 2w(0.5))\, D(t)\left(v(\overline{c}_t) - v(\underline{c}_t)\right) & \text{if} & \left(\overline{c}_t, \underline{c}_{t+k}\right) \prec \left(\underline{c}_t, \overline{c}_{t+k}\right) \\ (1 - 2w(0.5))\, D(t+k)\left(v(\overline{c}_{t+k}) - v(\underline{c}_{t+k})\right) & \text{if} & \left(\underline{c}_t, \overline{c}_{t+k}\right) \prec \left(\overline{c}_t, \underline{c}_{t+k}\right) \end{cases}.$$

In each case, the condition for intertemporal risk aversion, $V_R(L^-) > V_R(L^+)$, holds if

$$1 - 2w(0.5) > 0, \text{ or } w(0.5) < 0.5. \tag{2.156}$$

This condition is satisfied for most inverse S-shaped probability weight functions; see Epper and Fehr-Duda (2014b). For instance it is satisfied by the Prelec function for commonly used values of α, β. In a nutshell, a decision maker who follows RDU is also likely to exhibit intertemporal risk aversion if the condition in (2.156) holds.

2.12.3 *An agenda for the future*

In an insightful paper, Epper and Fehr-Duda (2014b) lay out the agenda for future research that wishes to explore the link between risk preferences and time preferences. They propose a general theoretical framework designed to address a set of stylized facts that any aspiring theory in this area may wish to take into account. The stylized facts can be organized as follows.

1. Empirically observed risk tolerance and patience are *delay dependent*: People appear more risk tolerant for events that are to happen in the more distant future.[90] An implication is that people may be more tolerant in facing risks relating to global warming or insuring against natural hazards if the consequences are in the more distant future. Hyperbolic discounting captures delay dependence of behavior but does not incorporate risk.

2. Behavior under risk and time is *process dependent*. There is a very large number of process dependent behaviors that have been observed. For instance, it matters whether we first reduce lotteries in a one-shot manner or sequentially (see, for instance, Figure 2.18). In other contexts, it matters if uncertainty is resolved gradually, or in the terminal period. For instance, a greater risk premium may be required on a portfolio whose returns are evaluated frequently rather than observed at the end of the period (Benartzi and Thaler, 1995; Barberis et al., 2001). More generally, in a range of contexts, people take on more risks if they are informed of the outcomes at the end rather than frequently over time.[91] We shall also consider process dependence of time behavior in Volume 3; in particular, we shall consider *subadditive discounting* in some detail.

3. The *timing of the resolution of uncertainty* affects behavior of subjects when they face situations that have a risk and time component: For instance, for negative news, people may prefer uncertainty to resolve later rather than sooner (e.g., is one affected by a genetic disorder that runs in the family?). For positive news, people may prefer uncertainty to resolve sooner rather than later (e.g., has the book that I ordered arrived?).[92]

4. Time discount differs in the presence of risk: For instance, risky future incomes are discounted less than safe future incomes (Ahlbrecht and Weber, 1997a; Weber and Chapman, 2005). This is in contrast to the exponential discounting utility model that applies the same discounting to safe and risky returns. A literature also examines the dynamic inconsistency of choices in the presence of risk.[93]

5. Behavior differs depending on whether we first reduce a lottery in the time dimension or in the risk dimension: It appears that the value assigned to prospects is lower if they are first

---

[90] See, for instance, Coble and Lusk (2010) and Abdellaoui, Diecidue, and Öncüler (2011).

[91] See for instance, Gneezy and Potters (1997), Thaler et al. (1997), Gneezy et al. (2003), and Bellemare et al. (2005).

[92] For the empirical evidence, see Ahlbrecht and Weber (1997b), Lovallo and Kahneman (2000), Eliaz and Schotter (2007), and von Gaudecker et al. (2011). For papers that propose a theoretical framework, see Kreps and Porteus (1978), Chew and Epstein (1989b), and Grant et al. (2000).

[93] See, for instance, Cubitt et al. (1998) and Busemeyer et al. (2000).

reduced for risk and then for time (as compared to the reverse case). See, for instance, the recursive case in Figure 2.18 and for the empirical evidence, see Öncüler and Onay (2009).

We now consider some of these issues.

2.12.4 *Delay dependence and probability weighting*

Suppose that we have a binary lottery

$$L = (x, 1-p; y, p), 0 \leq x < y. \tag{2.157}$$

An RDU decision maker evaluates the lottery L by and it is subproportional (Definition 2.6). v is a utility function such that $v(0) = 0$ and $v' > 0$.

$$V_R(L) = \left[1 - w(p)\right] v(x) + w(p)v(y). \tag{2.158}$$

In (2.158), w is the "true" weighting function of the decision maker.

Suppose that time is discrete, and the lottery L is paid out at time $t > 0$. We make two assumptions.

1. Utility is discounted back to time 0 using the exponential function

$$D(t) = e^{-\theta t},$$

   where $\theta > 0$ is the discount rate.

2. There is uncertainty about whether the payments will be made in the future. Suppose that one is promised a payment at time 0 of an amount $z > 0$ to be received at time t. Then the probability of receiving the payment at time t is s^t, $0 < s \leq 1$, where s is the per-period probability of the payment being honored. Hence, if the prospect L in (2.157) is to be realized at time t, it is viewed at time 0 as the prospect[94]

$$\widetilde{L} = (0, 1 - s^t; x, (1-p)s^t; y, ps^t), 0 \leq x < y, 0 < s \leq 1.$$

Under Assumptions 1 and 2, a decision maker, who uses RDU, evaluates at time 0 the lottery $\widetilde{L}$ to be received at time t, as follows (see Definitions 2.7 and 2.8),

$$V_R(\widetilde{L}; t = 0) = D(t) \left[\left(w(s^t) - w(ps^t)\right) v(x) + w(ps^t)v(y)\right], \tag{2.159}$$

where w is the *atemporal probability weighting function*. (2.159) can be rewritten as

$$V_R(\widetilde{L}; t = 0) = D(t)w(s^t) \left[\left(v(y) - v(x)\right) \frac{w(ps^t)}{w(s^t)} + v(x)\right]. \tag{2.160}$$

Suppose that an observer is unaware of Assumption 2. For example, experimenters (observers) may never wish to withhold future payments promised in lotteries but subjects (decision

---

[94] This assumption is motivated by the work of Halevy (2008) and Walther (2010); see Volume 3 of the book for more details.

makers) may nevertheless assign a positive probability, $s > 0$, to this event. The observer mistakenly believes that decision makers evaluate lottery $\widetilde{L}$ with $s = 1$, so, recalling $w(1) = 1$, he calculates

$$V_R(\widetilde{L}; t = 0) = \widehat{D}(t)\left[\left(v(y) - v(x)\right)\widehat{w}(p) + v(x)\right], \tag{2.161}$$

where $\widehat{w}$ and $\widehat{D}$ are, respectively, the probability weighting function and the discount function, which the observer believes are used by the decision maker. Suppose that the observer uses (2.161) to estimate the true weighting function and the discount function of the decision maker. Then, comparing (2.160) and (2.161), the relation between his estimates, $\widehat{w}$ and $\widehat{D}$, and the true functions w and D is

$$\widehat{w}(p) = \frac{w(ps^t)}{w(s^t)}. \tag{2.162}$$

$$\widehat{D}(t) = w(s^t)D(t). \tag{2.163}$$

Epper and Fehr-Duda (2014b) use this simple framework to address the five stylized facts in Section 2.12.3, above. Consider the first hypothesis on delay dependence.

> **Proposition 2.20**   *Let the true probability weighting function w be subproportional (Definition 2.6), and $s < 1$. Then the properties of the estimated function, $\widehat{w}$ (see (2.162)) are as follows.*
>
>   *(i) $\widehat{w}$ is a probability weighting function.*
>   *(ii) $\widehat{w}$ is subproportional.*
>   *(iii) $\widehat{w}$ is more elevated than w. The degree of elevation of $\widehat{w}$ increases with time delay, t, and survival risk, $1 - s$, but this increase is at a decreasing rate.*
>   *(iv) $\widehat{w}$ is less elastic than w.*
>   *(v) The increase in risk tolerance is greater when w is more subproportional.*

Proof: (i) Using (2.162), $\widehat{w}(0) = \frac{w(0)}{w(s^t)} = 0$, $\widehat{w}(1) = \frac{w(s^t)}{w(s^t)} = 1$, $\widehat{w}'(p) = s^t \frac{w'(ps^t)}{w(s^t)} > 0$, and $\widehat{w}$ is continuous, hence, $\widehat{w}$ is a probability weighting function.

(ii) Using the definition of subproportionality in Definition 2.6, and noting that w is subproportional, we have for $0 < \lambda < 1$ and $q < p \leq 1$,

$$\frac{\widehat{w}(p)}{\widehat{w}(q)} = \frac{w(ps^t)}{w(qs^t)} > \frac{w(\lambda ps^t)}{w(\lambda qs^t)} = \frac{\frac{w(\lambda ps^t)}{w(s^t)}}{\frac{w(\lambda qs^t)}{w(s^t)}} = \frac{\widehat{w}(\lambda p)}{\widehat{w}(\lambda q)},$$

which proves the result.

(iii) Using the definitions of $w(p)$, $\widehat{w}(p)$, and subproportionality, we get

$$\frac{1}{w(p)} = \frac{w(1)}{w(p)} > \frac{w(s)}{w(ps)} > \frac{w(s^2)}{w(ps^2)} > \ldots > \frac{w(s^t)}{w(ps^t)} = \frac{1}{\widehat{w}(p)},$$

hence, $w(p) < \widehat{w}(p)$. Thus, $\widehat{w}$ is more elevated than w. Differentiating $\widehat{w}$ with respect to t and s gives the remaining results.

(iv) The elasticity, ε_w, of the weighting function, w is defined as $\varepsilon_w(p) = \frac{w'(p)p}{w(p)}$. It can be shown that if w is subproportional, then $\varepsilon'_w(p) > 0$. Thus, by the definition of $\widehat{w}$, we have

$$\varepsilon_{\widehat{w}}(p) = \frac{\widehat{w}'(p)p}{\widehat{w}(p)} = \frac{w'(ps^t)ps^t}{w(ps^t)} = \varepsilon_w(ps^t) < \varepsilon_w(p),$$

where the last inequality follows from $ps^t < p$ and $\varepsilon'_w(p) > 0$.

(v) We leave the proof of this part to the reader. ■

From Proposition 2.20(iii), the estimated probability weighting function, $\widehat{w}$, is relatively more elevated; this is a central result. Hence, the observed risk tolerance of the decision maker is also relatively higher (see Example 2.5). Since the elevation of the estimated weighting function increases with the time delay, risk tolerance appears, to the observer, to also increase with the time delay. The empirical evidence is consistent with these findings. In particular, the utility function is not influenced by time delay, so this affect appears to arise through probability weighting;[95] see Figure 2.22 for an illustration of the delay effect that we discuss below.

From (2.163), $\widehat{D}(t) = w(s^t)D(t)$. D takes the exponential form. Suppose that w is the inverse S-shaped Prelec function with $\alpha = \beta = 1$ (Definition 2.4), so $w(s^t) = e^{(-\ln s^t)}$. Thus, $\widehat{D}(t) = e^{-\widehat{\theta}t}$ where $\widehat{\theta} = \theta - \ln(s) > \theta$. Thus, the presence of uncertainty increases the observed discount rates and increases the degree of observed impatience. However, this does not account for the typical finding of decreasing discount rates as, say, in hyperbolic discounting (because θ is independent of t). However, this can be accommodated if the probability weighting function is subproportional, an idea that is closely related to Halevy (2008) that we consider in more detail in Volume 3. We summarize the results in the next proposition and we leave the proof to the reader as an exercise.

Proposition 2.21 *(Epper and Fehr-Duda, 2014b): Suppose that w is subproportional.*

(i) *$\widehat{D}$ is a discount function if $1 < s \leq 1$, i.e., it is decreasing in t (impatience), $\lim_{t \to \infty} \widehat{D}(t) = 0$, and $\widehat{D}(0) = 1$.*

(ii) *When $s < 1$ we have $\widehat{\theta} > \theta$.*

(iii) *The observed discount rate $\widehat{\theta}$ is declining in t.*

(iv) *Greater risk of survival (lower s) results in more steeply declining discount rates.*

(v) *An increase in the degree of subproportionality of the weighting function leads to more steeply declining discount rates.*

For the Prelec probability weighting function with $\alpha = 0.5$ and $\beta = 1$, Figure 2.20 shows the effect of varying survival risk, s, on the observed discount rate, $\widehat{\theta}$ (vertical axis), while time t is on the horizontal axis. Thus, the estimated discount rate is hyperbolic and the degree of hyperbolicity is increasing with an increase in risk (lower s).

2.12.5 *Probability weighting and process dependence*

Empirical evidence suggests that the probability weighting function is more elevated when future rewards are received with a longer delay, while the utility function appears stable under delay; see Abdellaoui, Diecidue et al. (2011). Fehr-Duda and Epper (2012) give the example of a choice between a compound lottery and its equivalent simple lottery shown in Figure 2.21. The simple lottery is $L_s = (x_1, 1 - p; x_2, p)$, where $x_1 < x_2$, $p = rq$ and $1 - p = q(1 - r) + (1 - q) = 1 - rq$.

---

[95] See Epper and Fehr-Duda (2014b) for the references.

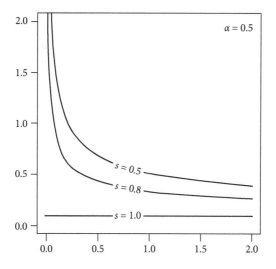

Figure 2.20 A plot of the estimated dicount rate, $\widehat{\theta}$ (vertical axis) and the time delay t (horizontal axis). The weighting function is a Prelec function with $\alpha = 0.5$ and $\beta = 1$.

Source: Epper and Fehr-Duda (2014b).

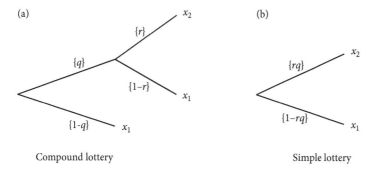

Figure 2.21 A choice between a compound lottery and its equivalent simple lottery.

Source: Reproduced with permission of Annual Review of Economics, Volume 4. Helga Fehr-Duda and Thomas Epper, "Probability and risk: foundations and economic implications of probability dependent risk preferences." © 2012 by Annual Reviews http://www.annualreviews.org.

The RDU of the simple lottery is

$$V_R(L_s) = \left[1 - w(rq)\right]u(x_1) + w(rq)u(x_2). \tag{2.164}$$

Suppose that the compound lottery is reduced recursively. Then with probability q, the RDU of the decision maker is $\left[1 - w(r)\right]u(x_1) + w(r)u(x_2)$, and with probability $1 - q$ it is $u(x_1)$. Hence, at the initial node, the decision maker faces the lottery

$$L_c = \left(u(x_1), 1 - q; \left[1 - w(r)\right]u(x_1) + w(r)u(x_2), q\right).$$

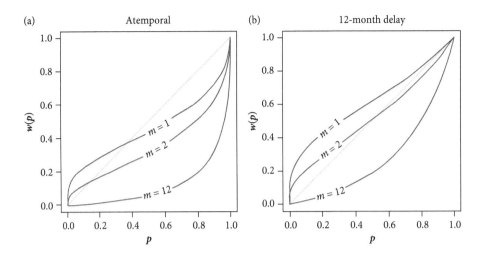

Figure 2.22 Estimated Prelec weighting functions.

Source: Reproduced with permission of Annual Review of Economics, Volume 4. Helga Fehr-Duda and Thomas Epper, "Probability and risk: foundations and economic implications of probability-dependent risk preferences." © 2012 by Annual Reviews http://www.annualreviews.org.

The RDU of the compound lottery (reduced recursively) is

$$V_R(L_c) = \left[1 - w(q)\right]u(x_1) + w(q)\left([1 - w(r)]u(x_1) + w(r)u(x_2)\right), \qquad (2.165)$$

which can be rewritten as

$$V_R(L_c) = \left[1 - w(r)w(q)\right]u(x_1) + w(r)w(q)u(x_2). \qquad (2.166)$$

Suppose that the weighting function is subproportional. Then, the certainty effect (Definition 2.6) implies $w(qr) > w(q)w(r)$. Comparing (2.164) and (2.166) we get that $V_R(L_s) > V_R(L_c)$, so the decision maker tolerates less risk in the compound case. Thus, although the simple and compound lotteries are equivalent in the classical sense, the timing of the resolution of uncertainty does matter for a decision maker who follows RDU, if the weighting function is subproportional. As the number of stages in the compound lottery increase, the decision maker exhibits less and less risk tolerance.

Figure 2.22 shows the estimated Prelec weighting functions. Panel (a) shows the atemporal probability weighting function when there is one stage, i.e., a simple lottery ($m = 1$), two stages ($m = 2$), and twelve stages ($m = 12$). Elevation falls as the number of stages increases, so risk tolerance falls, and for $m = 12$, the probability weighting function becomes convex; in Section 2.3, we classified such a decision maker as exhibiting pessimism.

In panel (b) of Figure 2.22 we assume that the uncertainty in compound lotteries is realized in 12 months time. Comparing the corresponding curves in the two panels, we can compare the effect of time delay. With time delay, each of the curves is more elevated than the corresponding curve in the atemporal case, hence, they exhibit greater risk tolerance.

As Fehr-Duda and Epper (2012, pp. 585–6) put it: "Extreme risk aversion can thus result from several different underlying mechanisms: loss aversion, disappointment aversion, and rank dependence with convex probability weighting or frequent compounding of originally inverse S-shaped probability weights."

CHAPTER 3

Applications of Behavioral Decision Theory

3.1 Introduction

Prospect theory (PT) has been successful in addressing a wide range of questions in almost all areas of economics. In this chapter we consider several applications of PT. Many applications rely on a subset of the components of PT (reference dependence, loss aversion, concavity of utility in gains and convexity in losses, and non-linear probability weighting). The vast majority of the applications invoke reference dependence and loss aversion, but omit non-linear weighting of probabilities. While this explains much human behavior, which is a testament to the importance of these features of human behavior, sometimes this is undesirable, for two reasons. First, the calibration of such models to the data might not be very successful, particularly if one arbitrarily picks and chooses among the components of PT. Second, while the evidence supports the fourfold classification of risk under PT, the omission of non-linear probability weighting can induce, at best, twofold risk aversion, which may reduce the scope of the models' predictions.[1] There is a strong case for giving more attention to non-linear probability weighting in applications of PT, than has traditionally been the case (Fehr-Duda and Epper, 2012).

The general psychological principles behind reference dependence and loss aversion have excellent foundations in experimental and field data.[2] An important test of these principles has come from an examination of the disparity between *willingness to accept, WTA,* and *willingness to pay, WTP,* for the same good. This disparity is sometimes known as the finding of *exchange asymmetry.* Since this finding arises from mere physical ownership of an object, it is also known as the *endowment effect.*

In Section 3.2 we begin by describing the early and pioneering evidence for exchange asymmetries (Kahneman et al., 1990). The endowment effect arises for physical goods but typically not for money, intrinsically worthless items, or items held for exchange only. This finding, which

---

[1] For a classic example, see Wakker (2003).

[2] For experimental evidence on loss aversion, see, for instance, Kahneman and Tversky (1979), Tversky and Kahneman (1992), Gneezy and Potters (1997), Thaler et al. (1997), and Kahneman and Tversky (2000). For the field evidence, see, for instance, Camerer et al. (1997), Odean (1998), Genesove and Mayer (2001), Mas (2006), and Fehr and Goette (2007).

has been replicated in a large number of experiments, survives controls for transaction costs of exchange, subject misconceptions, learning, and strategic concerns.

Section 3.2.1 considers the leading explanation of exchange asymmetries, loss aversion (Thaler, 1980). Parting with an object, when one is endowed with it, is coded as a loss by an individual. Hence, loss aversion applies to the act of parting with an object. But loss aversion does not apply to money, hence, the act of parting with the money to buy an object is not subject to loss aversion. In conjunction, this gives rise to the finding of $WTP < WTA$. Indeed, in a PT framework, it can be shown that loss aversion equals the ratio WTA/WTP. Kahneman et al. (1990) report an average value of $WTA/WTP \cong 2$, which is close to the typical values of loss aversion found in many experiments. One study reports the median estimate of WTA/WTP across 45 studies to be 2.6, although there is individual-level heterogeneity in estimates of loss aversion (Horowitz and McConnell, 2002). We also discuss, briefly, the dependence of loss aversion on a range of demographic, goods-specific, context-specific and emotional factors.

Typically, experiments on exchange asymmetries are conducted in riskless environments. In Section 3.2.2, we consider exchange asymmetries in risky environments (Novemsky and Kahneman, 2005), and pose a fundamental question: *Is there any risk aversion beyond loss aversion?* Loss aversion is found to be present in both conditions used to elicit exchange disparities: the risky and the riskless conditions. If there is any risk aversion beyond loss aversion, then one would expect, for instance, that WTA should be relatively higher in the risky situation. But this turns out not to be the case. Hence, there is no risk aversion beyond loss aversion.

Section 3.2.3 considers the effect of experience on the endowment effect. Some evidence suggests a slight reduction in the endowment effect from markets in sports cards memorabilia (List, 2003, 2004). However, this effect was found to be similar for lab subjects and market participants, so the conclusion that markets may eliminate behavioral features in humans is misleading. Furthermore, it is not surprising that one may find lower loss aversion among people who hold goods from trade because they are likely to be interested in making a profit from the goods and do not necessarily derive intrinsic satisfaction from owning the goods; this has been known since Kahneman et al. (1990). A comprehensive study based on more than 2.5 million data points from professional sports players shows that even experienced players exhibit loss aversion (Pope and Schweitzer, 2011). This ties in nicely with evolutionary explanations, which suggest that loss aversion may be hardwired in humans; see Section 3.3, below.

Section 3.2.4 considers the possibility that subject misinterpretation and the instructions themselves may be responsible for the endowment effect (Plott and Zeiler, 2005, 2007). However, using the altered instructions, and accounting for subject misperceptions in the suggested manner, it has not been possible to replicate these findings for the case of lotteries (Isoni et al., 2011), although they can be replicated for mugs. This suggests that it is not subject misperception that is the cause of the endowment effect but the particular context of the experiments.

Section 3.2.5 considers some implications and other explanations of exchange asymmetries. Indifference curves may cross over, depending on initial endowments, and the Coase theorem may be violated (Kahneman et al., 1990). We also consider some marketing implications of the endowment effect (Novemsky and Kahneman, 2005). *Stochastic reference points* may be a potential explanation of exchange asymmetries (Köszegi and Rabin, 2006); this is dealt with in more detail in Section 2.8.3. A potential explanation of exchange asymmetries is the *query theory of value construction* (Johnson et al., 2007), which is similar in spirit to the availability heuristic (see Volume 5). This is a promising line of work, which shows that the nature of queries that sellers and buyers of objects pose may influence the extent of exchange asymmetries. Yet another possible explanation that we consider is the role of uncertainty in explaining the endowment effect (Engleman and Hollard, 2008).

Non-human primates share a common evolutionary history with humans. If they were to exhibit the endowment effect or PT preferences, then this might be the result of an evolutionary process that precedes the separation of these primates and humans from a common ancestor. We consider this fascinating question in Section 3.3 (Chen et al., 2006; Brosnan et al., 2007; Lakshminarayanan et al., 2008, 2011). It turns out that capuchin monkeys have consistent preferences and they exhibit many of the features of PT that include reference dependence, loss aversion, and different risk attitudes in the domain of gains and losses. Chimpanzees exhibit an endowment effect for food items, but not for non-food items where they exhibit the reverse of the endowment effect (a preference for interacting with the experimenter makes them trade too much). This difference arises possibly because food is more salient for evolutionary success as compared to non-food items.

Section 3.4 considers the tendency of humans to evaluate gains and losses only over short horizons, even when the relevant horizons are longer. For instance, even if the returns on a portfolio are to materialize in two years, many individuals often check the market returns. Insofar as negative returns may lead to loss aversion, risky assets appear more aversive. Such a phenomenon is known as *myopic loss aversion*. This explains the *equity premium puzzle*, i.e., why the return differential on risky and riskless assets cannot be explained by any reasonable attitudes to risk under EU (Benartzi and Thaler, 1995). Myopic loss aversion is supported in experimental data on individual subjects (Gneezy and Potters, 1997), team experimental data (Sutter, 2007), and in artifactual field data (Haigh and List, 2005).

Section 3.5 considers the only application in Chapter 3 that uses all the components of PT in order to address the *tax evasion puzzles*. The classic analysis of tax evasion, based on EU (Allingham and Sandmo, 1971), gives rise to qualitative and quantitative puzzles. The quantitative puzzle is that given the return from tax evasion for an amateur tax evader of 91–98%, why should anyone bother to pay taxes?[3] The qualitative puzzle arises because, under the reasonable assumption of decreasing absolute risk aversion, EU predicts that evasion should fall as the tax rate goes up (Yitzhaki, 1974). However, the bulk of the evidence indicates that people attempt to evade more if the government tries to tax away more of their incomes.

We show that PT is able to address the quantitative and qualitative tax evasion puzzles (Dhami and al-Nowaihi, 2007, 2010b). Although the probability of an audit and the penalty rates for tax evaders are low, loss aversion from being caught, and overweighting of small probabilities of detection, ensure that only about a third of those who can evade, do evade. Using parameters of risk from generic situations of risk under PT, we can explain well the evidence from tax evasion. This provides independent confirmation of PT in a two-horse race with EU. By contrast, the predictions of EU are wrong up to a factor of up to 100.

We considered Rabin's paradox for EU in Section 1.5.4 in Chapter 1. Section 3.6 shows that this paradox can be resolved by using loss aversion (Rabin, 2000a). Several alternative explanations for Rabin's paradox turn out to rely on reference dependence, which is central to PT (Wakker, 2005, 2010).

---

[3] The probability, p, of audit for an amateur tax evader is 1–5 % and, if caught, the taxpayer has to pay back the evaded tax, plus a fine, θ, at the rate of 0.5 to 2 times the evaded tax. Thus, the return on one dollar of evaded tax is $(1 - p) - p\theta$.

Under EU, the carriers of utility are final wealth levels, so *goals* or *targets* should not alter behavior. However, the evidence suggests that goals and targets do influence behavior and outcomes. We begin, in Section 3.7, by considering the role that *goals* play as reference points and propose a simple theoretical model of goals under PT, using unpublished notes by al-Nowaihi and Dhami. This model is able to address some of the stylized facts in the literature (Heath et al., 1999) that show the following. First, goals partition the space of outcomes into gains and losses, thus, they serve as reference points. Second, individuals often work harder when they have a goal. Third, individuals work even harder as they get closer to a goal. Finally, we make some preliminary progress in the direction of determining *optimal goals*.

Section 3.8 provides an application of PT to labor economics, as encapsulated in the following question. Why is it hard to find a taxi on a rainy day in New York (Camerer et al., 1997)? The behavioral explanation is that taxi drivers have a target daily level of earnings (reference dependence), which is possibly a response to issues of *self-control*, particularly for drivers who are not highly experienced. If they quit before achieving their target, then they suffer loss aversion. On a rainy day, they are more likely to achieve their target early because the average waiting times between successive jobs is low. Hence, they are more likely to quit early. Thus, the labor supply curve is backward bending, although it is less pronounced for more experienced drivers. We review the relevant empirical evidence (e.g., Farber, 2005, 2008; Fehr and Goette, 2007). We also sketch out models of labor supply with a single target (earnings) and the more recent work in which there are multiple targets (earnings and hours worked) (Crawford and Meng, 2011).

One implication of the inverse S-shaped probability weighting functions is that the decision maker places higher decision weight on more extreme outcomes (Fehr-Duda and Epper, 2012). In Section 3.9, we briefly consider applications of this idea, mainly to issues in finance. For additional applications to finance, see the chapter on behavioral finance in Volume 5.

In Section 3.10, we consider sequential interaction between contracting parties who enter into a contract at date 0, and then engage in some economic transaction at date 1. At date 0, there is a competitive pool of contracting parties from which a pair (say, a buyer and a seller) are matched. The critical idea is that the date 0 contract may serve to define the *entitlements* of the two parties and, hence, serve as a reference point for decisions at date 1 (Hart and Moore, 2008). If the date 1 behavior of parties does not conform to their expected entitlements, then parties may shade their performance, and reduce the joint surplus. We consider the effect of these factors on the choice of optimal contracts. The empirical evidence is consistent with the model (Fehr et al., 2011).

Section 3.11 considers the effect of loss aversion on optimal contracts in the presence of moral hazard, in the standard principal–agent problem (De Meza and Webb, 2007). It turns out that loss aversion reduces the power of incentive schemes. If incentives schemes are too high powered, then loss aversion makes the satisfaction of the agent's individual rationality constraint too expensive for the principal. Thus, it is optimal for the principal to offer relatively flat segments in the optimal wage schedule. We then examine heuristically how loss aversion may explain some other observed contractual phenomena (Herweg et al., 2010).

Section 3.12 considers the issue of renegotiation of contracts under reference dependence and loss aversion (Herweg and Schmidt, 2013). The two main findings are that under loss aversion, renegotiation is sluggish and does not take place in all states of the world, although it would have, in the absence of loss aversion. The analysis also offers insights into the choice between long-term contracts and the use of spot markets.

This chapter explores only a very small set of the applications that have successfully applied PT. Some of the other successful applications include: prediction of complex states of health (Abellan-Perpiñan et al., 2009), life-cycle consumption savings models (Bowman et al., 1999), racetrack betting (Jullien and Selanié, 2000), crime and punishment (Dhami and al-Nowaihi, 2010a, 2014), asset market phenomena (Barberis et. al., 2001; Gurevich et al., 2009; Kliger and Levy, 2009), the disposition effect (Shefrin and Statman, 1985), and asymmetric price elasticities (Camerer, 2000).

3.2 The endowment effect and exchange asymmetries

The idea behind exchange asymmetries is that ownership confers a psychic benefit, which leads to an *endowment effect*. Kahneman et al. (1991) motivate the endowment effect through the following example. "A wine-loving economist we know purchased some nice Bordeaux wines years ago at low prices. The wines have greatly appreciated in value, so that a bottle that cost only $10 when purchased would now fetch $200 at auction. This economist now drinks some of this wine occasionally, but would neither be willing to sell the wine at the auction price nor buy an additional bottle at that price." Neoclassical economics predicts that, depending on his valuation $v \gtreqless 200$, either the seller would like to sell at a price of $200 or prefer to buy it.

Let us term the amount of money that *owners* of an object are willing to accept in exchange for the object as *the willingness to accept* (*WTA*). The *willingness to pay* (*WTP*) for the object is the amount of money that individuals are willing to pay to buy an extra unit of the object. Thaler (1980) noted the presence of *exchange asymmetries*, i.e., $WTP < WTA$; a phenomenon also known as the *endowment effect*. The effects of ownership need not be immediate, but could be gradual, increasing over time as the duration of ownership increases (Strahilevitz and Loewenstein, 1998). Ariely and Simonson (2003) also demonstrate a similar pattern for the case of bidding in auctions. The highest bidder at any stage (who has not won the auction yet) becomes partially attached to the object (a pseudo-endowment effect).

Thaler (1980) invoked *loss aversion* to explain the endowment effect. The act of giving up an object is coded as a *loss* by the owner, so *loss aversion* applies to sales of items. However, the endowment effect has been found to apply to goods but not to money or to goods purchased for resale (Kahneman et al., 1990).[4] Hence, loss aversion does not apply to the buyer's act of giving up cash, thus, $WTP < WTA$.

The endowment effect need not be limited to goods. It can also arise in the case of *perceived entitlements*, say, to a previously prevailing price. So, for instance, houses stay on the market longer in a period of falling prices. Sellers might be reluctant to sell at a lower price because they perceive that they are entitled to a previously prevailing, higher, price. There is also some evidence that the volume of stocks traded is lower for those stocks whose price is falling relative to those whose price is increasing (Shefrin and Statman, 1985).

We now describe a generic experiment in Kahneman et al. (1990), designed to test for the *endowment effect*. In order to control for factors such as subject misperception and transaction costs in potentially interfering with, or even causing, the endowment effect, Kahneman et al. (1990) first ran three markets in tokens. Tokens are intrinsically worthless and (in the absence of factors such as misperceptions and transactions costs) are not expected to induce an endowment effect, so $WTP = WTA$. The tokens can be redeemed from the experimenter for money at a pre-announced exchange rate.

---

[4] Using data from the TV show *Deal or no Deal*, Blavatskyy and Pogrebna (2009) raise the possibility that the endowment effect might be weakened when the stakes are very high.

We reproduce the instructions for sellers and buyers in some detail because these have played an important part in the debate on the explanation of the endowment effect. In the market for tokens, sellers receive the following instructions.

In this market, the objects being traded are tokens. You are an owner, so you now own a token which has a value to you of $x. It has this value to you because the experimenter will give you this much money for it. The value of the token is different for different individuals. A price for the tokens will be determined later. For each of the prices listed below, please indicate whether you prefer to: (1) Sell your token at this price and receive the market price. (2) Keep your token and cash it in for the sum of money indicated above. For each price indicate your decision by marking an X in the appropriate column.

The instructions for the buyers were as follows.

In this market, the objects being traded are tokens. You are a buyer, so you have an opportunity to buy a token which has a value to you of $x. It has this value to you because the experimenter will give you this much money for it. The value of the token is different for different individuals. A price for the tokens will be determined later. For each of the prices listed below, please indicate whether you prefer to: (1) Buy a token at this price and cash it in for the sum of money indicated above. (2) Not buy a token at this price. For each price indicate your decision by marking an X in the appropriate column.

This is followed by a list of prices, ranging from $0.25 to $8.75, increased in steps of $0.50. Sellers are asked to state their WTA, while buyers are asked to state their WTP. Subjects were made to alternate in the roles of buyers and sellers in three successive markets. The tokens were assigned a different individual redemption value in each trial. Once the subjects give their responses, the experimenter immediately computes the implied demand and supply schedules for each market as well as the market clearing price.

Three buyers and sellers are then selected and paid off in accordance with the market clearing price. The procedure described above is incentive compatible. The main finding was $WTP = WTA$. Hence, based on the trading in the market for tokens, one can rule out the presence of factors that might vitiate the endowment effect. These factors include subject misperception (e.g., confusing instructions), bargaining postures (sellers asking for more to strengthen their bargaining positions), and transactions costs of trade.

Kahneman et al. (1990) then gave Cornell coffee mugs to subjects on alternative seats (these mugs could be purchased from the university bookshop for $6.00 each). Subjects were given an opportunity to examine the mugs. Then, the experimental procedure for tokens was applied by replacing mugs with tokens; all subjects found the mugs to be desirable items because they placed a positive valuation on them. Subjects were told that it was in their best interests to answer questions truthfully and that of the four mug markets conducted, one market, *the binding market trial*, would be selected at random and played for real. The initial assignment of subjects in the roles of buyers or sellers was maintained throughout. Following the four markets for mugs, four more markets were conducted for boxed ballpoint pens, which sold for $3.98 in the university bookstore (the price tags were left visible to the subjects). This procedure is also incentive compatible.

The repetition of each of the markets for four times was designed to allow learning to take place. However, no learning effects were found in the experimental results (we comment more on these results below).

The results in the mugs and pens markets were very different from the results arising with tokens. In the markets for these objects, Kahneman et al. (1990) found that the median selling price was more than twice the median buying price. The actual volumes of trade were only 20% and 41%, respectively, of the predicted volumes.

Could sellers simply be inflating their WTA in order to get a higher equilibrium price? Kahneman et al. (1990) control for this objection by running another experiment in which the price is chosen randomly. Subjects are explicitly told that their decision will have no effect on the actual price chosen. From Becker et al. (1964), it is known that this elicitation mechanism ensures truthful reporting of valuations and willingness to pay for the good. Since strategic postures on the part of sellers and buyers have no bearing on the actual price in this case, it is always at least a weakly dominant strategy to tell the truth. The experimental results still showed a large endowment effect and were nearly identical to the ones obtained when actual market clearing prices were used.

Experiments 6 and 7 in Kahneman et al. (1990) added an extra group of experimental subjects. Sellers in the experiment were given a mug and asked if they would sell the mug at prices ranging from $0 to $9.25. The *buyers* were asked if they would buy the mug at these prices. The third subset of subjects, the *choosers*, were asked at each price, say x, if they would prefer to have a cash amount of x, or the mug (which is exactly the same choice as faced by a seller). The only difference between choosers and sellers is that the latter have physical possession of the good.

If the behavior of the choosers and the sellers is similar, then the endowment effect does not have any bite, because, in this case, it is not physical possession of the good, per se, that creates a higher WTA. In contrast, it was found that the behavior of choosers was similar to that of buyers, but not the sellers, which confirms the endowment effect. Median valuations of the mug for sellers, choosers, and buyers, were $7.12, $3.12, and $2.87, respectively.

By way of comparison, the earlier study of Knetsch (1989) used two objects (mugs and candy bars). Each object was, in turn, randomly allocated to some subjects (sellers) who had an opportunity to trade it for the other object. When endowed with the mug, 89% of the sellers preferred to keep the mug. When endowed with the candy bar, 90% of the sellers preferred to keep the candy bar. Since subjects are allocated randomly to the two treatments (i.e., mug ownership and candy ownership), in the absence of an endowment effect it is difficult to explain these results. An even earlier study by Knetsch and Sinden (1984) found the WTA to WTP ratio for lottery tickets to be about 4.[5]

The evidence for the endowment effect outlined in this section relied mainly on items such as mugs and pens. However, the endowment effect has also been documented for a range of other objects such as college basketball tickets (Carmon and Ariely, 2000), gift certificates (Sen and Johnson, 1997), choice of pizza toppings (Levin et al., 2002), hunting permits (Cummings et al., 1986), wine (Van Dijk and Van Knippenberg, 1996), and car attributes (Johnson et al., 2006). Kahneman et al. (1990) argue that the endowment effect is also likely to hold when the entities engaged in a transaction are firms rather than individuals. They conjecture that once firms obtain property rights over some economic asset (by accident of history, luck, or public policy) they might be reluctant to sell the asset, while at the same time being reluctant to buy such an asset at the market price.

---

[5] Perhaps one of the earliest studies to report a WTA–WTP gap was by Coombs et al. (1967). However, the experiment involved a hypothetical setting of lottery tickets without real exchange.

The endowment effect suggests that individuals are relatively more reluctant to give up objects they own, so they appear to have a bias towards the current allocation, i.e., a *status-quo bias*. Samuelson and Zeckhauser (1988) gave subjects a choice between investing in one of four possible investments: moderate risk, high risk, treasury bills, and municipal bonds. In the neutral treatment, the endowment of the subjects is just money. In the non-neutral treatments, the endowment is one of the possible investments themselves. A status-quo bias (a larger fraction of the final portfolio consisting of the investment one is endowed with) is found in the non-neutral treatment relative to the neutral treatment. Furthermore, the status-quo bias is found to be more pronounced when there is a larger number of alternatives.

3.2.1 *Loss aversion and the endowment effect*

To understand exchange asymmetries in terms of loss aversion, consider the following piecewise-linear Köszegi–Rabin type utility function,

$$v(x) = \begin{cases} m + (x - r) & if \quad x \geq r \\ m + \lambda(x - r) & if \quad x < r \end{cases}, \tag{3.1}$$

where x is the actual value of the consumption of the good, r is some "reference point" for this good, m is the amount of money received (this is negative if money is paid out), and λ is the coefficient of loss aversion.[6]

In most exchange experiments, sellers are endowed with one unit of an object, say, a mug, hence, assume that the reference point of the seller is $r = 1$. In (3.1), the separability in goods and money is motivated by experimental results (see above), which suggest that there is no endowment effect for money. Suppose that the seller is offered a price p for the mug. Using (3.1), and noting that $m = p$, if he does not sell the mug, then his utility is $v(x = 1) = 0$. If he sells the mug, his utility is $v(x = 0) = p - \lambda$. Hence, he sells the mug if and only if

$$p - \lambda \geq 0. \tag{3.2}$$

Notice that the coefficient of loss aversion, λ, plays a critical role in the decision to sell the mug. Higher loss aversion impedes sales, unless the price is high enough.

> **Definition 3.1** *(WTA): The WTA is the minimum price, $p = p_s$, that the seller is willing to accept in order to sell the mug. From (3.2)*

$$p_s = \lambda. \tag{3.3}$$

Consider now the buyer who is not endowed with the mug, so his reference point is $r = 0$. Using (3.1), and noting that at any price that he pays, p, we have $m = -p$. If the buyer does not buy the mug, then his utility is $v(x = 0) = 0$. If he buys the mug, then, his utility is $v(x = 1) = 1 - p$. Hence, the buyer buys the mug if and only if

$$1 - p \geq 0. \tag{3.4}$$

---

[6] Recall the first two lines of instructions above: "You are an owner, so you now own a token which has a value to you of $x. It has this value to you because the experimenter will give you this much money for it." This is the value of x in (3.1).

Definition 3.2   *(WTP): The WTP is the maximum price, $p = p_b$, that the buyer is willing to pay for the mug. From (3.4),*

$$p_b = 1. \tag{3.5}$$

From (3.3), (3.5), we get that:

$$\frac{WTA}{WTP} = \frac{p_s}{p_b} = \lambda. \tag{3.6}$$

Hence, the loss aversion parameter, λ, equals WTA/WTP. In Kahneman et al. (1990), the median values are $WTA = 7.12$ and $WTP = 2.87$, so median $\lambda \approx 2.5$. Across 45 studies surveyed in Horowitz and McConnell (2002), median WTA/WTP is 2.6.

What sort of factors does the endowment effect depend on? Insofar as the endowment effect is caused by loss aversion alone, one can equivalently ask, what factors does loss aversion depend on? Can the endowment effect be switched on and off, or be reduced/amplified? While more work remains to be done in this area, the literature already suggests several factors.

The endowment effect is reduced (equivalently loss aversion is reduced), when (1) the owned good and the unowned good are close substitutes (Van Dijk and Van Knippenberg, 1996; Chapman, 1998), (2) the duration of ownership is shorter (Strahilevitz and Loewenstein, 1998), (3) questions are framed in a way that directs sellers to the uses that money from sales can be put to and buyers to the benefits arising from ownership of the object (Carmon and Ariely, 2000), (4) a lesser proportion of money is earmarked for necessities (Wicker et al., 1995), (5) negative emotions such as disgust are invoked, prior to the elicitation of WTA and WTP,[7] (6) subjects are relatively younger or less educated individuals, and have greater knowledge of the attributes of a product (Johnson et al., 2006); the youngest subject had a loss aversion of 1.4, while the oldest subject had a loss aversion of 2.4, (7) there is a reduction in the ambiguity about the value of the good, and a reduction in the cost of gathering information (Kolstad and Guzman, 1999); explicit price information can reduce the ambiguity about value and reduce the WTA/WTP disparity (Zhao and Kling, 2001).

There is evidence of variability of loss aversion for an individual across different traits of a good or for different goods. Factors that could influence loss aversion for an individual include the following: whether the good is a health or a non-health good with greater variability for health related goods (Brown and Gregory, 1999; Sayman and Oncüler, 2005); whether the good is an environmental or a non-environmental good (Irwin, 1994); whether trade in the good is legitimate or not (Sayman and Oncüler, 2005); and whether the good has hedonic or utilitarian attributes (Dhar and Wertenbroch, 2000).

To get a feel for how loss aversion might vary with the attributes of a product, consider the empirical study by Johnson et al. (2006). They conducted a survey of 360 German car buyers who had recently purchased a mid-sized car. Four different attributes of the car were considered. The aim was to measure loss aversion (using appropriate lotteries) for each individual and for each car attribute. Across all individuals, and attributes, the average loss aversion was 1.85. On average, for any individual, loss aversion for the four attributes was not correlated. There was also significant

---

[7] See, for instance, Lerner et al. (2004). These authors find that when disgust is invoked, the endowment effect gets switched off. Peters et al. (2003) also point out the effect of emotionally difficult trade-offs on the WTA–WTP disparity. Boyce et al. (1992) find that the WTA–WTP disparity increases when the exchange of goods involves a degree of moral responsibility.

heterogeneity in measured loss aversion across individuals. The average coefficients of loss aversion across the four attributes were 1.66 (fuel consumption), 1.89 (comfort), 1.89 (safety), and 1.94 (information). One possible explanation is that people differ in their perceptions of the various attributes and loss aversion is context dependent. This supports a great deal of research elsewhere on the context dependence of preferences.

It is important to note that the same subjects who exhibit loss aversion in this study had recently engaged in a major purchase. This is a noteworthy point in the light of other studies (considered below) which push the alternative view that if subjects are sufficiently well trained, experienced, and briefed about strategies and equilibrium notions, then they might completely shed loss aversion. Johnson et al. (2006) conclude with the following: "Thus, we suggest that the question should not be whether or not loss aversion is important, but rather how important loss aversion is, and for which attributes and consumers."

Individual-level heterogeneity is found in another study by Gächter et al. (2010) who compare loss aversion for risky and riskless choice. The correlation in loss aversion between these two choices is 0.635, which is statistically significant at the conventional levels. Averaged across all individuals they get the classic figure of loss aversion of around 2. However, across individuals they found that for 78% of the individuals, the loss aversion parameter is between 1 and 4; for 10% of the individuals, it is above 4; and for 22% of individuals, it is around 1.

3.2.2 Is there any risk aversion beyond loss aversion?

Novemsky and Kahneman (2005) extend Thaler's (1980) idea of using loss aversion as an explanation of exchange disparities to risky choice. Their most important conclusion is that *there is no risk aversion beyond loss aversion* when subjects are presented with lotteries that have balanced risks (i.e., equal probability of all outcomes). The idea that the finding of risk aversion could, at least partly, be caused by loss aversion is well recognized.[8]

Definitions 3.1, 3.2, respectively, define WTA and WTP. We now give another useful definition that relies on the concept of "choosers" in Kahneman et al. (1990) that we have defined above.

> **Definition 3.3** *(Choice equivalent): The choice equivalent, CE, is defined as the minimum amount of money that "choosers" would accept in preference to the object.*

Novemsky and Kahneman (2005) motivate their ideas through a series of hypotheses. Recall that choosers do not actually have possession of the object, and they exhibit no endowment effects. Empirically, they behave like buyers and not sellers. For this reason, they are willing to accept a lower amount of money in preference to the object (CE) relative to the WTA of sellers, hence, we get hypothesis H1, below.

H1: $\frac{WTA}{CE} > 1$ (endowment effect).

A second finding is that for intrinsically useless assets such as money and tokens, one does not find the presence of an endowment effect. In this case $WTA = WTP$, but $WTA = CE$ for choosers, thus, we get H2.

H2: $\frac{CE}{WTP} = 1$ (no loss aversion in parting with money).

---

[8] See, for instance, Marquis and Homer (1996), Kahneman and Tversky (2000), Kahneman (2003), Rizzo and Zeckhauser (2003), and List (2004).

In Novemsky and Kahneman (2005), the first three conditions are identical to Kahneman et al. (1990), namely, *sellers*, *buyers*, and *choosers*. In order to take account of risk, two additional conditions are introduced. In the first of these conditions, the *risky seller condition*, sellers are endowed with a mug. In addition, they are asked if they would be willing to accept the following voluntary *balanced risk* lottery with two outcomes. (i) Retain the mug and gain an amount of money, *m*, with probability 0.5. (ii) Lose the mug and receive nothing with probability 0.5.

> **Definition 3.4** *(RWTA): The risky willingness to accept (RWTA) is the minimum sum of money, m_s, that the sellers require to accept the balanced risk gamble in the "risky seller condition."*

In the second additional condition, the *risky buying condition*, buyers face the following balanced risk gamble with two outcomes. (i) Receive the object and pay nothing with probability 0.5. (ii) Pay some amount of money, *m*, and not receive the object with probability 0.5.

> **Definition 3.5** *(RWTP): The risky willingness to pay (RWTP) is the maximum amount of money, m_b, that the buyer will pay to accept the balanced risk gamble in the "risky buying condition."*

We use the value function under PT (Definition 2.15) to calculate the relevant expressions for RWTA and RWTP. We use a probability weighting function $w(p)$ that has the same form for losses and gains. The decision maker's utility from an outcome is given by (3.1).

In the *risky seller condition*, consider the problem faced by a seller who owns a mug, so $r = 1$. If the seller accepts the balanced risk gamble, then there is one outcome each in the domain of gains and losses, and his utility, v_s, is given by

$$v_s = w(0.5)(1 - 1 + m) + w(0.5)\lambda(0 - 1). \tag{3.7}$$

If the seller does not accept the gamble, then he retains the mug but gets no money, so his utility is $v_s = 1 - 1 = 0$. Hence, the seller accepts the gamble if and only if

$$w(0.5)m - \lambda w(0.5) \geq 0 \Leftrightarrow m - \lambda \geq 0.$$

Using Definition 3.4, the RWTA is given by

$$m_s = \lambda. \tag{3.8}$$

Now consider the *risky buyer condition*. Since the buyer does not own the mug to begin with, so his reference point $r = 0$. If the buyer engages in the balanced risk gamble, there is one outcome each in the domain of gains and losses, and his utility, v_b, is given by

$$v_b = w(0.5)(1 - 0 - 0) + w(0.5)\lambda(0 - 0 - m). \tag{3.9}$$

If the buyer does not engage in the gamble, then his utility is $v_b = 0$. Hence, in the *risky buyer condition*, the buyer accepts the gamble if and only if

$$w(0.5) - w(0.5)\lambda m \geq 0 \Leftrightarrow 1 - \lambda m \geq 0. \tag{3.10}$$

Using Definition 3.5 and (3.10), we get that the RWTP is given by

$$m_b = \frac{1}{\lambda} < 1. \tag{3.11}$$

(3.8) and (3.11), in conjunction with Definitions 3.1 and 3.2, allow us to formulate the next two hypotheses.

H3: For balanced risks, $\frac{RWTA}{WTA} \equiv \frac{m_s}{p_s} = 1$ (no risk aversion beyond loss aversion).

Hypothesis H3 simply follows from (3.3), (3.8). Its consequences are profound for economics, namely, that for balanced risks there is no risk aversion beyond loss aversion. Loss aversion is present in the risky and the riskless conditions. If the individual feels any risk aversion beyond loss aversion, then it must be the case that $RWTA > WTA$ (i.e., the seller would require greater compensation for parting with the object in the risky condition). But $RWTA = WTA$. Hypothesis H3 shows that for balanced risks, the parameter of loss aversion is the same in risky and riskless situations.

From (3.5), $p_b = 1$ and from (3.11) $m_b = 1/\lambda$, hence, we get our final hypothesis, H4.

H4: For balanced risks $\frac{WTP}{RWTP} \equiv \frac{p_b}{m_b} > 1$.

Hypothesis H4 assumes that in riskless conditions, buyers do not have loss aversion for the money that they are spending. However, in the risky condition, buyers are gambling away their money. If buyers are loss averse with respect to money under risk, then their risky willingness to pay should be relatively smaller, giving rise to H4.

To recap, there are five conditions: sellers, choosers, buyers, risky sellers, and risky buyers. The objects used are chocolates, pens, and mugs. The elicitation mechanism ensured that there are no strategic responses. The median response by the appropriate subset of subjects is used to compute WTP, WTA. A bootstrapping method is used to estimate confidence intervals for the various ratios used in H1–H4. The aggregate estimates of these ratios were as follows,

$$\frac{WTA}{CE} = 1.85; \quad \frac{CE}{WTP} = 1.07; \quad \frac{RWTA}{WTA} = 0.91; \quad \frac{WTP}{RWTP} = 2.31, \tag{3.12}$$

which supports all of the hypotheses H1–H4. The experimental results can thus be summarized as follows.

1. Because $\frac{WTA}{CE} > 1$ and $\frac{CE}{WTP} \cong 1$, as in earlier studies, there is no loss aversion for money in riskless situations.[9] The 95% confidence interval for $\frac{WTA}{CE}$ included the number 2 (a commonly found magnitude for the parameter of loss aversion, λ) in five out of seven experiments.

2. Since $\frac{WTP}{RWTP} > 1$, there is loss aversion for money given up in risky situations. The ratio $\frac{WTP}{RWTP}$, however, turned out to be quite variable across experiments so there is need for more work in this area.

---

[9] Unlike most other studies, Bateman et al. (1997) report loss aversion of buyers for money in riskless situations; they find that $\frac{CE}{WTP} = 1.67$, which is statistically different from 1. They also find little loss aversion in selling. Novemsky and Kahneman (2005) conjecture that the source of the difference lies in different subject pools (US versus UK students) as well as the perception of the UK subjects that they did not have budget reserves (hence leading to loss aversion for money).

3. Since $\frac{RWTA}{WTA} \cong 1$ (the 95% confidence interval included the number 1 for all experiments), *there is no risk aversion beyond loss aversion.* This is a profound result for economics; indeed, economists who report risk aversion in their empirical studies, might actually be picking out loss aversion.[10]

Schunk and Winter (2009) provide more indirect support for these results. They look at problems which require the computation of optimal stopping times. Such models typically postulate risk-neutral decision makers. The observed stopping times fall short of the predictions under standard theory with risk-neutral decision makers. Schunk and Winter (2009) find that the optimal stopping times are based on search heuristics. Furthermore, these search heuristics are not correlated with risk attitudes but with attitudes towards loss aversion.

3.2.3 *Market experience and loss aversion*

In their experiments, Kahneman et al. (1990) (see above) conducted two sets of market trials, respectively, with mugs and pens. Each set of trials consisted of four successive markets. At the end of each market trial, full feedback was provided to all the participants in order to facilitate learning. They found that as the market trials progressed (from 1 to 4) there was no evidence of learning, and the disparity between WTP and WTA remained. In contrast, some earlier studies report that market experience in practice trials (typically hypothetical and non-binding trials) significantly reduces the WTP/WTA disparity.[11] Kahneman et al. (1990) argue that the source of the difference between the two sets of results arises from the fact that each of their market trials was potentially binding, which is not the case with earlier empirical studies.

One may wonder if the time span required for learning is longer than what Kahneman et al. (1990) allow for in their experiments? List (2003) seeks to address these issues using field data. In his first market, he used two sports memorabilia items, A and B.[12] A distinction is made between dealers and non-dealers in the sports memorabilia market. Dealers have greater experience of trades as compared to non-dealers. Both dealers and non-dealers could be buying and/or selling objects. The pooled sample contained both dealers and non-dealers. There were also separate samples of dealers and non-dealers.

Dealers/non-dealers were given possession of one of the two objects. They were then given the opportunity to trade the object for the other object. Both items are somewhat non-standard in the sports memorabilia market. However, a pre-test suggested that the preference between the two items is nearly equally split, so we should expect trade to take place about 50% of the time. In the exit interviews, 95% indicated that they would like to keep the object for their own collection, rather than intending to use it for resale.

In the pooled sample of dealers and non-dealers, there was too little trading (i.e., trades below 50%) as predicted by the endowment effect. For items A and B, the actual trades were 32.8% and

---

[10] An important condition for this result is that income effects must be small. Hence, for large stakes, this result might or might not hold.

[11] See, for instance, Knez et al (1985), Brookshire and Coursey (1987), and Coursey et al. (1987). Loomes et al. (2003) also find a disappearance of the systematic part of the WTA–WTP disparity with experience, although they cannot pinpoint the mechanism that leads to this disappearance. Shogren et al. (1994) find that exchange asymmetries disappear with repeated experimental interaction when there are close substitutes for market goods. But this result does not hold for non-market goods with imperfect substitutes. However, Morrison (1997) raises concerns about these results.

[12] Item A is a ticket stub in which Cal Ripken Jr. broke the world record for consecutive baseball games played. Item B was a dated certificate to commemorate the game in which Nolan Ryan achieved the distiction of winning 300 baseball games.

34.6%, respectively, which suggest that *WTA* > *WTP*. Despite the random allocation of objects, a Fisher exact test was used to control for the problem that more people than the average could have received their most preferred item (and so do not need to trade). The test rejected the null hypothesis of no-endowment effect.

Splitting the pooled sample into dealers and non-dealers reveals a different picture. Dealers trade objects A, B, respectively, 43.6% and 45.7% of the time. For non-dealers, these percentages lie between 20–25%. The Fisher test allows rejection of the null hypothesis (no-endowment effect) for non-dealers. However, the null hypothesis is accepted for dealers, i.e., dealers do not exhibit an endowment effect. When non-dealers are differentiated between experienced (who trade six or more items in a month) and inexperienced ones, it is found that for the latter category, the endowment effect is stronger. The nature of the results is similar when they are replicated with a different set of objects. A logit regression confirms that the propensity to trade is positively affected by trading experience, i.e., experience seems to mitigate the endowment effect.

An important issue is whether *selection effects* have been properly controlled for. Do dealers trade more because they are more experienced (treatment effect) or is it because the type of people who have lower loss aversion (and, so, a lower endowment effect) become dealers and trade more (selection effect)? To test for this effect, List followed up, a year later, the 148 people who participated in the earlier sports memorabilia experiment in 1999. Of these, he was able to meet 72 (less than half the original sample). The idea was that the subjects have had an extra year's experience and so would perhaps have shed their endowment effect even further. With this restricted set of subjects, two new A and B objects were introduced. The result was that the subjects, on average, engaged in slightly more trades in the year 2000 compared to the year 1999 (6.84 versus 5.66). List (2003) concludes that this demonstrates a reduction of the endowment effect with experience.

List (2004) seeks to address one possible criticism of List (2003). This is to take account of the possibility that no endowment effect should be observed if sellers hold a good for resale (e.g., Kahneman et al., 1990). Whilst the exit interviews in List (2003) suggested that subjects intended to keep the objects for personal consumption, List (2004) reverts back to the more traditional items used to test the endowment effect, such as mugs and Swiss chocolate bars. The expectation is that these items will not be used for resale. The other feature of List (2004) that is different from List (2003) is that experience in selling/buying one sort of item is expected to be transferred to selling/buying other objects (mugs, chocolates). The findings in List (2004) are similar to those of List (2003).

In conjunction, the findings in List (2003, 2004) have generated substantial interest. The skeptical view is that these findings have served to reject PT. A more balanced view is that the real contribution of List (2003) is to demonstrate that there are differences in the trading propensities of dealers and non-dealers. List (2003) is not alone in highlighting the role of experience in potentially affecting loss aversion. For instance, Camerer et al. (1997) find differences in loss aversion for experienced and inexperienced New York cab drivers. Similar evidence from the housing market comes from Genesove and Mayer (2001). However, we would urge caution in interpreting the List (2003) findings as a rejection of PT. We elaborate below.

1. Considerable experience is required in the market experiments of List for the endowment effect to diminish.[13] However, in a range of plausible and non-trivial real-world situations such as selling a car, a house or a consumer durable, and making decisions such as marriage

---

[13] In List (2003), experienced dealers carry out six or more trades per month, while in List (2004) the requirement increases to eleven or more trades per month. Furthermore, such intense trading is carried out by these dealers over several years.

and divorce, one typically does not have the benefit of learning from a large number of repetitions. In these cases, one is likely to exhibit loss aversion, like non-dealers in the List experiments.

2. There are other possible interpretations of the results in List (2003). In 1999, his sample had 148 individuals, while the latter sample in 2000 had 72. It is quite likely that the average trades of the two groups could differ by a relatively small amount (6.84 versus 5.66, as it turns out) for a variety of other reasons, e.g., a more pessimistic trading environment in 2000 as compared to 1999. Further, the 72 people out of 148 is not a random sample. It is possible that the 72 who agreed to participate in the experiment, a second time, are the more committed traders who regularly go to the annual sports trade shows. Hence, there is a selection issue involved. Others are even more skeptical about the attempts to control for selection issues in the context of List's work. For instance, Plott and Zeiler (2007, p. 1451) write: "One can formulate other candidate theories, based on various features of List's experiments, to explain his observation… Conducting experiments in the field makes it difficult, if not impossible to control for selection effects."

3. Several other studies that we review below suggest that in other important contexts, with higher stakes, and much larger datasets (in one case, more than 2.5 million data points), experienced subjects are also loss averse.

4. List (2003) also finds a reduction in the endowment effect for students who participate in a WTA/WTP experiment for four successive weeks. Students exhibit experience effects that are similar to these effects for dealers in the field. In the first week, 12% of the students trade their endowed good, but 26% do so in the fourth week, suggesting that experience may mitigate the endowment effect. In the light of these experiments, the title of List's paper "Does market experience eliminate market anomalies?" is misplaced. Going by the results of the paper, market experience appears to reduce loss aversion both in the lab and in the field. Yet the misleading inference that only market experience in the field is somehow effective is routinely drawn. Consider, for instance, the following quote from Haigh and List (2005, p. 525): "In light of some recent studies (e.g., List, 2002, 2003, 2004) that report market anomalies in the realm of riskless decision-making are attenuated among real economic players who have intense market experience, the current lot of experimental studies with MLA [myopic loss aversion] may be viewed with caution."[14]

A recent field study by Pope and Schweitzer (2011) finds that even experienced players on the PGA golf tour exhibit loss aversion. The stakes in this study, in contrast to the work by List (2003, 2004), are very large. In golf, on the PGA circuit, players play four rounds of 18 holes, for a total of 72 holes, over four days. The objective is to minimize the number of shots required to complete the 72 holes. In order to complete a hole, the golfer begins with a drive (or a *tee*) and then a series of shots that takes the golfer to the "green." At the green, the golfer engages in a series of sequential shots, until eventually the ball rolls into the targeted hole. Technically, the shots on the green are known as *putts* and the aim is to *sink the putt into the hole*.

Each hole in a golf course is associated with a number, called the *par*. The par is the minimum number of shots that a skilled golfer would take in order to sink the putt, starting with the drive. The par score can differ among the holes because of the distance from the tee to the hole, or the level of difficulty involved. On the PGA golf tour, the par scores for holes are typically 3, 4, or 5. The scores are recorded on score cards that measure the number of shots taken to sink the putt relative to the par score. Thus, if one sinks a putt using one stoke less than the par score, then one is said to have shot a *birdie*, and two strokes below par is an *eagle*. In these cases, the golfer is

---

[14] MLA in this quote refers to *myopic loss aversion*; see Section 3.4.

said to be *under par*. On the flip side, sinking the putt one stroke above par is called a *bogey* and two strokes above par is called a *double bogey*. In this case, the golfer is said to be *over par*. The third possibility is that the golfer might be *on par* (matching the par score).

Since all scores are measured relative to the par score, the authors make the plausible assumption that the par score for a hole acts as the reference point for that hole. It follows that if the golfer is *under par* (say, on a birdie or an eagle), he/she faces a different situation as compared to being *on* or *over par*. When on par, there is the possibility of missing the par score (reference point) so shots ought to be hit with relatively greater precision and accuracy, otherwise the golfer might be in the domain of losses and suffer loss aversion. Thus, we expect more successful par putts as compared to birdie putts.

Pope and Schweitzer (2011) explore this idea by using a sample in excess of 2.5 million data points with laser measurements of initial and final ball placements. They control for a large number of potentially relevant factors. These include the following. (i) The greater difficulty of birdie putt positions of the ball relative to the par putt positions. (ii) Information revealed by a birdie putt that helps the par putt. (iii) Player and tournament specific factors. The findings are as follows.

First, controlling for other factors, and consistent with a loss aversion account, golfers are less successful with their birdie putts, relative to comparable par putts, by 2–3 percentage points; see Figure 3.1. Second, the contrast between the birdie and par putts is even more noticeable on the first hole, where the par score is even more salient relative to subsequent holes.[15] Third, if the top 20 golf players on the PGA tour in 2008 were to shed the trait of loss aversion, then they would each stand to gain $1.2 million. Fourth, players are more risk averse in the gains domain than in

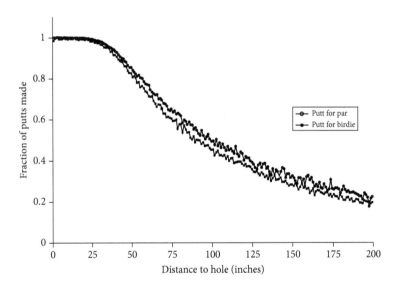

Figure 3.1 Fraction of successful par and birdie putts by distance to the hole.

Source: Pope and Schweitzer (2011) with permission from the American Economic Association.

---

[15] In subsequent holes, other factors such as competitor's scores also become important.

the loss domain. In conjunction, these results make a persuasive case that loss aversion persists even with experience when large stakes are involved.[16]

Using field data from school teachers in Chicago, Fryer et al. (2012) demonstrate that teachers, including experienced teachers, exhibit loss aversion. They distinguish between two treatments. In one treatment, teachers were promised an "end of year bonus" conditional on student grades. In a second treatment, teachers were given financial incentives in the form of money, up-front. However, they were told that the money would be clawed back from them at the end of the year if the students did not achieve the desired educational levels. In EU, RDU, the results should be identical under the two treatments assuming that the effects from discounting are small. However, if teachers follow PT, then in the second treatment, teachers who are already endowed with the money would be loss averse with respect to giving back the money at the end of the year. So, as expected from a loss aversion based explanation, the effect of the financial incentives on student grades was significantly larger in the second treatment.

Kliger and Levy (2009) put EU, RDU, and PT to the test, using real financial assets market data. Their findings provide strong support for the individual components of PT, which include reference dependence, diminishing marginal sensitivity, loss aversion, and non-linear weighting of probabilities in the domain of gains and losses. Gurevich et al. (2009) also find support for PT using US stock market data, although they find loss aversion that is asset specific and, on average, lower than that found in student populations.

The work of Abdellaoui et al. (2013) nicely complements these findings using as their subjects, finance professionals (private bankers and money managers handling $300 million on average). Unlike Gurevich et al. (2009) who use more aggregate data, Abdellaoui et al. (2013) are able to get data at the level of the individual finance professional, and observe if these "individual choices" are in accordance with PT. Almost all elements of PT find strong support (with the exception of loss aversion), and there is significant preference heterogeneity among the professionals. Furthermore, these professionals violate EU. These are significant findings because finance professionals are experienced and well trained in diversifying risk, and provided with extensive feedback on their performance.

3.2.4 *Subject misinterpretation as explanation of exchange asymmetries*

Plott and Zeiler (2007) (henceforth, PZ) conjecture that disparities between WTP and WTA are caused by the "procedure" that is used to elicit WTA and WTP. In the traditional experiments for exchange asymmetries, it was typical for the experimenter to announce the following; "I am giving you this object. It is a gift. You own it." The *language* used in these instructions potentially

---

[16] Readers, particularly golf enthusiasts, may wonder about the role of confounding factors in these results. Here we quote from the authors (p. 130): "Beyond controlling for distance, we consider and rule out several competing explanations for this finding. First, prior to hitting a par putt, players may have learned something about the green (by having already attempted a birdie putt). Second, birdie putts may start from a more precarious position on the green than par putts due to a longer approach shot. Third, player or Tournament-specific differences may bias our results. Using detailed data, we are able to rule out competing explanations with control methods and matching estimators. For example, we can match par and birdie putts attempted within one inch of each other on the exact same hole in the same Tournament. We are also able to rule out other psychological explanations. For example, we consider whether or not players become more nervous or overconfident when they shoot birdie putts relative to par putts."

creates problems.[17] In order to rectify this potential problem, PZ tell subjects that a coin is tossed to determine their endowment, which could be one of two objects. In the typical exchange asymmetry experiment, subjects make their choices publicly. To ensure that there are no spillover effects of such announcements, PZ asked subjects to report their choices privately, in writing.

In a control group under the standard procedure, they detected the presence of exchange asymmetries. However, having made the procedural changes, listed above, they find that the endowment effect is weakened or eliminated (depending on the treatment). PZ take their results as a challenge to the traditional explanations of exchange asymmetries. The explanations offered by PZ of their results are behavioral in nature, such as framing effects, reciprocity, and gift-exchange arguments. Some of these results have been replicated by Knetsch and Wong (2008).

In an earlier paper, Plott and Zeiler (2005) (henceforth, PZ1), examine the effect of subject mis-perceptions in generating exchange asymmetries. Subjects are extensively *tutored* in economic logic, prior to the conduct of actual experiments.[18] In a baseline experiment, absent these controls for subject misrepresentation, the phenomenon of exchange asymmetry is confirmed. However, in the presence of the controls, the means of the ordered (WTA, WTP) pairs for three different experiments were $(5.69, 5.60), (5.71, 7.88), (5.06, 7.29)$. The mean WTP exceeded the mean WTA for two out of three experiments. The authors conclude that the observed gaps are the result of subject "misconceptions about the nature of experimental tasks."

Like PZ, the major contribution of PZ1 is to bring out the importance of framing effects in the area of exchange asymmetries. Subjects in experiments alternate in the roles of sellers and buyers, which might alter attitudes that produce, say, the ownership effect that is important for exchange asymmetries. Furthermore, as PZ1 recognize, their procedures might have created a feeling on the part of subjects that the experimenter wishes to remove notions of ownership of the object. If this is the case (which cannot be rejected by the data from the experiment), then there could be a gap between the subject's stated and true preferences.

Isoni et al. (2011) question the results of PZ1 along the following lines. PZ1 first run lottery experiments for training purposes and then run their experiments using mugs. PZ1 find that controlling for subject misperceptions, no exchange asymmetries are found for the case of mugs. But they do not report the experimental results for the case of lotteries because these were subjected to two forms of contamination. The first problem was that the selling task preceded the buying task and the second problem was that the experimenter publicly corrected mistakes and gave public answers to questions. The result was that PZ1's influential results were based only on coffee mug experiments with 36 subjects reporting WTP and 38 reporting WTA.

The aim of the experiments by Isoni et al. (2011) is to report the results for the WTA/WTP for not only coffee mugs but also experiments based on lotteries that were not subjected to any con-taminating influences. Subjects were asked to report their WTA for the lottery $(x, p; y, 1 - p)$ and their WTP for the lottery $(x + c, p; y + c, 1 - p)$, where $c > 0$. Under EU, and constant absolute

---

[17] They also raise other potential confounds. One potential problem is asymmetric information about the quality of the object used. However, the objects are typically quite simple such as mugs and pens, so asymmetric information might not be a serious issue. Another potential confound is that sellers may have other-regarding preferences, so they could reciprocate a gift from the experimenter by placing a high value on it.

[18] As part of the tutorial, they are taught how and why economic mechanisms designed to elicit truthful preferences, such as the Becker DeGroot and Marshak (1964) mechanism, work. They are also taught about the cost and benefits of pursuing alternative strategies. Subjects could ask questions, which the experimenter would then clarify. Numerical examples with concrete illustrations were also provided. Each experimental session consisted of a detailed training session, two practice rounds (unpaid), followed by 14 paid rounds using lotteries and finally one paid round with mugs that tested for exchange asymmetries.

risk aversion, we have $WTP - WTA = c$, while the alternative hypothesis is $WTP - WTA < c$; this allowed for a within-subjects test of exchange disparities. The experimental formats are identical in Isoni et al. (2011) and PZ1, so both control for subject misrepresentations. The main finding in Isoni et al. (2011) is that no WTA/WTP disparities are found for mugs (as in PZ1), but significant exchange disparities were found for lotteries.

The exchange disparity is not mitigated as subjects gain more experience in successive rounds. If the elicitation procedure holds the key to explaining exchange asymmetries, then it should apply to both lotteries and mugs. But since exchange asymmetries are found for lotteries but not mugs, Isoni et al. (2010) conclude that the elicitation procedure is possibly a red herring in explanations of exchange asymmetries. It is an open question as to why exchange asymmetries are found for lotteries but not mugs. The authors offer some conjectures using the mental accounting literature, such as the *house money effect* caused by show-up fees.[19] Based on their results, the authors also conjecture that the difference between the results from lotteries and mugs are not due to the certainty/uncertainty dimension but due to the nature of money and consumption goods.

Fehr et al. (2015) suggest that if subject misconception is the cause of WTA/WTP anomalies, then we ought to separate subjects into those who understand the elicitation mechanism used in the experiments, and those who do not. When they make this separation, and use the experimental protocol in PZ1 and the insights of Isoni et al., they find that the WTA/WTP anomaly arises for both lotteries and mugs; the findings for mugs are also replicated for USB sticks. Hence the title of their paper: The Willingness to Pay–Willingness to Accept Gap: A Failed Replication of Plott and Zeiler.

3.2.5 *Other implications/explanations of the endowment effect*

PROPERTY RIGHTS AND EXCHANGE ASYMMETRIES

A basic lesson from microeconomics is that indifference curves can be specified in the absence of any information on endowments and the budget constraint. However, one implication of WTP and WTA disparities is that an individual's indifference curves might cross if their endowment changes.

Figure 3.2 shows indifference curves in the space of mugs (a commonly used object in experiments for which the endowment effect is found), and money (for which no endowment effect arises under certainty). For any individual in the respective roles of buyer (no mugs, no money) and seller (one mug, no money), the respective endowment points are $e_b = (0,0)$ and $e_s = (0,1)$. Starting from the endowment point, the evidence on exchange asymmetries shows that a seller places a greater marginal value on another unit of mug (in terms of money) as compared to a buyer. Thus, the indifference curves for a seller are relatively flatter, as shown in Figure 3.2; $I_b I_b$ is an indifference curve for a buyer and $I_s I_s$ for a seller. The implication is that the indifference curves of the seller and the buyer, who only differ in their endowment, can cross.

The Coase theorem states that in the absence of any frictions/transaction costs, the initial allocation of property rights is irrelevant to the efficiency of the eventual outcome. However, if the endowment effect is accepted, then the act of assigning ownership (i.e., property rights) alters one's valuation (for sellers) or willingness to pay for the good (for buyers). This, in turn, alters the

---

[19] The house money effect refers to the tendency to take greater risks in the presence of prior gains (Thaler and Johnson, 1990). For a form of the house money effect, based on a loss aversion explanation, and using stock market data, see Zhang and Semmler (2009).

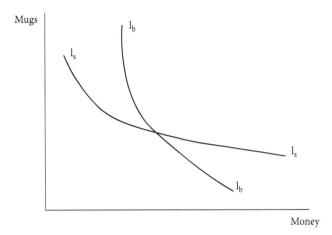

Figure 3.2 Crossing of indifference curves when there is an endowment effect.

efficient outcome before and after the allocation of property rights. Hence, the Coase theorem, as it is traditionally stated, does not hold, or has to be modified to take account of ownership effects.

The increase in the value of an object that arises purely from the act of ownership is also recognized in common law. For instance, the common perception that "possession is nine-tenths of the law" exemplifies this. Kahneman et al. (1991) credit the US Supreme Court justice, Oliver Wendell Holmes with the following quote: "It is in the nature of a man's mind. A thing which you enjoyed and used as your own for a long time, whether property or opinion, takes root in your being and cannot be torn away without your resenting the act and trying to defend yourself, however you came by it. The law can ask no better justification than the deepest instincts of man."

SOME MARKETING IMPLICATIONS OF EXCHANGE ASYMMETRIES

Novemsky and Kahneman (2005) give several implications of the endowment effect for marketing that are based on two premises.

1. When the benefits of the good whose ownership is about to be given up are similar to the benefits of the good to be acquired, then loss aversion with respect to the owned good is not likely to present. In this view, loss aversion operates along the benefits dimension of the good rather than along the attributes dimension.

2. Goods that are intended to be used only for exchange are not evaluated as losses. This assertion has two dimensions. First, firms or merchants that acquire a good with the sole intention of reselling it for money, do not experience loss aversion from the act of selling. This also potentially explains why List (2003, 2004) finds a lower degree of loss aversion for dealers relative to non-dealers. Second, some consumers/households may have a budget for miscellaneous items in order to cover for unforeseen expenditures. The goods acquired by spending money from this account might not be close substitutes for other goods. However, there is no loss aversion with respect to the money spent from this miscellaneous account. Other consumers may not have a miscellaneous account for unanticipated purchases, which typically are not substitutes for other goods. These consumers may suffer loss aversion for the money spent on making such unanticipated purchases.

Novemsky and Kahneman use these premises to offer the following applications. *Trial-offers*, which give consumers the opportunity to use a good for a limited period without making a payment, induce consumers to include the good as part of their endowment. Having used the good, the consumer experiences loss aversion by giving up the good at the end of the trial period. Such consumers may be willing to buy the good at the end of the trial period, but in the absence of the trail period, they might never have decided to buy. Yet another effect of the trial period is that the expenditure on the good could be transformed from being an unanticipated item, to which loss aversion applies, to being a part of the consumer's main budget for intended purchases. Thus, the money spent on such goods once the trial period expires may not be subjected to loss aversion.

Yet another marketing device is to trade in old cars for new ones. Consumers of older cars might be loss averse to selling their old cars (endowment effect), creating a trade friction. However, by trading-in their old car for another car, whose benefits are very similar, loss aversion is mitigated (premise 1 above). Consumers are then more likely to buy newer cars.

Another implication of the differing behavior of sellers and buyers in studies of the endowment effect is the following. Buyers consider the *opportunity cost* of buying objects such as mugs. Not buying the mug is a *reduction in gain*. If the endowment effect is accepted, then sellers on the other hand are worried about *out-of-pocket costs*; parting with the mug is an *actual loss*. Hence, the disparity between WTP and WTA can alternatively be viewed as a disparity between (1) opportunity costs versus out-of-pocket costs or, equivalently, as (2) reduction in gain versus actual loss.

Kahneman et al. (1986) test these ideas using telephone interviews conducted on Canadian subjects. Successive questions, which were designed to draw out the contrast between "opportunity costs versus out-of-pocket costs" or "reduction in gain versus actual loss" were posed to the subjects. These questions were as follows.

> Q.1a: (134 respondents) A shortage has developed for a popular model of automobile, and customers must now wait two months for delivery. A dealer has been selling these cars at list price. Now the dealer prices this model at $200 above list price.

71% found the dealer's action to be unfair and 29% found the action to be acceptable.

> Q.1b: (123 respondents) A shortage has developed for a popular model of automobile, and customers must now wait two months for delivery. A dealer has been selling these cars at a discount of $200 below list price. Now the dealer sells this model only at list price.

42% find the dealer's action to be unfair and 58% find it acceptable.

In Q.1b, the elimination of the discount is viewed as a "reduction in gain." This, we know, from the endowment effect, is less troubling for the individual relative to the imposition of the surcharge in Q.1a, which is viewed as an "actual loss." Hence, a larger percentage of subjects think of the dealer's action in Q.1a to be unfair. Along these lines, Thaler (1980) explains why firms that charge customers differently depending on whether they pay by cash or credit, frame the cash price as a discount (rather than saying that the credit price contains a surcharge).

Similar considerations might explain why it is easier to cut real wages during inflationary periods as the next two questions illustrate.

> Q.2a: (129 subjects) A company is making a small profit. It is located in a community experiencing a recession with substantial unemployment but no inflation. The company decides to decrease wages and salaries 7% this year.

63% consider the company's actions to be unfair, while the remaining 27% find the actions acceptable.

Q.2b: (129 subjects) A company is making a small profit. It is located in a community experiencing a recession with substantial unemployment and inflation of 12%. The company decides to increase salaries only 5% this year.

22% find the company's actions to be unfair, while 78% find those actions acceptable.

The only difference in questions Q.2a and Q.2b is that in the latter, inflation takes place at 12%. In both questions, the final outcome for the workers is a 7% cut in real wages. In Q.2a, the outcome is framed as a nominal wage decrease (which subjects in experiments interpret as an actual loss). In Q.2b, on the other hand, it is framed as a reduction in (wage) gains on account of inflation, which subjects find relatively more acceptable.[20]

STOCHASTIC REFERENCE POINTS

The exchange disparities between WTA and WTP can be explained if reference points are stochastic, say, in the Köszegi and Rabin (2006) framework; we do this in Section 2.8.3.

A QUERY THEORY OF VALUE CONSTRUCTION

Another explanation of the endowment effect, called the *query theory*, has been proposed by Johnson et al. (2007). The theory is based on four main premises, all grounded in well known psychological principles.[21]

(1) *Queries*: When subjects in experiments are asked how much they would accept, or pay, for an object, say, a mug, they decompose the question into a series of *queries* such as the following. What are the advantages of my status quo (mug for the seller, and money for the buyer)? What are the advantages of pursuing the alternatives (in this case, arising from trade)? Advantages and disadvantages are encapsulated by means of positive and negative *aspects* of a situation. For a seller, examples of the positive or value increasing aspects could be the following. "Nice memento from the experiment; can be used as a Christmas present; you can never have too many mugs." The negative, or value decreasing aspects could be things like the following. "This mug is ugly, I don't need a coffee mug, or this mug looks dirty." For a potential buyer, on the other hand, possible positive aspects could be: "I am a low-income student, a few extra dollars will be very valuable"; and negative aspects could be: "I could hardly buy anything with this amount of money." Queries could be automatic responses to questions that are unobservable to an outsider. Unlike queries, positive and negative aspects of a decision can be observed.

(2) *Sequential execution of queries*: Queries are executed *sequentially*. The order in which the queries are executed depends on the conditions in the experiment.

(3) *Competing memories*: Suppose that one is trying to recall some items from a list. Then the directed recall of some items in the list reduces the available memory for the unrecalled items in the list. In particular, when there are two main queries, then the recall of answers to one query suppresses recall of the answers to the second query; this is termed as *output interference*. In the particular context of this example, output interference implies that the retrieval of one source of

---

[20] While loss aversion can explain the outcome of these sets of questions, there are other competing behavioral explanations such as "money illusion" which is particularly relevant for Q.2a, Q.2b, and theories of reciprocity that take account of the role of intentions; see Volumes 2 and 4.

[21] We omit the references. The interested reader can directly look up the references in Johnson et al. (2007).

information such as the advantages of the mug, reduces the retrieval of information about what could be done with that money.

(4) *Dependence on the endowment state*: This premise implies that the order in which the queries are executed depends on one's endowment of the mug. So, if one is an owner of the mug, then the first executed query is the advantages of the mug. Alternatively, if the endowment is no mug, say, the subject is a buyer, then the first executed query is alternative uses of the money.

The first three of these premises have reasonably good psychological bases, while the fourth, which is specific to the exchange asymmetry problem, needs to be tested. An important motivation of Johnson et al. (2007) is to test this premise.

In order to perform these tests, the authors perform an exchange asymmetry experiment using mugs. However, in addition, they use the method of *aspect listing*. While queries used and the order in which they are executed is not observable, the *aspects* (positive or negative) used by subjects in experiments are observable and can be used to form inferences about the queries used. *Aspect listing* accomplishes this by asking subjects to list the aspects they consider when making their WTA and WTP decisions. Subjects are also asked to note down the order of these aspects as well as the salience of various aspects. Trading in mugs was real, actual money was exchanged, and tests were carried out to check for subject miscomprehension. Subjects were randomly assigned as either *sellers, choosers,* or *buyers* and an incentive compatible elicitation mechanism was used.

The results are as follows.

1. On average, the WTA for the mugs is $5.71, while the WTP is $3.42; the difference is statistically significant.
2. Sellers of the mugs produced more *value increasing aspects of mugs* that highlighted advantages of holding on to the mug. By contrast, buyers and choosers produced more *value increasing aspects of the alternative uses of money*. Furthermore, the order of queries was also in the expected sequential order. Sellers of mugs first produced value increasing aspects of the mugs before thinking about the value decreasing aspects of the mugs. In contrast, buyers first produced aspects relating to the alternative uses of the money.
3. Value increasing aspects increase the price and value decreasing aspects reduce the price of mugs.
4. Even stronger support for the theory is provided by an experiment in which the natural order of queries was reversed. Sellers were asked to first produce value decreasing aspects of the mugs, followed by the value increasing ones. Buyers were asked to produce value increasing, followed by value decreasing aspects of the mugs. This reversal of the natural order of queries eliminated exchange asymmetries entirely.

UNCERTAINTY AND EXCHANGE ASYMMETRIES

Engleman and Hollard (2008) distinguish between two alternative sources of uncertainty. *Choice uncertainty* refers to uncertainty about the object at the time of making the choice. For instance, the value of an object might be uncertain, or the individual might have incomplete preferences over objects in a set. On the other hand, *trade uncertainty* refers to uncertainty arising from the trading procedure and aspects of the trading partners. For instance, does the trading partner have "other-regarding preferences"? Is it morally appropriate to trade this object?

The authors conjecture that the endowment effect is caused by trade uncertainty. If true, then the presence of trade uncertainty causes people to trade less. In the words of the authors: "The market would thus be a poor teacher because traders will avoid those trades that would teach them the crucial lessons." In order to examine these ideas, two treatments are considered. In the first treatment, subjects are free to trade, as in the traditional experiments that test for exchange asymmetries. However, in the second treatment, subjects were forced to trade; if they did not trade, they lost their endowments. This allowed subjects to experiment in uncertain situations, where natural caution would have prevented them from trading. In subsequent rounds of the second treatment, subjects in experiments do not exhibit the endowment effect. The authors provide one possible resolution of the endowment effect by artificially inducing more trade.

Roca et al. (2006) find that the status-quo bias arising on account of the endowment effect persists when an individual is endowed with an ambiguous lottery that can be exchanged with a lottery that has no ambiguity.[22]

3.3 Prospect theory preferences in primates

Humans and other primate species share a common evolutionary history. Humans (genus Homo) and chimpanzees and bonobos (genus Pan) split from a common ancestor, the genus Hominini, about five to six million years ago. The two immediately previous temporal evolutionary splits from common ancestors gave rise to, respectively, the gorillas, orangutans, and the gibbons. Humans differ experientially from the other primates in having specific market experience; however, evolution is very slow and conservative. Hence, common evolutionary features are likely to be exhibited in shared behavior between humans and other primates in several domains; for a survey, see Santos and Platt (2014).

We focus on studies that have been done on two species of monkeys, capuchin and macaque.[23] Macaques are extremely spatially dispersed Old World monkeys that are found mainly in Africa and Asia. The most common species of macaques in neurophysiological studies is the rhesus macaque. In contrast, the most common species of monkeys used in experiments on economic preferences and risk is capuchin monkeys. The habitat of these monkeys is in South and Central America; these are also sometimes known as New World monkeys. There are several reasons why capuchin monkeys are particularly suitable for these studies. The ratio of their brain to body size is high, they live in social groups, are socially sensitive, can learn from others, share food, engage in using tools, and quickly learn to trade tokens for food with experimenters (Fragaszy et al., 2004). Humans, chimpanzees, bonobos, and gorillas are part of the genus Hominidae, but monkeys belong to a different genus. Macaques separated from the evolutionary line that led to humans about 25 million years ago, while capuchins separated about 35 million years ago.

Chen et al. (2006) is one of the first studies to test elements of prospect theory on capuchin monkeys. They used monkeys who were trained to exchange tokens for food rewards. Under certainty, the monkey offers a token to the experimenter, who simultaneously holds a food item in one hand; see Figure 3.3. On receiving the token, the experimenter gives the food item to the monkey. Under risk, the experimenter offers a probabilistic reward, as explained below. The monkeys were placed in an enclosure and given a budget of tokens. Two experimenters wearing different colored clothing then positioned themselves on different sides of the enclosure. The monkey could trade tokens for food with both experimenters using openings in the enclosure.

---

[22] The ambiguous lottery is simply a ticket that allows one to bet on the unknown urn in Ellsberg's experiments (see Chapter 4). The unambiguous lottery is a ticket to bet on the color of the ball from the known urn in Ellsberg's experiments.

[23] We ignore studies on pigeons and rats because they are more distant in evolutionary terms.

Figure 3.3 Tests of capuchin monkey preferences.
Source: Lakshminarayanan et al. (2008).

Two initial tests of consistency of capuchin preferences were conducted. In the first test, the monkeys' original allocation of budget on two food items (jello pieces and apple slices) was established after repeated trials. Then the monkeys were given a new budget but the price of one of the food items, in terms of tokens, was reduced. The monkeys substituted consumption towards the relatively cheaper item by spending a greater fraction of their budget on it. In fact, the choices of monkeys reliably satisfied the generalized axiom of revealed preference. As the authors note, many naive models and even some forms of random behavior can satisfy GARP.

In the second consistency test, experimenter 1 always offered and traded one apple slice in return for one token. However, experimenter 2 made a risky offering; he initially held out two apple slices to the monkey, but was equally likely to offer either two slices or one slice after receiving the token from the monkey. Thus, on average, experimenter 2 offered 1.5 slices, which is higher than the number offered by experimenter 1. Clearly, the offering of experimenter 2, first order stochastically dominates the offering of experimenter 1. Over 60 trials, spread over five sessions, 87% of the trading choices were directed towards experimenter 2. Thus, the vast majority of capuchins satisfied stochastic dominance.

In order to test for reference dependence, the offerings made by the two experimenters were as follows. In each case, the initial offer made by any experimenter, say, offering x slices of apples in return for a token, may be considered as the reference point. However, once a token is received from the monkey, the experimenter offers a trade in the following lottery in apple slices $(y, 0.5; z, 0.5)$. For experimenter 1, $x = y = 1$, $z = 2$ for an average offering of 1.5, while for experimenter 2, $x = y = 2$, $z = 1$, for an average offering of 1.5. The reference point is low for experimenter 1 and half the time his offering leads to a gain relative to the reference point. In contrast, the reference point for experimenter 2 is high and half the time his offering leads to a loss. Pooled across all monkey subjects, in the last five sessions, 71% of the monkeys traded with experimenter 1; the results are statistically different from an equal split in trading between the two experimenters. One cannot explain this result in a theory that ignores reference dependence of preferences. For instance, under EU this implies that $0.5u(1) + 0.5u(2) > 0.5u(2) + 0.5u(1)$, which is absurd.

In order to test for loss aversion, experimenter 1 always initially offered two pieces of apple but after receiving a token, always traded one piece in return. Experimenter 2 always initially offered one piece and always traded one piece in return for a token. The final choice is identical for both experimenters, however, under reference dependence, the offering of experimenter 1 invokes loss aversion. As expected, in nearly 80% of the trades, monkeys preferred to trade with experimenter 2, suggesting an explanation based on loss aversion.

Lakshminarayanan et al. (2011) test for different risk attitudes in the domain of gains and losses with capuchin monkeys. In one experiment, both experimenters framed their offerings as a gain. Experimenter 1, the safe experimenter, initially offered one piece of food, but on receiving the token always traded two pieces. Experimenter 2, the risky experimenter, initially offered one piece of food, but then was equally likely to trade either one or three pieces in exchange for a token. Most trades occurred with the safe experimenter. However, when the offerings were framed as losses, most trades occurred with the risky experimenter. These results are consistent with prospect theory preferences but are not immediately consistent with theories that do not have a reference point.

Brosnan et al. (2007) wonder if the endowment effect arises from the shared evolutionary history of humans and chimpanzees, on account of a common ancestor? To test this conjecture, they perform standard endowment effect experiments, using food and non-food items on 33 chimpanzees. They ran six trials with items that are familiar to chimpanzees. The food items were a frozen fruit juice stick and a PVC pipe filled with peanut butter (henceforth, juice and PB). The non-food items were a rubber-bone dog chew toy and knotted-rope dog toy (henceforth, bone and rope).

Three trials were run for each of the food and non-food items. The trials were similar to those run for human subjects with the difference that the exchange of an item by a chimpanzee takes place with a human at the other end (and not with another chimpanzee). Prior to the experiment, chimpanzees are trained to exchange items with an experimenter. If they wish to exchange an item for another, they must do so within two minutes, otherwise no exchange takes place. The results are shown in Figure 3.4.

In the food trial, it was found that 58% of the chimpanzees preferred PB to juice. When endowed with the PB, however, 79% of the chimpanzees preferred to keep it rather than exchange

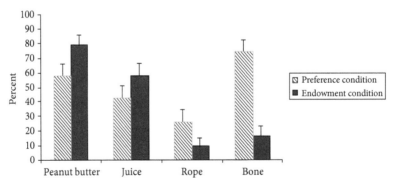

Figure 3.4 Choices made by chimpanzees in different conditions. Hatched bars represent the percentage of the population that preferred the object in a choice condition, and solid bars represent the percentage of the population that chose to maintain possession. Vertical bars show standard errors of means.

Source: Reprinted from Current Biology, 17(19): 1704–7. Brosnan, S. F., Jones, O. D., Lambeth, S. P. Mareno, M. C., and Schapiro, S. J., "Endowment effects in chimpanzees." © 2007, with permission from Elsevier.

it for juice. In another trial, when chimpanzees were endowed with juice, 58% of the chimpanzees preferred not to trade their juice for the PB.

For non-food items, the outcome was opposite to that predicted by the endowment effect: 74% of the chimpanzees preferred the bone over the rope. Despite this, when chimpanzees are given ownership of the bone, they prefer to keep it only 16% of the time. When endowed with the rope, they preferred to keep it only 10% of the time (rather than the predicted 26%). There are two possibilities for this difference in result between the food and non-food items. First, chimpanzees simply do not have a strong enough preference for non-food items. Second, they like interacting with the experimenter.

To test for the possibility that chimpanzees simply like interaction with the experimenter, further tests were carried out. For food items, no chimpanzee (with one exception) exchanged one food item with an identical item offered by the experimenter. However, for non-food items, the opposite result was found: 82% traded a bone for a bone, while 79% traded a rope for a rope.

In conjunction, these results suggest that chimpanzees exhibit the endowment effect for evolutionary salient items such as food, but there is no endowment effect for non-food items. The evolutionary explanation is that food has a greater bearing on the fitness (i.e., reproductive success) of the animal relative to non-food items. Since humans share a common evolutionary history with chimpanzees, the authors conjecture that it is also likely that humans too possess the endowment effect. Lakshminarayanan et al. (2008) showed that the results on endowment effect survive when one controls for transactions costs and timing issues.

3.4 Myopic loss aversion

Yet another determinant of loss aversion is the horizon over which a risky situation is to be evaluated. *Myopic loss aversion* (MLA) relies on two concepts. The first is loss aversion. The second is *mental accounting*, due to which individuals may evaluate the *return* on lotteries over very short horizons, even when the *actual return* accrues over a longer horizon.

> **Example 3.1**   *(Gneezy and Potters, 1997): Consider the following PT utility function that exhibits loss aversion.*
>
> $$v(x) = \begin{cases} x & if \quad x \geq 0 \\ 2.5x & if \quad x < 0 \end{cases}. \tag{3.13}$$
>
> *Suppose that the individual is offered two independent and identical prospects on two separate days. The prospect is $(200, 0.5; -100, 0.5)$. Assuming linear weighting of probabilities, the utility of the prospect on any day under PT is*
>
> $$0.5(200) - 0.5(250) = -25 < 0. \tag{3.14}$$
>
> *Now consider two individuals who use two different mental accounting procedures. Individual S uses a short horizon and evaluates the prospect on each day separately. From (3.14), his utility on each day is negative, so he refuses the prospect on each day. The other individual, L, who uses a long horizon, combines the two independent prospects on the two days to give the composite prospect $(400, 0.25; 100, 0.5; -200, 0.25)$. Using the utility function in (3.13), the utility of the combined prospect for individual L is*
>
> $$0.25(400) + 0.5(100) - 0.25(500) = 25 > 0.$$

MLA applies to individual S, who does not choose to invest in the gamble. Individual L, who does not use MLA, in contrast, prefers to invest in the gamble.

Gneezy and Potters (1997) provide direct evidence for MLA. They gave individuals an endowment of $e = 200$ cents; a part $x \in [0, 200]$ of the endowment could be invested. The individual was then offered a lottery $(-x, 2/3; 2.5x, 1/3)$ and asked to make an investment decision over nine rounds. The same level of endowment, e, is given at the beginning of each round. In any round, subjects could only bet using their endowment for that round.[24]

In one treatment, treatment S (short horizons), subjects were asked to make an investment decision, x, in every period, having observed the outcome of the lottery in the previous period. Thus, a total of nine investment decisions had to be made. In the second treatment, treatment L (long horizons), investment decisions are made in three rounds 1, 4, 7 and, in each case, the investment decision also applies for the following two periods. Individuals can observe their earnings in rounds 1–3 when they choose their investment in round 4, and observe earnings in rounds 4–6 when they choose their investment in round 7.

The average level of investment in treatment S is found to be significantly lower as compared to treatment L. On average, subjects bet about half their endowment in treatment S and about two-thirds of their endowment in treatment L. The basic result on MLA has proven to be robust to several changes in the experimental design, such as changing the number of rounds, and the number of lotteries.[25]

Haigh and List (2005) examine MLA for professional traders in finance, relative to a control group of undergraduate students. There were 32 students and 27 traders. They elicited, over several rounds, the amount of money each of the groups was willing to bet in two treatments. In one treatment (Treatment I) subjects were given "infrequent" feedback on the returns to their investment, while in the other (Treatment F) "frequent" feedback was given. The prediction of MLA that there should be less betting on the risky investment in Treatment F relative to Treatment I was confirmed for both subject groups. However, professional traders exhibited statistically significantly greater MLA as compared to students; see, Figure 3.5. Traders bet an average of 75 units in Treatment I but only 45 units in Treatment F. The corresponding numbers for students are 62.50 and 50.89. These results are in contrast to the ones by List (2003, 2004), reviewed above, that seek to demonstrate elimination or reduction in loss aversion with real-world experience.

Sutter (2007) uses the framework of Gneezy and Potters (1997) to determine if membership of a team weakens or strengthens MLA. Subjects were asked to make their decisions individually, or as part of a team of three individuals. The endowment was $e = 100$ euro-cents. The two conditions were short (S) and long (L) planning horizons. The results are shown in Figure 3.6. Two main findings emerge from Sutter's (2007) experiments. First, individuals invest more when they are part of a team. Second, individuals and teams invest more when the horizon is longer.

The frequency of the evaluation of a lottery and the horizon over which the return from the lottery accrues, play a similar role in determining the effect of MLA on the amount invested. So what is the relative contribution of each of these factors. The experimental results of Fellner and Sutter (2009) indicate that each of these factors contributes equally. They find that making subjects opt for either longer horizons or a lower frequency of evaluation leads to an increase in investment.

---

[24] Three more rounds were run after the ninth round. In each of these rounds, the money won in the first nine rounds divided by three became the new endowment level.

[25] See, for instance, Thaler et al. (1997), Barron and Erev (2003), Bellamare et al. (2005), and Langer and Weber (2008). But for evidence to the contrary, see Blavatskyy and Pogrebna (2009).

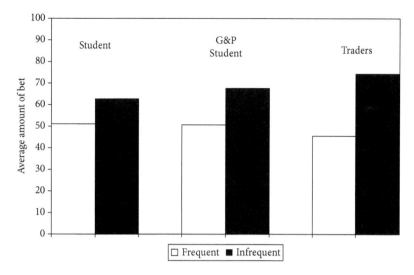

Figure 3.5 Average bets of students and professionals.

Source: "Do professional traders exhibit myopic loss aversion? An experimental analysis," Haigh,M. and List, J. A. The Journal of Finance, 60(1): 523–34. © 2005, John Wiley and Sons.

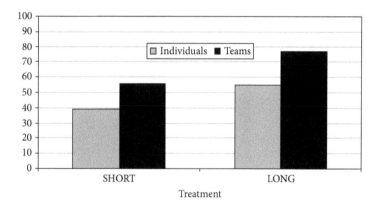

Figure 3.6 Amount invested in each treatment.

Source: Reprinted from Economics Letters, 97(2): 128–32. Sutter, M., "Are teams prone to myopic loss aversion? An experimental study on individual versus team investment behaviour." © 2007, with permission from Elsevier.

Benartzi and Thaler (1995, p. 73) make the following observation: "Since 1926 the annual real return on stocks has been about 7 percent, while the real return on treasury bills has been less than 1 percent." The difference in returns between the two assets is not explained by differences in the standard deviations; the annual standard deviation of stock returns over the period 1926–97 is about 20%. This is known as the *equity-premium puzzle*.

The main distinction between stocks and bonds in terms of their returns is the greater variability of returns on stocks. Risk averse individuals will naturally demand a greater return on stocks relative to bonds. However, Mehra and Prescott (1985) find that for EU to explain the equity premium puzzle, an unreasonably high coefficient of relative risk aversion of about 30 is required.[26] The actual coefficient of risk aversion is close to 1 (see Bombardini and Trebbi, 2012), and in some estimates, up to about 5.

Benartzi and Thaler (1995) seek to explain the equity premium puzzle by PT and narrow bracketing (stock returns are considered in isolation from all other returns and sources of wealth). They first ask, what planning horizon must investors be choosing so that they are indifferent between stocks that give a 7% return and bonds which give a 1% return? Their empirical results give a best estimate of one year. This is plausible, given that individuals prepare tax returns, and receive company annual newsletters over the same horizon. They term a one-year planning horizon as *myopic investor behavior*. Furthermore, most stock returns fluctuate a lot over a one-year horizon, hence, the investor potentially experiences repeated gains and losses. The resulting loss aversion accentuates the downward movements in returns, and ensures that the return on stocks must be sufficiently high if they are to be held in a portfolio that contains bonds. Under these assumptions, it turns out that a 7% return on stocks is indeed required to explain the observed compositions of portfolios between stocks and bonds.

> **Example 3.2** *Suppose that initial wealth I is 1 and the decision maker uses PT with linear probability weighting. The reference income, r, is the status quo, so it also equals 1. There are two assets, each with a maturity period of 1 year. A safe asset offers a return of 0.01. The value function is piecewise linear so it takes the form*
>
> $$v(x) = \begin{cases} x & \text{if} \quad x \geq 0 \\ -\lambda(-x) & \text{if} \quad x < 0 \end{cases}.$$
>
> *The coefficient of loss aversion $\lambda = 2.25$. The value function from holding the safe asset is*
>
> $$V_S = (1+0.01)I - r = (1+0.01) - 1 = 0.01. \qquad (3.15)$$
>
> *Assume that the return on the risky asset, θ, can take either of two values, a low level of return, $\theta_L = -0.06$ (with probability 0.8), or a high level of return θ_H (with probability 0.2). Hence, there is one outcome each in the domain of gains and losses. The value function in this case is given by:*
>
> $$V_R = 0.8(-2.25(0.06)) + 0.2\theta_H.$$
>
> *What level of return, θ_H, is required for the decision maker to be indifferent between the two assets? Setting V_S equal to V_R, we get that $\theta_H = 0.59$. Hence, the average return on the risky asset is*
>
> $$0.2(0.59) - 0.8(0.06) = 0.07 = 7\%,$$
>
> *which is seven times higher than the return on the riskless asset. Thus, relatively high average returns are required on the risky asset in the presence of loss aversion. This is the main insight of Benartzi and Thaler.*

---

[26] Mankiw and Zeldes (1991) illustrate the absurdity of such a high level of risk aversion. A decision maker with a relative risk aversion coefficient of 30 evaluates the certainty equivalent of the lottery (100,000,0.5;50,000,0.5) to be 51209.

The insights in the Benartzi–Thaler model were formalized more fully in Barberis et al. (2001). While there are no direct empirical tests of these insights, Barberis (2013) cites the empirical work of Dimmock and Kouwenberg (2010) that found a relation between loss aversion and stock market participation.

3.5 Why do people pay taxes?

So far, we have seen applications where researchers selectively choose the components of PT that they feel are most essential for explaining their research questions. We now consider one of the few applications that uses all the components of PT. Issues of tax evasion are extremely important and losses to society from tax evasion are huge.[27] The existing literature on tax evasion, since Allingham and Sandmo (1972) and Yitzhaki (1974), had largely assumed that taxpayers use EU. Dhami and al-Nowaihi (2007, 2010b) used, instead, all components of PT to model the tax evasion decision; a simplified version of the model is given below.[28]

An EU model of tax evasion leads to several puzzles.

1. Quantitative puzzle: Suppose that tax is not withheld at source, and taxpayers have a choice to report or evade their income. Consider a taxpayer who follows EU and evades \$1. With probability $1 - p$, he is not caught, so he can keep \$1. With probability p, he is caught, so he surrenders \$1 to the tax authorities, and, in addition, pays a fine at the rate $\theta > 0$ on \$1. Thus, under EU, the taxpayer will evade taxes if the expected return per dollar on evading the tax,

$$1 - p - p\theta > 0. \tag{3.16}$$

   In actual practice, for the amateur tax evader, the audit probability, p, ranges from 0.01 to 0.03, while the penalty rate, θ, on the amount evaded, ranges from 0.5 to 2.0. Using these values of p and θ, the expected return on tax evasion lies between 91% and 98.5%; it would be hard to find assets with such high rates of return. So, why do people pay taxes? This contradicts the empirical evidence in two ways. First, only about 40% of taxpayers who have a chance of evading, do evade. Further, experimental evidence suggests that at least 20% of taxpayers fully declare all their income, even when $p = 0$. Second, to make these results consistent with EU, taxpayers are required to be risk averse to an absurd degree.[29]

2. Qualitative puzzles: In addition to the quantitative puzzle, there are also qualitative puzzles arising from the application of EU to tax evasion. First, Yitzhaki (1974) showed that using EU, and under the reasonable assumption of decreasing absolute risk aversion (DARA), an increase in the tax rate leads to a decrease in tax evasion. However, most empirical evidence rejects this result; people try to hide more income if the government tries to extract greater tax revenues. Second, obligatory advance tax payments should not influence the taxpayer's evasion decision under EU. This is because under EU, the carriers of utility are final levels

---

[27] For the US, for example, Slemrod and Yitzhaki (2002) give a conservative estimate of the *tax gap* (difference between taxes paid and taxes owed) of the order of \$300 billion per year.

[28] We shall keep references to a minimum. The interested reader can look up Dhami and al-Nowaihi (2007, 2010b) for the references, the justification behind the assumptions, and robustness tests, etc.

[29] In one example, Skinner and Slemrod (1985) calculate that in order to square the observed tax evasion rates a coefficient of relative risk aversion (CRRA) of 70 is required, while realistic magnitudes of CRRA lie between 1 and 5.

of wealth (see Remark 1.1); final wealth is identical under advance tax payment or post tax payment. In contrast, obligatory advance payments alter tax evasion; see, for example, Yaniv (1999) for the evidence and an explanation based on PT.

Dhami and al-Nowaihi (2007) run a two-horse race that pits EU against PT. They show that these qualitative and quantitative paradoxes can be explained by PT.

THE BASIC SET UP

The government moves first and levies a tax at the constant marginal rate $t \in [0, 1]$ on the declared income of the taxpayer, D. Each taxpayer who has exogenous taxable income $W > 0$ can then choose to declare an amount $D \in [0, W]$; we focus only on those individuals for whom tax is not withheld at source. An exogenous fraction $p \in [0, 1]$ of the taxpayers are randomly audited, subsequent to the filing of tax returns, and the audit reveals the true taxable income; Dhami and al-Nowaihi (2007) consider the more general case where this probability is *endogenous* and it depends negatively on the amount of income declared. If caught, the dishonest taxpayer must pay the outstanding tax liabilities $t(W - D)$ and a penalty on the amount evaded, $\theta t(W - D)$, where $\theta > 0$ is the penalty rate. If evasion is discovered, the taxpayer also suffers some stigma costs $s(W - D)$, where $s \in [0, 1]$ is the stigma rate on evaded income.[30] There is a distribution of stigma rates over the taxpayers with density $\phi(s)$. Thus, our treatment of the stigma rate parallels the tax rate; both lie in the interval $[0, 1]$.

Denoting by Y_A and Y_{NA}, respectively, the income of the taxpayer when he is audited and when he is not, for any $D \in [0, W]$ we have

$$\begin{cases} Y_{NA} = W - tD, \\ Y_A = W - tD - t(1 + \theta)(W - D) - s(W - D). \end{cases} \tag{3.17}$$

Under EU, individuals derive utility from their final wealth. To enable comparison with the utility function under PT (see (2.19)) suppose that the utility function under EU is $v(Y) = Y^\beta$ for $Y \geq 0$ and $v(Y) = 0$ for $Y < 0$; $\beta \in (0, 1)$.[31] Thus, the EU of a taxpayer is given by

$$EU = (1 - p)Y_{NA}^\beta + pY_A^\beta. \tag{3.18}$$

Under PT, take the *legal after-tax income*, $R = (1 - t)W$, as the reference point of the taxpayer; this is in the spirit of the status-quo justification of reference points. A simple calculation shows that (provided R is independent of p) this is the *unique* reference income, that has the following desirable property. For any D, if the taxpayer is caught, he is in the domain of losses, and if he is not caught, he is in the domain of gains. Thus, it is an eminently sensible reference point.

The taxpayer's income relative to the reference point, in the two states, is $X_i = Y_i - R$, $i = A$, NA. Using (3.17), we get

$$\begin{cases} X_{NA} = t(W - D) \geq 0 \\ X_A = -(\theta t + s)(W - D) \leq 0 \end{cases}. \tag{3.19}$$

---

[30] The UK government initiative of naming and shaming tax offenders, spearheaded by the HMRC, is at least partly motivated by tapping into such stigma costs of the taxpayer.

[31] From (3.17) it is possible that $Y_A < 0$. Other possible formulations for utility when $Y_A < 0$ are $v(Y_A) = -v(-Y_A)$ and $v(Y_A) = -\infty$. None of our results depend on which specification we use for $v(Y_A)$ when $Y_A < 0$.

The taxpayer is in the *domain of gains* in the No Audit state, and the magnitude of the gains is the amount of the tax evaded. In the Audit state, the taxpayer is in the *domain of losses*; the magnitude of the loss equals the penalty on the evaded tax plus stigma costs. The taxpayer faces the following lottery in incremental form (or *prospect*), denoted by L.

$$L = \{-(\theta t + s)(W - D), p; t(W - D), 1 - p\}.$$

The *value function* under PT is given by (2.23), which in this case is

$$V(L) = \pi (1 - p) v(X_{NA}) + \pi (p) v(X_A),$$

where v is the utility function under PT. Substituting (3.19) in the value function, using the power form of utility in (2.19), and the decision weights in Definition 2.14, we get the objective function of the taxpayer under PT as

$$V(L) = w(1 - p)[t(W - D)]^{\gamma} - \lambda w(p)[(\theta t + s)(W - D)]^{\gamma}. \tag{3.20}$$

THE TAX EVASION DECISION UNDER EXPECTED UTILITY

Maximizing (3.18) by a choice of D, the solution to the declared income is

$$D^* = W \left[1 - (1 - t) \left[(t\theta + s) + t \left(\frac{(t\theta + s)p}{t(1 - p)} \right)^{\frac{1}{1-\gamma}} \right]^{-1} \right]. \tag{3.21}$$

Direct differentiation of (3.21) gives rise to all the comparative static results under EU, summarized in Proposition 3.1.

> **Proposition 3.1** *Under EU, tax evasion is decreasing in the probability of detection and conviction, p, the penalty rate, θ, and the rate of stigma, s. If preferences exhibit decreasing absolute risk aversion, then tax evasion is decreasing in the tax rate, t (Yitzhaki (1974) puzzle).[32]*

Simple calculations give the following result.

> **Proposition 3.2** *Suppose that the taxpayer follows EU. Consider the set of (θ, p) points implicitly generated by the inequality*

$$\theta \geq \frac{1 - p}{p} - \frac{s}{t}. \tag{3.22}$$

> *In (θ, p) space, (3.22) gives the loci of points such that a taxpayer with stigma $s \in [\underline{s}, \bar{s}]$ reports the full amount of income. At all points below this loci, the taxpayer chooses to evade some strictly positive fraction of income.*

---

[32] For the assumed utility function under EU, the coefficient of absolute risk aversion (for EU we need only consider the domain of gains) is given by $\frac{1-\gamma}{Y}$ which is decreasing in Y. Hence, the Yitzhaki (1974) result applies.

Using (3.22), in the absence of stigma costs, $s = 0$, the taxpayer will evade income when $1 - p - p\theta > 0$, as claimed in (3.16).

THE TAX EVASION DECISION UNDER PROSPECT THEORY

The taxpayer maximizes the value function in (3.20) by an appropriate choice of D, given the probability weighting function $w(p)$. Rewriting (3.20),

$$V(L) = (W - D)^\gamma h(\theta, p, s, t, \lambda, \alpha, \gamma),\qquad(3.23)$$

where,

$$h = h(\theta, p, s, t, \lambda, \alpha, \gamma) = t^\gamma \left(w(1 - p) - \lambda \left(\theta + \frac{s}{t}\right)^\gamma w(p) \right) \gtreqless 0.\qquad(3.24)$$

Since the value function in (3.23) is monotonic in D, the solution is given by:

$$D = \begin{cases} 0 & \text{if} \quad h > 0 \quad \Leftrightarrow \left(\frac{1}{\lambda}\right) \frac{w(1-p)}{w(p)} > \left(\theta + \frac{s}{t}\right)^\gamma \\ \in [0, W] & \text{if} \quad h = 0 \quad \Leftrightarrow \left(\frac{1}{\lambda}\right) \frac{w(1-p)}{w(p)} = \left(\theta + \frac{s}{t}\right)^\gamma \\ W & \text{if} \quad h < 0 \quad \Leftrightarrow \left(\frac{1}{\lambda}\right) \frac{w(1-p)}{w(p)} < \left(\theta + \frac{s}{t}\right)^\gamma \end{cases}\qquad(3.25)$$

(3.25) depicts a *bang–bang solution*, which might be descriptive of several forms of tax evasion that take the form of hiding certain activities completely from the tax authorities. For the general case considered in Dhami and al-Nowaihi (2007), in which the probability of detection is endogenous and depends on the amount declared, one gets continuous dependence of the solution on the parameters of the model. The bang–bang solution arises in the special case of an exogenous and fixed probability of detection.

In (3.25), a large enough change in the parameters can push the solution from one case to the other. Starting from the case $D = 0$, the following factors are conducive to completely eliminating tax evasion ($D = W$). (1) Low tax rate, t, (2) high levels of stigma, s, and high penalties for tax evasion, θ, (3) high levels of loss aversion, λ, and (4) overweighting of the probability of a loss, p, which leads to a decrease in $\frac{w(1-p)}{w(p)}$.

Under EU and PT, tax evasion decreases with an increase in p, θ, and s, although, as we shall see below, the quantitative effects under PT are in accord with the evidence, while those under EU are not. There is also no counterpart in EU to the effect on tax evasion of (i) loss aversion, and (ii) overweighting of small probabilities. The main qualitative difference between EU and PT is in the predicted effect of the tax rate on the amount evaded. The result under EU is given in Proposition 3.1. However, PT predicts the empirically supported result that tax evasion increases with an increase in the tax rate. This is formally stated in Proposition 3.3 below (the simple proof is omitted).

> **Proposition 3.3** *Ceteris paribus, $\exists\, t = t_c \in [0, 1]$ such that the individual does not evade taxes if $t < t_c$ but evades taxes if $t > t_c$.*

A rough but useful intuition about the effect of the tax rate can be given as follows (the actual results are more subtle). An increase in the tax rate makes the taxpayer poorer. Hence, under decreasing absolute risk aversion, EU predicts a taxpayer would become more risk averse, and so evade less. By contrast, under PT the utility function is convex for losses. So, if the reference point is such that an audited taxpayer finds himself in the domain of losses (as is indeed the case), then an increase in the tax rate causes him to be poorer and, hence, more risk seeking. So he evades more.

A comparative static result similar to the one in Proposition 3.3 can be stated with respect to the stigma rate s (the simple proof is omitted). If stigma is high enough, then people do not evade any taxes; a similar result can easily be seen to hold for EU.

Proposition 3.4 *Ceteris paribus, $\exists\, s = s_c \in [0,1]$ such that all individuals characterized by $s > s_c$ do not evade taxes, while all those with $s < s_c$ evade taxes.*

MODEL CALIBRATION

The analysis below provides simulation results in a calibrated model.[33] We use the Prelec probability function (see Definition 2.4) with $\alpha = 0.35$ and $\beta = 1$. For the utility function, we use the power form of utility in (2.19). From estimates in Tversky and Kahneman (1992), $\gamma \approx 0.88$ and $\lambda \approx 2.25$. Let us use a realistic tax rate of 30%, i.e., $t = 0.3$.

Based on TCMP (taxpayer compliance measurement program) data, Andreoni et al. (1998) report that about 40% of taxpayers report their incomes incorrectly in the US; see also Bernasconi (1998). Since these figures include those who unintentionally report incorrectly (about 7%), let us use the more conservative estimate that only about 30% of taxpayers who have a chance, do evade taxes. Assume that the density of the stigma rate, $\phi(s)$, is uniform. From Proposition 3.4, we know that under PT all individuals characterized by $s > s_c$ do not evade taxes, while all those with $s < s_c$ evade taxes. Given the assumption that the stigma rate is uniformly distributed over $[0,1]$, the hypothesis that approximately 30% of taxpayers evade taxes corresponds to $s_c = 0.3$, which is the value we shall use for the calibration exercise.

We ask the following question. Given realistic magnitudes of tax evasion, about 30%, how close are the predicted θ, p values under EU and PT, respectively, to their actual values?[34]

Under EU, using (3.22), and the calibration values, the locus of (θ, p) combinations that need to be consistent with the actual data is given by

$$\theta^{EU} = \frac{1-p}{p} - \frac{0.3}{0.3}, \tag{3.26}$$

where θ^{EU} may be taken to be the predicted value of θ under EU, conditional on all the other parameters of the model. Using (3.25), and the Prelec weighting function, a similar (θ, p) locus under PT is given by

$$\theta^{PT} = \left(\frac{1}{2.25}\right)^{\frac{1}{0.88}} \Gamma(p)^{\frac{1}{0.88}} - \frac{0.3}{0.3}, \tag{3.27}$$

where $\Gamma(p) = \exp\left[(-\ln p)^{0.35} - (-\ln(1-p))^{0.35}\right]$ and $\alpha = 0.35$. θ^{PT} may be taken to be the predicted value of θ under PT, conditional on all the other parameters of the model.

---

[33] For robustness tests with respect to changes in the calibration values, such as the parameters of the Prelec function and alternative assumptions about the rate of stigma, *s*, the reader can consult Dhami and al-Nowaihi (2007). All the results go through.

[34] We could have equivalently posed our question in many different ways. For example, given actual (θ, p) combinations, what level of tax evasion does each theory predict?

Table 3.1 Comparison of the predicted value of penalty rates under EU and PT.

	.005	.010	.015	.020	.025	.030	.035	.040	.045	.050
θ^{EU}	197.7	97.7	64.3	47.7	37.7	31.0	26.2	22.7	19.9	17.7
θ^{PT}	1.6	1.2	1.0	0.9	0.8	0.7	0.6	0.5	0.5	0.4

Source: Dhami and al-Nowaihi, 2007.

The numerical magnitudes of (θ,p) that correspond to the two loci in (3.26), (3.27) are shown in Table 3.1; in the top row, we use probabilities ranging from 0.005 to 0.050. For most realistic audit probabilities, i.e., $p \in [0.01, 0.05]$ the prediction of the penalty rate, θ, ranges from 0.66 to 1.21 for PT. This is consistent with actual values for the audit probabilities which range from 0.5 in the USA to 2.0 in Italy with several other Western countries in the middle (Bernasconi, 1998). On the other hand, EU predicts a penalty rate that is up to 100 times larger in this range and, on average, about 60 times higher.

It is sometimes argued that sufficiently high stigma can align the predictions of EU with the evidence. This is not correct. For instance, choose a middle probability of around 0.03 and increase the stigma rate from 30% (which forms the basis of the calculations in Table 3.1) to the maximum possible rate, 100%. The new value of $\theta^{EU} = \frac{1-0.03}{0.03} - \frac{1}{0.3} = 29.0$, which is nowhere near the 0.5–2 range that is observed in actual practice.

On the other hand, in PT, all components of the theory (reference dependence, diminishing sensitivity, loss aversion, non-linear probability weighting) were needed in order to explain the qualitative and quantitative tax evasion puzzles. While the penalty rate and the probability of detection may appear low, PT decision makers overweight the small probability of being caught and suffer loss aversion, which magnifies the penalty rate. This provides strong vindication for the choice of PT in explaining actual parameters of policy choice relevant for the tax evasion problem. It is remarkable that the predicted magnitudes of (θ,p) are so close to the actually observed values when one considers that the parameter values used for the calibration exercise were obtained from independent experimental evidence applied to generic situations of risk. This model also shows that PT is quite simple and tractable to apply.

3.6 Explanation of Rabin's paradox using PT

Rabin's paradox for EU was described in Section 1.5.4. We now show that the concepts of reference dependence and loss aversion, that are central to PT, can explain Rabin's results, an explanation that Rabin (2000a) favored. Recall the three lotteries in Section 1.5.4, L_0, L_1, L_2:

$$L_0 = (w, 1), \; L_1 = (w - 10, 0.5; w + 11; 0.5), \; L_2 = (w - 100, 0.5; w + m, 0.5), \qquad (3.28)$$

where m is any positive reward level, no matter how high. Under PT, lotteries are defined in incremental form. Assume that initial wealth, w, is the reference point. Redefine the three lotteries, L_0, L_1, L_2, in incremental form (or prospects) as follows

$$L_0 = (0, 1), \; L_1 = (-10, 0.5; 11; 0.5), \; L_2 = (-100, 0.5; m, 0.5). \qquad (3.29)$$

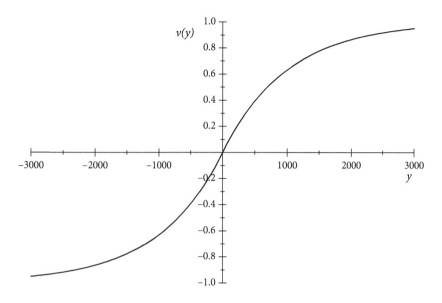

Figure 3.7 Plot of (3.30) for the case of $\lambda = 2$.

Let us continue with Example 1.4 from Section 1.5.4 and show that Rabin's paradox can be explained with PT. For any level of wealth x, let $y = x - w$ be the wealth relative to the reference point (initial wealth level, w). Adapt the utility function in (1.44) to define the reference dependent utility function of the individual as

$$v(y) = \begin{cases} 1 - e^{-y/1000} & \text{if } y \geq 0 \\ -\lambda(1 - e^{y/1000}) & \text{if } y < 0 \end{cases}, \tag{3.30}$$

where $\lambda > 1$ is the parameter of loss aversion. Figure 3.7 gives a plot of this function for $\lambda = 2$, which is the parameter value we shall use in the calculations below. We wish to show that Rabin's paradox can be explained by using reference dependence and loss aversion only, so we do not invoke non-linear probability weighting (but see Wakker (2005) who shows that the paradox can also be explained with non-linear probability weighting).

1. Let us first compare the two prospects in incremental form $L_0 = (0,1)$ and $L_1 = (-10, 0.5; 11, 0.5)$ when the decision maker follows PT. The preference $L_1 \prec L_0$ (see Assumption A1 in Section 1.5.4) implies that

$$V(-10, 0.5; 11, 0.5) < V(0, 1) = 0, \tag{3.31}$$

where V is the value function under PT. Using (3.30) and (3.31), we get

$$-(1 - e^{-.010}) + \frac{1}{2}\left(1 - e^{-.011}\right) < 0 \Leftrightarrow -4.4803 \times 10^{-3} < 0,$$

which is true. Thus, at all levels of initial wealth, a decision maker who follows PT prefers the prospect L_0 over L_1.

2. Let us now compare the two prospects $L_1 = (-10, 0.5; 11; 0.5)$ and $L_2 = (-100, 0.5; \infty, 0.5)$ when the decision maker follows PT. Rabin's paradox will arise if one now observes the preference $L_2 \prec L_1$. We now show that the preference $L_2 \prec L_1$ cannot arise. Using (3.30), we get that

$$L_2 \prec L_1 : -(1 - e^{-0.1}) + \frac{1}{2}\left(1 - e^{-\infty}\right) < -(1 - e^{-.010}) + \frac{1}{2}\left(1 - e^{-0.011}\right)$$

$$\Leftrightarrow 0.40484 < -4.4803 \times 10^{-3},$$

which is false. Thus, a decision maker who follows PT prefers the prospect L_2 over L_1, hence, Rabin's paradox does not arise for a decision maker who follows PT.

The Rabin paradox has elicited several responses. For a behavioral counter response, which argues that these responses are unsatisfactory, see Wakker (2005, 2010). Palacios-Huerta and Serrano (2006) and Watt (2002) argued that the preferences $L_1 \prec L_0$ need not hold at all wealth levels (see Assumption A1 in Section 1.5.4) if the decision maker follows EU. They do so by estimating the parameters of the power form of utility that allow for Assumption A1. They find that some of the parameters are unreasonable. But this only illustrates the difficulty in accounting for plausible preferences under EU, a point that Rabin had already made.

Cox and Sadiraj (2006), Watt (2002), Rubinstein (2006), and Samuelson (2005) propose to solve Rabin's paradox, not by abandoning EU but by defining utility over income. But doing so immediately imposes reference dependence because income arises over and above current wealth and so this simply assumes the reference point to be current wealth. For this reason, Wakker (2005, 2010) argues that these authors provide the same explanation as Rabin (2000a).

Consider, for instance, the explanation by Cox and Sadiraj (2006). They assume the following utility function.

$$v(y) = \begin{cases} 0.9y + 0.1 & \text{if } y < 1 \\ y^{0.9} & \text{if } y \geq 1 \end{cases}. \tag{3.32}$$

If we did not subtract the wealth level w from all the outcomes, then the relevant lotteries are given in (3.28). The variable y would then be the final wealth level. A simple calculation shows that this gives rise to Rabin's paradox under EU (as in Section 1.5.4). However, now suppose that utility in (3.32) is defined over income levels. So essentially, we subtract wealth, w, from all outcomes. This gives rise to the relevant lotteries in incremental form as in (3.29), exactly as under PT. Then, under EU, with the utility function in (3.32), the preference $L_1 \prec L_0$ implies that

$$0.5(0.9(-10) + 0.1) + 0.5(11^{0.9}) < v(0) = 0.1.$$

But $0.5(0.9(-10) + 0.1) + 0.5(11^{0.9}) = -0.12264 < 0.1$. Hence, the original preference $L_1 \prec L_0$ holds. Yet, a decision maker who has the utility function of income given in (3.32) will accept the lottery $(-1680, 0.5; 3412, 0.5)$ over the lottery $(0, 1)$, so $L_1 \prec L_0$ does not hold. But this means that Assumption A1 in Section 1.5.4 does not hold and Rabin's paradox does not arise in this case. Cox and Sadiraj propose an amendment to the expected utility function in which wealth directly enters the utility functions and attitudes to risk are dependent on initial wealth.

The Rabin paradox and the Cox and Sadiraj explanations are both results of the form, if A then B, and both results are technically sound. As noted earlier, reference dependence is not inconsistent with the axioms of EU, so the Cox and Sadiraj explanation is a feasible one. However, once again, it illustrates the difficulty in accounting for plausible preferences under EU without imposing reference dependence. Furthermore, simply imposing reference dependence in EU without a theory of how the behavior of decision makers differs in the domains of gains and losses is not entirely satisfactory either.

Neilson (2001) and Safra and Segal (2008) show that Rabin's puzzle also applies to other decision theory models based on final wealth levels. However, it is not clear that these two papers are based on empirically plausible assumptions; see Wakker (2010, p. 245).

3.7 Goals as reference points

Under EU, one typically derives utility from final levels of outcomes such as wealth, or if there are reference effects, then there is no difference in behavior in the domain of gains and losses (Remark 1.1). Thus, setting wealth targets or other goals should not, in the absence of auxiliary assumptions, have any influence on behavior. Yet, as we shall see below in Section 3.7.2, targets and goals influence human actions. The reason is that goals may serve as reference points and the decision maker may feel that he is in the domain of losses if he falls short of the goal. On account of loss aversion, this may induce the decision maker to exert even greater effort to achieve his goal. These effects have been found for human and non-human subjects and for cognitive and non-cognitive tasks.[35] Such reasoning is consistent with PT but not necessarily with other theories that lack a reference point.

3.7.1   A theory of goals in prospect theory

We first organize these ideas into a formal model, using unpublished notes by al-Nowaihi and Dhami.[36] An individual can exert effort $e \in [0, \bar{e}]$ at a cost $c(e)$ to produce output according to the production function $y(e)$. The properties of these functions are:

$$c(e) \geq 0, c(0) = 0, c'(0) \geq 0, c''(e) > 0; y(e) \geq 0, y(0) = 0, y'(e) > 0, y''(e) \leq 0. \quad (3.33)$$

Thus the cost function is positive, increasing, and convex, while the production function is positive, increasing, and concave.

The exogenously given *goal* of the individual is to produce a level of output $y = g \geq 0$. We assume that:

$$\text{for each } g \geq 0, y(e) = g \text{ for some level of } e. \quad (3.34)$$

The utility function of the individual, v, is separable in output and effort, and is defined separately for the domain of gains and losses, depending on whether the outcome $y(e)$ is larger or smaller relative to the goal, g.

$$v = \begin{cases} v_+(e,g) = u(y(e) - g) - c(e) & \text{if} \quad y(e) \geq g \\ v_-(e,g) = -\lambda u(g - y(e)) - c(e) & \text{if} \quad y(e) < g \end{cases}; \lambda > 1. \quad (3.35)$$

---

[35] See, for instance, Locke and Latham (1990) for a wide-ranging review of the laboratory and field studies in support of these stylized facts. For a more updated list of references, see Heath et al. (1999).

[36] This model was constructed circa 2010 and has been used by one of our Ph.D. students in his empirical research.

We assume that the functions u, y, c have continuous second order partial derivatives. We make the following standard assumptions.

$$u(x) \geq 0 \text{ for } x \geq 0; u(0) = 0; u'(x) > 0 \text{ for } x > 0; u''(x) < 0 \text{ for } x > 0. \qquad (3.36)$$

Further assumptions on the function u are as follows.

$$u'(x) \to \infty, \text{ as } x \to 0; u'(x) \to 0, \text{ as } x \to \infty. \qquad (3.37)$$

We consider separately, the domain of gains and losses.

I. Domain of gains: In the domain of gains, $y(e) \geq g$. Using (3.35), we get

$$\frac{\partial v_+}{\partial e} = y'(e) u' (y(e) - g) - c'(e), \qquad (3.38)$$

$$\frac{\partial^2 v_+}{\partial e^2} = y''(e) u' (y(e) - g) + [y'(e)]^2 u'' (y(e) - g) - c''(e) < 0. \qquad (3.39)$$

Thus, v_+ is continuous and strictly concave in e. Since $e \in [0, \bar{e}]$ is a compact interval, so v_+ has a unique (local and global) maximum. Let $e_+^* (g)$ be the (unique) function that assigns to each $g \geq 0$, the unique local maximum, e_+^*, corresponding to g in the domain of gains. In the domain of gains, $y(e) \geq g$, and from (3.37), (3.38), a corner solution cannot exist, hence, $e_+^* > 0$. We summarize these results in the next lemma.

Lemma 3.1 *Given $g \geq 0$, $\frac{\partial v_+}{\partial e} = 0$ at a unique maximum $e_+^* > 0$ and $y(e_+^*) > g$.*

Implicitly differentiating (3.38) we get

$$\frac{\partial^2 v_+}{\partial e \partial g} = -y'(e) u'' (y(e) - g) > 0, \qquad (3.40)$$

and, hence,

$$\frac{d e_+^* (g)}{dg} = -\left[\frac{\partial^2 v_+}{\partial e \partial g} \Big/ \frac{\partial^2 v_+}{\partial e^2} \right]_{e_+^*(g)} > 0. \qquad (3.41)$$

II. Domain of losses: We now turn to an analysis of the domain of losses, $y(e) < g$. Using (3.35), $v_- (e, g) < 0$, and we would like to maximize this function. We get

$$\frac{\partial v_-}{\partial e} = \lambda y'(e) u' (g - y(e)) - c'(e). \qquad (3.42)$$

$$\frac{\partial^2 v_-}{\partial e^2} = \lambda y''(e) u' (g - y(e)) - \lambda [y'(e)]^2 u'' (g - y(e)) - c''(e). \qquad (3.43)$$

$$\frac{\partial^2 v_-}{\partial e \partial g} = \lambda y'(e) u'' (g - y(e)) > 0. \qquad (3.44)$$

Unlike the domain of gains, we cannot sign the second derivative of v_-. Using (3.37), we get

$$\lim_{y(e) \uparrow g} \frac{\partial v_-}{\partial e} = \infty. \qquad (3.44)$$

Since the domain of losses is defined by $y(e) < g$, and since y is continuous, it follows that the domain of losses is open, i.e., v_- is not defined over a compact domain. In conjunction with the fact there is no guarantee that v_- is concave or convex, the analysis of the optimal solution in the domain of loss is less direct.

Let e_-^* be a local maximum in the domain of losses. It then follows that, necessarily, $\left[\frac{\partial v_-}{\partial e}\right]_{e=e_-^*} = 0$. Since $\frac{\partial v_-}{\partial e}$ is continuous, it follows that the set of all e such that $\frac{\partial v_-}{\partial e} = 0$ is closed. Finally, since y is strictly increasing, the set of feasible effort levels is bounded (by 0 below and $y^{-1}(g)$ above). Thus the set of all effort levels, e, such that $\frac{\partial v_-}{\partial e} = 0$ is closed and bounded, hence compact. It follows that, if this set is non-empty, then it contains a maximum. Choose the largest effort level associated with this maximum, and call it $e_-^*(g)$. If, in addition, $\left[\frac{\partial^2 v_-}{\partial e^2}\right]_{e=e_-^*(g)} < 0$, then

$$\frac{de_-^*(g)}{dg} = -\left[\frac{\partial^2 v_-}{\partial e \partial g} \Big/ \frac{\partial^2 v_-}{\partial e^2}\right]_{e=e_-^*(g)} < 0. \tag{3.45}$$

The existence of $e_-^*(g)$ is not guaranteed but $e_+^*(g)$ always exists. So we have two cases.

(1) For each $g \geq 0$, let $e^*(g) = e_+^*(g)$, if no $e_-^*(g)$ exist.

(2) Suppose one, or more, optimal effort levels exist in the domain of losses. By definition, each of these optimal effort levels give the same value of the objective function, hence, we need some tie breaking rule, which, given our convention, is to choose the highest of these, $e_-^*(g)$. In this case, let $e^*(g) = e_+^*(g)$ if $v_+\left(e_+^*(g), g\right) \geq v_-\left(e_-^*(g), g\right)$. Otherwise, set $e^*(g) = e_-^*(g)$.

From (3.41) we know that $\frac{de_+^*(g)}{dg} > 0$, and from (3.45) we know that $\frac{de_-^*(g)}{dg} < 0$. Define g^*, such that

$$v_+\left(e_+^*(g^*), g^*\right) = v_-\left(e_-^*(g^*), g^*\right),$$

in which case, given our convention, we would choose $e^*(g^*) = e_+^*(g^*)$. The next proposition shows that g^* is an optimal goal if the objective is to maximize the output y. The proof is left to the reader.

Proposition 3.5   *There exists a unique goal, g^*, such that the following holds.*

(a) *For $g < g^*$, $v_+\left(e_+^*(g), g\right) > v_-\left(e_-^*(g), g\right)$ and so $e^*(g) = e_+^*(g^*) < e^*(g^*)$.*
(b) *For $g > g^*$, $v_+\left(e_+^*(g), g\right) < v_-\left(e_-^*(g), g\right)$ and so $e^*(g) = e_-^*(g^*) < e^*(g^*)$.*
(c) *g^* is the goal that maximizes output, $y(e)$, when one restricts attention to the set of effort levels that maximize utility of the individual.*

A number of lessons can be drawn from Proposition 3.5.

1. If the objective is to maximize the output produced by an individual, then there exists an optimal goal, g^*.
2. For goals in the interval $[0, g^*]$, the optimal effort level of the individual is $e_+^*(g)$, which places the individual in the domain of gains, so $y(e_+) - g \geq 0$. Thus, the individual exceeds the goals that he sets.
3. Over the range $[0, g^*]$, $\frac{de_+^*(g)}{dg} > 0$, so the individual responds to an increase in goals by increasing effort.

Table 3.2 Some simulations for optimal goals and effort levels.

g	$e_+^*(g)$	$e_-^*(g)$	$e^*(g)$
0	0.908 66	n.a	0.908 66
1	1.116 2	n.a	1.116 2
2	2.000 3	n.a	2.000 3
$g^* = 2.391113282$	2.3912	1.956 4	2.391 2
2.5	2.5+	1.891 8	1.891 8
3	3+	1.762	1.762
4	4+	1.6528	1.6528

Source: unpublished notes by al-Nowaihi and Dhami.

4. For any goal that it too ambitious, i.e., in the range, $g > g^*$, the individual flips from being in the domain of gains to being in the domain of losses, i.e., $y(e_-) < g$. Indeed, $e_-(g)$ rather than $e_+(g)$ is optimal for goals in this range. Thus, the individual falls below the goal that he sets. Furthermore, because $\frac{de_-^*(g)}{dg} < 0$, the individual (at least locally in the neighborhood of $e_-^*(g)$) responds to an increase in goals by putting in even less effort.

Remark 3.1 *(Predictions under EU and RDU): Under EU and RDU, the utility function is defined over final levels of wealth (in this case $y(e)$) and is independent of g.*[37] *So goals are not predicted to have any effect on the effort levels of individuals. If goals do turn out to have an effect, then this finding would be inconsistent with EU and RDU.*

We now report a few simulations in Table 3.2 that illustrate the conclusions of the model. Let us assume that the production function is linear, i.e., $y = e$. Let the utility function for gains and losses be defined respectively by the following.

$$v_+ (y,g) = (y - g)^\beta - \frac{1}{2}y^2, y \geq g,$$

$$v_- (x,g) = -\lambda (g - y)^\beta - \frac{1}{2}y^2, \lambda > 1, x < g.$$

For simulation purposes, we use the values $\beta = 0.9$, $\lambda = 2$. We report for each value of the goal, g, the corresponding values of $e_+^* (g), e_-^* (g)$, and $e^* (g)$. The reader can verify observations 1–4 above.

3.7.2 The evidence on goals

We now consider the evidence on goals, based on experimental results from Heath et al. (1999). The results in Table 3.2 were results based on the calculation of optimal effort levels. The experiments, on the other hand, present hypothetical information that is not necessarily based on a calculation of the optimal solution.

---

[37] Even if we allowed for reference dependence under EU and RDU, then identical behavior in gains and losses (Remark 1.1) ensures that this is not a fruitful exercise.

The number of subjects in an experiment is denoted by N. One implication of goals as reference points is that it is possible that an individual with a higher goal performs better than an individual with a lower goal, yet feels less happy. This is supported by the following problem.

Problem 1. [$N = 60$] Alice typically scores around 80 on weekly 100-point quizzes in one of her classes. One week she sets a goal of scoring 90. She scores 87. Betty typically scores around 80 on weekly 100-point quizzes in one of her classes. One week she decides to do her best. She scores 83. Overall, who will be more satisfied with her performance?

Alice's performance is better than Betty's but because of her higher goal, a statistically significant majority of people respond that Alice should be less satisfied with her performance. This indicates that goals partition the domain of outcomes into gains and losses akin to the role of reference points in prospect theory. This result, and the next experiment which illustrates the role of loss aversion, is in conformity with the framework of our theoretical model.

Problem 2. [$N = 48$] Sally and Trish both follow workout plans that usually involve doing 25 sit-ups. One day, Sally sets a goal of performing 31 sit-ups. She finds herself very tired after performing 35 sit-ups and stops. Trish sets a goal of performing 39 sit-ups. She finds herself very tired after performing 35 sit-ups and stops. Who is experiencing more emotion?

Of the subjects 29% answer, Sally, while the remaining 71% answer, Trish. One plausible interpretation is that because Trish falls below the goal of 39 she experiences more emotion, on account of loss aversion.

Problem 3. [$N = 73$] Charles and David both follow workout plans that usually involve doing 25 sit-ups. One day, Charles sets a goal of performing 30 sit-ups. He finds himself very tired after performing 34 sit-ups and, at most, has the energy to perform one more. David sets a goal of performing 35 sit-ups. He finds himself very tired after 34 sit-ups and, at most, has the energy to perform one more. Who will work harder to perform the 35th sit-up?

Of the respondents 82% give the answer as David, which supports the prediction of PT. This can be seen from (3.42). As $y(e) \to g$, the marginal returns to effort, $\lambda y'(e) u'(g - y(e))$ increase rapidly and in the limit, (3.37) ensures that this marginal return is infinite. In other words, by doing just one more sit-up David can avoid falling into the domain of losses, so he should work harder.

Problem 4. [$N = 76$] Charles and David both follow workout plans that usually involve doing 25 sit-ups. One day, Charles sets a goal of performing 30 sit-ups. He finds himself very tired after performing 42 sit-ups and, at most, has the energy to perform one more. David sets a goal of performing 40 sit-ups. He finds himself very tired after 42 sit-ups and, at most, has the energy to perform one more. Who will work harder to perform one final sit-up?

Of the respondents 69% give David as the answer.

Problem 5. Same as problem 4, with 42 sit-ups replaced by 28 sit-ups.

Now 86% of the respondents give Charles as the answer.

In problem 4, both individuals exceed their goal. However, David has exceeded his goal by less than Charles. Since the effort level is held fixed for both (42 sit-ups), the marginal benefit for David of performing an extra sit-up is greater (because $u'(x) > 0$ $u''(x) < 0$). People exert greater effort when they are closer to their goals. The key is to invoke diminished sensitivity to gains and losses as one moves away from the reference point, a feature that is already incorporated into various versions of PT. The same reasoning explains the responses to Problem 5.

There are other emerging effects of goals that we have not touched on. For instance, there appears to be a strong effect of non-binding goals on performance and this effect appears to be much stronger for men relative to women (Smithers, 2015).

3.8 Why is it so hard to find a taxi on a rainy day in New York?

Consider the standard model of labor supply. Suppose that there is a small current transitory increase in wage. The decision maker would then smooth the transitory wage change over all future time periods so that income effects are negligible. In this case, we can concentrate solely on the substitution effects. Since wages are temporarily high, and so the opportunity cost of leisure is high, the individual engages in intertemporal substitution of labor, working relatively harder today. Hence, we can state the following well-known result.[38]

> **Remark 3.2** *Transitory increases in the real wage are predicted, under neoclassical economic theory, to produce an increase in hours worked.*

In the labor economics literature, there is little empirical consensus on the magnitude and sign of the labor supply elasticity. There are two main problems with estimating labor supply elasticities. First, actual wage changes are often not transitory in nature. Second, individuals often have limited control over hours worked. The modern literature has tried to address these issues.

Camerer et al. (1997) ask: *Why is it harder to find a taxi on a rainy day in New York?* The situation for cab drivers in New York is particularly interesting. First, it is possible to identify transitory wage changes. Second, by deciding when to quit for the day, cab drivers make a real "hour's worked" decision. The rate that cab drivers can charge per mile is fixed by law. However, on busy days, drivers have to spend less time searching for customers and, so, their (effective) real wage rate is higher.

Let h_{it} and Y_{it} denote hours worked and total daily earnings by driver i at date t. Hourly wage w_{it} is computed as Y_{it}/h_{it}. Let X_{it} denote a set of other independent variables; some are driver-specific, and others such as rain, temperature, and shift dummies, control for the difficulty of driving conditions and, hence, the opportunity cost of leisure. Camerer et al. (1997) estimate regression equations of the following form.

$$\log h_{it} = \beta_0 + \beta_1 w_{it} + \beta_2 X_{it} + \varepsilon_{it}, \tag{3.46}$$

where β_1 is a measure of labor supply elasticity and β_2 is a vector of coefficients. For the three sets of data in the sample, the inclusion of driver fixed effects gives the estimated labor supply

---

[38] For a simple, tractable, two-period model and discussion of these issues, see, for instance, Blanchard and Fischer (1989, section 7.2).

elasticities to be respectively, -1.86, -0.618, -0.355. These estimates suggest the presence of a *downward sloping labor supply curve* over the relevant range.

The construction of wages as $w_{it} \equiv Y_{it}/h_{it}$ raises two sets of issues. First, in the econometric model in (3.46), the labor supply decision responds to the average wage over the day, rather than fluctuations in the wage over the day. If the wage is negatively correlated over the day, then the intertemporal labor substitution model predicts that workers will work harder during the early part of the day when wages are relatively higher, and quit early. However, the authors find a positive autocorrelation in wages over the day, ruling out this problem. Second, h_{it} appears on the LHS as well as on the RHS because $w_{it} \equiv Y_{it}/h_{it}$. Hence, any model mis-specification or measurement errors will bias the estimates of β_1 downwards.

To control for these issues, the authors use the average daily wage rate of other drivers as an instrument. However, they find that this makes the estimate of β_1 even more negative. Another econometric issue is an identification issue. Are the authors picking out points along a downward sloping labor demand curve because of relatively greater variation in the labor supply curve? The authors report that they conducted personal interviews with cab drivers that led them to believe that the marginal cost of driving does not alter in a manner that might have an effect on the wage. However, the authors do not directly introduce an instrument for labor supply.

How does one explain the estimated labor supply elasticities? The authors favor an explanation that is based on reference dependence. Cab drivers have a daily target level of earnings. The target earnings level could be some fixed number (say, $150 per day) or be linked to the costs of leasing the cab (such as, twice the daily leasing fee). Drivers dislike falling below the daily target and the probability of quitting for the day increases as they approach the target.

Explanations based on daily income targeting are supported by interviews that the authors conducted with the fleet managers. For instance, six fleet managers chose the following response: "Drive until they make a certain amount of money." Five fleet managers chose: "Fixed hours." Only one fleet manager chose a response that is consistent with the intertemporal substitution model: "Drive a lot when doing well; quit early on a bad day." Daily income targeting is not a feature of standard labor economics models. However, it appears to be a sensible heuristic and is reminiscent of the short horizon of portfolio holders (one year) in the Benartzi and Thaler (1995) model and of the literature on goals and targets. A daily income target is also simple and computationally easy, say, relative to a monthly or a weekly income target.

Does experience make a difference? For instance, experienced drivers might realize that it pays to work longer on busy days. It is possible to split up the cab drivers' data into experienced drivers (greater than 3–4 year's experience), and inexperienced drivers. The elasticity of labor supply for inexperienced drivers is generally close to -1 (which is consistent with a daily income target). The corresponding elasticity for experienced drivers is much larger, and positive.

We now present a simple model of reference dependent preferences in labor supply, due to Farber (2008). Section 2.8.2 considers the optimality of income targeting in a similar model with Köszegi–Rabin preferences. Suppose that Y is income, $\overline{Y}$ is reference income, h is hours worked, and w is the wage rate (such that $w = Y/h$). Suppose that the reference dependent utility function is given by

$$U(Y, \overline{Y}) = \begin{cases} (Y - \overline{Y}) - \frac{\theta}{1+v}h^{1+v} & \text{if} \quad Y \geq \overline{Y} \\ -\lambda(\overline{Y} - Y) - \frac{\theta}{1+v}h^{1+v} & \text{if} \quad Y < \overline{Y} \end{cases}, \tag{3.47}$$

where λ is the parameter of loss aversion, v is the inverse of the elasticity of labor supply, θ is a parameter related to disutility of hours worked. Noting that $Y \equiv wh$, the conditions which separate the domain of income in (3.47) into losses and gains are

$$Y > \overline{Y} \Leftrightarrow w > \overline{Y}/h$$
$$Y < \overline{Y} \Leftrightarrow w < \overline{Y}/h \cdot$$

(3.48)

When $Y > \overline{Y}$, a simple calculation gives the interior solution to the hours worked,

$$h = \left(\frac{w}{\theta}\right)^{1/v}.$$

(3.49)

Analogously, when $Y \equiv wh < \overline{Y}$, from the second row of (3.47), a simple calculation gives the interior solution to the hours worked as

$$h = \left(\frac{\lambda w}{\theta}\right)^{1/v}.$$

(3.50)

When $Y \equiv wh = \overline{Y}$, the solution can be directly found as follows

$$h = \overline{Y}/w.$$

(3.51)

From (3.48), (3.49), (3.50), (3.51), we can summarize the solution in Table 3.3.

The labor supply curve has the following shape. For wage rates that are less that w_1 and those that are greater than w_2, the labor supply curve is upward sloping with elasticity of labor supply given by $1/v$. However, for intermediate ranges of wage rates, between w_1 and w_2, the individual finds that his income is at the reference point, so, as in (3.51), it is optimal simply to offset, one for one, an increase in the wage rate by the hours worked. Thus, the labor supply elasticity in the intermediate range is -1.

Having fixed the basic ideas, we now give a brief overview of the empirical evidence. Oettinger (1999) examines the labor supply decision of vendors in baseball stadiums. The vendors have a choice of working during a particular game by giving prior notice of their decision to their employers. Vendors receive a commission for their sales during the game. The effective wage depends on the attendance at a particular game; greater attendance reduces the time needed to search for the next customer. The level of attendance is a "demand shock," while the number of other vendors who have chosen to work at a particular game is the relevant "supply shock"

Table 3.3 A summary of the solution to the simple labor supply problem in Farber (2008).

Wage	Hours	Elasticity
$w < w_1 \equiv \left(\theta \overline{Y}^v\right)^{1/(1+v)}$	$h = \left(\frac{w}{\theta}\right)^{1/v}$	$1/v$
$w_1 \leq w \leq w_2 \equiv \left(\theta \overline{Y}^v\right)$	$h = \overline{Y}/w$	-1
$w_2 < w$	$h = \left(\frac{\lambda w}{\theta}\right)^{1/v}$	$1/v$

for a vendor. Using instrumental variables for the attendance at any game, they find positive and statistically significant wage elasticities (ranging from 0.53 to 0.64). This evidence does not contradict either the standard neoclassical model (see Remark 3.2 above) or the reference dependence model because most of the equilibrium points could be along the positive sloping part of the labour supply curve.

Fehr and Goette (2007) look at the labor supply decision of bicycle messengers in Zurich who are paid a commission for each successfully delivered message. Bicycle messengers have to work a given number of fixed shifts during a month, but can voluntarily sign up for more shifts. There are two groups of messengers (groups A and B). Group A members are first offered a 25% increase in the commission rate for a period of one month after which they revert back to the old rate. In the following month, group B members are offered the same temporary increase in the commission rate for a month. Fehr and Goette (2007) find that the probability of working on a given day is higher for the group that is currently a recipient of the increase in the commission rate. The wage elasticities are positive and have similar magnitudes to those in the Oettinger (1999) study, ranging from 0.72 to 0.82.

Fehr and Goette (2007) then regress the log of revenues earned by a messenger in each shift on a dummy for the treatment group that receives the 25% increase in commission rates. They also use other control variables that take account of daily fixed effects and individual fixed effects. They find that the revenues within a shift are lower for the group that has been offered the commission increase, and the implied labor elasticities are negative, ranging from −0.23 to −0.29. These results are consistent with the reference dependence model.

The Fehr–Goette results are not only consistent with those of Camerer et al. (1997), they also control for some of the objections that were raised against those results. For instance, the source of the variation in wage (25% increase for the control group) is exogenous, so the issue of instruments for labor supply is not a concern. Similarly, messengers sorted themselves into one of the two groups (A or B) prior to the announcement of the increase in the wage, hence, selection issues are controlled for. In an insightful extension, the authors perform a follow-up experiment, designed to elicit the loss aversion parameter of the bicycle messengers. It is found that the effort elasticity is negative and statistically significant only for those messengers who also exhibit loss averse behavior (others do not exhibit an elasticity that is statistically different from zero). This provides much stronger confirmatory evidence of reference dependent preferences in labor supply.

Farber (2005) examines the within-day labor supply decision of New York cab drivers. He uses a hazard model of quitting to test the prediction of the reference dependence model that higher wages during the early part of the day induce earlier quits. In the simplest model, Farber finds that holding fixed the hours worked, the probability of quitting early increases when the earnings for the day up to that point are higher. This is consistent with the reference dependence model. Next, Farber adds controls for driver fixed effects, which alters the result of the simple model; the probability of quitting now does not depend on earnings so far during the day. However, one of the controls used is clock hours, which is the most predictable source of variation in hourly wages; average hourly wages are positively correlated over the day, peaking at evening rush time. This control eliminates an important source of information that could have identified the reference dependence model; for a discussion of these points, see Goette et al. (2004).

Goette and Huffman (2003), like Farber (2005), consider the within-day labor supply decisions of bike messengers based on US and Swiss data. They test the following prediction of the reference dependence model. Suppose that there is a windfall gain in the morning (e.g., a bike messenger gets lucky). Then, reference dependence should predict an increasing effort, followed by decreasing effort. The reason is that when messengers are below the target earnings, they have an increasing incentive to provide effort. However, once this target is exceeded, their incentive to provide effort, falls. In order to isolate just the effect of luck in the morning, they introduce messenger fixed effects, fixed effects to control for the effects of firm, day of the week, and clock hour. The residual variation in earnings of the messenger is on account of luck. The authors verify the prediction of reference dependence that they start out to prove.

Some of the concerns with Farber (2005) that prevented reference dependence to be identified are addressed in Farber (2008) in a model of reference dependent preferences and a reference point that is stochastic. The evidence supports a finding of reference dependence. The model in which income is targeted, performs much better than the standard neoclassical model. However, the reference point is found to fluctuate too much from day to day. The author concludes that this limits the power of reference dependence theory to explain labor supply.

Crawford and Meng (2011) raise two objections to the Farber (2008) results. (1) Farber finds that the probability of stopping increases when the income target is reached. While the individual decisions seem to have these kinks, the aggregate relation between stopping probability and income is too smooth. How can these results be reconciled? (2) The randomness in reference points is large but imprecisely estimated.

Crawford and Meng (2011) propose a model of reference dependent preferences that relies on the Köszegi–Rabin framework (see Section 2.8). In this model (and unlike Faber's model) there are targets for both hours worked and income. These targets are determined endogenously as rational expectations equilibria. The rational expectations of the wage is operationalized by simply taking the average wage. As before, we denote hours worked by h, income by Y, the actual hourly wage rate by w and reference income by $\overline{Y}$. The new variables are average or expected wage (w^e), and reference numbers of hours worked ($\overline{h}$). Conditional on the reference points for income and hours ($\overline{Y}, \overline{h}$), which are themselves endogenous, the utility of the individual is given by a weighted combination of *consumption utility* and *gain–loss utility*, as follows.

$$U(Y,h,\overline{Y},\overline{h}) = (1-\eta)\,[u(Y)+v(h)] + \eta\mu(Y,h,\overline{Y},\overline{h}); \eta \in [0,1]. \tag{3.52}$$

In (3.52), consumption utility (first term) is additively separable in income and hours and given the weight $1-\eta \geq 0$. There is positive marginal utility from consumption $u'(Y) > 0$, negative marginal utility from hours worked, $v'(h) < 0$, and $u(Y), v(h)$ are both concave. Gain–loss utility, denoted by μ, is the second term in (3.52), and it has weight $\eta \in [0,1]$. This term is defined by partitioning all (Y,h) pairs into four domains. The income domain and the hours domain are both in gains when $Y \geq \overline{Y}$ and $h \leq \overline{h}$; both in loss when $Y < \overline{Y}$ and $h > \overline{h}$; one in loss and the other in gain if either of $Y < \overline{Y}$ and $h \leq \overline{h}$ or $Y \geq \overline{Y}$ and $h > \overline{h}$ holds. Formally

$$\mu = \begin{cases} \left[u(Y)-u(\overline{Y})\right]+\left[v(h)-v(\overline{h})\right] & \text{if } Y \geq \overline{Y}, h \leq \overline{h} \\[2mm] \lambda\left[u(Y)-u(\overline{Y})\right]+\lambda\left[v(h)-v(\overline{h})\right] & \text{if } Y < \overline{Y}, h > \overline{h} \\[2mm] \lambda\left[u(Y)-u(\overline{Y})\right]+\left[v(h)-v(\overline{h})\right] & \text{if } Y < \overline{Y}, h \leq \overline{h} \\[2mm] \left[u(Y)-u(\overline{Y})\right]+\lambda\left[v(h)-v(\overline{h})\right] & \text{if } Y \geq \overline{Y}, h > \overline{h} \end{cases}. \tag{3.53}$$

When drivers decide to work an extra hour, they know that their earnings are random. To simplify, it is assumed that they simply focus on the expected or average wage, w^e, and use it to

Table 3.4 Summary of the marginal rates of substitution between Y and h in various domains.

Income/Hours	Gain ($h \leq \overline{h}$)	Loss ($h < \overline{h}$)
Gain ($Y \geq \overline{Y}$)	$\frac{-v'(h)}{u'(Y)}$	$\frac{-v'(h)}{u'(Y)}(1 + \eta(\lambda - 1))$
Loss ($Y < \overline{Y}$)	$\frac{-v'(h)}{u'(Y)}\frac{1}{1+\eta(\lambda-1)}$	$\frac{-v'(h)}{u'(Y)}$

compute their hourly earnings. w^e is determined by rational expectations. The objective of the driver is to maximize (3.52), subject to the budget constraint

$$Y = w^e h. \tag{3.54}$$

We motivate a diagrammatic solution. In each of the four domains listed in (3.53), the marginal rate of substitution (MRS) between Y and h is computed using (3.52) and (3.53); Table 3.4 summarizes these calculations.

Since the coefficient of loss aversion $\lambda > 1$, we get that $1 + \eta(\lambda - 1) > 1$. From Table 3.4, when both income and hours are either in the domain of gains or losses, then the MRS is given as in the standard neoclassical model. However, in the other two cases, when both outcomes are in different domains, this is no longer true. When income is in gains and hours are in losses, then the MRS is magnified (i.e., the indifference curves are steeper). When income is in losses and hours in gains the MRS shrinks (indifference curves are flatter). Equilibrium labor supply can be found from the usual condition that equates MRS with the marginal rate of transformation, which from (3.54) is w^e, hence, $MRS = w^e$. Denote the actual wage of the taxi driver on trip by w^a.

> **Lemma 3.2** *(a) Suppose that $w^a > w^e$, i.e., the actual wage is greater than the expected wage. Then the income target, $\overline{Y}$, is reached first, followed by the hours target, $\overline{h}$.*
> *(b) Conversely, if $w^a < w^e$, then the hours target is reached first.*

Proof: By definition, on any trip, $w^a = Y/h$. Since $w^a > w^e$, we get $Y/h > w^e$. On account of rational expectations, $\overline{Y} = hw^e$, i.e., the endogenous reference income equals the expected income. Suppose that the hours target is reached, i.e., $h = \overline{h}$, then from $\overline{Y} = hw^e$ we get that

$$h = \overline{h} = \frac{\overline{Y}}{w^e}. \tag{3.55}$$

From (3.54), actual income is given by $Y = w^a h$. Substituting (3.55) we get

$$Y = w^a \frac{\overline{Y}}{w^e}.$$

But since $w^a > w^e$ we get that $Y > \overline{Y}$. Hence, when the hours target is reached, the income target is already exceeded. Part (b) of the lemma is analogously derived. ∎

Figure 3.8 gives insights into the equilibrium in (Y_t, h_t) space, where the subscript t denotes the time of the day during the trip. On the vertical axis, we measure Y_t (increasing upwards) and

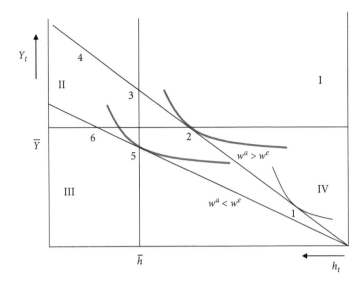

Figure 3.8 An illustration of the equilibrium in the Crawford–Meng (2011) model.

Source: Crawford and Meng (2011) with permission from the American Economic Association.

along the horizontal axis, h_t (increasing leftward). The space is truncated into four quadrants I, II, III, IV, based on the reference income and reference hours level, $\left(\overline{Y},\overline{h}\right)$, as the origin.

The driver begins at his endowment point of $(Y,h) = (0,24)$, assuming that the total time endowment is 24 hours. He begins with an expected wage w^e and then moves in the northwest direction along the line $Y = w^e h$. There are two possibilities, $w^a > w^e$ and $w^a < w^e$, both shown in the diagram. Having completed any single trip, the driver begins another trip starting from the last level of (Y,h), again moving in a northwest direction along the line $Y = w^e h$.[39] The key insight comes from Lemma 3.2; when $w^a > w^e$, the driver first reaches the income target, and when $w^a < w^e$ the driver first reaches the hours target.

Consider first the case $w^a > w^e$. We know from Table 3.4 that in quadrants I and III, the slope of the indifference curves is identical in neoclassical theory and in prospect theory (PT) with targets $\left(\overline{Y},\overline{h}\right)$. In quadrant II, the indifference curves are relatively steeper under PT as compared to neoclassical theory, while in quadrant IV, these indifference curves are relatively flatter. Let us concentrate only on quadrants I and IV.

Suppose that in the neoclassical model, the equilibrium is at point 1 (it could also be at other points such as 2, 3, and 4). However, because in quadrant IV the indifference curves under PT are flatter, so the equilibrium under PT could be at point 2, as shown in the figure. Starting at point 2, the individual will not like to enter quadrant I if the marginal rate of substitution, $\frac{-v'(h)}{u'(Y)}$ (see $(1,1)$th element in Table 3.4) exceeds the opportunity cost of leisure, w^e. Should this happen, then equilibrium is at point 2 and the income target is met before the hours target (see Lemma 3.2).

Conversely, when $w^a < w^e$, the relevant budget constraint is the lower of the two budget constraints in Figure 3.8. In this case, starting from the endowment point $(Y,h) = (0,24)$, an

---

[39] In practice, the budget line is random (because the wage is random) but for exposition, we consider that the driver takes account of only the wage w^e.

individual using PT may similarly find it optimal to be at point 5 (this turns out to be the empirically relevant case). But in this case, the hours target is reached before the income target.

Crawford and Meng (2011) estimate the probability of stopping, as in Farber (2005), with two main differences. First, targets are not treated as latent variables but rather as rational expectations (proxied by average sample realizations). Second, the sample is split into two parts $w^a > w^e$ and $w^a < w^e$, i.e., depending on whether the realized income is lower or higher than the (proxied) expected income. The authors find clear evidence of reference dependence.

The probability of stopping is heavily influenced by realized income when $w^a > w^e$. Conversely, when $w^a < w^e$, the probability of stopping is heavily influenced by hours worked. The cases $w^a > w^e$ and $w^a < w^e$ have almost equal weight in the sample. In the first case, the wage elasticity of hours is strongly negative, while in the second it is zero. Thus, in the aggregate, wage elasticity is negative, as in Camerer et al. (1997).

3.9 Some implications of inverse S-shaped weighting functions

Figure 2.5 in Section 2.3 considered the following important implication of inverse S-shaped probability weighting functions under rank dependent models. Extreme events (or tail events in finance) are more salient in the sense that such events are accorded higher decision weights. This is one possible explanation for why positively skewed portfolios and assets with positively skewed returns may be more attractive to investors, hence, driving up their prices (Barberis and Huang, 2008).[40] A related implication of a preference for positively skewed portfolios is that individuals may hold portfolios that are under-diversified; see Mitton and Vorkink (2007) for confirmatory evidence.

Another implication of the increased salience of tail events is that the decision maker is more averse to negatively skewed returns, which accords well with the actual shape of the average overall returns in the market (Fehr-Duda and Epper, 2012). This produces an even higher level of the equity premium, beyond that which can be explained by loss aversion alone (De Giorgi and Legg, 2012). This illustrates, once again, the importance of using the entire machinery of PT, particularly when one wishes to explain quantitative phenomena.

Salience of tail events may also explain why the volume of retirement annuities purchased is lower than the predicted volume in neoclassical theory. Suppose that the retirement age is 65. Hu and Scott (2007) present the problem as one in which if someone dies early, within a few years of 65 (small perceived probability of the event, hence, this is a tail event), then the annuity is not very useful. However, if tail events are overweighted, then the desirability of annuities falls, in line with the evidence.

A basic feature of the inverse S-shaped weighting functions is that low probabilities are overweighted. This has been used to explain why people choose low deductibles in insurance[41] even when the high deductibles are several times cheaper in expected value. In Sydnor (2010), potential insurees are given a menu of choices between four different levels of home insurance deductibles, $100, $250, $500, $1000. The most common choice was $500. However, in order to reduce the deductible from $1000 to $500, consumers typically paid an extra cost, in terms of the premium, of $100. The claim rate of this group of consumers was 5%. Thus, consumers are

---

[40] For related empirical evidence, see Ang et al. (2006), Boyer et al. (2010), Green and Hwang (2012), and Conrad et al. (2013).

[41] In the event of a loss, the loss of the consumer is capped at the level of the deductible that is chosen.

willing to pay an extra $100 to reduce the expected loss by $25. The implied coefficient of relative risk aversion is in triple and quadruple digits, which is unreasonably high. Sydnor's preferred explanation is that individuals must overweight the probability of tail events significantly, which is consistent with inverse S-shaped weighting functions.

The empirical tests in Barseghyan et al. (2013) discriminate among the Köszegi–Rabin framework, Gul's theory of disappointment aversion, and non-linear probability weighting. They show that it is non-linear probability weighting that accounts for the observed choice of low deductibles. Overweighting of low probabilities also explains the favorite long-shot *bias* in betting markets (e.g., in horse racing). This takes the form of over-betting on horses which have a small probability of winning and under-betting on horses which have a high chance of winning.[42]

A quick look at the literature suggests that loss aversion based explanations are more predominant in the literature as compared to those based on non-linear probability weighting. Fehr-Duda and Epper (2012) make a strong case for redressing this imbalance. They argue that (p. 589): "Probability dependence is the more fundamental of the two [loss aversion and non-linear probability weighting] because it is observed for all types of prospects: pure gain prospects as well as pure loss and mixed prospects. In contrast, loss aversion is effective for mixed prospects only. It is our impression that probability-dependent risk preferences have not received as much attention as loss aversion has, however."

3.10 Contracts as reference points

Suppose that a buyer and a seller write a contract at an initial stage in which the future cannot be perfectly anticipated. Hence, any contracts that they write have to be necessarily incomplete. At the initial stage, both parties (or just one party) sink relation-specific investment. Once the relevant uncertainty is resolved at a future date, then the two parties can renegotiate the terms of the contract. Under the assumptions of Coasian bargaining, renegotiation allows them to achieve an efficient outcome.

Renegotiation entails sharing, ex-post, the benefits of the relation-specific investment. Anticipating this hold up problem in the renegotiation stage, at the initial stage, each party invests an inadequate amount. This highlights an important *transaction cost* of using the market. The solution to the problem is the allocation of ownership rights and *residual control rights* in such a way that facilitates *efficient investment* (Grossman and Hart, 1986; Hart and Moore, 1990). Indeed, one possible solution is the *formation of firms* and entering into *long-term contracts*.

This account of the theory of the firm is restrictive in scope, because ex-ante investment in non-contractible relation-specific investments is the main driver in the formation of firms. In contrast, we often observe the existence of firms when such factors are absent. This explanation also does not shed light on the *internal organization of the firm* and the explanation of *authority*, *hierarchy*, and *delegation*.

In this section, we consider an alternative view of the firm, one that is based on the idea of reference dependence in prospect theory.

In a reference dependence-based explanation of firms, contracts establish a *reference point of entitlements* for the contracting parties. Initial contracts are typically written among parties

---

[42] See, for instance, Jullien and Salanié (2000) who show that prospect theory outperforms expected utility in explaining this phenomena. Snowberg and Wolfers (2010) are able to distinguish between the role of convex utility and probability weighting and find the latter to be the main source of the explanation.

chosen from a competitive pool of buyers and sellers. Hence, each party to the contract is likely to believe that the terms of the contract capture the market beliefs about its entitlements. Competition is critical to establishing entitlements. Lack of competition does not establish entitlements, hence, contracts that are signed in non-competitive conditions may not serve as a reference point; see Fehr et al. (2009) for the empirical evidence.

At a future date, once ex-ante uncertainty is resolved, parties to the contract evaluate the current outcomes, relative to the ex-ante entitlements established by the initial contract. If the outcomes are inferior to the entitlements, parties feel *aggrieved* and may *shade* their ex-post performance. Both parties need not share the same beliefs about their respective entitlements. For instance, there could be a *self-serving bias*, which leads each party to confound fairness with its selfishly preferred outcome. This self-serving bias in entitlements is analyzed in the context of bargaining models in Volume 4 (Babcock and Loewenstein, 1997).

Why is it typically difficult to specify ex-post performance in the ex-ante contract? Hart and Moore (2008) distinguish between *perfunctory performance* and *consummate performance*. The former refers to conformity with the *letter* of the contract (e.g., number of hours worked) and the latter with the *spirit* of the law (e.g., care and attention exercised during working hours). Perfunctory performance is observable and verifiable to a third party, so it can be specified in the ex-ante contract. By contrast, consummate performance is observable to both parties, but not verifiable to a third party, so it cannot be written down in the contract. Hence, the ex-post actions of the parties are only *partially contractible*. If, ex-post, parties to a contract feel aggrieved, based on a comparison with their entitlements based on the initial contract, then they can lower their consummate performance. This is the sense in which *shading of performance*, to the detriment of the other parties to a contract, can take place. In this framework, there is no loss aversion and there is no renegotiation.

In a buyer–seller framework, shading by the seller can take the form of reducing quality, or not agreeing to reasonable requests by the buyer that greatly enhance the utility of the buyer at zero or very low cost to the seller. Buyers can also engage in shading by, say, delaying payments, engaging in discourteous behavior, and writing bad references for future potential buyers.

These elements of the theory can be used to determine the choice between *rigid contracts* and *flexible contracts*. A rigid contract, such as an *employment contract*, rigidly fixes the wage at the initial stage in a competitive environment, and allows no ex-post flexibility in altering the wage. Hence, ex-post, parties have no opportunity to be aggrieved. However, such a contract lacks the ex-post flexibility to adapt to changing states of nature. For instance, demand might turn out to be surprisingly low, but the initially fixed wage cannot be lowered. By contrast, a flexible contract offers ex-post flexibility in adapting to the realized state of the world. However, it also creates an opportunity for aggrievement. As one of the parties adapts to the state of the world, the other party may feel unfairly treated relative to the entitlements and retaliate by reducing its consummate performance. This trade-off governs the choice between the rigid contract and the flexible contract. Under certain conditions that we specify below, the rigid contract may be optimal.

3.10.1 *A simple model*

Hart and Moore (2008) consider the following simple model of a long-term relation between a buyer, B, and a seller, S. A competitive pool of buyers and sellers meet at date 0. A matched buyer–seller pair then sign a contract at date 0, which structures their interaction at date 1. Once the two parties are matched, the competitive pool of market participants reduce to a bilateral monopoly situation; this is Williamson's well-known *fundamental transformation*. Both parties are risk neutral, all information is symmetric, there are no wealth constraints, and there are no non-contractible relation-specific investments.

There is potential uncertainty when parties sign contracts at date 0, but all uncertainty is resolved by date 1. At date 1, the parties act, in each state, as per the instructions in the date 0 contract. For instance, if the date 0 contract is a rigid contract, then parties make no active decisions. However, if the date 0 contract is a flexible contract, it might require one of the parties to the contract to choose a date 1 price, depending on which state of the world is realized. Trade then occurs and the two parties choose their consummate performance. In order to measure the degree of aggrievement, we make the simplifying assumption that each party feels entitled to the 'maximum outcome' that can arise for it in the date 0 contract (say, on account of self-serving bias).

Denote by Π_B, Π_S, the set of gross payoffs that are contractually feasible and let $\bar{u}_j = \max \Pi_j$ be the maximum possible payoff to party j as dictated by the date 0 contract. Suppose that at date 1, the gross payoffs of the buyer and seller are, respectively, u_B and u_S. Let the buyer and the seller be indexed, respectively, by $j = B, S$. The aggrievement of player j is given by

$$a_j = \bar{u}_j - u_j, u_j \in \Pi_j. \tag{3.56}$$

Being aggrieved causes a drop in consummate performance that causes a monetary loss to the other party (effort shading). Denote the monetary loss caused by the buyer and the seller, respectively, to the other party, on account of aggrievement, by l_B and l_S. The respective utilities of the buyer and the seller, U_B and U_S, are given by

$$U_B = u_B - l_S - \max\{\theta a_B - l_B, 0\}, \tag{3.57}$$
$$U_S = u_S - l_B - \max\{\theta a_S - l_S, 0\}, \tag{3.58}$$

where $\theta \in (0, 1]$. The third term on the RHS in each of (3.57) and (3.58) shows that being aggrieved leads to a loss in utility, the extent of which depends on θ. However, causing a monetary loss to the other party shades this loss in utility; this is viewed as "just retribution" inflicted on the other party when one perceives oneself to be unfairly treated. However, shading can never be used to increase one's own utility, although one can shade enough such that all aggrievement disappears (i.e., if $\theta a_B = l_B$ or $\theta a_S = l_S$). Each party simultaneously chooses $l_j, j = B, S$. Clearly, the utility maximizing choice of each party is $l_B = \theta a_B$ and $l_S = \theta a_S$. Substituting this solution in (3.57) and (3.58), the equilibrium utilities of the buyer and seller are, respectively,

$$U_B = u_B - \theta a_S \text{ and } U_S = u_S - \theta a_B. \tag{3.59}$$

Let us use this framework to find the optimal contracts for the following simple case. A buyer would like to enter into a date 0 contract with a seller to supply 1 unit of an object at date 1. It is common knowledge that the buyer's utility is $u_B = 100 - p$, where p is the date 1 price at which the object is exchanged. The seller's cost is zero, so $u_S = p$. The total surplus is $u_B + u_S = 100$. There are no ex-ante non-contractible investments. The results for this simple case are listed in the next proposition.

Proposition 3.6 *(i) In the neoclassical framework, the solution is identical in the absence or presence of an ex-ante contract.*

(ii) In the "contracts as reference points" framework, the total surplus is given by $(1 - \theta)\,100$, which is independent of p and there is a deadweight loss of 100θ.

(iii) Ex-post Coasian renegotiation does not alter the result in (ii).

(iv) A mechanism that gives residual control rights to the buyer to choose a date 1 price does not alter the result in (ii).

(v) Suppose that there is a competitive market for sellers or buyers. Consider a rigid contract at date 0 that fixes a date 1 price, p, determined by competitive contracts. Such a contract achieves a social surplus of 100.

(vi) Suppose that the date 0 market is imperfectly competitive and the contracting parties agree on some price interval $\left[\underline{p}, \overline{p}\right]$ for the date 1 trading price, such that $0 < \underline{p} < \overline{p} < 100$. Then the shading costs of aggrievement are $\theta\,(\overline{p} - \underline{p}) < 100\theta$.

Proof: (i) Consider the neoclassical framework in which there is absence of aggrievement and shading. Assume that there is a competitive supply of sellers but only one buyer, and lump-sum transfers are allowed. Suppose that the buyer writes a contract with one of the sellers from the competitive pool of sellers at date 0. All parties know that at date 1, there is bilateral monopoly between the contracting parties, so that the date 1 price is determined by bargaining. The total surplus from trading is $u_B + u_S = 100$, arising entirely from the buyer's valuation, because the seller's cost is zero.

Assume symmetric Nash bargaining among the two parties at date 1, thus, $p = 50$ and the gains from trade are shared equally. However, at date 0, since there is a competitive pool of sellers, the single buyer must get all the surplus. Anticipating ex-post opportunism, the seller who gets the contract at date 0, pays a lump-sum transfer to the buyer, equal to 50. Thus, the date 1 payoffs of the seller and the buyer are $u_B = 100$, $u_S = 0$. On the other hand if the parties had waited for date 1 to write a contract, then competition among the sellers would have driven the price to $p = 0$ so that $u_B = 100$, $u_S = 0$, which is identical to the outcome under a date 0 contract.

This result can also be shown to hold for other market configurations such as one buyer and one seller or many competitive buyers and one seller.

(ii) Consider one buyer and one seller. Suppose that the two parties do not write a date 0 contract and both realize that they will agree on some price p at date 1. At date 1, the maximum possible payoff of the buyer, as dictated by the date 0 contract, is $\overline{u}_B = 100$, so the buyer feels aggrieved if $p > 0$. Analogously, for the seller, $\overline{u}_S = 100$, so the seller feels aggrieved if $p < 100$. Thus, for any $0 < p < 100$ both parties will shade their consummate performance.

Since $a_j = \overline{u}_j - u_j$, $j = B, S$, we have that $a_B = 100 - (100 - p) = p$ and $a_S = 100 - p$. Thus, the buyer shades by $l_B = \theta a_B = \theta p$, and the seller shades by $l_S = \theta a_S = \theta(100 - p)$. Using (3.59), the final utilities of the buyer and the seller are, thus,

$$U_B = 100 - p - \theta(100 - p) = (1 - \theta)(100 - p).$$
$$U_S = p - \theta p = (1 - \theta)p.$$

The total surplus is $W = U_B + U_B = (1 - \theta)100$, which is independent of p. Thus, there is a deadweight loss of 100θ that is increasing in the weight that the two parties put on aggrievement.

(iii) Suppose that at date 1, the buyer pays an amount x to the seller to reduce the seller's shading. The seller will find that a_S falls (see (3.56)), so he indeed shades less. However, the buyer will find that a_B goes up, so he feels more aggrieved, thus, he will shade more. On net, given the linear, additive, structure of the model, there is no change to the result in (ii).

(iv) Part (ii) holds for any arbitrary date 1 price, p and there is a deadweight loss of 100θ, which is independent of p. In particular, this result holds for $p = 0$. In part (iv) we have a particular price p chosen by the buyer who makes a take it or leave it offer to the seller, hence, $p = 0$. So we get the same deadweight loss and same total surplus as in part (ii).

(v) Suppose that there is a competitive pool of suppliers and one buyer, so that the buyer has all the bargaining power. Then a rigid contract at date 0 must fix a date 1 price of $p = 0$. Conversely, if there are a large number of buyers and one seller, this price must be $p = 100$. Once the price is fixed at date 0, none of the parties feels aggrieved at date 1 from the implementation of the date 0 price. Since the date 0 price was competitively determined, each party realizes that this price fixes an objective, market determined, entitlement. Thus, no shading of consummate performance occurs and the total surplus is $100 - p + p = 100$.

(vi) In this case, given the definition of $\bar{u}$, the buyer feels entitled to $\bar{u}_B = 100 - p$ and the seller feels entitled to $\bar{u}_S = \bar{p}$. Suppose that trade takes place at some $p \in \left[\underline{p}, \bar{p}\right]$. Then $a_B = \left(100 - \underline{p}\right) - \left(100 - p\right) = p - \underline{p}$. Thus, the buyer shades his effort by $\theta a_B = \theta(p - \underline{p})$. For the seller, $a_S = \bar{p} - p$, thus, the seller shades by $\theta a_S = \theta\left(\bar{p} - p\right)$. Total shading is given by $\theta(p - \underline{p}) + \theta\left(\bar{p} - p\right) = \theta\left(\bar{p} - \underline{p}\right) < 100\theta$ because $0 < \underline{p} < \bar{p} < 100$. Hence, the deadweight loss in this case is lower and the social surplus is higher. ∎

Proposition 3.6 shows that rigid contracts that determine the date 1 terms of trade at date 0 are preferable to flexible contracts that leave price determination to date 1. This is because they lead to lower aggrievement and lower shading of effort. An extension of these results to the case of non-contractible ex-ante investment can be found in Hart (2009).[43]

In general, Proposition 3.6 need not hold when either the buyer's valuation of the object, v, or the seller's cost, c, are uncertain. Suppose that trading at date 1 is voluntary and a date 0 contract specifies a no-trade price p_0 (paid by the buyer to the seller in the event of no-trade) and a trade price, p_1, if trade occurs at date 1. We allow lump-sum transfers between the two parties and no renegotiation of contracts at date 1. Let $q = 1$ if trade occurs at date 1, and $q = 0$ if no trade occurs. The buyer and the seller voluntarily engage in trade at date 1 if, respectively, $v - p_1 \geq 0 - p_0$ and $p_1 - c \geq p_0$, which can be summarized by

$$q = 1 \Leftrightarrow v \geq p_1 - p_0 \geq c. \tag{3.60}$$

We normalize $p_0 = 1$ because lump-sum transfers are allowed. Thus, the relevant trade condition is $v \geq p_1 \geq c$. One may compare this with the first best condition for trade:

$$q = 1 \Leftrightarrow v \geq c. \tag{3.61}$$

Since condition (3.60) is more restrictive than (3.61), thus, in the second best, trade takes place less often as compared to the socially optimal level.

Suppose that we consider a slightly more general contract in which:

(i) p_1 is not a point price but it can be chosen from the interval $\left[\underline{p}, \bar{p}\right]$, and

(ii) the contract gives the buyer the right to choose the date 1 price, once any uncertainty has resolved.

[43] For an extension of the Hart–Moore framework to renegotiation, see Halonen-Akatwijuka and Hart (2013) and for an application to the scope of the firm, see Hart and Holmstrom (2010).

In this case, a generalized version of (3.60) can be written as

$$q = 1 \Leftrightarrow \exists p_1 \in \left[\underline{p}, \overline{p}\right] : v \geq p_1 - p_0 \geq c. \tag{3.62}$$

Normalizing $p_0 = 0$, a sufficient condition for (3.62) to hold for all $p_1 \in \left[\underline{p}, \overline{p}\right]$ is

$$q = 1 \Leftrightarrow v \geq \overline{p} \text{ and } c \leq \underline{p}. \tag{3.63}$$

This condition holds irrespective of whether the buyer or the seller has residual control rights to choose $p_1 \in \left[\underline{p}, \overline{p}\right]$.

Assume that each party recognizes that due to the voluntary trade assumption, they cannot get more than 100% of the trade surplus. Thus, each party feels an entitlement up to the maximum surplus within the contract, conditional on trade taking place. So long as they achieve this level of entitlement, they feel no aggrievement.

Definition 3.6 *An 'optimal contract' maximizes ex-ante expected surplus, net of shading costs.*

Example 3.3 *Suppose that there are two possible states of the world at date 1, s1 and s2, but at date 0 it is not known which state will arise. The buyer's valuation, v, and the seller's cost, c, are given in Figure 3.9. Suppose first that p_1 is a point price. Then, we need to find a single value for p_1 at date 0 such that $v \geq p_1 \geq c$ in each state (see (3.60) when $p_0 = 0$). From Figure 3.9 there exists no such price.*

Now consider a contract that specifies $p_1 \in \left[\underline{p}, \overline{p}\right] = [9, 10]$. Recall that the buyer has the right to choose the date 1 price, once the state of the world is known. In state s1, the buyer picks $p_1 = 9$. Since this is the lowest possible price in the range of feasible prices [9, 10], the buyer does not feel aggrieved. The seller too does not feel aggrieved because any higher price will exceed the buyer's valuation and prevent trade from taking place. When the state of the world is s2, the buyer picks $p_1 = 10$, which is the upper bound of the feasible set of prices. The buyer does not feel aggrieved because any lower price will lead to no trade. The seller does not feel aggrieved because he gets his maximum possible entitlement within the contract. Thus, in each state, we obtain an efficient outcome.

The outcome under uncertainty about v, c need not always be efficient (although it is efficient in Example 3.3). Consider, for instance, Figure 3.10, which augments an extra state to Example 3.3. We leave the proof of the following proposition as an exercise.

Proposition 3.7 *Consider Figure 3.10 and suppose that the three states, s1, s2, and s3 occur with respective probabilities π_1, π_2, and π_3. In all states, $v > c$ so it is socially optimal*

	s1	s2
v	9	20
c	0	10

Figure 3.9 Valuations and costs in two states of the world.

	s1	s2	s3
v	9	20	20
c	0	10	0

Figure 3.10 Valuations and costs in three states of the world.

to trade. Consider three possible contracts A, B, and C. In contract A, $\underline{p} = \bar{p} = 9$. In contract B, $\underline{p} = \bar{p} = 10$. In contract C, $\underline{p} = 9, \bar{p} = 10$.

(i) In contracts A and B, there is inefficient amount of trade.
(ii) Contract A is optimal if π_2 is small, contract B is optimal if π_1 is small, and contract C is optimal if π_3 is small or θ is small.

In Proposition 3.7, a contract is more likely to be optimal if the probability of the state in which it does not allow trade is also low. Of the available contracts, contract C allows trade in all states, yet in state 3, there are aggrievement costs, hence, contract C is likely to be optimal if state 3 is less likely and if aggrievement costs are small.

3.10.2 *Empirical evidence for contracts as reference points*

Fehr et al. (2011) test if ex-ante competition serves to create entitlements via the reference point effect, using a version of the Hart and Moore (2008) model with payoff uncertainty. Their aim is not to test if players choose their contracts optimally, but rather to test if the behavioral assumptions of the Hart–Moore framework are empirically relevant.

Groups of 2 sellers and 2 buyers interact over 15 periods; groups are randomly rematched in each round to minimize reputational concerns. Each seller can sell up to 2 units, while each buyer needs only 1 unit at date 1, so there is seller competition. Parties are matched at date 0. At date 1, the contracted seller not only supplies the contracted quantity of 1 unit, but also determines the quality, q, which can take two possible values, normal (q_n) or low (q_l). There are two states of the world, the good state ($s = s_g$) that occurs with probability 0.8 and the bad state ($s = s_b$) that occurs with probability 0.2.

The production cost of the seller at date 1 is given by $c(q,s)$, where s is the state of the world and $c(q_n,s) < c(q_l,s)$, i.e., it is more costly to produce low quality in any state. The intuition is that it might be costly to alter the production process to produce an altered, and shaded level of consummate effort that results in a lower quality. The seller's costs are higher in the bad state, relative to the good state, so $c(q,s_g) < c(q,s_b)$. The payoffs of the buyer and the seller are given, respectively, by

$$u_B = v(q) - p \text{ and } u_S = p - c(q,s),$$

where v gives the buyer's valuation, and $v(q_n) > v(q_l)$, i.e., the buyer prefers normal to low quality. The outside option of the seller for any unit that he is unable to sell is $x_s = 10$. The payoff relevant data used in the experiments is shown in the self-explanatory Figure 3.11.

The buyers choose among contracts. They can choose either a rigid contract (r), or a flexible contract (f). These contracts are then auctioned off to sellers. In a *rigid contract*, the contract price

$p_r \in \left[c(q_l, s_g) + x_s, 75 \right] = [35, 75]$ is determined in an auction where the sellers bid against each other. The lower bound of 35 ensures that in the good state, even with the low quality, the seller does not make losses by trading, relative to getting an outside option price of $x_s = 10$ for unsold units. The upper limit ensures that the seller is always better off exercising his outside option price of $x_s = 10$ if the state is bad, rather than engaging in trade. This captures the idea that contract rigidity does not allow the parties to adapt well, ex-post, to changes in circumstances.

A *flexible contract* vests residual control rights in the hands of the buyer to choose the price p_f at date 1, once the state of the world is revealed. In the good state, s_g, the price $p_f \in \left[\underline{p}, \overline{p} \right]$, where $\underline{p} \in [35, 75]$ as in the rigid contract, and $\overline{p} = v(q_n) = 140$. In the bad state, s_b, the buyer chooses a price $p_f \in \left[c(q_l, s_b) + x_s, v(q_n) \right] = [95, 140]$. This ensures that in the bad state, the buyer's price does not let the seller make a loss by trading relative to exercising the outside option of $x_s = 10$. Unlike a rigid contract, a flexible contract permits trade to take place in both states of the world.

In each of the two contracts, sellers observe the price and then choose their quality. If they decide to choose a lower quality, they incur an extra cost of 5 units (see Figure 3.11).

Let us first summarize the results for the case of purely self-regarding preferences. In this case, bygones are bygones, so each seller will always choose the normal quality to avoid reducing their own payoff by 5 units. Anticipating that the seller never engages in shading of consummate performance, buyers choose the smallest price allowed in their respective contracts. In the rigid contract, buyers choose a price of 35 in each state of the world. Thus, the buyer's payoff equals 105 in the good state but 0 in the bad state because at a price of 35, the seller prefers to exercise the outside option. By contrast, in the flexible contract, in the good state, the buyer chooses 35 (so his payoff is 105) but in the bad state the buyer is restricted to choose no lower than 95, so his payoff is 45. Clearly, the flexible contract dominates the rigid contract because the payoffs are identical in the good state but relatively higher in the bad state under a flexible contract. These results do not depend on the presence of ex-ante competition.

Now consider the predictions in the "contracts as reference points" framework. In the rigid contract, the prices are fixed up-front, so the seller does not feel aggrieved ex-post, thus, no shading takes place. Therefore, we do not expect low quality to be chosen. In a flexible contract, by contrast, both parties have different entitlements, so shading by the seller does take place. Such shading is personally not very costly for the seller (a loss of 5 units in terms of the cost), however, it is costly for the buyer (a loss of 40 units in terms of the valuation in each state). The higher the price, the lower is the expected shading on the part of the seller. In response, buyers will attempt to increase the price to reduce shading by the seller. But increasing the price reduces the buyer's profits under flexible contracts, so they might end up preferring rigid contracts.

	s_g		s_b	
	q_n	q_l	q_n	q_l
c	20	25	80	85
v	140	100	140	100

Figure 3.11 Quality dependent valuation and cost data in two states of the world.
Source: Fehr et al. (2011) with permission from the American Economic Association.

Table 3.5 Summary of the results for rigid and flexible contracts.

Contract type	Rigid contract		Flexible contract	
State of nature	Good	Bad	Good	Bad
Average price	40.7	—	51.1	98.4
Relative frequency of normal quality	0.94	—	0.75	0.70
Average auction outcome	40.7		40.2	
Average profit buyer (per state)	96.8	10	78.9	29.7
Average profit seller (per state)	20.4	10	29.8	16.9
Average profit buyer (over both states)	77.9		68.9	
Average profit seller (over both states)	18.1		27.2	
Relative frequency of contract	0.50		0.50	

Source: Fehr et al. (2011).

Recall that in a flexible contract, in the bad state, $p_f \in [95, 140]$. In an additional treatment, buyers are restricted to choose the date 1 price in the interval $[95, 95]$. Since there is no ex-post flexibility for the buyer in this case, we expect lower shading by the seller. Yet another treatment eliminates ex-ante seller-competition. In the absence of seller-competition, the sellers may increase their entitlements, so they may engage in more shading.

The empirical results confirm the predictions of the Hart–Moore model that are outlined above, but reject the model of purely self-regarding preferences. The results are summarized in Table 3.5.

The *competitive price* is simply the cost of the seller plus the outside option. Since trade never takes place in the bad state under rigid contracts, the competitive price in a rigid contract is 35 in the good state. Analogously, in a flexible contract that allows trade in the bad state, the competitive price is 95. From Table 3.5, the average prices in rigid and fixed contracts are 40.7 and 40.2, respectively, which are not statistically different.

Looking at the results in each state, although the lower bound for price is only 35 in the good state of a flexible contract, buyers use their residual control right over prices to offer a price of 51.1. This is significantly higher than the price of 40.7 in the good state of a rigid contract where no shading can occur. In a flexible contract, 75% of the prices are above the lower bound. The difference between actual prices and the lower bound is significant, stable, and persists over time. This is consistent with the prediction that in a flexible contract, buyers offer a higher price to take account of the possibility of shading by the sellers.

Sellers rarely shade in the rigid contract in the good state (no trade takes place, by design, in the bad state) and in 94% of the cases, sellers choose normal quality. However, the corresponding figure for flexible contracts is 75%. A non-parametric signed rank test confirms that the difference between the two figures is significant. This is consistent with the hypothesis that sellers are aggrieved when they receive a payoff below their entitlements.

As noted above, if all parties had self-regarding preferences, then buyers should always prefer the flexible contract. However, in the Hart–Moore framework, buyers may get a higher payoff from the rigid contracts on account of the shading behavior of sellers in a flexible contract. The data confirms this prediction. Average profit over both states in the rigid contract is 77.9, while it is 68.9 in the flexible contract. By contrast, the average profits of sellers are higher in the flexible contract relative to the rigid contract. It would seem that buyers may have conceded a higher price that more than offsets the higher costs of the sellers from shading in the flexible contracts.

Possibly in response to these differences in profits, on average, buyers choose the rigid contract in 50% of the cases. Over time, the share of rigid contracts increases from 38% in round 1 to 56% by the last round (round 15) and the time trend is statistically significant. These results provide insights about why some forms of rigid contracts such as the employment contract may be preferred in many cases.

3.11 Moral hazard, loss aversion, and optimal contracts

Consider a simple principal–agent model in which the principal is risk neutral and the agent has prospect theory preferences (de Meza and Webb, 2003, 2007). The outside option of the agent is zero. The agent chooses an action $a \in \{0,1\}$. Each action probabilistically determines one of three observable output levels, $0 \leq y_L < y_M < y_H$. Let P and Q be the distribution functions, respectively, under $a = 1$ and $a = 0$. Under action $a = 1$, the probability of outcome y_i is p_i, $i = L, M, H$, while under action $a = 0$, the corresponding probability is q_i. We make two assumptions about the probability distribution of outcomes.

A1. The distribution of outcomes under $a = 1$ first order stochastically dominates the distribution under $a = 0$, so $P_i \leq Q_i$ for $i = L, M, H$.

A2. The *monotone likelihood ratio property* (MLRP) holds, so

$$\frac{p_L}{q_L} < \frac{p_M}{q_M} < \frac{p_H}{q_H}.$$

Thus, the probability of a higher outcome under the higher action is higher. In other words, a higher output is more likely to have come from a higher effort level.

The only observable and verifiable signal of the agent's effort is the output level produced. Hence, the principal conditions the agent's reward scheme on the observed output level. The agent receives a wage w_i when the observed output level is y_i. The agent has limited liability ($w_j \geq 0$) and there is no renegotiation of contracts. For pedagogical ease, let the *reference wage* of the agent be w_M. Since the MLRP holds, the optimal wage is increasing in the observed output level, so w_M will also be the median wage. The utility function of the agent from the wage w_i and action a, is given by

$$v(w_i \mid w_M, a) = \begin{cases} u(w_i) - a & \text{if} \quad w_i > w_M \\ u(w_i) - \lambda (w_M - w_i) - a & \text{if} \quad w_i \leq w_M \end{cases},$$

where $u' > 0$, $u'' < 0$, and $\lambda > 0$ is the coefficient of loss aversion. Thus, when $w_i \leq w_M$ the decision maker suffers disutility from loss aversion that is linear in the distance $w_M - w_i$. This formulation is similar to the Köszegi–Rabin framework in which the individual derives consumption utility and gain–loss utility, except that here we only capture disutility from losses. In order to ensure an interior solution, we impose the Inada condition, $\lim_{x \to 0} u'(x) = -\infty$.

A contract is given by four parameters, (w_L, w_M, w_H, a), where w_i is the contractible wage level if the observed output is y_i, and a is the *non-contractible, desired action*. We assume that the principal always wishes to induce the higher action, $a = 1$. Thus, we wish to focus attention on contracts of the form $(w_L, w_M, w_H, 1)$ in which the principal optimally chooses w_L, w_M, w_H. Let $u_i = u(w_i)$ and define the expected utility of the agent under the utility function u, and the expected cost of the principal under the distribution P by

$$\overline{u}(P) = p_H u_H + p_M u_M + p_L u_L, \overline{C}(P) = p_H w_H + p_M w_M + p_L w_L. \tag{3.64}$$

One can analogously define $\overline{u}(Q)$ and $\overline{C}(Q)$ under the distribution Q. Define

$$\Delta \overline{u}(P) = \overline{u}(P) - \overline{u}(Q), \Delta p_i = p_i - q_i, \Delta w_M = w_M - w_L; i = L, M, H.$$

With this definition, we can write the MLRP in Assumption A2 as

$$\frac{\Delta p_L}{p_L} < \frac{\Delta p_M}{p_M} < \frac{\Delta p_H}{p_H}. \tag{3.65}$$

The expected utility of the agent when he chooses the action $a = 1$ and induces the distribution P over outcomes can be written as

$$E_P v(w_i \mid w_M, 1) = \overline{u}(P) - p_L \lambda \Delta w_M - 1.$$

Similarly, the agent's expected utility when he takes action $a = 0$ and induces the distribution Q over outcomes is

$$E_Q v(w_i \mid w_M, 0) = \overline{u}(Q) - q_L \lambda \Delta w_M.$$

In order to implement the action $a = 1$, the principal chooses w_L, w_M, w_H to solve Problem 1:

$$Min \ \overline{C}(P)$$

subject to:

$$0 \leq w_L \leq w_M. \tag{NDW}$$
$$E_P v(w_i \mid w_M, 1) \geq 0 \Leftrightarrow \overline{u}(P) - p_L \lambda \Delta w_M - 1 \geq 0. \tag{IR}$$
$$E_P v(w_i \mid w_M, 1) \geq E_Q v(w_i \mid w_M, 0) \Leftrightarrow \Delta \overline{u}(P) - \Delta p_L \lambda \Delta w_M - 1 \geq 0. \tag{IC}$$

The first constraint restricts attention to non-decreasing wage schemes (NDW); this is motivated by the MLRP assumption. The *individual rationality constraint* (IR) requires that the agent earns at least his outside option of zero when he takes the action $a = 1$. Since the reference point is w_M, the agent only experiences a loss when he receives a wage w_L. The *incentive compatibility constraint* (IC) requires that the agent gets at least as much expected utility from taking the action $a = 1$ as he does from the action $a = 0$. Setting $\lambda = 0$ recovers the no loss aversion case.

Letting $\phi \geq 0$, $\gamma \geq 0$, $\mu \geq 0$ be the Lagrangian multipliers on the constraints, NDW, IR, and IC, respectively, the Lagrangian for the minimization problem, Problem 1, can be written as:

$$\Gamma = \overline{C}(P) + \gamma \left[-\overline{u}(P) + p_L \lambda \Delta w_M + 1 \right] + \mu \left[-\Delta \overline{u}(P) + \Delta p_L \lambda \Delta w_M + 1 \right] - \phi \Delta w_M. \tag{3.66}$$

Our assumptions on preferences and constraints ensure that the Kuhn–Tucker conditions are necessary and sufficient for a minimum. The Kuhn–Tucker conditions are as follows.

$$\frac{\partial \Gamma}{\partial w_H} = p_H - \gamma p_H u'_H - \mu \Delta p_H u'_H \geq 0. \tag{3.67}$$

$$\frac{\partial \Gamma}{\partial w_M} = p_M - \gamma \left(p_M u'_M - p_L \lambda \right) - \mu \left(\Delta p_M u'_M - \Delta p_L \lambda \right) - \phi \geq 0. \tag{3.68}$$

$$\frac{\partial \Gamma}{\partial w_L} = p_L - \gamma \left(p_L u'_L + p_L \lambda \right) - \mu \left(\Delta p_L u'_L + \Delta p_L \lambda \right) + \phi \geq 0. \tag{3.69}$$

$$\frac{\partial \Gamma}{\partial \gamma} \leq 0; \frac{\partial \Gamma}{\partial \mu} \leq 0; \frac{\partial \Gamma}{\partial \phi} \leq 0. \tag{3.70}$$

$$w_i \frac{\partial \Gamma}{\partial w_i} = 0, i = L, M, H. \tag{3.71}$$

$$\gamma \frac{\partial \Gamma}{\partial \gamma} = 0; \mu \frac{\partial \Gamma}{\partial \mu} = 0; \phi \frac{\partial \Gamma}{\partial \phi} = 0. \tag{3.72}$$

The first order conditions with respect to the state-contingent wages are given in (3.67)–(3.69). The condition (3.70) recovers the three constraints. The two complementary slackness conditions are given in (3.71) and (3.72). Given the Inada condition, $\lim_{x \to 0} u'(x) = -\infty$, it must be the case that $w_i > 0, i = L, M, H$, otherwise, $\frac{\partial \Gamma}{\partial w_i} < 0$, which is not possible. But if $w_i > 0$, then we get from (3.71) that $\frac{\partial \Gamma}{\partial w_i} = 0, i = L, M, H$.

The decision maker feels loss averse whenever $\Delta w_M > 0$. On the one hand, as in classical agency theory, $\Delta w_M > 0$ helps the principal to counter the moral hazard problem by providing higher incentives for better outcomes. However, because the agent is loss averse, this also requires a higher wage compensation to the agent in order to fulfill his IR condition. The size of this compensation is directly proportional to the loss aversion parameter, λ. Indeed, if λ is high enough, the second effect is likely to dominate the first effect, and the firm may find it optimal to set $\Delta w_M = 0$. In this case, the agent does not face any downside risk. De Meza and Webb (2007) conjecture that this case applies to CEO salary compensation that takes the form of stock options, which protect the CEO from downside risk. The next proposition formalizes this idea.

Proposition 3.8 *There exists a critical value of the parameter of loss aversion, λ_c, such that $\lambda \geq \lambda_c$ is necessary and sufficient for $\Delta w_M = w_M - w_L = 0$.*

Proof: Here we prove the if part. Suppose that $\Delta w_M = w_M - w_L = 0$, so $u'_L = u'_M$. Recall that $\frac{\partial \Gamma}{\partial w_i} = 0, i = L, M, H$. Thus, from (3.67) we must have

$$\frac{1}{u'_H} = \gamma + \mu \frac{\Delta p_H}{p_H}. \tag{3.73}$$

Adding (3.68), (3.69), noting that $\Delta w_M = 0$ and $u'_L = u'_M$, and dividing by $p_L + p_M$ we have

$$\frac{1}{u'_M} = \gamma - \mu \frac{\Delta p_H}{1 - p_H}. \tag{3.74}$$

First we show that in this case, $\gamma > 0$ and $\mu > 0$. Suppose not. If $\gamma = 0$, then from (3.74) we get $u'_M < 0$, which is a contradiction. If $\mu = 0$, then, from (3.73), (3.74), we have $u'_M = u'_H$. Thus, in this case $w_L = w_M = w_H$. However, if the agent is paid a fixed wage, then this destroys incentives and he will choose the minimum action, $a = 0$.[44] This contradicts the desired implementation of $a = 1$. Thus, it follows that $\gamma > 0$ and $\mu > 0$.

From (3.69), $\frac{\partial \Gamma}{\partial w_L} = 0$ implies that

$$1 + \frac{\phi}{p_L} = \left(u'_L + \lambda\right)\left(\gamma + \mu \frac{\Delta p_L}{p_L}\right). \tag{3.75}$$

When $\phi = 0$, (3.75) implies $\lambda = \lambda_c = \left(\gamma + \mu \frac{\Delta p_L}{p_L}\right)^{-1} - u'_L$. Thus, when $\lambda = \lambda_c$ it is optimal for the principal to choose $\Delta w_M = 0$. But for any $\phi > 0$, (3.75) implies that $\lambda > \lambda_c$ to ensure that our maintained assumption $\Delta w_M = 0$, holds. Thus, for $\phi \geq 0$ we have $\lambda \geq \lambda_c$ and $\phi \frac{\partial \Gamma}{\partial \phi} = 0$ implies $\frac{\partial \Gamma}{\partial \phi} = -\Delta w_M = 0$, or $\Delta w_M = 0$. We leave the if and only if part to the reader. ∎

Corollary 3.1 $\lambda < \lambda_c$ *is necessary and sufficient for* $\Delta w_M = w_M - w_L > 0$.

Proof: Proposition 3.8 shows that $\lambda \geq \lambda_c \Leftrightarrow \Delta w_M = 0$. Thus, if $\lambda < \lambda_c$, then $\Delta w_M \neq 0$. But $w_M < w_L$ would violate the MLRP when used in conjunction with (3.68), (3.69). So the only possibility is $\Delta w_M > 0$. ∎

Classical moral hazard theory predicts *high-powered incentives*, i.e., wage schemes that are very sensitive to the observed and verifiable outcomes. In real life, one typically observes incentives that are *low-powered*, relative to these predictions.[45] High enough loss aversion, by leading to flat segments in the optimal incentive scheme ($\Delta w_M = 0$; see Proposition 3.8) provides one potential explanation.

In Proposition 3.8, the incentive scheme is flat at the bottom of the outcome range. However, when there are more than three states of the world, then it is possible that the incentive scheme may be flat in the intermediate ranges. Consider, for instance, four possible states of the world, in which the output levels are $0 \leq y_S < y_L < y_M < y_H$. In all other respects, the model is identical to the one with three states. In this case, suppose that the principal wishes to implement the high action, $a = 1$. Then the optimal contract specifies the wage levels (w_S, w_L, w_M, w_H). The main result is summarized in the next proposition. The proof is similar to that of Proposition 3.8, so we leave it as an exercise.

Proposition 3.9 *(de Meza and Webb, 2003): There exist critical values of the parameter of loss aversion,* $\lambda_1 \geq \lambda_2 \geq 0$, *such that:*

(i) $\lambda \geq \lambda_1$ *is necessary and sufficient for* $w_S = w_L = w_M$.
(ii) $\lambda_1 \geq \lambda \geq \lambda_2$ *is necessary and sufficient for* $w_L = w_M$ *but* $w_S < w_L$.
(iii) $\lambda_1 \geq \lambda_2 \geq \lambda$ *is necessary and sufficient for* $w_S < w_L < w_M < w_H$.

The main insight of this analysis is that, relative to the predictions of the classical agency model, loss aversion may lead to low-powered incentive schemes. This insight helps to explain several interesting economic phenomena. Herweg and Mierendorff (2013) show that if loss aversion of consumers is high enough, then a monopolist risk-neutral seller finds it optimal to offer a two-part tariff to the consumer. This involves a fixed charge to be paid by the consumer, and a variable charge that depends on the number of units consumed. The authors argue that their framework

---

[44] The IC then gives $-1 \geq 0$, which is a contradiction.
[45] See Volume 2 for the empirical evidence.

provides the rationale for a fixed payment in situations where the competing explanations are not very persuasive.

Heidhues and Kőszegi (2005, 2008) consider a model of monopolist competition in which consumers are loss averse and have a reference price. If the price is higher than the reference price, they suffer a gain–loss disutility. Thus, at prices that exceed the reference point, firms compete more aggressively in prices. The reason is that lowering prices towards the reference price contributes greatly to an increase in consumer utility by avoiding expensive loss aversion. The reference point might then serve as a *focal point* around which firms compete. Loss aversion, thus, leads to non-responsiveness of prices to changes in economic circumstances, particularly when the desired price exceeds the focal reference price. Interestingly, a single focal price may exist even when firms are asymmetric. Spiegler (2012) considers a simplified version of this model. See Spiegler (2011, Chapter 9) for a further discussion of optimal contracts under loss aversion.

Herweg et al. (2010) consider another implication of loss aversion. They seek to explain why most real-world incentive schemes are of a binary nature, i.e., they have a fixed wage and a bonus payment that is conditional on the observed outcome exceeding a certain threshold. They consider a principal–agent framework with moral hazard on the part of the agent. The agent has Kőszegi–Rabin preferences; see Section 2.8 above. As in de Meza and Webb (2007), Herweg et al. (2010) show that loss aversion leads to lower-powered incentive schemes. However, the main insights of their paper arise from the manner in which it is optimal for the principal to bundle different signals of the agent's effort level, when providing a bonus. While it is not possible to give an exposition of their model without a fuller specification of the details, we consider below a simple example of the sorts of issues that can arise; the interested reader should pursue the much richer model in Herweg et al. (2010).

Suppose that the observable and verifiable output levels are $0 \leq y_1 \leq y_2 \leq \ldots \leq y_n$. The principal is interested in eliciting a particular effort level from the agent that gives rise to a probability distribution P over outcomes. So the outcomes $y_1, y_2, \ldots, y_n$ occur with the respective probabilities $p_1, p_2, \ldots, p_n$. In order to explain the intuition behind the results, let us restrict attention to the case of increasing wage schemes, so $0 \leq w_1 \leq w_2 \leq \ldots \leq w_n$. Assume also that the material utility is given by $m(x) = x$ and gain–loss utility, μ, is linear and is operative only for losses as in (2.76). Suppose that the realized state is i, with the associated wage w_i. Then, the Kőszegi–Rabin utility of the agent (see Section 2.8) is

$$u(w_i \mid r) = w_i - \sum_{j=i+1}^{n} p_j \lambda \left(w_j - w_i \right).$$

Thus, given $m(x) = x$ and (2.76), the expected Kőszegi–Rabin utility of the agent, prior to the realization of the state of the world is

$$Eu = \sum_{j=1}^{n} p_j u(w_j \mid r) = \sum_{j=1}^{n} p_j w_j - \lambda \sum_{i=1}^{n-1} p_i \sum_{j=i+1}^{n} p_j (w_j - w_i). \tag{3.76}$$

We now consider a sequence of hypothetical incentive schemes to illustrate the intuition behind the results. Suppose that we begin with an initial fixed wage contract, $w_j = w, j = 1, 2, \ldots, n$; we call this the *baseline contract*. In the baseline contract, there is no gain–loss utility, so the Kőszegi–Rabin utility, in (3.76), denoted by Eu_0, is

$$Eu_0 = w.$$

The baseline contract illustrates the classic conflict between insurance and incentives. By putting zero risk on the agent, the contract eliminates incentives completely, so a self-regarding agent will put in the least amount of effort. In other words, this contract is not incentive compatible. Starting from the baseline contract, consider a $n - 1$ *perturbed contract* that offers the following incentive structure

$$w_1 = w \text{ and } w_j = w + b, j = 2, 3, \ldots, n,$$

where $b > 0$ is a credible bonus payment. Recall that the distribution function of outcomes for the desired effort level is P. The expected Köszegi–Rabin utility, in (3.76), for the $n - 1$ *perturbed contract*, Eu_1, can be written as

$$Eu_1 = w + b(1 - P_1)(1 - \lambda P_1),$$

where $P_1 = Prob(y \le y_1)$. Now consider a $n - 2$ *perturbed contract*

$$w_1 = w_2 = w \text{ and } w_j = w + b, j = 3, 4, \ldots, n.$$

The expected Köszegi–Rabin utility, (3.76), for this incentive scheme, Eu_2, can be written as

$$Eu_2 = w + b(1 - P_2)(1 - \lambda P_2),$$

where $P_1 = Prob(y \le y_2)$. These calculations reveal the pattern of recursion. In general, for any $n - k$ *perturbed contract*

$$w_1 = w_2 = \ldots = w_k = w \text{ and } w_{k+1} = w_{k+2} = \ldots = w_n = w + b,$$

we have that the expected Köszegi–Rabin utility is

$$Eu_k = w + b(1 - P_k)(1 - \lambda P_k), \tag{3.77}$$

where $P_k = Prob(y \le y_k)$.

In the absence of loss aversion ($\lambda = 0$), bonus payments always increase the expected utility of the agent, hence, they serve to loosen the individual rationality constraint of the agent. The exact bonus payment may be calculated in such a manner that the individual rationality constraint always holds. Now consider the presence of loss aversion ($\lambda > 0$). If loss aversion is low enough, in the sense that $\lambda < \frac{1}{P_k}$ for all $k = 1, \ldots, n$, then using (3.77), bonuses for performance that exceeds some threshold always improve expected utility.

The more interesting situation arises when $\frac{1}{P_{k+1}} < \lambda < \frac{1}{P_k}$. In this case, offering bonuses for equalling or exceeding the output threshold of y_{k+1} (a $n - (k + 1)$ *perturbed contract*) reduces the expected utility of the agent. This result is contrary to that obtained in the standard model. Thus, once this threshold is reached, the principal will have to increase the fixed wage, w, of the agent to implement the desired effort. On the other hand if the performance threshold is chosen to be below y_{k+1}, say at y_k then bonuses for performance that exceeds y_k increase the expected utility of the agent. Such an incentive scheme loosens the individual rationality constraint and makes implementation of the desired effort easier. On the other hand if k is very high, then $1 - P_k$ is very low, which reduces the marginal impact on the agent's utility from an increase in the bonus payment. For a characterization of the optimal contract under these sorts of considerations, see Herweg et al. (2010).

3.12 Renegotiation, long-term contracts, and loss aversion

In the traditional theory of the firm, once the state of the world is realized, parties that are bound by some initial contract use Coasian bargaining to renegotiate to an efficient outcome. Suppose that the terms of the initial contract serve to form a reference point for loss averse contracting parties, as in Hart and Moore (2008). However, parties write a contract with each other before the realization of state of nature. Once the state of nature is realized, the contracting parties can renegotiate the ex-ante reference contract to an efficient ex-post contract.

An ex-post change in the terms of the contract through renegotiation may improve the payoff of one of the parties, but reduce the payoff of the other party. If the harmed party is loss averse, the extent of the harm is magnified. The party that benefits may be able to compensate the harm caused to the other party, but might not be able to compensate the scaled-up harm that arises on account of loss aversion. In this case, ex-post renegotiation may only be partially successful in altering the original contract towards the efficient outcome.

Furthermore, this might lead to sticky ex-post renegotiation; such renegotiation may take place only for a restricted range of states of nature, while for all other states, it completely breaks down. Anticipating these ex-post problems, the parties may not wish to write long-term contracts, preferring instead to use the spot market, particularly if the spot market is fairly competitive. We consider below these issues in a model due to Herweg and Schmidt (2013).

Consider a buyer (B) and a seller (S) who agree at date 0 on two contractual features of one unit of a good/widget that they might trade in the future. These features are: a specification $x \in X$ of the good, where X is a compact, possibly multidimensional, space, and a price p chosen from some non-negative closed real interval. Denote the set of states by Θ.

The sequence of moves is shown in Figure 3.12. At date 0, the two parties sign a contract $(\bar{x}, \bar{p})$. At date 1, a state of the world, $\theta \in \Theta$ is realized. This state determines which specification $x \in X$ of the traded good is most appropriate. At date 0, the two parties know that θ is distributed with the distribution function $F(\theta)$. They also know that ex-post, the state of the world is not verifiable to a third party, so they cannot write state-contingent contracts at date 0. Having observed the state at date 1, the parties can renegotiate to another feasible contract, $(\hat{x}, \hat{p})$, at date 2. If they fail to renegotiate, the default contract, $(\bar{x}, \bar{p})$ is implemented. The valuation of the buyer and the

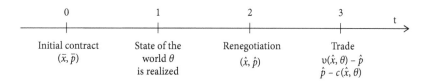

Figure 3.12 Sequence of moves in a bilateral trade model with renegotiation.

Source: Herweg, F. and Schmidt, K. M., "Loss aversion and inefficient renegotiation," Review of Economic Studies (2015) 82(1): 297–332, by permission of Oxford University Press.

cost of the seller are, respectively, $v(x,\theta)$ and $c(x,\theta)$. Their respective payoffs are $v(x,\theta) - p$ and $p - c(x,\theta)$, which are realized at date 3.

Define the joint surplus of the two parties as

$$W(x,\theta) = v(x,\theta) - c(x,\theta), x \in X, \theta \in \Theta.$$

We assume that $W(x,\theta)$ is strictly concave, so the first order conditions are sufficient. In any given state $\theta \in \Theta$, denote the socially optimum specification found by maximizing W with respect to $x \in X$ by $x^*(\theta)$. This is given by the solution to the following equation.

$$\frac{\partial W}{\partial x} = \frac{\partial v(x^*(\theta),\theta)}{\partial x} - \frac{\partial c(x^*(\theta),\theta)}{\partial x} = 0. \tag{3.78}$$

Both parties have Köszegi–Rabin utilities. Define gain–loss utility as in (2.76) by

$$\mu(z) = \begin{cases} 0 & \text{if } z > 0 \\ \lambda z & \text{if } z \leq 0 \end{cases}, \lambda > 0 \tag{3.79}$$

then the Köszegi–Rabin utilities of the buyer and the seller from the contract $(\widehat{x},\widehat{p})$, conditional on the state of the world $\theta \in \Theta$ are given, respectively, by

$$U_B(\widehat{x},\widehat{p};\theta) = v(\widehat{x},\theta) - \widehat{p} + \mu(\overline{p} - \widehat{p}) + \mu(v(\widehat{x},\theta) - v(\overline{x},\theta)). \tag{3.80}$$

$$U_S(\widehat{x},\widehat{p};\theta) = \widehat{p} - c(\widehat{x},\theta) + \mu(\widehat{p} - \overline{p}) + \mu(c(\overline{x},\theta) - c(\widehat{x},\theta)). \tag{3.81}$$

The original contract $(\overline{x},\overline{p})$ establishes the relevant entitlements that determine the subsequent gains and losses of the two parties. We assume a common or universal gain–loss function, so that the form of μ is identical for each party and in each dimension (price, valuation, or cost). Moreover, we assume that gain–loss utility from price variation and value/cost variation is additively separable. The buyer experiences a loss if the renegotiated price is higher than the date 0 price and the seller suffers a loss if it is lower. The buyer suffers a loss if the value of the renegotiated specification is lower than the date 0 specification and the seller suffers a loss if the cost of this specification is higher.

Clearly, if the original contract is not renegotiated, then there is no gain–loss utility, so

$$U_B(\overline{x},\overline{p};\theta) = v(\overline{x},\theta) - \overline{p} \text{ and } U_S(\overline{x},\overline{p};\theta) = \overline{p} - c(\overline{x},\theta). \tag{3.82}$$

Using (3.80)–(3.82) the buyer and the seller would wish to renegotiate if

$$B: v(\widehat{x},\theta) - v(\overline{x},\theta) + \mu(v(\widehat{x},\theta) - v(\overline{x},\theta)) \geq \widehat{p} - \overline{p} - \mu(\overline{p} - \widehat{p}). \tag{3.83}$$

$$S: c(\overline{x},\theta) - c(\widehat{x},\theta) + \mu(c(\overline{x},\theta) - c(\widehat{x},\theta)) \geq \overline{p} - \widehat{p} - \mu(\widehat{p} - \overline{p}). \tag{3.84}$$

Conditional on any initial contract, $(\overline{x},\overline{p})$, the set of contracts $(\widehat{x},\widehat{p})$ that satisfies (3.83), (3.84) is said to be *individually rational*. For a given initial contract, $(\overline{x},\overline{p})$, let the set of all individually rational contracts be denoted by $I(\overline{x},\overline{p})$. The *renegotiation set*, R, is simply the set of specifications of the good that the parties wish to voluntarily renegotiate to at some mutually agreed price, i.e.,

$$R(\overline{x},\overline{p}) = \{\widehat{x} \in X : \exists \widehat{p} \in P \text{ and } (\widehat{x},\widehat{p}) \in I(\overline{x},\overline{p})\}.$$

The next proposition summarizes the renegotiation possibilities.

Proposition 3.10 *Consider an initial contract $(\bar{x},\bar{p})$ at date 0, and the realization of a state $\theta \in \Theta$ at date 1. Then the renegotiation set $R(\bar{x},\bar{p})$ at date 2 is characterized as follows:*

(i) *For some $\hat{x} \in X$, if $v(\bar{x},\theta) \leq v(\hat{x},\theta)$ and $c(\bar{x},\theta) \geq c(\hat{x},\theta)$, then $\hat{x} \in R(\bar{x},\bar{p})$.*

(ii) *For some $\hat{x} \in X$, if $v(\bar{x},\theta) \leq v(\hat{x},\theta)$ and $c(\bar{x},\theta) \leq c(\hat{x},\theta)$, then $\hat{x} \in R(\bar{x},\bar{p})$ if and only if*

$$v(\hat{x},\theta) - v(\bar{x},\theta) \geq (1+\lambda)^2 \left[c(\hat{x},\theta) - c(\bar{x},\theta) \right]. \tag{3.85}$$

(iii) *For some $\hat{x} \in X$, if $v(\bar{x},\theta) \geq v(\hat{x},\theta)$ and $c(\bar{x},\theta) \geq c(\hat{x},\theta)$, then $\hat{x} \in R(\bar{x},\bar{p})$ if and only if*

$$c(\bar{x},\theta) - c(\hat{x},\theta) \geq (1+\lambda)^2 \left[v(\bar{x},\theta) - v(\hat{x},\theta) \right]. \tag{3.86}$$

Proof: (i) If there is a specification such that at date 2, the valuation of the buyer is higher and the cost of the seller is lower, then each party benefits by agreeing to renegotiate to this specification even if they kept the initial price $\bar{p}$, unchanged.

(ii) Since renegotiation is voluntary, the buyer will have to offer $\hat{p} \geq \bar{p}$ in order to cover the higher costs of the seller. Thus, the buyer suffers a loss in the price domain and a gain in the valuation domain. The seller suffers a loss in the cost domain and a gain in the price domain. From (3.79), (3.83), (3.84) we get that

$$v(\hat{x},\theta) - v(\bar{x},\theta) \geq (1+\lambda)(\hat{p} - \bar{p}) \Leftrightarrow \hat{p} \leq \bar{p} + \frac{v(\hat{x},\theta) - v(\bar{x},\theta)}{1+\lambda}. \tag{3.87}$$

$$(1+\lambda)(c(\bar{x},\theta) - c(\hat{x},\theta)) \geq \bar{p} - \hat{p} \Leftrightarrow \hat{p} \geq \bar{p} - (1+\lambda)(c(\bar{x},\theta) - c(\hat{x},\theta)). \tag{3.88}$$

Hence, we get

$$\bar{p} - (1+\lambda)(c(\bar{x},\theta) - c(\hat{x},\theta)) \leq \bar{p} + \frac{v(\hat{x},\theta) - v(\bar{x},\theta)}{1+\lambda}. \tag{3.89}$$

Simplifying (3.88), we get (3.85), as claimed. Thus, $\hat{x} \in R(\bar{x},\bar{p})$ for any $\hat{x}$ satisfying (3.85).

(iii) In this case, the seller must offer a price reduction to the buyer in order to induce him to voluntarily renegotiate. Thus, the buyer faces a loss in the value dimension and the seller faces a loss in the price dimension. Using (3.79), (3.83), (3.84) and proceeding as in the proof of part (ii), an easy calculation gives rise to the claimed result. ∎

Proposition 3.10 illustrates at least two ideas:

1. In the absence of loss aversion ($\lambda = 0$) each of the renegotiation conditions (3.85) and (3.86) is easier to satisfy. Consider, for instance, (3.85). It might be the case that $v(\hat{x},\theta) - v(\bar{x},\theta) \geq c(\hat{x},\theta) - c(\bar{x},\theta)$ but $v(\hat{x},\theta) - v(\bar{x},\theta) < (1+\lambda)^2 \left[c(\hat{x},\theta) - c(\bar{x},\theta) \right]$. Hence, the presence of loss aversion may create stickiness in renegotiation.

2. The results in Proposition 3.10 are independent of prices. This is because the utilities are quasilinear in prices and specifications.

Next, we need to specify how the two parties bargain at date 2. Herweg and Schmidt (2013) assume that the two parties bargain by using generalized Nash bargaining.[46] For expositional ease, we consider instead the two polar extremes in which either the buyer or the seller have all the bargaining power. In what follows, we consider the case where the buyer has all the bargaining power (as an exercise, the reader can work through the case where the seller has all the bargaining power).

To make further progress, let us consider the following example.

$$v(x,\theta) = \theta x, \quad c(x,\theta) = \frac{1}{2}x^2 + \frac{1}{3}\theta. \tag{3.90}$$

Using (3.78), we get the unique socially optimal (or first best) state-contingent solution

$$x^*(\theta) = \theta. \tag{3.91}$$

Suppose that the two parties have agreed to a contract $(\bar{x}, \bar{p})$ at date 0. For simplicity, let us normalize $\bar{x} = 1$. Define $\bar{\theta}$ such that

$$\frac{\partial v(1, \bar{\theta})}{\partial x} = \frac{\partial c(1, \bar{\theta})}{\partial x},$$

so, using (3.91), $\bar{\theta} = 1$.

Suppose that at date 1, the realized state of the world is $\theta_H > 1$. How should the two parties renegotiate at date 2? There are two possibilities.

I. For any $\hat{x} > 1$, $v(1, \theta_H) < v(\hat{x}, \theta_H)$ and $c(1, \theta_H) < c(\hat{x}, \theta_H)$. The buyer experiences an increase in value and the seller experiences an increase in cost. This is the case described in Proposition 3.10(ii), hence, $\hat{x} \in R(1, \bar{p})$ if and only if (3.85) holds. Using (3.90), we can write (3.85) as

$$\theta_H(\hat{x} - 1) \geq (1 + \lambda)^2 \frac{1}{2}(\hat{x}^2 - 1) \Leftrightarrow \lambda \leq \sqrt{\frac{2\theta_H}{(\hat{x} + 1)}} - 1. \tag{3.92}$$

In the absence of loss aversion ($\lambda = 0$), the condition in (3.92) is more likely to be satisfied. However, if loss aversion is high enough, then no renegotiation can take place. Using (3.92), $\hat{x} \in R(\bar{x}, \bar{p})$ if

$$\theta_H \geq \frac{(1 + \lambda)^2}{2}(\hat{x} + 1). \tag{3.93}$$

Thus, when, say, $\lambda = 1$, θ_H must exceed the critical value of 4 before any renegotiation can occur. So, we have that at date 3, $x = \bar{x} = 1$ for $1 \leq \theta \leq 4$. However, for any θ in this range, the socially efficient outcome is $x^*(\theta) = \theta$. Thus, loss aversion leads to rigidity in contract renegotiation, in the sense that there is a set of states for which it is socially optimal to renegotiate but privately suboptimal.

Since the buyer is assumed to have all the bargaining power, he ensures that the individual rationality constraint of the seller in (3.88) holds with equality. Thus,

---

[46] For various bargaining solutions, and the empirical evidence, see Volume 4.

$$\widehat{p}(\widehat{x}) = \overline{p} + (1+\lambda)\frac{1}{2}\left(\widehat{x}^2 - 1\right). \tag{3.94}$$

II. For any $\widehat{x} < 1$ we have $v(1,\theta_H) > v(\widehat{x},\theta_H)$ and $c(1,\theta_H) > c(\widehat{x},\theta_H)$. The buyer's value falls and the seller's cost also falls, so this is the case in Proposition 3.10(iii), hence, $\widehat{x} \in R(1,\overline{p})$ if and only if (3.86) holds. Using (3.90), we can write (3.86) as

$$\frac{1}{2}\left(1-\widehat{x}^2\right) \geq (1+\lambda)^2\theta_H(1-\widehat{x}) \Leftrightarrow \lambda \leq \sqrt{\frac{(1+\widehat{x})}{2\theta_H}} - 1. \tag{3.95}$$

Since λ is non-negative, $\widehat{x} < 1$ and $\theta_H > 1$, so (3.95) cannot hold. Thus, following a realization of any state $\theta_H > \overline{\theta} = 1$, the two contracting parties never reduce the specification of the good that they trade. The only relevant case, therefore, is Case I.

Substitute $\widehat{p}(\widehat{x})$ from (3.94) into (3.80) and use the assumed functional forms in (3.90) to get

$$U_B(\widehat{x},\widehat{p}(\widehat{x});\theta_H) = \theta_H\widehat{x} - \widehat{p}(\widehat{x}) - \lambda\left(\widehat{p}(\widehat{x}) - \overline{p}\right); \ 1 < \theta_H \in \Theta. \tag{3.96}$$

The buyer experiences a loss in the price dimension (last term in (3.96)) and a gain in the value dimension, but given (3.79), the gain is set to zero. Since the buyer has all the bargaining power, the ex-post solution $\widehat{x} = \widehat{x}^*$ maximizes $U_B(\widehat{x},\widehat{p}(\widehat{x});\theta_H)$.

$$\frac{\partial U_B(\widehat{x},\widehat{p}(\widehat{x});\theta_H)}{\partial \widehat{x}} = \theta_H - (1+\lambda)^2\widehat{x}.$$

It is immediate that U_B is strictly concave and the first order condition is sufficient. Thus,

$$\widehat{x}^* = \frac{\theta_H}{(1+\lambda)^2}. \tag{3.97}$$

There are two noteworthy features of the renegotiated solution under loss aversion. First, the socially optimal solution requires $x^*(\theta) = \theta$. But when renegotiation takes place, we have $\widehat{x}^* < x^*$, i.e., the specification is lower than the socially optimal specification. Second, the socially optimal solution requires a one for one adjustment of the specification to θ (because $x^*(\theta) = \theta$), while the renegotiated solution in (3.97) exhibits a less than one for one adjustment to θ. Coupled with the fact that renegotiation takes place for only some values of θ (see (3.93)) it follows that in the presence of loss aversion, renegotiation is inefficient and sluggish.

Substituting $\widehat{x}^*$ in (3.94) gives the optimal solution for the renegotiated price, $\widehat{p}^* = \widehat{p}(\widehat{x}^*)$. Thus, the utility of the buyer from the long-term contract in any state of the world, $\theta_H > 1$, is given by $U_B(\widehat{x}^*,\widehat{p}^*;\theta_H)$. One can proceed analogously to find the utility of the buyer from a long-term contract for any $\theta_L < 1$. Integrating over all states $\theta \in \Theta$ gives the expected utility of the buyer from a long-term contract, U_B^{LT}.

The other possibility is that the parties may not sign a long-term contract, but following the realization of θ at date 1, choose to trade on the spot market. Should the buyer prefer spot markets? The answer depends on three factors.

1. The degree of competition in the spot market: the greater the competition, the lower is the spot price, so the higher is the utility of the buyer.

2. Reference point of the buyer in the spot market: In a long-term contract, the initial contract serves as an entitlement. However, adjustment to the realized state is easier in a spot contract because there is no initial contract. In a simple class of models this may be mathematically similar to having a lower value of loss aversion in spot market contracts (see Herweg and Schmidt, 2013).

3. The degree of loss aversion in long-term contracts. The greater the loss aversion, the higher is the inefficiency and sluggishness of renegotiation in long-term contracts, which reduces their attractiveness.

We refer the reader to Herweg and Schmidt (2013) for a more detailed analysis of these factors.[47]

---

[47] The interested reader can also consult Herweg et al. (2014) for an application of the UPE concept to the incomplete contracts problem.

CHAPTER 4

Human Behavior under Ambiguity

4.1 Introduction

Ambiguity arises when individual choices depend on the *source* of the uncertain information, but within each source, the individual possesses reasonable subjective probabilities (non-negative probabilities that add to one). This is sometimes also referred to as *source-dependent uncertainty*. Ambiguity is a major topic, and deserves a book length treatment in its own right. However, the discussion in this chapter is relatively brief.[1] The reason is that the approach of most of the modern literature on ambiguity does not appear behavioral enough. A troubling feature of several of these models is that under pure risk they simply reduce to expected utility theory, which is not supported by the evidence.

For this reason, we have split this chapter into two parts. Section 4.3 outlines *neoclassical models of ambiguity*, and Section 4.4 considers *behavioral models of ambiguity*. There is, by no means, a neat or established separation between the two sets of models. However, the main difference is that all the models in Section 4.4 do not reduce to EU under pure risk, while many of the models in Section 4.3 do.[2] In order to maintain brevity of discussion, we focus almost exclusively on the *Ellsberg paradox* and consider its resolution in the different models.

In Section 4.2, we consider the classic Ellsberg paradox that illustrates the phenomenon of ambiguity in lab experiments. Suppose that one urn, the *known urn*, is known to have 50 red and 50 black balls. Another urn, the *unknown urn*, has 100 balls of only two colors, red and black, but their exact composition is unknown. As a first pass, one may appeal to the *principle of insufficient reason* to argue that the prior probability of a red and a black ball from the unknown urn is 0.5 each. Indeed, when individuals are asked to bet *separately* on the two urns, the evidence suggests that they assign equal probabilities to drawing either a red or a black ball from either urn. This is the sense in which they have reasonable subjective beliefs about each urn. However, individuals are unwilling to exchange a bet on any color on the known urn with the same bet on the unknown urn. This is the sense in which the subjective beliefs across the two urns are

---

[1] The reader can also consult Ch. 17 in Gilboa (2009), Ch. 11 in Wakker (2010), Etner et al. (2012), and Machina and Siniscalchi (2014) for more details.

[2] This is not true of several models. For instance, Choquet expected utility (CEU) that is considered in Section 4.3 does not reduce to EU for the case of risk.

not reasonable. The decision maker is then said to have a preference for avoiding ambiguity (or source-dependent uncertainty) associated with the unknown urn.[3] Thus, SEU cannot be applied because no consistent subjective probabilities exist. The Ellsberg paradox is also a violation of *probabilistic sophistication* (Definition 1.13).

Section 4.3 gives a brief discussion of the neoclassical models of ambiguity and outlines their explanation for the Ellsberg paradox. Section 4.3.1 discusses *non-additive probability measures* (or *capacities* or *Choquet capacities*). Choquet capacities are different from probabilities in that they need not be additive.[4] This framework gives rise to *Choquet expected utility* (CEU) and is able to explain the Ellsberg paradox.

Section 4.3.2 describes the *multiple priors model*. In this class of models, decision makers have probability distributions over their prior beliefs that reflect their uncertainty about the true model of the world (Gilboa and Schmeidler, 1989). We describe the *maximin model* and its two main axioms. The maximin model has a pessimistic attitude to uncertainty. Among the set of minimum outcomes achieved through all actions, the decision makers choose the action with the maximum outcome. None of the axioms used in deriving such a preference representation gives any explicit clue about this extreme degree of pessimism. We also describe another popular multiple priors model, the *α-MEU model* (Hurwicz, 1951; Ghirardato et al., 2004).[5] This class of models can also explain the Ellsberg paradox.

Section 4.3.3 considers the *failure of the reduction of compound lotteries axiom* as an explanation of the Ellsberg paradox in a *two-stage recursive model* (Segal, 1987, 1990). Section 4.3.4 considers the *smooth ambiguity aversion model* (Klibanoff et al., 2005). Unlike some models of multiple priors, such as the *maximin model*, the objective function here is differentiable. The two-stage recursive models and the smooth ambiguity aversion models are both multiple priors models. However, the main difference between the two is that the smooth ambiguity aversion model uses a different utility function at each stage. Ambiguity is captured by the concavity of the second stage utility function and the burden of explaining risk and ambiguity attitudes in this model lies with the utility function.

Section 4.3.5 gives a brief account of other models that can account for the Ellsberg paradox. Section 4.3.6 shows that the empirical evidence for neoclassical models of ambiguity aversion is mixed (Hey et al., 2010; Conte and Hey, 2013). No single model can account for all the experimental results. What causes ambiguity aversion? Some experimental evidence suggests that *fear of negative evaluation by others* and one's competence in the problem could be important explanations (Curley et al., 1986; Trautmann et al. 2008).

Section 4.4 considers the small literature on behavioral models of ambiguity. None of these models reduce to EU under pure risk. In Section 4.4.1, we consider promising work that was conducted in the 1990s on *support theory* but was ignored by the subsequent literature in economics. This work is associated most with the names of Amos Tversky and his collaborators. In *support theory*, the support for one hypothesis over another depends on how the two hypotheses are framed and how events are subdivided. For instance, the probability that one assigns to death by homicide in an area might be lower than the sum of probabilities that one assigns to homicide by friends and homicide by strangers, although classically the two

---

[3] It is possible to define ambiguity generally as a preference for information from one source relative to another; see Definition 11.1.1 in Wakker (2010).

[4] Lack of additivity means that for two disjoint events, E_i, E_j, in some well-defined sample space, the subjective probability $\mu(E_i \cup E_j)$ need not equal $\mu(E_i) + \mu(E_j)$.

[5] Luce and Raiffa (1957) already discuss multiple priors (maximin EU) and the α-maximin model (see their Ch. 13 on ambiguity, with §13.5 pp. 304–5). I am grateful to Peter Wakker for pointing this out.

answers should be identical. Splitting the event into its components, brings more such instances to mind (as in the *availability heuristic*), hence, increasing its perceived probability. In support theory, in the first stage, individuals form beliefs about events by using such considerations. Once these beliefs are formed, then one evaluates the uncertain situation using PT.

Section 4.4.2 considers the possibility that decision makers perceive information from different *sources* of uncertainty in a fundamentally different manner (Abdellaoui, Baillon et al., 2011). Applied to the Ellsberg paradox, in this view, each urn is a different source of uncertainty. This accounts for the unwillingness of decision makers to exchange bets on the known urn (first source) with bets on the unknown urn (second source). Empirical results presented by the authors confirm this view, although they also reveal a rich diversity in the attitudes of individuals to uncertainty. In particular, the differences in the two Ellsberg urns cannot be ascribed to differences in the utility functions but rather to the elicited probability weighting functions (or source functions) across them. In an important study that applies these concepts, PT outperforms all others in an 11-way horse race (Kothiyal et al., 2014). This strengthens the case for PT to apply to risk, uncertainty, and ambiguity, which is a central theme that runs through Wakker (2010).

The explanation of ambiguity in these behavioral models is different from neoclassical models, such as the smooth ambiguity aversion model. The neoclassical models locate the source of ambiguity aversion in the shape of the utility function. This is analogous to the feature of EU under risk and uncertainty, which places the entire burden of risk attitudes on the shape of the utility function; a finding that is rejected by the evidence. On the other hand, non-EU theories such RDU and PT rely jointly on the shapes of the utility function and the probability weighting function in capturing attitudes to risk; a finding that is consistent with the evidence.

4.2 A problem for SEU: The Ellsberg paradox

Under uncertainty, there is no problem in applying EU, RDU, or PT (see Sections 1.3, 2.3.2, and 2.4) provided that decision makers have well-defined subjective probabilities. However, evidence suggests that this assumption might not always hold. The most famous example of this is the Ellsberg (1961) paradox. We present two variants of the Ellsberg paradox below; the two-colors and the three-colors experiment.

Example 4.1 *(Two-colors experiment): Consider the simplest demonstration of the Ellsberg paradox, the two-colors experiment. Urn 1 has 50 red and 50 black balls, while Urn 2 contains 100 balls that are an unknown mixture of red and black balls.*

(1) *Suppose that subjects are asked to bet on a color (a red or a black ball) for each urn and they receive a monetary prize, z, if a ball of their chosen color is drawn. Subjects reveal, through their choices, that they are indifferent among the two colors for each urn.[6] Thus, they appear to assign equal probabilities to the two colors in both urns.*

(2) *Now suppose that subjects, in addition, are also asked which urn they would like to bet on. Irrespective of their chosen color, they typically choose Urn 1 over Urn 2.*
Let p_r and p_b represent the subjective probabilities of a red and a black ball, respectively, in Urn 2 such that $p_r + p_b = 1$. Then, the indifference in (1) implies that $p_r = 0.5$. However, if the chosen color is red, the preference for Urn 1

---

[6] The original Ellsberg experiments were not incentivized and are thought experiments. However, once these potential drawbacks are addressed by modern experimental methods (see below) the results still survive.

Table 4.1 Description of the four Savage acts in the three-colors experiment.

	r	b	y
f_1	100	0	0
f_2	0	100	0
f_3	100	0	100
f_4	0	100	100

implies that $0.5u(z) > p_r u(z) \Leftrightarrow p_r < 0.5$. Analogously if the chosen color is black, the stated preference implies $0.5u(z) > p_b u(z) \Leftrightarrow p_b < 0.5$. This contradicts $p_r = p_b = 0.5$ from (1). Hence, the subjects do not hold reasonable subjective beliefs.[7] Furthermore, this violates probabilistic sophistication (see Definition 1.13).

Example 4.2 *(Three-colors experiment) In the three-colors experiment, subjects are told that an urn contains 90 balls of 3 different colors: red, black, and yellow. There are 30 red balls and the remaining balls are either black or yellow. One ball is drawn at random from the urn. Let r, b, y be the events: red ball, black ball, and yellow ball. The minimum "reasonableness" that we might expect from subjective beliefs is that they should satisfy an additive probability measure, q, such that*

$$q(r) = \frac{1}{3}, \ q(b) = 1 - p - \frac{1}{3}; q(y) = p; \ p \in [0, 2/3]. \tag{4.1}$$

The decision maker is offered a choice between the following two pairs of lotteries or Savage acts (see Section 1.3).

$$f_1 = (r, 100; b, 0; y, 0) \ and \ f_2 = (r, 0; b, 100; y, 0), \tag{4.2}$$

$$f_3 = (r, 100; b, 0; y, 100) \ and \ f_4 = (r, 0; b, 100; y, 100). \tag{4.3}$$

Thus, for instance, the Savage act f_2 is the lottery that pays $100 if a black ball turns up but $0 if any other color comes up. Analogously, the Savage act f_4 is the lottery that pays $100 if either a black or a yellow ball is drawn and $0 if a red ball comes up. This information is summarized in Table 4.1.

Subjects in experiments, typically express the preferences $f_1 \succ f_2$ and $f_4 \succ f_3$. Assuming SEU preferences (see Section 1.3), these preferences imply the following inequalities.

$$f_1 \succ f_2 \Leftrightarrow \frac{1}{3}u(100) > \left(1 - p - \frac{1}{3}\right)u(100) \Leftrightarrow p > \frac{1}{3}. \tag{4.4}$$

$$f_4 \succ f_3 \Leftrightarrow \frac{1}{3}u(100) + pu(100) < \left(1 - p - \frac{1}{3}\right)u(100) + pu(100) \Leftrightarrow p < \frac{1}{3}. \tag{4.5}$$

From (4.4) and (4.5), the decision maker does not assign consistent subjective probabilities. This is an illustration of the Ellsberg paradox.

The examples suggest the following observations.

---

[7] This problem was also discussed by Keynes (1921).

1. The preferences $f_1 \succ f_2$ and $f_4 \succ f_3$ suggest that the decision maker tries to search for greater certainty in the probability of the outcome. For instance, the preference $f_1 \succ f_2$ may suggest that the decision maker wishes to avoid the possibility that the probability of the black ball is very small or zero. Similarly, in the preference $f_4 \succ f_3$, the decision maker knows that the probability of getting a prize of 100 under f_4 is 2/3, while under f_3 it might just be 1/3. This is the sense in which the individual is *ambiguity averse*.

2. From Table 4.1, the outcomes under the two Savage acts f_1, f_2 are identical if a yellow ball comes up but $f_1 \succ f_2$. Similarly, the outcomes under the two Savage acts f_3, f_4 are identical if a yellow ball comes up. If Savage's *sure thing principle* (see Definition 1.11) is applied we should observe $f_3 \succ f_4$. However, we observe $f_4 \succ f_3$. Hence, the Ellsberg paradox is essentially a violation of the sure thing principle. For this reason, explanations of the Ellsberg paradox have typically tried to relax this principle.

3. The Ellsberg paradox violates probabilistic sophistication (Definition 1.13). For instance, in the two-colors experiment in Example 4.1 above, for each urn, separately, $p_r = 0.5$ but when the two urns are compared, the decision maker does not behave as if $p_r = 0.5$. It is as if the probabilities depend on the act itself.[8] Suppose that an individual bets on the color red when presented with each urn separately. Let xi denote the event that a ball of color $x = $ Red, Black is drawn from urn $i = 1, 2$. Then for each urn, the expressed preference is $(Red1, z; Black1, 0) \sim (z, 0.5, 0, 0.5)$ and $(Red2, z; Black2, 0) \sim (z, 0.5, 0, 0.5)$, where $\sim$ is the indifference relation, so probabilistic sophistication holds for each urn separately. But $(Red1, z; Black1, 0) \succ (Red2, z; Black2, 0)$, so $(z, 0.5, 0, 0.5) \succ (z, 0.5, 0, 0.5)$, where $\succ$ is the strict preference relation; this is a contradiction of probabilistic sophistication.

We now consider alternative explanations of the Ellsberg paradox within two classes of models. The neoclassical approach and the behavioral approach.

4.3 Neoclassical models of ambiguity

In this section, we consider models of ambiguity that are based on the neoclassical tradition. There is no clear dividing line between models in the neoclassical and the behavioral traditions, so any such division is necessarily arbitrary. However, in the presence of pure risk, many of the models in this section collapse to expected utility, but clearly some such as Choquet expected utility do not. Given the refutations of EU (see Chapter 1), this is clearly a troublesome feature of many of these models (Wakker, 2010); and some may argue, a direct refutation of these models. By contrast, the behavioral models of ambiguity (see Section 4.4) do not typically reduce to EU under risk. Furthermore, the main difference between the neoclassical and the main behavioral models of ambiguity is that, in the behavioral models, ambiguity is *source-dependent*.

The following two comments on this class of models illustrate the reservations that many behavioral economists have with the neoclassical approach to ambiguity, despite its immense popularity and widespread acceptance. Hey (2014, p. 838) writes: "We remain agnostic as to whether these can be really considered as models of ambiguity." Kothiyal et al. (2014, p. 3) write: "Since 1990, quantitative ambiguity models have become available (Gilboa 1987; Gilboa & Schmeidler 1989; Schmeidler 1989), and many extensions have been proposed ... These models

---

[8] Probabilistic sophistication was originally introduced by Machina and Schmeidler (1992). For subsequent developments, see Grant (1995) and Chew and Sagi (2006). See also the exposition in Wakker (2010).

were all normatively motivated … assuming expected utility for risk, backward induction in an Anscombe-Aumann (1963) model, and (with α-maximin excepted) universal ambiguity aversion. These assumptions, even if accepted normatively, fail descriptively." For this reason, we provide a relatively brief treatment of these models, focusing mainly on their approach to the Ellsberg paradox.

4.3.1 Choquet expected utility

One resolution to the Ellsberg paradox is to employ non-additive probability measures. Consider a sample space, S and a sigma algebra Σ of the subsets of S.

> **Definition 4.1** *A sigma algebra Σ corresponding to a sample space S is a set of subsets of S such that the following hold. (i) The empty set $\varnothing \in \Sigma$. (ii) If $A \in \Sigma$, then $A^c \in \Sigma$, where A^c is the complement of A. (iii) For countably many sets $A_1, A_2, \ldots A_n, \ldots \in \Sigma$, the union $A_1 \cup A_2 \cup \ldots \cup A_n \cup \ldots \in \Sigma$.*

The non-additive measure, $\varsigma : \Sigma \to [0,1]$, also sometimes called a *capacity* or *Choquet capacity*, has the following properties.

1. $\varsigma(\varnothing) = 0$, where $\varnothing$ is the empty set.
2. If $A \subseteq B$, then $\varsigma(A) \leq \varsigma(B)$; $A, B \in \Sigma$.
3. $\varsigma(S) = 1$.

Thus, as with probability measures, the probability assigned to the empty set, $\varnothing$, is zero, while the probability assigned to the entire sample space, S, is one. However, the main difference lies in the weaker requirement in Property 2. For an additive probability measure, say, p, and for disjoint events A, B, $p(A \cup B) = p(A) + p(B)$. However, Property 2 does not impose any such condition for a non-additive probability measure. The triple (S, Σ, ς) is known as the *capacity space*.

Recall that for any partition of a sample space, S, into a set of *mutually exclusive* events $\{E_1, \ldots, E_n\}$, a Savage act $f : S \to X$. Suppose that the outcomes or prizes corresponding to the events $E_1, \ldots, E_n$ are, respectively, $z_1, \ldots, z_n$. We assume that the events are arranged, so that $0 < z_1 < \ldots < z_n$ and $f = \{E_1, z_1; \ldots; E_n, z_n\}$. Let F be the set of all Savage acts (or lotteries) under consideration. For non-additive measures, the Riemann integral is not adequate (Gilboa, 2009, pp. 148–9). The *Choquet integral* that we define next, turns out to be useful in this regard.

> **Definition 4.2** *(Choquet integral): Consider the capacity space (S, Σ, ς). Define a Savage act $f = \{E_1, z_1; \ldots; E_n, z_n\}$, $0 < z_1 < \ldots < z_n$, over a sigma algebra, Σ, of the sample space S. The Choquet integral of f with respect to the Choquet capacity ς is given by:*

$$\int_S f d\varsigma = \sum_{j=1}^{n} z_j \left[\varsigma\left(\cup_{k=j}^{n} E_k\right) - \varsigma\left(\cup_{k=j+1}^{n} E_k\right)\right]. \tag{4.6}$$

If ς were additive, then $\varsigma\left(\cup_{k=j}^{n} E_k\right) = \sum_{k=j}^{n} \varsigma(E_k)$, so (4.6) can be written as

$$\int_S f d\varsigma = \sum_{j=1}^{n} z_j \varsigma(E_j),$$

which is simply the Riemann integral.

> **Definition 4.3** *(Comonotonicity): Consider two Savage acts $f = (s_1, z_1; \ldots; s_n, z_n)$, and $g = (s_1, x_1; \ldots; s_n, x_n)$. Then f and g are comonotonic if for all i, j*

$$f(s_i) < f(s_j) \Rightarrow g(s_i) < g(s_j),$$

> *where $f(s_i) = z_i$ and $g(s_j) = x_j$ for all $i, j = 1, \ldots, n$.*

For our next definitions, we need to define mixtures over horse-roulette acts. Hence, we introduce the following terminology (Machina and Siniscalchi, 2014). Recall that we represented a lottery under objective probabilities in the *one-stage form* as $L = (x_1, p_1; \ldots; x_n, p_n)$. Consider a partition $E_1, \ldots, E_m$ of the sample space. A *horse-roulette act* or an *Anscombe–Aumann act* (or an *objective–subjective prospect*) takes the form, $(L_1, E_1; \ldots; L_m, E_m)$ with the interpretation that the decision maker plays the objective lottery L_i if the event E_i takes place. Thus, horse-roulette acts are mappings from the sample space to the objective, single-stage, lotteries. These sorts of lotteries were used by Anscombe and Aumann (1963) in providing an axiomatic derivation of subjective expected utility (SEU) that is simpler than the axiomatization in Savage (1954).

Recall that mixtures over objective one-stage lotteries are defined as follows. If $L_1 = (x_1, p_1; \ldots; x_n, p_n)$ and $L_2 = (y_1, q_1; \ldots; y_m, q_m)$, then for $\alpha \in (0, 1)$ the $\alpha : (1 - \alpha)$ probability mixture of L_1 and L_2, is denoted by

$$\alpha L_1 + (1 - \alpha)L_2 = (x_1, \alpha p_1; \ldots; x_n, \alpha p_n; y_1, (1 - \alpha)q_1; \ldots; y_m, (1 - \alpha)q_m).$$

If the reduction of compound lotteries axiom holds, then one can reduce the mixture lottery to an objective one-stage lottery such that for any common prize, $x_i = y_i$, in the two lotteries L_1 and L_2, the corresponding probability is $\alpha p_i + (1 - \alpha)q_i$.

In most models of ambiguity aversion, preferences are defined over horse-roulette acts (or simply "acts"). Probability mixtures over such acts are constructed as follows. Suppose that we have a common partition $\{E_1, \ldots, E_n\}$ of the sample space. For two acts $f = (L_1, E_1; \ldots; L_n, E_n)$ and $g = (L'_1, E_1; \ldots; L'_n, E_n)$, and $\alpha \in (0, 1)$, the $\alpha : (1 - \alpha)$ mixture of f and g, is defined as

$$\alpha f + (1 - \alpha)g = (\alpha L_1 + (1 - \alpha)L'_1, E_1; \ldots; \alpha L_n + (1 - \alpha)L'_n, E_n).$$

Definition 4.4 *(Comonotonic independence): Consider three acts f, g, h that satisfy pairwise comonotonicity and let $\succeq$ denote the decision maker's preference relation. Then comonotonic independence implies that*

$$f \succeq g \Leftrightarrow \alpha f + (1 - \alpha)h \succeq \alpha g + (1 - \alpha)h \text{ for all } \alpha \in (0, 1).$$

Schmeidler (1986, 1989) demonstrated axiomatically that if the relevant notion of independence is comonotonic independence, then,

$$f \succeq g \Leftrightarrow \int_S u(f)d\varsigma \geq \int_S u(g)d\varsigma,$$

where the relevant notion of integration is Choquet integration (Definition 4.2), ς is a capacity and u is a non-constant function such that $u : X \to R$. $\int_S u(f)d\varsigma$ is termed as the Choquet expected utility (CEU) of the act, f.[9]

Allowing for subjective, non-additive, beliefs raises problems for the Pareto criterion in welfare economics. Consider, for instance, the following hypothetical problem posed by Gilboa et al. (2004). In an age of chivalry, two gentlemen, A and B, are considering a resolution of a nagging dispute by engaging in a duel. The objective probability that A wins is p and that B wins is $1 - p$. However the two gentlemen do not know the objective probabilities. Given their tastes, each prefers to engage in the duel if their respective probability of winning is greater than 0.8. Suppose that A and B assign respective subjective probabilities of their winning the duel at 0.9. It is, therefore, privately optimal for each to fight the duel; indeed it is Pareto optimal to duel,

---

[9] For other axiomatizations of CEU, see Gilboa (1987), Nakamura (1990), Sarin and Wakker (1992), Ghirardato et al. (2003), and Lehrer (2009).

based on such subjective probabilities. However, there are no objective probabilities $p, 1 - p$ such that it is optimal to duel. Hence, it may not seem justified for society to accept the individual preferences for a duel, knowing that at least one of the gentlemen has got his beliefs wrong.

Let us now give an explanation of the preferences observed in the three-colors experiment in Example 4.2. Under the four acts in Example 4.2, the sample space is

$$S = \big\{\{r\}, \{b\}, \{y\}, \{r, b\}, \{r, y\}, \{b, y\}\big\}.$$

Suppose that we assign the following capacities to these events

$$\varsigma(r) = \varsigma(rb) = \varsigma(ry) = \frac{1}{3}; \varsigma(b) = \varsigma(y) = 0; \varsigma(by) = \frac{2}{3},$$

which satisfy the conditions for a capacity. Let us now compute the CEU corresponding to the two preferences and let $u(0) = 0$.

$$\int_S u(f_1)d\varsigma - \int_S u(f_2)d\varsigma = \frac{1}{3}u(100) - 0 > 0 \Leftrightarrow f_1 \succ f_2.$$

$$\int_S u(f_3)d\varsigma - \int_S u(f_4)d\varsigma = \frac{1}{3}u(100) - \frac{2}{3}u(100) < 0 \Leftrightarrow f_4 \succ f_3.$$

Thus, we are able to explain the observed preference patterns in the Ellsberg paradox if we allow for non-additive probability measures.

4.3.2 Models of multiple priors

Multiple priors models offer one way of capturing ambiguity. Instead of point estimates of the prior probability, decision makers might assign a probability distribution over the prior probabilities. This could arise because decision makers may not fully trust any particular prior or they may have many possible models of the world in mind, each model having some probability of being the true one.

Gilboa and Schmeidler (1989) propose the following axiomatized model, which can explain the Ellsberg paradox.[10] Consider some act $f \in F$, where F is the set of all acts under consideration. Suppose that the state space is $S = \{s_1, \ldots, s_n\}$ and let Δ be the set of possible subjective probability distributions over S. Let Λ be some closed and convex subset of Δ and denote a typical element of Λ by $\rho = (\rho(s_1), \ldots, \rho(s_n))$. The set Λ captures all priors that the decision maker has about the set of states; each prior may be taken to denote a different model of the world. Now consider two acts f, g. Then, under certain conditions (see below), Gilboa and Schmeidler (1989) showed that:

$$f \succeq g \Leftrightarrow \min_{\rho \in \Lambda} \int_S u(f(s))d\rho(s) \geq \min_{\rho \in \Lambda} \int_S u(g(s))d\rho(s), \tag{4.7}$$

where $u : X \to R$ is a non-constant function. In words, (4.7) says the following. For each possible act, compute the minimum expected utility for that act from the set of all possible priors under

[10] There are several axiomatizations of the multiple priors model. See also, Bewley (2002), Klibanoff et al. (2005), Maccheroni et al. (2006a,b).

consideration. Then choose the act which gives the maximum utility from the set of minimum expected utilities obtained in the first step. This is also called as the *maximin expected utility model* (MEU).[11]

In order to derive the representation in (4.7), Gilboa and Schmeidler (1989) weakened the independence axiom in the Anscombe–Aumann framework to *C-independence*, and they also required a notion of *uncertainty aversion*. We now define these concepts.

> **Definition 4.5** *(C-independence): Suppose that f, g are two acts and h is some constant act that gives the same outcome in each state of the world. Then C-independence requires that*
>
> $$f \succeq g \Leftrightarrow \alpha f + (1 - \alpha)h \succeq \alpha g + (1 - \alpha)h \text{ for all } \alpha \in (0, 1).$$

Notice the difference between C-independence and comonotonic independence: the acts here are not required to be pairwise comonotonic and h is a constant act.

> **Definition 4.6** *(Uncertainty aversion): Suppose that the decision maker is indifferent between two acts f, g, i.e., $f \sim g$, then*
>
> $$\delta f + (1 - \delta)g \succeq f \text{ for all } \delta \in (0, 1).$$

Roughly speaking, uncertainty aversion requires that the decision maker would like to hedge bets by preferring a combination of two equivalent acts to any one of the acts.

The representation in (4.7) exhibits extreme pessimism because the decision maker focuses on the worst possible expected utility under each prospect. However, the two conditions, C-independence and uncertainty aversion, do not directly suggest such pessimism.

Consider now the three-color Ellsberg experiment in Example 4.2. For the four lotteries in (4.2), (4.3), using the most pessimistic subjective probability distribution, we get that for $p \in [0, 2/3]$ (the joint probability of a black and yellow ball) the minimum expected utility for each of the four acts, f_1, f_2, f_3, f_4 is:

$$
\begin{cases}
f_1 : & \frac{1}{3}u(100) \\
f_2 : & \left(1 - p - \frac{1}{3}\right)u(100) = 0 \text{ for } p = 2/3 \\
f_3 : & \left[\frac{1}{3}u(100) + pu(100)\right] = \frac{1}{3}u(100) \text{ for } p = 0 \\
f_4 : & \left[\left(1 - p - \frac{1}{3}\right)u(100) + pu(100)\right] = \frac{2}{3}u(100) \text{ for any } p \in [0, 2/3]
\end{cases}
$$

It is clear from these calculations that

$$\min_{\rho \in \Lambda} \int_S u(f_1(s))d\rho(s) \geq \min_{\rho \in \Lambda} \int_S u(f_2(s))d\rho(s), \text{ so } f_1 \succ f_2,$$

$$\min_{\rho \in \Lambda} \int_S u(f_4(s))d\rho(s) \geq \min_{\rho \in \Lambda} \int_S u(f_3(s))d\rho(s), \text{ so } f_4 \succ f_3,$$

which is in agreement with the observed choices: f_1 over f_2 and f_4 over f_3.

---

[11] For a generalization of the maximin criteria, see Chateauneuf and Faro (2009). These authors restrict the set of allowable priors to only those on which the decision maker can put a certain minimum degree of confidence. One undesirable feature of MEU models is that they violate monotonicity (see exercise 11.10.1 in Wakker, 2010).

The models of multiple priors and the MEU approach has also been applied to macroeconomics in the work of Hansen and Sargent (2001a,b). Roughly speaking, the idea is as follows. Suppose that a policymaker has uncertainty about which model best describes the real world. For instance, the policymaker could be uncertain about the relevant coefficients of the expectations augmented Phillips curve. The policymaker must make a choice between $n > 1$ alternative policies. Then the policymaker computes, first, the maximum loss that could arise by using each of the policies. At the second stage, the policymaker chooses the policy that gives the least loss from among the set of losses computed in the first step. For more on the precise link between *robust control methods* of this sort on the one hand and the maximin model, see Maccheroni et al. (2006b).

Some of the assumptions behind the MEU model have been relaxed. For instance, Maccheroni et al. (2006a) relax C-independence. By relaxing the assumption of uncertainty aversion (Definition 4.6 above) in the MEU model, Ghirardato et al. (2004) obtained the α-MEU model. In this model, any act f is evaluated in the following manner:

$$V(f) = \alpha(f) \min_{\rho \in \Lambda} \int_S u(f(s)) d\rho(s) + [1 - \alpha(f)] \max_{\rho \in \Lambda} \int_S u(f(s)) d\rho(s), \qquad (4.8)$$

where Λ is some closed and convex subset of the set of possible probability distributions, Δ, over the set of states. The parameter $\alpha(f) \in [0,1]$ depends on the act, f, and it captures the decision maker's *ambiguity aversion* for the act. For $\alpha(f) = 1$, this is simply the MEU model. For $\alpha(f) = 0$, this representation turns out to be the same as that for a special case of incomplete preferences as in Bewley (2002), which we examine in Section 4.3.5. In this case, it is sometimes known as the maximax EU model. It has recently been shown that the preference foundations for the α-MEU model are quite restricted. Eichberger et al. (2011) show that the proposal by Ghirardato et al. (2004) holds only for $\alpha = 0$ and $\alpha = 1$. Siniscalchi (2006) shows that α cannot be interpreted as a parameter of ambiguity aversion.

We note that (4.8) is reminiscent of the *Arrow–Hurwicz criterion*, which preceded the axiomatic developments. Arrow and Hurwicz (1972) generalized in turn, the Wald criterion. The latter advocated looking at the worst possible outcome of an act. The generalization of Arrow–Hurwicz was to advocate a weighted average of the worst and best outcome under each act.

4.3.3 Two-stage recursive models and failure of compounding

Segal (1987, 1990) provided an explanation for the Ellsberg paradox within the class of two-stage recursive models where subjects violate the reduction of compound lotteries axiom.[12] Consider the following simplified Ellsberg setup.

> **Example 4.3** *Suppose that there are two urns. Urn 1 is known to contain 5 red and 5 black balls. Urn 2 has 10 balls that are either red or black, but their composition is not known. In this sense, as in the original setup of the Ellsberg paradox, there is ambiguity associated with Urn 2, while Urn 1 involves known risks.*

---

[12] For a list of two-stage models that preceeded the work of Segal and suggest giving up compounding so as to model ambiguity, see the annotated bibliography on Peter Wakker's homepage under the heading "second-order probabilities to model ambiguity."

The decision maker is offered a monetary prize, z, if a red ball comes up in a random draw. No prize is given if a black ball comes up. Suppose that the decision maker uses RDU. Then, the utility from betting on a red ball from Urn 1, denoted by RDU_1, is

$$RDU_1 = u(z)w(0.5), \qquad (4.9)$$

where $w(p)$ is a probability weighting function and u is a utility function such that $u(0) = 0$. Suppose the decision maker has the following *mental models* of the color composition of Urn 2.

Definition 4.7 *With probability $\rho > 0$, Urn 2 has 10 red balls (Model 1). With probability ρ, Urn 2 has 0 red balls (Model 2). Finally, with the complementary probability $1 - 2\rho$, Urn 2 has 5 red and 5 black balls (Model 3). We denote Model i by Mi, $i = 1, 2, 3$.*

The (ex-ante) probability of a red ball in the three models is, respectively, ρ, 0, $(1 - 2\rho)/2$. A decision maker who respects the reduction axiom, computes the total probability of a red ball to be $\rho + 0 + (1 - 2\rho)/2 = 0.5$, and the total probability of a black ball to be 0.5. Thus, such a decision maker evaluates Urn 2, based on his mental model in Definition 4.7, as the lottery

$$L = (0, 0.5; z, 0.5). \qquad (4.10)$$

If a decision maker who follows RDU did respect compounding, then he would evaluate the lottery in (4.10) drawn from Urn 2, and based on the mental models in Definition 4.7, as $RDU(L) = u(z)w(0.5)$.

Suppose now that the decision maker does not respect the reduction axiom, so is unable to reduce compound lotteries in the usual manner. Further, the decision maker follows RDU. Segal (1987, 1990) provided the following formalization of the departure from compounding, in the context of RDU. Assume that $w(p)$ is *convex*.[13] The certainty equivalent of the lottery $L = (0, 1 - p; z, p)$ is a prize, c, earned with probability 1, such that

$$u(c) = u(z)w(p). \qquad (4.11)$$
$$\Rightarrow c = u^{-1}\big(u(z)w(p)\big). \qquad (4.12)$$

The decision maker essentially faces a two-stage lottery when considering the draw of a ball from Urn 2. In the first stage, there is risk on account of three possible mental models described in Definition 4.7 (these occur with respective probabilities $\rho, 0, 1 - 2\rho$). For each mental model, in the second stage, he faces another risky situation because the prize z is won with some probability (only in the first mental model is it won with certainty).

Suppose the decision maker violates the reduction axiom in the following manner. For each mental model, he replaces the second stage lottery by its certainty equivalent, which violates compounding. Denote by c_i, $i = 1, 2, 3$, the certainty equivalent in model M_i, then

$$\begin{cases} c_1 = u^{-1}\left(u(z)w(1)\right) = u^{-1}\left(u(z)\right) = z, \\ c_2 = u^{-1}\left(u(z)w(0)\right) = u^{-1}\left(0\right) = 0, \\ c_3 = u^{-1}\left(u(0)[1 - w(0.5)] + u(z)w(0.5)\right) = u^{-1}\left(u(z)w(0.5)\right). \end{cases}$$

---

[13] Convexity of the weighting function has certain desirable properties under RDU. For instance, it is a necessary condition for risk aversion (see Chew et al., 1987). For other desirable properties, see Segal (1987).

By replacing the second stage lottery by its certainty equivalent, and rolling back the decision tree, the individual faces the following lottery. The outcomes are arranged in an increasing order, as required by RDU (w is convex, so $u^{-1}(u(z)w(0.5)) < u^{-1}(u(z)) = z$).

$$\left(0, \rho; u^{-1}(u(z)w(0.5)), 1 - 2\rho; z, \rho\right). \tag{4.13}$$

We can now compute the utility of a RDU decision maker, when faced with the lottery in (4.13). This is the utility of the decision maker from betting on a red ball from Urn 2 (the ambiguous urn in the classical terminology), when he employs the mental models in Definition 4.7, and reduces lotteries in the manner described above. Under RDU, this utility, denoted by RDU_2, is:

$$\begin{aligned} RDU_2 &= u\left(u^{-1}(u(z)w(0.5))\right)[w(1-\rho) - w(\rho)] + u(z)w(\rho) \\ &= u(z)[w(0.5)w(1-\rho) + w(\rho)(1-w(0.5))]. \end{aligned} \tag{4.14}$$

Using the assumed convexity of the weighting function we get that

$$\begin{aligned} w(0.5)w(1-\rho) + w(\rho)(1-w(0.5)) &< w(w(0.5)(1-\rho) + (1-w(0.5))\rho) \\ &= w(w(0.5)(1-2\rho) + \rho) \\ &< w(w(0.5)(1-2\rho)) \ (\because w \text{ is increasing}) \\ &< w(w(0.5)) \ (\because (1-2\rho) \in (0,1)) \\ &< w(0.5) \ (\because w(0.5) < 0.5). \end{aligned} \tag{4.15}$$

From (4.14), (4.15), and using (4.9), we get that

$$RDU_2 < u(z)w(0.5) = RDU_1. \tag{4.16}$$

From (4.16), the decision maker prefers to bet on a red ball from Urn 1 rather than Urn 2. Hence, using the classical terminology, one can explain a preference for the risky urn relative to the ambiguous urn, solely by a failure of a decision maker, using RDU, to understand or invoke compounding, when the decision maker has more than one model of the world as in Definition 4.7.

Halevy (2007) found evidence consistent with the predictions of models that allow for a failure of compounding. These models include those of Segal (1987, 1990), Klibanoff et al. (2005), and Halevy and Feltkamp (2005). Halevy found that most subjects in experiments who were able to reduce compound lotteries were ambiguity neutral. Conversely, most subjects who were ambiguity neutral were able to reduce compound lotteries. Over the entire population of subjects in experiments, none of the existing theories can explain all the experimental findings. However, the results do strongly suggest that the reduction of compound lotteries must be an important part of the explanation of the Ellsberg paradox.

4.3.4 *The smooth ambiguity aversion model*

The *smooth ambiguity aversion model* proposed by Klibanoff et al. (2005) belongs to a similar class of models as Segal (1987, 1990). The main differences are the nature of lotteries in the two frameworks (objective versus subjective lotteries) and the nature of preferences in the two stages (identical versus different preferences). Consider the three-colors Ellsberg experiment in Example 4.2. The decision maker has a set of priors, or initial belief, or *first order beliefs*, given in (4.1). These are given by the distribution function Q^1 with the associated probabilities: $q^1(r) = \frac{1}{3}$, $q^1(b) = \frac{2}{3} - p$; $q^1(y) = p$; $p \in [0, 2/3]$. There are an infinite number of such priors because $p \in [0, 2/3]$. Suppose that the decision maker has *second order beliefs* captured by the distribution Q^2 about the set of possible priors $p \in [0, 2/3]$.

Preferences over the initial or first order beliefs are represented by a von Neumann–Morgenstern utility function, u, and $u(0) = 0$. Preferences over second order beliefs are represented by an increasing transformation, ϕ, of u, i.e., $\phi(u) : \mathbb{R} \to \mathbb{R}$. Then, the observed preferences in the Ellsberg paradox (i.e., $f_1 \succ f_2$ and $f_4 \succ f_3$) are represented by:

$$f_1 \succ f_2 \Leftrightarrow \phi\left(\frac{1}{3}u(100)\right) > \int_{-\infty}^{\infty} \phi\left(\left(\frac{2}{3} - p\right)u(100)\right) dQ^2, \tag{4.17}$$

$$f_4 \succ f_3 \Leftrightarrow \phi\left(\frac{2}{3}u(100)\right) > \int_{-\infty}^{\infty} \phi\left(\frac{1}{3}u(100) + pu(100)\right) dQ^2. \tag{4.18}$$

In this framework, u captures the individual's attitudes to risk. However, ϕ measures attitudes to ambiguity, i.e., the uncertainty faced by the decision maker about the set of priors. Ambiguity aversion is associated with concavity of ϕ, i.e., $\phi' > 0$, $\phi'' < 0$. The preferences expressed in (4.17), (4.18) are reasonable; this is shown in the next example.

Example 4.4 *(Machina and Siniscalchi, 2014): Suppose that $u(100) = 1$, $u(0) = 0$, $\phi(u) = \sqrt{u}$. The distribution Q^2 assigns a probability 0.5 each to one of two possible Q^1 distributions. In the first distribution, $p = \frac{2}{3}$, and the second, $p = 0$. We can now rewrite (4.17), (4.18) as follows.*

$$f_1 \succ f_2 \Leftrightarrow \phi\left(\frac{1}{3}\right) > \frac{1}{2}\phi\left(\frac{2}{3}\right) \Leftrightarrow 0.5774 > 0.4083.$$

$$f_4 \succ f_3 \Leftrightarrow \phi\left(\frac{2}{3}\right) > \frac{1}{2}\phi(1) + \frac{1}{2}\phi\left(\frac{1}{3}\right) \Leftrightarrow 0.8165 > 0.7887.$$

Hence, there is no paradox in this case.

More generally, let the initial priors over the set of states in the sample space, S, be captured by the distribution, Q^1. An ambiguity averse decision maker's preferences over two acts f, g in the smooth ambiguity aversion model are represented by:

$$f \succ g \Leftrightarrow \int_{\Lambda} \phi\left(\int_S u(f(s))dQ^1\right) dQ^2 > \int_{\Lambda} \phi\left(\int_S u(g(s))dQ^1\right) dQ^2, \tag{4.19}$$

where u is a von Neumann–Morgenstern utility function, $\phi''(u) < 0$, the distribution Q^1 defined over S, captures prior beliefs, and the distribution Q^2 defined over Λ, captures uncertainty about prior beliefs. In a sense, the decision maker applies subjective expected utility twice; once over the prior distribution with von Neumann–Morgenstern preferences given by u and then over the posterior distribution with preferences given by $\phi(u)$.

In contrast to the MEU model of Gilboa and Schmeidler (1989), where the objective function is not differentiable, here it is differentiable. For this reason, when ϕ is smooth, the

Klibanoff et al. (2005) model is sometimes known as the *smooth ambiguity aversion model*. Insofar as expected utility is applied at each of the two stages, within each stage, the model is susceptible to the criticisms that have already been made of EU. Furthermore, the burden of explaining risk and ambiguity attitudes in this model lies on the utility function; in contrast the evidence indicates that the shape of the probability weighting function plays an important role in risk attitudes. Finally, the theory is not easy to test because second order acts are difficult to observe. Wakker (2010) gives a more detailed discussion of these criticisms; see also Baillon et al. (2012) for a further critical evaluation.

Related models can be found in Nau (2006) and Ergin and Gul (2009). The idea in Nau (2006) is that the state space can be partitioned in such a manner that each partition has a similar degree of uncertainty. In a similar framework, Ergin and Gul (2009) obtain a representation that is similar to (4.19). Epstein (2009) has criticized the smooth ambiguity aversion model of Klibanoff et al. (2005), raising concerns about its very foundations and interpretations. He also contests the claim that the model provides a separation between attitudes to ambiguity and to what one would reasonably agree to be an ambiguous situation.[14]

4.3.5 A brief note on the related literature

Bewley (2002) allowed for the possibility that one might not have complete preferences over acts. Thus, in the Ellsberg paradox, some of the acts may not be comparable. In this model, let Λ be the set of acts over which the preferences are complete. Then, using the same terminology that was used in (4.7),

$$f \succeq g \Leftrightarrow \int_{\Lambda} u(f(s))d\rho(s) \geq \int_{\Lambda} u(g(s))d\rho(s) \text{ for all } \rho \in \Lambda,$$

otherwise (for $\rho \notin \Lambda$), the acts f, g are simply non-comparable. In any non-comparable situation, it is assumed that the status quo is chosen. This framework can also be used to explain the Ellsberg paradox.

A range of other proposals can explain the Ellsberg paradox. We briefly note some of these. Siniscalchi (2009) proposes a model of *vector expected utility*. In this model, for any act, the individual computes his expected utility using a baseline probability distribution. However, the individual also makes an adjustment to utility which depends on a comparison of the act with similar acts, using a measure of statistical similarity. Maccheroni et al. (2006b) propose a representation that they call the *variational representation of preferences*. This is based on a weakening of C-independence (Definition 4.5). Their main axiom, *weak certainty independence*, requires that preferences over acts be invariant to changes in location, but not scale of utilities. Cerreia-Vioglio et al. (2011) propose a general model that provides a unified account of MEU and smooth ambiguity aversion models. Gul and Pesendorfer (2013) propose an axiomatization of their model, *expected uncertain utility*. Chew and Sagi (2006, 2008) propose a theory of "small worlds." The idea here is to divide the domain of possible events into groups of events. The decision maker has a good idea of probabilities within a group. However, he/she reveals ambiguity when asked to compare across the groups.

---

[14]   The criticisms also apply to the related representation by Ergin and Gul (2009). For a reply, see Klibanoff et al. (2009) who argue that Epstein's thought experiments either strenghten their smooth ambiguity aversion model, or point shortcomings that apply to a much wider range of ambiguity models.

We have already considered some definitions of ambiguity aversion. In Definition 4.6, we considered Schmeidler's definition. In Section 4.3.3 we considered the definition of ambiguity aversion given by Klibanoff et al. (2005). In the α-MEU model of Ghirardato et al. (2004) considered above, the magnitude of α is used to capture the degree of ambiguity (although we have also noted the problems with this approach). These definitions depend on the shape of the utility function. However, it is also possible to give definitions of ambiguity aversion that are independent of the shape of the utility function.[15]

Yet another definition of ambiguity aversion is due to Chateauneuf and Tallon (2002). Suppose that there are n acts $f_1, f_2, \ldots, f_n$ and the decision maker is indifferent between them, i.e., $f_1 \sim f_2 \sim \ldots \sim f_n$. Suppose also that there exist n real numbers $\alpha_1, \alpha_2, \ldots, \alpha_n$ with the property that $\sum_{i=1}^{n} \alpha_i = 1$ and $\sum_{i=1}^{n} \alpha_i f_i = x$, where X is an act. Notice that x could be considered to be a hedged bet relative to any of the acts, f_i. Then, ambiguity aversion requires that $x \succ f_i$, $i = 1, 2, \ldots, n$. This definition is similar in idea to Schmeidler's definition. It too relies on a taste for diversification; the decision maker prefers a hedged bet to an unhedged bet.

Some other definitions of ambiguity aversion include those by Epstein (1999) and Ghirardato and Marinacci (2002). An issue with these definitions is that they do not fully separate attitudes to ambiguity from attitudes to risk. For one such separation of ambiguity and risk preferences, see Gajdos et al. (2008).[16]

4.3.6 *Some empirical evidence on ambiguity aversion*

The experimental results (see Section 4.4.1) question some of the underlying premises of the modern ambiguity aversion literature; for a survey, see Trautmann et al. (2016). For instance, ambiguity disappears in Ellsberg style experiments when individuals bet on one urn at a time rather than across both urns. Knowledge/expertise in the sorts of questions asked could even create ambiguity-seeking behavior that is problematic for the modern theoretical models of ambiguity aversion. Furthermore, in the presence of losses or lower probabilities with which events occur, we may observe ambiguity neutrality or even ambiguity-seeking behavior.

Hey et al. (2010) use an experimental setup that modifies the one in Halevy (2007). The authors argue that the original Ellsberg paradox is subject to one important criticism. Namely, that the urn with the unknown composition of balls invites *suspicion*. Subjects in experiments could be suspicious that the experimenter wishes to reduce their total monetary payoff and could somehow have rigged the urns in his favor. Hence, the "ambiguous urn" could turn into a "suspicious urn". Subjects might even use the heuristic that they are playing a game against a *malevolent nature*. The very fact that someone offers you a bet, could make you suspicious. For instance, you might wonder if the other party has access to some information that you do not have.

The solution proposed by Hey et al. (2010) for the suspicious urn problem is to use a bingo-blower. This is a rectangular device with transparent glass walls that has a collection of balls being spun around in a continuous motion. In order to draw a ball from the box, the box is tilted and a ball is ejected randomly, and transparently, through a transparent tube. In this case, the balls

---

[15] See, for instance, Epstein and Zhang (2001), Nehring (2001), Ghirardato et al. (2004), and Ghirardato and Siniscalchi (2012). Tversky and Wakker (1995) define ambiguity aversion as source preference for risk, which does not involve any utility.

[16] Klibanoff et al. (2005) also claim a separation between attitudes to risk and to ambiguity. This claim is contested in Epstein (2009).

can be seen, but their proportions cannot be calculated on account of the continuous motion of the balls. The authors argue that this enables them to term the urn as "ambiguous" rather than "suspicious."

Hey et al. (2010) examine 12 alternative specifications. These include expected utility, the decision field theory (DFT) of Busemeyer and Townsend (1993), MEU and α-MEU models, the Hurwicz criterion, Choquet expected utility, a form of prospect theory that is not PT,[17] and minimum regret. Theories with second order beliefs (see, for instance, Sections 4.3.3 and 4.3.4) are not included because the experiments do not have the multiple stages required to test them. DFT and OPT emerge as the two best theories out of the 12. There is support for Gilboa and Schmeidler's (1989) MEU model and Ghirardato et al.'s (2004) α-MEU models.

Ahn et al. (2014) find greater support for multiple priors models and rank dependent models relative to smooth ambiguity aversion models. Hayashi and Wada (2010) reject multiple priors models on the grounds that priors that lead to intermediate values of expected utility also play a critical role. By contrast, from (4.8), only those priors that lead to maximum and minimum expected utility should matter.

Conte and Hey (2013) employ a new experimental setup that allows for the testing of theories that employ second order beliefs. They use a mixture model that considers five different theories. They find that the choices of 22% of the subjects are consistent with EU, 53% are consistent with the smooth ambiguity aversion model, 22% are consistent with the rank dependent model and 3% with the α-MEU model. There are vexed econometric issues in interpreting the results from any of these studies; see Hey (2014) for a discussion.

Recall that the Ellsberg paradox poses problems for Savage's SEU, because it rules out well-defined subjective probabilities in the sense of SEU. Machina (2009) proposes two-urn problems that give rise to a similar problem for models based on Choquet expected utility and axiomatized, for instance, by Gilboa (1987) and Schmeidler (1989).[18] Baillon et al. (2011) show in fact that Machina's results falsify four main models: maximin expected utility, variational preferences, α-maximin, and the smooth model of ambiguity aversion.[19]

Gilboa et al. (2009) illustrate a shortcoming of the Bayesian approach by asking the following hypothetical question. Suppose that you were to hear the title of a seminar in a university: "Are all cydophines, also abordites?" What probability do you assign to the event? As the authors say: "For all you know these could be enzymes, grammatical structures in an ancient language, or Abelian groups." So you cannot justifiably assign any probability. Using the principle of insufficient reason is not fully satisfactory either. The authors conclude: "The Bayesian approach is lacking because it is not rich enough to describe one's degree of confidence in one's assessments. For any probability question it requires a single probability number as an answer, excluding the possibility of replies such as 'I don't know' or 'I'm not so sure.'" In a similar vein, Gilboa et al. (2009) ask readers, what is the probability that the US president, six years from now, will be a Democrat?

These arguments rule out other possible solutions, particularly expert advice and the 'option value' of waiting for uncertainty to resolve. For instance, suppose that instead a non-economics

---

[17] It is an extension of OPT but Kothiyal et al. (2014) express reservations about using this variant in the domain of lotteries that they consider.

[18] Models based on Choquet expected utility violate *event separability* because the Choquet capacities involve other events on account of the cumulative treatment of events. A particular kind of separability, *tail separability*, still remains in such models. Machina (2009) exploits the notion of tail separability for his results.

[19] The vector expected utility model of Siniscalchi (2009) is, however, not subjected to the anomalies pointed out by Machina (2009).

scholar at a university were to see a seminar titled "Are Hicksian cross partial derivatives negative?" The scholar could ask a friend in the economics department for advice. In many situations of interest in real life, if it were terribly important for you to know the relevant probabilities, you would often ask someone who knows better. For instance, you would ask an expert for financial/insurance information. Or perhaps you might rely on some institutional solution; for instance you need not figure out the probability that the saturated fat content of a jar of powdered milk drink is high or low, you simply read information about the contents, which must be provided by law in most countries.

But in some situations, nobody might currently know the relevant probabilities, not even experts. The modern ambiguity aversion literature requires decision makers to form an immediate probability assessment of an event. In many relevant situations of interest to economics, there is substantial *option value of waiting*. The reason is that ambiguity can resolve as time passes. If you are not sure that you have met the right person for marriage, or you are not sure if this is the right time for having a child, or divorcing your partner, you can rationally wait for more information to unravel. Similarly, if you are not sure that this is the right time to make a particular investment, you can wait to see how events unfold. Countries might put off having a common currency, e.g., the euro, or defer on the death penalty, if they are not sure about the probabilistic merit of the case.

The findings of Halevy (2007), Hey et al. (2010), and Kothiyal et al. (2014) cast sufficient empirical doubt about some of the modern ambiguity aversion theories. The findings of Amos Tversky and colleagues that we outline in Section 4.4.1, question some of the central assumptions in all neoclassical theories of ambiguity.

The empirical literature on ambiguity aversion till about the mid 1990s is considered in Camerer (1995). We can summarize his stylized facts on ambiguity aversion as follows. First, subjects' aversion to more ambiguous choices does not vanish if one gives them written arguments to illustrate their paradoxical choices. Second, ambiguity and attitudes to risk are not correlated. So, for instance, someone who is more risk averse is not necessarily more ambiguity averse. Third, compound lotteries are considered to be more ambiguous, i.e., subjects are more keen to bet on lotteries with some unknown probability rather than a probability distribution over an unknown probability. Fourth, as one widens the domain of the probability distribution of unknown events (for instance, the range of probabilities p in Example 4.2), choices are considered by subjects to be more ambiguous. Fifth, ambiguity aversion is not caused by a belief on the subjects' part that the odds are stacked against them in the ambiguous choice.

There is also some evidence that ambiguity aversion might be more relevant in the domain of gains rather than in the domain of losses (Cohen et al., 1987). Similar findings can be found in Du and Budescu (2005) who find decision makers to be nearly ambiguity-neutral in the loss domain. Furthermore, while there appears to be some correlation between risk and ambiguity attitudes in the domain of gains, there is none in the domain of losses (Chakravarty and Roy, 2009). Gender differences in ambiguity aversion have also been documented. Women are relatively more ambiguity averse in situations where the degree of ambiguity is high (Borghans et al., 2009). Using data from trainee truck drivers, Burks et al. (2008) find that attitudes to risk and ambiguity can be separated in their data. Furthermore, indices of ambiguity aversion are found to be negatively correlated with cognitive skills (measured through, say, non-verbal IQ tests).

Several field experiments illustrate the effect of ambiguity aversion in real-world choice. Investors have a home country bias, investing far more in home country securities relative to diversifying by using international securities (French and Poterba, 1991). Referees are more willing to accept papers when refereeing is single-blind rather than double-blind (Blank, 1991).[20] Insurance contracts can charge an ambiguity premium (Hogarth and Kunreuther, 1992). Furthermore, even professionals such as actuaries and insurance underwriters exhibit ambiguity aversion (Hogarth and Kunreuther, 1989; Kunreuther et al., 1995).

What causes ambiguity aversion? This remains an intriguing question. One possible explanation is that people take account of the negative evaluation of their decision by others (Curley et al., 1986). Hence, if they are being directly observed by others, they are found to be more ambiguity averse. This is sometimes referred to as the *fear of negative evaluation*, FNE. When the perception is that others are more competent, then FNE (and, hence, ambiguity aversion) might be enhanced even more.[21] Trautmann et al. (2008) introduce an experimental design which is able to control for FNE. They find that this leads to the disappearance of ambiguity aversion. The authors conjecture that FNE might be a necessary condition for the presence of ambiguity aversion.

4.4 Behavioral models of ambiguity

In this section, we consider behavioral models of ambiguity. Under pure risk, this class of models does not reduce to EU. We consider two classes of models. The common theme running through these models is that the individual's attitudes towards ambiguity are influenced by the *source of information*.

4.4.1 *Support theory*

In a series of papers, Amos Tversky and several collaborators examine the nature of ambiguity within and outside the Ellsberg context. We now examine this line of work which is influential in psychology, and its decision theoretic foundations have recently been articulated by Ahn and Ergin (2010).[22]

Fox and Tversky (1998) begin with the observation that subjective expected utility (SEU) determines beliefs and tastes in one fell swoop. SEU is agnostic on what the decision maker forms first: beliefs or preferences. However, beliefs may precede preferences. For instance, a punter might bet on team A rather than on team B because he believes the former is more likely to win. Punters do not, however, infer this belief from the observation that they prefer betting on team A.

In the first step, individuals form beliefs about events using the *support theory* of Tversky and Koehler (1994). The starting point of support theory is the empirical observation that *procedure invariance* is violated when one elicits beliefs using different methods. Suppose that $E_1, E_2, \ldots, E_n$ are disjoint events, then we typically observe the following form of subadditivity (Teigen, 1974; Fischhoff et al., 1978).

$$P(E_1 \cup E_2 \cup \ldots \cup E_n) < P(E_1) + P(E_2) + \ldots + P(E_n).$$

---

[20] These experiments used data on referees from the *American Economic Review*. In single blind refereeing, the identity of the author is known to the referee (but not vice versa). In double blind refereeing, the identity of each is private knowledge (so this is a more ambiguous situation).

[21] See for instance, Heath and Tversky (1991), Fox and Tversky (1998), and Fox and Weber (2002).

[22] These authors derive a partition dependent expected utility representation of preferences. The same sample space can be finely or coarsely partitioned. The decision maker then has non-additive weights over events in any partition. Also see Cohen and Jaffray (1980) for an earlier attempt along this direction.

Motivated by this finding, support theory assumes that individuals do not attach probability to events, but rather to the "description of events" or "hypotheses." So depending on how the same event is described or framed, the individual could assign different probabilities to it.

If only two possible hypotheses, A and B, hold, then the subjective probability that A rather than B holds, denoted by $P(A,B)$, is given by:

$$P(A,B) = \frac{s(A)}{s(A) + s(B)} \in [0,1], \tag{4.20}$$

where, for any hypothesis, A, $s(A) \geq 0$ is the "support value" of the hypothesis. This reflects the strength of evidence for this hypothesis. It is obvious from (4.20) that $P(A,B) + P(B,A) = 1$; this is known as *binary complementarity*. For $A = A_1 \cup A_2$, the support value satisfies:

$$s(A) \leq s(A_1 \text{ or } A_2) \leq s(A_1) + s(A_2). \tag{4.21}$$

The first inequality in (4.21) implies that by unpacking an event into its constituent parts increases the support for the event. The second inequality implies that this, in turn, is dominated by the sum of support for the individual constituents. The idea behind this kind of *subadditivity* is that by breaking an event into its sub-parts, one increases the salience of the event; quite possibly, one might be able to recall a greater number of instances of the event. For instance, it is likely that the support value for homicide (event A) is lower than the support value for the two constituent events, homicide by strangers (A_1) and homicide by acquaintances (A_2), simply because the latter two might bring to mind more instances of such events and thereby increase their salience. This intuition is borne out by evidence, which includes field studies of the behavior of experienced physicians.[23]

Once beliefs consistent with (4.20), (4.21) are allowed for, one transforms an uncertain situation (what is the probability of events A and B that lack an objective probability?) into a risky one (well-defined probabilities $P(A,B), P(B,A)$ can be formed). Such probabilities are said to be consistent with support theory.

For n possible events $E_1, E_2, \ldots, E_n$ that represent a partition of the sample space S, denote the associated subjective probabilities that are consistent with support theory by $p_1, p_2, \ldots, p_n$. One can then move on to the second stage. In this stage, the decision maker simply uses prospect theory to evaluate what has, in effect, become a risky prospect.

Tversky and Wakker (1995) extend the weighting function under risk, $w(p)$, to uncertainty, $W(E)$, as follows.

1. (Weight on extreme events) $W(\phi) = 0$, $W(S) = 1$.
2. (Bounded subadditivity) Denote by E_i, E_j, two events in the sample space such that $i, j = 1, 2, \ldots, n$, $i \neq j$ and $E_i \cap E_j = \phi$, then:[24]
2a. (Possibility effect or lower subadditivity) $W(E_i) \geq W(E_i \cup E_j) - W(E_j)$ whenever $W(E_i \cup E_j) \leq W(S - E)$ for some event E. The possibility effect captures the idea that increasing the probability of winning a prize from 0 to p has a larger effect than increasing the probability from $q > 0$ to $q + p \leq 1$. This is seen by considering successively the cases $E_j = \phi$ (where the inequality binds) and $E_j \neq \phi$ (where it need not bind).

---

[23] For the evidence, see, for instance, Tversky and Koehler (1994) and Rottenstreich and Tversky (1997). For the specific case of experienced physicians exhibiting the ideas in (4.21), see Redelmeier et al. (1995).
[24] Support for the bounded subadditivity hypothesis can be found in Tversky and Fox (1995).

2b. (Certainty effect or upper subadditivity) $W(S) - W(S - E_i) \geq W\left(E_i \cup E_j\right) - W(E_j)$ whenever $W(E_j) \geq W(E')$ for some E'. The certainty effect shows that the impact of an event E_i is greater when it is subtracted from a certain event (S) rather than an uncertain event.

Consider simple prospects of the form (E_i, x) that offer a monetary prize x if the event E_i occurs. Denote the reference point by $\bar{x}$. Then the value of the prospect (E_i, x) is given by

$$V = v(x - \bar{x})W(E_i) = v(x - \bar{x})w(p_i),$$

where p_i is the subjective probability associated with the event E_i and it is consistent with support theory. The function $v(x - \bar{x})$ is as defined in prospect theory.

Heath and Tversky (1991) introduce the *competence hypothesis*. The competence hypothesis requires that an individual's propensity to bet on a lottery depends on how knowledgeable or competent the individual feels in that context. Several cognitive explanations for this hypothesis are suggested. For instance, people learn from experience that they perform better in challenges where they have better knowledge, skill, or competence. Another possibility is that in addition to the monetary consequences from betting, there are also psychic consequences, e.g., credit or blame for an outcome, lowered or improved self esteem, and approval or condemnation from others. In pure games of chance, one does not expect these psychic payoffs to be very important. However, in games involving skill, judgment, or knowledge, they are likely to be far more important. Competent people can take credit when they succeed in games of skill and can sometimes be insulated from blame ("the expert's prediction was incorrect but the expert is very competent, so it must be a very noisy environment, making predictions too difficult"). On the other hand, if a non-expert gets it correct he gets no credit ("succeeded by chance") and if he fails he might get the blame ("he had no expertise; failure was expected"). Hence, we would expect people with the relevant knowledge and competence to be more likely to bet on games that involve knowledge/competence.

In the context of the Ellsberg paradox, people might dislike betting on the "vague" urn for fear of being shown up to be less knowledgeable or competent. Indeed, Curley et al. (1986) show that aversion to ambiguity increases if others can observe one's decision and the actual outcome ("fear of negative evaluation"). The Ellsberg paradox is not, however, a particularly good application of the competence hypothesis because it is not clear what knowledge or competence is involved.

Fox and Tversky (1995) made the important observation that the literature following the Ellsberg paradox typically invoked a *within-subjects design* of experiments. In these experiments, subjects always compared clear and vague bets; for instance, a comparison of two urns, one with a known composition of balls and another with an unknown composition. They propose, instead, a *between-subjects design* in which subjects compare either one or the other urn at a time. Their main experimental finding is that ambiguity aversion no longer exists in a between-subjects design.

Consider, for instance, the following experiment reported in Fox and Tversky (1995). Bag A has 50 red chips and 50 black chips. Bag B has 100 red and black chips, but the exact proportion is unknown. A "ticket" to a bag entitles the holder to play the following game. First, choose a color, then draw randomly a chip from the bag. If the chip is of the same color as the chosen color, then the ticket holder wins $100, otherwise he/she wins nothing. Experimental subjects are asked how much they would pay for a "ticket" to each bag?

Two conditions were identified and the subjects were split roughly evenly between the two conditions. In the *comparative condition* (67 subjects) the two bags were simultaneously

Table 4.2   Results from the Fox and Tversky (1995) study.
Standard errors in parantheses.

	Clear bet	Vague bet
Comparative condition	$24.34	$14.58
	(2.21)	(1.80)
Non-comparative condition	$17.94	$18.82
	(2.50)	(2.87)

presented to the subjects and they had to state a price they were willing to pay for a ticket for each bag. The other half of the subjects (74 subjects) played the *non-comparative condition* and they were split into two groups. One group (35 subjects) had to state the price they were willing to pay for the ticket to Bag A only and the remaining (39 subjects) had to state the price they were willing to pay for Bag B only.

The results are shown in Table 4.2 for the case of the *clear bet* (betting on bag A) and the *vague bet* (betting on bag B). The results are in line with the conjecture made by the authors. Ambiguity aversion, as traditionally understood, arises in the comparative condition; subjects are willing to pay significantly more for a ticket to Bag A. However, in the non-comparative condition, such ambiguity aversion completely disappears. This result is unaltered when the authors introduce real monetary stakes.

Subjects do seem aware that relevant information is missing in the case of Bag B. However, unless there is a direct comparison between the clear bet and the vague bet, ambiguity aversion does not arise, so missing information is not a sufficient condition for ambiguity aversion. These results are problematic for neoclassical theories of ambiguity.

4.4.2 *Prospect theory, source-dependent uncertainty, and ambiguity*

We have briefly alluded to the work of Chew and Sagi (2008) above. They partition the domain of events into groups such that there is homogeneity in uncertainty within each group, yet heterogeneity between the groups. Section 4.4.1 also alluded to the *source of information* in influencing the beliefs of individuals about uncertain events (Tversky and Fox, 1995; Fox and Tversky, 1995).

In an important breakthrough, Abdellaoui, Baillon et al. (2011) formalize some of these ideas and also present evidence for their insights. The central idea is that the decision maker distinguishes between information from difference *sources* of uncertainty. The authors (p. 699) give an informal definition of a *source*: "A source of uncertainty concerns a group of events that is generated by a common mechanism of uncertainty." Consider the two-colors example of the Ellsberg paradox (Example 4.1) in which there is a known urn (K) and the unknown urn (U). Decision makers are indifferent between the two colors in each urn when the urns are presented separately. Yet, they are not willing to exchange a bet on a color in urn K with a bet on the same color in urn U. Thus, it appears that each urn constitutes a separate source of uncertainty.

We have outlined PT under uncertainty in Section 2.4.1. We now employ similar machinery to develop the ideas here. Let $f = (E_1, x_1; E_2, x_2; \ldots; E_n, x_n)$ be a Savage act, as in (1.6), that gives a prize x_i if event E_i occurs and $\cup_{i=1}^{n} E_i = E$, where E is the universal event. The decision maker does not known which of the n events will occur. Let $P(E_i)$ be the subjective probability of the event E_i, which can be elicited from the choices made by the subjects. Suppose that the decision maker has complete and transitive preferences $\succeq$ over F, the set of all Savage acts. Under SEU (see Section 1.3) the decision maker evaluates the act f by the functional

$$SEU(f) = \sum_{i=1}^{n} P(E_i)u(x_i), \tag{4.22}$$

where u is a continuous and strictly increasing utility function.

In the empirical tests undertaken by Abdellaoui, Baillon et al. (2011), $n = 2$. Thus, they have prospects of the form $(E_1, y; E_2, x)$, where $y \le x$. The reader should have no problems with the next two definitions.

Definition 4.8 *(Weighting function for uncertainty): A weighting function under uncertainty is a mapping $\widetilde{w} : S \to [0,1]$ such that:*

(i) $\widetilde{w}(\varnothing) = 0$, where $\varnothing$ is the empty set.
(ii) $\widetilde{w}(E) = 1$, where E is the universal event.
(iii) If $E_i \subseteq E_j$, then $\widetilde{w}(E_i) \le \widetilde{w}(E_j)$.

Definition 4.9 *(Binary rank dependent utility): The utility representation of the prospect $(E_1, y; E_2, x)$ under rank dependent utility is given by*

$$RDU(E_1, y; E_2, x) = [1 - \widetilde{w}(E_2)]u(y) + \widetilde{w}(E_2)u(x). \tag{4.23}$$

We now wish to define the sense in which two events are perceived to be equally likely.

Definition 4.10 *(Exchangeable events):*

(i) Two disjoint events E_1 and E_2 are exchangeable if permuting their respective prizes has no effect on preferences, i.e.,

$$(E_1, x_1; E_2, x_2; \ldots; E_n, x_n) \sim (E_1, x_2; E_2, x_1; \ldots; E_n, x_n).$$

(ii) An entire partition $(E_1, E_2, \ldots, E_n)$ of the universal event is exchangeable if all pairs of events in it are exchangeable.

Definition 4.11 *(Source; Abdellaoui, et al., 2011, p. 699): A source, S is an algebra. It contains the universal event (certain to happen), the vacuous event (certain not to happen), the complement of each element in the set, and the union of each pair of elements in the set.[25]*

We distinguish between the various sources of uncertainty (such as the single urn and the two urns in the Ellsberg paradox) by giving the following definition of a uniform source.

Definition 4.12 *(Uniform sources): A source S is said to be uniform if for any partition of events in S, $(E_1, E_2, \ldots, E_n)$, probabilistic sophistication (Definition 1.13) holds. In other words, choices among prospects of the form $(E_1, x_1; E_2, x_2; \ldots; E_n, x_n)$ can equivalently be expressed as choices over prospects of the form $(x_1, P(E_1); x_2, P(E_2); \ldots; x_n, P(E_n))$ where $P(E_i)$ is the subjective probability of the event E_i. The decision maker is indifferent between two event-contingent prospects "from the same source" that lead to the same probability-contingent prospect. This property need not hold if we were to change the source.*

---

[25] Thus sources also contain every finite union and intersection of their elements.

If any finite partition of a source is exchangeable (Definition 4.10), then the source is a uniform source.

Example 4.5 *(Source Preference; Wakker, 2010, p. 318): Suppose that **A** and **B** are two sources and we have*

$$A \succeq B \text{ and } A^c \succ B^c \text{ for all } A \in \mathbf{A} \text{ and } B \in \mathbf{B}$$

*but it is never the case that $B \succeq A$ and $B^c \succ A^c$, then we say that the decision maker prefers the source **A** to **B**.*

Definition 4.13 *(Source functions): Since probabilistic sophistication holds in any uniform source, S, so for any $E_i \subseteq S$ we have*

$$\widetilde{w}(E_i) = w_s(P(E_i)),$$

where w_s is known as a source function. In this case we can write (4.23) as

$$RDU(E_1, y; E_2, x) = [1 - w_s(P(E_2))] u(y) + w_s(P(E_2))u(x).$$

Example 4.6 *Consider the prospect $(E_1, x_1; E_2, x_2; \ldots; E_n, x_n)$ in which the probabilities of all events are "objective probabilities" and $\cup_{i=1}^n E_i = S$. Then S is a uniform source. In this case we have the standard situation of choice under risk in which the source function w_s is written as a standard probability weighting function w without a subscript.*

To check if the behavior of decision makers differs when they receive information from non-uniform sources, Abdellaoui, Baillon et al. (2011) propose the following modification of the Ellsberg experiments. They consider urns K and U as in the Ellsberg paradox. Urn K is known to contain 8 balls of different colors, while urn U is also known to have 8 balls; the color composition in urn U is unknown, but it contains no new colors relative to urn K. So urn U may contain one ball each of the 8 colors, or all 8 balls of the same color, or any combinations of the 8 colors that are present in urn K.

To test for uniformity, events E_2, E_2', E_2'', ... have the same number of winning colors (e.g., E_2 could be: win a prize if the ball drawn is of color red, black, or cyan), for each urn. The decision maker then states certainty equivalents, CE, for the prospects $(E_1, 0; E_2, 25)$, $(E_1, 0; E_2', 25)$, $(E_1, 0; E_2'', 25)$, ... from each urn. Since each urn is hypothesized to be a uniform source, one would expect the events in each urn to be exchangeable, hence, the CE for each prospect in each urn should be identical. However, if the K and U urns are different sources, then a comparison of the CE for each prospect across the two urns should reveal a difference.

Utility elicitation was carried out by using the method of Abdellaoui et al. (2008) (see Section 2.5). Certainty equivalents, CE, were elicited for prospects of the form $(E_1, 0; E_2, x)$, where x varied from 0 euros to 25 euros, and the event E_2 specified balls of 4 colors, red, blue, yellow, cyan, $E_2 = \{R_s, B_s, Y_s, C_s\}$; the sources being $s = K, U$. Since the event E_2 specifies 4 out of 8 colors, so we expect the subjective probability of the event to be 0.5 for each urn, i.e., $P(E_2) = 0.5$. A power form of utility was assumed, so $u(x) = \left(\frac{x}{25}\right)^{\rho_s}$, where $\rho_s > 0$ is a parameter. Using the definition of certainty equivalent, this implies that $\left(\frac{CE_s}{25}\right)^{\rho_s} = w_s(0.5)\left(\frac{x}{25}\right)^{\rho_s}$, where CE_s is the certainty equivalent when $s = K, U$. Non-linear least squares is then used to estimate the utility function and the source function at the probability 0.5.

For probabilities different from 0.5, we obtain the source function by varying the number of colors j in the event E_2, $j = 1, 2, 3, 4, 5, 6, 7, 8$. Once we obtain the 8 values of the source function

$(w_s\left(\frac{1}{8}\right), w_s\left(\frac{2}{8}\right),\ldots, w_s\left(\frac{8}{8}\right))$, a two-parameter Prelec function, $w(p) = e^{-\beta(-\ln p)^{\alpha}}$ (Definition 2.4), is fitted through them.

The results are as follows.

1. Uniformity is not rejected for each of the two urns separately. This result holds at the aggregate and the individual-level data.
2. The estimates of ρ_s, $s = K, U$ are indistinguishable. Hence, potential explanations for the Ellsberg paradox should not rely on the differences in the utility functions across the two sources.
3. The most telling differences between the two urns come from the fitted source functions, w_s, $s = K, U$. The Prelec parameters for urn K are $\alpha = 0.85$, $\beta = 0.93$, and for urn U these are $\alpha = 0.64$, $\beta = 1.03$; Figure 4.1 plots the two source functions. The diagonal line corresponds to EU, the dotted curve to the source function for urn K and the heavy curve for urn U. Both parameter estimates for the source functions are significantly different from 1, hence, EU cannot explain the data (recall that for EU, $\alpha = \beta = 1$). A plausible interpretation is that each urn is viewed as a different source of uncertainty by the decision maker. The difference between the source functions for the two urns may be taken as a measure of the *ambiguity attitudes* of the decision maker. A measure of pessimism, that is developed by the authors, is significantly higher for urn U relative to urn K.
4. There is significant heterogeneity among the decision makers, as shown by the source functions for three subjects in Figure 4.2. Subject 2 is most pessimistic; subject 44 is most likely to be insensitive (flattest middle segment of the source function for urn U); subject 66 is *ambiguity seeking* because the source function for urn K lies outside the source function for urn U. Thus, subjects are characterized by a rich range of behaviors in the domain of uncertainty.

We have noted earlier that PT can be applied to risk, uncertainty, and ambiguity. An important empirical test of PT in this regard is provided by Kothiyal et al. (2014). These authors offer a more satisfactory treatment of PT relative to that reported in the tests of Hey et al. (2010). These

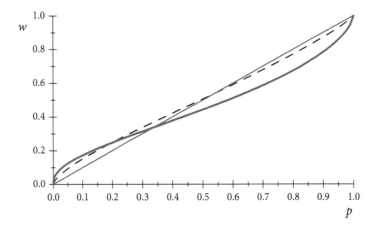

Figure 4.1 Source-dependent probability weighting functions. Plots of the diagonal line (solid thin line) and the source functions for urn K (dashed curve) and urn U (solid line).

Source: Abdellaoui, Baillon et al. (2011).

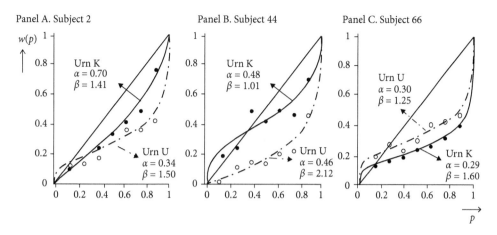

Figure 4.2 Subject heterogeneity for three subjects expressed in terms of their source functions.
Source: Abdellaoui, Baillon et al. (2011).

tests involve a combination of two major advances: the source method employed in Abdellaoui, Baillon et al. (2011) and the experimental implementation of the method for testing multiple prior models in Hey et al. (2010).

The device of a three-color (pink, blue, and yellow) bingo blower (see discussion above in Section 4.3.6) is used to ensure that the *ambiguous urn* does not turn into a *suspicious urn*. The total number of balls was varied to be 10, 20, and 40. Three-event prospects of the form $(E_1, 100; E_2, 10; E_3, -10)$ are presented. An example is: $E_1 = \{pink\}$, $E_2 = \{yellow, blue\}$ and $E_3 = \varnothing$ (an impossible event that never occurs). In most alternatives to EU, the decision maker maximizes an objective function of the form

$$V = \pi_1 u(100) + \pi_2 u(10) + \pi_3 u(-10),$$

where π_i is the decision weight associated with event E_i, $i = 1, 2, 3$ and u is a utility function. Under SEU, the decision maker evaluates utility as shown in (4.22). *Subjective expected value* (EV) is similar except that $u(x) = x$. Under *Choquet expected utility* (CEU) described in Section 4.3.1, the weighting function, $\widehat{w}$, has the properties: (i) $\widehat{w}(\varnothing) = 0$, where $\varnothing$ is the empty set; (ii) if $E_i \subseteq E_j$, then $\widehat{w}(E_i) \le \widehat{w}(E_j)$; (iii) $\widehat{w}(\cup_i E_i) = 1$. The decision weights in this case are given as in cumulative transformations of probabilities under PT, i.e.,

$$\pi_1 = \widehat{w}(E_1), \pi_2 = \widehat{w}(E_1 \cup E_2) - \widehat{w}(E_1), \pi_3 = 1 - \widehat{w}(E_1 \cup E_2).$$

The decision weights under PT are similar except that we allow for different weighting functions in the domains of gains and losses; in this example, only event E_3 pushes the decision maker into the domain of losses. Thus, in PT, unlike CEU, the decision weights need not add up to 1. For estimation purposes, the parameters of the models need to be reduced. We leave the reader to pursue the details on this issue from the original paper.[26]

---

[26] For instance, the weighting functions for gains and losses under PT are treated to be identical, and the Prelec weighting function is used. The authors also examine the implications of relaxing some of these assumptions.

A tournament is then run among 11 competing models (as in Hey et al. 2010); this list does not include models with second order beliefs. On most yardsticks, PT beats every other theory. These yardsticks include log likelihoods and the number of subjects conforming to the theory. Among the other rank dependent theories, α-MEU with $\alpha = 1$ does best. The authors conclude (p. 16): "This facilitates the study of ambiguity (the difference between uncertainty and risk), where prospect theory, unlike most other ambiguity theories today, need not commit to the descriptively failing expected utility for risk."

So far, we have considered the two-colors and three-colors Ellsberg experiments (see Examples 4.1 and 4.2). However, in order to consider the effect of the size of probabilities on ambiguity attitudes, we need to introduce more colors.

> **Example 4.7** *(n colors Ellsberg experiments, $n = 1, 2, 3, \ldots$) In the experiments of Dimmock et al. (2015), the known urn (K) contains kn balls of n different colors and k balls of each color. The unknown urn (U) also contains kn balls of the same n colors as urn K but in unknown proportions. The subject wins a prize if a randomly drawn ball from an urn is of the winning color. The experimenter chooses l of the n colors to be the winning colors, so urn K is known to contain kl balls of the winning colors. Which of the two urns (K or U) should the subject choose to bet on?*

Subjects do not know the proportions of the different colors in urn U, yet, if they use the *principle of insufficient reason*, they have no reason to favour one proportion over another. Hence, they should assign the same probability, $p = \frac{kl}{kn} = \frac{l}{n}$, to drawing a ball of a winning color from urn U. They should, thus, be indifferent to betting on K or U on probabilistic grounds (*ambiguity neutral*). Keeping unchanged the contents of urn U, construct a new known urn, K_i, with a known number, M_i, of balls of the l winning colors such that subject i is elicited to be indifferent between urns K_i and U. Then $m_i(p) = \frac{M_i}{kn} = \frac{M_i}{k(l/p)}$ is the *matching probability* of p for subject i.

Note that the definition of $m_i(p)$ does not depend on the particular decision theory assumed for the subjects. Let there be N subjects and let $m(p) = \frac{1}{N} \sum_{i=1}^{N} m_i(p)$ be the average of matching probabilities across all subjects. In their empirical exercise Dimmock et al. (2015) find $m(0.1) = 0.22$, $m(0.5) = 0.40$, $m(0.9) = 0.69$. Thus, on average, subjects are ambiguity seeking for low probabilities ($m(0.1) > 0.1$) but ambiguity averse for medium and high probabilities ($m(0.5) < 0.5$, $m(0.9) < 0.9$). This finding is difficult to account for in the neoclassical theories of ambiguity. However, these findings can be accounted for by new advances in *quantum decision theory* (al-Nowaihi and Dhami, 2017) and the empirical evidence is supportive of this explanation (Wei et al., 2018).

CHAPTER 5

A Guide to Further Reading

I include here brief notes on a few key papers that were published after I submitted my book draft to OUP in September 2015.[1] This is not merely an addendum to Volume 1. It contains critical new advances in the literature. As such, it is an essential requirement for developing a more complete understanding of the subject. We organize the readings below in the same order as the material presented in this book.

5.1 Evidence on decision making under risk and uncertainty

Baillon et al. (2016) consider if departures from EU are influenced by the contrast between individual and group decision making. They find that group decision making is more conducive to spotting stochastic dominance (when dominance is not obvious); in this sense groups lead to greater conformity with the axioms of rationality. On the other hand, groups enhance departures from EU in the context of the Allais paradox in its common ratio and common consequence violation forms.

Neoclassical economics and a great deal of behavioral economics are based on the assumption of stable risk preferences. However, are risk preferences really stable? We have considered in Section 1.5.6, the phenomenon of preference reversals, which suggest that such preferences might depend on the frame of the problem. Pedroni et al. (2017) consider six different elicitation methods (EMs) for measuring risk preferences across 1507 participants. The six EMs are drawn from across the social sciences and include Holt–Laury gambles, the balloon analogue risk task (BART), multiple price lists, the adaptive lottery method, the Columbia card task, and the marbles task. The main finding is that risk preferences are not stable across the EMs when measured by either the absolute levels of risk aversion or the ranks of individuals who are risk averse across the tasks. Measured preference parameters of PT are also not stable across tasks (although PT does better than EU).

These results are valuable and must be replicated. Even more important, the reasons for instability across the EMs, if successfully replicated, must be explored in depth. One possible

---

[1] I am very grateful to Peter Wakker for suggesting many of these papers and sharing his comments on the papers with me.

confound in the experiment is that the experiments took an entire day for each subject and there is likely to have been significant cognitive burden imposed on the subjects, possibly leading to noise in the data. One potential clue to this possibility is that contrary to the widespread finding of loss aversion, some EMs in this study (e.g., BART) find the opposite, i.e., gain seeking. The authors appear to favor an explanation based on the 'EM–specific construction of preferences' by subjects and reject the notion of stable preferences.

The work by Pedroni et al. (2017) speaks to the question of stability of preferences across different elicitation mechanisms. However, there is a different sense in which the stability of preferences may be studied. This has to do with aversion to risk before and after some cataclysmic natural event. We have already considered a few of the papers on this topic in this book. Hanaoka et al. (2018) consider the stability of risk preferences following the Great East Japan earthquake of 2011. Their findings are as follows. There are gender differences in the risk preferences when measured about one year from the earthquake. Men become more risk tolerant (their already low risk aversion decreases further). Many women, in contrast, become more risk averse. These effects are even more pronounced in regions in which the intensity of the earthquake was higher. The second main finding is that this effect persists in men, when measured five years from the earthquake, and the risk tolerance is about the same as it was, one year after the earthquake. This suggests that there are long-term and persistence effects on risk preferences of such natural events.

On the one hand these studies are valuable because they question the basic assumption of temporally stable preferences. On the other hand, they continue to use the expected utility framework, which implies that risk attitudes are captured entirely by the shape of the utility function. We know that this is not the case when we consider the alternatives such as RDU and PT. Not only are risk attitudes much richer in PT, but it might also be the case that what we believe to be risk aversion under EU might well be loss aversion instead (see Sections 2.4.2 and 3.2.2). There is still imperfect awareness and acknowledgment of these critical issues in the literature.

Countercyclical risk aversion has been offered as an explanation of several puzzles (e.g., measured equity risk premium is relatively higher in a recession as compared to a boom). However, measuring such risk aversion using field data is problematic because depending on the economic circumstances (boom or bust conditions) the expected rates of return on assets may also change. For instance, investors may invest less in a bust condition because risk aversion is higher, or because they expect low returns in the future. Cohn et al. (2015) find a way out of this measurement confound by priming finance professionals for boom and bust conditions; they find that their measured risk aversion is countercyclical. Thus, in a bust condition they are more risk averse, and in a boom condition they are relatively less risk averse. Investment in risky assets is also about 22% lower in a bust condition. A similar finding of lower investment in the risky asset in a bust condition also arises when subjects face a situation of ambiguity rather than risk. These results are not mitigated by taking account of the experience of the subjects; in fact, more experienced subjects exhibit even more countercyclical risk aversion. The authors identify 'fear' as an underlying explanatory mechanism; subjects are more fearful in a bust condition that potentially makes them more cautious and reduces investment in risky assets.[2]

---

[2] Fear is induced by the threat of a random electric shock while the subjects make their investment decision. Two treatments, high and low electric shock, were run to induce high and low levels of fear and the contrast between these conditions is used to make the relevant inferences.

5.2 Models of behavioral decision theory

In Section 2.6.2 we outlined the axiomatic foundations of the Prelec probability weighting function and we noted that three axiomatic foundations have been proposed. In Theorem 2.2, we noted that these three are equivalent. Aydogan et al. (2016) test empirically for one of these, reduction invariance, and find that their tests support it (although they do not show awareness of the result in Theorem 2.2). By implication, from Theorem 2.2, all three of the axiomatic foundations must be supported. In Section 1.5.7, we noted that the evidence does not support the reduction of the compound lotteries axiom. The authors replicate this finding at the aggregate level, although 60% of the subjects behave in conformity with it.

Most existing axiomatizations of prospect theory use an exogenously given reference point. Werner and Zank (2018) propose an axiomatization that has an endogenous reference point. The method relies on the idea that probability midpoints are influenced as one shifts some probability mass in a lottery from losses to gains—this reveals the location of the reference point.

In Section 2.8.3, while examining the empirical evidence for Köszegi–Rabin reference points, I stressed the need for more stringent tests of the theory. Gneezy et al. (2017) extend the method of Abeler et al. (2011), described in Section 2.8.3. The prediction of the Köszegi–Rabin reference point is a monotone response in behavior to changes in expectations in the real effort task experiment. However, this is found to be violated.

Models of stochastic utility are often used to infer attitudes to risk. These models are also used extensively in the learning literature (see Volume 6). Apesteguia and Ballester (2018) highlight an important limitation of these models. Suppose that an individual is given two gambles, one riskier than the other. One would then expect most reasonable models to predict that as risk aversion increases, the probability of choosing the riskier gamble should fall (monotonicity property). In contrast, the authors show that an implication of the random utility model when the gambles are chosen using a logistic model is that the monotonicity property is violated. In one of their results, the authors show that there is a level of risk aversion beyond which the probability of choosing the riskier gamble actually increases. Finally, a modification of the random utility model is proposed that is not subject to this criticism.

At the end of Section 2.9, we have briefly alluded to the correlation between cognitive ability and risk taking. In their survey, Dohmen et al. (2018) review the relevant literature and the difficulties in establishing causality. One of the main findings is that in the domain of harmful decisions (substance abuse, unsafe sexual practices, criminal behavior) people with greater cognitive ability undertake less risky activities (so risk aversion and cognitive ability are positively correlated in the harmful activities domain). In contrast, in the domain of advantageous activities (financial decision making, stock market participation), the correlation between cognitive ability and risk aversion is negative. Another finding is that the precise measure of cognitive ability is important. Thus, risk preferences are better correlated with those aspects of cognitive ability that are specific to quantitative problem solving.

Case based decision theory (CBDT) was discussed in Section 2.10.4. One advantage of the theory is that relative to subjective expected utility, it does not require knowledge of all probabilities and all outcomes, so it can deal with true uncertainty (or Knightian uncertainty). However, the use of a similarity function in comparing the current situation to ones that exist in memory involves the measurement of the parameters of the similarity function. Bleichrodt et al. (2017) propose a nonparametric estimation that obviates the need for measuring such parameters. They find support for CBDT but also one violation of CBDT (cases are not separable in memory).

In Section 2.10.1, we considered regret theory, due to Bell (1982) and Loomes and Sugden (1982). We gave the choice criterion under regret theory in (2.105) using a regret function R. In this formulation, utility and regret functions are not separable. Consider now a slightly different formulation that allows such a separation. Assume the same setup as in the first two paragraphs of Section 2.10.1. Given actions A_1 and A_2, a decision maker who follows regret theory satisfies

$$A_1 \succeq A_2 \text{ if and only if } \sum_{i=1}^{n} p_i Q\left(u\left(x_i\right) - u\left(y_i\right)\right),$$

where u is a utility function and Q is a regret function. Comparing (2.105) with this formulation, we see that $R\left(x_i, y_i\right) = Q\left(u\left(x_i\right) - u\left(y_i\right)\right)$. This is the sense in which the regret and utility functions may be separated. The main insight of regret theory is that one's enjoyment from an outcome may be reduced by the emotion of regret if one contemplates the foregone outcome from an action that was not taken. Clearly, if Q is a convex function, as the size of the utility difference grows, so does the magnitude of regret. In other words, regret simply corresponds to a convex Q. If Q is linear then EU can be seen to be a special case of regret theory.

As noted in Section 2.10.1, regret theory does not impose transitivity, which makes it difficult to accommodate it within other decision theories in economics that require transitivity. However, we also noted that the measurements of Bleichrodt et al. (2010), based on the trade-off method, support a convex Q, which is a central implication of regret theory.

The available axiomatizations of regret theory were available for the form given in (2.105). Diecidue and Somasundaram (2017) propose an axiomatization of the newer form given above, based on tradeoff consistency (Definition 2.20 in the text) that takes account of the measurement method employed in Bleichrodt et al. (2010). Their key new axiom is *d-transitivity*. This axiom only kicks in if in a set of three Savage acts, one act dominates others or is dominated by the others.[3] It requires that if one act dominates the others then improving its outcomes in all states does not alter the preference relation. Or if one act is dominated by others, then reducing its outcomes in all states does not alter the preference relation either.

5.3 Behavioral economics of ambiguity

Ambiguity attitudes are typically measured only for lab events, such as lab experiments on the Ellsberg paradox. Why? The reason is that lab events allow one to invoke plausible auxiliary assumptions, such as the principle of insufficient reason, to infer the likelihood of events. This may be difficult for natural events. Consider a Savage act K that promises a reward of $\$z$ in the two-colors Ellsberg experiment (Example 4.1) if the outcome of a random draw is a 'red ball' from the known urn. We now form a field analogue of the unknown urn, U, in a lab Ellsberg experiment as follows.

Let E be the event that the market price of silver (a very volatile market) changes within $\pm 5\%$ of its current price in the next four months, and E^c the complementary event. Consider the Savage act $U = (E, z; E^c, 0)$ that pays $\$z$ if event E occurs. Suppose that the decision maker reveals a preference for K over U. Is the decision maker ambiguity averse/seeking, or does he simply assign too low a subjective probability to the event E? Without knowing the likelihood of the event E it

---

[3] Our exposition in Section 2.10.1, and above, is in terms of actions, not Savage acts. However, it is not difficult to convert our discussion in terms of Savage acts.

is difficult to give an answer. By contrast, the principle of insufficient reason suggests that in the two-colors Ellsberg lab experiment, one may assign a probability of 0.5 to a red ball being drawn from the unknown urn.

The contribution of Baillon et al. (2018) is to suggest a method of measuring ambiguity attitudes for natural events without the need to invoke likelihoods. They use the method of matching probabilities that is outlined at the end of Chapter 4. The proposed method applies to all theories of ambiguity that evaluate the Savage act U, as described above (but potentially extended to more than two events), by $W(E)u(z)$, where W is a probability weighting function defined over events and u is a utility function that is invariant to risk and any type of uncertainty (e.g., it is identical under risk and ambiguity). Some of the ambiguity theories that we considered in Chapter 4, notably the smooth ambiguity aversion model, do not fit into this framework.

Suppose that the decision maker expresses the following indifference in the context of the two Savage acts K and U, as described above: "I am indifferent between betting on the Savage act U and the Savage act K provided that the probability of drawing a red ball from the known urn is $m \in [0,1]$." Here m is the matching probability. Let probabilistic sophistication hold so that the likelihood assigned to event E, in the mind of the individual, is $\mu(E)$. The revealed indifference implies that $W(m)u(z) = W(\mu(E))u(z)$, from which it follows that $\mu(E) = m \equiv m(E)$; this allows us to drop subjective likelihoods. Let the matching probability of event E^c be likewise $m(E^c)$.

A decision maker is said to be ambiguity neutral if $m(E) + m(E^c) = 1$ and ambiguity averse if $m(E) + m(E^c) < 1$; indeed this leads to the following natural definition of the ambiguity aversion index.

Definition 5.1   *The ambiguity aversion index is $b = 1 - (m(E) + m(E^c))$.*

Ambiguity aversion is the highest when $m(E) = 0$ and $m(E^c) = 0$ so that b takes its highest possible value of 1. Conversely, ambiguity aversion is the lowest when $m(E) = 1$ and $m(E^c) = 1$, so $b = 0$. There is a range of intermediate cases when $b \in (-1,1)$.

The ambiguity aversion index does not alone capture the richness of ambiguity attitudes. It does not, for instance, capture *a-insensitivity*, which requires the use of at least three events, E_1, E_2, E_3. As above, we can find matching probabilities of these events $m(E_1)$, $m(E_2)$, $m(E_3)$ and the matching probabilities of the complements of these events, $m(E_1^c)$, $m(E_2^c)$, $m(E_3^c)$. Define the averages, $\overline{m}_E = \frac{1}{3}(m(E_1) + m(E_2) + m(E_3))$ and $\overline{m}_{E^c} = \frac{1}{3}(m(E_1^c) + m(E_2^c) + m(E_3^c))$. The ambiguity aversion index is now defined as $b = 1 - \overline{m}_E - \overline{m}_{E^c}$. Under ambiguity neutrality, $\overline{m}_E = \frac{1}{3}$, $\overline{m}_{E^c} = \frac{2}{3}$ and $b = 0$. However, departures from ambiguity neutrality lead to $b \in [-1, 0)$.

The a-insensitivity index captures the extent to which low likelihoods (low values of subjective likelihoods $\mu(E_i)$, $i = 1, 2, 3$) are overweighted and high likelihoods are underweighted.[4] This can be shown to reduce the difference $\overline{m}_{E^c} - \overline{m}_E$. Complete insensitivity to the events takes place when a decision maker assigns a 50–50 chance to an event and its complement (in this case $\overline{m}_{E^c} - \overline{m}_E = 0$). As noted above, under ambiguity neutrality, $\overline{m}_E = \frac{1}{3}$, $\overline{m}_{E^c} = \frac{2}{3}$ so that $\overline{m}_{E^c} - \overline{m}_E = \frac{1}{3}$. Departures from $\frac{1}{3}$ are measured by the ambiguity generated insensitivity (or a-insensitivity) index.

Definition 5.2   *The a-insensitivity index is given by $a = 3\left[\frac{1}{3} - (\overline{m}_{E^c} - \overline{m}_E)\right]$.*

---

[4] The corresponding finding of inverse S-shaped probability weighting functions under risk (see Section 2.2) is sometimes termed *risk insensitivity*.

The multiplication by 3 in the definition of a-insensitivity index is a convenient normalization which bounds its maximal value to 1 (when $\overline{m}_{E^c} - \overline{m}_E = 0$). The common finding is one of a-insensitivity, i.e., $a > 0$. When the experiments are conducted under time pressure, there is no effect on ambiguity aversion, but a-insensitivity is affected.

We have considered the fourfold classification of risk attitudes in Section 2.4.2. Does a similar classification exist under ambiguity? Kocher et al. (2018) consider this question for gain/loss outcomes, low/moderate likelihoods of events and for mixed prospects that have both gain and loss outcomes. They find that the majority of their subjects are ambiguity neutral. Of the remaining subjects, they find a fourfold pattern of ambiguity attitudes. Ambiguity aversion is found for moderate likelihood gains and low likelihood losses. In contrast, ambiguity seeking is found for low likelihood gains and moderate likelihood losses. No clear pattern emerges for mixed prospects. This evidence calls into further focus the assumption of universal ambiguity aversion that is found in many models of ambiguity.

Measuring loss aversion is a non-trivial problem in PT because PT allows the utility function and the probability weighting function to differ in the domain of gains and losses. Thus, most measurements of loss aversion impose either piecewise linear utility or linear probability weighting. For this reason, Abdellaoui et al. (2007) came up with a method of measuring loss aversion that did not require these simplifying conditions; see Section 2.5 above. However, there existed no method of measuring loss aversion under ambiguity.

In light of this discussion, the main contribution of Abdellaoui et al. (2016) is as follows. (1) They propose a parameter-free method to measure loss aversion under ambiguity. This is achieved through an extension of the trade-off method of Wakker and Deneffe (1996) to mixed prospects. With this contribution one can now measure loss aversion under risk, uncertainty, and ambiguity. (2) Measured utility does not depend on the source when tested with the classical Ellsberg known/unknown urn experiments. Yet, subjects exhibit ambiguity aversion, which rejects most utility-based neoclassical theories of ambiguity. (3) Subjects exhibit identical levels of loss aversion for risk and ambiguity, suggesting that it is a deep parameter of preferences that is independent of the underlying situation. (4) Sign-comonotonic trade-off consistency is a necessary and (under richness assumptions) sufficient preference condition for PT. It is satisfied by the data. Furthermore, utility is found to be concave in gains and convex in losses with significant loss aversion. These findings give strong support to PT.

Consider the matching probabilities described at the end of Chapter 4. Dimmock, Kouwenberg, and Wakker (2015) find that these matching probabilities are inverse S-shaped, with a relatively flat middle segment, so there is ambiguity insensitivity for probabilities in the middle range. This they term as *a-insensitivity*. While a-insensitivity has been documented in experiments on the student population (e.g., Trautmann and van de Kuilen, 2016), this is the first paper to report such a finding for the general population. Subjects who exhibit a-insensitivity are less likely to participate in the stock market (non–participation puzzle). However, ambiguity aversion has only a weaker link with stock market participation.

In section 4.4.2 we outlined the source dependence approach to an explanation of the Ellsberg paradox. Chew and Sagi (2008) informally defined a source as: "a group of events that is generated by a common mechanism of uncertainty." In Section 4.4.2, the basic approach relied on identifying the known and the unknown urns as two different sources. Armantier and Treich (2016) take this idea further. They consider three kinds of urns, a known urn (K) and an unknown urn (U) as in the classical Ellsberg experiments, and, in addition, a *complex urn under risk* (K_1). There are balls of eight colors in known proportions in urns K and K_1 (hence, these are risky urns) but the proportion of the eight colors in urn U is unknown. Thus, as explained at the end of

Chapter 4, this allows us to conduct Ellsberg experiments for different levels of probabilities. Urn K_1 is complex in the following sense. It is composed of two transparent urns (K_{1A} and K_{1B}), which have eight balls each. The subject wins a prize if a pair of balls drawn randomly from urns K_{1A} and K_{1B} are of a certain color (or colors). For instance, a prize may be conditional on drawing a red ball from each of the two urns K_{1A} and K_{1B}; the probability of this event is $1/64$.

The results are as follows. (1) For probabilities greater than $1/4$, the certainty equivalents of events (an event specifies a prize for drawing a set of winning colors from an urn) for urns U and K_1 are similar, but both are statistically different from urn K. (2) Fitting a power form of utility and a generalization of the Prelec weighting function, the utility functions from the three urns K, U, and K_1 are, on average, indistinguishable. (3) The α and β parameters in the Prelec function are indistinguishable between urns U and K_1 but both parameters are lower when compared with urn K. (4) The contrast in certainty equivalents between urns K, U captures ambiguity premium, while a similar contrast between urns K, K_1 captures complexity premium. The ambiguity and complexity premia are significantly positively correlated ($\rho = 0.714$). The paper concludes that the domain of risk is also rich and depending on the distinction between simple and complex tasks in this domain, there could be multiple sources within the risk domain.

Experiments on the Ellsberg paradox and the attempt to correlate ambiguity attitudes with financial decisions are typically undertaken in a lab environment. In contrast, Dimmock, Kouwenberg, Mitchell et al. (2016) undertake this exercise with US households by paying them real monetary incentives. The objective is to elicit their ambiguity attitudes and then correlate them with financial market variables that include the following: Stock market participation; fraction of financial assets held in stocks; foreign stock ownership; ownership of stocks in own-company; and selling behavior of stocks in the financial crises. This follows a similar methodology and theory (despite the contrary claim by the authors) as done for Dutch households in the study by Dimmock, Kouwenberg, and Wakker (2015). The experiments are conducted with 50–50 likelihoods, so they are not suitable to study ambiguity attitudes for different levels of probabilities. However, the study breaks new ground in the literature because it is large scale, fully incentivized, and contributes towards establishing the external validity of lab experiments in this area.

The main findings are as follows. (1) As in many earlier studies, there is heterogeneity in ambiguity attitudes; 52% are ambiguity averse, 10% are ambiguity neutral, and 38% are ambiguity seeking. These attitudes are not due to a misunderstanding of probabilities, i.e., they are not mistakes. (2) Greater ambiguity aversion reduces three of the financial variables considered (stock market participation, fraction of financial assets held in stocks, and foreign stock ownership) but increases ownership of own-company stock. The first of these results implies that risk aversion and ambiguity aversion are different because risk aversion implies a different effect (diversification of portfolio) relative to the other. (3) We have already noted the competence hypothesis in Section 4.3.6; namely, that people appear more ambiguity averse in domains in which they believe that they have a lower competence. This is confirmed in the experiments here. Stock market competence is measured in terms of self-assessed stock market knowledge and financial literacy. Lack of competence enhances the negative effect of ambiguity aversion on stock market participation.

Does ambiguity aversion vary with income? Is ambiguity aversion in developing countries comparable with that in developed countries? These questions are answered in Li (2017) who studies the ambiguity attitudes of poor and rich rural and urban Chinese adolescents. The particular ambiguity considered is linguistic ambiguity in terms of the ability to identify foreign-sounding words. The results are as follows. (1) In the group of rural subjects, ambiguity aversion and a-insensitivity decrease with an increase in income. (2) In the urban group, a-sensitivity increases with an increase in income but there is no effect of income on ambiguity aversion (which ties in with findings from developed countries). (3) Comparing the two groups, on average, the urban group is less ambiguity averse as compared to the rural group.

5.4 Exercises for Volume 1

1. Using the reduction axiom, show that Proposition 1.1 holds for the case of any finite number of outcomes.

2. Using Definition 1.5, show that risk neutrality, risk aversion, risk seeking are equivalent, respectively, to a linear, concave, convex utility function.

3. (St. Petersburg paradox) Suppose that a decision maker were to accept the following gamble. A fair coin is tossed repeatedly in independent trials until a head comes up. If a head comes up on the nth toss, then the payoff from this gamble is 2^n. Show that the expected value of this gamble is infinite. People are typically willing to pay only about $20 for this gamble. How much would a decision maker who followed the expected value criterion (EV) pay for this lottery? Show that a sufficient condition to reconcile the EV criterion with the empirical findings is to have a sufficiently concave utility function, $u(x)$, where x is an outcome.

4. (Affine transformations) Let $F : \mathcal{L} \to \mathbb{R}$ and $G : \mathcal{L} \to \mathbb{R}$, where $\mathcal{L}$ is the set of all simple lotteries. We say that G is a positive affine transformation of F if, and only if, there are real numbers, α, β, with $\beta > 0$, such that $G = \alpha + \beta F$. Show that $G : \mathcal{L} \to \mathbb{R}$ is a positive affine transformation of $F : \mathcal{L} \to \mathbb{R}$ if, and only if, F is a positive affine transformation of G.

5. Given two functions, $F : \mathcal{L} \to \mathbb{R}$ and $G : \mathcal{L} \to \mathbb{R}$, let the respective induced preferences on $\mathcal{L}$, be denoted by $\preceq_F$ and $\preceq_G$. Let the two functions, $F : \mathcal{L} \to \mathbb{R}$ and $G : \mathcal{L} \to \mathbb{R}$, satisfy, for all $L_1, L_2, L \in \mathcal{L}$, and all $p \in [0, 1]$,
   (i) $F(x_1) \leq F(L) \leq F(x_n)$ and $F(x_1) < F(x_n)$,
   (ii) $G(x_1) \leq G(L) \leq G(x_n)$ and $G(x_1) < G(x_n)$.
   (iii) $F(L_1, p; L_2, 1-p) = pF(L_1) + (1-p)F(L_2)$,
   (iv) $G(L_1, p; L_2, 1-p) = pG(L_1) + (1-p)G(L_2)$.
   Show that the induced orders, $\preceq_F$ and $\preceq_G$, are identical if, and only if, G is a positive affine transformation of F.

6. Show that Example 1.3 can be recast as a common consequence violation, as defined in Definition 1.15.

7. Prove Propositions 1.6 and 1.7.

8. Draw a probability triangle to explain the common consequence violation corresponding to Example 1.3 and show that the indifference curves in the triangle must *fan out* for consistency with the evidence.

9. (Probabilistic insurance; Wakker et al., 1997) Suppose that a decision maker has wealth, $W > 0$. With some probability $0 < p < 1$, the decision maker incurs a monetary loss, $L < 0$. In effect, the decision maker faces the lottery $(W - L, p; W, 1 - p)$. The utility function of the risk averse decision maker is given by $u(z)$, which is increasing and concave. Since utility is measured on an ordinal scale, we can, for pedagogical simplicity, choose the following normalization $u(W) = 1$, $u(W - L) = 0$.

Suppose that the decision maker is offered a hypothetical insurance contract that charges a premium, $P > 0$, so that he just prefers to buy the insurance contract. The insurance contract offers the following lottery, $(W - P, p; W - P, 1 - p) \equiv (W - P, 1)$. Now, suppose that the decision maker is offered *probabilistic insurance*. Under this form of insurance contract, the decision maker will pay a premium of θP, $0 \leq \theta \leq 1$. Should a loss occur, then (1) with probability $1 - \theta$, the loss will not be covered, and the premium θP will be returned, and (2) with probability θ, the loss will be fully covered, but the decision maker will have to pay an extra premium of $(1 - \theta) P$ (so in effect, a total premium of P in that state). All this is summarized in the following lottery under probabilistic insurance.

$$\left(W - L, (1 - \theta) p; W - P, \theta p; W - \theta P, 1 - p\right). \tag{5.1}$$

Show that conditional on just accepting the insurance contract at a premium P, an EU decision maker will prefer probabilistic insurance.
10. Prove Proposition 2.1.
11. Prove Proposition 2.2.
12. Consider the probability weighting function $w(p) = p^\gamma$, where $\gamma > 1$. Is this probability weighting function subproportional? Can it capture the certainty effect?
13. Check that the weighting functions in (2.5), (2.6), and (2.7) satisfy the conditions of a probability weighting function. Also check the conditions under which these functions are subproportional.
14. (al-Nowaihi and Dhami, 2011): Let $w(p)$ be the Prelec function. Suppose $\alpha \neq 1$. Then prove the following:
    (a) $w''(\widetilde{p}) = 0$ for some $\widetilde{p} \in (0, 1)$ and, for any such $\widetilde{p}$:
        (i) For $\alpha < 1 : p < \widetilde{p} \Rightarrow w''(p) < 0, p > \widetilde{p} \Rightarrow w''(p) > 0$.
        (ii) For $\alpha > 1 : p < \widetilde{p} \Rightarrow w''(p) > 0, p > \widetilde{p} \Rightarrow w''(p) < 0$.
    (b) The Prelec function has a unique inflexion point, $\widetilde{p} \in (0, 1)$, and is characterized by $\alpha\beta \left(-\ln\widetilde{p}\right)^\alpha + \ln\widetilde{p} + 1 - \alpha = 0$.
    (c) $\beta = 1 \Rightarrow \widetilde{p} = e^{-1}$.
    (d) $\frac{\partial \widetilde{p}}{\partial \beta} = \frac{\alpha\widetilde{p}(-\ln\widetilde{p})^{1+\alpha}}{(\alpha-1)(\alpha-\ln\widetilde{p})}$.
    (e) $\frac{\partial[w(\widetilde{p})-\widetilde{p}]}{\partial\beta} = \frac{\widetilde{p}(-\ln\widetilde{p})^{1+\alpha}}{(\alpha-1)(\alpha-\ln\widetilde{p})}\left(e^{\frac{1-\alpha}{\alpha}}(\widetilde{p})^{\frac{1-\alpha}{\alpha}} - \alpha\right)$.
    (f) $\widetilde{p} \lessgtr w(\widetilde{p}) \Leftrightarrow \beta \lessgtr 1$.
15. Prove Propositions 2.3, 2.4, and Corollary 2.1.
16. Prove Proposition 2.5.
17. Prove Proposition 2.6.
18. Consider the lottery $L = (15, 0.8; 0, 0.2)$ that captures the risky returns associated with a financial decision. The utility function of the decision maker satisfies $u(0) = 0$. The individual uses RDU to evaluate lotteries and has the probability weighting function $w(p) = p^2$. Relative to a decision maker who follows expected utility (EU), is this decision maker optimistic or pessimistic?
19. Consider the lottery $L = (9, \frac{1}{3}; 16, \frac{1}{3}; 25, \frac{1}{3})$ that captures the discounted risky returns associated with the purchase of a financial security. The utility function of the decision maker is $u(x) = \sqrt{x}$. [Restrict calculations to four decimal places.]
    (a) Suppose that the decision maker follows EU. Compute the expected utility of the lottery. Is the decision maker risk averse, risk neutral, or risk loving?

(b) Suppose that the decision maker uses RDU to evaluate lotteries and has the probability weighting function $w(p) = \sqrt{p}$. Is this decision maker risk averse, risk neutral, or risk loving?

(c) If there is a difference in the risk attitudes found in parts (a) and (b), what accounts for the difference?

20. (RDU can explain the Allais paradox) Suppose that the utility function is $u(x) = x^{0.6} - x_0^{0.6}$, where x is the (final) level of wealth and x_0 is the initial level of wealth. The constant $-x_0^{0.6}$ is added, so that $u(x_0) = 0$ (as was assumed in Example 1.2). Take the Prelec (1998) probability weighting function with $\alpha = 0.15$, $\beta = 0.5$. Show that RDU is able to predict the "common ratio violation" in Example 1.2.

21. Let a decision maker have initial wealth, x_0, and utility function, u. Now consider problems 1 and 2 from Kahneman and Tversky (1979) that were given to 72 subjects. All lotteries are in units of Israeli pounds.

Problem 1: (72 subjects) Choose between

$$L_1 = (x_0, 0; x_0 + 2400, 1) \text{ and } L_2 = (x_0, 0.01; x_0 + 2400, 0.66; x_0 + 2500, 0.33).$$

Problem 2: (72 subjects) Choose between

$$L_3 = (x_0, 0.66; x_0 + 2400; 0.34) \text{ and } L_4 = (x_0, 0.67; x_0 + 2500, 0.33).$$

The data shows that 82% of the subjects chose L_1 in problem 1 and 83% of subjects chose L_4 in problem 2. Each of these preferences was significant at the 1% level.

(a) Is the choice data of the majority of subjects consistent with expected utility?

(b) Assume that $u(x_0) = 0$, and the weighting function is very steep in the neighborhood of $p = 1$, and flat in the middle, which, for instance, is the case with the Prelec function. Is the choice data of the majority of subjects consistent with rank dependent utility?

22. Prove Proposition 2.7.

23. Construct an example, analogous to Example 2.7 to illustrate Claim 2.2.

24. (Huber et al., 1982; Ok et al., 2015) Consider three alternatives, x, y, z. Each alternative has two dimensions (say, price and quality). Alternative x dominates y in one dimension and is dominated in the other. Alternative z (i) is dominated by x in both dimensions, and (ii) dominates y in one dimension, while being dominated in the other dimension. When given a choice from the set $\{x, y\}$ the decision maker chooses y and when given a choice from the set $\{x, y, z\}$ he chooses x. This is known as the *asymmetric dominance effect* or the *attraction effect*.

(a) Within the neoclassical framework, does such an individual have a well-defined utility function?

(b) How can you explain this effect using prospect theory?

25. Suppose that a decision maker who uses prospect theory faces the following lottery with two outcomes $0, x$ such that $x < 0$.

$$L = \left(0, 1 - p; x, p\right) \text{ where } x < 0.$$

Suppose that the utility function for losses is given by $u(x) = -2.5\sqrt{-x}$ and we treat the reference point r as zero wealth (so $u(0) = 0$). Let us use the Prelec weighting function, $w\left(p\right) = e^{-\beta(-\ln p)^{\alpha}}$ with $\alpha = 0.5$, $\beta = 1$. Show that depending on the value of p, such a decision maker can be both risk loving and risk averse. In particular, show that there is a cutoff point $p^* = 0.0183$ such that $w(p^*)^2 = p^*$, and (i) for $p^* < 0.0183$, the decision maker is risk averse, while (ii) for $p^* > 0.0183$, the decision maker is risk averse.

26. (Loomes et al., 1992) This exercise highlights various features of regret theory.

    (a) (Violation of transitivity under regret theory) Suppose that we have three states of the world, s_1, s_2, and s_3; each occurs with probability $\frac{1}{3}$. There are three actions, A_1, A_2, and A_3; outcomes ($x_1 < x_2 < x_3$) corresponding to these actions in the various states are given in the following table.

	$s_1 \left(\frac{1}{3}\right)$	$s_2 \left(\frac{1}{3}\right)$	$s_3 \left(\frac{1}{3}\right)$
A_1	x_1	x_2	x_3
A_2	x_3	x_1	x_2
A_3	x_2	x_3	x_1

Actions A_1, A_2, A_3 are said to be *stochastically equivalent* because the three states are equiprobable. Suppose that $A_1 \prec A_2$, $A_2 \prec A_3$ and $A_3 \prec A_1$, which violates transitivity. Can regret theory account for this pattern of intransitivity?

(b) (Violation of monotonicity) Suppose that we have only two actions, A_1, A_2. The outcomes are shown in the following table:

	$s_1 \left(\frac{1}{3}\right)$	$s_2 \left(\frac{1}{3}\right)$	$s_3 \left(\frac{1}{3}\right)$
A_1	x_1	$x_2 + \epsilon$	x_3
A_2	x_3	x_1	x_2

where $\epsilon > 0$ is a sufficiently small number, so that $x_2 + \epsilon < x_3$ and

$$\frac{1}{3}R(x_3, x_1) + \frac{1}{3}R(x_1, x_2 + \epsilon) + \frac{1}{3}R(x_2, x_3) > 0. \tag{5.2}$$

Show that $A_1 \prec A_2$ but A_1 first order stochastically dominates A_2.

27. (al-Nowaihi and Dhami, 2010a,b) Suppose that a decision maker suffers loss, $L > 0$, with a small probability $p > 0$. He/she can buy coverage, $C \in [0, L]$, at the cost rC, where $r \in (0, 1)$ is the *premium rate* (which is *actuarially fair* if $r = p$). Hence, with probability, $1 - p$, the decision maker's wealth is $W - rC$, and with probability p, her wealth is $W - rC - L + C \leq W - rC$. Suppose that the reference point of the individual is the status quo, i.e., $y_0 = W$, the utility function is the power form in Equation (2.19) with $\gamma^+ \simeq \gamma^- = \gamma$, and the objective function is given in Definition 2.15. Assume that we have actuarially fair premium, $r = p$.

    (a) Show under RDU, with the Prelec function, and $p \to 0$, optimal $C^* = 0$ or $C^* = L$.

    (b) What is the predicted insurance purchase under PT?

    (c) What is your conjecture of insurance behavior under composite prospect theory (CPT)?

    (d) Two kinds of insurance behavior are observed for low probability losses. Kunreuther et al. (1978) report little or no take-up of insurance for many individuals. However, Sydnor (2010) reports over-insurance for modest risks for many individuals. Conjecture if CPT can account for these conflicting findings?

28. (al-Nowaihi and Dhami, 2010a) Consider the same setup as in Problem 27:

(a) Suppose that a decision maker faces a loss, L, with probability $p = 0.001$. Recall the formal definition of CPT in Section 2.11.3. Motivated by the insurance data from Kunreuther et al. (1978), suppose that the CPF is given by

$$w(p) = \begin{cases} e^{-0.61266(-\ln p)^2}, & \text{i.e., } \alpha = 2, \beta = 0.61266, & \text{if} \quad 0 \le p < 0.25, \\ e^{-(-\ln p)^{\frac{1}{2}}}, & \text{i.e., } \alpha = 0.5, \beta = 1, & \text{if} \quad 0.25 \le p \le 0.75, \\ e^{-6.4808(-\ln p)^2}, & \text{i.e., } \alpha = 2, \beta = 6.4808, & \text{if} \quad 0.75 < p \le 1. \end{cases} \quad (5.3)$$

In this case (i.e., $p = 0.001$) the findings of Kunreuther et al. (1978) show that only 20% of the decision makers insure. Suppose that the utility function of the decision maker is given in (2.19) with $\gamma^+ \simeq \gamma^- = \gamma = 0.88$.

(a1) For decision makers who use PT, the probability weighting function is the standard Prelec function with $\beta = 1$ and $\alpha = 0.50$, i.e., $w(p) = e^{-(-\ln p)^{0.50}}$. Show that such a decision maker will fully insure.

(a2) Consider decision makers who use CPT. Decision makers who belong to the fraction $1 - \mu$ use PT and so, as in (a), will fully insure. Now consider those who belong to the fraction μ. They use the composite Prelec function given in (5.3). Show that these individuals will not insure.

(b) Let the probability of the loss be $p = 0.25$ (instead of $p = 0.001$). Kunreuther's (1978) data shows that 80% of subjects in experiments took up insurance in this case. Show that the predictions of both PT and CPT are in close (but not perfect) conformity with the evidence.

(c) What do we learn from comparing the (correct) answers to parts (a) and (b)?

29. (Dhami and al-Nowaihi, 2013) Suppose that income from legal activity is $y_0 \ge 0$ and income from an illegal activity is $y_1 \ge y_0$. Hence, the benefit, b, from the illegal activity is $b = y_1 - y_0 \ge 0$. If engaged in the illegal activity, the individual is caught with some probability p, $0 \le p \le 1$. If caught, the individual is asked to pay a fine F. Assume that we have the *hyperbolic punishment function* $F = \varphi(p) = b/p$.[5]

(a) Consider a decision maker with continuously differentiable and strictly increasing utility of income, u. Show that under EU, if the decision maker is risk neutral, or risk averse, then the hyperbolic punishment function $\varphi(p) = \frac{b}{p}$ will deter crime. It follows that given any probability of detection and conviction, $p > 0$, no matter how small, crime can be deterred by a sufficiently large punishment. This is the *Becker proposition* alluded to in the text (see Proposition 22).

(b) Now suppose that the decision maker uses PT or CPT and that the reference incomes from the two activities, crime and no-crime, are, respectively, y_R and y_r. If a decision maker commits a crime, and is caught, then assume that the outcome $(y_1 - F)$ is in the domain of losses (i.e., $y_1 - F - y_R < 0$). If he commits a crime and is not caught, then assume that the outcome, y_1, is in the domain of gains (i.e., $y_1 - y_R > 0$). The recent literature has sometimes made the case for the reference point to be the rational

---

[5] al-Nowaihi and Dhami (2012) show that the hyperbolic punishment function is optimal for a wide class of cost of deterrence and damage from crime functions. Furthermore, it provides an upper bound on punishments for a large and sensible class of cost and damage functions. Thus, if the hyperbolic punishment function cannot deter crime, then neither can the optimal punishment function, if different from the hyperbolic.

expectation of income and also the state-dependent reference point.[6] In the spirit of these suggestions, suppose that the expected income from each activity is the reference point. Thus, $y_r = y_0$ and $y_R = y_1 - p\varphi(p)$. Assume the power form of utility in (2.19) with $\gamma^+ = \gamma^- = \gamma$.

(b-1) Show that as the probability of detection approaches zero, a decision maker using PT does not engage in the criminal activity.

(b-2) Show that as the probability of detection approaches zero, under CPT, the fraction μ of individuals is not deterred from the criminal activity (which is consistent with the empirical evidence reviewed in the text). Why does CPT give a better account of criminal behavior?

30. (al-Nowaihi and Dhami, 2010a) Rieger and Wang (2006) show that the St. Petersburg paradox re-emerges under PT. How can the St. Petersburg paradox be resolved under CPT?

31. Prove Proposition 3.5.

32. (Loss aversion as an explanation of the St. Petersburg paradox; Camerer, 2005) Consider the gamble set out in the St. Petersburg paradox in Exercise 3. Bernoulli explained this paradox by using a concave utility function with EU.[7] Camerer (2005) showed that the paradox could also be explained by using loss aversion and OPT/PT.

Suppose that a casino, which offers the gamble has a budget of $\$b$, which is the maximum possible payout. Let m be the number of trials such that if a head first came out on the mth trial, the maximum possible payout would be just about exhausted. Suppose that $b = \$1$billion (check this implies $m = 30$). Thus, if the first heads came up on any trial beyond the 30th, then the casino will not be able to honor the terms of the gamble. Suppose that the gamble is purchased for a price equal to P and the decision maker has the piecewise linear utility function,

$$u(x) = \begin{cases} (2^j - P) & if \quad 2^j \geq P \\ \lambda(2^j - P) & if \quad 2^j < P \end{cases} \tag{5.4}$$

For some n, let $2^n < P < 2^{n+1}$ and use the identity weighting function $w(p) = p$.

Show that the imposition of a concave utility function is not a necessary condition for resolving the St. Petersburg paradox. Loss aversion provides a sufficient condition for the resolution of the paradox.

33. (Birnbaum, 2008) Consider the Birnbaum critique of PT in Section 2.9.1. Suppose that decision makers obeyed the three principles—transitivity, coalescing, restricted branch independence (RBI). Then show that there can be no Allais paradox.

34. Prove Proposition 2.9(b).

35. Prove Proposition 3.7.

36. Prove Proposition 3.9.

37. Consider the Bayesian approach to uncertainty (SEU). In SEU, beliefs are required to be updated using Bayes' rule. However, Bayesian analysis is agnostic as to the source of beliefs. Evaluate the implications for SEU of the following two scenarios.

---

[6] See, for instance, Koszegi and Rabin (2006, 2009). The act dependence of the reference point that we use is also consistent with the third generation prospect theory of Schmidt et al. (2008).

[7] Bernoulli used the logarithmic function.

(a) Consider two alternative ways of forming subjective beliefs, $\mu(E_i)$. In one case, the decision maker uses an actual accurate historical record to construct $\mu(E_i)$. In another, the decision maker is ignorant of any data and merely uses a hunch to construct $\mu(E_i)$. For instance, the decision maker can use the *principle of insufficient reason* and simply assign each of the n outcomes a subjective probability equal to $1/n$.[8] Schmeidler (1989) argued that the two probabilities feel very different.

(b) Beliefs can sometimes be updated without any apparently new information being available as, for instance, in the *fact-free learning theory* of Aragonés et al. (2005).

---

[8] The principle of insufficient reason may be more reasonable to apply in problems where the alternatives appear to be relatively more symmetric.

REFERENCES FOR VOLUME 1

Abdellaoui, M. A. (2000). Parameter-free elicitation of utility and probability weighting functions. *Management Science* 46(11): 1497–512.

Abdellaoui, M. A. (2002). A genuine rank-dependent generalization of the Von Neumann–Morgenstern expected utility theorem. *Econometrica* 70(2): 717–36.

Abdellaoui, M. A., Baillon, A., Placido, L., and Wakker, P. P. (2011). The rich domain of uncertainty: source functions and their experimental implementation. *American Economic Review* 101(2): 695–723.

Abdellaoui, M. A. and Bleichrodt, H. (2007). Eliciting Gul's theory of disappointment aversion by the tradeoff method. *Journal of Economic Psychology* 28(6): 631–45.

Abdellaoui, M. A. Bleichrodt, H., and Kammoun, H. (2013). Do financial professionals behave according to prospect theory? An experimental study. *Theory and Decision* 74(3): 411–29.

Abdellaoui, M. A., Bleichrodt, H., and L'Haridon, O. (2008). A tractable method to measure utility and loss aversion in prospect theory. *Journal of Risk and Uncertainty* 36(3): 245–66.

Abdellaoui, M. A., Bleichrodt, H., and Paraschiv, C. (2007). Loss aversion under prospect theory: a parameter-free measurement. *Management Science* 53(10): 1659–74.

Abdellaoui, M., Bleichrodt, H., L'Haridon, O., and van Dolder, D., (2016). Measuring loss aversion under ambiguity: a method to make prospect theory completely observable. *Journal of Risk and Uncertainty* 52(1): 1–20.

Abdellaoui, M. A., Diecidue, E., and Öncüler. A. (2011). Risk preferences at different time periods: an experimental investigation. *Management Science* 57(5): 975–87.

Abdellaoui, M. A., Klibanoff, P., and Placido, L. (2014). Experiments on compound risk in relation to simple risk and to ambiguity. Forthcoming in *Management Science*.

Abdellaoui, M. A. Vossmann, F., and Weber, M. (2005). Choice-based elicitation and decomposition of decision weights for gains and losses under uncertainty. *Management Science* 51(9): 1384–99.

Abdellaoui, M. A. and Wakker, P. P. (2005). The likelihood method for decision under uncertainty. *Theory and Decision* 58(1): 3–76.

Abeler, J., Altmann, S., Kube, S., and Wibral, M. (2010). Gift exchange and workers' fairness concerns: when equality is unfair. *Journal of the European Economic Association* 8(6): 1299–324.

Abeler, J., Falk, A., Goette, L., and Huffman, D. (2011). Reference points and effort provision. *American Economic Review* 101(2): 470–92.

Abellan-Perpiñan, J. M., Bleichrodt, H., and Pinto-Prades, J. L. (2009). The predictive validity of prospect theory versus expected utility in health utility measurement. *Journal of Health Economics* 28(6): 1039–47.

Ahlbrecht, M. and Weber, M. (1997a). An empirical study on intertemporal decision making under risk. *Management Science* 43(6): 813–26.

Ahlbrecht, M. and Weber, M. (1997b). Preference for gradual resolution of uncertainty. *Theory and Decision* 43: 167–84.

Ahn, D., Choi, S., Gale, D., and Kariv, S. (2014). Estimating ambiguity aversion in a portfolio choice experiment. *Quantitative Economics* 5(2): 195–223.

Ahn, D. and Ergin, H. (2010). Framing contingencies. *Econometrica* 78(2): 655–95.

Allais, M. (1953). Le comportement de l'homme rationnel devant le risque: critique des postulats et axiomes de l'Ecole Americaine. *Econometrica* 21(4): 503–46.

Allais, M. and Hagen, O. (eds.) (1979). *Expected Utility Hypotheses and the Allais Paradox*. Dordrecht: Reidel.

Allingham, M. G. and Sandmo, A. (1972). Income tax evasion: a theoretical analysis. *Journal of Public Economics* 1(3–4): 323–38.

al-Nowaihi, A., Bradley, I., and Dhami, S. (2008). A note on the utility function under prospect theory. *Economics Letters* 99(2): 337–9.

al-Nowaihi, A. and Dhami, S. (2006). A simple derivation of Prelec's probability weighting function. *Journal of Mathematical Psychology* 50(6): 521–4.

al-Nowaihi, A. and Dhami, S. (2010a). Composite prospect theory: a proposal to combine prospect theory and cumulative prospect theory. University of Leicester. Discussion Paper 10/11.

al-Nowaihi, A. and Dhami, S. (2010b). The behavioral economics of the demand for insurance. University of Leicester. Discussion Paper.

al-Nowaihi, A. and Dhami, S. (2011). Probability weighting functions. In *Wiley Encyclopaedia of Operations Research and Management Science*. Hoboken, NJ: John Wiley and Sons.

al-Nowaihi, A. and Dhami, S. (2012). Hyperbolic punishment functions. *Review of Law and Economics* 8(3): 759–87.

al-Nowaihi A. and Dhami, S. (2017). The Ellsberg paradox: a challenge to quantum decision theory? *Journal of Mathematical Psychology* 78: 40–50.

Andersen, S., Cox, J. C., Harrison, G. W., et al. (2012). Asset integration and attitudes to risk: theory and evidence. Georgia State University, Experimental Economics Center. Working Paper 2012–12.

Andreoni, J., Erard, B., and Feinstein, J. (1998). Tax compliance. *Journal of Economic Literature* 36(2): 818–60.

Andreoni, J. and Sprenger, C. (2012a). Estimating time preferences from convex budgets. *American Economic Review* 102(7): 3333–56.

Andreoni, J. and Sprenger, C. (2012b). Risk preferences are not time preferences. *American Economic Review* 102(7): 3357–76.

Ang, A., Hodrick, R. J., Xing, Y., and Zhang, X. (2006). The cross-section of volatility and expected returns. *Journal of Finance* 61(1): 259–99.

Anscombe, F. J. and Aumann, R. J. (1963). A definition of subjective probability. *Annals of Mathematical Statistics* 34(1): 199–205.

Apesteguia, J. and Ballester, M. A. (2018). Monotone stochastic choice models: the case of risk and time preferences. *Journal of Political Economy* 126(1): 74–106.

Aragones, E., Gilboa, I., Postlewaite, A., and Schmeidler, D. (2005). Fact-free learning. *American Economic Review* 95(5): 1355–68.

Ariely, D. and Simonson, I. (2003). Buying, bidding, playing, or competing? Value assessment and decision dynamics in online auctions. *Journal of Consumer Psychology* 13(1–2): 113–23.

Armantier, O. and Treich, N. (2016). The rich domain of risk. *Management Science* 62, 1954–69.

Arrow, K. and Hurwicz, L. (1972). An optimality criterion for decision making under ignorance. In C. Carter and J. Ford (eds.), *Uncertainty and Expectations in Economics*. Oxford: Blackwell, pp. 1–11.

Aydogan, I., Bleichrodt, H., and Gao, Y. (2016). An experimental test of reduction invariance. *Journal of Mathematical Psychology* 75: 170–82.

Babcock, L. and Loewenstein, G. (1997). Explaining bargaining impasse: the role of self-serving biases. *Journal of Economic Perspectives* 11(1): 109–26.

Baillon, A., Bleichrodt, H., Liu, N., and Wakker, P. P. (2016). Group decision rules and group rationality under risk. *Journal of Risk and Uncertainty* 52(2): 99–116.

Baillon, A., Driesen, B., and Wakker, P. P. (2012). Relative concave utility for risk and ambiguity. *Games and Economic Behavior* 75(2): 481–9.

Baillon, A., L'Haridon, O., and Placido, L. (2011). Ambiguity models and the Machina paradoxes. *American Economic Review* 101(4): 1547–60.

Baillon, A., Zhenxing H., Selim, A., and Wakker, P. P. (2018). Measuring ambiguity attitudes for all (natural) events. *Econometrica*, forthcoming.

Bar-Ilan, A. (2000). The response to large and small penalties in a natural experiment. University of Haifa, Department of Economics. Working Paper.

Bar-Ilan, A. and Sacerdote, B. (2001). The response to fines and probability of detection in a series of experiments. National Bureau of Economic Research. Working Paper 8638.

Bar-Ilan, A. and Sacerdote, B. (2004). The response of criminals and noncriminals to fines. *Journal of Law and Economics* 47(1): 1–17.

Barberis, N. C. (2013). Thirty years of prospect theory in economics: a review and assessment. *Journal of Economic Perspectives* 27(1): 173–96.

Barberis, N. C. and Huang, M. (2008). Stocks as lotteries: the implications of probability weighting for security prices. *American Economic Review* 98(5): 2066–100.

Barberis, N., Santos, T., and Huang, M. (2001). Prospect theory and asset prices. *Quarterly Journal of Economics* 116(1): 1–53.

Barberis, N. and Thaler, R. H. (2003). A survey of behavioral finance. In G. M. Constantinides, M. Harris, and R. M. Stulz (eds.), *Handbook of the Economics of Finance, Volume 1*. 1st edition. Amsterdam: Elsevier, ch. 18, pp. 1053–128.

Barron, G. and Erev, I. (2003). Small feedback-based decisions and their limited correspondence to description-based decisions. *Journal of Behavioral Decision Making* 16(3): 215–33.

Barseghyan, L., Molinari, F., O'Donoghue, T., and Teitelbaum, J. C. (2013). The nature of risk preferences: evidence from insurance choices. *American Economic Review* 103(6): 2499–529.

Bateman, I., Munro, A., Rhodes, B., Starmer, C., and Sugden, R. (1997). A test of the theory of reference-dependent preferences. *Quarterly Journal of Economics* 112(2): 479–505.

Battalio, R. C., Kagel, J. H., and Jiranyakul, K. (1990). Testing between alternative models of choice under uncertainty: some initial results. *Journal of Risk and Uncertainty* 3(1): 25–50.

Battalio, R. C., Kagel, J. H., and MacDonald, D. N. (1985). Animals' choices over uncertain outcomes: some initial experimental results. *American Economic Review* 75(4): 597–613.

Baucells, M. and Heukamp, F. H. (2012). Probability and time trade-off. *Management Science* 58(4): 831–42.

Beattie, J. and Loomes, G. (1997). The impact of incentives upon risky choice experiments. *Journal of Risk and Uncertainty* 14(2): 155–68.

Becker, G. S. (1968). Crime and punishment: an economic approach. *Journal of Political Economy* 76(2): 169–217.

Becker, G. S., DeGroot, M. H., and Marschak, J. (1964). Measuring utility by a single-response sequential method. *Behavioral Science* 9(3): 226–32.

Bell, D. (1982). Regret in decision making under uncertainty. *Operations Research* 30(5): 961–81.

Bell, D. (1985). Disappointment in decision making under uncertainty. *Operations Research* 33(1): 1–27.

Bellemare, C., Krause, M., Kroger, S., and Zhang, C. (2005). Myopic loss aversion: information feedback vs. investment flexibility. *Economics Letters* 87(3): 319–24.

Benartzi, S. and Thaler, R. H. (1995). Myopic loss-aversion and the equity premium puzzle. *Quarterly Journal of Economics* 110(1): 73–92.

Bernasconi, M. (1998). Tax evasion and orders of risk aversion. *Journal of Public Economics* 67(1): 123–34.

Bernasconi, M. and Loomes, G. (1992). Failures of the reduction principle in an Ellsberg-type problem. *Theory and Decision* 32(1): 77–100.

Berns, G. S., Capra, C. M., Chappelow, J., Moore, S., and Noussair, C. (2008). Nonlinear neurobiological probability weighting functions for aversive outcomes. *Neuroimage* 39(4): 2047–57.

Bewley, T. F. (2002). Knightian decision theory. Part I. *Decisions in Economics and Finance* 25(2): 79–110.

Billot, A., Gilboa, I., Samet, D., and Schmeidler, D. (2005). Probabilities as similarity-weighted frequencies. *Econometrica* 73(4): 1125–36.

Binswanger, H. P. (1981). Attitudes toward risk: theoretical implications of an experiment in rural India. *Economic Journal* 91(364): 867–90.

Birnbaum, M. H. (1997). Violations of monotonicity in judgment and decision making. In A. A. J. Marley (ed.), *Choice, Decision, and Measurement: Essays in Honor of R. Duncan Luce*. Mahwah, NJ: Erlbaum, pp. 73–100.

Birnbaum, M. H. (1999). Testing critical properties of decision making on the Internet. *Psychological Science* 10(5): 399–407.

Birnbaum, M. H. (2001). A Web-based program of research on decision making. In U.-D. Reips and M. Bosnjak (eds.), *Dimensions of Internet Science*. Lengerich: Pabst Science Publishers, pp. 23–55.

Birnbaum, M. H. (2004a). Causes of Allais common consequence paradoxes: an experimental dissection. *Journal of Mathematical Psychology* 48(2): 87–106.

Birnbaum, M. H. (2004b). Tests of rank-dependent utility and cumulative prospect theory in gambles represented by natural frequencies: effects of format, event framing, and branch splitting. *Organizational Behavior and Human Decision Processes* 95(1): 40–65.

Birnbaum, M. H. (2005). Three new tests of independence that differentiate models of risky decision making. *Management Science* 51(9): 1346–58.

Birnbaum, M. H. (2007). Tests of branch splitting and branch-splitting independence in Allais paradoxes with positive and mixed consequences. *Organizational Behavior and Human Decision Processes* 102(2): 154–73.

Birnbaum, M. H. (2008). New paradoxes of risky decision making. *Psychological Review* 115(2): 463–501.

Birnbaum, M. H. and Chavez, A. (1997). Tests of theories of decision making: violations of branch independence and distribution independence. *Organizational Behavior and Human Decision Processes* 71(2): 161–94.

Birnbaum, M. H. and Navarrete, J. B. (1998). Testing descriptive utility theories: violations of stochastic dominance and cumulative independence. *Journal of Risk and Uncertainty* 17(1): 49–79.

Birnbaum, M. H., Patton, J. N., and Lott, M. K. (1999). Evidence against rank-dependent utility theories: violations of cumulative independence, interval independence, stochastic dominance, and transitivity. *Organizational Behavior and Human Decision Processes* 77(1): 44–83.

Birnbaum, M. H. and Stegner, S. E. (1979). Source credibility in social judgment: bias, expertise, and the judge's point of view. *Journal of Personality and Social Psychology* 37(1): 48–74.

Blanchard, O. J. and Fischer, S. (1989). *Lectures on Macroeconomics* Cambridge, MA: MIT Press.

Blank, R. M. (1991). The effects of double-blind versus single-blind reviewing: experimental evidence from The American Economic Review. *American Economic Review* 81(5): 1041–67.

Blavatskyy, P. R. (2007). Stochastic expected utility theory. *Journal of Risk and Uncertainty* 34(3): 259–86.

Blavatskyy, P. R. (2010). Reverse common ratio effect. *Journal of Risk and Uncertainty* 40(3): 219–41.

Blavatskyy, P. R. (2011). Loss aversion. *Economic Theory* 46(1): 127–48.

Blavatskyy, P. and Pogrebna, G. (2009). Myopic loss aversion revisited. *Economics Letters* 104(1): 43–5.

Bleichrodt, H., Abellan-Perpiñan, J. M., Pinto-Prades, J. L., and Mendez-Martinez, I. (2007). Resolving inconsistencies in utility measurement under risk: tests of generalizations of expected utility. *Management Science* 53(3): 469–82.

Bleichrodt, H., Cillo, A., and Diecidue, E. (2010). A quantitative measurement of regret theory. *Management Science* 56(1): 161–75.

Bleichrodt, H., Filko, M., Kothiyal, A., and Wakker, P. P. (2017). Making case-based decision theory directly observable. *American Economic Journal: Microeconomics* 9(1): 123–51.

Bleichrodt, H. and Pinto, J. L. (2000). A parameter-free elicitation of the probability weighting function in medical decision analysis. *Management Science* 46(11): 1485–96.

Bleichrodt, H. and Pinto, J. L. (2002). Loss aversion and scale compatibility in two-attribute trade-offs. *Journal of Mathematical Psychology* 46(3): 315–37.

Bleichrodt, H., Pinto, J. L., and Wakker, P. P. (2001). Making descriptive use of prospect theory to improve the prescriptive use of expected utility. *Management Science* 47(11): 1498–514.

Bleichrodt, H. and Wakker, P. P. (2014). Regret theory: a bold alternative to the alternatives. *Economic Journal* in press.

Bombardini, M. and Trebbi, F. (2012). Risk aversion and expected utility theory: an experiment with large and small stakes. *Journal of the European Economic Association* 10(6): 1348–99.

Bommier, A. (2007). Risk aversion, intertemporal elasticity of substitution and correlation aversion. *Economics Bulletin* 4(29): 1–8.

Booij, A. S. and van de Kuilen, G. (2009). A parameter-free analysis of the utility of money for the general population under prospect theory. *Journal of Economic Psychology* 30(4): 651–66.

Bordalo, P., Gennaioli, N., and Shleifer, A. (2012). Salience theory of choice under risk. *Quarterly Journal of Economics* 127(3): 1243–85.

Bordalo, P., Gennaioli, N., and Shleifer, A. (2013a). Salience and asset prices. *American Economic Review* 103(3): 623–8.

Bordalo, P., Gennaioli, N., and Shleifer, A. (2013b). Salience and consumer choice. *Journal of Political Economy* 121(5): 803–43.

Borghans, L., Golsteyn, B. H. H., Heckman, J. J., and Huub, M. (2009). Gender differences in risk aversion and ambiguity aversion. *Journal of the European Economic Association* 7(2–3): 649–58.

Bosch-Domènech, A. and Silvestre, J. (1999). Does risk aversion or attraction depend on income? An experiment. *Economics Letters* 65(3): 265–73.

Bowman, D., Minehart, D., and Rabin, M. (1999). Loss aversion in a consumption-savings model. *Journal of Economic Behavior and Organization* 38(2): 155–78.

Boyce, R. R., Brown, T. C., McClelland, G. H., Peterson, G. L., and Schulze, W. D. (1992). An experimental examination of intrinsic environmental values as a source of the WTA–WTP disparity. *American Economic Review* 82(5): 1366–73.

Boyer, B., Mitton, T., and Vorkink, K. (2010). Expected idiosyncratic skewness. *Review of Financial Studies* 23(1): 169–202.

Brookshire, D. S. and Coursey, D. L. (1987). Measuring the value of a public good: an empirical comparison of elicitation procedures. *American Economic Review* 77(4): 554–66.

Brosnan, S. F., Jones, O. D., Lambeth, S. P. et al. (2007). Endowment effects in chimpanzees. *Current Biology* 17(19): 1704–7.

Brown, T. C. and Gregory, R. (1999). Why the WTA–WTP disparity matters. *Ecological Economics* 28(3): 323–35.

Bruhin, A., Fehr-Duda, H., and Epper, T. (2010). Risk and rationality: uncovering heterogeneity in probability distortion. *Econometrica* 78(4): 1375–412.

Buffon, G. L. L. (1777). Essai d'Arithmétique Morale, Supplément à l'Histoire naturelle, vol. IV.

Burks, S., Carpenter, J., Götte, L., Monaco, K. et al. (2008). Using behavioral economic field experiments at a large motor carrier: the context and design of the truckers and turnover project. In S. Bender, J. Lane, K. Shaw, F. Anderson, and T. von Wachter (eds.), *The Analysis of Firms and Employees: Quantitative and Qualitative Approaches*. Chicago, IL: University of Chicago Press.

Busemeyer, J. R. and Townsend, J. T. (1993). Decision field theory: a dynamic-cognitive approach to decision making in an uncertain environment. *Psychological Review* 100(3): 432–59.

Busemeyer, J. R., Weg, E., Barkan, R., Li, X., and Ma, Z. (2000). Dynamic and consequential consistency of choices between paths of decision trees. *Journal of Experimental Psychology* General 129(4): 530–45.

Camerer, C. F. (1989). An experimental test of several generalized utility theories. *Journal of Risk and Uncertainty* 2(1): 61–104.

Camerer, C. F. (1992). Recent tests of generalizations of expected utility theory. In W. Edwards (ed.), *Utility: Theories, Measurement, and Applications*. Norwell, MA: Kluwer, pp. 207–51.

Camerer, C. F. (1995). Individual decision making. In J. Kagel and A. E. Roth (eds.), *The Handbook of Experimental Economics*. Princeton, NJ: Princeton University Press.

Camerer, C. F. (2000). Prospect theory in the wild: evidence from the field. In D. Kahneman and A. Tversky (eds.), *Choices, Values and Frames*. Cambridge: Cambridge University Press, pp. 288–300.

Camerer, C. F. (2005). Three cheers—psychological, theoretical, empirical—for loss aversion. *Journal of Marketing Research* 42(2): 129–33.

Camerer, C. F., Babcock, L., Loewenstein, G., and Thaler, R. H. (1997). Labor supply of New York City cabdrivers: one day at a time. *Quarterly Journal of Economics* 112(2): 407–41.

Camerer, C. F. and Ho, T.-H. (1994). Violations of the betweenness axiom and nonlinearity in probability. *Journal of Risk and Uncertainty* 8(2): 167–96.

Camerer, C. F. and Hogarth, R. M. (1999). The effects of financial incentives in experiments: a review and capital-labor-production framework. *Journal of Risk and Uncertainty* 19(1–3): 7–42.

Carbone, E. and Hey, J. D. (1994). Estimation of expected utility and non-expected utility preference functionals using complete ranking data. In B. Munier and M. J. Machina (eds.), *Models and Experiments on Risk and Rationality*. Amsterdam: Kluwer, pp. 119–39.

Carmon, Z. and Ariely, D. (2000). Focusing on the forgone: how value can appear so different to buyers and sellers. *Journal of Consumer Research* 27(3): 360–70.

Cerreia-Vioglio, S., Ghirardato, P., Maccheroni, F., Marinacci, M., and Siniscalchi, M. (2011). Rational preferences under ambiguity. *Economic Theory* 48(2–3): 341–75.

Chakravarty, S. and Roy, J. (2009). Recursive expected utility and the separation of attitudes towards risk and ambiguity: an experimental study. *Theory and Decision* 66(3): 199–228.

Chapman, G. (1998). Similarity and reluctance to trade. *Journal of Behavioral Decision Making* 11(1): 47–58.

Charness, G. and Gneezy, U. (2012). Strong evidence for gender differences in risk taking. *Journal of Economic Behavior and Organization* 83(1): 50–8.

Chateauneuf, A. and Cohen, M. (1994). Risk seeking with diminishing marginal utility in a non-expected utility model. *Journal of Risk and Uncertainty* 9(1): 77–91.

Chateauneuf, A. and Faro, J. H. (2009). Ambiguity through confidence functions. *Journal of Mathematical Economics* 45(9–10): 535–58.

Chateauneuf, A. and Tallon, J.-M. (2002). Diversification, convex preferences and non-empty core in the Choquet expected utility model. *Economic Theory* 19(3): 509–23.

Chateauneuf, A. and Wakker, P. P. (1993). From local to global additive representation. *Journal of Mathematical Economics* 22(6): 523–45.

Chateauneuf, A. and Wakker, P. P. (1999). An axiomatization of cumulative prospect theory for decision under risk. *Journal of Risk and Uncertainty* 18(2): 137–45.

Chen, M. K., Lakshminarayanan, V., and Santos, L. (2006). How basic are behavioral biases? Evidence from capuchin monkey trading behavior. *Journal of Political Economy*. 114(3): 517–32.

Cheung, S. (2014). On the elicitation of time preference under conditions of risk. Forthcoming in *American Economic Review*.

Chew, S. H. (1983). A generalization of the quasilinear mean with applications to the measurement of income inequality and decision theory resolving the Allais paradox. *Econometrica* 51(4): 1065–92.

Chew, S. H. (1989). Axiomatic utility theories with the betweenness property. *Annals of Operations Research* 19(1): 273–98.

Chew, S. H. and Epstein, L. G. (1989a). A unifying approach to axiomatic non-expected utility theories. *Journal of Economic Theory* 49(2): 207–40.

Chew, S. H. and Epstein, L. G. (1989b). The structure of preferences and attitudes towards the timing of the resolution of uncertainty. *International Economic Review* 30(1): 103–17.

Chew, S. H. and Epstein, G. L. (1990). Non-expected utility preferences in a temporal framework with an application to consumption-savings behaviour. *Journal of Economic Theory* 50(1): 54–81.

Chew, S. H., Epstein, L. G., and Segal, U. (1991). Mixture symmetry and quadratic utility. *Econometrica* 59(1): 139–63.

Chew, S. H., Karni, E., and Safra, Z. (1987). Risk aversion in the theory of expected utility with rank-dependent preferences. *Journal of Economic Theory* 42(2): 370–81.

Chew, S. H. and MacCrimmon, K. R. (1979). Alpha-nu choice theory: a generalization of expected utility theory. University of British Columbia. Working Paper 669.

Chew, S. H. and Sagi, J. S. (2006). Event exchangeability: small worlds probabilistic sophistication without continuity or monotonicity. *Econometrica* 74(3): 771–86.

Chew, S. H. and Sagi, J. (2008). Small worlds: modeling attitudes toward sources of uncertainty. *Journal of Economic Theory* 139(1): 1–24.

Chew, S. H. and Waller, W. S. (1986). Empirical tests of weighted utility theory. *Journal of Mathematical Psychology* 30(1): 55–72.

Coaubs, C. H., Bezembinder, T. G., and Goode, F. M. (1967). Testing expectation theories of decision making without measuring utility or subjective probability. *Journal of Mathematical Psychology* 4(1): 72–103.

Coble, K. H. and Lusk, J. L. (2010). At the nexus of risk and time preferences: an experimental investigation. *Journal of Risk and Uncertainty* 41(1): 67–79.

Cohen, M. and Jaffray, J.-Y. (1980). Rational behavior under complete ignorance. *Econometrica* 48(5): 1281–99.

Cohen, M., Jaffray, J.-Y., and Said, T. (1987). Experimental comparison of individual behavior under risk and under uncertainty for gains and for losses. *Organizational Behavior and Human Decision Processes* 39(1): 1–22.

Cohn, A., Engelmann, J., Fehr, E., and Maréchal, M. A. (2015). Evidence for countercyclical risk aversion: an experiment with financial professionals. *American Economic Review* 105 (2): 860–85.

Conlisk, J. (1989). Three variants on the Allais example. *American Economic Review* 79(3): 392–407.

Conrad, J., Dittmar, R. F., and Ghysels, E. (2013). Ex ante skewness and expected stock returns. *Journal of Finance* 68(1): 85–124.

Conte, A. and Hey, J. D. (2013). Assessing multiple prior models of behaviour under ambiguity. *Journal of Risk and Uncertainty* 46(2): 113–32.

Conte, A., Hey, J. D., and Moffatt, P. G. (2011). Mixture models of choice under risk. *Journal of Econometrics* 162(1): 79–88.

Coursey, D. L., Hovis, J. L., and Schulze, W. D. (1987). The disparity between willingness to accept and willingness to pay measures of value. *Quarterly Journal of Economics* 102(3): 679–90.

Cox, J. C. and Sadiraj, V. (2006). Small- and large-stakes risk aversion: implications of concavity calibration for decision theory. *Games and Economic Behavior* 56(1): 45–60.

Crawford, V. P. and Meng, J. (2011). New York City cab drivers' labor supply revisited: reference-dependent preferences with rational-expectations targets for hours and income. *American Economic Review* 101(5): 1912–32.

Croson, R. and Gneezy, U. (2009). Gender differences in preferences. *Journal of Economic Literature* 47(2): 448–74.

Cubitt, R. P., Starmer, C., and Sugden, R., (1998). Dynamic choice and the common ratio effect: and experimental investigation. *Economic Journal* 108(450): 1362–80.

Cummings, R. G., Brookshire, D. S., and Schulze, W. D. (eds.) (1986). *Valuing Environmental Goods: An Assessment of the Contingent Valuation Method.* Totowa, NJ: Rowman and Allanheld.

Curley, S. P., Yates, J. F., and Abrams, R. A. (1986). Psychological sources of ambiguity avoidance. *Organizational Behavior and Human Decision Processes* 38(2): 230–56.

de Finetti, B. (1937). La prevision: ses lois logiques, ses sources subjectives. *Annales de l'Institute Henri Poincare* 7(1): 1–68.

De Giorgi, E. G. and Legg, S. (2012). Dynamic portfolio choice and asset pricing with narrow framing and probability weighting. *Journal of Economic Dynamics and Control* 36(7): 951–72.

de Meza, D. and Webb, D. C. (2003). Principal agent problems under loss aversion: an application to executive stock options. Mimeo, London School of Economics.

de Meza, D. and Webb, D. C. (2007). Incentive design under loss aversion. *Journal of the European Economic Association* 5(1): 66–92.

Dekel, E. (1986). An axiomatic characterization of preferences under uncertainty: weakening the independence axiom. *Journal of Economic Theory* 40(2): 304–18.

Dhami, S. and al-Nowaihi, A. (2007). Why do people pay taxes? Expected utility versus prospect theory. *Journal of Economic Behavior and Organization* 64(1): 171–92.

Dhami, S. and al-Nowaihi, A. (2010a). The behavioral economics of crime and punishment. University of Leicester. Discussion Paper 1014.

Dhami, S. and al-Nowaihi, A. (2010b). Optimal income tax taxation in the presence of tax evasion: expected utility versus prospect theory. *Journal of Economic Behavior and Organization* 75(2): 313–37.

Dhami, S. and al-Nowaihi, A. (2013). An extension of the Becker Proposition to non-expected utility theory. *Mathematical Social Sciences* 65(1): 10–20.

Dhami, S. and al-Nowaihi, A. (2014). Prospect theory, crime and punishment. Forthcoming in K. Zeiler and J. C. Teitelbaum (eds.), *Research Handbook on Behavioral Law and Economics.* Cheltenham: Edward Elgar.

Dhami, S., al-Nowaihi, A., and Sunstein, C. R. (2018). Heuristics and Public Policy: Decision Making Under Bounded Rationality. Mimeo.

Dhar, R. and Wertenbroch, K. (2000). Consumer choice between hedonic and utilitarian goods. *Journal of Marketing Research* 37(1): 60–71.

Diecidue, E. and Somasundaram, J. (2017). Regret theory: a new foundation. *Journal of Economic Theory* 172: 88–119.

Diecidue, E., Ulrich, S., and Horst, Z. (2009). Parametric weighting functions. *Journal of Economic Theory* 144(3): 1102–18.

Dimmock, S. G. and Kouwenberg, R. (2010). Loss-aversion and household portfolio choice. *Journal of Empirical Finance* 17(3): 441–59.

Dimmock, S. G., Kouwenberg, R., Mitchell, O. S., and Peijnenburg, K. (2016). Ambiguity aversion and household portfolio choice puzzles: empirical evidence. *Journal of Financial Economics* 119: 559–77.

Dimmock, S. G., Kouwenberg, R., and Wakker, P. P. (2015). Ambiguity attitudes in a large representative sample. *Management Science* 62(5): 1363–80.

Dohmen, T., Falk, A., Huffman, D., and Sunde, U. (2010). Are risk aversion and impatience related to cognitive ability? *American Economic Review* 100(3): 1238–60.

Dohmen, T., Falk, A., Huffman, D., and Sunde, U. (2012). The intergenerational transmission of risk and trust attitudes. *Review of Economic Studies* 79(2): 645–77.

Dohmen, T., Falk, A., Huffman, D., and Sunde, U. (2018). On the relationship between cognitive ability and risk preference. *Journal of Economic Perspectives* 32(2): 115–34.

Dohmen, T., Falk, A., Huffman, D., et al. (2011). Individual risk attitudes: measurement, determinants and behavioral consequences. *Journal of the European Economic Association* 9(3): 522–50.

Du, N. and Budescu, D. (2005). The effects of imprecise probabilities and outcomes in evaluating investment options. *Management Science* 51(12): 1791–803.

Eckel, C. C. and Grossman, P. J. (2008). Men, women and risk aversion: experimental evidence. In C. R. Plott and V. L. Smith (eds.), *Handbook of Experimental Economics Results, Volume 1*. Amsterdam: Elsevier, ch. 113, pp. 1061–73.

Edwards, W. (1954). The theory of decision making. *Psychological Bulletin* 51(4): 380–417.

Edwards, W. (1962). Subjective probabilities inferred from decisions. *Psychological Review* 69(2): 109–35.

Eichberger, J., Grant, S., Kelsey, D., and Koshevoy, G. A. (2011). The α-MEU model: a comment. *Journal of Economic Theory* 146(4): 1684–98.

Eliaz, K. and Schotter, A. (2007). Experimental testing of intrinsic preferences for non-instrumental information. *American Economic Review* 97(2): 166–9.

Ellsberg, D. (1961). Risk, ambiguity, and the Savage axioms. *Quarterly Journal of Economics* 75(4): 643–69.

Engelmann, D. and Hollard, G. (2008). A shock therapy against the endowment effect. Mimeo, Royal Holloway, University of London.

Epper, T. and Fehr-Duda, H. (2014a). Balancing on a budget line: comment on Andreoni and Sprenger (2012)'s "Risk preferences are not time preferences." Forthcoming in *American Economic Review*.

Epper, T. and Fehr-Duda, H. (2014b). The missing link: unifying risk taking and time discounting. Mimeo, University of Zurich.

Epstein, L. G. (1999). A definition of uncertainty aversion. *Review of Economic Studies* 66(3): 579–608.

Epstein, L. G. (2009). Three paradoxes for the smooth ambiguity model of preference. Mimeo, Boston University.

Epstein, L. G. and Le Breton, M. (1993). Dynamically consistent beliefs must be Bayesian. *Journal of Economic Theory* 61(1): 1–22.

Epstein, L. G. and Zhang, J. (2001). Subjective probabilities on subjectively unambiguous events. *Econometrica* 69(2): 265–306.

Epstein, L. G. and Zin, S. E. (1989). Substitution, risk aversion, and the temporal behavior of consumption and asset returns: a theoretical framework. *Econometrica* 57(4): 937–69.

Erev, I., Ert, E., and Roth, A. E. (2010) A choice prediction competition: choices from experience and from description. *Journal of Behavioral Decision Making* 23: 15–47.

Ergin, A. and Gul, F. (2009). A theory of subjective compound lotteries. *Journal of Economic Theory* 144(3): 899–929.

Ericson, K. M. M. and Fuster, A. (2011). Expectations as endowments: evidence on reference-dependent preferences from exchange and valuation experiments. *Quarterly Journal of Economics* 126(4): 1879–907.

Etchart-Vincent, N. (2004). Is probability weighting sensitive to the magnitude of consequences? An experimental investigation on losses. *Journal of Risk and Uncertainty* 28(3): 217–35.

Etner, J., Jeleva, M., and Tallon, J.-M. (2012). Decision theory under ambiguity. *Journal of Economic Surveys* 26(2): 234–70.

Fafchamps, M., Kebede, B., and Zizzo, D. J. (2014). Keep up with the winners: experimental evidence on risk taking, asset integration, and peer effects. University of East Anglia, CBESS. Discussion Paper 14–03.

Falk, A. and Knell, M. (2004). Choosing the Joneses: endogenous goals and reference standards. *Scandinavian Journal of Economics* 106(3): 417–35.

Farber, H. S. (2005). Is tomorrow another day? The labor supply of New York City cabdrivers. *Journal of Political Economy* 113(1): 46–82.

Farber, H. S. (2008). Reference-dependent preferences and labor supply: the case of New York City taxi drivers. *American Economic Review* 98(3): 1069–82.

Fehr, D., Hakimova, R., and Kübler, D. (2015). The willingness to pay–willingness to accept gap: a failed replication of Plott and Zeiler. *European Economic Review* 78: 120–8.

Fehr, E. and Goette, L. (2007). Do workers work more if wages are higher? Evidence from a randomized field experiment. *American Economic Review* 97(1): 298–317.

Fehr, E., Hart, O., and Zehnder, C. (2011). Contracts as reference points—experimental evidence. *American Economic Review* 101(2): 493–525.

Fehr, E., Zehnder, C., and Hart, O. (2009). Contracts, reference points, and competition—behavioral effects of the fundamental transformation. *Journal of the European Economic Association* 7(2–3): 561–72.

Fehr-Duda, H., Bruhin, A., Epper, T., and Schubert, R. (2010). Rationality on the rise: why relative risk aversion increases with stake size. *Journal of Risk and Uncertainty* 40(2): 147–80.

Fehr-Duda, H. and Epper, T. (2012). Probability and risk: foundations and economic implications of probability-dependent risk preferences. *Annual Review of Economics* 4: 567–93.

Fehr-Duda, H., Epper, T., Bruhin, A., and Schubert, R. (2011). Risk and rationality: the effects of mood and decision rules on probability weighting. *Journal of Economic Behavior and Organization* 78(1–2): 14–24.

Fellner, G. and Sutter, M. (2009). Causes, consequences, and cures of myopic loss aversion: an experimental investigation. *Economic Journal* 119(537): 900–16.

Fennema, H. and van Assen, M. (1998). Measuring the utility of losses by means of the trade-off method. *Journal of Risk and Uncertainty* 17(3): 277–96.

Fischhoff, B., Slovic, P., Lichtenstein, S., Read, S., and Combs, B. (1978). How safe is safe enough? A psychometric study of attitudes towards technological risks and benefits. *Policy Sciences* 9(2): 127–52.

Fishburn, P. C. (1978). On Handa's "New theory of cardinal utility" and the maximization of expected return. *Journal of Political Economy* 86(2): 321–4.

Fishburn, P. C. (1982a). Nontransitive measurable utility. *Journal of Mathematical Psychology* 26(1): 31–67.

Fishburn, P. C. (1982b). *The Foundations of Expected Utility*. Dordrecht: Reidel.

Fishburn, P. C. (1983). Transitive measurable utility. *Journal of Economic Theory* 31(2): 293–317.

Fishburn, P. C. and Kochenberger, G. A. (1979). Two-piece von Neumann–Morgenstern utility functions. *Decision Sciences* 10(4): 503–18.

Fox, C. R. and Tversky, A. (1995). Ambiguity aversion and comparative ignorance. *Quarterly Journal of Economics* 110(3): 585–603.

Fox, C. R. and Tversky, A. (1998). A belief-based account of decision under uncertainty. *Management Science* 44(7): 879–95.

Fox, C. R. and Weber, M. (2002). Ambiguity aversion, comparative ignorance, and decision context. *Organizational Behavior and Human Decision Processes* 88(1): 476–98.

Fragaszy, D. M., Visalberghi, E., and Fedigan, L. M. (2004). *The Complete Capuchin: The Biology of the Genus Cebus*. Cambridge: Cambridge University Press.

French, K. R. and Poterba, J. M. (1991). Investor diversification and international equity markets. *American Economic Review* 81(2): 222–6.

Friedman, M. and Savage, L. (1948). The utility analysis of choices involving risk. *Journal of Political Economy* 56(4): 279–304.

Fryer, R. G., Levitt, S. D., List, J. A., and Sadoff, S. (2012). Enhancing the efficacy of teacher incentives through loss aversion: a field experiment. NBER. Working Paper 8237.

Gächter, S., Johnson, E. J., and Herrmann, A. (2010). Individual-level loss aversion in riskless and risky choices. University of Nottingham, CeDEx. Discussion Paper 1749–3293.

Gajdos, T., Hayashi, T., Tallon, J.-M., and Vergnaud, J.-C. (2008). Attitude toward imprecise information. *Journal of Economic Theory* 140(1): 27–65.

Genesove, D. and Mayer, C. (2001). Loss aversion and seller behavior: evidence from the housing market. *Quarterly Journal of Economics* 116(4): 1233–60.

Gennaioli, N. and Shleifer, A. (2010). What comes to mind. *Quarterly Journal of Economics* 125(4): 1399–433.

Ghirardato, P., Maccheroni, F., and Marinacci, M. (2004). Differentiating ambiguity and ambiguity attitude. *Journal of Economic Theory* 118(2): 133–73.

Ghirardato, P., Maccheroni, F., Marinacci, M., and Siniscalchi, M. (2003). A subjective spin on roulette wheels. *Econometrica* 71(6): 1897–908.

Ghirardato, P. and Marinacci, M. (2002). Ambiguity made precise: a comparative foundation. *Journal of Economic Theory* 102(2): 251–89.

Ghirardato, P. and Siniscalchi, M. (2012). Ambiguity in the small and in the large. *Econometrica* 80(6): 2827–47.

Gilboa, I. (1987). Expected utility with purely subjective non-additive probabilities. *Journal of Mathematical Economics* 16(1): 65–88.

Gilboa, I. (2009). *Theory of Decision under Uncertainty*. Cambridge: Cambridge University Press.

Gilboa, I., Lieberman, O., and Schmeidler, D. (2006). Empirical similarity. *Review of Economics and Statistics* 88(3): 433–44.

Gilboa, I., Postlewaite, A., and Schmeidler, D. (2009). Is it always rational to satisfy Savage's axioms? *Economics and Philosophy* 25(3): 285–96.

Gilboa, I., Samet, D., and Schmeidler, D. (2004). Utilitarian aggregation of beliefs and tastes. *Journal of Political Economy* 112(4): 932–8.

Gilboa, I. and Schmeidler, D. (1989). Maxmin expected utility with a non-unique prior. *Journal of Mathematical Economics* 18(2): 141–53.

Gilboa, I. and Schmeidler, D. (1995). Case-based decision theory. *Quarterly Journal of Economics* 110(3): 605–39.

Gilboa, I. and Schmeidler, D. (1997). Act similarity in case-based decision theory. *Economic Theory* 9(1): 47–61.

Gilboa, I. and Schmeidler, D. (2001). *A Theory of Case-Based Decisions*. New York: Cambridge University Press.

Gill, D. and Prowse, V. (2012). A structural analysis of disappointment aversion in a real effort competition. *American Economic Review* 102(1): 469–503.

Gintis, H. (2009). *The Bounds of Reason: Game Theory and the Unification of the Behavioral Sciences*. Princeton, NJ: Princeton University Press.

Gneezy, U., Goette, L., Sprenger, C., and Zimmermann, F. (2017). the limits of expectations-based reference dependence. *Journal of the European Economic Association* 15(4): 861–76.

Gneezy, U., Kapteyn, A., and Potters, J. J. M. (2003). Evaluation periods and asset prices in a market experiment. *Journal of Finance* 58(2): 821–38.

Gneezy, U. and Potters, J. (1997). An experiment on risk taking and evaluation periods. *Quarterly Journal of Economics* 112(2): 631–45.

Goette, L. and Huffman, D. (2003). Reference dependent preferences and the allocation of effort over time: evidence from natural experiments. Mimeo, Institute for Empirical Research in Economics, University of Zurich.

Goette, L., Huffman, D., and Fehr, E. (2004). Loss aversion and labor supply. *Journal of the European Economic Association* 2(2–3): 216–28.

Goldstein, W. M. and Einhorn, H. J. (1987). Expression theory and the preference reversal phenomena. *Psychological Review* 94(2): 236–54.

Gonzalez, R. and Wu, G. (1999). On the shape of the probability weighting function. *Cognitive Psychology* 38(1): 129–66.

Grant, S. (1995). Subjective probability without monotonicity: or how Machina's mom may also be probabilistically sophisticated. *Econometrica* 63(1): 159–89.

Grant, S., Kajii, A., and Polak, B. (2000). Temporal resolution of uncertainty and recursive non-expected utility models. *Econometrica* 68(2): 425–34.

Grant, S., Özsoy, H., and Polak, B. (2008). Probabilistic sophistication and stochastic monotonicity in the Savage framework. *Mathematical Social Sciences* 55(3): 371–80.

Green, J. R. and Jullien, B. (1988). Ordinal independence in nonlinear utility theory. *Journal of Risk and Uncertainty* 1(4): 355–87.

Green, T. and Hwang, B.-H. (2012). Initial public offerings as lotteries: expected skewness and first-day returns. *Management Science* 58(2): 432–44.

Grossman, S. J. and Hart, O. D. (1986). The costs and benefits of ownership: a theory of vertical and lateral integration. *Journal of Political Economy* 94(4): 691–719.

Guerdjikova, A. (2008). Case-based learning with different similarity functions. *Games and Economic Behavior* 63(1): 107–32.

Gul, F. (1991). A theory of disappointment aversion. *Econometrica* 59(3): 667–86.

Gul, F. and Pesendorfer, W. (2013). Expected uncertainty utility theory. Mimeo, Princeton University.

Gurevich, G., Kliger, D., and Levy, O. (2009). Decision-making under uncertainty: a field study of cumulative prospect theory. *Journal of Banking and Finance* 33(7): 1221–9.

Haigh, M. S. and List, J. A. (2005). Do professional traders exhibit myopic loss aversion? An experimental analysis. *Journal of Finance* 60(1): 523–34.

Halevy, Y. (2007). Ellsberg revisited: an experimental study. *Econometrica* 75(2): 503–36.

Halevy, Y. (2008). Strotz meets Allais: diminishing impatience and the certainty effect. *American Economic Review* 98(3): 1145–62.

Halevy, Y. and Feltkamp, V. (2005). A Bayesian approach to uncertainty aversion. *Review of Economic Studies* 72(2): 449–66.

Halonen-Akatwijuka, M. and Hart, O. (2013). More is less: why parties may deliberately write incomplete contracts. Mimeo, Harvard University.

Hanaoka, C., Shigeoka, H., and Watanabe, Y. (2018). Do risk preferences change? Evidence from the great East Japan earthquake. *American Economic Journal: Applied Economics* 10(2): 298–330.

Handa, J. (1977). Risk, probability, and a new theory of cardinal utility. *Journal of Political Economy* 85(1): 97–122.

Hansen, L. P. and Sargent, T. J. (2001a). Acknowledging misspecification in macroeconomic theory. *Review of Economic Dynamics* 4(3): 519–35.

Hansen, L. P. and Sargent, T. J. (2001b). Robust control and model uncertainty. *American Economic Review* 91(2): 60–6.

Harbaugh, W. T., Krause, K., and Vesterlund, L. (2002). Risk attitudes of children and adults: choices over small and large probability gains and losses. *Experimental Economics* 5(1): 53–84.

Harbaugh, W. T., Krause, K., and Vesterlund, L. (2010). The fourfold pattern of risk attitudes in choice and pricing tasks. *Economic Journal* 120(45): 595–611.

Harless, D. W. (1992). Predictions about indifference curves inside the unit triangle: a test of variants of expected utility. *Journal of Economic Behavior and Organization* 18(3): 391–414.

Harrison, G. W., Humphrey, S. J., and Verschoor, A. (2010). Choice under uncertainty: evidence from Ethiopia, India and Uganda. *Economic Journal* 120(543): 80–104.

Harrison, G. W., Martínez-Correa, J., and Swarthout, J. T. (2012). Reduction of compound lotteries with objective probabilities: theory and evidence. Andrew Young School of Policy Studies, Experimental Economics Center. Working Paper 2012–04.

Harrison, G. W. and Rutström, E. E. (2009). Expected utility theory and prospect theory: one wedding and a decent funeral. *Experimenta Economics* 12(2): 133–58.

Hart, O. (2009). Hold-up, asset ownership, and reference points. *Quarterly Journal of Economics* 124(1): 267–300.

Hart, O. and Holmstrom, B. (2010). A theory of firm scope. *Quarterly Journal of Economics* 125(2): 483–513.

Hart, O. and Moore, J. (1990). Property rights and the nature of the firm. *Journal of Political Economy* 98(6): 1119–58.

Hart, O. and Moore, J. (2008). Contracts as reference points. *Quarterly Journal of Economics* 123(1): 1–48.

Hayashi, T. and Wada, R. (2010). Choice with imprecise information: an experimental approach. *Theory and Decision* 69(3): 355–73.

Heath, C., Larrick, R. P., and Wu, G. (1999). Goals as reference points. *Cognitive Psychology* 38(1): 79–109.

Heath, C. and Tversky, A. (1991). Preference and belief: ambiguity and competence in choice and uncertainty. *Journal of Risk and Uncertainty* 4(1): 5–28.

Heffetz, O. and List, J. A. (2014). Is the endowment effect an expectations effect? *Journal of the European Economic Association* 12(5): 1396–422.

Heidhues, P. and Kőszegi, B. (2005). The impact of consumer loss aversion on pricing. CEPR. Discussion Paper 4849.

Heidhues, P. and Kőszegi, B. (2008). Competition and price variation when consumers are loss averse. *American Economic Review* 98(4): 1245–68.

Heiner, R. A. (1983). The origin of predictable behavior. *American Economic Review* 73(4): 560–95.

Helson, H. (1964). *Adaptation Level Theory: An Experimental and Systematic Approach to Behavior.* New York: Harper and Row.

Hershey, J. C. and Schoemaker, P. J. H. (1985). Probability vs. certainty equivalence methods in utility measurement: are they equivalent? *Management Science* 31(10): 1213–31.

Herweg, F. (2013). The expectation-based loss-averse newsvendor. *Economics Letters* 120(3): 429–32.

Herweg, F., Karle, H., and Müller, D. (2014). Incomplete contracting, renegotiation, and expectation-based loss aversion. CEPR. Discussion Paper 9874.

Herweg, F. and Mierendorff, K. (2013). Uncertain demand, consumer loss aversion, and fiat rate tariffs. *Journal of the European Economic Association* 11(2): 399–432.

Herweg, F., Müller, D., and Weinschenk, P. (2010). Binary payment schemes: moral hazard and loss aversion. *American Economic Review* 100(5): 2451–77.

Herweg, F. and Schmidt, K. M. (2013). Loss aversion and inefficient renegotiation. Mimeo, University of Munich.

Hey, J. D. (2014). Choice under uncertainty: empirical methods and experimental results. In M. J. Machina and W. K. Viscusi (eds.), *Handbook of the Economics of Risk and Uncertainty, Volume 1*. Amsterdam: North Holland, pp. 809–50.

Hey, J. D., Lotito, G., and Maffioletti, A. (2010). The descriptive and predictive adequacy of theories of decision making under uncertainty/ambiguity. *Journal of Risk and Uncertainty* 41(2): 81–111.

Hey, J. D. and Orme, C. (1994). Investigating generalizations of expected utility theory using experimental data. *Econometrica* 62(6): 1291–326.

Hogarth, R. M. and Einhorn, H. J. (1990). Venture theory: a model of decision weights. *Management Science* 36(7): 780–803.

Hogarth, R. M. and Kunreuther, H. (1989). Risk, ambiguity and insurance. *Journal of Risk and Uncertainty* 2(1): 5–35.

Hogarth, R. M. and Kunreuther, H. (1992). Pricing insurance and warranties: ambiguity and correlated risks. *The Geneva Papers on Risk and Insurance Theory* 17(1): 35–60.

Holt, C. A. (1986). Preference reversals and the independence axiom. *American Economic Review* 76(3): 508–15.

Holt, C. A. and Laury, S. K. (2002). Risk aversion and incentive effects. *American Economic Review* 92(5): 1644–55.

Holt, C. A. and Laury, S. K. (2005). Risk aversion and incentive effects: new data without order effects. *American Economic Review* 95(3): 902–12.

Horowitz, J. K. and McConnell, K. E. (2002). A review of WTA/WTP studies. *Journal of Environmental Economics and Management* 44(3): 426–47.

Hu, W.-Y. and Scott, J. S. (2007). Behavioral obstacles in the annuity market. *Financial Analysts Journal* 63(6): 71–82.

Huber, J., Payne, J. W., and Puto, C. (1982). Adding asymmetrically dominated alternatives: violations of regularity and the similarity hypothesis. *Journal of Consumer Research* 9(1): 90–8.

Humphrey, S. J. (1995). Regret aversion or event-splitting effects? More evidence under risk and uncertainty. *Journal of Risk and Uncertainty* 11(3): 263–74.

Humphrey, S. J. (1998). More mixed results on boundary effects. *Economics Letters* 61(1): 79–84.

Humphrey, S. J. (2000). The common consequence effect: testing a unified explanation of recent mixed evidence. *Journal of Economic Behavior and Organization* 41(3): 239–62.

Hurwicz, L. (1951). Some specification problems and applications to econometric models. *Econometrica* 19: 343–4.

Irwin, J. R. (1994). Buying/selling price preference reversals: preference for environmental changes in buying versus selling modes. *Organizational Behavior and Human Decision Processes* 60(3): 431–57.

Isoni, A., Loomes, G., and Sugden, G. (2011). The willingness to pay–willingness to accept gap, the "endowment effect," subject misconceptions, and experimental procedures for eliciting valuations: comment. *American Economic Review* 101(2): 991–1011.

Johnson, E. J., Gächter, S., and Herrmann, A. (2006). Exploring the nature of loss aversion. CeDEx. Discussion Paper 2006–02.

Johnson, E. J., Haeubel, G., and Anat, K. (2007). Aspects of endowment: a query theory of loss aversion. *Journal of Experimental Psychology: Learning Memory and Cognition* 33(3): 461–74.

Johnson, E. J. and Schkade, D. A. (1989). Bias in utility assessments: further evidence and explanations. *Management Science* 35(4): 406–24.

Jullien, B. and Salanié, B. (2000). Estimating preferences under risk: the case of racetrack bettors. *Journal of Political Economy* 108(3): 503–30.

Kachelmeier, S. J. and Shehata, M. (1992). Examining risk preferences under high monetary incentives: experimental evidence from the People's Republic of China. *American Economic Review* 82(5): 1120–41.

Kagel, J. H., MacDonald, D. N., and Battalio, R. C. (1990). Tests of "fanning out" of indifference curves: results from animal and human experiments. *American Economic Review* 80(4): 912–21.

Kahneman, D. (2003). Maps of bounded rationality: psychology for behavioral economics. *American Economic Review* 93(5): 1449–75.

Kahneman, D. (2012). *Thinking Fast and Slow.* London: Penguin.

Kahneman, D., Knetsch, J. L., and Thaler, R. H. (1986). Fairness as a constraint on profit seeking: entitlements in the market. *American Economic Review* 76(4): 728–41.

Kahneman, D., Knetsch, J. L., and Thaler, R. H. (1990). Experimental tests of the endowment effect and the Coase Theorem. *Journal of Political Economy* 98(6): 1325–48.

Kahneman, D., Knetsch, J. L., and Thaler, R. H. (1991). Anomalies: the endowment effect, loss aversion, and status quo bias. *Journal of Economic Perspectives* 5(1): 193–206.

Kahneman, D. and Tversky, A. (1979). Prospect theory: an analysis of decision under risk. *Econometrica* 47(2): 263–91.

Kahneman, D. and Tversky, A. (2000). *Choices, Values and Frames.* Cambridge: Cambridge University Press.

Karmarkar, U. S. (1979). Subjectively weighted utility and the Allais paradox. *Organizational Behavior and Human Performance* 24(1): 67–72.

Karni, E. (2003). On the representation of beliefs by probabilities. *Journal of Risk and Uncertainty* 26(1): 17–38.

Karni, E. and Safra, Z. (1987). "Preference reversal" and the observability of preferences by experimental methods. *Econometrica* 55(3): 675–85.

Keynes, J. M. (1921). *A Treatise on Probability.* London: Macmillan.

Kilka, M. and Weber, M. (2001). What determines the shape of the probability weighting function under uncertainty? *Management Science* 47(12): 1712–26.

Klibanoff, P., Marinacci, M., and Mukerji, S. (2005). A smooth model of decision making under ambiguity. *Econometrica* 73(6): 1849–92.

Klibanoff, P., Marinacci, M., and Mukerji, S. (2009). On the smooth ambiguity aversion model: a reply. Oxford University. Discussion Papers in Economics 449.

Kliger, D. and Levy, O. (2009). Theories of choice under risk: insights from financial markets. *Journal of Economic Behavior and Organization* 71(2): 330–46.

Knetsch, J. L. (1989). The endowment effect and evidence of nonreversible indifference curves. *American Economic Review* 79(5): 1277–84.

Knetsch, J. L. and Sinden, J. A. (1984). Willingness to pay and compensation demanded: experimental evidence of an unexpected disparity in measures of value. *Quarterly Journal of Economics* 99(3): 507–21.

Knetsch, J. L. and Wong, W.-K. (2009). The endowment effect and the reference state: evidence and manipulations. *Journal of Economic Behavior and Organization* 71(2): 407–13.

Knez, P., Smith, V. L., and Williams, A. W. (1985). Individual rationality, market rationality, and value estimation. *American Economic Review* 75(2): 397–402.

Knight, F. J. (1921). *Risk, Uncertainty, and Profit.* Boston, MA: Houghton Mifflin Company.

Köbberling, V. and Wakker, P. P. (2003). Preference foundations for non-expected utility: a generalized and simplified technique. *Mathematics of Operations Research* 28(3): 395–423.

Köbberling, V. and Wakker, P. P. (2005). An index of loss aversion. *Journal of Economic Theory* 122(1): 119–31.

Kocher, M. G., Lahno, A. M., and Trautmann, S. T. (2018). Ambiguity aversion is not universal. *European Economic Review* 101(C): 268–83.

Kolm, S.-C. (1973). A note on optimum tax evasion. *Journal of Public Economics* 2(3): 265–70.

Kolstad, C. D. and Guzman, R. M. (1999). Information and the divergence between willingness to accept and willingness to pay. *Journal of Environmental Economics and Management* 38(1): 66–80.

Köszegi, B. and Rabin, M. (2006). A model of reference-dependent preferences. *Quarterly Journal of Economics* 121(4): 1133–65.

Köszegi, B. and Rabin, M. (2007). Reference-dependent risk attitudes. *American Economic Review* 97(4): 1047–73.

Köszegi, B. and Rabin, M. (2009). Reference-dependent consumption plans. *American Economic Review* 99(3): 909–36.

Kothiyal, A., Spinu, V., and Wakker. P. P. (2011). Prospect theory for continuous distributions: a preference foundation. *Journal of Risk and Uncertainty* 42(3): 195–210.

Kothiyal, A., Spinu, V., and Wakker. P. P. (2014). An experimental test of prospect theory for predicting choice under ambiguity. *Journal of Risk and Uncertainty* 48(1): 1–17.

Kreps, D. M. (1990). *A Course in Microeconomic Theory*. Princeton, NJ: Princeton University Press.

Kreps, D. M. and Porteus, E. L. (1978). Temporal resolution of uncertainty and dynamic choice theory. *Econometrica* 46(1): 185–200.

Kunreuther, H., Ginsberg, R., Miller, L. et al. (1978). *Disaster Insurance Protection: Public Policy Lessons*. New York: Wiley.

Kunreuther, H., Meszaros, J., Hogarth, R. M., and Spranca, M. (1995). Ambiguity and underwriter decision processes. *Journal of Economic Behavior and Organization* 26(3): 337–52.

Kunreuther, H. and Pauly, M. (2004). Neglecting disaster: why don't people insure against large losses? *Journal of Risk and Uncertainty* 28(1): 5–21.

Kunreuther, H. and Pauly, M. (2005). Insurance decision making and market behaviour. *Foundations and Trends in Microeconomics* 1(2): 63–127.

Lakshminarayanan, V., Chen, M. K., and Santos, L. R. (2008). Endowment effect in capuchin monkeys. *Philosophical Transactions of the Royal Society B* 363: 3837–44.

Lakshminarayanan, V., Chen, M. K., and Santos, L. R. (2011). The evolution of decision-making under risk: framing effects in monkey risk preferences. *Journal of Experimental Social Psychology* 47(3): 689–93.

Langer, T. and Weber, M. (2008). Does commitment or feedback influence myopic loss aversion? An experimental analysis. *Journal of Economic Behavior and Organization* 67(3–4): 810–19.

Lehrer, E. (2009). A new integral for capacities. *Economic Theory* 39(1): 157–76.

Lerner, J. S., Small, D. A., and Loewenstein, G. (2004). Heart strings and purse strings: carry-over effects of emotions on economic transactions. *Psychological Science* 15(5): 337–41.

Levin, I., Schreiber, J., Lauriola, M., and Gaeth, G. J. (2002). A tale of two pizzas: building up from a basic product versus scaling down from a fully loaded product. *Marketing Letters* 13(4): 335–44.

Levitt, S. D. (2004). Understanding why crime fell in the 1990's: four factors that explain the decline and six that do not. *Journal of Economic Perspectives* 18(1): 163–90.

Li, C., (2017). Are the poor worse at dealing with ambiguity? Ambiguity attitude of urban and rural Chinese adolescents. *Journal of Risk and Uncertainty* 54: 239–68.

Lichtenstein, S. and Slovic, P. (1971). Reversals of preference between bids and choices in gambling decisions. *Journal of Experimental Psychology* 89(1): 46–55.

Lichtenstein, S. and Slovic, P. (eds.) (2006). *The Construction of Preferences*. Cambridge: Cambridge University Press.

List, J. A. (2003). Does market experience eliminate market anomalies? *Quarterly Journal of Economics* 118(1): 41–71.

List, J. A. (2004). Neoclassical theory versus prospect theory: evidence from the marketplace. *Econometrica* 72(2): 615–25.

List, J. A. and Haigh, M. S. (2005). A simple test of expected utility theory using professional traders. *Proceedings of the National Academy of Sciences* 102(3): 945–8.

Locke, E. A. and Latham, G. P. (1990). *A Theory of Goal Setting and Task Performance*. Englewood Cliffs, NJ: Prentice-Hall.

Loewenstein, G. F., Weber, E. U., and Hsee, C. K. (2001). Risk as feelings. *Psychological Bulletin* 127(2): 267–86.

Loomes, G. (2008). Modelling choice and valuation in decision experiments. University of East Anglia. Working Paper.

Loomes, G., Starmer, S., and Sugden, R. (1989). Preference reversal: information-processing effect or rational non-transitive choice? *Economic Journal* 99(395): 140–51.

Loomes, G., Starmer, C., and Sugden, R. (1991). Observing violations of transitivity by experimental methods. *Econometrica* 59(2): 425–39.

Loomes, G., Starmer, C., and Sugden, R. (1992). Are preferences monotonic? Testing some predictions of regret theory. *Economica* 59(233): 17–33.

Loomes, G., Starmer, C., and Sugden, R. (2003). Do anomalies disappear in repeated markets? *Economic Journal* 113(486): C153–C166.

Loomes, G. and Sugden, R. (1982). Regret theory: an alternative theory of rational choice under uncertainty. *Economic Journal* 92(368): 805–24.

Loomes, G. and Sugden, R. (1986). Disappointment and dynamic consistency in choice under uncertainty. *Review of Economic Studies* 53(2): 271–82.

Loomes, G. and Sugden, R. (1987). Some implications of a more general form of regret theory. *Journal of Economic Theory* 41(2): 270–87.

Lovallo, D. and Kahneman, D. (2000). Living with uncertainty: attractiveness and resolution timing. *Journal of Behavioral Decision Making* 13(2): 179–90.

Luce, R. D. (1991). Rank- and sign-dependent linear utility models for binary gambles. *Journal of Economic Theory* 53(1): 75–100.

Luce, R. D. (2000). *Utility of Gains and Losses: Measurement-Theoretical and Experimental Approaches.* Mahwah, NJ: Erlbaum.

Luce R. D. (2001). Reduction invariance and Prelec's weighting functions. *Journal of Mathematical Psychology* 45(1): 167–79.

Luce, R. D. and Fishburn, P. C. (1991). Rank- and sign-dependent linear utility models for finite first-order gambles. *Journal of Risk and Uncertainty* 4(1): 29–59.

Luce, R. D. and Marley, A. A. J. (2005). Ranked additive utility representations of gambles: old and new axiomatizations. *Journal of Risk and Uncertainty* 30(1): 21–62.

Luce, R. D. and Raiffa, H. (1957). *Games and Decisions.* New York: Wiley.

Maccheroni, F., Marinacci, M., and Rustichini, A. (2006a). Ambiguity aversion, robustness, and the variational representation of preferences. *Econometrica* 74(6): 1447–98.

Maccheroni, F., Massimo, M., and Rustichini, A. (2006b). Dynamic variational preference. *Journal of Economic Theory* 128(1): 4–44.

McClelland, G. H., Schulze, W. D., and Coursey, D. L. (1993). Insurance for low-probability hazards: a bimodal response to unlikely events. *Journal of Risk and Uncertainty* 7(1): 95–116.

McCord, M. and de Neufville, R. (1986). Lottery equivalents: reduction of the certainty effect problem in utility assessment. *Management Science* 32(1): 56–60.

MacCrimmon, K. and Larsson, S. (1979). Utility theory: axioms versus paradoxes. In M. Allais and O. Hagen (eds.), *Expected Utility Hypotheses and the Allais Paradox.* Dordrecht: Reidel.

MacDonald, D. N., Kagel, J. H., and Battalio, R. C. (1991). Animals' choices over uncertain outcomes: further experimental results. *Economic Journal* 101(408): 1067–84.

Machina, M. J. (2009). Risk, ambiguity, and the rank-dependence axioms. *American Economic Review* 99(1): 385–92.

Machina, M. J. and Schmeidler, D. (1992). A more robust definition of subjective probability. *Econometrica* 60(4): 745–80.

Machina, M. J. and Siniscalchi, M. (2014). Ambiguity and ambiguity aversion. In M. J. Machina and W. K. Viscusi (eds.), *Handbook of the Economics of Risk and Uncertainty, Volume 1.* Oxford Amsterdam: North-Holland.

Mankiw, N. G. and Zeldes, S. P. (1991). The consumption of stockholders and nonstockholders. *Journal of Financial Economics* 29(1): 97–112.

Markowitz, H. (1952). The utility of wealth. *Journal of Political Economy* 60(2): 151–8.

Marley, A. A. J. and Luce, R. D. (2001). Rank-weighted utilities and qualitative convolution. *Journal of Risk and Uncertainty* 23(2): 135–63.

Marley, A. A. J. and Luce, R. D. (2005). Independence properties vis-à-vis several utility representations. *Theory and Decision* 58(1): 77–143.

Marquis, M. S. and Holmer, M. R. (1996). Alternative models of choice under uncertainty and demand for health insurance. *Review of Economics and Statistics* 78(3): 421–7.

Mas, A. (2006). Pay, reference points, and police performance. *Quarterly Journal of Economics* 121(3): 783–821.

Mas-Colell, A., Whinston, M. D., and Green, J. R. (1995). *Microeconomic Theory.* New York: Oxford University Press.

Mehra, R. and Prescott, E. C. (1985). The equity premium: a puzzle. *Journal of Monetary Economics* 15(2): 145–61.

Miao, B. and Zhong, S. (2012). Separating risk preference and time preference. National University of Singapore, Department of Economics. Working Paper.

Mitton, T. and Vorkink, K. (2007). Equilibrium underdiversification and the preference for skewness. *Review of Financial Studies* 20(4): 1255–88.

Morrison, G. C. (1997). Resolving differences in willingness to pay and willingness to accept: comment. *American Economic Review* 87(1): 236–40.

Nakamura, N. (1990). Subjective expected utility with non-additive probabilities on finite state spaces. *Journal of Economic Theory* 51(2): 346–66.

Nau, R. F. (2006). Uncertainty aversion and second-order utilities and probabilities. *Management Science* 52(1): 136–45.

Nehring, K. (2001). Ambiguity in the context of probabilistic beliefs. Mimeo, University of California, Davis.

Neilson, W. S. (1992). A mixed fan hypothesis and its implications for behavior toward risk. *Journal of Economic Behavior and Organization* 19(2): 197–211.

Neilson, W. S. (2001). Calibration results for rank-dependent expected utility. *Economics Bulletin* 4(10): 1–5.

Neilson, W. S. (2002). Comparative risk sensitivity with reference-dependent preferences. *Journal of Risk Uncertainty* 24(2): 131–42.

Noussair, C. and Wu, P. (2006). Risk tolerance in the present and the future: an experimental study. *Managerial and Decision Economics* 27(6): 401–12.

Novemsky, N. and Kahneman, D. (2005). The boundaries of loss aversion. *Journal of Marketing Research* 42(2): 119–28.

Ober, J. (2012). Thucydides as prospect theorist. Princeton/Stanford. Working Papers in Classics.

Odean, T. (1998). Are investors reluctant to realize their losses? *Journal of Finance* 53(5): 1775–98.

Oettinger, G. S. (1999). An empirical analysis of the daily labor supply of stadium vendors. *Journal of Political Economy* 107(2): 360–92.

Ok, E. A., Ortoleva, P., and Riella, G. (2015). Revealed (P)Reference Theory. *American Economic Review* 105(1): 299–321.

Öncüler, A. and Onay, S. (2009). How do we evaluate future gambles? Experimental evidence on path dependency in risky intertemporal choice. *Journal of Behavioral Decision Making* 22(3): 280–300.

Orwin, C. (1994). *The Humanity of Thucydides*. Princeton, NJ: Princeton University Press.

Page, L., Savage, D. A., and Torgler, B. (2012). Variation in risk seeking behavior in a natural experiment on large losses induced by a natural disaster. CESifo. Working Paper 3878.

Palacios-Huerta, I. and Serrano, R. (2006). Rejecting small gambles under expected utility. *Economics Letters* 91(2): 250–9.

Pape, A. D. and Kurtz, K. J. (2013). Evaluating case-based decision theory: predicting empirical patterns of human classification learning. *Games and Economic Behavior* 82: 52–65.

Pedroni, A., Frey, R., Bruhin, A., Dutilh, G., Hertwig, R., and Rieskamp, J. (2017). The risk elicitation puzzle. *Nature Human Behaviour* 1: 803–9.

Pennings, J. M. E. and Smidts, A. (2003). The shape of utility functions and organizational behavior. *Management Science* 49(9): 1251–63.

Peters, E., Slovic, P., and Gregory, R. (2003). The role of affect in the WTA/WTP disparity. *Journal of Behavioral Decision Making* 16(4): 309–30.

Peters, H. J. M. (2012). A preference foundation for constant loss aversion. *Journal of Mathematical Economics* 48(1): 21–5.

Pfanzagl, J. (1968). *Theory of Measurement*. New York: John Wiley and Sons.

Plott, C. R. and Zeiler, K. (2005). The willingness to pay–willingness to accept gap, the "endowment effect", subject misconceptions, and experimental procedures to eliciting valuations. *American Economic Review* 95(3): 530–45.

Plott, C. R. and Zeiler, K. (2007). Exchange asymmetries incorrectly interpreted as evidence of endowment effect theory and prospect theory? *American Economic Review* 97(4): 1449–66.

Polinsky, M. and Shavell, S. (2007). The theory of public enforcement of law. In M. Polinsky and S. Shavell (eds.), *Handbook of Law and Economics, Volume 1*. Amsterdam: Elsevier, ch. 6.

Pope, D. and Schweitzer, M. (2011). Is Tiger Woods loss averse? Persistent bias in the face of experience, competition, and high stakes. *American Economic Review* 101(1): 129–57.

Post, T., van den Assem, M. J., Baltussen, G., and Thaler, R. H. (2008). Deal or no deal? Decision making under risk in a large-payoff game show. *American Economic Review* 98(1): 38–71.

Pöystia, L., Rajalina, S., and Summala, H. (2005). Factors influencing the use of cellular (mobile) phone during driving and hazards while using it. *Accident Analysis and Prevention* 37(1): 47–51.

Prelec, D. (1990). A "Pseudo-endowment" effect, and its implications for some recent nonexpected utility models. *Journal of Risk and Uncertainty* 3(3): 247–59.

Prelec, D. (1998). The probability weighting function. *Econometrica* 66(3): 497–527.

Quiggin, J. (1981). Risk perception and risk aversion among Australian farmers. *Australian Journal of Agricultural Economics* 25(2): 160–9.

Quiggin, J. (1982). A theory of anticipated utility. *Journal of Economic Behavior and Organization* 3(4): 323–43.

Quiggin, J. (1993). *Generalized Expected Utility Theory*. Dordrecht: Kluwer.

Rabin, M. (2000a). Risk aversion and expected-utility theory: a calibration theorem. *Econometrica* 68(5): 1281–92.

Rabin, M. (2000b). Diminishing marginal utility of wealth cannot explain risk aversion. In D. Kahneman and A. Tversky (eds.), *Choices, Values and Frames*. Cambridge: Cambridge University Press.

Radelet, M. L. and Ackers, R. L. (1996). Deterrence and the death penalty: the views of the experts. *Journal of Criminal Law and Criminology* 87(1): 1–16.

Ramsey, F. P. (1931). Truth and probability. In *The Foundation of Mathematics and Other Logical Essays*. New York: Harcourt, Brace.

Redelmeier, D. A., Koehler, D. J., Liberman, V., and Tversky, A. (1995). Probability judgment in medicine: discounting unspecified causes. *Medical Decision Making* 15(3): 227–30.

Richard, S. F. (1975). Multivariate risk aversion, utility independence and separable utility functions. *Management Science* 22(1): 12–21.

Rieger, M. O. and Wang, M. (2006). Cumlative prospect theory and the St. Petersburg paradox. *Economic Theory* 28(3): 665–79.

Rieger, M. O., Wang, M., and Hens, T. (2014). Prospect theory around the world. Forthcoming in *Management Science*.

Rizzo, J. A. and Zeckhauser, R. J. (2003). Reference incomes, loss aversion, and physician behaviour. *Review of Economics and Statistics* 85(4): 909–22.

Roca, M., Hogarth, R. M., and Maule, A. J. (2006). Ambiguity seeking as a result of the status-quo bias. *Journal of Risk and Uncertainty* 32(3): 175–94.

Rottenstreich, Y. and Hsee, C. K. (2001). Money, kisses, and electric shocks: on the affective psychology of risk. *Psychological Science* 12(3): 185–90.

Rottenstreich, Y. and Tversky, A. (1997). Unpacking, repacking, and anchoring: advances in support theory. *Psychological Review* 104(2): 406–15.

Routledge, B. R. and Zin, S. E. (2010). Generalized disappointment aversion and asset prices. *Journal of Finance* 65(4): 1303–32.

The Royal Society for the Prevention of Accidents (2005). The risk of using a mobile phone while driving. Available at http: //www.rospa.com/roadsafety/info/mobile_phone_report.pdf.

Rubinstein, A. (2006). Dilemmas of an economic theorist. *Econometrica* 74(4): 865–83.

Rutten-van Mölken, M. P., Bakker, C. H., van Doorslaer, E. K., and van der Linden, S. (1995). Methodological issues of patient utility measurement. Experience from two clinical trials. *Medical Care* 33(9): 922–37.

Safra, Z. and Segal, U. (2008). Calibration results for non-expected utility theories. *Econometrica* 76(5): 1143–66.

Samuelson, L. (2005). Economic theory and experimental economics. *Journal of Economic Literature* 43(1): 65–107.

Samuelson, W. F. and Zeckhauser, R. (1988). Status quo bias in decision making. *Journal of Risk and Uncertainty* 1(1): 7–59.

Santos, L. R. and Platt, M. L. (2014). Evolutionary anthropological insights into neuroeconomics: what non-human primates can tell us about human decision-making strategies. In P. W. Glincher and E. Fehr (eds.), *Neuroeconomics: Decision Making and the Brain*. London: Elsevier Inc.

Sarin, R. and Wakker, P. P. (1992). A simple axiomatization of nonadditive expected utility. *Econometrica* 60(6): 1255–72.

Sarin, R. and Wakker, P. P. (2000). Cumulative dominance and probabilistic sophistication. *Mathematical Social Sciences*. 40(2): 191–6.

Savage, L. J. (1954). *The Foundations of Statistics*. New York: Wiley and Sons.

Sayman, S. and Öncüler, A. (2005). Effects of study design characteristics on the WTA–WTP disparity: a meta analytical framework. *Journal of Economic Psychology* 26(2): 289–312.

Schmeidler, D. (1986). Integral representation without additivity. *Proceedings of the American Mathematical Society* 97(2): 255–61.

Schmeidler, D. (1989). Subjective probability and expected utility without additivity. *Econometrica* 57(3): 571–87.

Schmidt, U. (2003). Reference-dependence in cumulative prospect theory. *Journal of Mathematical Psychology* 47(2): 122–31.

Schmidt, U., Starmer, C., and Sugden, R. (2008). Third-generation prospect theory. *Journal of Risk and Uncertainty* 36(3): 203–23.

Schmidt, U. and Traub, S. (2002). An experimental test of loss aversion. *Journal of Risk and Uncertainty* 25(3): 233–49.

Schmidt, U. and Zank, H. (2005). What is loss aversion? *Journal of Risk and Uncertainty* 30: 157–67.

Schmidt, U. and Zank, H. (2007). Linear cumulative prospect theory with applications to portfolio selection and insurance demand. *Decisions in Economics and Finance* 30(1): 1–18.

Schmidt, U. and Zank, H. (2008). Risk aversion in cumulative prospect theory. *Management Science* 54(1): 208–16.

Schmidt, U. and Zank, H. (2012). A genuine foundation for prospect theory. *Journal of Risk and Uncertainty* 45(2): 97–113.

Schunk, D. and Betsch, C. (2006). Explaining heterogeneity in utility functions by individual differences in decision modes. *Journal of Economic Psychology* 27(3): 386–401.

Schunk, D. and Winter, J. (2009). The relationship between risk attitudes and heuristics in search tasks: a laboratory experiment. *Journal of Economic Behavior and Organization* 71(2): 347–60.

Segal, U. (1987). The Ellsberg paradox and risk aversion: an anticipated utility approach. *International Economic Review* 28(1): 175–202.

Segal, U. (1988). Does the preference reversal phenomenon necessarily contradict the independence axiom? *American Economic Review* 78(1): 233–6.

Segal, U. (1989). Anticipated utility: a measure representation approach. *Annals of Operations Research* 19(1): 359–73.

Segal, U. (1990). Two-stage lotteries without the reduction axiom. *Econometrica* 58(2): 349–77.

Segal, U. (1993). The measure representation: a correction. *Journal of Risk and Uncertainty* 6(1): 99–107.

Sen, S. and Johnson, E. J. (1997). Mere-possession effects without possession in consumer choice. *Journal of Consumer Research* 24(1): 105–17.

Shefrin, H. and Statman, M. (1985). The disposition to sell winners too early and ride losers too long: theory and evidence. *Journal of Finance* 40(3): 777–90.

Shogren, J. F., Shin, S. Y., Hayes, D. J., and Kliebenstein, J. B. (1994). Resolving differences in willingness to pay and willingness to accept. *American Economic Review* 84(1): 255–70.

Siniscalchi, M. (2006). A behavioral characterization of plausible priors. *Journal of Economic Theory* 128(1): 91–135.

Siniscalchi, M. (2009). Vector expected utility and attitudes toward variation. *Econometrica* 77(3): 801–55.

Skinner, J. and Slemrod, J. (1985). An economic perspective on tax evasion. *National Tax Journal* 38(3): 345–53.

Slemrod, J. and Yitzhaki, S. (2002). Tax avoidance, evasion and administration. In A. J. Auerbach and M. Feldstein (eds.), *Handbook of Public Economics, Volume 3*. Amsterdam: Elsevier Science.

Smith, A. (2008). Lagged beliefs and reference-dependent utility. Department of Economics, University of Arizona, Working Paper 08–03.

Smithers, S. (2015). Goals, motivation and gender. *Economics Letters* 131: 75–7.

Snowberg, E. and Wolfers, J. (2010). Explaining the favorite-longshot bias: is it risk-love or misperceptions? *Journal of Political Economy* 118(4): 723–46.

Spiegler, R. (2011). *Bounded Rationality and Industrial Organization*. Oxford: Oxford University Press.

Spiegler, R. (2012). Monopoly pricing when consumers are antagonized by unexpected price increases: a "cover version" of the Heidhues–Koszegi–Rabin model. *Economic Theory* 51(3): 695–711.

Stalmeier, P. F. and Bezembinder, T. G. (1999). The discrepancy between risky and riskless utilities: a matter of framing? *Medical Decision Making* 19(4): 435–47.

Starmer, C. (1992). Testing new theories of choice under uncertainty using the common consequence effect. *Review of Economic Studies* 59(4): 813–30.

Starmer, C. (2000). Developments in non-expected utility theory: the hunt for a descriptive theory of choice under risk. *Journal of Economic Literature* 38(2): 332–82.

Starmer, C. and Sugden, R. (1989a). Violations of the independence axiom in common ratio problems: an experimental test of some competing hypotheses. *Annals of Operations Research* 19(1): 79–102.

Starmer, C. and Sugden, R. (1989b). Probability and juxtaposition effects: an experimental investigation of the common ratio effect. *Journal of Risk and Uncertainty* 2(2): 159–78.

Starmer, C. and Sugden, R. (1993). Testing for juxtaposition and eventsplitting effects. *Journal of Risk and Uncertainty* 6(3): 235–54.

Starmer, C. and Sugden, R. (1998). Testing alternative explanations of cyclical choices. *Economica* 65(259): 347–61.

Stott, H. P. (2006). Choosing from cumulative prospect theory's functional menagerie. *Journal of Risk and Uncertainty* 32(2): 101–30.

Strahilevitz, M. A. and Loewenstein, G. (1998). The effect of ownership history on the valuation of objects. *Journal of Consumer Research* 25(3): 276–89.

Sugden, R. (1986). New developments in the theory of choice under uncertainty. *Bulletin of Economic Research* 38(1): 1–24.

Sugden, R. (2003). Reference-dependent subjective expected utility. *Journal of Economic Theory* 111(2): 172–91.

Sugden, R. (2004). Alternatives to expected utility: foundations. In S. Barbera, P. Hammond, and C. Seidl (eds.), *Handbook of Utility Theory, Volume 2: Extensions*. Dordrecht: Kluwer, pp. 685–755.

Sutter, M. (2007). Are teams prone to myopic loss aversion? An experimental study on individual versus team investment behavior. *Economics Letters* 97(2): 128–32.

Sydnor, J. (2010). (Over)insuring modest risks. *American Economic Journal: Applied Economics* 2(4): 177–99.

Taylor, S. E. and Brown, J. D. (1988). Illusion and well-being: a social psychological perspective on mental health. *Psychological Bulletin* 103(2): 193–210.

Teigen, K. H. (1974). Overestimation of subjective probabilities. *Scandinavian Journal of Psychology* 15(1): 56–62.

Thaler, R. H. (1980). Toward a positive theory of consumer choice. *Journal of Economic Behavior and Organization* 1(1): 39–60.

Thaler, R. H. and Johnson, E. (1990). Gambling with the house money and trying to break even: the effects of prior outcomes on risky choice. *Management Science* 36(6): 643–60.

Thaler, R. H., Tversky, A., Kahneman, D., and Schwartz, A. (1997). The effect of myopia and loss aversion on risk taking: an experimental test. *Quarterly Journal of Economics* 112(2): 647–61.

Trautmann, S. T. and van de Kuilen, G. (2016). Ambiguity attitudes. In G. Keren and G. Wu (eds.), *Blackwell Handbook of Judgment and Decision Making, Volume 1*. Chichester: Wiley Blackwell, pp. 89–116.

Trautmann, S. T., Vieider, F. M., and Wakker, P. P. (2008). Causes of ambiguity aversion: known versus unknown preferences. *Journal of Risk and Uncertainty* 36(3): 225–43.

Trautmann, S. T., Vieider, F. M., and Wakker, P. P. (2011). Preference reversals for ambiguity aversion. *Management Science* 57(7): 1320–33.

Tversky, A. and Fox, C. R. (1995). Weighing risk and uncertainty. *Psychological Review* 102(2): 269–83.

Tversky, A. and Kahneman, D. (1981). The framing of decisions and the psychology of choice. *Science* 211(4481): 453–8.

Tversky, A. and Kahneman, D. (1992). Advances in prospect theory: cumulative representation of uncertainty. *Journal of Risk and Uncertainty* 5(4): 297–323.

Tversky, A. and Koehler, D. J. (1994). Support theory: a nonextensional representation of subjective probability. *Psychological Review* 101(4): 547–67.

Tversky, A. Slovic, P., and Kahneman, D. (1990). The causes of preference reversal. *American Economic Review* 80(1): 204–17.

Tversky, A., and Thaler, R. H. (1990). Anomalies: preference reversals. *Journal of Economic Perspectives* 4(2): 201–11.

Tversky, A. and Wakker, P. P. (1995). Risk attitudes and decision weights. *Econometrica* 63(6): 1255–80.

van de Kuilen, G. and Wakker, P. P. (2011). The midweight method to measure attitudes towards risk and ambiguity. *Management Science* 57(3): 582–98.

van Dijk, E. and van Knippenberg, D. (1996). Buying and selling exchange goods: loss aversion and the endowment effect. *Journal of Economic Psychology* 17(4): 517–24.

Varian, H. (1992). *Microeconomic Analysis*. New York: W. W. Norton.

Viscusi, K. W. (1998). *Rational Risk Policy: The 1996 Arne Ryde Memorial Lectures*. Oxford: Oxford University Press.

von Gaudecker, H.-M., van Soest, A., and Wengstrom, E. (2011). Heterogeneity in risky choice behaviour in a broad population. *American Economic Review* 101(2): 664–94.

von Neumann, J. and Morgenstern, O. (1944). *Theory of Games and Economic Behavior*. Princeton, NJ: Princeton University Press.

Wakker, P. P. (1994). Separating marginal utility and probabilistic risk aversion. *Theory and Decision* 36(1): 1–44.

Wakker, P. P. (2001). Testing and characterizing properties of nonadditive measures through violations of the sure-thing principle. *Econometrica* 69(4): 1039–59.

Wakker, P. P. (2003). The data of Levy and Levy (2002) "Prospect theory: much ado about nothing?" actually support prospect theory. *Management Science* 49(7): 979–81.

Wakker, P. P. (2005). Formalizing reference dependence and initial wealth in Rabin's calibration theorem. Mimeo, Econometric Institute, Erasmus University Rotterdam, The Netherlands.

Wakker, P. P. (2010). *Prospect Theory for Risk and Ambiguity*. Cambridge: Cambridge University Press.

Wakker, P. P. and Deneffe, D. (1996). Eliciting von Neumann–Morgenstern utilities when probabilities are distorted or unknown. *Management Science* 42(8): 1131–50.

Wakker, P. P., Thaler, R. H., and Tversky, A. (1997). Probabilistic insurance. *Journal of Risk and Uncertainty* 15(1): 7–28.

Wakker, P. P. and Tversky, A. (1993). An axiomatization of cumulative prospect theory. *Journal of Risk and Uncertainty* 7(2): 147–75.

Wakker, P. P. and Zank, H. (2002). A simple preference foundation of cumulative prospect theory with power utility. *European Economic Review* 46(7): 1253–71.

Walther, H. (2003). Normal-randomness expected utility, time preference and emotional distortions. *Journal of Economic Behavior and Organization* 52(2): 253–66.

Walther, H. (2010). Anomalies in intertemporal choice, time-dependent uncertainty and expected utility—a common approach. *Journal of Economic Psychology* 31(1): 114–30.

Watt, R. (2002). Defending expected utility theory. *Journal of Economic Perspectives* 16(2): 227–9.

Weber, B. J. and Chapman, G. B. (2005). Playing for peanuts: why is risk seeking more common for low-stakes gambles? *Organizational Behavior and Human Decision Processes* 97(1): 31–46.

Wei, M., al-Nowaihi A., and Dhami, S. (2017). Can quantum decision theory explain the Ellsberg paradox? Division of Economics, University of Leicester, Working Paper No. 17/07.

Weinstein, N. D. (1980). Unrealistic optimism about future life events. *Journal of Personality and Social Psychology* 39(5): 806–20.

Werner, K. M. and Zank, H. (2018). A Revealed Reference Point for Prospect Theory. *Economic Theory*, forthcoming.

Wicker, F., Hamman, D., Hagen, A. S., Reed, J. L., and Wieche, J. A. (1995). Studies of loss aversion and perceived necessity. *Journal of Psychology* 129(1): 75–89.

Williams. A. F. and Lund, A. K. (1986). Seat belt use laws and occupant crash protection in the United States. *American Journal of Public Health* 76(12): 1438–42.

Wu, G. (1994). An empirical test of ordinal independence. *Journal of Risk and Uncertainty* 9(1): 39–60.

Wu, G. and Gonzalez, R. (1996). Curvature of the probability weighting function. *Management Science* 42(12): 1676–90.

Wu, G. and Markle, A. B. (2008). An empirical test of gain–loss separability in prospect theory. *Management Science* 54(7): 1322–35.

Yaari, M. E. (1987). The dual theory of choice under risk. *Econometrica* 55(1): 95–115.

Yaniv, G. (1999). Tax compliance and advance tax payments: a prospect theory analysis. *National Tax Journal* 52(4): 753–64.

Yitzhaki, S. (1974). A note on income tax evasion: a theoretical analysis. *Journal of Public Economics* 3(2): 201–2.

Zank, H. (2001). Cumulative prospect theory for parametric and multiattribute utilities. *Mathematics of Operations Research* 26(1): 67–81.

Zhang, W. and Semmler, W. (2009). Prospect theory for stock markets: empirical evidence with time-series data. *Journal of Economic Behavior and Organization* 72(3): 835–49.

Zhao, J. and Kling, C. L. (2001). A new explanation for the WTP/WTA disparity. *Economics Letters* 73(3): 293–300.

AUTHOR INDEX

Note: Tables are indicated by an italic *t* following the page number.

SUBJECT INDEX

Note: Tables and Figures are indicated by an italic *t* and *f*, respectively, following the page number.